CORRECTIONAL CONTEXTS

CORRECTIONAL CONTEXTS

CONTEMPORARY AND CLASSICAL READINGS

FOURTH EDITION

Edward J. Latessa
UNIVERSITY OF CINCINNATI

Alexander M. Holsinger
UNIVERSITY OF MISSOURI-KANSAS CITY

NEW YORK OXFORD
OXFORD UNIVERSITY PRESS
2011

Oxford University Press, Inc., publishes works that further Oxford University's objective of excellence in research, scholarship, and education.

Oxford New York
Auckland Cape Town Dar es Salaam Hong Kong Karachi
Kuala Lumpur Madrid Melbourne Mexico City Nairobi
New Delhi Shanghai Taipei Toronto

With offices in
Argentina Austria Brazil Chile Czech Republic France Greece
Guatemala Hungary Italy Japan Poland Portugal Singapore
South Korea Switzerland Thailand Turkey Ukraine Vietnam

Published by Oxford University Press, Inc.
198 Madison Avenue, New York, NY 10016
www.oup.com

Library of Congress Cataloging-in-Publication Data

ISBN 978-0-19-975146-4

Printing number: 9 8 7 6 5 4 3

Printed in the United States of America
on acid-free paper

To our families

Sally, Amy, Jennifer, Michael, and Allison

and

Kristi, Jordan, Lucas, and Elijah

CONTENTS

PART VI REENTRY INTO THE COMMUNITY *301*

---

* Denotes new chapter for this edition

PREFACE

This anthology traces the history and development of corrections and punishment as it has evolved in the United States over the past few centuries. This collection of articles and essays offers the reader a critical review of where "corrections" in the United States has been in the past, how various facets of the system operate today, and where as a country we may be headed regarding the confinement, control, and treatment of our correctional populations.

We have tried to combine some classical writings with more contemporary works throughout this volume. We believe that it is important to understand where we started in order to appreciate where we are today. We have tried to update this volume by providing relevant articles on some of the pressing issues facing corrections: renewed debate about the effectiveness of treatment and rehabilitation, how to improve reentry and transition back into the community, and some of the realities of a social policy that has led to record numbers of our citizens being under correctional sanctions. Included are entire sections that contain essays highlighting the rehabilitative treatment efforts within and outside of institutions, the increasingly critical role of reentry, and the sources for future major influences in corrective efforts. This collection of essays is designed to offer the reader a comprehensive and relevant review and critical analysis of the many issues that concern our corrective efforts. We hope that you find this anthology interesting and informative and a starting point in your studies and work in the field of corrections.

NEW TO THE FOURTH EDITION

In addition to revising the part summaries and introductory sections for the new articles, eleven new readings have been included in the fourth edition of Correctional Contexts:

- "Prison Guard Predators: An Analysis of Inmates who Established Inappropriate Relationships with Prison Staff, 1995-1998" by Robert Worley, James W. Marquart, and Janet L. Mullings (Reading 11)
- "Job Stress and Burnout Among Correctional Officers: A Literature Review" by Wilmar B. Schaufeli and Maria C. W. Peeters (Reading 12)
- "Sex Offender Laws: Can Treatment, Punishment, Incapacitation, and Public Safety be Reconciled?" by Mary Ann Farkas and Amy Stichman (Reading 15)
- "The Experiences and Attitudes of Registered Female Sex Offenders" by Richard Tewkesbury (Reading 16)

- "Psychopathy: Etiology, Diagnosis and Treatment" by Gary Zajac (Reading (21)
- "Equal or Equitable: An Exploration of Educational and Vocational Program Availability for Male and Female Offenders" by Karen F. Lahm (Reading 22)
- "How to Prevent Prisoner Reentry Programs from Failing: Insights from Evidence Based Correction" by Shelley Johnson Listwan, Francis T. Cullen, and Edward J. Latessa (Reading 24)
- "Parole Violations and Revocations in California: Analysis and Suggestions for Action" by Ryken Grattet, Joan Petersilia, and Jeffrey Lin, and Marlene Beckman (Reading 27)
- "Putting Public Safety First: 13 Strategies for Successful Supervision and Reentry" from the Pew Center on the States (Reading 28)
- "One in 100: Behind Bars in America" from the Pew Center on the States (Reading 29)
- "Social Consequences of the War on Drugs: The Legacy of Failed Policy" by Eric L. Jensen, Jerg Gerber, and Clayton Mosher (Reading 30)

In addition, the following chapter has been updated for the fourth edition: "Halfway Houses," by Edward J. Latessa, Lawrence F. Travis, III, and Christopher Lowenkamp (Reading 25)

ACKNOWLEDGMENTS

We wish to express our sincere appreciation to those who gave their time and effort in many different capacities to assist us in assembling this anthology.

First, to the many reviewers of previous editions who took the time to provide feedback and critiques—thank you. We read each review carefully and tried our best to incorporate the suggestions offered. We hope that this edition meets your needs and appreciate your help in improving this manuscript.

Further, we wish to express our sincere appreciation to those who gave their time and effort in many different capacities to assist us in assembling this anthology: Janice Miller of the University of Cincinnati, Kristi Holsinger of the University of Missouri–Kansas City, and Sherith Pankratz of Oxford University Press. Finally, we would like to thank the following scholars who reviewed the manuscript for this edition for their insights: Natasha A. Frost, Northeastern University; Dena Hanley, University of Akron; Andrea Leverentz, University of Massachusetts—Boston; Shannon Womer Phaneuf, Indiana University of Pennsylvania; and Deborah Koetzle Shaffer, University of Nevada—Las Vegas. Thank you.

ABOUT THE EDITORS

Edward J. Latessa, Ph.D.

Edward J. Latessa received his Ph.D. from the Ohio State University in 1979 and is a Professor and Director of the School of Criminal Justice at the University of Cincinnati. Dr. Latessa has published over 110 works in the area of criminal justice, corrections, and juvenile justice. He is coauthor of seven books, including Corrections in the Community and Corrections in America. Professor Latessa has directed over 100 funded research projects, including studies of day reporting centers, juvenile justice programs, drug courts, intensive supervision programs, halfway houses, and drug programs. He and his staff have also assessed over 550 correctional programs throughout the United States, and he has provided assistance and workshops in over 40 states. Dr. Latessa served as President of the Academy of Criminal Justice Sciences (1989–1990). He has also received several awards, including The Mark Hatfield Award for contributions in public policy research by The Hatfield School of Government at Portland State University (2009), the Outstanding Achievement Award by the National Juvenile Justice Court Services Association (2007), the August Vollmer Award from the American Society of Criminology (2004), the Simon Dinitz Criminal Justice Research Award from the Ohio Department of Rehabilitation and Correction (2002), the Margaret Mead Award for dedicated service to the causes of social justice and humanitarian advancement by the International Community Corrections Association (2001), the Peter P. Lejins Award for Research from the American Correctional Association (1999), an ACJS Fellow Award (1998), an ACJS Founders Award (1992), and the Simon Dinitz award by the Ohio Community Corrections Organization.

Alexander M. Holsinger, Ph.D.

For the last several years Alexander M. Holsinger has been conducting research, teaching, and training in the areas of offender classification, risk prediction, correctional program effectiveness, and criminological theory. He received his Ph.D. in Criminal Justice from the University of Cincinnati, School of Criminal Justice (1999). His research areas include offender assessment and classification, gun violence reduction strategies, offender reentry, community corrections, and program effectiveness. He has assisted several municipal, county, and state agencies with the implementation of the best practices in offender assessment and classification and correctional treatment intervention. His teaching consists of several different corrections-based courses as well as statistics and research methods. He is currently an Associate Professor in the Department of Criminal Justice and Criminology at the University of Missouri–Kansas City. In addition to his academic pursuits, he serves as President of the Inmate Services Advisory Board for the Jackson County Detention Center and is a member of the Missouri Department of Corrections' Citizen Advisory Board.

ABOUT THE CONTRIBUTORS

Don A. Andrews is Emeritus Professor of Psychology at Carleton University.

Marlene Beckman is at the National Institute of Justice.

Tim Bynum is Professor of Criminal Justice at Michigan State University.

Jack E. Call is Professor of Criminal Justice at Radford University.

Madeline Carter is a Principle with the Center for Effective Public Policy.

Donald Clemmer completed pioneering research in 1940 on the prison inmate subculture in his book *The Prison Community.*

Terry Conover is the author of *Newjack: Guarding Sing Sing.*

Francis T. Cullen is Distinguished Research Professor of Criminal Justice at the University of Cincinnati.

Mary Ann Farkas is Associate Professor in Criminology and Law Studies at Marquette University.

Paul Gendreau is Emeritus Professor of Psychology at the University of New Brunswick and Visiting Professor of Criminal Justice at the University of Cincinnati.

Jurg Gerber is Professor in the College of Criminal Justice at Sam Houston State University.

Ryken Grattet is Professor of Sociology at the University of California at Davis.

Craig Haney is director of the Program in Legal Studies at the University of California in Santa Cruz.

Eliot S. Hartstone is President of Spectrum Research Associates.

Victor Hassine was an inmate in the Pennsylvania Department of Corrections. In 2008 he died in prison under unusual circumstances.

Rodney J. Henningsen is on the faculty in the College of Criminal Justice at Sam Houston State University.

Eric L. Jenson is Professor of Sociology at the University of Idaho.

Robert Johnson teaches in the Department of Justice, Law, and Society at The American University.

W. Wesley Johnson is Professor in the School of Criminal Justice, Southern Mississippi State University.

Karen F. Lahm is Assistant Professor of Sociology at Wright State University.

Edward J. Latessa is Professor and Director of the School of Criminal Justice at the University of Cincinnati.

Thomas P. LeBel is Assistant Professor of Criminal Justice at the University of Wisconsin at Milwaukee.

Jeffrey Lin is Assistant Professor of Sociology and Criminology at the University of Denver.

Shelley Johnson Listwan is Associate Professor of Justice Studies at Kent State University.

Christopher T. Lowenkamp is Director of Research for the U.S. Administrative Office of the Courts.

James W. Marquart is Professor in the School of Economic, Political, and Policy Sciences at the University of Texas at Dallas.

Robert Martinson was a member of the New York State Governor's Special Committee on Criminal Offenders, which was responsible for the analysis of the effectiveness of treatment programs that resulted in the publication of the infamous *Martinson Report*.

Shadd Maruna is Professor of Justice and Human Development at the School of Law at Queens University of Belfast.

Scott Matson is an Associate of the Center for Effective Public Policy.

John Monahan is Professor of Law at the University of Virginia.

Clayton Mosher is Associate Professor in the Department of Sociology at Washington State University at Vancouver.

Janet L. Mullings is Associate Dean in the College of Criminal Justice at Sam Houston State University.

Charles Onley is an Associate of the Center for Effective Public Policy.

Maria C. W. Peeters is on the faculty in the Department of Psychology at Utrecht University in the Netherlands.

Joan Petersilia is a Professor in the School of Social Ecology at the University of California at Irvine.

Nicole Hahn Rafter teaches in the College of Criminal Justice at Northeastern University.

Pamela Clark Robbins is Vice President of Policy Research Associates in Delmar, New York.

David J. Rothman is Bernard Schoenberg Professor of Social Medicine and Professor of History at Columbia University.

Wilmar B. Schaufeli is Professor of Work and Organizational Psychology at Utrecht University in the Netherlands.

Thorsten Sellin was Emeritus Professor of Sociology at the University of Pennsylvania.

Pieter C. Spierenburg teaches in the Department of History at Erasmus University in Rotterdam, Holland.

Henry J. Steadman is President of Policy Research Associates in Delmar, New York.

Amy Stichman is Assistant Professor of Criminal Justice at North Dakota State University.

Richard Tewksbury is Professor of Administration of Justice at the University of Louisville.

Lawrence F. Travis III is Professor of Criminal Justice and Director of the Center for Criminal Justice Research at the University of Cincinnati.

Terry Wells is in the Department of Government, Georgia College and State University **in Milledgeville, Georgia.**

Robert Worley is on the faculty at Pennsylvania State University at Altoona.

Gary Zajac is Director of Research and Evaluation for the Pennsylvania Department of Corrections.

Philip Zimbardo is a Professor of Psychology at Stanford University.

INTRODUCTION

Prior to the nineteenth century in the United States, facilities designed to hold offenders were largely regarded as a vehicle toward an ultimate end—punishment of some form or another for persons who had committed a crime against another individual. Detainment was merely a means of holding an individual while he or she awaited "real" punishment. The punishment to be carried out was often a publicly held flogging, branding, disfigurement, a lengthy term in the stocks, or execution. Realization of the brutality of these punishments, coupled with a societal philosophical shift (embodied by the Enlightenment), led to the birth of the penitentiary. From that point forward, punishment in the United States has mainly comprised a term in an institution, living in congregate style with many other individuals who have met a similar fate. This is not to say, however, that the birth of the prison meant an end to somewhat brutal practices within the walls of the institution.

The original purpose of early penitentiaries was to instill repentance in the offender (hence, the root of the term, *penitent*). Reform was certainly the goal, but primarily by way of the errant offenders seeking forgiveness from God, through the (at times silent) contemplation of their "sins."

Since that time, the penitentiary has undergone many changes in both form and philosophy. Religious atonement was put aside, and a concentration on skill development (through educational and vocational programming) took its place. Other changes occurred in the U.S. sentencing structure, perhaps most notably with the advent of the indeterminate sentence. This paved the way for what came to be known as the medical model. Offenders would be housed in prison until they "became better" or had been "healed." Not surprisingly, this model rested on the assumption that the prison was indeed *able* to identify, target, and change the factors that had led someone into criminal activity. Because of disparities in sentencing, the indeterminate sentence has largely been replaced by determinate sentencing structures (along with the instigation of the "justice model"). Part I of this text explores the origins of punishment and charts the development of the institution as a form of punishment. In addition, trends in sentencing as well as the evolution of treatment and correctional policy are presented and analyzed.

Life inside an institution (regardless of its size) provides a unique set of parameters around which the individual must conform. As such, much study during the twentieth century was directed toward the effect that the institution has on individuals and groups. Similarly, researchers have studied how individuals and groups affect and shape the institution. This inquiry has motivated the study of both inmates and correctional workers. Several hypotheses have been formulated and investigated regarding what the most important factors are in the prison environment. Because the prison is a "total institution," it has provided a somewhat self-contained laboratory for the student of human interaction. Until the mid-twentieth century, many never imagined that the offender could have an impact on the day-to-day routine within the institution in the long term. Part I in this new fourth edition has remained unchanged, presenting important classic works that explore the development of the institution as a punitive concept, as well as the important changes that have occurred in sentencing in the United States. Specifically, two pieces document changes in sentencing practices and how they have been influenced by the philosophies of punishment. Part II focuses solely on living within the prison environment with three pieces that each deal with a different aspect of prison life. The chosen articles represent a collection of pieces rich in depth and detail regarding the first-hand experience of being an inmate inside a prison. The "convict code" as well as the development of "supermax" prisons are explored.

Working inside a secure environment represents a unique experience that few if any other occupations simulate. As such, this fourth edition includes a new part that focuses solely on working within the prison environment. Part III contains two new articles—one of which focuses on correctional officers dealing with inmates who target them, as well as one that presents an analysis of correctional officer stress and burnout—subject matter of increasing importance as prison populations continue to increase. Also included is a reading rich in detail representing one man's experience as a new officer in the storied Sing Sing prison.

Although some have argued about the details of the true beginning of significant inmate litigation (i.e., the prisoners' rights movement), some important changes occurred during the twentieth century that have influenced both prisons and the numbers of individuals sent to them. Perhaps most notably, courts have shown a willingness to check the conditions inside an institution. This refers to both physical and procedural conditions. The advent of these rights has served to change the prison experience for many offenders and has also brought forth issues regarding the institutions' ability to modify behavior in the long term (post-release). Legislation has also developed in recent years requiring offenders to register with local law enforcement offices, which in turn place this information in the public domain (particularly in the case of sex offenders). In response to these important old issues as well as new developments, Part IV contains two new articles that deal with sex offenders. The effect of sex offender registries on the female offender population is examined, as is the extent to which treatment, punishment, incapacitation, and public safety can be reconciled in light of this special population. Also presented are two pieces taking a broad historical and future look at U.S. prison policy, as well as the evolution of the Supreme Court's position on prisoner rights.

Several studies of offender treatment within institutions and in the community have revealed the efficacy of correctional treatment, provided it is the correct treatment directed toward the correct populations. Advances have been made in the areas of offender classification and treatment mechanisms, for instance. Treatment programs regarding substance abuse, sexual offending, and educational/vocational training have been examined to specify in detail what works and how. In addition, specific populations, such as mentally disordered offenders and the growing number of female offenders, have been scrutinized in the same way. Part V provides a broad and detailed examination of the history and current state of correctional treatment intervention within both the institutional correctional setting and corrections in general. Two new articles have been added to this fourth edition, one of which deals with an increasingly critical issue to correctional settings—the etiology, diagnosis, and treatment of the psychopathic offender. The other new piece examines the extent and types of treatment that are available to the female offender population and the male offender population. The result is a series of readings that explore the most pertinent issues when considering what is necessary to produce long-term change in an offender. Simultaneously, several specific issues, including treating the female offender population and special needs populations (such as the mentally disordered offender), are also examined. The origin of well-intentioned but ill-designed (and at times damaging) programming is explored as well.

Offender reentry into the community has moved to the forefront of correctional policy debate over the last several years. An increasing amount of attention has been devoted to all issues relating to the offender who spends some time in prison and then reenters society. Just as prison populations have continued to increase, so too have the populations of former inmates who are residing in the community (either completely on their own or under the supervision of a parole officer). Three new articles have been added to this fourth edition and constitute the majority of Part VI, "Reentry into the Community." One policy piece deals specifically with the best way for agencies to respond to parole violations and revocations. One article also deals broadly with the 13 strategies for successful supervision and reentry. In addition, since many offenders reenter the community with unmet needs, a new article in this part explores ways, from an evidence-based perspective, to prevent reentry programs from failing. Also explored in this part are the historical significance and effectiveness of halfway houses in America, as well as the "reentry courts"—a programming strategy that is experiencing increasing popularity.

Part VII, "Contemporary Issues," includes two new articles that explore two pertinent and dynamic issues within corrections: America's ever-increasing prison population and the net consequences of the "war on drugs." Some have argued that this war planted seeds that have finally come to fruition in the form of burgeoning prison populations—as evidenced by a recently released Pew Report revealing that for the first time in history America's incarceration rate was greater than 1 in 100 persons. These two readings, combined with an article reprinted from the previous edition, provide food for thought as the correctional system in the United States continues to grow and change at an increasing rate. When considering the history and the present state of corrections in America, the only constant appears to be dynamic change.

PART

I

HISTORY AND PURPOSE OF PUNISHMENT AND IMPRISONMENT

Perhaps one of the greatest and most complex social dilemmas has been the processing and treatment of the social deviant. Members of any society who do not follow rules and norms pose a natural threat to the group as a whole. Mechanisms and strategies have long been in place to deal with the errant, but the form and reason behind them have varied greatly over the centuries. However, the underlying goal has remained constant—finding ways to respond to and correct what can be a complex set of problems within each individual.

Although the traditional Auburn-style prison is perhaps the most common image representing punishment in the United States, dealing with offenders has a somewhat varied past. Prior to the nineteenth century, for instance, confinement was viewed as a means to an end, rather than an end in and of itself. Large-scale facilities designed to meet any correctional goal did not exist to any great degree. Instead, confinement occurred briefly, prior to the actual punishment, which was often.

Pre-Enlightenment punishments were often biblically based and corporal in nature. Brandings, whippings, stocks and pillories, ducking stools, thumbscrews, and execution were fashioned and performed to humiliate offenders publicly. Through pain and public humiliation, offenders were expected to atone for their social sins—sins committed against God, a monarch, and/or society. This served an assumed secondary goal of general deterrence. Public punishment was in part a warning to others of their potential fate should they commit similar offenses.

There is no dispute that pre-Enlightenment punishment in general was severe. What often compounded the severity of the punishment were instances where the punishment clearly did not fit the crime. It was not uncommon for petty thefts, adultery, or vagrancy (just to name a few examples) to carry disproportionate and permanently (physically) disfiguring government responses. One of the social forces that created a correctional conversion was quite possibly public outrage at this disproportionate sentencing structure. Perhaps the desired effect of general deterrence created an unintended consequence of raising public awareness (and outcry) to what was perceived as an unfair state response to relatively minor behavior.

The Enlightenment brought about great change in the application of punishment, in large part because of thinkers such as Beccaria, Bentham, and Voltaire. The net effect of the writings of these philosophers and others was to draw attention to the brutality meted out by the state at that time. As a result, confinement itself was identified as a new "end" in the punishment spectrum. Housing offenders together in large-scale, secure facilities would allow for the accomplishment of different and apparently more humane goals.

In the United States, 1819 saw the birth of the penitentiary in Auburn, New York, with many other states soon implementing this correctional strategy. Although public floggings, drawing and quartering, and other forms of torture were placed aside, the conditions inside this first American prison were in many respects no less destructive.

Originally, prisoners were not afforded opportunities for activity (leisure or labor); they were kept in total isolation from one another, and total silence was enforced. Provisions were minimal, conditions were dreary, and offenders were required to contemplate a sin-free (i.e., crime-free) lifestyle. The unfair humiliation and cruel disfiguring punishments largely criticized by Enlightenment philosophers had become a thing of the past. The alternative, however, resulted in punishment turning into a much longer, drawn-out affair with its own set of drawbacks, despite the overarching goal that offenders should contemplate and ultimately reject a sinful lifestyle. Nevertheless, the Auburn-style prison set the stage for a new era in corrections—one that still determines practices of imprisonment.

In addition to a reconsideration of the delivery of punishment, the Enlightenment brought about other changes in the criminal justice system—principally, the seeds of due process. The nineteenth century also ushered in questions regarding the causation of crime (at both the individual and the societal levels). The belief that human beings are indeed free to choose a criminal lifestyle further opened up the possibility that they can just as well choose a crime-free lifestyle.

Although the housing of offenders in large-scale penitentiaries was designed to invoke positive change, offenders were nonetheless viewed largely as slaves of the state.

Issues arose throughout the nineteenth and twentieth centuries regarding the value of prison industrial labor, the management of increasing populations of offenders, and the challenges of handling a more diverse population with complex needs.

At several points during the nineteenth and twentieth centuries, the purposes and practices of imprisonment were reviewed and critiqued. Propositions were put forth questioning practices that inhibit offender reform. This is of particular importance (even today), since correctional options have been reduced to essentially one—imprisonment.

Over the past 200 years, the United States has relied heavily on imprisonment as the general population has swelled and as new crime enforcement strategies (e.g., the war on crime, the war on drugs, and three-strikes legislation) have boosted prisoner populations. The dilemma of overcrowded prisons that may not be capable of rehabilitating prisoners has called into question the true utility of such a strategy. Hence, America's imprisonment binge is under consideration in hopes of revealing pathways toward improvement. The reader of the following selections is encouraged to take note of the true origins of modern-day punishment, especially the contributions from Enlightenment thinkers. The movement from arbitrary corporal punishment to methods of mass confinement may be viewed as an improvement in some respects. However, the long-term consequences brought on by the accompanying set of problems caused by large-scale imprisonment are deserving of more thought.

1
THE SPECTACLE OF SUFFERING

PIETER C. SPIERENBURG

Pieter C. Spierenburg reveals the origins of the criminal justice system through an investigation of the beginnings of state-enforced punishment. The feudal system in Western Europe provides the backdrop for what ultimately represents a shift away from personal vengeance as the primary impetus for punishment. Criminal behavior came to be viewed as a sin against the state, rather than a sin against another individual. As such, it became the state's responsibility to regulate the processing of offenders. Secondary to the rise of the nation-state as a precursor of state-enforced punishment is urbanization. Although urbanization may have provided an initial opportunity for greater public display of punishment that was rooted in general deterrence, it was ultimately the revulsion of the public that led to what Spierenburg calls the privatization of repression. Above all else, Spierenburg highlights the importance of considering the greater social context when analyzing major changes in a society's punishing mechanisms.

THE EMERGENCE OF CRIMINAL JUSTICE

From the way in which I have defined repression, it is obvious that its evolution should be intimately connected with the development of the state. The practice of criminal justice was one of the means by which authorities, with or without success, attempted to keep the population in line. As the position of these authorities changed, the character of criminal justice changed. However, before we can speak of criminal justice in any society, at least a rudimentary state organization has to be present. A system of repression presupposes a minimal level of state formation. Differentiation of this system, moreover, also presupposes the rise of towns. This . . . is an attempt to trace the origins of preindustrial repression. . . . It focuses on repression as a system of control, the emergence of which was a function of the rise of territorial principalities and of urbanization.

At the height of the feudal age in Western Europe the state hardly existed at all. Violent entrepreneurs were in constant competition; from his castle a baron would dominate the immediate surroundings and de facto recognize no higher authority. His domain may be called a unit of attack and defense but not a state. Essentially it comprised a network of ties of affiliation and bondage. But in the violent competition between the numerous chiefs of such networks the mechanism was imminent which would eventually lead to the emergence of states. The first units with the character of a state were the territorial principalities which appeared from the twelfth century onwards.

As it happens, the emergence of criminal justice also dates from the twelfth century. Several legal historians have studied the "birth of punishment" or "emergence of public penal law." The most detailed work is by P. W. A. Immink. This author also comes closest to a sociological-historical view of the subject. He placed the origins of punishment in the context of changing relationships of freedom and dependence in feudal society. Thus he avoided presenting an analysis of legal texts alone, which can be very misleading especially for the period in question. From a sociological-historical perspective, the essence of criminal justice is a relationship of subordination. This was noted by Immink: "In common parlance the term 'punishment' is never used unless the person upon whom the penalty is inflicted is clearly subordinate to the one imposing the penal act." This is the crucial point. This element distinguishes punishment from vengeance and the feud, where the parties are equal. If there is no subordination, there is no punishment.

The earliest subordinates in Europe were slaves. In that agrarian society, from Germanic times up into the feudal period, freemen were not subject to a penal system, but unfree persons were. The lord of a manor exercised an almost absolute authority over his serfs. When the latter were beaten or put to death "or maybe even fined" for some illegal act, this can certainly be called punishment. The manorial penal system of those early ages belonged to the realm of custom and usually did not form part of written law. Therefore we do not know much about it. The Barbarian Codes (*Leges Barbarorum*) were meant for freemen. They only referred to unfree persons in cases where their actions could lead to a conflict between freemen.

Free persons, on the other hand, settled their conflicts personally. There were a few exceptions to this, even in Germanic times. In certain cases, if a member was held to have acted against the vital interests of the tribe, he could be expelled from the tribal community (branded a "wolf") or even killed. But on the whole, as there was no arbiter strong enough to impose his will, private individuals settled their own conflicts. A settlement could be reached through revenge or reconciliation. Vengeance and the feud were accepted forms of private retaliation, but they did not necessarily follow every injury. In a situation where violence is not monopolized, private violence is potentially omnipresent but does not always manifest itself in practice. Notably, it can be bought off. Reconciliation through payment to the injured party was already known in Tacitus' time.

To the earliest powerful rulers who represented an embryonic public authority, encouragement of this custom was the obvious road to be taken if they wished to reduce private violence. This is in fact what the Barbarian Codes are all about. In every instance they fix the amount which can buy off vengeance. These sums are not fines in the modern sense, but indemnities. They were either meant as compensation when a person had been killed, wounded or assaulted (*wergeld*) or as a form of restitution when property had been stolen, destroyed or damaged. Among freemen this remained the dominant system well into the twelfth century.

Criminal justice, however, slowly developed alongside this system. Its evolution during the feudal period was construed by Immink as one argument against the thesis put forward by Viktor Achter. The latter had argued that punishment suddenly emerged in Languedoc in the middle of the twelfth century, from where it spread to the rest of Europe. Although Immink placed the definite breakthrough around the same time, he believed the evolution of punishment was inextricably linked with feudalism. The feudalization of Western Europe had brought about a fundamental change in the notion of freedom. This change eventually led to the emergence of criminal justice.

Before the feudal age the notion of freedom was closely connected to the allod. An allod should not be considered as a piece of property in the modern sense, but rather as an estate which is free from outside interference. Its occupant is completely his own master. His freedom implies a total independence from any worldly power and is similar to what later came to be called sovereignty. Hence the relationship of a freeman with the unfree persons subject to him, and over whom he exercises a right of punishment, is not one of owner-owned but one of ruler-ruled. The development of the institution of vassalage slowly put an end to the notion of freedom based on the allod. The Frankish kings and their successors attached freemen to themselves in a relationship of lord and *fideles*. Hence the latter were no longer entirely independent. By the time the whole network of feudal ties had finally been established, the notion of freedom had been transformed. Freedom meant being bound directly to the king, or to be more precise, there were degrees of freedom depending on how direct the allegiance was.

The feudal transformation of the notion of freedom formed the basis of the emergence of a penal system applied to freemen. The king remained the only free person in the ancient allodial sense, the only sovereign. His reaction to a breach of faith by his vassal (*infidelitas*, felony), usually the imposition of death, can truly be called punishment. The king himself never had a *wergeld*, because no one was his equal. His application of punishment for *infidelitas* resembled the exercise of justice by a master over his serfs. When more and more illegal acts were defined as felonies, the emergence of a penal system with corporal and capital punishments applied to freemen became steadily more apparent.

The implication of Immink's analysis for the study of state formation processes is evident. Absence of a central authority is reflected in the prevalence of private vengeance, the feud or voluntary reconciliation. The development of criminal justice runs parallel to the emergence of slightly stronger rulers. Originally it is only practiced within the confines of a manor; later it is applied by the rulers of kingdoms and territories. But we do not have to accept every part of Immink's story. For one thing, in his description the evolution of criminal justice and the parallel decline of the feud appeared too much as an unlinear process. This follows partly from his criticism of Achter. The latter, for instance, saw the legal reforms of the Carolingian period as a precocious spurt in the direction of a breakthrough of a modern notion of punishment. This would be in line with the fact that this period also witnessed a precocious sort of monopoly of authority. Achter considered the spurt as an isolated episode followed by centuries of silence. This may be too crude. Immink, however, with his conception of an ultimate continuity, seems to go too far in the other direction, playing down the unsettled character of the ninth and tenth centuries. These were certainly times when the vendetta was prevalent, despite whatever intentions legislators might have harbored. On the other hand, we should not overestimate the degree of monopolization of authority around AD 800. The Carolingian Empire and its successor kingdoms were no more than temporary sets of allegiances over a wide geographic area, held together by the personal prestige of an individual king or by a military threat from outside. From Roman times until the twelfth century Europe witnessed nothing approaching a state, but there were certainly spurts in that direction.

In the middle of the twelfth century the first territorial principalities made their appearance and a penal system applied to freemen was established. The symbiosis is evident. Criminal justice emerged because the territorial princes were the first rulers powerful enough to combat private vengeance to a certain degree. The church had already attempted to do so, but largely in vain. I leave aside the question of whether its representatives were motivated by ideological reasons or by the desire to protect ecclesiastical goods. In any case they needed the strong arm of secular powers in order to succeed. The *treuga Dei* only acquired some measure of effectiveness when it became the "country's peace." Two of the earliest regions to witness this development were Angevin England "which can also be seen as a territorial principality" and the duchy of Aquitaine.

Incidentally, the South of France is also the region where, according to Achter, the concept of punishment originated. It is interesting that he reached this conclusion even though he used quite different sources and from a different perspective. Achter considered the element of moral disapproval as the essence of punishment. This notion was largely absent from Germanic law, which did not differentiate between accidents and intentional acts. If a felled tree accidentally killed a man the full *wergeld* still had to be paid. Immink criticized this view and it may be another point where his rejection is too radical. He indicated, in fact, how Achter's view can be integrated into an approach focusing on state-formation processes. For the private avenger redressing a personal wrong, the wickedness of the other party is so self-evident that it need not be stated. As long as the law merely attempts to encourage reconciliation, it is likewise indifferent to a moral appreciation of the acts which started the conflict. When territorial lords begin to administer punishments to persons who have not wronged them personally, their attitudes to the law change as well. Theorizing about the law increases. The beginnings of a distinction between civil and criminal cases become apparent. The latter are *iniquitates,* acts that are to be disapproved of morally and which put their author at the *misericordia* of his lord.

Thus it is understandable that a new emphasis on the moral reprehensibility of illegal acts also dates from the middle of the twelfth century. Indeed this period witnessed an early wave of moralization-individualization, connected to what medievalists have long been accustomed to call the Renaissance of the twelfth century. And yet we should not overestimate this spurt towards individualization, certainly not with regard to penal practice. Before the twelfth century there may have been even less concern for the motives and intentions of the perpetrators of illegal acts, but...the practice of criminal justice continued to focus on crimes and their impact on the community rather than on the criminal's personality and the intricacies of his guilt. Up into the nineteenth century repression was not primarily individualized.

There is another aspect of the transformation under discussion which merits attention. When a malefactor finds himself at the mercy (*misericordia*) of a prince, the implication is that a religious notion has entered criminal justice. Mercy was an attribute of God, the ultimate judge. The relationship of all people with God had always been viewed as one of subordination. Hence God was indeed able to punish. Any wrong suffered, such as the loss of a combat, could be seen as a divine punishment, of which another man was merely the agent. Heavenly justice was never an automatic response. The Lord could be severe or show mercy. By analogy this line of thought was also applied to human justice practiced by a territorial lord.

Several authors discussed the "sacred quality" of preindustrial punishment and even considered it an explanatory factor for its character. According to this view, executions, especially capital ones, were a sort of sacrifice, an act of expiation. They reconciled the deity offended by the crime and restored the order of society sanctioned by heaven. This notion may have been part of the experience of executions, although there is little direct evidence for it. But it would certainly be incorrect to attribute an explanatory value to it as being in some way the essence of public punishment. For one thing, during and after the Middle Ages *every* social event also had a religious element. In the absence of a division between the sacred and the profane, religion pervaded life entirely. To note the sacred quality of executions in this context is actually redundant. If a religious view of the world has to "explain" public punishment in any way, it should do so in a more specific sense. But the evolution which gave rise to criminal justice hardly lends support to this view. Criminal justice arose out of changing relationships of freedom and dependence in the secular world. It was extended by powerful princes at the expense of vengeance and the feud. Ecclesiastics had indeed already advocated harsh corporal penalties in the tenth century. But they too favored these merely as alternatives to the vendetta. Their wishes were realized by the territorial princes of the twelfth century. Only then, when powerful lords applied a new form of justice, did notions of mercy, guilt and moral reprehensibility enter the picture; rather as a consequence than as a cause of the transformation. That clergymen should figure in the drama on the scaffold during the next centuries is only natural. As will be argued in this study, the role of the church remained largely instrumental in a spectacle which primarily served the purposes of the secular authorities.

The transformation during the twelfth century was only a small beginning. First, private vengeance had been pushed back to a certain degree, but continued to be practiced throughout the later Middle Ages. Second, generally the various courts were not in a very powerful position. Often they acted merely as mediators facilitating the reconciliation of the parties involved. A resolute practice of criminal justice depended as before on a certain measure of state power and levels of state power continued to fluctuate. But state formation is not the only process to which the further development of criminal justice was linked. A new factor entered the stage: urbanization. During the later Middle Ages the peculiar conditions prevailing in towns increasingly made their mark on the practice of justice. This situation was not equally marked everywhere. In a country such as France alterations in criminal procedure largely ran parallel with the growth of royal power. In the Netherlands, on the other hand, the towns were the major agents of change.

During the early stages of urban development the social context actually formed a counter-influence to the establishment of criminal justice. Originally, relationships of subordination did not prevail in cities. The charters of most towns recognized the inhabitants as free citizens. It has long been commonplace in historiography to note that the urban presence was encapsulated into feudal society. The body of citizens became the vassal, as it were, of the lord of the territory. The town was often a relatively independent corporation, a *coniuratio*. *Vis-à-vis* each other the citizens were equal. The councils ruling these cities were not very powerful. There were hardly any authorities in a real sense, who could impose their will and control events.

This situation left plenty of room for private violence. As the degree of pacification around the towns was still relatively low, so was the degree of internal pacification. To be sure, the vendetta might be officially forbidden. In the Northern Netherlands the prohibition was legitimized by the notion of a quasi-lineage: the citizens were held to be mutual relatives and a feud cannot arise among relatives. But the fiction of lineage could never prevent actual feuds from bursting out, as the prohibitions, reiterated well into the fifteenth century, suggest. Similarly, proclamations ordering a truce between parties were frequent until the middle of the sixteenth century. An early seventeenth-century commentator gives a good impression of the situation. Speaking of the 1390s, he denounces the lawlessness of the age:

> The people were still rough and wild in this time because of their newly won freedom and practically everyone acted as he pleased. And for that reason the court had neither the esteem nor the power which it ought to have in a well-founded commonwealth. This appears from the homicides, fights and wanton acts which occurred daily and also from the old sentences, in which one sees with what kind of timidity the Gentlemen judged in such cases: for they bargained first and took an oath from the criminals that they would not do *schout, schepenen* and burgomasters harm because of whatever sentence they would pass against them. And the most severe, almost, which they imposed on someone, was a banishment or that the criminals would make a pilgrimage here or there before they came in [to town] again, or that they would give the city money for three or four thousand stones. They also often licensed one or the other, if he was under attack from his party, that he might defend himself with impunity, even if he killed the other in doing so. These are things which have no place in cities where the law is in its proper position of power.

Apart from the fact that this situation was considered abnormal in the seventeenth century, we note an acceptance of forms of private violence and the predominance of a reconciliatory stand instead of serious punishment. Towards the end of the fifteenth century, however, this began to change. The ruling elites finally became real authorities. Patriciates emerged everywhere, constituting a socially superior group. The towns became increasingly stratified. The patrician courts could act as superiors notably towards the lower and lower-middle class citizens. In the towns of the Netherlands this development is clearly reflected in their ways of dealing with criminal cases. For a long time the main business of the courts had been to mediate and register private reconciliations. Around 1500 "corrections" gradually outnumbered reconciliations. The former were measures expressing a justice from above and often consisted of corporal punishment.

Another development in criminal law which took place during the same period, was even more crucial. A new procedure in criminal trials, the inquisitorial, gradually superseded the older, accusatory procedure. This change occurred throughout Continental Europe, but not in England. The accusatory trial, when nothing else existed, was geared to a system of marginal justice. Where the inquisitorial trial prevailed, a justice from above had been established more firmly.

The contrast between the two procedures is a familiar item in legal history. Here it suffices to review briefly the relevant characteristics. The inquisitorial procedure had been developed in ecclesiastical law, and was perfected by the institution which took its name from it. From the middle of the thirteenth century onwards it entered into secular law. Generally speaking, the rules of the accusatory trial favored the accused, while the rules of the inquisitorial one favored those bent on condemning him. The former procedure was much concerned with the preservation of equality between the parties. Thus if the accused was imprisoned during the trial "which was not usually the case" the accuser was often imprisoned as well. Moreover, if the latter could not prove his case, he might be subjected to the *talion:* the same penalty which the former would have received if he had been convicted. While the proceedings in the older trial were carried out in the open, the newer one was conducted in secrecy. Publicity was only sought after the verdict had been reached.

The most important element of the inquisitorial procedure, however, was the possibility of prosecution *ex officio.* The adage of the older procedure, "no plaintiff, no judge," lost its validity. If it wished to, the court could take the initiative and start an investigation (*inquisitio*). Its officials would collect denunciations and then arrest a suspect, if they could lay hands on him. The court's prosecutor acted as plaintiff. Thus an active prosecution policy was possible for the first time. In the trial the authorities and the accused faced each other and the power distribution between the two was unequal, favoring the former. Under the accusatory procedure the authorities had hardly been more than bystanders. Consequently the rise of the newer form of trial meant a further spread of a system of justice from above.

This is also implicit in the final element to be noted. The inquisitorial procedure brought the introduction of torture. An accused who persisted in denial, yet was heavily suspect, could be subjected to a "sharper examination." It is evident that the principle of equality between parties under the accusatory procedure would have been incompatible with the practice of torture. Torture was not unknown in Europe before the thirteenth century. It had long been a common feature of the administration of justice by a lord over his serfs. Under the inquisitorial procedure torture could for the first time also be applied to free persons. The parallel with the transformation discussed above is obvious.

The retreat of the accusatory before the inquisitorial procedure did not occur at the same pace everywhere. That the older one was originally more common is reflected in the names of "ordinary" and "extraordinary" procedure which the two forms acquired and often retained throughout the *ancien regime*. The gradual establishment of the primacy of the latter took place between the middle of the thirteenth and the beginning of the sixteenth century. Its use in France by Philip the Fair against the Templars paved the way for its further spread. Prosecution *ex officio* increased in importance from the fourteenth to the sixteenth centuries. The growth of royal power was the main force behind it. In the Netherlands, North and South, the cities formed the most important theater. The formation of patrician elites facilitated the shift. But here too the central authorities confirmed it. In 1570, when the Dutch Revolt was already in the process of breaking out, Philip II issued his criminal ordinances, which clearly favored the inquisitorial trial.

In the Dutch towns non-residents were the first to be tried according to the inquisitorial procedure. As outsiders they were more easily subjected to justice from above. Citizens occasionally put up resistance to it, in Malines, for example. In France it was the nobles of Burgundy, Champagne and Artois who protested. Louis X granted them privileges in 1315 which implied a suspension of inquisitorial proceedings. In the end they were unsuccessful. The forces of centralization and urbanization favored the development of a more rigorous penal system.

England forms a partial exception. Criminal procedure in that country remained largely accusatory throughout the preindustrial period. Nevertheless, essentially these developments can be observed there too, and in the end processes of pacification and centralization brought about a firmer establishment of criminal justice. Originally there had been plenty of room for private violence, just as on the Continent. An outlaw or "wolf," for instance, could be captured by any man and be slain if he resisted. This right was abrogated in 1329, but as late as 1397 a group of men who had arrested and beheaded an outlawed felon, were pardoned because they had thought it was lawful. Around 1400 it was not uncommon for justices to be threatened with violence by the parties in a lawsuit. The power of the courts went up and down with the fluctuations in the power of a central authority. It was the Tudors, finally, who gradually established a monopoly of violence over most of England. Consequently, except in border areas, the feud definitely gave way to litigation. The available literature on crime and justice in early modern England suggests that a system of prosecution of serious crimes, physical punishment and exemplary repression prevailed there, which was basically similar to that on the Continent.

Thus, the emergence and stabilization of criminal justice, a process going on from the late twelfth until the early sixteenth centuries, meant the disappearance of private vengeance. Ultimately vengeance was transferred from the victims and their relatives to the state. Whereas formerly a man would kill his brother's murderer or beat up the thief he caught in his house, these people were now killed or flogged by the authorities. Legal texts from late medieval Germany sometimes explicitly refer to the punishments imposed by the authorities as "vengeance." Serious illegal acts, which up until then had been dealt with in the sphere of revenge and reconciliation, were redefined as being directed not only against the victims but also against the state. In this process the inquisitorial procedure was the main tool. Its increase in frequency in fourteenth-century Venice, for instance, went hand in hand with the conquest of the vendetta. Private violence by members of the community coming to the assistance of a victim was similarly pushed back. In the Netherlands a thief caught redhanded could be arrested by anyone. His captors were obliged to hand him over to the court, but they might seriously harass him and were often excused if they killed him. This "right" retreated too before the increase of prosecution *ex officio*.

It would be incorrect to assume that the state's arm was all-embracing during the early modern period. An active prosecution policy remained largely confined to the more serious crimes. Private vengeance had been conquered, but reconciliation survived in cases of petty theft and minor violence. The mediators were no longer the courts but prestigious members of local communities. The infra-judicial resolution of conflicts prevailed beneath the surface of justice from above. Historians have only recently come to realize this and the phenomenon has only been studied in detail in France.

This "subterranean stream" was kept in motion from two sides. The authorities, though able to take the initiative, restricted their efforts to specific cases. Prosecution policy was often concentrated on vagrants and other notorious groups. The near-absence of a professional police force further limited the court's scope. Hence many petty offenders were left undisturbed. The attitude of local residents also contributed to this situation. Victims of thefts and acts of violence did not often take recourse to the judiciary. One reason was that a trial might be too costly for the potential plaintiff. Another reason was that numerous conflicts arising from violent exchanges or disputes over property were not viewed in terms of crime and the court was not considered the most appropriate place to settle them. Mediation was sought from non-judicial arbiters. This form of infra-judicial reconciliation survived until the end of the *ancien regime.* Thus preindustrial repression was never an automatic response to all sorts of illegal acts.

Relics of private vengeance can also be observed in the early modern period. This is attested by the public's reaction to property offenders in Republican Amsterdam. The archival sources regularly make mention of a phenomenon called *maling.* From it a picture emerges of communal solidarity against thieves. Events always followed a similar pattern. A person in the street might notice that his pocket was picked or he might be chasing after someone who had intruded into his house. Soon bystanders rushed to help him and the thief was surrounded by a hostile crowd. The people harassed and beat him and forced him to surrender the stolen goods. The thief was then usually thrown into a canal. Servants of justice were often said to have saved his life by arresting him, which meant getting him out of the hands of the crowd or out of the water. Memories of the medieval treatment of thieves caught red-handed were apparently still alive. The authorities tolerated it but did not recognize a form of popular justice. In 1718 a man was condemned for throwing stones at servants of justice when they were busy saving a woman, who was in the *maling,* from her assailants. Comparable forms of self-help by the community against thieves existed in eighteenth-century Languedoc.

...[T]he emergence of criminal justice was not a function of changing sensibilities. These only started to play a role later. If corporal and capital penalties increased in frequency from the twelfth to the sixteenth centuries, this certainly cannot be taken as reflecting an increased taste for the sight of violence and suffering. It was primarily a consequence of the growth and stabilization of a system of criminal justice. Conversely, whatever resistance may have been expressed against the transformation...did not spring from an abhorrence of violent dealings as such. Physical punishment was simply introduced into a world which was accustomed to the infliction of physical injury and suffering. In that sense it was not an alien element. The authorities took over the practice of vengeance from private individuals. As private retaliation had often been violent, so was the penal system adopted by the authorities. Similarly, as the first had always been a public affair, so was the second. Attitudes to violence remained basically the same. Huizinga demonstrated the medieval acceptance of violence more than sixty years ago and recent research confirms his view. Thus "to mention only a few" Barbara Hanawalt gets the "impression of a society in which men were quick to give insult and to retaliate with physical attack." Norman Cohn recalls the violent zeal with which self-appointed hunters of heretics proceeded, such as the two who managed to reverse God's dictum at the destruction of Sodom and Gomorrah: "We would gladly burn a hundred, if just one among them were guilty."

It is understandable that in such a climate of acceptance of violence no particular sensitivity prevailed towards the sufferings of convicts. This arose only later. Urban and territorial rulers had to ensure that people accepted the establishment of criminal justice. But once they had accomplished that, they did not encounter psychological barriers against the full deployment of a penal system based on open physical treatment of delinquents. By the middle of the sixteenth century a more or less stable repression had been established in most of Western Europe. It did not exclusively consist of exemplary physical punishments. Banishment was important as well and confinement would soon appear on the scene. From that time on it was possible for changing sensibilities within society to affect the modes of repression. From that time too the development of states and the ensuing pacification produced domesticated elites and changed mentalities. These would eventually lead to a transformation of repression....

STATE FORMATION AND MODES OF REPRESSION

Modes of repression belong to the history of mentalities. They reflect the elites' willingness to deal in one way or another with persons exhibiting undesirable behavior. The sort of repression which is advocated or tolerated in a particular society is an indication of the psychic make-up of its members. Publicity and the infliction of physical suffering were the two main elements of the penal system of the *ancien regime*. They should be understood as part of the mental atmosphere prevailing in preindustrial Western Europe. Many events in social life, from childbirth to dying, had a more open character, while with regard to physical suffering in general, a greater lack of concern prevailed than is current today. This mentality was never static; it began to crumble from the seventeenth century onwards. Simultaneously, repression was changed too.

In this study the routine character of seventeenth- and eighteenth-century executions has been demonstrated. From about 1600 the seeds of the later transformation of repression were manifest. The two elements, publicity and suffering, slowly retreated. The disappearance of most forms of mutilation of non-capital convicts constituted the clearest example. An equally important expression of the retreat was the spread of houses of correction; a theme which could not be discussed here. A slight uneasiness about executions among the elites in the second half of the seventeenth century has also been shown. These developments all anticipated the more fundamental change in sensibilities which set in after the middle of the eighteenth century: an acceleration which led to the privatization of repression. The acceleration after the middle of the eighteenth century had a parallel in other areas of the history of mentalities. Processes of privatization are notably reflected in the rise of the domesticated nuclear family.

I am explaining the evolution of modes of repression with reference to processes of state formation. The latter do not of course belong to the history of mentalities; we enter the field of human organization. State formation and such events as the rise and fall of social strata comprise a separate area of societal development.... Norbert Elias offered a model for the interdependence of developments in the two fields. I indicate the revisions to be made in the model: notably the shift in emphasis from single states to the rise of a European network of states. In early modern Europe this network extended its influence to areas, such as the Dutch Republic, which lagged behind in centralization. There too a relative pacification produced domesticated elites. On the other hand, the stability of the early modern states remained vulnerable, and this holds true for both patrician republics and absolute monarchies. Ultimately, however, the early modern state was transformed almost everywhere into the nation-state; in Britain, France and the Netherlands among others. These developments provide the key for understanding the evolution of repression in Europe.

This study has continually emphasized the functions which public executions had for the authorities.... [L]ate medieval and early modern executions served especially to underline the power of the state. They were meant to be an exemplary manifestation of this power, precisely because it was not yet entirely taken for granted. This explains the two basic elements of the preindustrial penal system. Publicity was needed because the magistrates' power to punish had to be made concretely visible: hence the ceremony, the display of corpses and the refusal to refrain from executions in the tense situation after riots. That public penalties usually involved the infliction of physical suffering is in tune with their function as a manifestation of the power of the magistrates. Physical punishment achieved a very direct sort of exemplarity. The authorities held a monopoly of violence and showed this by actually using it. The spectators, who lived in a relatively pacified state but did not yet harbor a modern attitude towards the practice of violence, understood this. Public executions represented *par excellence* that function of punishment which later came to be called "general prevention."

So far the relationship has been demonstrated largely in a static context: It can be further clarified if we consider the dynamics.... [T]he beginnings of criminal justice were intertwined with the beginnings of state formation and, to a lesser extent, with urbanization. Gradually urban and territorial authorities conquered the vendetta and limited private reconciliation. They started to protect their servant, the executioner, and attempted "though unsuccessfully" to raise his status. The magistrates became the agents who exercised justice.

Public executions first served to seal the transfer of vengeance from private persons to the state. The justice which the authorities displayed served to bolster up their precarious position. They were preoccupied with the maintenance of a highly unstable and geographically limited monopoly of violence well into the sixteenth century. When these monopolies became slightly more stable and crystallized into dynastic states or oligarchic republics uniting a larger area, new considerations came to the fore. Control of the monopoly had to be defended against real or imagined incursions. Bandits and armed vagabonds were still omnipresent. Maintaining the dominance over lower strata and marginal groups was another pressing concern.

Thus, the display of physical punishment as a manifestation of authority was still considered indispensable in the early modern period, because the existing states were still relatively unstable in comparison to later times. In other words, the spectacle of suffering was to survive until a certain degree of stability had been reached. The spectacle was part of the *raison d'etat*. I note this in connection with the penalty of sword over head for semi-homicide in the Netherlands. The peace of the community stood more centrally in dealing with crime than today. Hence the existence of a category such as "half guilty," which would be inconceivable in modern criminal law. Similar considerations applied to torture. In the second half of the eighteenth century, when opinions *pro* and *contra* were both expressed, this becomes eminently clear. The reformers, placing an individual person at the center of their considerations, argued that he could be either guilty or innocent. It made torture unnecessary since innocent persons should not be hurt and those found guilty should simply receive their punishment. The defenders of torture argued from a different point of view. They stuck to an intermediate category of serious suspicion. The heavily suspect were dangerous to the community, so that it was lawful to subject them to torture. This argument is based on the *raison d'etat*, where the security of the community takes precedence.

The relative instability was not the sole characteristic of early modern states that explains the nature of repression. A second one, also inherited from the later Middle Ages, was equally important. It is the personal element in wielding authority.... In the later Middle Ages the preservation of authority was often directly dependent on the person of the ruler. This was illustrated by urban ordinances which put a higher penalty on acts of violence if committed when the lord was in town. In the early modern period this personal element was not as outspoken as it had been before, but it continued to make its mark on the character of the state. A crime was a breach of the king's peace. Public executions constituted the revenge of the offended sovereign.

The personal element should not be viewed as referring exclusively to the king or sovereign. If that were the case, the fact that public executions in countries ruled by patrician elites "such as the Dutch Republic and eighteenth-century England" did not differ significantly from those in France and in German principalities, would be inexplicable. In France the state meant the king and his representatives; judges in the royal courts, for instance. In the Netherlands the state meant the gentlemen assembled in The Hague, the Prince of Orange or the burgomasters of Amsterdam. Foucault's image of physical punishment as the king's branding-mark is relatively well known. But the marks usually represented the jurisdiction. The symbol was equally forceful in a patrician republic. The reaction to the removal of a body from Amsterdam's gallows field... is revealing. The magistrates considered such a body as the property of the city and saw the removal as a theft. The inhabitants of urban and rural communities, also in dynastic states, must have associated authority—perhaps even in the first place—with local magistrates. The conspicuous presence of these magistrates at executions sealed the relationship.

These observations, finally, bring a solution to the problem of the disappearance of public executions. They suggest that a transformation of the state constitutes the explanatory factor. Indeed other transformations are less likely candidates. It would be futile, for instance, to relate the change to industrialization. In many countries the privatization of repression preceded the breakthrough of an industrial society. This chronology is evident in the case of the Netherlands. In England, on the other hand, public executions were still a common spectacle when industrialism was already fully developed. The situation produced hybrid combinations of modern transport and traditional punishment, especially in the larger cities. For a hanging in Liverpool the railway company advertised special trains ("parties of pleasure"), departing from the manufacturing towns. The chronology of industrialization varied from country to country, while the retreat of public executions took place almost everywhere between about 1770 and about 1870. Similarly, the transition from the early modern to the nation-state also occurred in most Western European countries in this period.

Thus, the closing of the curtains can be explained with reference to state formation processes as well. We may schematically divide the inherent transformation of sensibilities into two phases. The first comprised the emergence of an aversion to the sight of physical punishment and a consequent criticism of the penal system among certain groups from the aristocracy and the bourgeoisie. This aversion became manifest in the late eighteenth century and was a result of processes of conscience formation. The relative pacification reached in the early modern states cleared the way for the appearance of domesticated elites. The psychic changes which they underwent first found an expression in a refinement of manners and restraints in social intercourse. But the slight sensitivity to public justice that was already manifest before 1700 prefigured later developments. Originally, psychic controls were largely confined to a context of one's own group. Emotions and aggressive impulses were hardly restrained with regard to inferior classes. This situation altered gradually. In the course of the early modern period mutual dependence between social groups increased. Consequently, the context of psychic controls widened. Once more I should note the importance of the identification aspect: an increase in mutual identification between social groups took place. This increase certainly had its setbacks.... [T]he Amsterdam magistrates became "within the confines of the general standard of the period" slightly harsher towards delinquents between 1650 and 1750 due to their increasing social distance from the classes they ruled. This can also be understood as a temporary decrease in identification of rulers with the ruled. But in the long run this identification grew stronger. By the end of the eighteenth century an unknown number of individuals among the elites had reached a new stage and identified to a certain degree with convicts on the scaffold. These delicate persons disliked the sight of physical suffering: even that of the guilty. The first phase of the transformation of sensibilities had set in.

This first phase, so it appeared, resulted from developments that took place within the context of the early modern state. It did not immediately produce a major reform of the penal system. Two ancient features of repression disappeared though: torture and exposure of corpses. Abolition of the latter custom was often part of revolutionary measures. The gallows field symbolized a monopoly of justice particularly within an urban or regional context. The image of the individual city or county as a relatively independent entity had eroded during the seventeenth and eighteenth centuries. The final blow was long overdue. It came everywhere as a direct consequence of the downfall of the *ancien regime.*

The early modern state, however, did not disappear overnight in the Revolutionary period. The final establishment of the nation-state in Western Europe took most of the nineteenth century. The second phase of the transformation of sensibilities set in parallel to it. Repugnance to the sight of physical punishment spread and intensified. In the end the "political conclusion" was drawn and public executions were abolished. The privatization of repression had been completed. It could be completed because the nation-state lacked the two essential elements of which public executions had been a function. The nation-state, because of closer integration of geographic areas and wider participation of social groups, was much more stable than the early modern state. And the liberal/bourgeois regimes, with their increasingly bureaucratized agencies, had a much more impersonal character. Hence the later nineteenth century witnessed more impersonal and less visible modes of repression. Public executions were not only felt to be distasteful; they were no longer necessary. In its internal affairs the nation-state could largely do without the *raison d'etat.* Beccaria had anticipated the transformation a century earlier. His often-quoted saying that effective prevention of crime depends on the certainty of being caught rather than on the severity of punishment was actually a plea for a stronger state, and in particular for a police force. This was realized in the nation-state. Consequently the authorities could afford to show a milder and more liberal face.

Once more it should be emphasized that absolutes do not exist. Even the privatized repression which emerged in the course of the nineteenth century needed a minimum of exemplarity. We find it expressed, for instance, in the location of prisons on a conspicuous spot where a road or railway entered a town. In an indirect way punishment remained public. L. O. Pike, writing in 1876, reminded his readers that a secondhand impression of a whipping indoors was occasionally brought home to the public by the press. Indirect knowledge of the death penalty, executed within prison walls, remained alive.

National variations in the chronology of the disappearance of public executions must be related to national singularities. The relative importance of the two elements, stability and impersonal rule, may also have varied. In England, for instance, the first half of the nineteenth century was the period of the great public order panic. Thereafter only occasional outbursts of fear occurred and a relative orderliness prevailed. No doubt this situation made the completion of the privatization of repression easier. The kingdom of the Netherlands, on the other hand, was relatively peaceful. The old patrician elites, however, largely dominated the scene until the middle of the nineteenth century. Shortly thereafter the abolition of public executions was a fact. Around the same time the system of public order maintenance was also depersonalized and acquired a more bureaucratic character. These remarks about the specifics of the transformation are of a hypothetical nature and call for detailed research. The continuation of public guillotining in France until 1939 likewise needs a separate explanation.

The fact that the completion of the privatization of repression took about two-thirds of the nineteenth century in most Western European countries adds up to a critique of Foucault's views. He pictures early nineteenth-century imprisonment as suddenly and almost totally replacing a penal system directed at the display of the human body. The new penal system, and especially solitary confinement, was also directed at the mind. It is true that a widespread enthusiasm for "moral treatment" prevailed in the first half of the nineteenth century. But the penitentiary cannot be considered as the successor to public executions. The observations of the present study make the conclusion inescapable: classical nineteenth-century imprisonment represented an experimental phase contemporary to the last days of public executions. Several authors emphasize that the middle of the nineteenth century was the heyday of the penitentiary and solitary confinement, after which the enthusiasm declined. Of course executions were less frequent at the time, but this is not relevant to the argument. From a quantitative viewpoint they had always been in the minority, though they were the pearl in the crown of repression. In the course of the nineteenth century public physical punishment was increasingly questioned. This coincided with experiments in new penal methods such as solitary confinement. The experiments were discontinued and public executions disappeared. Routine imprisonment succeeded "with capital punishment indoors for a few heinous offenses" to the top of the penal system.

Modern imprisonment would need another story. The penal system of today, however, bears the mark of the developments that gave rise to it. On the one hand, it has retained its ancient characteristics to a certain degree. Everyone still has to realize that punishment exists, and this is the essence of the notion of general prevention. And a penalty still involves, in one way or another, the infliction of injury. Feelings of sensitivity, on the other hand, did not vanish after their appearance in the late eighteenth century. Time and again those concerned with the condemned have looked inside prisons and told the public the painful story. The result is a permanent tension. Every modern Western society witnesses the conflict between a perceived necessity of punishment and an uneasiness at its practice. Perhaps this remains inevitable, unless we find a way to do without repression entirely.

STUDY QUESTIONS

1. How did relations among the governing and the governed change between the Germanic and the feudal periods?
2. During this time period, how did inquisitorial procedures change power relations among individuals and between individuals and the state?
3. What purpose did repression, especially caused by the spectacle of public physical suffering, serve in the early modern states?
4. Exactly how did the transition from an early modern to a nation-state transform sensibilities and make the spectacle of suffering unnecessary?

2
THE DISCOVERY OF THE ASYLUM

DAVID J. ROTHMAN

In yet another historical account of the development of the penitentiary, David J. Rothman explores the development of the institution from colonial America to the 1820s. Again, the reader should observe a societal shift from a system based largely on interpersonal settling of disputes in an agrarian setting to an urbanized nation that requires state intervention for punishment. The reader should also take note that, in addition to the rise of the penitentiary, representing confinement as an end in and of itself, society held a belief that the institution could indeed change the individual for the better. Thus, penal institutions were designed to confine the offender while leading him to the skills necessary for a law-abiding life.

THE BOUNDARIES OF COLONIAL SOCIETY

The colonial attitudes and practices toward...the criminal...were in almost every aspect remarkably different from those Americans came to share in the pre-Civil war decades. Almost no eighteenth-century assumption about the origins or nature of...deviancy survived intact into the Jacksonian era, and its favorite solutions to these conditions also became outmoded. In fact, the two periods' perspectives and reactions were so basically dissimilar that only a knowledge of colonial precedents can clarify the revolutionary nature of the changes that occurred.

Eighteenth-century Americans did not define... crime as a critical social problem....They devoted very little energy to devising and enacting programs to reform offenders and had no expectations of eradicating crime. Nor did they systematically attempt to isolate the deviant....While they excluded some persons, they kept others wholly inside their communities. At times they were...willing to allow offenders another chance; but they could also show a callousness and narrow-mindedness that was utterly cruel. From the viewpoint of nineteenth-century critics, their ideas and behavior seemed careless and inconsistent, irrational and injurious, but within their social and intellectual framework, the colonists followed clear and well-established guidelines....

The colonists judged a wide range of behavior to be deviant, finding the gravest implications in even minor offenses. Their extended definition was primarily religious in origin, equating sin with crime. The criminal codes punished religious offenses, such as idolatry, blasphemy, and witchcraft, and clergymen declared infractions against persons or property to be offenses against God. Freely mixing the two categories, the colonists proscribed an incredibly long list of activities. The identification of disorder with sin made it difficult for legislators and ministers to distinguish carefully between major and minor infractions. Both were testimony to the natural depravity of man and the power of the devil—sure signs that the offender was destined to be a public menace and a damned sinner....

To counteract the powerful temptations to misconduct and the inherent weakness of men, the colonists looked to three critical associations. They conceived of the family, the church, and the network of community relations as important weapons in the battle against sin and crime. If these bodies functioned well, the towns would be spared the turbulence of vice and crime and, without frequent recourse to the courts or the gallows, enjoy a high degree of order and stability. To these ends, families were to raise their children to respect law and authority, the church was to oversee not only family discipline but adult behavior, and the members of the community were to supervise one another, to detect and correct the first signs of deviancy....

These attitudes did not stimulate the colonists to new ways of controlling crime. The broad definition of potential offenders and improper behavior did not spur attempts to revise the patently inadequate formal mechanisms of law enforcement. Assemblies created a militia to contain mass disturbances and repel enemy forces but they did not intend it or use it for day-to-day supervision. Towns designated constables to protect their peace, but the force was inadequate both in the number and physical condition of its men. It was understaffed, poorly supervised, and filled with the elderly. Rather, the colonists' perspective on deviancy encouraged a dependence upon informal mechanisms which promoted a localism in many settlements. To an important degree the community had to be self-policing. The citizens themselves would be on guard to report and even apprehend the offender. Just as churchgoers were to be diligent about one another's salvation, so too residents were to protect one another's lives and property. And given the popular sense of man's proclivities to sin and crime, they expected to be busy....

CHARITY AND CORRECTION IN THE EIGHTEENTH CENTURY

Eighteenth-century criminal codes fixed a wide range of punishments. They provided for fines, for whippings, for mechanisms of shame like the stocks, pillory and public cage, for banishment, and for the gallows. They used one technique or a combination of them, calling for a fine together with a period in the stocks, or for a whipping to be followed by banishment. The laws frequently gave the presiding magistrate discretion to choose among alternatives "to fine or to whip" or directed him to select the applicable one "to use the stocks if the offender could not pay his fine." They included some ingenious punishments, such as having a convicted felon mount the gallows, remain for an hour with a noose around his neck, and then go free....The statutes defined a large number and variety of capital crimes and the courts were not reluctant to inflict the penalty. The gallows was the only method by which they could finally coerce obedience and protect the community. In the absence of punishments in the middle range, they depended extensively upon the discipline of the hangman....

Local jails were found throughout the colonies, and in decent repair. Some towns utilized part of the courthouse building, others erected a separate structure. But regardless of form, these institutions had only limited functions. They held persons about to be tried or awaiting sentence or unable to discharge contracted debts. They did not, however, except on rare occasions, confine convicted offenders as a means of correction. The jails facilitated the process of criminal punishment but were not themselves instruments of discipline. They did not expand in function during the course of the eighteenth century to become a method for penalizing as well as detaining offenders.

The colonists might have adopted a penitentiary system in order to reform the criminal, or to terrify him, or simply to confine him. They could have attempted to mold him into an obedient citizen, or to frighten him into lawful conduct or, at least, to prevent him, if for only a limited period, from injuring the community. But given their conception of deviant behavior and institutional organization, they did not believe that a jail could rehabilitate or intimidate or detain the offender. They placed little faith in the possibility of reform. Prevailing Calvinist doctrines that stress the natural depravity of man and the powers of the devil hardly allowed such optimism. Since temptations to misconduct were not only omnipresent but practically irresistible, rehabilitation could not serve as the basis for a prison program. Moreover, local officials believed that a policy of expulsion offered the community some protection against recidivism. Institutionalization seemed unnecessary when numerous offenders could be marched beyond the town line and not be seen again.

The failure to broaden the functions of the jail also revealed the colonists' dependence upon the family model for organizing an institution. Since life in a prison would perforce duplicate that in a large household, they saw no reason to believe institutionalization would discourage the criminal or even offer the community a temporary respite. A household existence did not seem either painful or corrective....

The institutions already functioning in the colonies did not substantially depart from the family model. The almshouse ran like a large household. Since officials appropriately considered admission a privilege, penalizing anyone who tried to enter it illegally, the poorhouse was hardly an inspiration for a prison system. The occasional workhouse was not a more useful guide; the few to be found in America had not established a disciplinary or punitive routine....

Eighteenth-century jails in fact closely resembled the household in structure and routine. They lacked a distinct architecture and special procedures....True to the household model, the keeper and his family resided in the jail, occupying one of its rooms; the prisoners lived several together in the others, with little to differentiate the keeper's quarters from their own. They wore no special clothing or uniforms and usually neither cuffs nor chains restrained their movements. They walked "not marched" about the jail. The workhouse model was so irrelevant that nowhere were they required to perform the slightest labor.

Jail arrangements so closely replicated the household that some colonists feared that prisons would be comfortable enough to attract inmates. Far from striking terror, they would build a clientele willing to be decently supported in return for a temporary deprivation of liberty. This is why towns frequently required prisoners to provide their own food and "to use such bedding, linen and other necessaries as they think fit, without their being purloined, detained, or they paying [the jailer] for the same." So long as they did not cost the town money, inmates could make living arrangements as pleasant and as homelike as they wished....

The colonial jails were not only unlikely places for intimidating the criminal, but even ill-suited for confining him. Security was impossible to maintain, and escapes were frequent and easy. Conditions were sometimes so lax that towns compelled a prisoner to post a bond that he would remain in the jail, especially if he wished the privilege of exercising in the yard....

No one placed very much confidence in these structures. Even at the close of the colonial period, there was no reason to think that the prison would soon become central to criminal punishment....

THE CHALLENGE OF CRIME

Eighteenth-century notions of...deviancy did not survive for very long into the nineteenth, nor did its methods of dispensing...correction. The social, intellectual, and economic changes that differentiated the states of the new republic from the several colonies prompted a critical reappraisal and revision of the ideas and techniques of social control. Americans felt compelled to rethink inherited procedures and devise new methods to replace old ones. They devoted extraordinary attention to this issue, hoping to establish quickly and effectively alternatives to the colonial system.

Between 1790 and 1830, the nation's population greatly increased and so did the number and density of cities. Even gross figures reveal the dimensions of the change. In these forty years, the population of Massachusetts almost doubled, in Pennsylvania it tripled, and in New York it increased five times; border and midwestern states, practically empty in 1790, now held over three million people. At Washington's inauguration, only two hundred thousand Americans live[d] in towns with more than twenty-five hundred people; by Jackson's accession, the number exceeded one million. In 1790, no American city had more than fifty thousand residents. By 1830, almost half a million people lived in urban centers larger than that. During these same years factories began to dot the New England and mid-Atlantic rivers. The decade of the 1830s witnessed the first accelerated growth of manufacturing in the nation. At the same time, Enlightenment ideas challenged Calvinist doctrines; the prospect of boundless improvement confronted a grim determinism. But these general trends are not sufficient to explain the very specific reactions to the issue of deviant...behavior. To them must be added Americans' understanding of these changes. Under the influence of demographic, economic and intellectual developments, they perceived that the traditional mechanisms of social control were obsolete. The premises upon which the colonial system had been based were no longer valid.

Each change encouraged Americans to question inherited practices and to devise new ones. Inspired by the ideals of the Enlightenment, they considered older punishments to be barbaric and traditional assumptions on the origins of deviant behavior to be misdirected. Movement to cities, in and out of territories, and up and down the social ladder, made it difficult for them to believe that a sense of hierarchy or localism could now stabilize society. When men no longer knew their place or station, self-policing communities seemed a thing of the past. Expanding political loyalties also made colonial mechanisms appear obsolete. Citizens' attachment to state governments promoted a broader definition of responsibility, so that a sentence of banishment seemed a parochial response. The welfare of the commonwealth demanded that towns no longer solve their problems in such narrow and exclusive ways.

This awareness provoked at least as much anxiety as celebration. Americans in the Jacksonian period could not believe that geographic and social mobility would promote or allow order and stability. Despite their marked impatience and dissatisfaction with colonial procedures, they had no ready vision of how to order society. They were still trapped in many ways in the rigidities of eighteenth-century social thinking. They knew well that the old system was passing, but not what ought to replace it. What in their day was to prevent society from bursting apart? From where would the elements of cohesion come? More specifically, would...criminals roam out of control?...This question became part of a full, intense, and revealing investigation of the origins of deviant...behavior. To understand why men turned criminal...would enable reformers to strengthen the social order. To comprehend and control abnormal behavior promised to be the first step in establishing a new system for stabilizing the community, for binding citizens together. In this effort, one finds the clearest indications of how large-scale social changes affected thinking and actions of Americans in the Jacksonian period. And here one also finds the crucial elements that led to the discovery of the [penitentiary].

In the immediate aftermath of independence and nationhood, Americans believed that they had uncovered both the prime cause of criminality in their country and an altogether effective antidote. Armed with patriotic fervor, sharing a repugnance for things British and a new familiarity with and faith in Enlightenment doctrines, they posited that the origins and persistence of deviant behavior would be found in the nature of the colonial criminal codes. Established in the days of oppression and ignorance, the laws reflected British insistence on severe and cruel punishments....

These conceptions had an immediate and widespread appeal. The reform seemed worthy of the new republic, and feasible, so that by the second decade of the nineteenth century, most of the states had amended their criminal codes. The death sentence was either abolished for all offenses save first-degree murder or strictly limited to a handful of the most serious crimes. Instead, the statutes called for incarceration, the offender to serve a term in prison. Construction kept apace with legal stipulations. Pennsylvania led the way, turning the old Philadelphia jail at Walnut Street into a state prison. In 1796, the New York legislature approved funds for building such institutions, and soon opened the Newgate state prison in Greenwich Village. The New Jersey penitentiary was completed in 1797, and so were others in Virginia and Kentucky in 1800. That same year, the Massachusetts legislature made appropriations for a prison at Charlestown, and in short order Vermont, New Hampshire, and Maryland followed suit. Within twenty years of Washington's inaugural, the states had taken the first steps to alter the traditional system of punishment.

In this first burst of enthusiasm, Americans expected that a rational system of correction, which made punishment certain but humane, would dissuade all but a few offenders from a life in crime. They located the roots of deviancy not in the criminal, but in the legal system. Just as colonial codes had encouraged deviant behavior, republican ones would now curtail, or even eliminate it. To pass the proper laws would end the problem.

This perspective drew attention away from the prisons themselves. They were necessary adjuncts to the reform, the substitutes for capital punishment, but intrinsically of little interest or importance. A repulsion from the gallows rather than any faith in the penitentiary spurred the late-eighteenth-century construction. Few people had any clear idea what these structures should look like or how they should be administered—or even addressed themselves seriously to these questions. To reformers, the advantages of the institutions were external, and they hardly imagined that life inside the prison might rehabilitate the criminal. Incarceration seemed more humane than hanging and less brutal than whipping. Prisons matched punishment to crime precisely: the more heinous the offense, the longer the sentence. Juries, fully understanding these advantages, would never hesitate to convict the guilty, so that correction would be certain. The fact of imprisonment, not its internal routine, was of chief importance.

By the 1820s, however, these ideas had lost persuasiveness. The focus shifted to the deviant and the penitentiary, away from the legal system. Men intently scrutinized the life history of the criminal and methodically arranged the institution to house him. Part of the cause for this change was the obvious failure of the first campaign. The faith of the 1790s now seemed misplaced; more rational codes had not decreased crime. The roots of deviancy went deeper than the certainty of a punishment. Nor were the institutions fulfilling the elementary task of protecting society, since escapes and riots were commonplace occurrences. More important, the second generation of Americans confronted new challenges and shared fresh ideas. Communities had undergone many critical changes between 1790 and 1830, and so had men's thinking. Citizens found cause for deep despair and yet incredible optimism. The safety and security of their social order seemed to them in far greater danger than that of their fathers, yet they hoped to eradicate crime from the new world. The old structure was crumbling, but perhaps they could draw the blue prints for building a far better one.

...Although the colonists had blamed inadequate parental and religious training for crime, they were preoccupied with the sinner himself. Convinced that the corrupt nature of man was ultimately at fault, they did not extensively analyze the role of the criminal's family or the church or the general society. Furthermore, they shared a clear understanding of what the well-ordered community *ought to* look like, and this too stifled any inclination to question or scrutinize existing arrangements. Their religious and social certainty covered the discrepancies between ideas and realities, obviating new approaches and theories. Americans in the Jacksonian period stood in a very different position. They learned that men were born innocent, not depraved, that the sources of corruption were external, not internal, to the human condition. Encouraged by such doctrines to examine their society with acute suspicion, they quickly discovered great cause for apprehension and criticism....

Holding such a position, American students of deviant behavior moved family and community to the center of their analysis. New York officials accumulated and published biographies because this technique allowed them to demonstrate to legislators and philanthropists the crucial role of social organizations. Accordingly, almost every sketch opened with a vivid description of an inadequate family life and then traced the effects of the corruptions in the community....

The pessimism and fear underlying this outlook pointed to the difficulty Americans had in fitting their perception of nineteenth-century society as mobile and fluid into an eighteenth-century definition of a well-ordered community. Their first reaction was not to disregard the inherited concept but to condemn present conditions. Hence, in these biographies a dismal picture emerged of a society filled with a myriad of temptations. It was almost as if the town, in a nightmarish image, was made up of a number of households, frail and huddled together, facing the sturdy and wide doors of the tavern, the gaudy opening into a house of prostitution or theater filled with dissipated customers; all the while, thieves and drunkards milled the streets, introducing the unwary youngster to vice and corruption. Every family was under siege, surrounded by enemies ready to take advantage of any misstep. The honest citizen was like a vigilant soldier, well trained to guard against temptation. Should he relax for a moment, the results would be disastrous. Once, observers believed, neighbors had disciplined neighbors. Now it seemed that rowdies corrupted rowdies.

Yet for all the desperation in this image, Americans shared an incredible optimism. Since deviant behavior was a product of the environment, the predictable result of readily observable situations, it was not inevitable. Crime was not inherent in the nature of man, as Calvinists had asserted; no theological devils insisted on its perpetuation. Implicit in this outlook was an impulse to reform. If one could alter the conditions breeding crime, then one could reduce it to manageable proportions and bring a new security to society.

One tactic was to advise and warn the family to fulfill its tasks well. By giving advice and demonstrating the awful consequences of an absence of discipline, critics would inspire the family to a better performance. (The biographical sketches, then, were not only investigations but correctives to the problem.) One might also organize societies to shut taverns and houses of prostitution, an effort that was frequently made in the Jacksonian period. But such measures, while important, were slow-working, and by themselves seemed insufficient to meet the pressing needs of this generation. Another alternative then became not only feasible but essential: to construct a special setting for the deviant. Remove him from the family and community and place him in an artificially created and therefore corruption-free environment. Here he could learn all the vital lessons that others had ignored, while protected from the temptations of vice. A model and small-scale society could solve the immediate problem and point the way to broader reforms....

THE INVENTION OF THE PENITENTIARY

Americans' understanding of the causes of deviant behavior led directly to the invention of the penitentiary as a solution. It was an ambitious program. Its design "external appearance, internal arrangement, and daily routine" attempted to eliminate the specific influences that were breeding crime in the community, and to demonstrate the fundamentals of proper social organization. Rather than stand as places of last resort, hidden and ignored, these institutions became the pride of the nation. A structure designed to join practicality to humanitarianism, reform the criminal, stabilize American society, and demonstrate how to improve the condition of mankind, deserved full publicity and close study.

In the 1820s New York and Pennsylvania began a movement that soon spread through the Northeast, and then over the next decades to many midwestern states. New York devised the Auburn or congregate system of penitentiary organization, establishing it first at the Auburn state prison between 1819 and 1823, and then in 1825 at the Ossining institution, familiarly known as Sing-Sing. Pennsylvania officials worked out the details of a rival plan, the separate system, applying it to the penitentiary at Pittsburgh in 1826 and to the prison at Philadelphia in 1829....

The doctrines of separation, obedience, and labor became the trinity around which officials organized the penitentiary. They carefully instructed inmates that their duties could be "comprised in a few words"; they were *"to labor diligently, to obey all orders,* and preserve an *unbroken silence."* Yet to achieve these goals, officers had to establish a total routine, to administer every aspect of the institution in accord with the three guidelines, from inmates' dress to their walk, from the cells' furnishings to the guards' deportment. The common solution was to follow primarily a quasi-military model. The regulations based on this model promised to preserve isolation, to make labor efficient, and to teach men lacking discipline to abide by rules; this regimented style of life would inculcate strict discipline, precision, and instantaneous adherence to commands. Furthermore, a military model in a correctional institution seemed especially suitable for demonstrating to the society at large the right principles of organization. Here was an appropriate example for a community suffering a crisis of order....

Reformers never spelled out the precise nature and balance of this reformation. They hoped that families, instead of overindulging or neglecting their children, would more conscientiously teach limits and the need for obedience to them. Assuming that social stability could not be achieved without a very personal and keen respect for authority, they looked first to a firm family discipline to inculcate it. Reformers also anticipated that society would rid itself of corruptions. In a narrow sense this meant getting rid of such blatant centers of vice as taverns, theaters, and houses of prostitution. In a broader sense, it meant reviving a social order in which men knew their place. Here sentimentality took over, and critics in the Jacksonian period often assumed that their forefathers had lived together without social strain, in secure, placid, stable, and cohesive communities. In fact, the designers of the penitentiary set out to re-create these conditions. But the results, it is not surprising to discover, were startlingly different from anything that the colonial period had known. A conscious effort to instill discipline through an institutional routine led to a set work pattern, a rationalization of movement, a precise organization of time, a general uniformity. Hence, for all the reformers' nostalgia, the reality of the penitentiary was much closer to the values of the nineteenth than the eighteenth century.

STUDY QUESTIONS

1. How did the American colonists' views on the nature of man and crime shape punishment?
2. Why didn't the colonists conceive of incarceration as a form of punishment?
3. Discuss social changes occurring at the turn of the nineteenth century that would change Americans' thoughts on crime and punishment within a generation or two.
4. How did Americans' views on the nature of man, crime, and punishment during the Jacksonian era differ from the views of their colonial counterparts?
5. In what way did Jacksonian Americans believe that the trinity of the penitentiary (separation, obedience, and labor) would act as an appropriate example for a community in crisis?

3
A LOOK AT PRISON HISTORY

THORSTEN SELLIN

Thorsten Sellin traces the history of punishment and imprisonment from approximately the Reformation forward. However, Sellin focuses on the historically relevant view of Radbruch's theory,* which states that punishments were designed to control the underclass, which in many cases meant slaves. As such, prison inmates came to be viewed as slaves of the state. This historical analysis does an excellent job of detailing and describing the societal shift that moved confinement from occurring prior to the "real" punishment (which generally involved severe if not deadly corporal punishment) to actually being the punishment. Although Sellin views moving away from corporal (and public) punishment as a positive shift, he concludes by noting some of the unanticipated consequences that arose from this country's willingness to house offenders of all types en masse. Not the least of these problems are the issues of prison labor and of inmates' grotesque mistreatment within institutions.

In his symposium, *Elegantiae Juris Criminalis,* Gustav Radbruch published in 1938 an article entitled "Der Ursprung des Strafrechts aus dem Stande der Unfreien." It is a brilliant exposition of a theory which had been advanced many decades earlier by scholars like Köstlin, von Bar, and Jastrow and it makes the origin of penal imprisonment comprehensible. Rejecting, as illogical or unproved, various explanations of the origin of punishment, Radbruch maintained that the common punishments which came to be introduced in law and applied to all offenders had once been used only for slaves or bondsmen.

> Especially the mutilating penalties. Applied earlier almost exclusively to slaves, they became used more and more on freemen during the Carolingian period and specially for offenses which betokened a base and servile mentality. Up to the end of the Carolingian era, punishments "to hide and hair" were overwhelmingly reserved for slaves. Even death penalties occurred as slave punishments and account for the growing popularity of such penalties in Carolingian times. The aggravated death penalties, combining corporal and capital punishments, have their roots in the penal law governing slaves.[1]

Radbruch believed that earlier penal customs, like feud or compensation, were natural for equals and propertied people who could demand satisfaction or make payments. But the social class system changed greatly during the Frankish era and with it the character of criminality. "Vulgar crime" became looked upon as low-class crime, "vulgar both in the sense of its origin in baseborn people and in its appraisal as being infamous—the crime of another, uncomprehended and despised social layer....The aim of punishment had been clearly stated, in a capitulary of Childebert II in 596 A.D., to be 'to ensure by every means the control of the lower classes.' It was natural that the best means to that end were the punishments that were earlier applied to the very lowest layer of the people—the class of slaves."[2]

The evolution of the penal law until the old slave punishments—death, mutilation, whipping, etc.—were gradually incorporated in the penal law and applied generally needs no further elaboration here.

> The criminal law...to this very day reflects its origin in slave punishments. Even now, punishments mean a *capitis deminutio* because it presumes the *capitis deminutio* of those for whom it was originally designed. Being punished means being treated like a slave. This was symbolically underscored in earlier times when whipping was accompanied by the shaving of the head, for the shorn head, was the mark of the slave.[3]

PENAL SLAVERY

Being concerned mostly with corporal and capital punishments, Radbruch made no mention of penal imprisonment in his essay, yet his theory applies perfectly to that punishment which in its primitive form was slavery of a most abject kind, called penal servitude. Penal servitude was in use in Imperial Rome. Von Bar says that

> since it was customary to punish slaves by hard labor and since the lowest class of freemen were in reality little more respected than were slaves, by the all powerful imperial officials, the idea easily arose of making use of the toil of convicts in the great works being undertaken by the state. This idea was perhaps furthered by an acquaintance with the custom of states annexed to Rome. Thus even Pliny the Younger speaks of the employment of convicts in public works (*opus publicum*), such as cleaning sewers, mending highways, and working in the public baths. A more severe type of this kind of punishment was a sentence "ad metalla"—labor in the mines—and in "opus metalli." The convicts in each of these instances wore chains and as "servi poenae" lost their freedom. For this reason the punishment was always for life....These punishments were properly regarded as sentences to a slow and painful death.[4]

It is significant that in Imperial Rome the *condamnatio ad opus publicum* was reserved for the *personae humiles*, the humble class of people; it was not applicable to the upper class or *honestiores*. The more severe forms of the *condemnatio* deprived the offender of his liberty (*capitis deminutio maxima*) and hence of his citizenship, reducing his status to that of a penal slave. These punishments, together with exile and death, were classed by the legists as capital punishments because they incurred civil death. Sentences *ad metalla* meant hard labor, while in chains, in stone quarries, such as the Carrara marble ones, in metal mines, or in sulphur pits. It is obvious that in order to exploit the manpower of these penal slaves it was necessary to keep them imprisoned in some way. Here, then, we find punitive imprisonment in its original form, even though the Romans may not have been its inventors. Therefore, it is curious to be told by George Ives, in his interesting *History of Penal Methods* (1914) that

> imprisonment as a punishment in itself, to be endured under rules made expressly punitive and distressful, may be described as essentially modern and reached its worst phase in the nineteenth century.[5]

"Imprisonment as a punishment in itself" would thus be something new and in essence different from the primitive penal servitude just described. To be sure, historians seem to have adopted that view, but I propose to show that this judgment is questionable.

Parenthetically speaking, it is puzzling to find the great Roman jurist Ulpian categorically declaring that prisons existed only for detention and not for punishment, a phrase which was accepted as a correct definition of prisons until the 18th century. Considering the sentences *ad metalla* common in Ulpian's own day; the later use, mainly in the Mediterranean sea, of convicts as oarsmen in war galleys; the working of convicts in the Spanish mines of northern Africa by the banking house of Fugger to secure repayment of immense loans made to Charles V; the use of convict labor in the arsenals of France and Spain; the transportation of convicts to work in the Siberian mines and lumber camps of Russia; the common use of convicts during the 16th and 17th centuries to build fortifications, etc., one can only conclude that, despite the complete deprivation of liberty characterizing such punitive enterprises, jurists did not look on that element in these punishments as being their distinguishing mark, but placed them, instead, in another category of punishment, that of forced or compulsory labor, to which the deprivation of liberty was merely incidental. As late as 1771, the great French jurist Daniel Jousse still classed penal servitude among the capital punishments. This probably accounts for the view expressed by George Ives that imprisonment as an end in itself is a modern invention.

You will recall that Radbruch claimed that corporal and capital punishments originally imposed only on slaves and bondsmen gradually came to be used for freemen. The same holds true for imprisonment. Originally applied as a punishment for slaves in connection with hard labor, it came to be used for humble folk, who for crime were reduced to penal slaves. In the middle of the 15th century, when France found the supply of free and slave labor on its galley fleets dwindling, beggars and vagrants were first sent to fill the galley crews and later sturdy felons who had merited the death penalty or corporal punishments. When imprisonment later was applied to all serious offenders, it turned out, on close examination, to be only a variant of the original form of penal servitude.

PUNITIVE IMPRISONMENT

The credit for the gradual substitution of imprisonment for corporal and capital punishments must go to the political philosophers of the 18th century. Experimentation with punitive imprisonment had occurred earlier in the monastic orders and in the houses of correction in many countries, but this involved mostly errant clerics or petty misdemeanants and had not greatly changed the ways of dealing with more serious criminals, who were still being whipped, broken on the wheel, maimed, and hanged. Now the demand arose that nearly all such criminals be sentenced to imprisonment. The most influential voice, so far as penal reform was concerned, was that of Beccaria, who crystallized ideas he had gleaned from the French philosophers, especially Montesquieu.

Beccaria's great essay *On Crimes and Punishments* (1764) is too well-known to you to require any extensive commentary. You will recall that he opposed the death penalty and advocated substituting imprisonment for it, but what may have passed notice is the reason for his proposal and the nature of the substitute. No sentimentality dictated his opposition to capital punishment. As a firm believer in Rousseau's version of the theory of the social contract, he denied the *right* of the state to execute anyone with the possible exception of the leader of a revolt threatening to overthrow the government. No citizen, he said, would have voluntarily agreed to surrender to the state his right to live. When using the death penalty a state was not exercising a right it was not entitled to possess but was engaging in a war against a citizen, whose destruction it believed to be necessary and useful. Beccaria then proceeded to demonstrate the falsity of such beliefs.

Why should imprisonment be preferred to capital punishment? Because

> it is not the intensity but the duration of punishment which has the greatest effect upon man's mind.... It is not the terrible but fleeting spectacle of the execution of a scroundrel that is the strongest deterrent to crime but rather the long and painful example of a man deprived of his freedom and become a beast of burden, repaying with his toil the society he has offended.... Therefore the intensity of the punishment of perpetual servitude as substitute for the death penalty possesses that which suffices to deter any determined soul. I say that it has more. Many look on death with a firm and calm regard... but neither fanaticism nor vanity dwells among fetters and chains, under the rod, under the yoke, or in the iron cage.... Were one to say that perpetual servitude is as painful as death and therefore equally cruel I would reply that, adding all the unhappy moments of servitude together, the former would be even worse.[6]

In the last analysis, then, Beccaria, who clearly stated in his essay that the aim of punishment should be to prevent a criminal from repeating crime and to deter others from crime by the example of punishment, did not ask for the abolition of the death penalty for humanitarian reasons but because it (a) had no logical place in a political society based on a social contract and (b) was less of a deterrent than life imprisonment. Such imprisonment was to be served in a prison where the inmate led the existence of a penal slave. Since scores of crimes in the penal laws of his day were made punishable by death, his reform proposal, if accepted, would require the creation of prisons to house large numbers of inmates. It is noteworthy also that Beccaria rarely mentioned imprisonment in his essay except as a substitute for capital punishment. He referred to it in connection with thefts committed with violence, for instance, but when he did mention it he called it temporary or perpetual slavery. Nor was he opposed to corporal punishments.

It is important to remember that Beccaria's essay was, first and foremost, a political tract announcing the principles of a penal code based on the new democratic philosophy of the political equality of men. Older penal law had reflected the views dominant in societies where slavery or serfdom flourished, political inequality was the rule, and sovereignty was assumed to be resting in absolute monarchs. Now the most objectionable features of that law, which had favored the upper classes and had provided often arbitrary, brutal and revolting corporal and capital punishments for the lower classes, were to be removed and equality before the law established. Judicial torture for the purpose of extracting evidence was to be abolished, other than penal measures used to control some conduct previously punished as crime, and punishments made only severe enough to outweigh the gains expected by the criminal from his crime. This meant a more humane law, no doubt, applied without discrimination to all citizens alike in harmony with the new democratic ideas. There was nothing startlingly new, however, in the aims of punishment as advocated by Beccaria. Myuart de Vouglans, who wrote a polemic against him in 1766 and was a leading defender of the old system, believed that the aim of punishment should be (a) to correct the offender; (b) repair the wrong caused by the crime if possible; and (c) deter the evilminded by the example and fear of similar punishments. The aims of these two defenders of different penal philosophies were essentially the same; only the means they advocated differed.

The governments who were influenced by the new philosophy created prison systems that incorporated Beccaria's ideas. Emperor Joseph II of Austria, hailed as a reformer for having eliminated the death penalty from his code of 1787, substituted horrible varieties of imprisonment in dungeons, where prisoners were chained and loaded with irons while working. At about the same time, John Howard observed in a Viennese prison prisoners chained together and awaiting transportation to Hungary where they were to draw barges up the Danube, a task so exhaustive that few survived it. When the French Constituent Assembly in 1791 translated Beccaria's principles into a penal code, different varieties of imprisonment were substituted, the most severe of which provided that the criminal was to have a chain with an iron ball attached to his legs, be confined at hard labor in security prisons, ports or arsenals, or at other public works, and work for the profit of the state. This was, in fact, the way galley slaves had been treated ever since the galleys had been decommissioned as outmoded.

PRISON REFORM

Concern about the sufferings of prisoners had been expressed in many ways since ancient times. There is both a literature to demonstrate it and organized efforts of relief, engaged in mainly for religious and humanitarian reasons. The outstanding work of John Howard need only be mentioned; it coincided with the period we have just been discussing. But now a new generation of writers appeared. The effects of the movement to make prisons places of punishment rather than of mere detention required not only justification but inventiveness. How should such prisons be organized, what should be the regime, how would they most effectively serve the aims of punishment? The last decade of the 18th and the first half of the 19th century produced an impressive list of writers on prison reform as well as impressive efforts to convert their ideas into practice.

But the roots of imprisonment in penal servitude could not be easily eradicated. When the young American states built penitentiaries for serious offenders who would formerly have been executed, mutilated, or whipped, the law provided that prisoners confined in them should perform labor of the "most harsh and servile kind" (a phrase borrowed from John Howard). The prisons operated on the Auburn plan, in particular, were, most of them, notorious for the maltreatment of prisoners and for the excessive labor required of them in an attempt to meet the demand of legislators that the prisons be self-supporting and even show a profit if possible. These conditions were not reflected in the glowing reports that often emanated from the wardens or overseers of the prisons, but they were amply proved by the many investigations of abuses made from time to time by official commissions. Quite early—in New York in 1817, for instance—the practice began of selling the labor of prisoners to private contractors. This contract system of prison labor spread rapidly to other states and was not completely eliminated until 1934, by act of Congress. As late as 1919 a committee of the American Prison Association reported, after a national survey, that most prisons worked their prisoners in a manner reminiscent of the early forms of penal servitude and that reformation was an empty word.

Let me return to Radbruch for a moment and his theory that in a society where slaves existed, the punishments for slaves tended to be adopted for freemen sooner or later; that, in other words, the institution of slavery placed its stamp on the penal law. Consider the fact that the ancient societies of Greece and Rome were built on a foundation of slavery; that Plato said that all manual labor should be done by slaves; that Aristotle regarded it as an established law of nature that slavery was just and even agreeable to those subjected to it; and that there were times during the Roman Empire when the number of slaves almost equalled the number of free citizens. Consider also that wherever slavery existed the status of a slave was that of chattel property, useful and necessary to his owner, but not permitting the slave to be treated like a free man. In societies where the debtor could be enslaved by his creditor or where the serf was considered practically as a slave, the rise of penal slavery, to use Beccaria's term, and its gradual extension to the members of the lower orders of society who committed crimes and finally to all persons convicted of serious crimes would seem to be a natural evolution. The demonstration of the accuracy of this contention can best be made in the study of the evolution of punishment in the southern states of the United

States where slavery was legal until abolished one century ago. Two illustrations will suffice:

The entire history of punishment can almost be said to be recapitulated in the State of Florida in the brief period of a century and a half. Prior to the 1860's punishments were capital, corporal, and financial and the local county jails were detention houses with the kind of inmates that have in historical times been found in such places. There was no interest in prison reform; the State itself had no prison. In 1869 a penitentiary act was adopted by the legislature providing for a state prison to be operated by the Commissioners of Public Institutions. The act authorized the Commissioners to enter into contracts with private persons for the labor of the prisoners. The act emphasized the need to make the prison self-supporting; this nullified another provision of the act, namely, that the contractors must insure the health and safety of the prisoners working for them.

The state penitentiary was located in an arsenal belonging to the Federal Government and for 2 years was governed as a military post where, for the lack of a work program, the prisoners were controlled by chains, muskets, and bayonets. In 1871 the prison was removed from the military, and 6 years later the State transferred the control and custody of the prisoners to private contractors who could now employ them anywhere in the State. Prisoners were leased to individuals and corporations and set to work in phosphate mines and in turpentine camps in the forests. By 1902 there were 30 such convict camps.

"The leasing of convicts," according to a report recently issued by the Florida Division of Correction, from which these data have been culled,

> resulted in incredible acts of brutality to prisoners. The atrocities of the system seem obvious to a modern observer, yet, state officials, conditioned by their culture, could observe that frequent convict camp investigations always found the convicts "well treated and cared for." ... In 1917, the legislature created the State Road Department and also the State Road Convict Force. The Board of Commissioners was authorized to allocate up to 300 convicts for use on the road force (the old *opus publicum*) ... the remaining convicts were leased to the counties and to private lessees.[7]

LEASING OF PRISONERS

Prisoners unable to do manual labor—mostly the aged, crippled, and deformed—had to be placed in a state prison, of course. In 1919 the Board of Commissioners were forbidden to lease convicts because public opinion had been aroused and outraged by some of the incidents that had occurred in the convict camps. Now these prisoners had to be placed in state prisons where they worked on large attached plantations under the guard of specially selected fellow-prisoners, who carried arms. It was not until 1957 that Florida adopted a Correctional Code and set up a State Division of Correction. Since then the State has rapidly joined the mainstream of modern penology.

The particular form of the contract system, known as the lease system described above, flourished in the old slave states of the South after the Civil War, when the slaves had been freed. Can anyone doubt that this kind of penal slavery was not only reminiscent of its most primitive forms but also was adopted as a suitable way of punishing former slaves, their descendants, and poor whites by a dominant group of former slaveowners and their sympathizers? The last state to abolish this system was Alabama, in 1928.

A RECENT PRISON SCANDAL

Penal slavery did not disappear when the lease system of prison labor was abandoned; it was merely transplanted into the state penitentiaries. The most recent prison scandal in the United States has just erupted in an old slave state, Arkansas. In 1897 the legislature of that State acquired a large plantation, which ... [had] 15,000 acres and later a subsidiary farm of 4,500 acres, which together constitute[d] the state penitentiary. The aim was to develop a self-supporting institution. That this aim...[was] realized is shown by the fact that in 1964, the penitentiary showed a net profit from its livestock and its cotton and vegetable acres of nearly half a million dollars. The major cost items were about $91,000 for feeding 1,900 prisoners and $57,000 for feeding the cattle.

This financial success...[was] achieved by working the prisoners from dawn to dusk, guarded by inmate guards, on foot or mounted, and armed with shotguns and rifles. There...[were] only 35 salaried employees in the two institutions combined, including the superintendent and his staff, chaplains, doctors, bookkeepers, and a chief warden and 18 so-called field wardens. Whipping...[was] authorized as disciplinary punishment for a variety of offenses including failure to perform one's quota of work. Nearly half of the inmates...[were African American] guarded by inmates of their race. The sentences served...[were] to hard labor and hard labor it...[was], and unpaid at that. No shops or prison industries exist[ed] except those necessary for the maintenance of the buildings, the agricultural machinery, and the trucking equipment.[8]

...[C]ertain incidents at the subsidiary farm known as the Tucker farm resulted in a thorough investigation by the state police of Arkansas. The investigation revealed conditions of corruption, maltreatment, and brutality that...[were] unbelievable. The...state administration...attempt[ed] to remedy the situation.[9]

CONCLUSION

These examples have not been chosen in order to denigrate the 52 prison systems of the United States, many of which are today acknowledged at home and abroad to be in the forefront of modern correctional treatment methods. I have chosen them to substantiate Radbruch's theory by showing that the primitive form of punitive imprisonment referred to as penal servitude or penal slavery, originally used for slaves (*servi poenae*) and later applied to free men, has not yet been completely stamped out despite the reforms in correctional treatment. I am, of course, aware that I have focused on perhaps the darkest side of the history of punitive imprisonment. Even so, much has been left unsaid. I have made no reference to the prison hulks of England, the treadmills and cranks, the British and French transportation systems, these variants of penal slavery which caused a British judge to say to a convicted murderer: "I shall pass upon you a sentence...which in my opinion will be a greater punishment than the momentary pain of death, for you will live like a slave laboring for others and have no reward for your labors. That sentence is that you be kept in penal servitude for life." Shades of Beccaria!

Nor have I referred to the innovations during the 19th century that have generally been regarded as progressive, such as the institutions governed by Obermayer in Bavaria, Montesinos in Spain, or Brockway's reformatory at Elmira, for instance, or the institutions for delinquent children or women that arose in the 19th century on both sides of the Atlantic and even earlier in Europe. From our present viewpoints, most of them were pale shadows of what we regard today as appropriate correctional institutions, even though at the time of their founding they were indeed trailbreakers.

One is tempted to speculate on the motive forces that have operated in producing the gradual progress toward the kind of correctional system we are today visualizing. Improvements in earlier times were and are to some degree even today motivated by humanitarian and religious feelings, but I believe that for penological progress in the last hundred years, slow at first and accelerated only since the second world war, we are indebted chiefly to the behavioral scientists—the psychiatrists, psychologists, and social scientists—whose studies and findings have gradually changed, generation after generation, the intellectual climate into which people, including legal scholars, legislators, correctional administrators, and the behavioral scientists themselves are born.

New ideas do not find easy acceptance, especially when they concern treatment of criminals and therefore meet emotional barriers. Max Planck once said that the only reason a scientific truth is accepted is not that its opponents are converted to it but that they die off and a new generation is born that takes that truth for granted. Perhaps this explains our presence here... discussing this week discussing correctional methods which a generation or two ago would have been considered unacceptable.

STUDY QUESTIONS

1. As a policy "thinker," Beccaria is often portrayed as a benevolent reformer advocating for mercy on the offender. Make a case for, and against, this portrayal.
2. What were the primary reasons behind the move from public torture and corporal punishment to imprisonment occurring as punishment?
3. What is meant by the phrase "penal slavery"?
4. What were some of the major consequences of moving to a correctional system based on confinement and imprisonment?

INTRODUCTION NOTE

*An address delivered at a Colloquium of the International Penal and Penitentiary Foundation at Ulm, West Germany, April 19, 1967.

NOTES

1. Gustav Radbruch, *Elegantiae Juris Criminalis* (2d Ed.). Basel: Verlog fur Recht und Gesellschaft A. G., 1950, p. 5.
2. *Ibid.*, pp. 8–9.
3. *Ibid.*, pp. 11–12.
4. Carl Ludwig von Bar, *A History of Continental Criminal Law.* Boston: Little, Brown & Co., 1916, p. 36.
5. George Ives, *A History of Penal Methods.* London: Stanley Paul & Co., 1914, p. 1.
6. Cesare Beccaria, *Dei delitti e delle pene,* xvi.
7. Florida Division of Corrections, *5th Biennial Report, July 1, 1964–June 30, 1966.* Tallahassee, Florida, 1966, p. 5.
8. Robert Pearman, "The Whip Pays Off," *The Nation*, 203: 701–704, December 26, 1966.
9. *Tucker Prison Farm Case.* Report No. 916–966, Criminal Investigations Division, Arkansas State Police, Little Rock, Arkansas.

4
PARTIAL JUSTICE

WOMEN, PRISONS, AND SOCIAL CONTROL

NICOLE HAHN RAFTER

Much of what is known regarding the structure and function of the corrective institution has focused on male offenders. Although male offenders make up the majority of the offending population, a very real need exists for more exploration of female offending. Nicole Hahn Rafter's essay provides a historical analysis of an institution designed to house female offenders during the nineteenth and early twentieth centuries. The Albion institution in New York, although housing serious female offenders, also may have served as an extension of formal social control for nonserious female offenders who, for various reasons, did not conform to proper norms. Such women were taught the virtues of a "good, womanly life." This essay provides yet another example of how important the greater social context is when studying institutional evolution.

Over the last several decades, historians and sociologists have devoted increasing attention to the phenomenon of social control—the mechanisms by which powerful groups consciously or unconsciously attempt to restrain and to induce conformity, even assent, among less powerful but nonetheless threatening segments of society. Laws, institutions such as schools and prisons, medical policies, informal gestures of approbation or displeasure, even forms of language—all may constitute forms of social control. (Social control in this sense should not be confused with criminological control theory . . . which offers an explanation for law-violating behaviors; through a complicated and terminologically unfortunate series of developments in social science, similar terms have been adopted to label different concepts.) The control achieved may be merely external, as when people are forced to do things against their wills; or it may be internal, so thoroughly absorbed by its subjects that they come to monitor and correct their own deviations from prescription. In recent years, research in social control has moved in two directions particularly germane to the study of women's prisons. First, it has come to focus sharply on the political implications of coercion. As David Rothman puts it, "A social control orientation . . . suggest[s] that [institutional] innovations were likely to confer benefits somewhere, and so the question becomes, where? If the prison did not serve the prisoner, then whom did it serve?" In other words, historians and sociologists no longer assume that the narratives of social controllers (who often speak sincerely of the benefits they expect to confer on prisoners and the like) tell the whole story; the picture has been broadened to include the political ramifications of extended controls for both reformers and the subjects of reform. Second, feminist theorists have become sensitive to ways in which social controls are exercised on women *as women*, to encourage conformity to prescribed gender roles.

This chapter analyzes an aspect of the social control of women by focusing on a particular type of prison, the women's reformatory. It explores the conjunction between formal vehicles of social control (in this case the laws establishing reformatories and the institutions themselves) and the internalization of their social control "messages" by the targeted group of inmates. The chapter also deals with social control in terms of social class—the process by which, through establishment and operation of women's reformatories, middle-class crusaders came to impose their definition of womanliness on working-class inmates. This chapter...is concerned with the movement's political implications. Without denying the benevolence of the reformers' aims, it attempts to look beyond good intentions to the movement's methods of social control and their results.

The women's reformatory, as we have seen, was unique as an institution for adults. Founded by middle- (often upper-middle-) class social feminists, reformatories extended government control over working-class women not previously vulnerable to state punishment. In addition, the reformatories institutionalized bourgeois standards for female propriety, making it possible to "correct" women for moral offenses for which adult men were not sent to state penal institutions. And reformatories feminized prison discipline, introducing into state prisons for women a program of rehabilitation predicated on middle-class definitions of ladylike behavior. For these reasons, the women's reformatory served special, female-specific functions with regard to social class and social control.

In this chapter, New York's Western House of Refuge at Albion, operated between 1894 and 1931, is used as a case study. Albion built upon experiments by its forerunners to become the first women's prison to realize completely the reformatory plan in architecture, administrative structure, type of inmates and sentence, and program. It established the model adopted by many women's reformatories opened in the early twentieth century. Additionally, Albion adhered to the goals of the women's reformatory movement more consistently than many sister institutions that succumbed to overcrowding, inadequate financing, and routinization. Although it was atypical in this respect, Albion provides a good case for analyzing the ways in which the reformatory movement extended social control just because it did manage to remain relatively "pure." The detailed nature of Albion's prisoner registries and the survival of case files on individual inmates, moreover, make it possible to follow in some depth the events that brought women to this prison, their institutional treatment, and their reactions to it.

SOCIAL CONTROL FUNCTIONS OF THE ALBION REFORMATORY

Records of the Albion reformatory indicate that in terms of social control, the institution served two primary functions: sexual and vocational regulation. It attempted the first by training "loose" young women to accept a standard of propriety that dictated chastity until marriage and fidelity thereafter. It tried to achieve the second by training charges in homemaking, a competency they were to utilize either as dutiful daughters or wives within their own families or as servants in the homes of others. In operation, techniques used to achieve these ends were usually indistinguishable. Although they are separated here for analytical purposes, in actuality tactics used to realize the dual goals of sexual and vocational regulation worked together, coalescing and mutually reinforcing one another.

FROM SEXUAL AUTONOMY TO PROPRIETY: PREPARATION FOR THE "TRUE GOOD WOMANLY LIFE"

To control the sexual activities of "promiscuous" women, the Albion reformatory used several approaches. One was the initial act of incarcerating women who had violated standards of sexual conduct for the "true woman." Second was parole revocation if a prisoner showed signs of lapsing back into impropriety while out on conditional release. Third was transfer of intractables to a custodial asylum for "feebleminded" women at Rome, New York, where they could be held indefinitely.

Over the thirty-seven years of its operation as a reformatory, Albion received about 3,150 prisoners. The menial nature of the jobs at which their parents ware employed and their own previously high rates of employment at poorly paid, low-skilled jobs indicate that most of these prisoners were working-class women. Three-quarters of them were between fifteen and twenty-one years old, the rest under thirty. The vast majority—over 95 percent—were white. Most had been born in New York State (particularly in the rural western area where the institution was located) of native-born parents; one-third were Catholic, while nearly all the rest were Protestant; and most were single. The composition of the population reflected the desire of Albion's officials to work with cases who appeared malleable and deserving. The institution's commitment law authorized it to receive women convicted of petit larceny, habitual drunkenness, common prostitution, frequenting a disorderly house, or any other misdemeanor. Originally, it could hold them for up to five years; later, the maximum number of years was reduced to three. Less than 2 percent of the prisoners were convicted of violent crimes (and these were mainly second or third degree assault) and but another 14 percent of property offenses (mainly petit larceny). The great majority (over 80 percent) had been sentenced for public order offenses—victimless crimes such as public intoxication, waywardness, and vagrancy.

... [F]or at least half (and perhaps up to three-quarters) of Albion's inmates, the act that led to incarceration had actually been sexual misconduct. Some of these women were apprehended for prostitution. Most, however, were merely sexually active, engaging in flirtations and affairs for pleasure instead of money. The efforts of Albion and other reformatories to curb sexual independence by women occurred within the wider context of antiprostitution and other social purity campaigns. Members of the middle and upper classes increasingly committed themselves to the cleansing of society. At the same time, however, some working women became indifferent to traditional definitions of virtue. In rapidly growing numbers, they left home to join the paid labor force. By 1910, a record high of 27 percent of all New York State women were gainfully employed. Even more significantly, nearly 80 percent of Albion's inmates had previously worked for wages. As they acquired a degree of independence, working women turned to new amusements. To smoke cigarettes, frequent dance halls, and become involved in sexual relationships did not strike *them* as depravity; but their disinterest in the ideals of "true" womanhood evoked alarm in those dedicated to the battle against vice. Reformers came to consider any deviation from female sexual propriety, even when it did not involve a financial transaction, as a form of "prostitution."

The sexual misconduct for which women were incarcerated at Albion came to the attention of authorities through a variety of routes. Sometimes irate parents reported sexually active daughters to the police; at others, cuckolded husbands complained to court officials. Premarital pregnancies alerted social control agents in many cases. In yet others, discovery of venereal diseases led to commitment. For many women, a sign of sexual impurity in combination with some other suspicious circumstance seems to have precipitated arrest. For example, Anna H., one of Albion's few black inmates, evidently came to the attention of police when her husband was arrested for attempted burglary. Anna was examined, found to have venereal disease, and sentenced to Albion for vagrancy. There was no question of her fidelity to her husband: reformatory officials accepted Anna's statement that it was he who had infected her, and they later refused to release her on the theory that she would return to him ("the combination is a very bad one"). But Anna had been living apart from her husband, supporting herself as a waitress, and this irregular arrangement may have increased officials' consternation.

Ostensibly, venereal disease was also the ground on which Lillian R., a Coney Islander of orthodox Jewish background, was originally committed; but in her case, too, unseemly independence and bad associates may have contributed to authorities' concern. Having quit school after the seventh grade to help her widowed mother support a large family, Lillian had been variously employed as a messenger, box factory worker, and forewoman in an artificial flower shop. At the age of sixteen she ran off with a soldier for a week and contracted venereal disease. She and her mother decided (according to her record) that "it would not be right for her to remain in her home with the other children. She was... put into the Magdalene home. [She] was there one week when sent to the City Hospital for treatment." At the hospital Lillian was charged with "contracting an infectious disease in the practice of debauchery" and sentenced to the Bedford reformatory, from which she was later transferred to Albion.

Some women committed to Albion for sexual misbehavior had in fact been sexually victimized. Such was the case with Anna B., who at the age of fourteen had been charged with ungovernability and sent to the Salvation Army Home in Buffalo, where she bore her first child. Not long after she returned home, her father was sentenced to prison for rape. Anna's case file strongly suggests that she was the victim. While her father was still on trial, Anna was sent to Pennsylvania to live with a grandmother. Within a month, she became pregnant by the sixty-year-old man for whom her grandmother kept house. Anna returned home, where she went to work in a restaurant. Convicted of "running around" when she was seven months into this second pregnancy, Anna seems actually to have been exploited twice by much older men.

Although a handful of cases were, like Anna B., "led astray," most of Albion's inmates appear to have been rebels of some sort—against the double standard of sexual morality; against their families or husbands; or against public regulations such as that prohibiting disorderly conduct. But perhaps "rebels" is not the most accurate term: in officials' view, they defied conventions, but many of these young women may have been acting in accordance with other standards that they themselves considered legitimate. Despite their youth, the majority were independent at the point when police officers plucked them from saloons, hotel rooms, and street corners to be sent to the reformatory. Four-fifths of them held jobs. Although over 70 percent had not yet married, they were no longer under their parents' control. Whether reacting defiantly against conventional concepts of morality or simply behaving in ways they regarded as acceptable, most clearly had not internalized a view of themselves as "proper" women, demure and asexual. It was this situation that the reformatory, with its goal of imposing and teaching sexual control, sought to remedy.

If incarceration and training within the institution did not teach the prisoner to conform, the reformatory employed another means: parole revocation. Most of Albion's inmates were released on parole before their sentences expired. During the period of parole their behavior was scrutinized by the institution's parole officers, community officials, and employers.... When parole was revoked, the violation was frequently sexual in nature.

Some women had parole revoked for overt returns to vice. Such was the case with inmate No. 1899, recalled to Albion after "an officer of Endicott, N.Y., arrested her in a questionable resort." Similarly, inmate No. 1913 was forced to return when, after marrying during parole, she was reported by her husband "for misconduct with men." Women who became pregnant during parole were returned to the institution—unless they quickly married someone "respectable." At other times revocation was triggered not by blatant signs of immorality but rather by indications that a lapse was imminent. One woman was returned to the reformatory because she "became infatuated with a married man named L___. Mrs. L___wrote us" and, after investigating, reformatory officials decided to recall her. Another parolee was revoked for associating with the father of her child ("they were not married and Washington is a most disreputable character"), and No. 1313 barely escaped revocation when "two former inmates report[ed] seeing her frequently at night with different conductors on the Genesee St. line."

In cases that appeared hopeless to Albion's administrators, a third step was sometimes taken to ensure against relapse: transfer to the State School at Rome or another of New York's institutions for the feebleminded. Such transfers carried an automatic extension of sentence up to life, for according to popular theory of the time, the feebleminded never improve. At the turn of the century, the feebleminded were considered innately promiscuous, so Albion's authorities easily assumed that women who would not reform were feebleminded "defective delinquents." Because intelligence testing was still in a primitive stage, it was not difficult to confirm "scientifically" a suspicion of feeblemindedness and thus establish the basis for a transfer. These transfers, which occurred in cases of women who were disciplinary problems within the institution as well as in instances of overt sexuality while on parole, constituted the final disposition for forty-eight of the sampled cases, or 3 percent of all first releases. In addition, thirteen women who were returned to the reformatory for parole violation (5.2 percent of those who were released a second time), and two women (5.6 percent of the thirty-six sampled cases who returned twice to the reformatory and then discharged a third time) were transferred to institutions for the feebleminded. Case file documents such as school records and letters written by these supposedly feebleminded women indicate that they were not in fact mentally retarded. They were, however, noncompliant. The lesson of their transfer to civil institutions was probably not lost on those left behind at the reformatory.

FROM SAUCINESS TO SUBSERVIENCE: PREPARATION FOR DOMESTIC SERVICE

The second central social control function of the Albion reformatory was to train inmates to become competent housekeepers in either their own homes or those where they were placed as domestics. The institution aimed, in the words of its managers, to reform "unfortunate and wayward girls" by giving them "moral and religious training... and such training in domestic work as will eventually enable them to find employment, secure good homes and be self-supporting." To the achievement of this end, the managers viewed the cottage system, with its "plan of ordinary domestic life," as crucial. Acquisition of decorum was also considered critical; the institution emphasized gentility in all aspects of its program. Within this institutional facsimile of the genteel home, inmates received both academic and domestic training, with by far the heavier emphasis falling on the latter. Albion seldom educated inmates beyond the sixth grade level, but it provided abundant opportunities for perfection of domestic skills, instructing prisoners in dressmaking, plain and fancy sewing, knitting, crocheting, "cookery," cleaning, and "ventilation." A steam-operated washing machine was purchased for the institution's laundry, but the sight of it made visiting prison commissioner Sarah L. Davenport "sorry," for it was "not educating the women...for the homes they will go to when they leave Albion." Thereafter, the laundry was washed by hand. A "finely equipped domestic science department," outfitted with dining room furniture, coal and gas burners, and kitchen utensils, was added in 1912, and from then on inmates received instruction in:

> manufacture and source of food supplies, relative cost, and nutritive values; the care of the kitchen, pantry, and dining room; construction and care of the sinks, stoves, (both gas and coal) and refrigerators; table etiquette; the planning and serving of meals; and waitress' duties.

When members of the board of managers met at the reformatory, inmates practiced for future employment by waiting on their table. As Elliott Curie has put it in writing of the Massachusetts reformatory, the institution "trained women to be women."

For middle-class women who lived in its vicinity, Albion provided trained, inexpensive household help. It was the institution's policy "to place our girls in the home of a woman who will take a motherly interest in them." One-quarter of the prisoners were paroled directly to live-in domestic positions. Of the 50 percent paroled to members of their own families, another sizeable proportion also took jobs as domestics. Housekeeping was familiar to Albion's prisoners, many of whom reported their previous occupation as "domestic" or "houseworker." But the reformatory's records suggest that some, at least, had been less than satisfactory servants, given to carelessness, impudence, filching, and running off with young men. The institution tried to turn these and other inmates into competent, submissive domestics.

Attempts by Albion and other reformatories to train domestics took place at a time when the "servant problem" was particularly intense. Difficulties in finding suitable servants became acute after the Civil War and continued to be so well into the twentieth century. As the number of families that could afford servants increased, the interest of working-class women in domestic service declined. The latter came to prefer factory jobs that offered more money, shorter hours, and greater autonomy. Those who had no alternative to domestic service resented the power of the mistress; they also objected to the social restrictions of live-in positions and to expectations of servility. Many reacted to such conditions with impertinence and petty theft. The distaste of working women for domestic service created a predicament for would-be employers. Servants were necessary for the operation of their households, and (equally important) they were a sign of status. Thus in increasing the supply of well-trained domestics, reformatory officials supported the interests of other middle-class women.

Nearly 20 percent of Albion's prisoners had worked before arrest in mills or factories. But as noted earlier, the frequent economic crises of the late nineteenth and early twentieth centuries led to widespread unemployment, and serious labor unrest. Insofar as reformatories removed women from the industrial labor force, they made more jobs available for men. In view of these circumstances, the reformatory's refusal to provide training in industrial skills deemed "unfit" for women, and the promotion of skills geared toward domestic service is especially significant. "No industries are maintained," one Albion report declared, "but every inmate is taught to cook and care for a home. This is the most important thing in the work of the institution. Most of the girls when paroled go into homes where this knowledge is necessary." Thus Albion not only provided rigorous training in housekeeping but also tended to discourage inmates from moving beyond the home and earning higher wages. It reinforced the point that women's place was in the home by paroling most women to family situations where they were needed as paid or unpaid domestic help.

Employers and the institution formed a symbiotic alliance over the discipline of women paroled as servants. The reformatory required women released to domestic positions to sign a form agreeing to

> accept the wages agreed upon between the Superintendent...and her employer...her wages to be retained by employer, excepting such amount as the latter thinks necessary for [the] girl.... [C]onsult employer as to her amusements, recreation, and social diversions. To form no friendships, not to visit or receive visits from members of her own family unless approved by the Superintendent. Is not to go out nights excepting when accompanied by a responsible person, and to go very seldom at night. To have one afternoon a week....

Paroled women were also required to send monthly reports to the reformatory, and they were further supervised through visits from a parole officer. If despite these controls a domestic became difficult, the reformatory could revoke parole, a threat that no doubt helped employers maintain discipline. These restraints notwithstanding, many women paroled to domestic positions behaved noncompliantly. Revocations were occasioned by "sauciness," "obscenity," failure to work hard enough, and other demonstrations of independence. Inmate No. 13, for example,

> went to Rochester to work for Mrs....J___ and for a time did very nicely but finding some girls of her acquaintance she began to visit them too often and to neglect her work. She came back to the institution in Aug. 1897 and there remained till [sentence] expiration.

Inmate No. 2585 was originally paroled to a Mrs. F___of Rochester. But, "Jane was a slow worker and very untidy and shiftless. She was very fond of reading. Returned [to the reformatory] for a change of place...." Next Jane was sent to a Mrs. S___of Buffalo. This time, "On Oct. 11 went to a movie and did not return until eleven o'clock when she was expected at nine." When Mrs. S___ threatened to return her to Albion, Jane fled. She was not recaptured, but others on domestic parole were returned to the institution for laziness, disobedience, and running away.

In return for the institution's help with disciplining difficult domestics, employers supervised prisoners. They were "authorized and requested to open and read all mail sent and received by girl" and further charged "to guard her morals, language and actions, and aid her as much as possible by advice as to her present and future conduct...." In the course of aiding fallen women, employers were also aiding themselves by maintaining the quality of the services they received. The entire arrangement, in fact, seems to have been one from which employers benefitted greatly, receiving trained and supervised servants who promised to consult them in all matters and work six and one-half days a week. If the servant became shiftless or impudent, the criminal justice system would step in to do the necessary disciplining.

TECHNIQUES OF SOCIAL CONTROL

Albion developed a variety of techniques to encourage reform. Some have already been identified: the initial act of incarcerating women for sexual misconduct and other petty offenses; intensive training in domesticity and gentility; a policy of parole to domestic positions; community surveillance; parole revocation; and transfer of the most uncooperative to civil institutions where they could be held indefinitely. Implicit in many of these techniques was another: from the moment of arrest, Albion's inmates were reduced to the standing of children. Like juvenile delinquents, many were detained for status offenses—immorality, waywardness, keeping bad company—for which men the same age were not arrested. At the reformatory they were supervised by motherly matrons, and at parole they were usually released to family situations in which they had a dependent position. Indeed, the very concept of an institution dedicated to the rescue and reform of women under the age of thirty, and operated with an extremely high level of discretionary authority, was rooted in a view of women as childlike creatures. Appropriately, like institutions for juvenile delinquents, Albion was titled a "refuge."

Disruption of inmates' ties with their families was another mechanism used by the reformatory to encourage inmates to conform to its values. Some prisoners, to be sure, had already separated from their families; but being independent through one's own choice was not the same as being severed from one's family by others—and at a time of crisis. Familial disruption was a technique to which women were especially susceptible, their roles being so intimately involved with domestic life. Disconnected from their own families, Albion inmates were more likely to identify with the surrogate "families" of their cottages and, on parole, with those to which they were sent as servants.

Disruption of family life is an inevitable by-product of incarceration, but Albion developed policies relating to mail and visitors that intensified the break. Once in custody, women had immense difficulty contacting families and friends. They were permitted to write letters only once every two months, and these were censored. If the Superintendent decided that either the contents or the designated recipient was unsuitable, she would file the letter in the inmate's folder—quite probably without notifying the writer and certainly without notifying the intended recipient, both of whom might therefore wait in vain anticipation. Incoming mail was also censored and often filed away undelivered. Visits were permitted, but only four times a year. A further restriction limited the pool of potential visitors to close relatives, and even these might be banned if deemed bad influences. Moreover, some approved visitors doubtless were discouraged from visiting by the institution's geographical isolation. For all these reasons, commitment to the reformatory resulted in nearly total severance of ties to former support groups. Isolated in this fashion, prisoners became more susceptible to the institution's staff and its moral advice.

Another aspect of familial disruption, separation from children, was sometimes traumatically final. When women were committed, their children might be sent to orphanages or put up for adoption. Such removals occurred even in instances when inmates had husbands living at home. Thus not only were young mothers severed from their children; they also had to suffer the knowledge that their families had been dissolved. In such cases, moreover, the children were now being cared for by strangers. To judge from Albion's records, its inmates were not informed of the welfare of institutionalized or adopted children.

Occasionally ultimate disposition of children would be left undecided and used to induce the mother to conform. Of a woman committed for vagrancy, for instance, the registry reports,

> Edna made a splendid record while on parole. Mr. Angel, Humane Officer of Courtland County[,] was so well pleased with her that he returned her children to her.

Not to please Mr. Angel, it seems, would have resulted in loss of her children. Another example is provided by the case of Martha, a mother of four, sentenced to Albion for public intoxication. Threat of removal of her children kept Martha sober even in times of great stress:

> Martha returned [on parole] to her husband who had promised every[thing] in the way of reform but who is the veriest hypocrite [*sic*]. She continued leading a true good womanly life hoping to be worthy of her children, as the authorities had promised to restore them when they were satisfied that she would hold out.

In instances like these, there was the initial familial disruption occasioned by commitment and then a threat of farther disruption—total loss of children—if the prisoner did not comply with the institution's requirements.

Similar methods of control involved babies who stayed with mothers at the institution. If a woman was nursing at commitment, she was allowed to bring the child with her. Those women who gave birth at Albion were permitted to keep infants. But reformatory policy decreed that all babies had to leave when they reached the age of two. Sometimes the institution decided not to parole a woman until after the baby had been sent away. Mary P___, for example, bore a child a few days after her arrival at Albion in 1922, and in September 1924, two years having expired, the child was sent to the Delaware County Superintendent of the Poor. Mary was paroled just a month later to work in her father's cigar factory. Mary's parents may have refused to let her bring home an illegitimate child. Whatever the reason, the effect of holding her slightly beyond the mandatory release date for the baby was to cut Mary off from the only family she had for two years. She was, moreover, returned to a situation in which she herself was the child.

Some babies brought into or born at the prison were sent to adoption agencies or other institutions before they reached the age of two. How long their mothers might keep them was a matter of administrative discretion, and like all such matters, liable to be used as a mechanism of control. Albion's records do not refer to the practice of using children to coerce institutionalized mothers, but this form of social control is described in a letter from the Superintendent of Maine's State Reformatory for Women to a journalist who had requested information on babies in prison. "The conduct of the mothers," the superintendent informed him,

> decides in a measure the time they are allowed to spend with their babies.... They dress and undress and feed their own babies after the baby is six months old. They always have the privilege to kiss them goodnight and to spend an hour in the afternoon with them, unless their conduct precludes the loss [*sic*] of this privilege.

Restricting access to children was probably used as a social control device at Albion and other reformatories as well.

Despite its emphasis on the home as woman's place, Albion developed parole policies that further disrupted some inmates' ties to their former homes. Women who before incarceration lived in stable family situations were frequently paroled not to their own families but to domestic positions in the homes of others. In some instances, the institution deemed the original family unsuitable and wanted to keep the woman away from it as long as possible. In others, officials seem simply to have decided that for a woman to work and save money was the best way for her to pass parole. Often the domestic jobs were in towns distant from the prisoners' families. Women could take infants with them to some domestic live-in positions, but others required them to leave their babies behind.

Many of these dislocating factors were present in the case of Marjorie M., a twenty-year-old of German extraction who, before commitment, lived with her parents and seven siblings in Batavia, where she was employed as a domestic. The mother of a three-year-old and again pregnant, Marjorie was convicted of disorderly conduct in 1917 and sent to Albion. There she gave birth to her second daughter, Helen. Paroled to a domestic position in Rochester, Marjorie sent five dollars of her eight-dollar weekly salary to the home where Helen was boarded. After parole, she found employment as assistant housekeeper at the Rochester Orphan's Asylum, where Helen was now living. Helen died of diphtheria in the winter of 1920. At this point Marjorie, who at the time of arrest had been living with ten members of her immediate family, was left entirely alone.

The reformatory's policies also perpetuated familial disruption in the case of Henrietta S., a Binghamton woman with two children. After serving time at Albion for intoxication, Henrietta was paroled to a domestic position in Lyndonville, where she earned four dollars a week. When her term was up, she returned to her family with $154 she had managed to save from her wages. The institution interpreted the large sum as a sign of success, but Henrietta and her family paid a high psychological price in return: their family life had been interrupted for three years, and while a Mrs. F___ of Lyndonville had cheap use of her services, Henrietta's own children had been deprived of her care.

The reformatory's parole policies were not disruptive of family life in all instances, and perhaps some women who *were* returned to parents or husbands would have preferred a less restrictive arrangement. In either case, the institution exercised tremendous control over inmates' social contacts (probably more than any contemporary prison for men), and it used this control to induce conformity. Denying inmates access to mail and visitors, institutionalizing their children or threatening to do so, on occasion probably blocking access to infants within the prison, developing parole policies that frequently prevented contact with families—through such means the prison demonstrated its power and often disrupted the continuity of whatever family life had existed. The effect was to encourage dependency on the institution and increase the likelihood that inmates would internalize the reformatory's teachings about how women like themselves should behave.

"THE BEST PLACE TO CONQUER GIRLS": THE REFORMATORY'S SUCCESS

Many women incarcerated at Albion went on to lead lives that met the institution's criteria for success, marrying and maintaining homes of their own or remaining for long terms in domestic placements. No doubt many former inmates would have become more sedate in their mid-twenties or early thirties even without the moral influence of the prison, just as more serious offenders outgrow crime. But the reformatory does seem to have set some formerly wayward women on the path to propriety— to have served, in the words of one inmate's sister, as "the only and best place to conquer girls." Albion appears, that is, to have achieved its goals in some, perhaps even a majority, of cases.

The reformatory worked through kindness as well as coercion, and therein lay the key to its success. Had it merely punished, it would have antagonized; but Albion also performed extensive nurturing functions, alleviating some of the harsher aspects of poverty. It served as a hospital where the diseased could receive treatment, the malnourished food, the pregnant decent care at delivery. It also functioned as a shelter to which women could turn from incestuous fathers and brutal husbands. The superintendent and other staff offered counseling in careers, marriage, and child-rearing. Moreover, the institution provided training in manners that many working-class women may have considered valuable: refined behavior was widely regarded as a sign of female superiority, particularly by people with authority and status.

To be sure, the reformatory did not bring every case to the desired conclusion. It tended to be least successful with women whose families had resisted their commitment. In the case of Anna H., the black woman sentenced for vagrancy, for instance, the reformatory was bombarded with appeals for release from the inmate's frantic parents and their lawyer, the mayor of Newport, Rhode Island; the latter also elicited requests for Anna's discharge from the offices of New York's State Board of Charities and Governor Alfred E. Smith. When the superintendent refused to heed these appeals, Anna attempted to escape. Lillian R., the inmate originally sentenced to the Bedford reformatory for "debauchery," was similarly unappreciative of institutionalization. At Bedford she participated in the July 1920 riots against cruelty to inmates. Subsequently, Bedford's matrons told her she was to be paroled, but as Lillian explained in a letter to her mother, "I knew that parole talk was all a frameup"; she realized she was really being transferred to Albion, at the other end of the state. "[I]f they were any kind of women they would tell us just where we are going and not say that we were paroled.... [T]hen they wonder why the girls don't respect them." Lillian's later letters show that she was equally critical of the matrons at Albion. Other inmates demonstrated resistance by misbehaving on parole:

> Julia was a great care throughout her parole... deceitful & deceptive. [No. 1581]
>
> She was arrested while on parole and sentenced again to the W.H. of R. But we refused to take her again. [No. 1355]
>
> Minnie gave entire satisfaction [while on domestic parole] for several months[,] saved her money[,] was quiet and unobtrusive....The spirit of unrest [then] took possession of her and she absconded, and no trace of her has been found. [No. 89]

When No. 61 sold her discharge clothes, "bought a telescope," and ran away from the Wayfarers' Lodge in Buffalo, reformatory officials resignedly observed, "[A] perverse nature and bad blood [had] proved too strong for human endeavor."

On the other hand, Albion's records also provide evidence that numerous inmates were grateful for its help. Some, especially those who were very young, alone in the world, or in poor health, seem not to have found incarceration onerous. A few, for example, requested to stay for their full terms, without parole. Inmate No. 1257 resisted leaving Albion for an unpleasant home situation: her mother had been committed to an insane asylum, and there were small children whose care would fall on her. "When it came time for her to go... she cried and it was with difficulty that the Parole Officer persuaded her to go." Some parolees ran back to the institution from uncongenial domestic placements. One woman, after having been paroled twice, returned "and asked to be admitted. She was a wreck, physically and morally—her clothing torn and soiled and evidently [she] had no place to go for the night nor money to pay her way." The reformatory gave her medical attention and sheltered her for another six months. After marrying, some former inmates brought their husbands to visit the reformatory and meet its superintendent. A woman who had escaped later wrote from a distant state to announce that she was happily married; her resentment at being confined, in other words, was not incompatible with a desire to demonstrate that she could achieve the institution's ideals. Many women wrote back after release. "My dear Mrs. Boyd," began a letter received by superintendent Boyd in 1907,

> [H]ave [you] entirely forgotten Nellie that one time lived in your pleasant Home for Homeless Girls.
>
> I have been thinking for some time that I would write to you....Of course you have heard from Mrs. Green that I am married and have a good Husband....Are any of the Ladies [officers] with you now that were in the years of 1894 or 95...how I would like to see them as well as your self..... I have a very pleasant home and appreciate it I think as I ought to. Yours in haste and with love,
>
> Nellie (I am Ever) L___

Albion succeeded in persuading inmates like Nellie to identify with its standards for correct female behavior. These were, essentially, middle-class standards. While many members of the working class may also have endorsed them, women sentenced to Albion had not—deviations from these values had led to their incarceration. In reforming (and in wanting to demonstrate reformation), successful cases had by definition come to identify with middle-class concepts of female propriety. Class identification was very much in flux at the turn of the century. As Charles Rosenberg has explained,

> [S]tatus definitions in 19th century America were...particularly labile....A good many Americans must, it follows, have been all the more anxious in their internalization of those aspects of life-style which seemed to embody and assure class status. And contemporaries clearly regard overt sexuality, especially in women, as part of a life-style demeaning to middle-class status.

When women who had been apprehended for sexual misconduct and other signs of independence from middle-class "status definitions" became chaste or sober or (like Nellie) "appreciative" of husband and home, the middle-class won an ideological victory. Its values had been affirmed; its symbols of status had been accorded validity by women of the working-class.

The reformatory probably influenced the values not only of those sentenced to it but also of women in the broader community. Albion's records show that some inmates knew each other before commitment and continued to associate after release. But to be a prisoner was unusual; since acquaintanceship networks existed among inmates, these networks must have been even more extensive between inmates and women never incarcerated. Through such connections, Albion would have come to play a role in the consciousness of working-class women in its area. Women who never set foot inside it would have been aware, through word of mouth, that there existed a state institution prepared to punish them for deviations from middle-class definitions of womanliness.

Informal as well as formal police actions reinforced the social values endorsed by Albion, reminding women in the community of the institution's potential for punishment. This kind of informal social control is almost invisible today since it was seldom noted in official records. Yet glimpses of it can be caught from time to time in reformatory documents. One hint appears in the registry record of inmate No. 2441, a woman confined for vagrancy. She had no previous arrests, according to the registry, but had been "taken to the Police Station twice and talked to for being out late, attending dances." Whereas this particular woman was evidently not influenced by police efforts to get her to behave properly (she did, after all, end up at the reformatory), others so treated may have been. Of No. 1775, paroled in 1919, we are told,

> Edna was very erratic and unreliable during her parole. She was reported [to the reformatory] by the Binghamton police as being on the streets at a late hour very frequently with different men. Chief Cronin was asked several times [by reformatory officials] to arrest her and instructed his men to that effect.

Other police chiefs probably also ordered their men to keep women like Edna in line. Thus, through informal procedures as well as formal arrests, the police helped uphold the reformatory's values; they, too, gave women incentives to submit and behave.

THE DEFINITION OF GENDER

Most other women's reformatories also aimed at rescue and reform and used techniques of social control similar to those of Albion. From Maine to North Carolina, New York to Nebraska, reformatories for women removed errant women from the streets, trained them in domestic skills, and returned them to the home. Through parole supervision they also encouraged inmates on conditional release to maintain "self-control" at work and in sexual relationships; and if located in states with facilities for the feebleminded, they also used transfers to such institutions as an auxiliary disciplinary measure. All prisons of the reformatory type seem to have exercised tight control over mail, visitors, and disposition of children. Like Albion, most other reformatories were multifunctional institutions that served as hospitals, refuges, schools, vocational training and placement agencies, and counseling centers—as well as prisons. Officials at many were rewarded by former inmates who returned, after discharge, to give thanks and demonstrate that they had indeed reformed.

The prisoners of these institutions were burdened by multiple disadvantages. They and their families fell near the bottom of the class hierarchy. In addition to being poor, the prisoners suffered the disability of being women in a society that barred women from many occupations, paid them less than male workers, and imposed male authority everywhere. Race was yet another factor relegating black or Indian women to the base of the social structure, while nativist prejudices pushed the foreign-born toward the margins of society. Most reformatory prisoners were young, a further drawback in terms of status. Those who were single—and they were probably in the majority at other reformatories as well as at Albion—were at another disadvantage in a society that placed a premium on marriage for women.

The prisoners were, then, located at the bottom of many power dimensions in their society, those defined by social class, sex, age, marital status, and (for some) race or ethnicity. But they did not stay put in these lowly positions. They had no authority, yet as the many cases of incorrigible daughters, wandering wives, and unreliable servants in reformatory reports indicate, they balked at obedience. Lacking autonomy, they nonetheless acted independently. Bereft of status, many refused to behave as inferiors. Their very handicaps, in fact, created a situation of some fluidity. As women who had to work, they had achieved a degree (albeit minimal) of economic self-sufficiency. Denied the luxury of being kept, they were to some extent freed from cultural imagery that associated "good" women with fragility and submissiveness. Youth in combination with physical maturity and lack of marital attachment probably encouraged them to seek sexual pleasure outside marriage. Thus their characteristics and situations promoted disengagement from their era's standards for propriety.

Among the factors that fostered establishment of woman's reformatories, two were of special importance: changes in gender roles in nineteenth- and early twentieth-century America and the simultaneous widening of divisions between social classes. During the nineteenth century, as production came to be located outside the family, women were increasingly isolated within the home. Their labor was devalued and a premium came to be placed on feminine characteristics such as domesticity, demureness, purity, and piety. But the ideal of true womanhood was more easily approximated by women of the middle than of the working class. The former were likely to have servants and other aids to gentility, and if they became restless they could take up causes like temperance and prison reform.

Intensification of gender roles had different implications for working-class women, however. For them, true womanhood was more difficult to achieve and less rewarding. As the nineteenth century flowed into the twentieth, some middle-class women (including those who founded and ran reformatories) participated in the gradual break from traditional roles. But for them, activity in the world was more likely to be compatible with respectability; charitable work, for instance, had long been a hallmark of the lady, and social feminism posed no real threat to male authority. But activities available to working-class women in search of self-fulfillment meshed less well with traditional notions of rectitude. Indeed, some of them, such as drinks in saloons, late night cigarettes with sailors, and casual affairs, became grounds for imprisonment.

Persuaded of innate temperamental differences between the sexes, the reformers naturally set about establishing separate prisons for women run by women; and believing that woman's mission included rescue of the unfortunate, they naturally focused on fallen women—not serious felons or confirmed prostitutes but wayward "girls" who might be saved. Those among them active in social purity campaigns argued against the double standard of sexual morality for men and women. Yet all the reformers worked to found or operate prisons that in fact institutionalized the double standard. Their understanding of "woman's nature" led logically to advocacy of special help for the frailer sex.

This understanding was embodied in laws establishing reformatories that could incarcerate women for minor offenses, mainly "moral" in nature. In many cases, apparently, the understanding came to be internalized by inmates. This internalization provides an instance of the ability of law to perform hegemonic functions—to reproduce the ideological and political conditions of social hierarchy. As Diane Polan has explained, "In respect to patriarchy, a set of ideas... operate[s] hegemonically to the extent it succeeds in convincing women that their inferior political, economic, and social status is a result of a *natural* division of the world into separate spheres and *natural* differences between male and female personalities... rather than the result of exploitation and domination." From this perspective, inmates' acceptance of reformatory values can be seen as a phase in the process that another writer describes as "the *embourgeoisement* of the working class," its absorption of middle-class attitudes toward status, security, property, the family—and gender roles.

Two groups of women—the working-class offenders and the middle-class reformers—met, so to speak, at the gate of the women's reformatory. The struggle between them was economically functional to the reformers: it helped maintain a pool of cheap domestic labor for women like themselves and, by keeping working women in the surplus labor force, it undergirded the economic system to which reformers owed their privileged positions. But a purely economic explanation does not adequately account for the dedication with which the reformers went about their tasks of rescue and reform. The struggle also involved the definition of gender. The reformers had already absorbed the social controls they sought to instill. These reformers hoped to recast offenders in their own image, to have them embrace the values (though not assume the social station) of the lady. And through reformatories like Albion, some working-class women were taught to accept a new concept of womanhood that restricted their sexual and vocational choices. They were, in fact, reformed.

STUDY QUESTIONS

1. What is meant by social control, and how does it apply to the women's reformatory movement?
2. For what types of offenses were women incarcerated in Albion? By whom? Why?
3. Discuss the types of sexual activities that were likely to land young women in reformatories. How was such promiscuity curtailed by the institution?
4. How did Albion prepare women for their domestic roles?
5. What types of coercive power did reformatories exert on their charges to gain compliance?
6. Discuss the relationship between social class and the reformatory movement.

5

SENTENCING IN THE UNITED STATES

LAWRENCE F. TRAVIS III

Sentencing is perhaps the point at which decision making in the criminal justice system has the most direct impact on U.S. prisons. The type and length of sentence imposed directly affect the size of the prison population, the characteristics of the prison population, and, ultimately, the overall conditions of prisons themselves (both socially and physically). In this piece by Lawrence Travis III, many aspects of sentencing in the United States are examined. First (and perhaps foremost), the base purposes and philosophies of punishment itself are reviewed. The author reveals the distinctiveness of each of the four philosophies, as well as their respective influences on sentencing in the United States. After presenting the philosophies of punishment, the reading then explores several technical aspects of sentencing that have been affecting the correctional system for the past several decades—specifically, the task of "risk prediction" (risk of future offending), the trend toward truth in sentencing, and various types of disparity in sentencing. Ultimately the reader should be challenged to consider what the most important purposes of punishment are, as well as how best to apply sentencing in an ever-expanding and increasingly diverse system.

In the year 2000, state courts imposed sentences on over 900,000 persons convicted of felonies (Durose and Langan 2003). More felons were sentenced in federal courts, and even greater numbers of persons convicted of misdemeanors were sentenced in state and local courts. Each year, criminal penalties are imposed on millions of persons in the United States. Of all punishments, those imposed on felons are the most severe and can include the death penalty for those convicted of capital crimes such as aggravated murder.

The sentencing decision, normally made by a judge, represents a determination of what to do about crime and, specifically, what to do with the convicted criminal. Sentencing is the choice of punishment. Punishment is the imposition of consequences, usually unpleasant consequences, for the commission of crime (von Hirsch 1976). Graeme Newman (1983, 6) writes, "Punishment, above all else, must be painful." Sentencing involves the imposition of harm (pain or unpleasant consequences) on persons convicted of crimes. The choice of punishment that is at the heart of the sentencing decision seems to require justification.

While there may be some element of reflex in punishment and sentencing (Mackie 1982), we tend to feel that government actions that hurt citizens must be justified and explained. What are the reasons that make it acceptable for agents of the government to cause harm to citizens? Justifications for criminal penalties are the goals of sentencing. They are the purposes that criminal sentences are expected to serve.

GOALS OF SENTENCING

There are four traditional goals of sentencing; deterrence, incapacitation, treatment, and desert. Of these four, the first three define sentencing as serving a utilitarian future purpose. The point of punishment is to prevent or reduce crime in the future. The fourth seeks to restore a balance by returning harm for harm. If the crime is harmful, the criminal deserves to receive harm in return. Let's look at each of these goals in more detail.

DETERRENCE

Deterrent penalties are expected to prevent future crime by "scaring" would-be offenders with the consequences of crime. A deterrent penalty provides an example of what awaits the offender should she or he commit a crime. In theory, the fear of punishment will cause the offender to "think twice" about crime.

There are two distinct types of deterrent penalties or purposes. The first is general deterrence, where the goal of the punishment is to influence the behavior of the general public. The second, known as specific deterrence, is aimed at the offender alone and tries to convince him or her to avoid future crime. In both cases, deterrent penalties rely on a theory of human behavior that assumes that people are rational and seek to avoid pain (Paternoster 1987).

For deterrence to work, potential offenders must view the penalty as unpleasant and, in fact, as unpleasant enough to outweigh the benefits to be gained by crime. If one could steal $1,000 and be fined only $500, the punishment produces less harm (loss of $500) than the gain of the crime ($1,000). In this case, the crime results in a net gain, even with the penalty, and we would not expect to deter theft. The second requirement of deterrence is that the penalty must be imposed. If a $1,000 theft carried a $10,000 fine, the punishment outweighs the gain of the crime. However, if the offender is not caught, or the punishment is not imposed, the reality is that the crime still "pays."

In the language of deterrence, these conditions represent severity and certainty. Severity relates to the level of pain or harm imposed by the punishment. More severe penalties impose greater harm. Penalty severity must outweigh the benefits of crime. Certainty relates to the likelihood of the penalty being imposed. If every offender who commits a crime is punished, then there is total or 100 percent certainty. The higher the certainty of punishment, the less likely it is that offenders will commit the crime.

A final part of a deterrent sanction relates to the speed with which a penalty is imposed, or the celerity of punishment. In theory, the more quickly punishment follows the crime, the more effective it will be in preventing future crime. The idea is that an immediate punishment clearly links the penalty to the criminal behavior, so that everyone can see that crime is punished. It may also help in conditioning the offender to associate the penalty with the criminal act so that, like Pavlov's dogs, the offender eventually becomes conditioned to avoid criminal acts.

Of these three conditions, research suggests that the certainty of punishment is much more important than either the severity or celerity of the sanction. With a rational offender, uncertainty of punishment means the offender will calculate the odds of being caught, will take steps to avoid detection, and may calculate that the odds of avoiding punishment make the crime worth the risk. It may also be that, as Paternoster

(1987) warned, offenders are not rational in their thinking. Piquero and Rengert (1999) found that the potential payoff of a burglary was a more important factor in the minds of burglars than the chance of punishment. Nagin and Pogarsky (2001) found that offenders differ in their willingness to take risks. What deters one person may not have the same effect on another.

INCAPACITATION

Like deterrence, incapacitation justifies the imposition of a penalty on the promise of reduced future crime. Unlike deterrence, incapacitation seeks to limit the offender's chance to commit future crimes rather than his or her decision to commit crime. A punishment for incapacitation reduces future crime by a particular offender by removing the opportunity for crime. An imprisoned offender is unable to commit a crime against people in free society, at least until released.

The biggest problem with incapacitation as a reason for punishment is the difficulty of predicting who is likely to commit future crimes and the costs of incarcerating or otherwise monitoring potential offenders. Given current levels of sophistication, it is not possible to correctly identify specific individuals who will commit crimes in the future.

Efforts to predict who will commit crimes run the risk of making one of two different mistakes. First, we might predict someone will commit a crime who actually will not. Alternatively, we might predict someone will not commit a new crime who actually does. Since we are predicting new crime, someone who commits a new crime is *positive,* and those who do not commit new crimes are *negative.* Our erroneous predictions are either *false positives,* where we wrongly predict an offender will commit a new crime, and *false negatives,* where we wrongly predict an offender will not commit a new crime.

False positives are incapacitated when there is no need to do so, while false negatives are allowed to commit new crimes. We have to decide how much of which type of error we can tolerate (Smith and Smith 1998). Largely as a result of the large number of false positives compared with true positives (most people do not commit crimes), we tend to overestimate the population of future criminals. This means we incapacitate many more offenders than need to be controlled. If we do that by imprisonment, at $25,000 or more per person per year, each false positive is expensive. If we need to incarcerate for at least ten years to prevent a future crime, then we waste a quarter of a million dollars, if not more, for each false positive. Incapacitation is a very rational policy, but unfortunately we do not yet have the expertise to accurately predict the danger of new crime.

TREATMENT

Sometimes also known as *rehabilitation,* punishment based on treatment is expected to reduce the chances of future crime by changing the offender's need or desire to commit crime. Treatment sentences are based on the individual needs or characteristics of the offender. Treatment is based on the notion that individuals commit crimes for a number of reasons and the solution to the crime problem lies in attacking those reasons. Successful treatment results in individuals who no longer wish or need to commit crimes. The treatment rationale demonstrates concern for the individual offender and establishes an obligation on the part of the state to provide aid and care for criminal offenders (Cullen and Gilbert 1982).

As with incapacitation, the behavioral sciences have not reached a point where they can provide completely successful treatment programs. Programs that are available to offenders are limited, partly in response to pragmatic concerns about cost and safety and partly from an inability to fully diagnose or respond to the criminogenic (crime-producing) needs of offenders. Often offenders receive some sort of counseling that is applied to a wide range of offenders. While theoretically aimed at individuals, the fact is that most treatment programs are applied to large groups of offenders and not often tailored to individuals. Adams (1961) discovered that such programming can result in harmful effects for some, positive effects for others, and no effects for still others. In the end, the positive and harmful effects cancel each other out, showing no benefit from treatment. Doris MacKenzie (1997, 9–16) phrased the issue when she wrote, "The important issue is not whether something works but what works for whom?" Like deterrence and incapacitation, the theory of treatment is eminently plausible, but may require more sophistication than is currently available.

Despite discouraging findings from a number of treatment program evaluations, attempts to improve treatment continue and are increasing (Gendreau and Ross 1987). There is evidence to support the positive impact of treatment programs. Among others, Taxman and Piquero (1998) reported that treatment sentences for drunk drivers were more successful in reducing repeat offending than were sentences that were simply punitive (i.e., deterrent or incapacitation based). Within the past two decades, a number of "problem-solving courts" have developed to focus on specific offenses and offenders. These courts work to insure that those convicted of drug offenses, domestic violence, or other identified crimes receive, participate in, and complete treatment programming (Casey and Rottman 2003).

DESERT

Also known as *retribution* or *just deserts,* sentences based on a desert rationale do not seek to reduce future crime. Desert sentencing is concerned with the imposition of fair punishment for past crime. The principal goal is not to prevent or control future crime but to insure justice in punishing the present offense. Those who break the law deserve to be punished, regardless of whether the punishment changes future crime.

Desert works to put limits on criminal punishment. A penalty is expected to balance the criminal act. More serious crimes deserve more severe punishment. Punishment is based on two criteria. First is the amount of harm caused by the crime. The more harm done, the greater the pain of the penalty. Second, the culpability of the offender plays a role in determining the level of a penalty. The more culpable (blameworthy) an offender, the more pain is deserved. Still, no matter how culpable an offender might be, desert recognizes real limits on the severity of punishment.

Desert might define burglary as requiring punishment by imprisonment of no more than ten years. A less culpable burglar (perhaps an 18-year-old, first-time offender who was influenced by an older partner) might be justly punished with a sentence of five years. If a life sentence would deter enough other possible burglars, deterrence would allow the imposition of life imprisonment. If the offender needed treatment that would take 20 years to complete, a treatment rationale would allow a 20-year term. If we thought the offender would repeat his crime by the age of 50, incapacitation would allow a sentence of 32 years (until age 50). Desert would not allow any sentence in excess of ten years. In contrast, if the offender posed no risk of future crime, deterrence, treatment, and incapacitation provide no justification for imprisonment. Desert requires imprisonment (but not more than ten years) for burglary, and it sets both a bottom and a top to punishment based on the seriousness of the crime.

While each of these purposes of punishment is separate and distinct, in practice it is common for legislatures and those who impose sentences to try to serve several purposes at once. As mentioned, using desert as a boundary, sentencing laws often provide utilitarian (crime prevention) justifications for punishment. In this way, while a burglary may deserve prison, we recognize that while in prison the offender is incapacitated, that imprisonment may deter others, and that we should strive to provide treatment to the burglar. The existence of multiple goals of sentencing coupled with attempts to achieve them at the same time helps make sentencing and punishment very complex parts of the justice system. In this complexity, a number of issues emerge.

SENTENCING ISSUES

It seems there has always been controversy and debate over criminal sentencing. Some disagreement exists about which of the purposes of punishment are most important, but other sentencing issues have also proven to be controversial. Among several, concern about prediction, truth in sentencing, and disparity are important sentencing issues.

PREDICTION

Prediction is a central concern in almost all criminal justice decisions (Clear and O'Leary 1983). Michael and Donald Gottfredson (1988) reported that concern about the prior criminal record of offenders was present at almost every decision point in the criminal justice process. We are, naturally, interested in the likelihood that someone will continue to commit crimes, and the best predictor of future behavior is past behavior. Society expects its criminal justice system to take steps to prevent future crime.

Any prediction of future crime risks the prediction errors discussed above. We may predict someone will be safe who will actually commit new crimes (false negative). Alternatively, we may predict someone will commit new crimes who actually will be safe (false positive). As we saw, we expend punishment resources unnecessarily on false positive errors and fail to protect society with false negative errors.

Assuming that prediction is appropriate and necessary in sentencing, we still have a few unresolved issues. Suppose we sentence someone to additional time in prison because we predict that he or she will commit another crime. Upon release, sure enough, this individual does commit a new crime. The question that emerges is whether he or she has already been punished for that new offense. Do we need to punish this person some more after we have already imposed a predicted sentence?

Even if we could accomplish complete accuracy in predictions, some people would argue that it is inappropriate to punish for crimes not yet committed. Like the offender in *Alice in Wonderland,* with prediction the punishment comes first and if there is no future offense, "so much the better." Predictive sentencing supports practices like habitual offender and *three strikes* laws that impose long sentences on repeat offenders. The issue around prediction in sentencing has to do with balancing the need to protect society from future harm with the need to protect the individual rights and interests of the criminal (and potential criminal) offender.

TRUTH IN SENTENCING

"The amount of time offenders serve in prison is almost always shorter than the time they are sentenced to serve by the court" (Ditton and Wilson 1999, 1). As a result of sentence reductions for good behavior, early release due to prison crowding, or discretionary parole release, most prisoners serve substantially less time than that to which they were sentenced. A study of prisoners admitted in 1994 estimated that the average prisoner would serve less than 40 percent of the court-imposed sentence

(Langan and Brown 1997). That those sent to prison typically serve sentences far shorter than what is announced in court led to a federal effort to achieve "truth in sentencing."

The Violent Crime Control and Law Enforcement Act of 1994 created funding for additional state prisons and jails. To qualify for federal funds, state laws must insure that those convicted of Part I violent crimes serve at least 85 percent of their prison sentence. In 1998, more than half the states and the District of Columbia qualified for this funding. States have abolished discretionary parole release, reduced or eliminated sentence reductions for good behavior, and created diversionary programs to keep nonviolent offenders out of prison to achieve longer terms of incarceration for those convicted of violent crimes.

Early release of prison inmates (before the expiration of their court-imposed term) has been criticized on a number of grounds. Some contend that early release undermines the deterrent effect of the law because it means that the sentence imposed is not certain, and that the offender can always hope for early release. Others argue that early release does not allow the sentence to achieve full incapacitation effects because offenders are returned to the community earlier than expected. Finally, still others argue that such dishonesty in sentencing undermines respect for the law and citizen confidence in the criminal justice system. When citizens learn that they have been misled about sentencing, they may question the integrity of the entire justice system.

Assuming that truth in sentencing is desirable, it is a complicated goal. One way to achieve truthful sentences is simply to keep offenders in prison longer, until they have served their full terms. Of course, doing so will greatly increase prison populations and drive correctional costs to levels that are probably beyond the reach of most states. A second approach is to reduce the maximum terms imposed on offenders so that prisoners will serve the same sentences as today, but the sentences announced in court will be lower. If the typical offender serves two years of a five year sentence, change the sentence to two years and make the prisoner serve it all.

More common are hybrid efforts that distinguish between types of offenders and that increase time to be served for those convicted of more serious crimes. What appears to have happened is that offenders sentenced for violent crimes are being required to serve longer terms than in the past. At the same time, offenders sentenced for nonviolent crimes are serving shorter terms. This "solution" to the truth in sentencing dilemma raises its own issues.

First, depending upon what changes are made to sentencing laws, these efforts result in more truth in the sentencing of violent offenders, but less truth in the sentencing of nonviolent offenders. In the end, the truthfulness of the entire sentencing system may not be affected at all. Second, adaptations that focus on longer terms for violent offenders and shorter or no prison terms for nonviolent offenders can change the dynamics of life inside prisons. Prisons have always housed a relatively violent population, but under truth in sentencing the prison population will increasingly come to be composed of serious, violent offenders. Prisons may become more dangerous as a result.

Beyond changes in prison population, the imposition of long terms complicates efforts to develop and provide treatment programs, as offenders will be spending substantially longer times in prison, making it more difficult to maintain contact with the outside world and to provide a smooth reentry to society on release. In addition, prisoners facing long terms with little hope of sentence reductions will be less inclined to obey prison rules. Ohio attempted to deal with this part of the truth in sentencing dilemma (how does one motivate prisoners to behave?) by creating the concept of *bad time.* The courts declared that bad time violated due process protections (Holcomb and Williams 2003).

The bad time provisions of Ohio law were akin to an inverse of traditional *good time.* For decades, prison administrators have been empowered to grant reductions in prison terms for good behavior. In most cases, reductions are automatically awarded to inmates, and misbehavior is punished by withholding a reduction. With bad time, prison administrators (and the parole authority) were authorized to increase the length of a sentence when inmates engaged in acts that violated the criminal law. The Ohio Supreme Court ruled that the imposition of additional prison time in the absence of a trial was unconstitutional, and bad time was abandoned. The problem of controlling inmate behavior is serious and is one of the most important explanations for a lack of truth in sentencing.

The sentencing decision is tightly bound to correctional programming and treatment. Changes in who gets sentenced to what dispositions will influence the composition of correctional populations, the implementation and effectiveness of treatment programs, and the ability of correctional officials to manage offenders. At the same time, sentencing is the decision of what to do about a criminal offender and is important to victims and others. There is a need for honesty in sentencing. It may be, though, that the best way to achieve truth in sentencing is not necessarily through changing the sentencing process but rather by better explaining sentencing to the public.

DISPARITY

Sentencing disparity is the term used to describe the unequal treatment of similar offenders (Gottfredson 1979). Most people would agree that persons who have similar criminal histories and are convicted of similar offenses should receive similar penalties. Two first-time offenders convicted of burglary should, we tend to think, receive the same punishment. When different sentences are imposed on similar offenders, the differences are called *disparity.* Yet sentencing disparity really relates to unwarranted differences (Gottfredson et al. 1978).

If we are trying to accomplish treatment and one of our first-offender burglars is diagnosed as needing employment training while the other needs no assistance, it would be acceptable to require the first offender to complete a training program or even spend time in a confinement facility that offered such training. So, too, a repeat offender can be given a punishment more severe than a first offender and most people would think that was acceptable. In both those cases the offenders are not "similar," in the sense that the differences in punishment are "warranted" by differences in treatment need or prior record. The controversy over disparity hinges in large part on the definition of *similar* (Vining 1983).

Beginning in the mid-1970s, several states and the federal government enacted legislation to reform criminal sentencing. One of the goals of almost all of these reforms was to increase consistency and fairness in sentencing (Ulmer 1997; Anspach and Monsen 1989; Goodstein and Hepburn 1983). That is, for three decades we have been trying to control or reduce sentencing disparity.

The culprit in sentencing disparity was identified as the individual whims of justice system officials. The attitudes and interests of judges, probation officers, parole authority members, and so on were felt to cause the imposition of different sentences on similar offenders. To reduce the impact of individual decision makers on sentences, a variety of sentencing reforms were enacted. Some states developed determinate sentencing that eliminated parole authority discretion. In some cases, the range of discretion granted to judges was greatly reduced by requiring mandatory prison terms or reducing the gap between minimum and maximum terms. In some jurisdictions, the legislature authorized the creation of sentencing guidelines that defined the purpose of punishment and directed sentencing judges to consider specific factors in deciding on a sentence. These guidelines helped reduce variation in sentences and thus increased consistency in punishment.

The effects of reform are unclear and may include increases in the rate of imprisonment and changes in the length of prison terms imposed (Tonry 1999). Concern over disparity was driven by suggestions that differences in sentences were a product of discrimination based on race, sex, age, or other social characteristics of offenders and not on offense seriousness, risk, culpability, or other legally relevant factors (Spohn 2000). Daly and Bordt (1995) reported that women tend to receive less severe sentences than men, but that this is probably due to differences in the kinds of offenses committed by women and men. Spohn (1994) compared sentences of blacks and whites, and, while persistent differences exist, she suggests that differences in types of offenses may account for different punishments. In addition to different types of offenses, blacks and whites tend to differ in terms of prior convictions, which also influences sentences (Pratt 1998). While differences in offense seriousness and prior record explain much of the difference in criminal sentences, it is also likely that sentencing decisions reflect the disadvantaged status of minority group members in American society.

Attempts to increase equity and fairness in sentencing, including determinate sentencing, presumptive sentencing, and sentencing guidelines, may have reduced the incidence of disparity in criminal punishments. Still, there is variation in sentences imposed on criminal offenders, and the differences in sentences appear to be related to the social and demographic characteristics of offenders. Disparity in sentencing remains an important unresolved issue in criminal punishment.

CONCLUSION

Even a cursory examination of criminal sentencing such as this indicates that there are many unanswered questions and that sentencing in practice is a complex process. What can or should be done to improve or change sentencing remains a judgment call determined in part by the goals of sentencing and conditioned by the constraints of the operating justice system. Improvements in prediction and treatment effectiveness, or changes in prison capacity, can influence decisions about what are appropriate and desirable sentences.

Efforts to increase consistency and reduce disparity in sentencing show the complexity of the topic. At the same time that legislatures around the country were moving to reduce sentencing discretion to reduce disparity, they were also adopting intermediate sanctions and alternatives to incarceration. While we may have reduced the range of prison sentences, we have added a range of sentencing options from electronic surveillance to community service orders (Morris and Tonry 1990). Increasing sentencing options runs the risk of increasing sentencing disparity. The more choices available to sentencing decision makers, the more different kinds of sentences can be imposed on similar offenders.

While we need to determine what are just punishments and how we can impose just sentences, we must also recognize that we often disagree about the requirements of justice. We may never be able to reach agreement about the justice of criminal punishments. Nonetheless, it is incumbent on us to understand sentencing and to strive to improve the process.

STUDY QUESTIONS

1. Describe and define the four major philosophies of punishment presented by the author. Which

one is the most valid? Offer details as to why you chose the philosophy that you did.

2. Combine your opinion with the information presented in this chapter, and determine why you feel the prison system may not be effective at deterring offenders from committing crime.
3. What role does "prediction" play in the sentencing decision? Should prediction have a role when judges make sentencing decisions?
4. For what reasons presented in this chapter has there been a push toward "truth in sentencing" legislation?
5. Based on your reading of the chapter, for what reason(s) does sentencing disparity exist in the criminal justice system?

REFERENCES

Adams, S. 1961. *Effectiveness of Interview Therapy with Older Youth Authority Wards: An Interim Evaluation of the PICO Project.* Sacramento, CA: California Youth Authority.

Anspach, D., and S. Monsen. 1985. "Determinate Sentencing, Formal Rationality, and Khadi Justice in Maine: An Application of Weber's Typology." *Journal of Criminal Justice* 17(6): 471–485.

Casey, P., and D. Rottman. 2003. *Problem-Solving Courts: Models and Trends.* Williamsburg, VA: National Center for State Courts.

Clear, T., and V. O'Leary. 1983. *Controlling the Offender in the Community.* Lexington, MA: Lexington Books.

Cullen, F. T., and K. E. Gilbert. 1982. *Reaffirming Rehabilitation.* Cincinnati, OH: Anderson.

Daly, K., and R. Bordt. 1995. "Sex Effects and Sentencing: An Analysis of the Statistical Literature." *Justice Quarterly* 12(1):141–175.

Ditton, P., and D. Wilson. 1999. *Truth in Sentencing in State Prisons.* Washington, DC: Bureau of Justice Statistics.

Durose, M., and P. Langan. 2003. *Felony Sentences in State Courts, 2000.* Washington, DC: Bureau of Justice Statistics.

Gendreau, P., and R. Ross. 1987. "Revivification of Rehabilitation: Evidence from the 1980s." *Justice Quarterly* 4(3):349–407.

Goodstein, L., and J. Hepburn. 1983. *Determinate Sentencing and Imprisonment.* Cincinnati, OH: Anderson.

Gottfredson, D., C. Cosgrove, L. Wilkins, J. Wallerstein, and C. Rauh. 1978. *Classification for Parole Decision Policy.* Washington, DC: U.S. Government Printing Office.

Gottfredson, M. 1979. "Parole Guidelines and the Reduction of Sentencing Disparity: A Preliminary Study." *Journal of Research in Crime and Delinquency* 23(4):218–231.

Gottfredson, M., and D. Gottfredson. 1988. *Decisionmaking in Criminal Justice,* 2nd ed. New York: Plenum.

Holcomb, J., and M. Williams. 2003. "From the Field: 'Bad Time': The Rise and Fall of Penal Policy in Ohio." *Journal of Crime and Justice* 26(2): 153–175.

Langan, P., and J. Brown. 1997. *Felony Sentences in State Courts, 1994.* Washington, DC: Bureau of Justice Statistics.

MacKenzie, D. 1997. "Criminal Justice and Crime Prevention," in L. Sherman, D. Gottfredson, J. Eck, P. Reuter, and S. Bushway (eds.) *Preventing Crime: What Works, What Doesn't, What's Promising.* Washington, DC: National Institute of Justice, Chapter 9.

Mackie, J. 1982. "Morality and the Retributive Emotions." *Criminal Justice Ethics* 1(1):3–10.

Martinson, R. 1974. "What Works?" *The Public Interest* (Spring):22.

Morris, N., and M. Tonry. 1990. *Between Prison and Probation.* Oxford, UK: Oxford University Press.

Nagin, D. S., and G. Pogarsky. 2001. "Integrating Celebrity, Impulsivity, and Extralegal Sanction Threats into a Model of General Deterrence: Theory and Evidence." *Criminology* 39(4):404–430.

Newman, G. 1983. *Just and Painful.* New York: MacMillan.

Paternoster, R. 1987. "The Deterrent Effect of the Perceived Certainty and Severity of Punishment: A Review of the Evidence and Issues." *Justice Quarterly* 4(2):173–217.

Piquero, A., and G. Rengert. 1999. "Studying Deterrence with Active Residential Burglars." *Justice Quarterly* 16(2):451–471.

Pratt, T. 1998. "Race and Sentencing: A Meta Analysis of Conflicting Empirical Research Results." *Journal of Criminal Justice* 26(6):513–523.

Smith, W., and D. Smith. 1998. "The Consequences of Error: Recidivism Prediction and Civil-Libertarian Ratios." *Journal of Criminal Justice* 26(6):481–502.

Spohn, C. 1994. "Crime and the Social Control of Blacks: Offender/Victim Race and the Sentencing of Violent Offenders," in G. Bridges & M. Myers (eds.) *Inequality, Crime, and Social Policy*. Boulder, CO: Westview.

Spohn, C. 2000. "Thirty Years of Sentencing Reform: The Quest for a Racially Neutral Sentencing Process," in J. Horney (ed.) *Policies, Processes, and Decisions of the Criminal Justice System*. Washington, DC: National Institute of Justice, Criminal Justice 2000, Vol. 3:427–501.

Taxman, F., and A. Piquero. 1998. "On Preventing Drunk Driving Recidivism: An Examination of Rehabilitation and Punishment Approaches." *Journal of Criminal Justice* 26(2):129–143.

Tonry, M. 1999. "The Fragmentation of Sentencing and Corrections in America." *Sentencing and Corrections Issues for the 21st Century* (September). Washington, DC: National Institute of Justice.

Ulmer, J. 1997. *Social Worlds of Sentencing: Court Communities Under Sentencing Guidelines*. Albany, NY: SUNY Press.

Vining, A. 1983. "Developing Aggregate Measures of Disparity." *Criminology* 21(2):233–252.

Von Hirsch, A. 1976. *Doing Justice*. New York: Hill & Wang.

Zatz, M. 2000. "The Convergence of Race, Ethnicity, Gender, and Class on Court Decision-making: Looking Toward the 21st Century," in J. Horney (ed.) *Policies, Processes, and Decisions of the Criminal Justice System*. Washington, DC: National Institute of Justice, Criminal Justice 2000, Vol. 3:503–552.

6
ASSESSING THE PENAL HARM MOVEMENT

FRANCIS T. CULLEN

Part I concludes with a review of the "penal harm" movement. Through historical analyses, the readings in this part have reviewed the origins and evolution of punishment as well as the ultimate rise of the institution as punishment. Similarly, the preceding readings have revealed some of the consequences of a society that places so much emphasis on confinement. The United States has been described as engaging in an "imprisonment binge." Cullen reviews what has occurred as a result of this binge. The author defines precisely what is meant by "penal harm" and documents major movements resulting from this phenomenon, such as the decline of rehabilitation, the abolition of parole release, and the proliferation of "three-strikes" legislation. The utility of penal harm is reviewed, along with its unintended consequences, such as a widening of the racial disparity in U.S. prison populations. Ultimately, one of the components of confinement that remains missing in action is identified as effective efforts toward rehabilitation.

In the aftermath of the Civil War, American corrections had devolved into a state of crisis. Prisons were filled to the brim, populated by the domestic and immigrant poor. Inmates increasingly were seen as coming from the left tail of the bell curve and from the bottom of the evolutionary ladder, and they stood as clear evidence that urban slums were producing a "dangerous class." The idea that prisons should serve the larger social purpose of changing offenders—as the founders of the penitentiary had argued convincingly to a receptive audience only a few decades earlier—was losing credibility. More affluent citizens were tempted to see prisons as effecting "a policy of exclusion and banishment, so the public might be rid of the offender" (Rothman 1980, pp. 24–25). Although "the promise of reform had built the asylums," observes Rothman (1971, p. 240), "the functionalism of custody perpetuated them."

Each historical era has its unique conversation about corrections, but these themes voiced in post-Civil War America resonate remarkably with contemporary discourse about crime and punishment. For over a decade, virtually every contemporary commentary on corrections in the United States has reminded us that the system is in crisis (see, e.g., Blumstein 1989; Colvin 1992; Cullen and Gilbert 1982; Selke 1993; Sherman and Hawkins 1981). Institutions are crowded with at-risk young adults—some would say the less intelligent among us (Herrnstein and Murray 1994)—drawn from the urban underclass. Indeed, it

Excerpts from "Assessing the Penal Harm Movement" by Francis T. Cullen. *Journal of Research in Crime and Delinquency*, Volume 32, Number 3 (August 1995), 338–358.

is not uncommon to hear talk of the "return of the dangerous classes" (Gordon 1994; Simon, p. 253). Doubts abound about the reformative powers of correctional facilities. Jails and prisons are now seen as performing a "waste management function" (Feeley and Simon 1992; Irwin 1985; Simon, pp. 259–60) or, in more sanitized language, as "selectively incapacitating the wicked" (Wilson 1983).

The response to the prison crisis—then and now—has been decidedly different, however. In 1870, the leading correctional thinkers and practitioners (the overlap in the groups being considerable at that time) gathered in Cincinnati at the National Prison Congress to design a "new penology" that would rectify correctional failures and challenge the prevailing notion that prisons should function as warehouses with bars or, still worse, as instruments of harm. In issuing their famous "Declaration of Principles," the Congress asserted that "the supreme aim of prison discipline is the reformation of criminals, not the infliction of vindictive suffering" ("Declaration of Principles" 1910 [1870], p. 39).

These new penologists were not moral relativists and did not idealize offenders ("Declaration of Principles" 1910 [1870]): They were defenders of Christian morality and believed in character education; they embraced middle-class values and thought inmates would benefit from them too; they did not mind transforming the urban poor into disciplined workers (though they did reject as exploitive both purposeless hard labor and contract labor in prison); they believed that recalcitrant inmates should not be spared the rod (though they also felt that "rewards, more than punishments, are essential to every good prison system") ("Declaration of Principles" 1910 [1870], p. 39); and they were prepared in defense of public safety to incarcerate incorrigible inmates indeterminately. They also were optimistic that the state could be "changed from its former vengefulness to that of dignified serenity, neither vindictive nor lovelorn, but firmly and nobly corrective" (Brockway 1910, p. 88). Later commentators would criticize them for being class biased and for their naïveté in not anticipating that state power, exercised unfettered behind the high walls of the prison, could be abused and cause more harm than good (Platt 1969; Rothman 1980). I would debate these claims on the grounds that the new penology exerted a restraining influence on punitive sentiments—that the alternative would have been worse (as I believe is now the case). But it is hoped that we can agree not to deconstruct the new penologists' words to the point of ignoring their intent to better, not to hurt, offenders (see Garland 1990).

Today, however, the response to the corrections crisis has turned ugly. In the 1990s, the term *new penology* no longer refers to a correctional philosophy that rejects vengeance in favor of offender reformation, but to an administrative style that seeks depersonalized efficiency in processing increasingly large hordes of inmates in and out of the system (Feeley and Simon 1992). More disquieting, we have entered a "mean season" in which it has become politically correct to build prisons and to devise creative strategies to make offenders suffer. In Todd Clear's words, we are witnessing a movement whose supreme aim is the infliction of "penal harm."

The field of criminology is one of the few remaining bastions in American society in which the advent of the penal harm movement has not been greeted warmly. A few bold colleagues defend the use of prisons (see, e.g., Logan and DiIulio 1992; Wright 1994), but most of us (including me) are sufficiently liberal, fearful of professional disapproval, or (I hope) criminologically astute to caution about the "limits of imprisonment" (see, e.g., Currie 1985; Gordon 1991; Irwin and Austin 1994; Selke 1993; Zimring and Hawkins 1995; see also Forer 1994). We often fret that our research and commentary are ignored by policymakers who seemingly succeed in purchasing the votes of citizens uneasy about crime by offering to effect law and order (see Kaminer 1995). But we are able to console ourselves at conferences through a shared and cathartic excoriation of the get-tough crowd, knowing that their panaceas are doomed to failure and that we stand for truth and justice.

There is a risk, however, that liberal criminologists (like me) will become too professionally insular and complacent in our thinking about corrections—that we will take turns preaching to, and being in, the choir. It is wise, I suspect, to reflect on assumptions that are held too uncritically and to check our biases with some good positivist criminology. An indispensable first step in this intellectual housecleaning is to read the three books informing this essay. Although clearly progressive in orientation, these works are sophisticated attempts to understand and to undermine the penal harm movement. They retain a humanity, which is an integral and worthy side of liberal criminology, but ultimately their strength comes from their rejection of ideology in favor of sharp logic and hard data.

I should warn that these exemplars of liberal correctional thinking—Clear's *Harm in American Penology*, Simon's *Poor Discipline*, and Tonry's *Malign Neglect*—are not immune to reasonable rejoinders by those who see benefits in penal harm; the debates are wonderfully engaged but perhaps not fully settled. But I have a more serious concern about these works: They reflect the tendency in contemporary progressive commentaries to provide incisive criticism of conservative crime policies but then to stop short of articulating a *coherent* alternative *correctional* agenda. Unlike the new penologists of the 1870s, whose "Declaration of Principles" mapped out such an agenda, they thus provide only limited guidance on how to move beyond penal harm—a point I return to at the end of this essay.

IS THERE A PENAL HARM MOVEMENT?

Clear does a service in reminding us that an integral part of state punishment is inflicting "penal harm." The "essence of the penal sanction," he observes, is that "it harms... it is supposed to hurt" (p. 4). Penal harm is a "planned governmental act, whereby a citizen is harmed, and implies that harm is justifiable precisely because it is an offender who is suffering" (p. 4). We often clothe this reality with respectable sounding euphemisms, such as "correctional interventions," "offender processing," and "incapacitation." Clear's insistent use of "penal harm" as his organizing concept strips away this comforting language, and forces us to confront the naked truth that corrections is, to a greater or lesser extent, a mean-spirited enterprise.

I suspect that only the culturally illiterate would be unaware that a movement has been afoot to expand the use of penal harm in the United States. In the past 2 years, for example, various versions of "three strikes and you're out" laws, which mandate life sentences for a third felony conviction, have been implemented in 15 states and are under consideration in 22 more (Turner, Sundt, Applegate, and Cullen forthcoming; see also Benekos and Merlo 1995). Legislators also have publicized their attempts to intensify the pains of imprisonment by reducing such inmate amenities as grants for college education, television privileges, computers in cells, and exercise through weight lifting. Alabama enthusiastically has reinstituted chain gangs. Offenders don white uniforms that display the stigmatizing label "chain gang," are shackled together, and conduct "stoop labor" for 12 hours a day (Bragg 1995; Cohen 1995). Modern technology, it must be admitted, has allowed some escape from penal harm; Alabama officials are able to point "proudly to a new, specially designed toilet that allows the men to relieve themselves in privacy while still linked to their colleagues" (Cohen 1995, p. 26).

Three-strikes laws and chain gangs might merely be part of a symbolic crusade that has affected corrections in visible, but marginal, ways. Is there evidence that penal harm has increased substantively, not just symbolically, in recent years? Clear, with help from Tonry, makes a strong case in the affirmative.

Given the ubiquity of the current get-tough talk about crime, it is easy today to forget that penal harm was not always on the rise. In the half century following 1925, imprisonment rates per 100,000 averaged under 108 per 100,000 citizens, and the number of inmates rose roughly in proportion to the growth in the general population (Clear, p. 44; see also Cullen, Van Voorhis, and Sundt forthcoming). In fact, this remarkable "stability of punishment" was the object of theoretical inquiry (Blumstein and Cohen 1973; see also Blumstein 1995; Scull 1977). Beginning in the early 1970s, however, a sea change in punishment occurred: The era of stability suddenly ended as the population of offenders under correctional supervision began a rapid, seemingly intractable rise.

Although establishing causal links between policy reforms and correctional populations is difficult (Zimring and Hawkins 1991), over the past two decades politicians certainly intended for penal harm to worsen. Clear documents that between 1972 and 1982, a majority of states restricted or abolished parole release, and mandatory or minimum sentences were widely implemented. "In one way or another," he concludes, "every state altered its penal policy in the direction of greater punitive severity" (p. 50; see also Cullen and Gilbert 1982).

To Clear, the figures on the use of prisons are "astounding": Between 1973 and the beginning of the 1990s, the number of prisoners increased by 332%, and the incarceration rate per 100,000 citizens jumped over 200% (p. 43). The growing punitiveness of sentencing also is apparent: Between 1981 and 1987, the time served for burglary rose 53% and for rape rose 129%; since 1975, the time served for violent offenses has tripled (pp. 54–55).

Michael Tonry echoes these themes and provides a useful cross-cultural perspective (see also Currie 1985). "Americans have a remarkable ability to endure suffering by others," he observes. "We lock up our citizens at rates 5 to 15 times higher than those in other Western countries" (p. 197). He claims that these incarceration rates cannot be explained by America's higher offense rate. Recently conducted international victimization surveys show that crime in the United States is not markedly higher than in other advanced industrial nations, although gun-related violence is a notable exception. Even so, the proclivity to lock up offenders seems less a product of having a larger pool of criminals and more a product of our "national character" (pp. 197–200).

Consider, however, DiIulio's (1994, p. 15) starkly different claim that the "justice system is a revolving door for convicted predatory street criminals"—not a potent instrument for inflicting penal harm—and that "America has not been on an imprisonment binge" (see also Wilson 1995; cf. Irwin and Austin 1994). How can intelligent scholars read the evidence so differently? In fact, there are two divergent cases to be made, and a scholar's intellectual and/or ideological preferences shape which position he or she embraces.

Liberals prefer to cite raw numbers of people in prison and incarceration rates per 100,000 citizens; they also read trends beginning in the early 1970s (Clear, p. 43). In contrast, conservatives, such as John DiIulio (1994) and James Q. Wilson (1995), prefer to cite the amount of punishment meted out per offense committed and to read trend lines dating back to 1960, if not before. This latter methodology reveals that the punishment-per-offense rate declined rapidly throughout the 1960s and 1970s, only to rebound partially in the 1980s.

According to DiIulio (1994, p. 16), for example, the number of people in prison per 1,000 violent crimes dropped from 738 in 1960 to 227 in 1980, only to increase in the 1980s to 423—a point still "42 percent lower than it was in 1960." Wilson's (1995, p. 499) analysis paints a similar portrait: In 1945, the sentence served for all crimes was 25 months, but by 1984 had decreased to 13 months. These statistical patterns, contends DiIulio (1994, p. 16), do not indicate an imprisonment binge, but rather that America "has been recovering from the starvation diet it went on in the late 1960s and stayed on throughout the 1970s."

Using this general approach, the cross-cultural case for America's exceptionalism as a punitive nation also is complicated. Lynch (1995) found that offenders in the United States receive longer sentences than in other advanced industrial nations. In time actually spent in prison, however, the findings were less consistent: Compared to offenders in other nations, offenders in the United States served longer sentences for property and drug offenses but served similar sentences for homicide and serious violence (see also Farrington and Langan 1992).

Where do these competing commentaries leave us? At the very least, we know that in raw numbers, the prison population has grown in the past two decades from about 200,000 to over 1 million inmates. It also is clear that in the past decade, punishment levels have increased considerably. But whether one considers current trends to constitute penal harm or a much-needed, if not overdue, redistribution of governmental resources depends on more than incarceration statistics. In the end, assessing whether penal harm is beneficial or wasteful, and deciding appropriate levels of penal harm, will be influenced by considerations of utility: What does penal harm accomplish?...

THE DIFFERENTIAL EFFECTS OF PENAL HARM

"No problem haunts the United States' sense of identity more intractably than race relations," comments Clear (p. 174). "The penal system," he adds, "is part of the problem, because penal harms are inequitably distributed among our racial and ethnic populations." In *Malign Neglect,* Tonry seeks to document how policies central to the ongoing penal harm movement not only have perpetuated but, more significantly, have exacerbated the concentration of punishment on African Americans.

Tonry does not deny that behavioral differences in crime exist between Black and White Americans, and although not dismissing the existence of ill and inequitable treatment of minorities, he does not contend that the racial gap in offending can be explained by the discriminatory practices of criminal justice officials.... Even so, he is adamant that "American crime policies since 1980 have had disastrous consequences for Black Americans" and that the penal harms visited on African Americans "do not result from increases in the proportions of serious crimes committed by Blacks" (p. 28).

Indeed, incarceration statistics paint a disquieting portrait: In both 1979 and 1990, African Americans accounted for about 44% of arrests for violent crimes. The Black proportion of admissions to state prisons, however, jumped in this period from 39% to 53% (p. 49). In fact, between 1986 and 1991, the racial mix in prison admissions flip-flopped from 53% White (and 46% Black) to 53% Black (p. 58). By 1991, African Americans were 6.47 times more likely than White Americans to be incarcerated (1,895 to 293 per 100,000) (p. 29). These figures mean that 1 in 50 Blacks are imprisoned on any given day. When the data are disaggregated by gender and age, we learn that 1 in 12 African American men between the ages of 18 and 54 are confined (p. 130). Further, nearly 1 in 4 Black men in their 20s are either behind bars or on probation or parole (p. 4; see also Tonry 1994).

"The rising levels of Black incarceration did not just happen," argues Tonry, but were due to "malign neglect"; indeed, the increased penal harms suffered by African Americans after 1980 were the "*foreseeable* effects of *deliberate* policies spearheaded by the Reagan and Bush administrations and implemented by many states" (p. 4, italics added). He indicts politicians for using race-based stereotypes about crime (Willie Horton and the like) as a means of stirring up racial enmity, polarizing the electorate, and capturing White votes. "The text may be crime," notes Tonry (p. 6), but "the subtext is race." Most important, he details how the "War on Drugs," which virtually no serious observer felt could be won, was used to increase political capital even though it served to "ruin countless lives and weaken numerous communities" (p. vii; see also Currie 1993; Gordon 1994).

In chapter 3, "Race and the War on Drugs," Tonry details the war's "foreseeable disparate impact on Blacks" (p. 104). The "major fronts in the drug wars were located in minority neighborhoods," in large part because trafficking occurred on the street and officers could more easily make arrests (pp. 105–7). Further, the focus on crack cocaine was especially consequential, because this drug was sold and used disproportionately by minorities and carried substantially longer penalties than powder cocaine—a drug used mainly by Whites. The result of targeting low-level, inner-city, street-level drug dealers and attaching harsh punishments to crack was predictable: In 1985, Blacks made up 30% of drug arrests; by 1989, this figure had jumped to 42%—even though African Americans' use of drugs generally is lower than that of White Americans. Numerically, Black drug arrests more than doubled from 210,298 to 452,574, whereas the number of arrests for Whites increased only 27% (pp. 107–9).

In turn, "drug arrests are a principal reason that the proportions of Blacks in prison... have risen rapidly in recent years to... extraordinary levels" (p. 110). Data from Pennsylvania are instructive. Between 1980 and 1990, drug commitments rose 1,613% for African American males but only 477% for White males (p. 115). And penal harms such as these have had disturbing consequences. "Poor minority communities cannot prosper," warns Tonry (p. vii), "when so many young men are prevented from settling into long-term personal relationships, getting or keeping jobs, and living conventional lives."

But is the disproportionate allocation of criminal justice resources to minority communities a form of spatial injustice, as Tonry claims, or of spatial justice? In 1989, George Rengert raised this issue, when he used the concept of "spatial justice" to refer "to whether or not citizens are placed at equal risk of victimization as a result of criminal justice practices regardless of where their communities are located—center city, suburb, or rural area" (p. 544). His analysis revealed that burglars received shorter sentences in Philadelphia than in other areas in Pennsylvania and that these offenders were poorly supervised by probation and parole officers burdened with caseloads of 100 to 200 persons. The decisions of officials not to incarcerate or adequately supervise burglars resulted in higher victimization rates for residents of inner-city neighborhoods—those "least able to bear the high physical, economic, and emotional burden of property crime" (p. 557).

Rengert (1989, p. 560) believed that addressing the issue of spatial injustice through imprisonment was the "easy" answer, but "also naive" (he favored intermediate sanctions and crime prevention). Not so for DiIulio (1994), who recently has taken up the issue of "saving Black lives" through penal harm. "If White suburbanites were victimized in disproportionate numbers by convicted criminals out on probation or parole," his essay begins, "then there would be little policy debate about keeping violent or repeat offenders locked up" (p. 3). But this is not the case, he claims. Affluent Whites have the luxury of moving to safer communities in the suburbs and of paying for security devices. Inner-city minorities do not have these options. They must reside, largely unprotected, in neighborhoods populated with predatory criminals whose victimization is mostly intraracial.

To DiIulio, the malign neglect lies in the failure of the criminal justice system to end "revolving door" justice and to lock up these predatory offenders. "No group of Americans would stand to benefit more from policies that kept convicted felons, adult and juvenile, behind bars for all or most of their terms," says DiIulio (p. 15), "than crime-plagued Black inner-city Americans and their children."

I have no reason to doubt DiIulio's sincerity. But his personal character and intent aside, I find it more than a little disingenuous when conservative commentators use the victimization of African Americans to argue for less welfare and more prisons. This new-found concern does not seem to extend to capital investment in inner-city areas; they do not want to improve the "barrel," only take out the "bad apples." I also feel compelled to add a rejoinder to the quote initiating DiIulio's essay: "If White suburbanites were in prison in disproportionate numbers, then there would be little policy debate about reducing imprisonment and investing resources to improve the quality of life in suburban communities."

Tonry (p. 36) takes up the justification of penal harm that he calls the "We are concerned about Black victims and Black communities' defense." His rebuttal is weakened, I believe, by his firm stance that incapacitation has few meaningful effects on crime—an issue discussed above. But his insights on what African Americans want strike a chord. Tonry agrees that Blacks often want the criminal justice system to crack down on crime when it is an "acute" problem that poses an immediate threat to community order. Blacks also understand, however, that crime is a symptom of "chronic social and economic conditions shaping disadvantaged inner-city communities and the life chances of the people in them" (p. 36). And in large percentages, they endorse social welfare policies that address crime's root causes. Somehow it is no surprise that conservatives hear calls for more police and prisons but turn a deaf ear to calls for help and hope.

MANAGING PENAL HARM

In *Poor Discipline,* Jonathan Simon contributes further to our understanding of the character of the current penal harm movement. Using parole in California as a vehicle for illuminating the larger correctional process, he traces the changing penological models used to control the underclass. He reminds us that "however general the formal commands of the criminal law, the power to punish has always been primarily directed at the poor" (p. 5). A particular strength of his analysis is that he links the meaning and practice of parole to the wider material conditions of the disadvantaged. "The massive expansion of criminal custody over the last decade in the United States," observes Simon, "must be seen in relationship to changes in political economy," including in particular "the restructuring of the labor force away from industrial employment" and "the emergence of an urban underclass living in zones of hardened poverty and made up primarily of minorities" (p. 5).

The emergence and growth of parole release in the late 1800s into the Progressive Era depended on furnishing a persuasive answer—or "narrative" or "account" as Simon would call it—to how it would be possible "to provide control in the community over those defined as dangerous to the community" (p. 38). The response, says Simon, was "disciplinary parole": Make community release contingent on securing and maintaining labor. This narrative (or account) should not strike us as unusual, says Simon, because it is so compatible with long-standing American thinking on corrections (see also Cullen and Travis 1984). "Wherever you look in the development of modernist penality you will find labor," says Simon. "Exhort offenders with religious tracts, but make them work. Subject them to silence, but make them work. Educate them as citizens, but make them work. Treat their pathological features, but make them work" (p. 39).

Having parolees work served to normalize them through the discipline of labor; it provided a test of character, for those who could not keep a job proved their essential criminality; and it implicated private networks of control, because employers had to agree to provide work and to certify that offenders remained on the job in good standing. The plausibility of the disciplinary parole model, of course, rested on having a labor market that could accommodate poor offenders on parole. Until the 1950s, these structural conditions obtained: With the exception of the Depression years, the cities provided a "large labor market...for unskilled and semi-skilled labor" (p. 50).

By the 1950s, however, America's deindustrialization undermined the coherence of disciplinary parole: Low-skilled jobs were declining in number, especially for minorities, who, simultaneously, were becoming a growing proportion of the correctional population. We now had offenders who were largely unemployable, who could not be "normalized" by the discipline of the changing workplace but who "must be altered before they could be moved in the labor force" (p. 100). The initial institutional response was the trumpeting of "clinical parole," in which parole officers would function as caseworkers delivering treatment and linking offenders to needed social services. In this narrative, crime was rooted not simply in the failure to work or "idleness," but in a "maladjustment between the individual and the institutions of the community....Such degeneration," continues Simon (p. 104), "could be halted by counseling and treatment which addressed the underlying pathologies that discouraged identification with conventional norms."

The clinical model, however, was rendered implausible by the intersection of three factors. First, the correctional crisis was exacerbated by the continued "hardening of urban poverty" in the inner cities caused by the erosion of the non-skilled labor market in an increasingly postindustrial America. Parole as normalization became "less coherent" when the project of reintegration meant returning underclass offenders to communities burdened by the "tangle of urban pathology" and with "fewer and fewer resources to sustain them."...

Second, at the same time, legal interventions by the court mandated due process rights for parolees, especially at the revocation hearing. Because discretionary decisions previously made without scrutiny now were rendered visible, pressures emerged to rationalize and introduce uniformity into the application of power (see chapter 4). The need to justify decisions to an external environment was increased further by a third condition: increasing public fears of violent crime and a loss of confidence in criminal justice officials. The challenge was to construct a correctional system in which accountability in the defense of public safety could be demonstrated.

The response to this context over the past two decades has been to rationalize procedures in the pursuit of "risk management" (p. 169). This "managerial model" stands traditional parole on its head by embracing the core principle of the penal harm movement that "custody is the necessary and sufficient solution to criminal risk" (p. 229). The task for parole officers thus becomes not assisting in the community reintegration of offenders but in discerning which offenders in the community should be reincarcerated. "New technologies of control"—risk classification systems, computerized databases, drug testing—increase the capacity for surveillance and for detecting dangerous parolees (see chapter 6). The logical conclusion of the managerial model is the primacy given to the "revocation hearing." Resources are concentrated on administering procedurally correct hearings in which parole's accountability is established by sending risky offenders back to prison at unprecedented rates (see chapter 7).

As Simon recognizes, the success of the managerial model is not complete (see also Cullen, Wright and Applegate forthcoming). It contains the fundamental inconsistency of exacerbating the fiscal crisis in corrections. "Parole has been successful in transforming itself from a system of rehabilitative discipline to one of risk management," observes Simon (p. 229), "and now finds itself criticized for that accomplishment." Further, there is danger in reifying Simon's managerial model to the point of being blinded to the continuing allegiance to offender rehabilitation that exists both among correctional personnel in California and in states that have been less quick to embrace control as the only goal of the criminal sanction.

Still, Simon's *Poor Discipline* is perceptive in identifying the forces that are helping to fuel the penal harm movement. Most disquieting, he reveals that no plausible narrative or account for the correctional enterprise currently exists to challenge the widening hegemony of penal harm. Criminologists, I believe, share a measure of responsibility for this state of affairs. Clear's analysis of "penal science" is sobering (see chapter 3). In recent decades—as authors and as consultants—we have played a large role in delegitimizing the rehabilitative ideal and in providing the intellectual justification and technology for managing penal harm. The challenge now is to help fashion an alternative plausible narrative that can move us beyond harm as the organizing principle of corrections.

BEYOND PENAL HARM

Unfortunately, the authors stop short of providing a coherent and compelling penological model that rivals the power of get-tough thinking. Let me hasten to blunt this criticism by noting that the books provide useful ideas on how to minimize harm in corrections and, taken together, succeed mightily in showing the importance of engaging in a conversation about the future of corrections. But unlike the "new penologists" who came to Cincinnati in 1870, they do not vigorously advocate the kind of optimistic and confident "Declaration of Principles" that might serve as an alternative narrative to penal harm.

I would like to claim that I do not have the space to outline such a new penological model, but my reticence lies more in a fear that the task is too daunting. Even so, I will take the risk of arguing—as I have for over a decade—in favor of reaffirming rehabilitation as a model to rival penal harm (Cullen and Gendreau 1989; Cullen and Gilbert 1982; Cullen, Van Voorhis, and Sundt forthcoming; Cullen and Wright forthcoming; Gendreau et al. 1994).

A whole generation of criminologists were raised to mistrust state power to do good, to believe that "nothing works" to change offenders, and to embrace "doing justice" as a means of "doing less harm." This pessimistic narrative, which seeks to restrain abuse and not to accomplish good, remains plausible to many criminologists, but it sparks little response from the public and has largely lost its power to humanize corrections. Most important, it fails to capitalize on the generous side of the public's sentiments about corrections; as Tonry (p. 9) notes, "large majorities of Americans...want prisons to rehabilitate offenders" (see also Cullen, Cullen, and Wozniak 1988; Cullen, Skovron, Scott, and Burton 1990; McCorkle 1993). In short, rehabilitation is the one liberal correctional narrative that citizens still find plausible.

I would warn, however, that rehabilitation as a form of pure-hearted benevolence is vulnerable to attack. Instead, as the new penologists of the 1870s understood, the *utility* of treatment interventions for the public good must be a central principle if the rehabilitative ideal is to achieve support. Like it or not, American culture is decidedly utilitarian (Bellah et al. 1985), and the failure to take this factor into account will render any liberal correctional model irrelevant. It is instructive that DiIulio and similar advocates of incapacitation do not make this mistake. Indeed, their persuasiveness comes from giving a plausible account of how prisons increase safety while portraying liberal naysayers as having no interest in protecting innocent citizens. The challenge of the utility of penal harm thus must be confronted, not just dismissed. Fortunately, science is on the side of treatment: The research is mounting that shows that rehabilitation "works better" than penal harm in reducing recidivism (see, e.g., Andrews and Bonta 1994; Andrews et al. 1990; Cullen, Wright, and Applegate forthcoming; Lipsey 1992; Palmer 1992; Tonry, pp. 201–3).

Second, rehabilitation should be framed not as a form of governmental entitlement but as a utilitarian exchange. Simon (p. 263) captures this insight with his call for "investing penal resources in community discipline"—a situation in which governmental rewards are tied to offender performance in programs (such as work) that encourage individual responsibility, normalize deviant tendencies, and contribute to the commonweal (such as by providing payment for victims or for the offender's family). Of course, reward systems must be backed up by the threat of negative reinforcement—"behave or you'll suffer the consequences"—which raises the sticky issue of how far to go in enforcing therapy. Although I am not unmindful of the potential for abuse (see Rothman 1980), no liberal correctional narrative will have credibility if offenders are not held accountable for their actions. And consistent with the principles of the 1870 new penologists, it is not clear that offender reform can be effective unless we are willing to assert values and to use "effective disapproval" to encourage conformity (Andrews and Bonta 1994, pp. 202–7).

Third, the rehabilitative narrative should trumpet early intervention. This strategy—a means of diverting much-needed services to vulnerable populations—has marked advantages: It forces attention on conditions, such as the capital disinvestment in inner cities (Currie 1985; Hagan 1994; Short 1991), that place families and children at risk; it focuses on a "deserving" object of attention—children born into difficult circumstances through "no fault of their own"; it embraces the persuasive logic that "you can pay me now or pay me later"; and there is evidence that such interventions can be successful (Greenwood 1995, pp. 112–17).

Some criminologists, I suspect, will find my proposal for reaffirming "utilitarian" rehabilitation misguided. But if so, it is incumbent on these critics and like-minded scholars to move beyond preaching to the criminological choir about the disutility of punishment and to declare their principles for designing a *plausible* and *positive* correctional model. The time for taking up this task is overdue. In chilling detail, Todd Clear, Jonathan Simon, and Michael Tonry illuminate the ideological power and the human costs of penal harm. Unless a better answer can be put forth, this movement promises to gain strength and to permeate more deeply the fabric of the correctional enterprise.

STUDY QUESTIONS

1. Specifically, how does Cullen define the penal harm movement in the United States?
2. What is the primary "utility" of the penal harm movement (from a conservative vantage point), according to Cullen?
3. What is the primary "detriment" of the penal harm movement (from a liberal vantage point)?
4. According to this article, what are the three ways in which the United States should move beyond the penal harm movement?

REFERENCES

Andrews, D. A. and James Bonta. (1994). *The Psychology of Criminal Conduct.* Cincinnati, OH: Anderson.

Andrews, D. A., Ivan Zinger, R. D. Hoge, James Bonta, Paul Gendreau, and Francis T. Cullen. (1990). "Does Correctional Treatment Work? A Clinically-Relevant and Psychologically-Informed Meta-Analysis." *Criminology,* 28:369–404.

Bellah, Robert N., Richard Madsen, William M. Sullivan, Ann Swidler, and Steven M. Tipton. (1985). *Habits of the Heart: Individualism and Commitment in American Life.* Berkeley: University of California Press.

Benekos, Peter J. and Alida V. Merlo. (1995). "Three Strikes and You're Out!: The Political Sentencing Game." *Federal Probation,* 59 (March):3–9.

Blumstein, Alfred. (1989). "American Prisons in a Time of Crisis." Pp. 13–22 in *The American Prison: Issues in Research and Policy,* edited by L. Goodstein and D. L. MacKenzie. New York: Plenum.

———. (1995). "Prisons." Pp. 387–419 in *Crime,* edited by James Q. Wilson and Joan Petersilia. San Francisco: ICS.

Blumstein, Alfred and Jacqueline Cohen. (1973). "A Theory of the Stability of Punishment." *Journal of Criminal Law and Criminology,* 64:198–206.

Bragg, Rick. (1995). "Chain Gangs to Return to Roads of Alabama: States Hopes Revival Will

Deter Crime." *New York Times,* March 26, p. Y9.

Braithwaite, John. (1989). *Crime, Shame and Reintegration.* Cambridge, UK: Cambridge University Press.

Brockway, Zebulon R. (1910). "The American Reformatory Prison System." Pp. 88–107 in *Prison Reform: Correction and Prevention,* edited by Charles Richmond Henderson. New York: Russell Sage Foundation.

Bureau of Justice Statistics. (1994). *Criminal Victimization in the United States, 1992.* Washington, DC: U.S. Department of Justice.

Byrne, James M. and April Pattavina. (1992). "The Effectiveness Issue: Assessing What Works in the Adult Community Corrections System." Pp. 81–303 in *Smart Sentencing: The Emergence of Intermediate Sanctions,* edited by James M. Byrne, Arthur J. Lurigio, and Joan Petersilia. Newbury Park, CA: Sage.

Clear, T. R. (1994). *Harm in American Penology: Offenders, Victims, and Their Communities.* West Sacramento, CA: California Correctional Peace Officers Association.

Cohen, Adam. (1995). "Back on the Chain Gang." *Time,* May 15, p. 26.

Cohen, Jacqueline and José A. Canela-Cacho. (1994). "Incarceration and Violent Crime: 1965–1988." Pp. 296–388 in *Understanding and Preventing Violence: Consequences and Control,* Vol. 4, edited by Albert J. Reiss, Jr. and Jeffrey A. Roth. Washington, DC: National Academy Press.

Colvin, Mark. (1992). *The Penitentiary in Crisis: From Accommodation to Riot in New Mexico.* Albany: SUNY Press.

Cullen, Francis T., John B. Cullen, and John F. Wozniak. (1988). "Is Rehabilitation Dead? The Myth of the Punitive Public." *Journal of Criminal Justice,* 34:379–92.

Cullen, Francis T. and Paul Gendreau. (1989). "The Effectiveness of Correctional Rehabilitation: Reconsidering the 'Nothing Works' Debate." Pp. 23–44 in *The American Prison: Issues in Research and Policy,* edited by L. Goodstein and D. L. MacKenzie. New York: Plenum.

Cullen, Francis T. and Karen E. Gilbert. (1982). *Reaffirming Rehabilitation.* Cincinnati, OH: Anderson.

Cullen, Francis T., Sandra Evans Skovron, Joseph E. Scott, and Velmer S. Burton, Jr. (1990). "Public Support for Correctional Rehabilitation: The Tenacity of the Rehabilitative Ideal." *Criminal Justice and Behavior,* 17:6–18.

Cullen, Francis T. and Lawrence F. Travis, III. (1984). "Work as an Avenue of Prison Reform." *New England Journal of Criminal and Civil Confinement,* 10:45–64.

Cullen, Francis T., Patricia Van Voorhis, and Jody L. Sundt. (1996). "Prisons in Crisis: The American Experience." In *Prisons 2000: An International Perspective on the Current State and Future of Imprisonment,* edited by Roger Matthews and Peter Francis. New York: Macmillan.

Cullen, Francis T. and John P. Wright. (1996). "The Future of Corrections." In *The Past, Present, and Future of American Criminal Justice,* edited by Brendan Maguire and Polly Radosh. New York: General Hall.

Cullen, Francis T., John P. Wright, and Brandon K. Applegate. (1996). "Control in the Community: The Limits of Reform?" In *Choosing Correctional Interventions That Work: Defining the Demand and Evaluating the Supply,* edited by Alan T. Harland. Newbury Park, CA: Sage.

Currie, Elliott. (1985). *Confronting Crime: An American Challenge.* New York: Pantheon.

———. (1993). *Reckoning: Drugs, the Cities, and the American Future.* New York: Hill and Wang.

"Declaration of Principles Promulgated at Cincinnati, Ohio, 1870." 1910 [1870], Pp. 39–63 in *Prison Reform Correction and Prevention,* edited by Charles Richmond Henderson. New York: Russell Sage Foundation.

DiIulio, John J., Jr. (1994). "The Question of Black Crime." *Public Interest,* 117 (Fall):3–32.

Farrington, David P. and Patrick A. Langan. (1992). "Changes in Crime and Punishment in England and America in the. 1980s." *Justice Quarterly,* 9:5–31.

Federal Bureau of Investigation. (1994). *Uniform Crime Reports: Crime in the United States, 1993.* Washington, DC: U.S. Government Printing Office.

Feeley, Malcolm M. and Jonathan Simon. (1992). "The New Penology: Notes on the Emerging Strategy of Corrections and Its Implications." *Criminology,* 30:449–74.

Forer, Lois G. (1994). *A Rage to Punish: The Unintended Consequences of Mandatory Sentencing.* New York: W. W. Norton.

Garland, David. (1990). *Punishment and Modern Society: A Study in Social Theory.* Chicago: University of Chicago Press.

Gendreau, Paul, Francis T. Cullen, and James Bonta. (1994). "Intensive Rehabilitation Supervision: The Next Generation in Community Corr-ections?" *Federal Probation,* 58 (March): 72–78.

Gordon, Diana R. (1991). *'The Justice Juggernaut: Fighting Street Crime, Controlling Citizens.* New Brunswick, NJ: Rutgers University Press.

—— (1994). *The Return of the Dangerous Classes: Drug Prohibition and Policy Politics.* New York: W. W. Norton.

Gramm, Phil. (1993). "Drugs, Crime and Punishment: Don't Let Judges Set Crooks Free." *New York Times,* July 8, pp. B1–B2.

Greenwood, Peter W. (1995). "Juvenile Crime and Juvenile Justice." Pp. 91–117 in *Crime,* edited by James Q. Wilson and Joan Petersilia. San Francisco: ICS.

Hagan, John. (1994). *Crime and Disrepute.* Thousand Oaks, CA: Pine Forge.

Herrnstein, Richard J. and Charles Murray. (1994). *The Bell Curve: Intelligence and Class Structure in American Life.* New York: Free Press.

Irwin, John. (1985). *The Jail: Managing the Underclass in American Society.* Berkeley: University of California Press.

Irwin, John and James Austin. (1994). *It's About Time: America's Imprisonment Binge.* Belmont, CA: Wadsworth.

Kaminer, Wendy. (1995). *It's All the Rage: Crime and Culture.* Reading, MA: Addison-Wesley.

Lipsey, Mark W. (1992). "Juvenile Delinquency Treatment: A Meta-Analytic Inquiry Into the Variability of Effects." Pp. 83–127 in *Meta-Analysis for Explanation: A Casebook,* edited by Thomas D. Cook, Harris Cooper, David S. Cordray, Heidi Hartmann, Larry V. Hedges, Richard J. Light, Thomas A. Louis, and Frederick Mosteller. New York: Russell Sage Foundation.

Logan, Charles H. and John J. DiIulio, Jr. (1992). "Ten Myths About Crime and Prisons." *Wisconsin Interest,* 1:21–35.

Lynch, James. (1995). "Crime in International Perspective." Pp. 11–38 in *Crime,* edited by James O. Wilson and Joan Petersilia. San Francisco: ICS.

Marvell, Thomas B. and Carlisle E. Moody, Jr. (1994). "Prison Population Growth and Crime Reduction." *Journal of Quantitative Criminology,* 10:109–40.

McCorkle, Richard C. (1993). "Punish and Rehabilitate? Public Attitudes Toward Six Common Crimes." *Crime & Delinquency,* 39:240–52.

Palmer, Ted. (1992). *The Re-Emergence of Correctional Intervention.* Newbury Park, CA: Sage.

Paternoster, Raymond. (1987). "The Deterrent Effect of Perceived Certainty and Severity of Punishment: A Review of the Evidence and Issues." *Justice Quarterly,* 4:173–217.

Petersilia, Joan. (1992). "California's Prison Policy: Causes, Costs, and Consequences." *The Prison Journal,* 72:8–36.

Petersilia, Joan and Susan Turner. (1993). "Intensive Probation and Parole." Pp. 281–335 in *Crime and Justice: A Review of Research,* Vol. 17, edited by Michael Tonry. Chicago: University of Chicago Press.

Platt, Anthony M. (1969). *The Child Savers: The Invention of Delinquency*. Chicago: University of Chicago Press.

Reiss, Albert J., Jr. and Jeffrey A. Roth, eds. (1993). *Understanding and Preventing Violence*. Washington, DC: National Academy Press.

Rengert, George F. (1989). "Spatial Justice and Criminal Victimization." *Justice Quarterly*, 6: 543–64.

Roth, Jeffrey A. (1995). "Achievements to Date and Goals for the Future: New Looks at Criminal Careers." *Journal of Quantitative Criminology*, 11:97–110.

Rothman, David J. (1971). *The Discovery of the Asylum: Social Order and Disorder in the New Republic*. Boston: Little, Brown.

——— (1980). *Conscience and Convenience: The Asylum and Its Alternatives in Progressive America*. Boston: Little, Brown.

Sampson, Robert J. and John H. Laub. (1993). *Crime in the Making: Pathways and Turning Points Through Life*. Cambridge, MA: Harvard University Press.

Scull, Andrew. (1977). *Decarceration: Community Treatment and the Deviant—A Radical View*. Englewood Cliffs, NJ: Prentice Hall.

Selke, William L. (1993). *Prisons in Crisis*. Bloomington: Indiana University Press.

Sherman, Lawrence W. (1993). "Defiance, Deterrence, and Irrelevance: A Theory of Criminal Sanctions." *Journal of Research in Crime and Delinquency*, 30:445–73.

Sherman, Michael and Gordon Hawkins. (1981). *Imprisonment in America: Choosing the Future*. Chicago: University of Chicago Press.

Short, James F., Jr. (1991). "Poverty, Ethnicity, and Crime: Change and Continuity in U.S. Cities." *Journal of Research in Crime and Delinquency*, 28:501–18.

Simon, J. (1993). *Poor Discipline: Parole and the Social Control of the Underclass*. Chicago: University of Chicago Press.

Spelman, William. (1994). *Criminal Incapacitation*. New York: Plenum.

Steffensmeier, Darrell and Miles D. Harer. (1993). "Bulging Prisons, an Aging U.S. Population, and the Nation's Crime Rate." *Federal Probation* 57 (June):3–10.

Tonry, Michael. (1994). "Racial Disproportion in US Prisons." *British Journal of Criminology*, 34: 97–115.

Tonry, Michael. (1995). *Malign Neglect: Race, Crime, and Punishment in America*. New York: Oxford University Press.

Turner, Michael G., Jody L. Sundt, Brandon K. Applegate, and Francis T. Cullen. (1995). "'Three Strikes and You're Out' Legislation: A National Assessment." *Federal Probation*.

Walker, Samuel. (1989). *Sense and Nonsense About Crime: A Policy Guide*, 2nd ed. Pacific Grove, CA: Brooks/Cole.

Wilson, James O. (1983). *Thinking About Crime*, rev. ed. New York: Random House.

———. (1995). "Crime and Public Policy." Pp. 489–507 in *Crime*, edited by James Q. Wilson and Joan Petersilia. San Francisco: ICS.

Wright, Richard A. (1994). *In Defense of Prisons*. Westport, CT: Greenwood.

Zedlewski, Edwin W. (1987). *Research in Brief: Making Confinement Decisions*. Washington, DC: National Institute of Justice.

Zimring, Franklin and Gordon Hawkins. (1991). *The Scale of Imprisonment*. Chicago: University of Chicago Press.

———. (1995). *Incapacitation: Penal Confinement* and the Restraint of Crime. New York: Oxford University Press.

PART

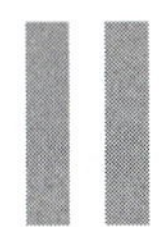

LIVING IN PRISON

By the turn of the twentieth century, the use of the prison as the primary form of punishment in the United States was well established. The general public was satisfied to allow government agencies to punish offenders with confinement, separated by sight and sound from most free people. During the early 1900s, incarceration also came to the attention of many sociologists who examined prisons as "total institutions."

Prisons attempt to maintain total control at all times. Studies have indicated that by and large both inmates and guards desire the same outcome at the end of the day—a peaceful ending. Much research has gone into studying every aspect of the prison as a total institution and the varied and complex systems and subgroupings that make up the total institution.

It is important to remember that the prison is designed to control virtually every aspect of the offender's life. While the overarching goal of incarceration is confinement of the offender, prisons also must meet many needs of inmates—most notably, housing, feeding, clothing, educating, and rehabilitating those within their walls. Inmates respond to this total control in a number of ways. Some have argued that while the prison administration holds sway over the "official" functioning of the institution, the "unofficial" functioning (which in some ways might be as or more influential at times), is up to the inmates. By "unofficial" functioning we mean the development of subculture, social and physical adaptation, economic proliferation, and uprisings. Often these aspects of prison life are governed by powerful subgroups within the general offender population.

The selections in this part are designed to present a detailed view of the prison subculture and the extent to which an inmate can experience "prisonization"—an orientation that has been so influenced by the confines of the institution for so long that successful readjustment to life outside the institution seems unlikely. This is an important construct to understand in light of the fact that the vast majority of offenders who are incarcerated will indeed come back to their communities at some point—perhaps greater than 95 percent.

In addition to the prison community, the advent and use of the "supermax" prison is explored in this part. "Supermax" prisons were originally designed to house the "worst of the worst"—meaning inmates who had severe behavioral problems within a maximum security environment. As such, "supermax" prisons were not originally intended to hold any one inmate for an extended (i.e., years-long) period of time. Rather, these institutions were designed to create total isolation for a short period of time, presumably while the inmate's behavior stabilized, after which point the prisoner would be returned to the prison system from which he came. Despite initial intentions, "supermax" prisons have to some degree become part of the lexicon of the "get-tough movement" and in many respects have simply come to be known as "level 6" security in what are normally five-level prison systems. Due to the single celling, extreme isolation, and the typical lack of stimulation, "supermax" prisons have had dire consequences, particularly for those inmates who spend extended periods of time in them. The Supreme Court has heard and will continue to hear cases involving the net effects of this very specific type of incarceration.

In light of the problems related to total isolation that can occur in a "supermax" environment, it is important to point out that the inmate population is perhaps the most important subgroup within a prison environment with which a prisoner will interact. A close second in importance would be the correctional officers that are also a constant part of the inmates' environment. As such, this part also explores, from an inmate's perspective, the intricacies of the relationships that develop between inmates and guards.

7
THE PRISON COMMUNITY

DONALD CLEMMER

In this article by Clemmer, the process of "prisonization" is examined closely. After considering the possible effects of the "total institution," the reader should consider how those effects may influence the culture (or subculture) within the walls of the prison. The author describes *prisonization* as "the process through which an individual will take on the values and mores of the penitentiary." In other words, the prison is seen as a world in and of itself—a world with unique characteristics and internal forces that at times mimic the outside world, but in many ways are completely different. Because the prisoners, through processes inherent within the prison, have been cut off from outside influences, the potential for the development of new rules, expectations, and economies presents itself. In responding to these new rules, inmates develop ways in which they modify their behavior to fit in and adapt. Such adaptation may help inmates survive in a number of ways. As you read, however, consider whether these behavior modifications inhibit the achievement of any other correctional goals.

ASSIMILATION OR PRISONIZATION

When a person or group of ingress penetrates and fuses with another group, assimilation may be said to have taken place. The concept is most profitably applied to immigrant groups and perhaps it is not the best term by which to designate similar processes which occur in prison. Assimilation implies that a process of acculturation occurs in one group whose members originally were quite different from those of the group with whom they mix. It implies that the assimilated come to share the sentiments, memories, and traditions of the static group. It is evident that the men who come to prison are not greatly different from the ones already there so far as broad culture influences are concerned: All speak the same language, all have a similar national heritage, all have been stigmatized, and so on. While the differences of regional conditioning are not to be overlooked, it is doubtful if the interactions which lead the professional offender to have a "we-feeling" with the naive offender from Coalville can be referred to as assimilation—although the processes furnishing the development of such an understanding are similar to it.... [T]he term assimilation describes a slow, gradual, more or less unconscious process during which a person learns enough of the culture of a social unit into which he is placed to make him characteristic of it. While we shall continue to use this general meaning, we recognize that in the strictest sense assimilation is not the correct term. So as we use the term Americanization to describe a greater or lesser degree of the immigrant's integration into the American scheme of life, we may use the term *prisonization* to indicate the taking on in greater or lesser degree of the folkways, mores, customs, and general culture of the penitentiary. Prisonization is similar to assimilation, and its meaning will become clearer as we proceed.

Every man who enters the penitentiary undergoes prisonization to some extent. The first and most obvious integrative step concerns his status. He becomes at once an anonymous figure in a subordinate group. A number replaces a name. He wears the clothes of the other members of the subordinate group. He is questioned and admonished. He soon learns that the warden is all-powerful. He soon learns the ranks, titles, and authority of various officials. And whether he uses the prison slang and argot or not, he comes to know its meanings. Even though a new man may hold himself aloof from other inmates and remain a solitary figure, he finds himself within a few months referring to or thinking of keepers as "screws," the physician as the "croaker" and using the local nicknames to designate persons. He follows the examples already set in wearing his cap. He learns to eat in haste and in obtaining food he imitates the tricks of those near him.

After the new arrival recovers from the effects of the swallowing-up process, he assigns a new meaning to conditions he had previously taken for granted. The fact that food, shelter, clothing, and a work activity had been given him originally made no especial impression. It is only after some weeks or months that there comes to him a new interpretation of these necessities of life. This new conception results from mingling with other men and it places emphasis on the fact that the environment *should* administer to him. This point is intangible and difficult to describe insofar as it is only a subtle and minute change in attitude from the taken-for-granted perception. Exhaustive questioning of hundreds of men reveals that this slight change in attitude is a fundamental step in the process we are calling prisonization. Supplemental to it is the almost universal desire on the part of the man, after a period of some months, to get a good job so, as he says, "I can do my time without any trouble and get out of here." A good job usually means a comfortable job of a more or less isolated kind in which conflicts with other men are not likely to develop. The desire for a comfortable job is not peculiar to the prison community, to be sure, but it seems to be a phase of prisonization in the following way. When men have served time before entering the penitentiary they look the situation over and almost immediately express a desire for a certain kind of work. When strictly first offenders come to prison, however, they seldom express a desire for a particular kind of work, but are willing to do anything and frequently say, "I'll do any kind of work they put me at and you won't have any trouble from me." Within a period of a few months, however, these same men, who had no choice of work, develop preferences and make their desires known. They "wise up," as the inmates say, or in other words, by association they become prisonized.

In various other ways men new to prison slip into the existing patterns. They learn to gamble or learn new ways to gamble. Some, for the first time in their lives, take to abnormal sex behavior. Many of them learn to distrust and hate the officers, the parole board, and sometimes each other, and they become acquainted with the dogmas and mores existing in the community. But these changes do not occur in every man. However, every man is subject to certain influences which we may call the *universal factors of prisonization*.

Acceptance of an inferior role, accumulation of facts concerning the organization of the prison, the development of somewhat new habits of eating, dressing, working, sleeping, the adoption of local language, the recognition that nothing is owed to the environment for the supplying of needs, and the eventual desire for a good job are aspects of prisonization which are operative for all inmates. It is not these aspects, however, which concern us most but they are important because of their universality, especially among men who have served many years. That is, even if no other factor of the prison culture touches the personality of an inmate of many years residence, the influences of these universal factors are sufficient to make a man characteristic of the penal community and probably so disrupt his personality that a happy adjustment in any community becomes next to impossible. On the other hand, if inmates who are incarcerated for only short periods, such as a year or so, do not become integrated into the culture except insofar as these universal factors of prisonization arc concerned, they do not seem to be so characteristic of the penal community and are able when released to take up a new mode of life without much difficulty.

The phases of prisonization which concern us most are the influences which breed or deepen criminality and antisociality and make the inmate characteristic of the criminalistic ideology in the prison community. As has been said, every man feels the influences of what we have called the universal factors, but not every man becomes prisonized in and by other phases of the culture. Whether or not complete prisonization takes place depends first on the man himself, that is, his susceptibility to a culture which depends, we think, primarily on the type of relationships he had before imprisonment, i.e., his personality. A second determinant effecting complete prisonization refers to the kind and extent of relationships which an inmate has with persons outside the walls. A third determinant refers to whether or not a man becomes affiliated in prison primary or semi-primary groups and this is related to the two points already mentioned. Yet a fourth determinant depends simply on chance, a chance placement in [a] work gang, cellhouse, and with [a] cellmate. A fifth determinant pertains to whether or not a man accepts the dogmas or codes of the prison culture. Other determinants depend on age, criminality, nationality, race, regional conditioning, and every determinant is more or less interrelated with every other one.

With knowledge of these determinants we can hypothetically construct schemata of prisonization which may serve to illustrate its extremes. In the least or lowest degree of prisonization the following factors may be enumerated:

1. A short sentence, thus a brief subjection to the universal factors of prisonization.
2. A fairly stable personality made stable by an adequacy of positive and socialized relationships during pre-penal life.
3. The continuance of positive relationships with persons outside the walls.
4. Refusal or inability to integrate into a prison primary group or semiprimary group, while yet maintaining a symbiotic balance in relations with other men.
5. Refusal to accept blindly the dogmas and codes of the population, and a willingness, under certain situations, to aid officials, thus making for identification with the free community.
6. A chance placement with a cellmate and workmates who do not possess leadership qualities and who are also not completely integrated into the prison culture.
7. Refraining from abnormal sex behavior, and excessive gambling, and a ready willingness to engage seriously in work and recreative activities.

Other factors no doubt have an influencing force in obstructing the process of prisonization, but the seven points mentioned seem outstanding.

In the highest or greatest degree of prisonization the following factors may be enumerated:

1. A sentence of many years, thus a long subjection to the universal factors of prisonization.

2. A somewhat unstable personality made unstable by an inadequacy of socialized relations before commitment, but possessing, nonetheless, a capacity for strong convictions and a particular kind of loyalty.
3. A dearth of positive relations with persons outside the walls.
4. A readiness and a capacity for integration into a prison-primary group.
5. A blind, or almost blind, acceptance of the dogmas and mores of the primary group and the general penal population.
6. A chance placement with other persons of a similar orientation.
7. A readiness to participate in gambling and abnormal sex behavior.

We can see in these two extremes the degrees with which the prisonization process operates. No suggestion is intended that a high correlation exists between either extreme of prisonization and criminality. It is quite possible that the inmate who fails to integrate in the prison culture may be and may continue to be much more criminalistic than the inmate who becomes completely prisonized. The trends are probably otherwise, however, as our study of group life suggests. To determine prisonization, every case must be appraised for itself. Of the two degrees presented in the schemes it is probable that more men approach the complete degree than the least degree of prisonization, but it is also probable that the majority of inmates become prisonized in some respects and not in others. It is the varying degrees of prisonization among the 2,300 men that contribute to the disassociation which is so common. The culture is made complex, not only by the constantly changing population, but by these differences in the tempo and degree of prisonization.

Assimilation, as the concept is customarily applied, is always a slow, gradual process, but prisonization, as we use the term here, is usually slow, but not necessarily so. The speed with which prisonization occurs depends on the personality of the man involved, his crime, age, home neighborhood, intelligence, the situation into which he is placed in prison and other less obvious influences. The process does not necessarily proceed in an orderly or measured fashion but tends to be irregular. In some cases we have found the process working in a cycle. The amount and speed of prisonization can be judged only by the behavior and attitudes of the men, and these vary from man to man and in the same man from time to time. It is the excessive number of changes in orientation which the men undergo which makes generalizations about the process so difficult.

In the free communities where the daily life of the inhabitants is not controlled in every detail, some authors have reported a natural gravitation to social levels. The matter of chance still remains a factor, of course, in open society but not nearly so much so as in the prison. For example, two associates in a particular crime may enter the prison at the same time. Let us say that their criminality, their intelligence, and their background are more or less the same. Each is interviewed by the deputy warden and assigned to a job. It so happens that a certain office is in need of a porter. Of the two associates the man whom the deputy warden happens to see first may be assigned to that job while the one he interviews last is assigned to the quarry. The inmate who becomes the office porter associates with but four or five other men, none of whom, let us suppose, are basically prisonized. The new porter adapts himself to them and takes up their interests. His speed of prisonization will be slow and he may never become completely integrated into the prison culture. His associate, on the other hand, works in the quarry and mingles with a hundred men. The odds are three to five that he will become integrated into a primary or semi-primary group. When he is admitted into the competitive and personal relationships of informal group life we can be sure that, in spite of some disassociation, he is becoming prisonized and will approach the complete degree.

Even if the two associates were assigned to the same work unit, differences in the tempo of prisonization might result if one, for example, worked shoulder to shoulder with a "complete solitary man," or a "hoosier." Whatever else may be said of the tempo of the process, it is always faster when the contacts are primary, providing the persons contacted in a primary way are themselves integrated beyond the minimal into the prison culture. Other factors, of course, influence the speed of integration. The inmate whose wife divorces him may turn for response and recognition to his immediate associates. When the memories of prepenal experience cease to be satisfying or practically useful, a barrier to prisonization has been removed.

Some men become prisonized to the highest degree, or to a degree approaching it, but then reject their entire orientation and show, neither by behavior nor attitudes, that any sort of integration has taken place. They slip out of group life. They ignore the codes and dogmas and they fall into a reverie or stupor or become "solitary men." After some months or even years of playing this role they may again affiliate with a group and behave as other prisonized inmates do.

Determination of the degree of prisonization and the speed with which it occurs can be learned best through the study of specific cases. The innumerable variables and the methodological difficulties which arise in learning what particular stage of prisonization a man has reached, prohibit the use of quantitative methods. It would be a great help to penology and to parole boards in particular, if the student of prisons could say that inmate so-and-so was prisonized to $x^3 + 9y$ degrees, and such a degree was highly correlated with a specific type of criminality. The day will no doubt come when phenomena of this kind can be measured, but it is not yet here. For the present we must bend our efforts to systems of actuarial prediction, and work for refinements in this line. Actuarial procedures do not ignore criteria of attitudes, but they make no effort as yet to conjure with such abstruse phenomena as prisonization. It is the contention of this writer that parole prediction methods which do not give as much study and attention to a man's role in the prison community as is given to his adjustment in the free community cannot be of much utility.

STUDY QUESTIONS

1. What is meant by the term *prisonization*, and what are some of its universal factors?
2. What characteristics of inmates determine the degree and speed with which prisonization occurs?
3. How do the features of the total institution, referred to by Goffman, relate to the process of prisonization?

8

SUPERMAX PRISONS

PANACEA OR DESPERATION?

RODNEY J. HENNINGSEN
W. WESLEY JOHNSON
TERRY WELLS

Most penal institutions have dedicated a portion of their buildings to inmates who are experiencing within-institutional punishment, those who are unable to control themselves satisfactorily in the general prison population. These sections of prisons are generally referred to as "administrative segregation" units. As a recent development, the "supermax" prison represents an institution designed to house nothing but offenders who are not able to control themselves within a general inmate population. The authors discuss how popular these institutions have become within the political realm, as they represent the ultimate "get-tough" strategy. Supermax prisons are characterized by solitary confinement, near 24-hour lockdown, and a total lack of congregation and severely limited interaction with other human beings. As such, the model has experienced criticism, particularly regarding the effects of extended solitary confinement. Although true "total control" does appear to be achieved in the supermax institution, the control comes at a cost. The authors identify the costs, including accusations of human rights violations, and describe a "psychologically assaultive" environment that creates long-term damage. The reader is encouraged to contemplate the problems inherent in the creation of a "supermax" prison, while simultaneously considering what "ordinary" prisons should do with those who simply cannot conform, even in a maximum-security setting.

For over a century Americans have sought to find the silver bullet to solve its crime problems. Fads and experiments in corrections have included public humiliation, single-celling, silent systems, 12-step recovery programs, boot camps, electronic surveillance, and now, supermax. Supermax prisons have evolved out of America's love-hate relationship with crime and punishment. A supermax

Excerpts from "Supermax Prisons: Panacea or Desperation?" by Rodney J. Henningsen, W. Wesley Johnson, and Terry Wells. *Corrections Management Quarterly*, Volume 3, Number 2: 53–59.

prison has been defined as:

> A free-standing facility, or distinct unit within a facility, that provides for the management and secure control of inmates who have been officially designated as exhibiting violent or seriously disruptive behavior while incarcerated. Such inmates have been determined to be a threat to safety and security in traditional high-security facilities, and their behavior can be controlled by separation, restricted movement, and limited access to staff and other inmates.[1]

At least in theory, this type of prison unit can and should be distinguished from administrative segregation (ad-seg). While most every prison has administrative segregation cells used for holding prisoners in short-term disciplinary or protective custody, supermax units are designed to house prisoners for a much longer period of time. Proponents of supermax prisons contend that they warehouse the worst of the worst, the most violent prisoners who threaten the security of guards and other prisoners while undermining the moral fabric of American society.

While the American public has increasingly turned to government for solutions to its social problems in the last 30 years, its perceptions of the criminal justice system have remained jaundiced. Over 75 percent of respondents in a recent national survey reported only "some" or "very little" confidence in state prison systems.[2] Similarly, over 80 percent of people surveyed each year since 1980 have indicated that the courts are too soft on crime.[3]

The American judiciary has responded to public concerns that they are soft on crime and cries for vengeance by placing more people under correctional supervision than ever before. To accommodate the increases in new prison admissions and increases in time served by prisoners, some 168 state and 45 federal prisons have been built since 1990. Today, there are a total of approximately 1,500 state and federal prisons. Between 1990 and 1995, the number of prison beds increased by 41 percent. Despite this tremendous fiscal investment, there are both state and federal prisons that operate in excess of their design capacity, state prisons by 3 percent and federal prisons by 24 percent.[4]

While there are more prisons and prisoners than ever before, there is sustained interest in making prisons even "tougher."[5] This interest may be based on the notion, not strongly supported in the criminological research on recidivism, that prisons deter. Another reason may be simply that victims of crime, and those that see themselves as potential victims, want prisoners to suffer. While harm is a critical component of punishment, its generic application to prison life creates unique challenges for correctional officers, staff, and correctional executives.[6]

POLITICAL POPULARITY OF SUPERMAX PRISONS

Getting tough on crime has become an increasingly popular campaign platform among elected officials, and support of supermax institutions is a politically popular position in many areas across the country. The American judiciary has also supported the need for supermax prison environments. In *Bruscino v. Carlson*, federal prisoners at Marion, Illinois, sought compensation for the attacks on them by correctional officers during the October 1983 shakedown and relief from the ongoing conditions created by the subsequent lockdown. A 1985 U.S. Magistrate's Report approved by the U.S. District Court for Southern Illinois in 1987 indicated that 50 prisoners who testified to beatings and other brutalities were not credible witnesses, and that only the single prisoner who testified that there were no beatings was believable.[7] When the prisoners appealed the decision, the ruling of the Fifth Circuit Court of Appeals described conditions at Marion as "ghastly," "sordid and horrible," and "depressing in extreme," but the court maintained that they were necessary for security reasons and did not violate prisoners' constitutional rights.[8]

THE "NEW" CONTROVERSIAL CONTROL MODELS

Today, control units go by many different names. They have been referred to as adjustment centers, security housing units, maximum control complexes, administrative maximum (Ad-Max), special housing units, violence control units, special management units, intensive management units, management control units, or "supermax" prisons. These new units are designed to subdue any and all resistance to order. A survey by the Federal Bureau of Prisons conducted in 1990 found that 36 states operated some form of supermax security prison or unit within a prison.[9] At that time, another six states were planning to build supermax prisons. By 1993, 25 states had specialized control units and control unit prisons were in operation in every part of the country.

The new model for high-security prisons is the security housing unit (SHU) at Pelican Bay Prison in California. Pelican Bay opened in December 1989.[10] Prisoners in such units are kept in solitary confinement in relatively small cells between 22 and 23 hours a day. There is no congregate dining or congregate exercise, and there are no work opportunities or congregate religious services. Prisoners are denied standard vocational, educational, and recreational activities.

The conditions are officially justified not as punishment for prisoners, but as an administrative measure. Prisoners are placed in control units as a result of an administrative decision. Because such moves are a result of an administrative decision, prisoners' ability to challenge such changes in imprisonment is severely limited. Today, throughout the country, conditions in "new" supermax prisons closely resemble those set forth at Pelican Bay.

Since their inception, supermax prison units have had their opponents. Typically, opponents have focused upon conditions that allegedly are illegal or inhumane. In some reports, prison guards have testified to shackling prisoners to their beds and spraying them with high-pressure fire hoses. Other criticisms have centered on issues surrounding

- arbitrary placement/assignment to control unit
- the long-term psychological effects from years of isolation from both prison and outside communities while being housed in solitary or small group isolation (celled 22.5 hours/day)
- denial of access to educational, religious, or work programs
- physical torture, such as forced cell extractions, four-point restraint and hog- tying, caging, beating after restraint, back-room beatings, and staged fights for officer entertainment
- denial of access to medical and psychiatric care
- mental torture, such as sensory deprivation, forced idleness, verbal harassment, mail tampering, disclosing confidential information, confessions forced under torture, and threats against family and visitors[11]

ARBITRARY PLACEMENT

Prisoners are placed in high-security units for administrative and/or disciplinary reasons.

Such decisions are based on results during (re-) classification hearings. Critics have called the hearings a kangaroo court claiming prisoners are being denied due process. What is called misbehavior is (arbitrarily) decided by the guard on duty and has been known to include refusing to make beds or complaining about clogged and overflowing toilets.[11]

VIOLATIONS OF HUMAN RIGHTS AND ABUSES

There are many claims of human rights violations and abuses in control units, including denial of medical care to injured and/or sick prisoners (including diabetics and epileptics), extremely cold cells during winter months and extremely hot cells during summer months, arbitrary beatings, psychological abuse of mentally unstable prisoners, illegal censorship of mail, extended isolation and indoor confinement, denial of access to educational programs, and administrative rather than judicial decisions about punishment for misbehaved prisoners.[12, 13]

ABILITY TO REDUCE VIOLENCE IN PRISONS AND SOCIETY

Prison officials claim that Marion, Pelican Bay, and the other supermax-type control units reduce violence in the rest of the prison system. All the evidence points to the opposite being true. The creation of control units and increased use of administrative segregation have not reduced the level of violence within general prison populations. In fact, assaults on prison staff nationwide rose from 175 in 1991 to 906 [in] 1993.[14] The number of inmate assaults on prison employees reached 14,000 in 1995. That was up 32 percent from 1990. The number of assaults per 1,000 employees remained stable at 15. It may also be that the potential of supermax prisons to reduce overall prison violence has yet to be realized. As more disruptive inmates are placed in supermax prison cells, assaults in prisons may decline.

While supermax prisons provide correctional executives with another weapon to facilitate order in prison, most supermax prisoners are released back into the general prison population or into society. Conditions in control units produce feelings of resentment and rage and exacerbate mental deterioration.[15] It is anticipated that control unit prisoners who re-enter the general prison population or society will have even greater difficulty coping with social situations than in the past.

THE TEXAS EXPERIENCE

Overcrowding and the control of violence are critical issues in correctional management, especially in states like Texas where the federal government, in *Ruiz v. Texas,* declared the entire department of corrections unconstitutional. As a result of the *Ruiz* decision, the federal government actively monitored virtually every facet of the Texas Department of Corrections-Institutional Division for over 20 years. In attempts to shed federal control over Texas prisons, relieve massive prison overcrowding, and avoid future lawsuits, an unprecedented number of new prisons were built in a relatively short period of time. In August 1993, the Texas Department of Criminal Justice, one of the largest correctional systems in the world, operated 54 inmate facilities.[16] By August 1998, the number of correctional facilities in Texas doubled, housing prisoners in 107 correctional facilities.[17]

According to David Stanley, of the Executive Services, Texas Department of Criminal Justice-Institutional Division, Texas prisons will soon be at maximum capacity again. In August 1997, Texas's men's prisons were at 98 percent of their capacity, while women's prisons approached 85 percent of their design capacity. Currently, there are about 126,000 men and 10,000 women incarcerated in Texas prisons. Estimates are that maximum design capacity for housing male inmates will be reached in little more than a year. If current inmate population trends continue, many institutions across the country will be operating above design capacity. These factors, combined with the fact that more violent offenders are now entering prisons at an earlier age for longer periods of time than just a decade ago, affect correctional administrators' ability to maintain order and protect their own staff from assaults.[14]

In attempts to keep the lid on a more volatile prison population, Texas has been one of the first states to make a commitment to new prison construction and new state-of-the-art high-security, supermax correctional facilities. This commitment has required an investment of substantial tax revenues. The new high-security prisons, according to a spokesman for the Texas Department of Criminal Justice-Institutional Division, Larry Fitzgerald, are being built and designed with efficiency and economy in mind. The estimated cost of the some 1,300 beds (double-celled) in the new control units will be a mere $19,000 compared to the current national average of $79,770 per maximum-security bed. Costs are being reduced by using inmate labor for nonsecurity tasks, such as masonry, painting, and welding.

Currently, one high-security unit has been completed near Huntsville, Texas and construction on two other similar units has already begun. Officials estimated that inmate labor saved Texas taxpayers over 2 million dollars in the construction of the new control unit near Huntsville, Texas. Currently, high-security inmates are housed in single-cells.[18]

On August 4, 1997, inmates began arriving at the new $25 million high-security unit of the Texas prison system. The high-security unit is located on the grounds of the Estelle Unit near Huntsville. Similar to high-security units in other states, Texas inmates who are placed in the new high-security unit are put there for one of three reasons: (1) they have tried to escape; (2) they pose a physical threat to staff or inmates; or (3) they are members of disruptive groups, such as an organized gang. Approximately 50 percent to 60 percent of the current residents have been officially classified as belonging to a particular gang.

The Gilbane Corporation, with the help of inmates, began construction on the 65,780 square foot facility in October 1995. Outside, two motion detector fences surround the prison. The exterior of the new unit, although secured by electronic surveillance of the outer fence and certain portions of the building and a patrol vehicle, ironically gives less of the appearance of a traditional fortress prison in that there is no guard tower. Some have likened its appearance to that of a modern high school gym.

Despite its relative benign external appearance, its overall design seeks to provide an alternative for the most recalcitrant inmates. Although two beds per cell are still found in accordance with the original plan, a change from the original purpose of the facility now calls for one inmate per cell. While it would be possible to house 1,300 inmates, the current plan is to house only 650 inmates.

The building has a central corridor with two-story wings on the east and west sides. The east wings contain 63 cells with two beds per cell. The east side recreation yard is 22,451 square feet with 42 individual yards. The west wings have 67 cells with two beds per cell. The west side recreation yard is 24,857 square feet and contains 40 individual yards.

The concern for security prompted the design to establish 8 x 10-foot cells. Unlike the traditional cell with barred doors, all doors on this unit consist of a solid sheet of steel. A slot in the door allows officers to pass items to inmates. An inmate can contact an officer by using an intercom system in his cell. The unit's supporters champion these new doors, convinced that officers will no longer need to fear being assaulted by inmates or their waste products as they walk the unit.[19]

The computerized high-tech design is used to monitor staff as well as inmates. All of the projected 246 employees are required to go through extensive security checks upon entering the building. They are required to place their right hands into a palm print recognition station and then enter their four-digit code. Their name and time of entrance into the unit are recorded and stored digitally.

Once access is authorized, a steel door is opened and shut electronically. The computer keeps a log of all times the door was opened and closed. This feature serves as a source of information for administrators to monitor employee traffic and as an additional source of information when prisoners file allegations of abuse or neglect. All incoming on-duty officers then proceed to a central room near the facility's entrance where monitors with split screens transmit views from the many cameras providing surveillance everywhere both inside and outside the unit.

The central control room, which contains several split-screen monitors, is the hub for internal surveillance. Smaller versions of these computerized nerve centers are found in all prison wings and in the hallways. The setup makes it possible for one officer to monitor each wing.

OPERATIONAL CONDITIONS IN THE TEXAS HIGH-SECURITY UNIT

Most of the conditions found in other control units are also found in the new unit in Texas as well. As in other such units the main objective is to minimize/eliminate an inmates' contact with staff and other prisoners. Such isolation is routine and can be up to 24 hours a day. The inmates in the new Texas control unit will spend most of their time alone in cells. Virtually all their activities both day and night take place in their cells. They eat, shower, and use the restroom in their own cells. The ability to shower the entire unit within a few hours is a major cost- and time-savings procedure, especially compared to showering individual ad-seg inmates under double and sometimes triple custody.

Each cell contains a steel toilet, sink, and showerhead. These are all bolted into the wall. Inmates have the opportunity to shower daily; at other times showers are turned off. Water for the sink and toilet is made available at all times. However, like other "amenities," they can be shut off by the central control system should the cell occupant try to flood his cell block. Inmates receive daily meals in their cells. The food is prepared within the unit by inmates from another institution and is delivered to the inmates by officers.

The high-security unit has no day rooms or television sets other than computer monitors. It does have a visitation room, however, where inmates and their visitors are separated by a thick, impact-resistant glass wall. A steel stool bolted to the floor and a two-way telephone are the only items in the room. No physical contact is possible between inmates and visitors. Likewise, inmates approved for legally prescribed visits may visit other inmates under similar conditions. Such visits are generally conducted in holding cells. Here a wall with a small window, criss-crossed by bars for communication, separates the two inmates who are seated on either side of the wall on a single steel stool bolted to the floor.

Inmates, depending on their level of classification, receive from one hour, three days a week to one hour, seven days a week outdoor recreation time. Often-times the only real reprieve from their nearly total isolation takes place at these times. During this time, inmates arc moved to individual "cages" where they are separated physically from other inmates by (only) fences. There they are able to see and talk to other inmates. The 18′ x 20′ enclosed recreation yards include a basketball court, a chin-up bar, and a hard wall on which inmates can play handball. Each "cage" is secured by a floor-to-ceiling 35-foot-high mesh steel fence. If other inmates are nearby, they can converse.

While out-of-cell programming is available to supermax inmates in 13 states, in Texas, the intense physical limitations are compounded by the absence of educational, training, or recreational programs. Thus far, supermax imprisonment in Texas has not attempted to include formal rehabilitation programs as part of its daily routine.[20]

CONSEQUENCES OF TOTAL CONTROL

As a result, control unit inmates live in a psychologically assaultive environment that destabilizes personal and social identities. While the same can be said of the prison system as a whole, in control units mind control is a primary weapon, implemented through architectural design and a day-to-day regimen that produces isolation, inwardness, and self-containment. Within this severely limited space, inmates are under constant scrutiny and observation. In the unit, cameras and listening devices ensure constant surveillance and control of not only the inmate but also every movement of the staff.

The rural location of control units increases (or supplements) isolation and makes contact with family and community difficult for many. The difficulty for inmates in maintaining contacts with the outside world is exacerbated by the unit's isolation from major urban centers. This alienation heightens inmate frustration, deprivation, and despair. Over long periods of time, the inevitable result is the creation of dysfunctional individuals who are completely self-involved, socially neutered, unable to participate in organized social activities, and unprepared for eventual reintegration into either the general prison population, or life on the outside. Those inmates who resist less, demand less, and see each other as fierce competitors for the few privileges allowed will fare best in the system. Programs that normally exist in other prisons to rehabilitate are deemed frivolous here.

DISCUSSION

The present system of mass incarceration accompanied by the specter of more and more control units can only be maintained with at least the tacit approval of society as [a] whole. In times of relative economic prosperity, America has had the luxury of focusing its resources on crime reduction. As the new millennium approaches, crime and its control has become a major industry. Despite the lack of valid scientific evidence that massive imprisonment reduces crime, billions of dollars have been spent to build new prisons and satisfy the American public's growing desire for vengeance. While there is some scientific evidence that there is a (weak) negative *correlation* between imprisonment and crime rates, the vast majority of studies indicate that imprisonment is *not causally related* to the variability in crime.[21–24] Critics of current imprisonment trends have argued that imprisoning large numbers of people in order to stop crime has been a spectacular and massively expensive failure.[25] Even prison officials sometimes admit to the reality of the situation.[26]

Supermax prisons, perhaps our most costly prison experiment ever, have been promoted as the new panacea for correctional management problems, a form of deterrence that is guaranteed to work. On the other hand, supermax prisons are symbolic of the desperation Americans face in trying to take out crime using traditional formal control methods. The efficacy of such approaches is generally limited by their reactive nature. As the cost of incarceration continues to increase, public officials may be forced to consider a more balanced approach incorporating a more holistic view of crime control; one which focuses more on community and restoration and less on imprisonment. The challenge of the future lies in the creation of a society and a criminal justice system that is able to thwart violence with less violent means.

What we need, in all seriousness, is a better class of inmates. Such change will take time and substantial resources. As we approach the next century, we have the luxury of a relatively strong economy. While many planners have their eye on the future of the global market, failure to learn from our mistakes of the past and strategically invest in proactive crime control strategies in local communities, will eventually limit our ability to compete with other countries and life in America will become, in the words of Hobbes, even more "short, brutish, and nasty."

STUDY QUESTIONS

1. What are some of the ways in which the supermax prison provides political appeal?
2. What were cited as some of the primary advantages that may have been brought about by the development of the supermax prison?
3. What are some of the primary inmate disadvantages created by being housed in a supermax prison?
4. Does the proliferation of supermax prisons have the potential for reducing violent behavior in general population prisons? In greater society?
5. What were identified as some of the primary consequences of "total control" as exemplified by the development of the supermax prison?

NOTES

1. National Institute of Corrections. (1997). *Supermax Housing: A Survey of Current Practice.* Washington, DC: Government Printing Office.
2. Flanagan, T. J., and Longmire, D., eds. (1996). *Americans View Crime and Justice.* Newbury Park, CA: Sage.
3. Maguire, K., and Pastore, A. L., eds. (1995). *Bureau of Justice Statistics Sourcebook of Criminal Justice Statistics.* Albany, NY: The Hindelang Criminal Justice Research Center.
4. U.S. Department of Justice. (1997). "Correctional Populations in the United States." *Bureau of Justice Statistics Bulletin.* Office of Justice Programs, June.
5. Johnson, W. W., Bennett, K., and Flanagan, T. J. (1997). "Getting Tough on Prisoners: A National Survey of Prison Administrators." *Crime and Delinquency,* 43(1):24–41.
6. Clear, T. (1994). *Harm in American Penology: Offenders, Victims, and Their Communities.* Albany: State University of New York Press.
7. "Bruscino v. Carlson." (1985). *In Marion Penitentiary—1985.* Oversight Hearing before the Subcommittee on Courts, Civil Liberties, and the Administration of Justice, August 15. Washington, DC: U.S. Government Printing Office.
8. Landis, T. (1988). "Marion Warden Praises Decision." *Southern Illinoisan,* July 28.
9. Lassiter, C. (1990). "Roboprison." *Mother Jones,* September/October.
10. Wilson, N. K. (1991). "Hard-Core Prisoners Controlled in Nations High-Tech Prisons." *Chicago Daily Law Bulletin,* April 25.
11. Prison Activist Resource Center. (1998). "National Campaign to Stop Control Unit Prisons." *Justice Net Prison Issues Desk,* http://www.igc.apc.org/justice/issues/control-unit/ntscup.html [*sic*].
12. Human Rights Watch. *Cold Storage: Super-Maximum Security Confinement in Indiana.* New York: HRW, 1997.
13. *Madrid v. Gomez,* 889 F. Supp. 1146 N.D. Calif. (1995).
14. Prendergast, A. (1995). "End of the Line: In the New Alcatraz, Prisoners Do the Hardest Time of All." *Westword,* 18(46) July:12.
15. Korn, R. (1988). "The Effects of Confinement in the High Security Unit at Lexington." *Social Justice,* 15(1):13–19.
16. Teske, R. H., ed. (1995). "Corrections." *Crime and Justice in Texas.* Huntsville, TX: Sam Houston Press.
17. Stanley, D. (1998). Executive Services, Texas Department of Criminal Justice Institutional Division. Telephone Interview. Huntsville, Texas.
18. *Huntsville Item,* 26 June 1997, p. 1, 6A.
19. *Huntsville Item,* 3 August 1997, p. 1, 10A.
20. Johnson, W. W., Henningsen, R. J., and Wells, T. (1998). *National Corrections Executives Survey (1998).* Unpublished Survey Research. Huntsville, Texas: College of Criminal Justice, Sam Houston State University.
21. Blumstein, A., Cohen, J., and Daniel, N., eds. (1978). *Deterrence and Incapacitation: Estimating the Effects of Criminal Sanctions on Crime Rates.* Washington, DC: National Academy of Sciences.
22. Visher, C. A. (1986). "Incapacitation and Crime Control: Does a 'Lock 'Em Up' Strategy Reduce Crime?" *Justice Quarterly,* 4(4):513–514.
23. Krajick, K., and Gettinger, S. (1982). *Overcrowded Time.* New York: The Edna McConnell Clark Foundation.
24. Zimring, F. E., and Gordon, H. (1996). "Lethal Violence and the Overreach of American Imprisonment." Presentation at the 1996 Annual Research and Evaluation Conference, Washington, DC.
25. Irwin, J., and Austin, J. (1994). *It's About Time: America's Imprisonment Binge.* Belmont, CA: Wadsworth.
26. Ticer, S. (1989). "The Search for Ways to Break Out of the Prison Crisis." *Business Week,* May 8.

9
RELATIONSHIPS BETWEEN INMATES AND GUARDS

VICTOR HASSINE

Editor's Note from Life Without Parole

Prisoners and their keepers have little in common. Yet as Victor Hassine notes, routine personal relationships between prisoners and guards are an important component of the larger social system within prisons. These institutions run primarily on social control, which in turn requires relationships. When prisons are overcrowded and understaffed, social control is compromised, because the relationships that hold a prison together are compromised. Officers turn to snitches to maintain order, setting in motion a process that corrupts daily life in the prison and promotes widespread violence.

—R. J.

The complexity of running a prison is revealed in this brief piece by Victor Hassine. Two distinct worlds are clearly revealed—one composed of inmates and a substantially less populated one composed of guards. Both of these populations have common goals, but by definition must go about achieving them in different ways. The role that the prison "snitch" has within the institution is highlighted as well. Many correctional professionals, including high-placed administrators, may consider snitches to be a sort of necessary evil that ultimately contributes to the peace within an institution. The relationship between a correctional officer and inmate snitch is by definition an informal arrangement that may indeed be necessary to promote informal social control. On the other hand, the existence of snitches also may force correctional officers—particularly young or inexperienced officers—to manage a vast and growing gray area, creating a gulf between the ordinarily "black-and-white" rules of a large institution. The reader is encouraged to keep in mind the ultimate goals of correctional institutions when considering the complexities that are discussed in this revealing piece.

When I first entered prison, 1 was surprised to discover that there was no open hostility between guards and inmates. As a matter of fact, many inmates and guards went out of their way to establish good relationships with each other. Inmates befriended guards in the hope that they would get such benefits as an extra phone call, special shower time, or the overlooking of some minor infraction. In turn, guards befriended inmates because they wanted to get information or just to keep the peace and make it through another day without getting hurt.

From what I have observed, most guards who have been attacked were attempting to enforce some petty rule. Over time, guards have learned that it doesn't always pay to be too rigid about prison regulations. Thus, an unwritten agreement has been established between inmates and guards: inmates get what they want by being friendly and nonaggressive, while guards ensure their own safety by not strictly enforcing the rules. For the most part, inmates manipulate the guards' desire for safety, and guards exploit the inmates' need for autonomy.

By the mid-1980s, things changed with overcrowding and the influx of new prison subcultures. Administrators could not hire new guards fast enough to keep pace with the flood of inmates, so the practice of overtime was employed. Any guard who was willing to work overtime could get it, with the result that on any given day a large percentage of guards were on overtime. This phenomenon had the immediate impact of introducing many exhausted, irritable guards into the work force, often on shifts with which they were not familiar.

These two factors virtually destroyed all sense of continuity and uniform treatment that the prison had established over the years. The most important element needed to maintain a workable relationship between inmates and staff is a continuity of treatment. Disturb the inmates' expectation of that continuity, and you destroy the delicate balance between them and the staff.

A tired, overworked guard on an unfamiliar shift tends to be unwilling to offer any assistance. Being a stranger to the unique inmate hierarchy of his newly assigned unit, he is unable to conform to longstanding customs and practices. This often spells disaster, as once workable relations between keeper and kept deteriorate into anger, distrust, and hatred. It has been my experience that this breakdown in relations inevitably provokes an upsurge of violence, disorder, and rioting.

There is an even more insidious consequence of excessive overtime that undermines inmate and guard relationships. In every prison there is a percentage of guards who are so rigid and unpopular with inmates, or so incompetent, that they are given work assignments that keep them away from contact with prisoners, such as tower duty or the late-night shift. Any prison administrator of intelligence knows that these kinds of guards can jeopardize the tenuous order and operation of a prison. With the advent of unlimited overtime, however, these guards have found their way into the prison mainstream. As expected, their presence has further exacerbated an already tense and uncertain environment.

The overexposure of tired, irritable, overworked, and sometimes inexperienced and antagonistic guards to the population has created an inconsistent and unpredictable prison environment, especially because guards know much less about what inmates are thinking, and vice versa. With all the new inmates coming in and out of prisons every year, it is becoming increasingly difficult for the staff to keep track of who is who and who is doing what, and even harder for a prison security force trying to employ traditional investigative and intelligence methods. In the old days, everyone knew each other in a prison and knew pretty well what everyone else was up to. Not so today.

The only way the security system can effectively operate in a prison today is by soliciting the services of snitches. Guards maintain a legion of snitches and openly advertise that fact to the inmate population. In order to keep their informants in force, prison administrators have gone overboard to reward and protect them. Their rationale is that every informant constitutes an unpaid member of the security force that helps to compensate for understaffing. This almost exclusive reliance on informants for information and intelligence creates several conditions, including:

1. Keeping the inmate population at odds with each other over who is the informant in their midst.
2. Elevating snitches in the prison hierarchy, since they are often rewarded with the best jobs, highest pay and best living conditions.
3. Increasing the growing antagonism between long-term inmates and parole violators, who are more likely to become informants in order to gain early parole and relative comfort during their brief stay in prison.
4. A proliferation of drugs entering the prison, as informants act as conduits for drug smuggling while looking for information.
5. Providing prison administrators with distorted images of inmate activity, as informants become less credible the more they are used.

This last condition often occurs because an informant is pursuing his own interests and therefore will only inform on those activities that do not affect his particular business. Such self-serving information is only as accurate as the informant needs it to be. Sometimes it is a fabricated reflection of what he knows the administration wants to hear. Thus, many informants provide the kind of information that sacrifices the truth in order to conform to some preexisting view.

To use a classic example of this, I knew an ambitious guard in 1983 who told me he used his overtime to ensure himself a more substantial pension benefit. (In those days, pensions were based on the three highest annual salaries rather than on base salary.) So he worked double shifts seven days a week for three years. But as a result, he became useless. He was either too listless and irritable or falling asleep all the time. In order to convince his superiors of his efficiency, he would reward informants who gave him information that he could use to issue misconducts. Consequently, his informants were in turn able to operate a massive drug and homosexual prostitution ring under his protection. Administrators ended up buying a nickel's worth of information for $1,000's worth of corruption.

Another example involved a prison murder. One day in the yard, two inmates fought over drugs until one of them was stabbed to death in plain view of dozens of witnesses. Subsequently, the prison security officer received numerous notes from inmates wishing to give eyewitness accounts. This enabled the authorities to quickly identify the culprit. But the informants all gave self-serving details of the crime and its motives, until there were so many contradicting versions of what happened that all their testimony was rendered worthless. Without enough evidence, the state was forced to offer the murderer five to ten years in return for a guilty plea. Such a sentence for a murder committed in a public prison yard is so lenient that it could be considered a license to kill. This failure of justice on the part of the prison administration was precipitated by its exclusive reliance on unreliable informants.

The end result is that today's prisons have become even more violent. Inmates do not trust each other, because informants call the shots and even initiate or encourage most of the crimes they report. Guards are overworked and increasingly alienated from the mainstream of prison life. And finally, a new breed of criminals—young, violent, ignorant, drug-addicted, and completely self-absorbed—is pouring in and leaving even the most veteran inmates and staff scared to death.

STUDY QUESTIONS

1. What effect do overworked guards have on the overall prison environment?
2. For what reason(s) may overworked guards exist, according to the author?
3. Consider whether you feel that snitches are a necessary evil within the prison environment. List the reasons you support or disapprove of the use of snitches.

4. In light of what correctional officers are trying to accomplish via the use of informants, can you think of any alternative solutions to meet those goals?
5. What was meant by the author's assertion that "the most important element needed to maintain a workable relationship between inmates and staff is a continuity of treatment"? What sorts of threats to that continuity are introduced by the existence of guards striving for more overtime and/or the use of snitches?

PART

WORKING IN PRISON

Working as a correctional officer inside a secure facility can be a stressful, boring, and even dangerous endeavor. Despite many state correctional systems not requiring more than a high school diploma as a credential for entry-level correctional officer positions, long-term success at the job often requires good communication skills, savvy, and a highly functional relational style. Reactions to stress and even burnout are not uncommon with correctional officers.

Correctional officers often have to interact with three different subcultures—the inmate subculture, the officer subculture, and the institution's administration subculture. Further, it is not uncommon for the news to highlight stories of inappropriate relationships developing between inmates and correctional officers, not to mention the occasional story about institutional corruption that can leave the public wondering how effectively its tax dollars are being spent. When considering the difficulty of the job, the pay level (which is often quite low), and the potential threat of violence, it should come as no surprise that many have studied correctional officers and the factors that shape their profession.

Part III contains three articles that highlight different themes within correctional officers' work. Much like Victor Hassine's "inmates' view" piece from Part II, the first reading in Part III shares detailed information about what the first year on the job was like for one new prison guard at the infamous Sing Sing prison in New York. This ethnographic piece shares information about the three groups mentioned here with whom a new correctional officer has to work—inmates, guards, and administrators—and highlights coping strategies and negative consequences. In addition, an often overlooked phenomenon in institutional correctional research—inmates targeting correctional officers—is analyzed in a qualitative study by Worley, Marquart, and Mullings. Also contained in Part III is a comprehensive literature review that presents a cross-national investigation of correctional officer stress and burnout. The reader will learn about many different types and sources of officer stress and will discover how correctional officers in the United States fare when compared to correctional workers in other countries. Through these three pieces, the student of corrections will gain much insight into what it means to work within a secure environment and will discover some of the more critical forces and dynamics with which professionals within prison walls have to contend.

10
A-BLOCK

TED CONOVER

Ted Conover presents the reader with a window into the life of a brand-new correctional officer in one of the most notorious prisons in the United States—Sing Sing. At the outset, the many risks of holding the position of correctional officer may not appear surprising. How some of these risks originate, however, may indeed be startling. The author presents an additional account that details the complexity of the relationships that exist within the prison environment. This time, though, the nuances of the relationships between "old guards" and "new guards" are highlighted, as are the relationships between guards and inmates. Despite the adversarial and subordinate nature of "the keeper and the kept," there may indeed be many avenues whereby the inmates have the upper hand within an institution. Literature regarding institutional corrections often centers on the inmate subculture that exists and investigates the sources of that subculture (e.g., importation versus deprivation as the primary pressures shaping subculture). Conover's piece reminds the reader that there may also be a very active and complex guard subculture that has advantages and disadvantages for pursuing what may be the ultimate goal of institutional corrections—peace within the walls.

Many times during those first months I was assigned to A-block. The mammoth cellblock required more officers to run it than any other building—around thirty-five during the day shift—but the senior officers there seemed particularly unfriendly to new officers, offering little encouragement and lots of criticism. The best way to fend off their comments, I decided, would be to try and enforce the rules as strictly as I could.

But, assigned to one of the vast eighty-eight-cell galleries for the first time, I found it hard to know where to begin. With the sheets hanging from the bars like curtains? The clothes drying on the handrails? The music blaring from several cells? I decided to start with the annoyance closest at hand: an inmate's illegal radio antenna.

Inmates were allowed to have music. Each cell had two jacks in the wall for the headphones its occupant was issued upon arrival. Through one jack was transmitted a Spanish-language radio station; through the other, a rhythm-and-blues station, except during sporting events, when the games were transmitted instead. Inmates could have their own radios, too, but the big steel cellblock made reception very difficult. Telescoping antennas were forbidden, because they might be turned into "zip guns." By inserting a bullet into the base of an extended antenna and then quickly compressing it, an inmate could fire the inaccurate but still potentially deadly gun. The approved wire dipole antennas were supposed to be placed within a two-by-four-foot area on the wall—where, apparently, they did no good at all.

To improve their chances of tuning in to a good station, inmates draped wires over their bars and across the gallery floor. Some even tied objects to the end of a bare strand of copper wire and flung it toward the outside wall, hoping that it would snag on a window and that they would win the reception jackpot. (When you looked up from the flats on a sunny day, you could sometimes see ten or twenty thin wires spanning the space between the gallery and the exterior wall, like the glimmering work of giant spiders.)

Antennas strewn across the gallery floor could cause someone to trip, and if they seemed likely to do so, I'd have the inmates pull them in. But the inmate in question on my first day as a regular officer in A-block— a short, white-haired man in his sixties—had gotten his off the floor by threading wire through a cardboard tube, the kind you find inside wrapping paper. One end of the tube was wedged between his bars at stomach level, and the other protruded halfway into the narrow gallery space between cell bars and fence, like a miniature bazooka.

"You're gonna have to take this down," I advised him the first time I brushed against it.

"Why's that?"

"Because it's in my space."

"But I can't hear if it's in my cell."

"Sorry. Try stringing it up higher on your bars."

"Sorry? You ain't sorry. Why say you sorry if you ain't sorry? And where'd you get to be an authority on antennas? They teach you that in the Academy?"

"Look, you know the rule. No antenna at all outside the cell. I could just take it if I wanted. I'm not taking it. I'm just telling you to bring it in."

"You didn't tell that guy down there to bring his in, did you? The white guy?"

I looked in the direction he indicated. There were no other antennas in tubes, and I said so.

"You're just picking on the black man, aren't you? Well, have a good time at your Klan meeting tonight," he spat out. "Have a pleasant afternoon. You've ruined mine."

All this over an antenna. Or, rather, all brought into focus by an antenna. In prison, unlike in the outside world, power and authority were at stake in nearly every transaction.

The high stakes behind petty conflict became clear for me on the night during my first month when Colton and I were assigned to work M-Rec, one of the kinds of recreation that Sing Sing relied upon heavily in order to give the prisoners something to do. After dinner, instead of the gym or the yard, inmates could gather at the gray-metal picnic-style tables bolted to the floor along M-gallery, on the flats, to play cards or chess or dominoes, or watch the television sets mounted high on the walls.

"The rule is that they can't be leaning against the bars of the cells," the regular officer said to us, "and the cell gates are supposed to be closed." You could tell from his "supposed" that this rule was not strictly enforced. Still, Colton, a lieutenant's son, seemed strangely zealous. I think he couldn't stand the laxity around us. As we walked along the dimly lit gallery, he challenged one inmate after another. I decided that to keep his respect, I had better do the same. At varying volumes, they objected. "What is this, newjack rec?" asked one older man in a kufi who was sitting right outside his own open cell. I gestured toward the door. He told me that he was *always* allowed to leave the cell door open during M-Rec. Well, not tonight, I said. He yelled and screamed. I closed the gate. He walked right up to me, stood less than a foot from my face, and, radiating fury, said, "You're going to learn, CO, that some things they taught you in the Academy can get you killed."

I would hear inmates utter these exact words several times more in the incoming months at Sing Sing, a threat disguised as advice. (The phrasing had the advantage of ambiguity, and thus could steer the speaker clear of rule 102.10: "Inmates shall not, under any circumstances, make any threat.") But I hadn't heard those words spoken to me before, and that, in combination with the man's standing so close, set my heart racing. I tried staring back at him as hard as he was staring at me, and didn't move until he had stepped back first.

Some of the conflict we saw, of course, wasn't only a fixed feature of prison life; it had roots in Sing Sing's frequent changes of officers. New officers, as we'd already learned, irritated inmates in much the same way that substitute teachers irritate school children. To try to lessen these effects, the chart office would often "pencil in" a resource officer to the post of a senior officer who was sick or on vacation. That way, there wouldn't be a different substitute every day.

One day in A-block, however, I was assigned to run the gallery temporarily assigned to one of my classmates, Michaels, whom I knew to be particularly lax. It was Michaels's day off, which made me the substitute for a substitute. I knew before I even arrived that things would be chaotic.

My first problem came at count time, 11 A.M. Inmates generally began to return to their cells from programs and rec at around 10:40 or 10:45 A.M. The officers would encourage them to move promptly to their cells. By 11, anyone not in his cell and ready to be counted was technically guilty of delaying the count and could be issued a misbehavior report. Few galleries, therefore, had inmates at large after 11 A.M.

But on this day, Michaels's gallery had a dozen still out. Michaels had grown up in Brooklyn and, more than most officers from the city, considered the inmates to be basically decent guys, his "homies." He wanted them to like him. Once penciled in to this post, he had quickly learned all their names. I had helped him at count time once before, and when I complained about two inmates who were slow to lock in, Michaels replied that they were good guys. Though I had seen sergeants chew him out for looseness, he had told me privately that the sergeants could "suck my dick in Macy's window" for all he cared.

I liked Michaels for acknowledging the inmates' humanity. He had told me how much he hated A-block's usual OIC, a big, pugnacious slob I'll call Rufino, who told jokes such as "How do you know when an inmate is lying? When you see him open his mouth." But I didn't appreciate Michaels's legacy of chaos that morning.

A group of three or four senior officers strolled by, to my relief—I was sure they'd been sent to help me usher in the stragglers. But they had no such plan. A couple of them glanced disapprovingly at their watches and then at me. They didn't have to help, so they weren't going to. Thanks, guys, I muttered to myself.

About an hour later, a couple of keeplocks returned from disciplinary hearings. The block's keeplock officer, instead of borrowing my keys and ushering the inmates to their cells, called, "They're back," when he came through the gate and then disappeared. One of the keeplocks returned to his cell without trouble, but the second had other plans. It was Tuesday, he told me, and Michaels always let him take a shower on Tuesdays.

"Keeplock showers are Mondays, Wednesdays, and Fridays," I said. "And Michaels isn't here today."

"C'mon, CO, don't play tough. I'll be out in a second."

"No," I said. He acted as though he hadn't heard, grabbed a towel from his cell, and strode quickly down the gallery to the shower stall. I wasn't overly concerned: I always kept the showers locked, just in case something like this came up, and felt confident that once I reminded him he would miss keeplock rec today if he didn't go back, he'd turn around. Then I remembered. On this gallery, the lock mechanism was missing from the shower cell door. The shower was always open. Sing Sing. The inmate was a good foot taller than me and well muscled. I yelled through the bars into the shower that he'd lost his rec. He said, "Fuck rec." I put the incident into the logbook, then wrote up a Misbehavior Report and had his copy waiting in the cell when he got back. He shrugged it off.

"I don't give a fuck, CO," he explained. "I got thirty years to life, right? And I got two years' keeplock. Plus today, I got another three months. When they see this lame-ass ticket, they're gonna tell you to shove it up your ass."

The frustration was, he was probably right. Of all the inmates on a gallery, keeplocks were the hardest to deal with. There were no carrots left to tempt them with, and few sticks—especially for the long-termers. And now it was time for keeplock rec. I tried to match faces with cells as they headed out to the yard on that hot June day—it could help me when it came time to lock them back in. I was in the middle of letting them out when the keeplock officer reappeared. He gestured in the direction I was walking.

"Forty-three cell?" he said. "Hawkins? No rec today."

"No rec for forty-three? Why's that?"

"He doesn't get it today," he said, and disappeared.

I knew there could be several reasons for the inmate not receiving rec. He might have committed an infraction within the past twenty-four hours. Or he might have a deprivation order pending against him; in cases of outrageous misbehavior, a keeplock who was a "threat to security" could have his rec taken away for a day by a sergeant. Or—what I worried about in this situation—he might have pissed off the officer but *not* had a deprivation order pending. In that case, another officer was asking me to burn the keeplock's rec as an act of solidarity. I hoped it wasn't the last possibility and went on down the gallery, passing up forty-three cell.

The inmate called out to me shortly after I went by.

"Hey, CO! Aren't you going to open my cell?" I ignored him until I was on my way back. He stood up from his bed as I approached.

"Open my cell, CO! I'm going outside."

"Not today," I said.

"What? Why not today?"

"No rec today."

"Why not?"

"That's what they told me."

"Who told you that?"

I didn't answer him, but I immediately felt I'd done something wrong. I returned to the office and tried to get the keeplock officer on the phone. I was going to insist on knowing his reason. What was up with this guy? The phone rang and rang. I called the office of the OIC and asked for him. He was outside now; couldn't be reached, Rufino said. But Rufino was always unhelpful. I called the yard. He'd had to go somewhere, wasn't there now. Shit, I thought.

Meanwhile, three keeplocks on their way out to the yard stopped separately to advise me that "forty-three cell needs to come out, CO." I looked down the gallery. He was waving his arm madly through the bars, trying to get my attention. I walked down to talk to him.

"You're not letting me out?"

I shook my head.

"Who said so?" He was angry now.

"I don't know his name," I lied.

"Well, what did he look like?" I declined to help out. "Then what's your name? I'm writing up a grievance." I told him my name. When I passed by the cell again an hour later, he had a page-long letter written out.

Instead of the classic newjack mistake of enforcing a rule that nobody really cared about, I had just enforced a rule that wasn't a rule, for my "brother in gray." I knew that many police admired that kind of thing. But it made me feel crummy. And with the grievance coming, I was going to have to answer for it.

I thought about how the senior officers hadn't helped me during the count, how the keeplock officer hadn't helped me when the two inmates came back, and how the same keeplock officer hadn't explained to me the deal with forty-three, even when I asked. More than once at the Academy, I'd heard the abbreviation CYA—cover your ass. I knew how to do it, though I also knew there could be consequences. In the logbook, I made note of the time and wrote, "No rec for K/L Hawkins, per CO X"—the keeplock officer. And then I waited.

The chicken came home to roost about a month later. I knew it when I arrived at work and approached the time clock. Officer X, instead of ignoring me as usual, gave me a cold, hard stare. His partner, Officer Y, stopped me and asked if I was Conover. Yes, I said, and he gave me the same stare and walked away. It was because inmate Hawkins in cell 43 had slugged Officer Y the day before (as I'd since learned) that Officer X had wanted to send him a message that day.

A sergeant who was unaware of all of this approached me with a copy of the inmate's grievance letter in the mess hall at lunch-time that same day. "Do you remember this incident?" he asked. I said yes. "You'll just need to respond with a To/From," he said, using department slang for a memo. "Do you remember why you didn't let him out? Probably forgot, right?"

"Well, no, the keeplock officer told me not to."

The sergeant wrinkled his brow. "Well, probably best just to say you forgot," he said cheerily, and turned away.

"Sarge," I said. "It's in the logbook. I wrote in the logbook that he told me."

"You're kidding," he said. "Why'd you do that?"

I shrugged. "I was new."

"I'll get back to you," he said.

I wrote the memo the sergeant had asked for, told the truth, and felt conflicted. Days went by. Another sergeant called me in and told to me to see a lieutenant in the Administration Building. My memo was on the lieutenant's desk, and he was poring over it. "So you say you logged this part about Officer X, right?" he asked. I nodded, expecting to receive a stern, quiet lecture on how not to fuck my fellow officer. But the lieutenant just nodded, cogitated a bit, and then picked up the phone.

I heard him greet a sergeant in A-block. "So Officer X remembers saying that to Conover now, is that right? And he's going to write a new To/From? And you'll take care of the deprivation order? Okay, fine." And hung up.

He passed my memo to me over the desk. "Just write this up again, but leave out the name of Officer X," he told me.

"And then we're set?"

"All taken care of."

I was relieved. Officer X was off the hook, which meant that maybe he wouldn't hate me more than he already did. Apparently, a deprivation order would be backdated to cover *his* ass. And I had learned an important lesson: If you were going to survive in jail, the goody-goody stuff had to go. Any day in there, I might find myself in a situation where I'd need Officer X to watch my back, to pry a homicidal inmate off of me, at his peril. The logic of the gray wall of silence was instantly clear, as clear as the glare of hate that Officer X had sent my way when he heard what I'd done.

* * *

The single most interesting word, when it came to the bending and ignoring of rules, was *contraband.* To judge by the long list of what constituted contraband, its meaning was clear. In practice, however, contraband was anything but.

The first strange thing about contraband was that its most obvious forms—weapons, drugs, and alcohol—could all be found fairly readily inside prison. Some of the drugs probably slipped in through the Visit Room, but most, it seemed, were helped into prison by officers who were paid off. The Department had a special unit, the Inspector General's Office, which followed up on snitches' tips and tried to catch officers in the act; the union rep had even warned us about the "IG" at the Academy. A couple of times a year, I would come to find, a Sing Sing officer was hauled off in handcuffs by the state police.

But even in its lesser forms, contraband had many interesting subtleties. As officers, we were not allowed to bring through the front gate glass containers, chewing gum, pocket knives with blades longer than two inches, newspapers, magazines, beepers, cell phones, or, obviously, our own pistols or other weapons. A glass container, such as a bottle of juice, might be salvaged from the trash by an inmate and turned into shards for weapons. The chewing gum could be stuffed into a lock hole to jam the mechanism. The beepers, newspapers, and magazines were distractions—we weren't supposed to be occupied with any of that while on the job. Nor could we make or receive phone calls, for the same reason. Apart from inmates smoking in their cells, smoking was generally forbidden indoors.

And yet plenty of officers smoked indoors. Many chewed gum. The trash cans of wall towers were stuffed with newspapers and magazines.

A much longer list of contraband items applied to inmates. As at Coxsackie, they couldn't possess clothing in any of the colors reserved for officers: gray, black, blue, and orange. They couldn't possess cash, cassette players with a record function, toiletries containing alcohol, sneakers worth more than fifty dollars, or more than fourteen newspapers. The list was very long—so long, in fact, that the authors of *Standards of Inmate Behavior* found it easier to define what *was* permitted than what wasn't. Contraband was simply "any article that is not authorized by the Superintendent or [his] designee."

You looked for contraband during pat-frisks of inmates and during random cell searches. One day in A-block, I found my first example: an electric heating element, maybe eight inches wide, such as you'd find on the surface of a kitchen range. Wires were connected to the ends of the coil, and a plug was connected to the wires. The inmate, I knew, could plug it into the outlet in his cell, place a pan on it, and do some home cooking. I supposed it was contraband because of the ease with which it could start a fire, trip the cell's circuit breaker, burn the inmate, or burn someone the inmate didn't like. And it must have been stolen from a stove somewhere inside the prison.

I was proud of my discovery and asked a senior officer on the gallery how to dispose of it and what infraction number to place on the Misbehavior Report.

"Where'd you find this?" he asked.

"Cell K-twelve, in a box behind the locker," I said.

"K-twelve—yeah, he's a cooker," the officer said. "Cooks every night. Can't stand mess-hall food. I don't blame him."

"Yeah? So what's the rule number?"

The other officer said he didn't know, so I made some phone calls, figured it out, and did the paperwork during lunch. While I was at it, an inmate porter stopped by and pleaded on behalf of the cooker. "He's a good guy, CO. He needs it." A few minutes later, to my amazement, a mess-hall officer called.

"You the guy who found that heating element?" he asked.

"Yeah. Why?"

"What are you going to do with it?"

"Turn it in."

"Oh really?"

"Yeah. Why?"

There was a long pause. "Oh, nothing." He hung up.

I finished my Misbehavior Report and stepped out of the office to let inmates back into their cells from chow. When I returned to the office, the coil, which 1 had placed on the desk, was gone.

"Where'd it go?" I asked the senior officer. "Did you move it?"

"What—oh, that heating thing?" he said offhandedly. "I gave it back to him."

"Gave it back? Why'd you do that? I just wrote up a report."

"Look, he's a good guy. Never gives any trouble. I think he's vegetarian. He really can't eat that stuff they serve down there. Why don't you go talk to him?" He made for the door.

I stared at him skeptically. He shrugged and was gone.

Unsure exactly why I did so, I went to talk to the inmate. He did seem like a nice guy, and thanked me profusely for not turning him in. Oh what the hell, I thought.

Not long afterward, I found another heating coil during a cell search in B-block. This time my sergeant, Murphy, saw it in my hands and insisted I turn it in. The paperwork that Murphy told me to fill out was even more elaborate than what I had imagined. Specifically, he said, I'd need to make an entry in the B-block cell-search logbook; to write a contraband receipt for the inmate, with copy stapled to a misbehavior report, to be signed by a supervisor in the Watch Commander's Office, where I would submit all the paperwork and get the key to the contraband locker in the hospital basement, where I would also sign the logbook. Oh, and on the way to the Watch Commander's Office, I should stop and pick up an evidence bag from the disciplinary office, in which to place the burner.

It was the end of my day. I knew that many officers, rather than plow through all this when their shift was over, would just drop the contraband in a trash can by the front gate and be done with it. Sergeant Murphy would never follow up. But some contrarian impulse drove me on. I finally made it to the Watch Commander's Office and waited twenty minutes for my turn with the lieutenant. He looked at the heating element, then at my paperwork.

"Do you think this is a good use of the Adjustment Committee's time?" he asked.

I shrugged and said I supposed it was. My sergeant must have thought so when he told me to write all this up, I added. The lieutenant blathered on about major versus minor offenses, the need to make judgments, and so on, apparently expecting me to say, "Oh, I get it!" and withdraw from his office. But it had been a lot of work. I had stayed late. I was pissed off about this and other things. I didn't move.

"Okay," the lieutenant finally said. "Leave it with me." I stood to leave, wondering how to take this. The lieutenant hadn't signed a thing. A CO at a desk near the lieutenant's translated for me as I walked out. "If in doubt, throw it out!" he said with a big smile. And that was that....

* * *

In July, I was penciled in for two weeks as officer in charge of the A-block gym. This huge room was filled morning, afternoon, and evening with inmates, and my day shift spanned two of those times. It was regarded as a fairly good post in that you generally didn't have to spend a lot of time telling people what to do. The regular officer, presently on vacation, had had it for years. Its main downside was risk. On a cold or rainy day, the gym could fill with upward of four hundred inmates, and there were moments when I would be the only officer there with them.

Depending on the time of day, eight to twelve porters were assigned to the gym. I had to put through their payroll, I was told, and therefore to keep porter attendance. (The twelve to fifteen cents an hour they earned was credited to their commissary accounts.) Because I knew the B-block porters to be a tight and surly bunch, I thought I'd better let the crew know right away who was in charge.

They arrived before rec was called, supposedly to get a jump on the cleaning. There was a lot to do, because an inspection of the block was scheduled for the next day. The gym had a full-size basketball court with a spectator area around it, a weights area the size of a half court, a table-and-benches zone for cards, chess, dominoes, and similar games, and two television areas. There was also a locked equipment room in front of which sat my desk, on an elevated platform, with a microphone on top. Instead of hopping to work, the porters turned on the TVs and sat down. I turned off the one most of them were watching.

"Gentlemen, I'm going to be here for the next two weeks and I want to talk with you about when the cleaning gets done and who does what."

They sat silently.

"For example, who normally cleans today?"

At first, nobody said anything. There were stares of indifference and defiance. A pudgy inmate whose nickname, I would later learn, was Rerun finally spoke. "Don't nobody normally clean today," he said. "Tuesday's the day off."

"The day off. So when do you clean?"

"Mondays, Wednesdays, and Fridays. We know what to do."

I tried wresting more details out of them, but they wouldn't say more. Firing porters, I knew, was a bureaucratic procedure that took weeks; I'd be working elsewhere in the prison before the wheels had even begun to turn. And evidently the regular officer was satisfied with these men. Wishing I'd never started down this path, I finally had to settle for a plea dressed up as an order. "Those ledges up there? They're covered with dust, and the inspectors will be looking. So tomorrow, make sure somebody takes care of that along with all the rest."

"They don't never check those ledges," came the quick reply as I walked to my desk. And the TVs went back on.

The next day, somewhat to my surprise, six or seven of the porters set to work in earnest upon their arrival. For half an hour, they swept and mopped and picked up trash. As promised, they skipped the ledges. The place looked pretty good, and the inspectors never came.

I began to relax, and as I did, I began to understand the complex culture of the gym. There was, naturally, a big basketball scene—a league, in fact, with prison-paid inmate referees and a scoreboard and games that took place about every other day. The games were often exciting to watch—sometimes even a few officers would attend—but also nervous-making, as the crowds that gathered for matches between popular teams were partisan and players would sometimes get into fights.

Weight lifting was also popular, and when I was new at Sing Sing, it was intimidating to be faced with the huge, muscle-bound inmates who took it seriously. But soon I noticed that these purposeful, self-disciplined inmates were almost never the ones who gave us problems, and I came to agree with the opinion, generally held among officers, that the weights and machines were valuable. The only complaint I ever heard from officers was that inmates' weight equipment was much better than what was provided to officers in the small weight room in the Administration Building.

Beyond these activities, the gym held many surprises. On a busy day, it seemed almost like a bazaar. A dozen fans of *Days of Our Lives* gathered religiously every day for the latest installment of their favorite soap. Behind them, regular games of Scrabble, chess, checkers, and bridge were conducted with great seriousness. (One of the bridge players, known as Drywall—a white-bearded man with dreadlocks—came from 5-Building; more than once when he was late, his partners asked me to call the officers over there and make sure he'd left so they could start their game.) At the table next to the games, an older man sold hand-painted greeting cards for all occasions to raise money for the Jaycees, one of Sing Sing's "approved inmate organizations." In a far corner behind the weight area, at the bottom of a small flight of stairs, a regular group of inmates practiced some kind of martial art. Martial arts were forbidden by the rules, but these guys were so pointedly low-key, and the rule seemed to me so ill conceived, that I didn't break it up. In the men's bathroom, inmates smoked—also against the rules but, from what I could tell, tacitly accepted.

A floor-to-ceiling net separated these areas from the basketball court. At court's edge, a transvestite known as Miss Jackson would braid men's hair as they watched the game or press their clothing with one of the electric irons inmates were allowed to use in the gym. She received packs of Newport cigarettes—the commissary's most popular brand—as payment. Miss Jackson seemed a sweet man who was at pains to be noticed: She stretched the collar of her sweatshirt so that it exposed one shoulder, and cut scallop-shaped holes in the body so that it held some aesthetic interest. She often wore Walkman headphones, disconnected, just for the look. She must have been rich in cigarettes, and I wondered how she spent them.

Out on the court one day, just a few yards from Miss Jackson's enterprise, four short-haired, long-sleeved, bow-tied members of the Nation of Islam stood in a close circle, sternly chastising another member of the group, who must have somehow strayed. One of them was also a gym porter, among those most courteous to me. The juxtaposition of such opposites—the ideologues of the Nation and the would-be sexpot— reminded me of street life in New York City.

I walked the floor every fifteen or twenty minutes, making sure no one was smoking too openly, telling those inmates who had put on do-rags to take them off (it violated the rule against wearing hats inside), and making announcements when there was room at the bank of inmate phones that were lined up on the flats near the front gate. (Inmates who had signed up on a list could be excused from the gym to make a call.) It wasn't a bad job overall, and I suppose I should have been sad to see it go. But, as usual, I was simply relieved that nothing awful had happened under my watch....

STUDY QUESTIONS

1. What similarities might there be between the author's experiences as a brand-new correctional officer and those of a brand-new inmate?
2. In what ways might inmates in some prisons have the upper hand regarding prison management?
3. Most organizations depend on (and even demand) very clear, precise, and detailed communication at all levels. In this piece by Conover, the prison guards seemed to benefit from a *lack* of this type of communication. For what reasons might this dynamic exist within the prison guard culture?
4. Why did the author state that the resolution of very small conflicts is as important as or even more important than resolving the bigger issues within a prison environment?

11
PRISON GUARD PREDATORS

AN ANALYSIS OF INMATES WHO ESTABLISHED INAPPROPRIATE RELATIONSHIPS WITH PRISON STAFF, 1995–1998

ROBERT WORLEY
JAMES W. MARQUART
JANET L. MULLINGS

Despite many images in the popular media, correctional officers working within a prison environment rarely if ever carry weapons. This fact may be surprising considering the very high inmate-to-guard ratio that is typically maintained in state prison systems. Nonetheless, correctional security officers are charged with maintaining a peaceful environment and with ensuring that the prison runs smoothly on a day-to-day basis. As a result, many correctional officers rely on their relational skills when interacting with prison inmates. Because of the conditions of confinement and the proximity in which inmates and guards find themselves, it is not uncommon for real (and often inappropriate) relationships to develop between the "keeper" and the "kept." The news media often carry stories about inappropriate relationships that develop between guards and inmates; most commonly these relationships appear to be initiated by the staff, who are perceived to have the majority of the power. A new perspective on the inmate–guard dynamic is offered in this unique piece of qualitative research by Worley, Marquart, and Mullings. The authors build on research initiated by Allen and Bosta (1981) that explored the extent to which inmates actually target correctional workers and their numerous reasons for doing so. Worley and colleagues present the reader with a rich and detailed exploration into the complicated dynamics that exist between inmates and guards and offer a new framework for considering inmates who initiate inappropriate relationships and their motivations for doing so.

Recently, media accounts have shed light on a number of correctional employees who were terminated for engaging in "inappropriate relationships" with prisoners. This study employed face-to-face interviews of 32 inmate "turners" who were investigated for engaging in inappropriate relationships with security officers. We found that many inmate manipulators share similar attitudes

Excerpts from "Prison Guard Predators: An Analysis of Inmates Who Established Inappropriate Relationships with Prison Staff, 1995–1998," by Robert Worley, James W. Marquart, and Janet L. Mullings. *Deviant Behavior: An Interdisciplinary Journal*, 24:175–194, 2003.

and beliefs regarding inappropriate relationships. Our findings indicate that there are three distinct types of inmate "turners," each exhibiting an entirely different set of motivations and behavior from one another. We conclude that inmates are very persistent in attempting to initiate an inappropriate relationship with prison employees.

Despite formal policies prohibiting familiarity between offenders and prison staff members, infractions occur that range from "serious (e.g., love affairs)" to "unserious (e.g., giving or receiving a candy bar or soda to/from an inmate)" (Marquart, Barnhill, and Balshaw-Biddle 2001). In the past, scholars have attributed this rule-breaking behavior to the nature of the prison environment. Sykes (1958), for example, contends that the "deal-making" that occurs between guards and inmates is due to prolonged periods of interaction, which may often be quite intense. Prison administrators argue that any type of familiarity between officers and offenders constitutes a major breach of professional work values and ethics (Strom-Gottfried 1999). News reports also suggest that inappropriate relationships occur when employees work closely with incarcerated individuals (Hanson 1999). Finally, the literature suggests that security officers who work with inmates of the opposite gender may be susceptible to engaging in unprofessional sexual relationships and risk losing their jobs (Strom-Gottfried 1999).

Sexual misconduct, primarily by male staff against female prisoners, has prompted lawsuits against 23 prison systems and jails (Siegal 1999; National News Brief 1999; Hanson 1999; National Institute of Corrections 1996). Recently the child killer Susan Smith admitted to having four sexual encounters with a high ranking male security officer (Geier 2000). Staff caught having sex with an inmate in South Carolina are charged with a felony. To deter this problem, 42 states, the District of Columbia, and the federal government have enacted laws to prohibit staff sexual misconduct with inmates (National Institute of Corrections 2000).

Contemporary prisons are no longer sex segregated and female security officers work in male penitentiaries. This situation also allows for different types of inappropriate relationships to occur. In 1998, women comprised 22 percent of the American correctional officer work force. Eight in ten female prison officers now work in male prisons. Male officers comprised 78 percent of the correctional officer work force in 1998, however; only 4 percent were assigned to female institutions (Camp and Camp 1998). According to Marquart and colleagues (2001), for example, in addition to inappropriate relationships that occur between male staff and female inmates, "three other combinations are possible (male staff-male prisoner, female staff-male prisoner, and female staff-female prisoner" (p. 5).

Currently it is unknown whether or not staff members initiate relationships with offenders. Indeed, the literature in most instances portrays male guards as sexual predators and victimizers that abuse female inmates (Siegal 1999). The news media also tend to focus exclusively on only those relationships in which the officer is at fault or is responsible for initiating an inappropriate encounter (*New York Times* 1999). Scholars, such as Bowker (1980:126), also attribute considerable blame to prison staff members who "act in sexually suggestive ways" and entice offenders. Moreover, little systematic research has examined the process by which incarcerated individuals solicit correctional staff to break the rules and make attempts to develop relationships, which could only be deemed as improper.

Correctional employees hold a high degree of control over offenders and are guided by norms and regulations as to how they should use their power in a manner that is safe, just, and professional (Dilulio 1987). As mentioned before, a prison staff member can act inappropriately in many ways when dealing with offenders. For example, employees can mistreat offenders, provide inmates with contraband, or exploit inmates for sexual favors. In all of these instances, staff members fail to respect the level of power that they are entrusted with and abandon their role as professionals. Marquart and colleagues (2001) developed Goffman's (1974) study of "social frames" to advance the notion that particular roles require distinct patterns of behavior if they are to truly remain professional. Rather than being model employees, staff members who behave inappropriately with offenders become deviant and engage in what Goffman (1974) refers to as "breaking frame."

Although there are explicit rules and policies designed to prohibit personal interactions between staff members and inmates, there are nevertheless offenders who persist in attempting to minimize the social boundary between themselves and prison employees. Allen and Bosta (1981) suggest five varieties of offenders that attempt to form inappropriate relationships with correctional staff members: "observers," "contacts," "runners," "point-men," and "turners." Observers were inmates who watched (e.g., personal mannerisms, body language, facial expressions) and listened to staff members to determine which employees might be susceptible to manipulation. These offenders in turn provided crucial information to other inmates who actually initiated the manipulation. "Contacts" were prisoners that ascertained personal details about an employee's life and passed on this "intelligence" to other inmates. "Runners" tested staff members by purposely violating the rules (e.g., asking the officer for a candy bar) to gauge the employee's reaction and willingness to enforce the rules or use discretion. "Point-men" functioned as lookouts to alert other inmates who were attempting to manipulate staff. Finally, these researchers stated that some offenders acted as "turners," or inmates who befriended employees and used that friendship to ultimately coerce employees into rule infractions. "Runners" also went to great lengths to gain an employee's trust, which was used later to corrupt the staff member. This typology illustrates that inmates can be the aggressor or the initiator of an inappropriate relationship with a staff member. This typology has, however, not been subjected to testing.

The present analysis focuses exclusively on inmate "turners"—offenders identified by Allen and Bosta (1981) as the most likely to develop inappropriate relationships with staff members. Although Allen and Bosta (1981) have identified this inmate "type," they did not examine fully the process by which "turners" manipulate staff. Which staff members are targeted for manipulation? Who initiated the relationship? What does the inmate hope to gain from the relationship? Answers to these questions will fill a gap in our present knowledge about inappropriate relationships and deviant behavior in prison settings. At a larger level, findings from our analyses will clearly illustrate that inmates are not docile or pliant actors. Rather, prisoners can, through staff manipulation, actively exert control over their personal situation to mediate or lessen the pains of imprisonment (Sykes 1958).

METHODOLOGY

The data for the present paper were collected as part of a larger project on staff-inmate boundary violations within the Texas prison system, which is the second largest prison system in the world, houses over 150,000 offenders, and employs over 41,000 people (Texas Department of Criminal Justice [TDCJ-ID], 2000). In addition, there are presently 105 different custodial units within the Texas prison system, which includes seven private prisons; 13 transfer facilities, and 12 state jails (TDCJ-ID, 2000). The primary data sources for the analysis of inmate "turners" were personal observations and inmate interviews.

PERSONAL OBSERVATIONS

In January 1999, the first author began working as a correctional officer in the Texas prison system and saw first hand the unusually high degree of sociability, over-familiarization, and friendliness between offenders and prison staff. It was not uncommon to observe employees and inmates laughing together, shaking hands, and conversing for long periods of time. Some offenders also were found to be especially successful at compromising staff members. This author personally knew seven staff members who were terminated within 12 months of employment for engaging in inappropriate relationships with prisoners. He wanted to know from an inmate's perspective how and why some staff members were targeted for manipulation and others were not.

TARGET POPULATION

Inappropriate relationships are defined by Texas prison officials as personal relationships between employees and inmates/clients or with family members of inmates/clients. This is behavior that is usually sexual or economic in nature and has the potential to jeopardize the security of a prison institution or compromise the integrity of a correctional employee (Marquart et al. 2001). Texas prison employees are required by policy to report to agency officials any inmate that actively engages in or attempts to engage in an inappropriate relationship.

In October 2000, prison personnel provided the authors with a list of 508 correctional employees disciplined (between 1995 and 1998) for engaging in inappropriate relationships with prisoners. The database also contained the names of 508 prisoners who partook in these relationships. Further analysis revealed that of 508 prisoners. 225 were still incarcerated in October of 2000. Upon approval from prison officials, we sent a letter to each of the 225 prisoners and asked them to voluntarily participate in a research project on deviant relationships between inmates and staff. Each letter detailed the research objectives (as well as a commitment from the prison system not to further investigate their cases) and also contained a stamped postcard with our address that indicated whether or not they wished to be interviewed about their particular incident.

We received positive responses from 82 (36 percent) prisoners and three offenders who heard of the study by "word of mouth." These respondents indicated that they had initiated the inappropriate relationship. Though only 36 percent of the inmates consented to an interview, scholars such as Miller (1991) have found this to be an acceptable rate for sensitive topics. Statistically, the average age of the respondents we interviewed was 36. Forty-one percent were African-American, 38 percent were Caucasian, and 21 percent Hispanic. We selected these 32 inmates for interviewing based on their unit location, which was within a 100 miles radius of Huntsville, Texas. All of the inmates that were interviewed resided in state, rather than private correctional facilities.

INTERVIEWS

Each inmate was contacted and arrangements were made for an interview. Based on our prior research on staff disciplined for engaging in inappropriate relationships with inmates, we developed 11 general questions for the inmates. Table 11.1 shows the 11 questions and each of the four related research topics.

We pre-tested the interview guide with several inmates at a local Texas prison. Between December 2000 and March 2001, we interviewed the inmates who were housed at 17 different prison units. The interviews were "unstructured," which provided the respondents with ample opportunity to elaborate on the questions. All responses were handwritten and the interviews averaged 90 minutes. The interviews took place in the inmate visitation room. We typed the inmate responses and then content analyzed their responses looking for themes related to staff manipulation.

FINDINGS

We uncovered three types of "turners": (1) heartbreakers, (2) exploiters, and (3) hell-raisers. There were no statistically significant differences in either the age or race among these three types of "turners." These types represent a contribution to the literature on inappropriate relationships between prison staff and prisoners. Table 11.2 illustrates the three types of "turners" and their characteristics.

HEART-BREAKERS

Of the 32 "turners," we identified eight as "heart-breakers," or inmates who initiated a relationship with a security officer to establish a long-term romantic relationship. Five heart-breakers claimed to be married to former correctional employees, though this was never verified. Of the eight respondents that were heart-breakers, two were White, two were Hispanic, and four were African-American. Also, seven were male and one was female. The female interviewee was the only heart-breaker who had a relationship with a staff member of the same sex. Heart-breakers typically formed strong emotional bonds with prison employees, and it was not uncommon for a lengthy courtship to unfold prior to any romantic involvement. It was also not usual for ex-staff members to

TABLE 11.1 RESEARCH TOPICS AND INTERVIEW QUESTIONS

Research Area	Interview Questions
Attitudes toward prison employees and inappropriate relationships	• What kinds of employees engage in inappropriate relationships? • How common is it for guards to engage in these types of relationships? • What does an inmate gain by engaging in an inappropriate relationship?
Inappropriate relationships and changes in the work environment	• Are officers different today, than 15–20 years ago? • How have changes in the work environment affected staff–inmate relations? • Has there been an increase or decrease in staff relationships?
How do inappropriate relationships begin?	• Who initiated the relationship? • Are there different forms of entrapment?
What are the consequences of inappropriate relationships?	• What impact does this behavior have on staff? Other inmates? • How can inappropriate relationships be stopped? • How did your inappropriate relationship become detected?

TABLE 11.2 TYPOLOGY OF INMATE "TURNERS"

Type of Inmate Turner	Characteristics
Heart-breakers ($n=8$)	• Seek to form emotional bond with staff member, which can lead to marriage • May spend several months courting an employee • Act alone, without the help of a "look-out" or "pointman"
Exploiters ($n=16$)	• Uses an employee as a means for contraband or fun and excitement • Perceptive, initiate a relationship very quickly • Usually act with the help of other offenders • Most manipulative, likely to use a "lever" on prison employees
Hell-raisers ($n=8$)	• Have relationships as a way to create problems and disruptions • Most likely to be severely disciplined, employee will help Internal Affairs Division • Most likely to target non-security staff members

reside with the family or close friends of heart breakers. As one male inmate explained:

> After we got busted, she went and lived with my family for a little while. But then she left, and now my mom is mad at her. I guess my mom just figured she was freeloading, but I really loved that girl.

In a related example, another informant made the following statement:

> Right now my old lady is shacking up with my parents and her two kids. But as soon as I get out we're gonna get our own place.

These "turners" stated that they pursued the relationship because of a romantic interest in a particular employee. They initiated the contact, typically through casual conversation that progressed to the exchange of details about one's self, and attempted to "date" the employees. Many heart-breakers held important jobs, such as a clerk or hall porter, which provided them with mobility and a limited amount of supervision. They could therefore search out their romantic interest under the cover of their institutional job.

It also was not unusual for heart-breakers to wait several months before becoming physically intimate with a staff member. One offender described his sexual encounter with a female kitchen sergeant in the following manner:

> We met through the "word of God." Every day, we would share scriptures with one another and we bonded as Christians. It took six to eight months before things became romantic and then sexual, if ya know what I'm talking 'bout. We kept things very quiet from everyone.

It was noteworthy that the above speaker mentioned that efforts were made to keep the relationship private. All of these offenders stated that they told no one, including their cellmate or closest friends about their personal involvement with a correctional employee. The heart-breakers did not utilize "point men," which according to Allen and Bosta (1981), were other offenders that helped "turners" conceal their inappropriate relationships with security, rather than non-security employees. We do not know how many of the heart-breakers engaged in sexual relations with staff members.

When these offenders were asked why they formed relationships mainly with guards, they gave a variety of different reasons. One respondent expressed his opinion in the following way:

> We mainly have relationships with C.O.s because they have less education and much poorer people skills than other employees. Guards relate better with inmates because they come from a lower-middle class background, the same way the convicts do. People in non-security jobs are better educated and don't socialize and mingle with prisoners the way guards do.

Another offender stated:

> If I was dating a nurse, I'd have to get a lay-in to see her. And if I kept getting lay-ins, sooner or later this would begin to look suspicious and some snitching inmate might find out about this and tell the rank.

Heart-breakers also engaged in an activity that Allen and Bosta (1981) referred to as the "touch game," which consisted of "innocent" touches (e.g., patting the staff member on the back, touching a staffing member on the hand) initiated by the inmate that seemed accidental. Simple touching breaks down the social distance between the keepers and kept. Touching humanizes an otherwise harsh and inhuman environment. One respondent explained his actions in the following way:

> When a boss is opening a door, we might grab for it too and touch hands for a moment. After a while we might be touching something else.

The interviewee claimed that inmates use "touching" to assess a staff member's vulnerabilities, as well as how open he or she would be in forming an unauthorized relationship. Heart-breakers also use such techniques "note-swapping" (e.g., sending love letters) and "holding jiggers," or acting as a lookout to establish contacts with staff members. When one respondent was asked how he held "jiggers," he gave a detailed account of the following scenario:

> At the time this boss lady was going through a lot with her family and didn't have any time to sleep. I told her that she could take a nap and I would just "watch her back." Pretty soon we become good friends and we would just stay up all night talking, even though I was supposed to be cleaning the wing and she was supposed to be guarding the other inmates.

In both the cases of the note-swapping and holding-jiggers, the respondents articulated that this was intended to develop a sense of trust between the inmate and employee. Although some of these offenders admitted that this trust was ultimately for manipulative purposes, there were also heart-breakers who insisted that they were truly in love and never intended to take advantage of their relationship. One interviewee argued that the agency should not be surprised that inmates desperately seek to establish romantic relationships with prison staff members, given the offender's lack of legitimate alternatives. The following quote from a prisoner illustrates that in some cases prisoner–staff contact was initiated to overcome institutional deprivation in the form of a lack of heterosexual relationships:

> TDCJ tries hard to keep inmates from society. Instead it needs to make an effort to let an inmate cultivate and maintain the relationships that he has out in the free world. If this was properly done, then, inmates would stop worrying about starting relationships with female officers because they'd have more contact with their wives and girlfriends on the outside.

EXPLOITERS

We uncovered 16 turners who were "exploiters" or inmates who aggressively forged inappropriate relationship with staff members to make illicit profits in the underground prison economy. We found 16 exploiters (14 male and 2 female inmates) of which there were seven Whites, three Hispanics, and seven African-Americans. Exploiters initiated the relationship and befriended staff for economic reasons. Male inmates exploited female staff and the two females exploited male staff. One African-American male prisoner explained it this way:

> When I first got here in '89 all I wanted was to do my time and be left alone. But when this place [TDCJ] did away with smoking, I said bullshit on this I'm gonna make me some money. So I hooked up with some ole ugly ass boss lady and I told her how great she looked and how she needed a strong dude like me to be her partner. Shit, she fell for that real fast. Next thing you know I got her bringing in cigarettes by the carton. I was making good money and living good. Hell you give' em a line a B.S. and you got' em hooked. We eventually got busted. Ha, she told me how much she loved me. I told her you a fool who was a mule.

A White female prisoner had this to say,

> I started talking real nice to the officer where I worked, in the laundry. He was married but I told him how his old lady didn't pay him enough attention. You know that if he was my man how I would treat him. He started writing me notes and cards. Pretty soon I got him to bring in eyeliner, perfume, and some cigarettes. I sold the stuff. Oh it was fun to talk to him and stuff but I never let it get any further. I mean I never let him touch me or anything. I used him to make my life easier in here. Why not? You'd do the same thing.

To obtain contraband, "exploiters" develop a "lever" or "hold" over security officers. Levers, according to Allen and Bosta (1981), were ploys that offenders use to manipulate staff members into violating organizational policies and procedures. In our study, the inmates were asked about the types of levers they used to manipulate correctional employees, and one of the exploiters responded as follows:

> If we see an officer that is dipping or smoking, we can use this against him. Also, if a boss tears up

> another officer's disciplinary case, we might use this to get the boss to do us a favor.

Another exploiter expressed a similar sentiment but also claimed to use tactics that were much more extreme and intimidating. When the respondent was asked what he would do if an employee wanted to terminate an inappropriate business relationship, the offender stated:

> If a boss wants to stop, I'll give her a couple of months. But you never let them quit. An inmate can always threaten to go to rank, and if that don't work then I tell him something like, "I ain't got but 15 months to go before I discharge. I know you love your kids. I'd hate to see them get hurt." Bosses with kids won't want anything to happen to their family.

Respondents also stated that it was not uncommon for inmates to intimidate staff members into engaging in inappropriate relationships, and these threats were often physical or psychological in nature. An example given of a psychological threat was a situation where a staff member was led to believe by a group of offenders that she had misplaced the inmates' mail, even though she had not. One interviewee suggested that naive employees could be "strong-armed" into bringing in tobacco, especially if enough inmates threatened to write a grievance or go to Internal Affairs to report fabricated wrongdoing.

Interestingly enough, the most common entrapment technique among exploiters involved the exchange of small items with prison staff members, like food or reading materials. Exchange of these minor items was used to establish an inappropriate relationship. One interviewee, for example, stated:

> Here a boss may go a whole shift and not get a lunch break. We can take advantage of them because of this. You know, we might offer a boss a candy bar or a soda on a hot day. Sometimes we might offer them a sandwich or something, and this can lead to all kinds of things. Sometimes they take it and sometimes they don't. When they do, it's like a fish on a hook. You just got to reel them in slow. It takes patience. Hey all I got is time, man, so time is on my side.

Other exploiters claimed to provide staff members with newspaper or "jack books" (pornography) to develop a unique type of rapport. Interestingly, both female exploiters stated that it was not unusual for inmates to solicit staff members to put money in their trust funds. One female exploiter stated:

> TDCJ doesn't require people to put their name on trust fund slips. So all a boss has to do is send in a money order and an inmate can get money added to their books. This happens a lot.

Exploiters used these transactions to develop "levers," which often led to inappropriate business relationships (Allen and Bosta 1981). Although exploiters were primarily motivated by profit and the need to dominate the prison marketplace, the vast majority of these offenders also claimed to have engaged in sexual relationships with prison staff members. There was, however, at least one instance where an exploiter chose not to mix "business with pleasure," and abstained from having sex with a female staff member who was supplying him with contraband. As the respondent stated:

> My cellmate used me as a contact with a female laundry officer. He and I were working together to bring tobacco in and were making good money. I was just happy to be involved and didn't want to do anything stupid to bring down any heat. Also, at the time, I was married to someone in the free world and didn't want to mess that up either.

In the above cases, the respondents indicated that levers were necessary to coerce staff members into illegal business arrangements. Some interviewees, however, stated that occasionally staff members are more than anxious to make extra money by bringing in contraband. This may be especially true, given that prison staff members are enormously underpaid and in dire need of additional money. In Texas, for example, a starting correctional officer grosses a modest income of $1,716 per month (Broddy 2002). Many inmates explained that because of the low pay, employees often enjoyed earning the extra money, which could be more than the income they earned with the prison system. One offender stated:

> Soon bosses start to feel pretty good once they see that they are making some real money by bringing in tobacco. If things are good, and I want other things, I might say something like, "so what else do you play with?" An officer can make $1,000 a week by bringing in cocaine. A nickel, which is $20 worth of coke out in the free world, goes for $1,000 in here.

Finally, most exploiters were very perceptive and quickly took advantage of any opportunity derived by chance. One offender explained how he became involved with a female correctional officer and made the following statement:

> She got on to me for no good reason, so I cussed her out and next thing I knew she started crying. After a while, we started talking and she began telling me things. I loved this and just listened. She said that her husband was abusing her mentally and then she began telling me what a whore she could be. She even showed me her tattoos and said she got them for free because she screwed the guy. Pretty soon, I knew she'd be screwing me too. I mean I wanted her to get me stuff and then I'd screw her later.

The exploiter immediately began talking to the guard in the above situation after seeing her cry. This led to a series of conversations in which she revealed aspects about her personal life, which included an abusive marriage. This was consistent with Marquart and colleagues' (2001) research, which found that in many cases involving employee-inmate relationships, the staff member often "suffered from domestic trouble, or recently finalized a divorce, or separated from a spouse" (p. 31). The inmate realized that the officer was in an unfortunate predicament, and he exploited this weakness to gain a sexual conquest.

Exploiters were inmates who were exceptionally skilled at targeting staff members who often appeared vulnerable and had what Cressey (1973) referred to as "non-sharable problems." Although Sykes (1958) and other early prison researchers delineated several inmate roles or types, these studies did not consider argot roles that involved inmate-staff interactions. In other words, our research extends the old prison sociology by uncovering exploiters or inmates who systematically seek out staff to manipulate for personal gain and/or to normalize the prison experience. Exploiters cultivated staff to establish heterosexual relations or to obtain contraband.

HELL-RAISERS

Last were "hell-raisers," or inmates who engaged in a unique kind of psychological warfare. As many of these offenders admitted, they simply wanted to cause trouble and create hell for the prison system. These "rebels with a cause" (or "ballbusters" in Sykes' (1958) terminology), "were consumed with the idea of creating havoc and trouble for an institution for the sake of it. There were eight inmates in this group, and all were male: three were White, two Hispanic, and three were African-American. It was not unusual for these inmates to have long histories of personal involvement with correctional employees and many hell-raisers claimed to presently be engaged in a least one inappropriate relationship with staff members. In addition, these respondents admitted that they actually thrived on putting staff members into situations that compromised their jobs as well as the facility's security. All eight hell-raisers aimed to embarrass correctional administrators, and many claimed they enjoyed the notoriety that followed after their relationship was exposed. As one offender explained, having an inappropriate relationship with a prison staff member was the "ultimate way to out-con the law."

Hell-raisers focused on staff members, not security officers. Of these eight offenders, six stated that they had engaged in at least one inappropriate relationship with an employee other than a correctional officer. It could be that hell-raisers perceived non-security staff members to be a challenge, and they may have enjoyed the pursuit as much as the actual relationship. In one interview, the respondent claimed to have had several sexual relationships with non-security employees, including both a chaplain's secretary and warden's wife. When asked to describe his most recent alleged relationships, the offender offered:

> I've had sex with the wives of two different wardens. One night around Christmas, I went over to the house of one warden and his wife asked me to put her son's bicycle together. You know it was a Christmas present. Then she cooked dinner for me and we had sex right there in the kitchen, on the floor. I can talk my way into any woman's panties. I did it 'cause I could. You know what I am saying? Man when they busted me for that, all hell broke loose. It was hilarious. Yeah, I lost my outside trusty job but it was worth it 'cause I embarrassed the shit out of that warden and his family. I still can't stop laughing 'bout it.

Hell-raisers also claimed that they used the act of masturbation to gauge whether or not an employee was likely to participate in a relationship with an inmate. The hell-raisers suggested that female employees who ignored masturbation were either weak or enjoyed this type of behavior. One interviewee, who later married a former prison employee, expressed himself in the following way:

> Before I married my wife, I used to always jack off for her and do a little show whenever she walked her runs. She used to love it too.

It was not uncommon for hell-raisers to suggest that women who decided to work in a prison were looking to "find a man." One hell-raiser was particularly adamant in his belief that female guards worked in correctional facilities as a way to be around male inmates. As this respondent stated:

> Women guards work here, so they can look at a bunch of dicks. That's one of the main reasons why they come here. That and the fact that they can't get welfare.

The previous statement by a hell-raiser also suggests that these inmates "condemned their condemners" and blamed the staff for their actions. In almost all of the instances involving hell-raisers, the inappropriate relationships were terminated by the employees, rather than by both participants being caught by other personnel. In one instance, a staff member wrote a letter to the unit warden detailing her sexual involvement with an offender and even testified later against the "turner" during his disciplinary hearing. It may be that employees who involved themselves with hell-raisers came to find that they actually shared very little with these types of inmates "turners," who seemed to hold values that were both anti-social and very detrimental to the institution.

CONCLUSION

While the research literature and popular media have reported on prison staff engaging in inappropriate relationships with prisoners, we hear very little about the reverse situation. Allen and Bosta (1981) developed a typology of four inmates, over 20 years ago, who manipulate correctional staff. The present paper focused on inmates types who established inappropriate relationships with staff members for deviant purposes. These inmates utilized such tactics as addressing employees by their first name or a nickname, offering staff members' food items, requesting special favors, or through touching the employee (Allen and Bosta 1981). Over an extended period of time, this type of behavior ultimately led to boundary violations or at least a profound sense of familiarity between staff members and inmates (Marquart et al. 2001).

The 32 inmate manipulators who participated in this study by no means represent the entire number of inmate turners that are presently incarcerated within Texas prisons or other penal institutions.

Nevertheless, despite the obvious limitations with regard to its external validity, this research validates the typology designed by Allen and Bosta (1981), and it supports the notion that it is often the inmate, rather than the staff member, who initiates inappropriate relationships. Offenders were found to be much more likely than staff members to initiate inappropriate relationships. Of the 32 turners, 25 stated that inmates were more likely to initiate the relationship. Two stated that staff members were more likely to initiate the relationship and five respondents suggested that staff members and offenders were equally likely to initiate the relationship.

This article extends Allen and Bosta's (1981) concept of an inmate turner and suggests that turners can also be "heart-breakers," "exploiters," or "hell-raisers." Each type was fundamentally different from one another and carried its own set of rationalizations and motivations for engaging in deviant behavior with staff members. Heart-breakers sought out and established inappropriate romantic relationships with staff members. The relationships had romantic overtures and broke down the barriers between the keepers and the kept, and facilitated heterosexual relationships in response to institutional deprivations. Hell-raisers established inappropriate relationships for "the hell of it," to throw a wrench into the institutional regimen. For heart-breakers and exploiters the relationship served as a means to an end. On the other hand, for hell-raisers the relationship was an end in itself. Prison staff members were often the "victims" of inappropriate relationships, and it was not uncommon for these interactions to be carefully orchestrated and initiated by inmates.

The interactions between inmates and prison employees seem to have become more complex in recent years, especially as prisons have reduced the amount of single-sex staff members. Not too long ago, in Texas prisons, it was almost unheard of for guards to fall prey to inmate manipulators, namely because of the largely informal control mechanisms which were implemented by an all male staff (Marquart 1983). This is not to say that there has not always been corruption in Texas prisons. It is likely, however, that the addition of female guards has provided inmates with more opportunities to engage in inappropriate relationships. Also, Texas penitentiaries no longer exert the same type of heavy-handed control over inmates which was once employed in the "building tender" days, and this undoubtedly has shed more light on the nature of inappropriate relationships.

Today, it is not unusual for staff members to unwittingly become the target of inmate manipulators. This is especially true because of the enormous shortage of guards in Texas facilities, which has caused prison officials to hire virtually anyone possessing the minimal job requirements (Broody 2002). This is disheartening because employees with a low level of education and job experience have been found to be the most likely to engage in inappropriate relationships with inmates (Marquart et al. 2001). Also because Texas correctional employees continue to be underpaid, this exacerbates any tendencies that a staff member might have toward engaging in an inappropriate business transaction with an offender. Some employees may in fact see nothing wrong with smuggling in tobacco, since it is not a mind-altering substance and has only recently become restricted. As Silverman (2001:240) argues,

> Since the ban in Texas, tobacco has become the number one contraband item. Moreover, many C.O.'s and other staff members are smokers, and some do not feel that bringing tobacco in is "really a violation," because they disagree with the ban. For some, throwing a carton of cigarettes over the wall to make an extra $100 is more of a game than a law violation. It presents staff with an easy way to supplement their income without really feeling guilty or that they are violating the law.

This is not to say that such behavior has become the rule rather than the exception in penal environments. Nevertheless, prison administrators everywhere must understand that offenders are very persistent in initiating interactions with employees for a variety of reasons.

STUDY QUESTIONS

1. What policy changes might be necessary in light of the findings of this article?
2. Are there any conditions under which a "friendship" between a correctional officer and an inmate would be acceptable?
3. For what reasons—individual/personal or institutional—might correctional officers be motivated to engage in relationships with inmates?
4. For what reasons might inmates be motivated to engage in relationships with correctional officers?
5. What similarities (e.g., background, social class) might inmates have with correctional officers, and how might this impact the likelihood that relationships will develop?
6. What uses—prison policy or other uses, such as further research—might the typologies ("heartbreakers," "exploiters," "hell-raisers") developed by these authors have?

REFERENCES

Allen, B. and D. Bosta, 1981. *Games Criminals Play.* Susanville, CA: Rae John Publishers.

Bowker, L. H. 1980. *Prison Victimization.* New York: Elsevier.

Broody, M. 2002. "Prisons in Neighboring Brazoria County Finding Filling Job Openings to Be Difficult." *Houston Chronicle,* This Week, p. 20.

Camp, G. M. and Camp, C. G. 1998. *The Corrections Yearbook.* South Salem, NY: Criminal Justice Institute.

Cressey, D. R. 1973. *Other People's Money.* Montclair, NJ: Patterson Smith.

Dilulio, J. J., Jr. 1987. *Governing Prisons.* New York: McMillan.

Geier, A. 2000. "Smith Says She Had Sex with a Guard." *Associated Press.* Thursday, August 31.

Goffman, E. 1974. *Frame Analysis.* Cambridge, MA: Harvard University Press.

Hanson, E. 1999, October 27. "Prisoner Who Said Deputy Raped Her Wins Suit." *Houston Chronicle,* Section 2, p. 3.

Holmes, S. 1996. "With More Women in Prison, Sexual Abuse by Guards Becomes a Greater Concern." *New York Times,* December 27:A180.

Marquart, J. 1983. "Coopting the Kept." Unpublished dissertation, Department of Sociology, Texas A & M University.

Marquart, J. W., Barnhill, M. B., and Balshaw-Biddle, K. 2001. "Fatal Attraction: An Analysis of Employee Boundary Violations in a Southern Prison System, 1995–1998." *Justice Quarterly* 18:878–910.

Miller, D. C. 1991. *Handbook of Research Design and Social Measurement,* 5th ed. New York: McKay.

National Institute of Corrections. 1996. *Sexual Misconduct in Prisons: Law, Remedies, and Incidence.* United States Department of Justice. Information Center, Longmont, Colorado.

New York Times. 1999. "Virginia Governor Orders Prison-Sex Abuse Inquiry." October 13, pp. 013, A22.

Siegal, N. 1999. "Stopping Abuse in Prison." *The Progressive* 63:31–33.

Silverman, I. J. 2001. *Corrections: A Comprehensive View.* Belmont, CA: Wadsworth-Thomson Learning.

Strom-Gottfried, S. 1999. "Professional Boundaries: An Analysis of Violations by Social Workers." *Families in Society.* 80:439–49.

Sykes, G. M. 1958. *The Society of Captives: A Study of a Maximum Security Prison.* Princeton, NJ: Princeton University Press.

Texas Department of Criminal Justice—ID. 2000. *Unit Profiles.* Huntsville, TX.

12

JOB STRESS AND BURNOUT AMONG CORRECTIONAL OFFICERS

A LITERATURE REVIEW

WILMAR B. SCHAUFELI
MARIA C. W. PEETERS

Positive changes within correctional officers' jobs have emerged in recent decades. Symbolically, many states have changed the job title of prison security personnel from "prison guard" to "correctional officer," for example. Along with this nominal change, increasing attention has been paid at times to work load, inmate-to-staff ratio, and other factors that contribute to the difficulty many correctional officers encounter in their day-to-day activities. Nonetheless, being a correctional officer remains one of the most stressful jobs in the "human service" realm. Research continues to reveal that correctional officers have higher than average rates of absenteeism, higher rates of job-related stress disorders, and overall lower job satisfaction. As a result, state prison systems suffer, since these job-related problems lead to very high rates of turnover compared to other professions. Prison systems with high turnover rates have correctional staff who are less experienced and more likely to make mistakes that threaten security. Job stress and burnout among correctional officers are explored in depth in this comprehensive cross-national literature review by Schaufeli and Peeters. While correctional officers across the board are shown to suffer from more negative job-related factors than those in other professions, it appears that officers in the United States have particularly high rates of professional difficulties. Many factors are examined in an effort to uncover the reasons for such high rates of burnout and job-related stress, which prompted one study subject to state that "we're just paid inmates."

This literature review presents an overview of occupational stress and burnout in correctional institutions, based on 43 investigations from 9 countries. First, the prevalence of various stress reactions among correctional officers (COs) is discussed: turnover and absenteeism rates, psychosomatic diseases, and levels of job dissatisfaction and burnout. Next, empirical evidence is summarized for the

Excerpts from "Job Stress and Burnout Among Correctional Officers: A Literature Review," by Wilmar B. Schaufeli and Maria C. W. Peeters. *International Journal of Stress Management*, Vol. 7, No. 1, 2000.

existence of 10 specific stressors in the CO's job. It appears that the most notable stressors for COs are role problems, work overload, demanding social contacts (with prisoners, colleagues, and supervisors), and poor social status. Finally, based on 21 articles, individual-oriented and organization-oriented approaches to reduce job stress and burnout among COs are discussed. It is concluded that particularly the latter (i.e., improving human resources management, professionalization of the CO's job, and improvement of the social work environment) seems to be a promising avenue for reducing job stress and burnout in correctional institutions.

Working in a prison as a correctional officer (CO) is a stressful job. At least this seems to be the prevailing opinion among professionals and the lay public alike. This current literature review seeks to find empirical support for this assertion by trying to answer three related specific questions: (1) What kinds of stress reactions are observed among correctional officers (COs)? (2) What kinds of job stressors are found among COs? (3) What preventive measures can be taken in order to reduce job stress among COs? Special attention is paid to burnout since this is considered a long-term stress reaction that occurs among professionals who, like COs, do "people work."

The majority (about 55%) of studies to be reviewed were conducted in the United States. Relatively few were carried out in Europe, most notably in Britain, Sweden, and the Netherlands, or in other countries such as Israel, Canada, or Australia. This might complicate the interpretation of the results since the situation in prisons in the United States differs greatly from those in other countries, particularly in Sweden and in the Netherlands. For instance, in the United States institutions with 1,500 prisoners are not uncommon, whereas in Sweden and in the Netherlands the maximum number of inmates is about 250. In addition, in the United States inmates may have to share cells whereas in Sweden and the Netherlands every inmate has a private cell. Also, the ratio of officers to inmates is less favorable in the United States than in these European countries. Finally, it is likely that COs' personal characteristics differ between countries since recruitment and selection policies vary considerably. In the United States selection criteria are rather broad (e.g., high school education, particular size and weight, good sense of sight) whereas, for example, in the Netherlands psychological criteria are included as well (e.g., a particular level of intelligence, certain skills, and personality characteristics). Accordingly, it can be hypothesized that job stress is more common among COs in the United States because of higher workload (i.e., larger institutions and more inmates to deal with) and fewer personal coping resources (i.e., less adequate skills and personality characteristics).

Despite these differences similar developments can be observed between countries as well. Most notably, there is a tendency toward further professionalization of the CO's job, which is well illustrated by the fact that the old-fashioned "prison guard" in most countries is replaced by the modern "correctional officer." Not only has the job title changed, but so has the content of the job. The most important changes include (Stalgaitis, Meyers, & Krisak, 1982; Jacobs & Crotty, 1983; Kommer, 1993): (1) growing size and changing composition of the inmate population (i.e., increasing number of drug addicts, mentally ill, and aggressive inmates); (2) introduction of new rehabilitative programs, (3) liberalization (e.g., conjugal visits, inmate access to telephones); (4) influx of new treatment professionals; (5) growth of more middle-level supervisory positions, which provides better opportunities for career advancement; (6) recruitment of better-educated officers; (7) an increased sense of professionalism through improved pay and fringe benefits, increased training in legal matters and inmates' rights, and stricter adherence to written policy and procedures. Therefore, as a result of these recent developments COs' jobs may have changed likewise in various countries....

REVIEW: CO STRESS AND BURNOUT

THE NATURE OF THE REVIEWED STUDIES

Typically, empirical studies on job stress and burnout among COs use cross-sectional study designs and self-report questionnaires. Of all 43 studies that were reviewed only one used a prospective design in order to predict future turnover (Jurik & Winn, 1987) and one was longitudinal in nature in the sense that questionnaire data was collected at two waves. The remaining 41 studies employed one-shot designs that do not allow one to disentangle cause and effect. Moreover, with one notable exception (Lombardo, 1981) *all* studies used questionnaires: 33 (80%) used exclusively questionnaires; two studies also used interviews (Poole & Regoli, 1981; Hughes & Zamble, 1993); four studies included administrative records (Verhagen, 1986a,b; Junk & Winn, 1987; Härenstam, Palm, & Theorell, 1988; Augestad & Levander, 1992); two studies used physiological measures in addition (Härenstam et al., 1988; Härenstam & Theorell, 1990); and finally, one study also used a daily event-recording approach in addition to questionnaires (Peeters, Buunk, & Schaufeli, 1995). Only the Swedish study of Härenstam et al. (1988) is truly multimethodological in nature because in addition to a questionnaire, data administrative records, physiological measures, and a physical health examination are included. Finally, with three exceptions that used large representative samples (Härenstam & Theorell, 1990; Saylor & Wright, 1992; Britton, 1997) all studies employed small and/or convenience samples. Thus, the results of the empirical studies to be reviewed should be interpreted with caution because: (1) cross-sectional designs do not allow drawing of conclusions about the causal direction of the relationship between stressors and strains; (2) self-reports are known to be sensitive to all kinds of response biases; and (3) results obtained in small and nonrepresentative samples cannot be generalized (see Frese & Zapf, 1988, for a methodological discussion of these three issues).

WHAT KINDS OF STRESS REACTIONS ARE OBSERVED AMONG COS?

Broadly speaking, four kinds of stress reactions can be distinguished among COs: (1) withdrawal behaviors; (3) psychosomatic diseases; (3) negative attitudes; and (4) burnout. Behavioral stress reactions (i.e., turnover and absenteeism) that are documented by archival data suggest that COs work in stressful jobs. This is illustrated by alarmingly high *turnover* rates. For instance, recent figures from a national survey of correctional facilities in the United States reveal an average turnover rate among COs of 16.2% with some states reporting turnover rates as high as 38% (Corrections Compendium, 1996). Needless to say, such rates are likely to create administrative nightmares, desperate recruiting, and much overwork. Most turnover in the United States occurs in young, inexperienced COs within six months after beginning their jobs. Likewise, in Israel 50% of the COs leave correctional service within 18 months of being hired (Shamir & Drory, 1982). Obviously, initial expectations of neophytes do not correspond with the everyday reality of the job. Probably, the less rigorous personnel selection in these countries explains these high turnover rates relative to the Netherlands, about 4–5% annually, where more strict criteria are applied than in the United States (Greuter & Castelijns, 1992).

In addition, *absenteeism* is also quite high among COs. For instance, absenteeism rates among New York COs are 300% higher than the average rate of all other occupations in that state (Cheek & Miller, 1983). In the Netherlands, absenteeism rates among COs are not as high as in the United States, but are nevertheless nearly twice as high as the country's average (Greuter & Castelijns, 1992). In the mid-eighties, the absenteeism rate among Dutch COs was 15% against 8.5% for all other occupations. It was calculated that on average, a Dutch CO was absent for two months per year. These alarming figures prompted the Dutch Ministry of Justice to grant a number of studies to investigate the causes of absenteeism. It appeared from these studies that about one-third of the COs' absenteeism was stress-related (Verhagen, 1986a). More than half of the Dutch COs receive their work disablement pensions on mental grounds. That is, they are work incapacitated because of the stressful nature of their jobs. This disablement rate is well above the Dutch average; about one-third of the disabled workers in the Netherlands leave their jobs for psychological reasons (Houtman, 1997).

It has been observed in the United States that *psychosomatic diseases* are more common among COs than among members of most other occupations, including police officers—a comparable profession (Cheek & Miller, 1983). In the period up to six months prior to the United States survey, 17% of the COs reported that they visited a physician because of hypertension (vs. 10% of police officers and 9% of other professions). Another 3.5% suffered from heart disease, which is rather high compared to police officers (1.4%) and members of the other occupations (2.1%). These figures agree with a carefully designed Swedish study that shows that COs are at higher risk to develop cardiovascular diseases (Härenstam et al., 1988). It appears from this study that COs not only had significantly higher levels of blood pressure compared to the control group, consisting of physicians, engineers, traffic controllers, and musicians, but also their levels of the stress hormone plasma Cortisol, were much higher (Härenstam, 1989).

Perhaps most typically, COs report a number of *negative job-related attitudes.* For instance, their level of job dissatisfaction is remarkably high compared to a dozen occupations that arc quite similar with respect to levels of pay and education (Cullen, Link, Cullen, & Wolfe, 1990). Moreover, abundant empirical evidence suggests that COs experience alienation (Lombardo, 1981; Toch & Klofas, 1982), occupational tedium (Shamir & Drory, 1982) and powerlessness, and are characterized by cynicism, authoritarianism, skepticism, and pessimism (for a review see Philliber, 1987). For instance, in the study of Toch and Klofas (1982) about 70% of COs in the United States agree with the statement: "We're damned if we do, and we're damned if we don't." Many officers viewed their work as dull, tedious, and meaningless. As one CO put it, "We're paid prisoners." Their skepticism and cynicism is nourished by the repeated failure to successfully rehabilitate prisoners, which is illustrated by high relapse rates. Research has shown that cynicism is more prevalent in treatment settings than in custodial settings where the accent is less on rehabilitation (Philliber, 1987). Moreover, cynicism is more common among officers who are in the middle of their careers. Younger COs are still idealistically motivated, whereas only those of the older COs have survived who did cope well in their jobs—this survival bias is also called the "healthy worker effect" (Karasek & Theorell, 1990).

How many COs are *burned out*? Although a valid and reliable burnout measure exists—the Maslach Burnout Inventory (Maslach, Leiter, & Jackson, 1996)—this question cannot be answered straightforwardly since it is wrongly posed; like length, burnout is a continuous variable. Obviously, the answer to this question depends on the criterion that is used, and the criterion for burnout is arbitrary. For instance, Lindquist and Whitehead (1986) used as a criterion for each dimension of burnout that one crucial symptom should occur at least once a week. Based on this arbitrary criterion they estimated that one-third of the COs experiences considerable emotional exhaustion, approximately one-fifth treated prisoners in an impersonal manner (depersonalization), and about one-quarter evaluated themselves negatively (reduced personal accomplishment). Schaufeli, Van den Eijnden, and Brouwers (1994) found that burnout among COs was particularly characterized by feelings of depersonalization and reduced personal accomplishment. These findings are in line with other empirical findings that suggest that, in comparison with other occupational groups, COs experience more feelings of alienation, cynicism, pessimism, skepticism, and powerlessness

(Philliber, 1987; see also the previous discussion about negative job-related attitudes). In a similar vein it has been observed that the level of psychological distress—as measured with the General Health Questionnaire—was significantly higher for Australian COs than in a national sample of that country (Dollard & Winefield, 1994). A recent Canadian study by Pollack and Sigler (1998), however, reported that compared to United States inner-city teachers and police officers, Canadian COs experience exceptionally low levels of job stress. The authors explain this finding by pointing to the harsh environment of northern Ontario that might have produced a selection effect: COs with a weaker constitution have left the service or did not apply for a job in this area in the first place.

Do differences in gender, race, and age exist as far as stress reactions in COs are concerned? Although many would probably expect that, for instance, women, non-whites, and older COs report higher strain levels, this is not supported by empirical results. Huckabee (1992) reviewed the literature and found that the effect of gender, race, ethnicity, and age on stress reactions "remains unclear" (p. 483). More recent research confirms that no significant *direct* relationship exists between gender and age on the one hand and job dissatisfaction (Cullen et al., 1990; Dollard & Winefield, 1995, 1998; Morrison, Dunne, Fitzgerald, & Cloghan, 1992), depression, boredom, trait anxiety, and minor psychiatric symptoms (Dollard & Winefield, 1995, 1998), physical health (Morrison et al., 1992), burnout (Hurst & Hurst, 1997), and stress symptoms (Triplett & Mullings, 1996) on the other hand. Race and ethnicity have been studied much less in relation with stress and burnout. Triplett and Mullings (1996) did not find significant relationships between stress reactions and race and Shamir and Drory (1981) who studied COs with Druze, Jewish North African and Jewish Georgian backgrounds in Israeli prisons, concluded that "the realities of the job are clear enough to be perceived in a similar manner by people with different cultural backgrounds and the pattern of relationships among perceptions and evaluations of the job is also generally similar across cultures" (p. 280). However, the fact that no direct relationships exist does not mean that gender, race, ethnicity, and age do not play a role at all; it seems that their role is more subtle. For instance, Britton (1997) found that among minority male COs, greater efficacy in working with inmates was associated with lower job stress, while white female COs' higher levels of overall job satisfaction were mediated by quality of supervision. Furthermore, Härenstam et al. (1988) found that understimulation was associated with a high sick leave rate for male prison staff and high mean levels of Cortisol and symptoms of ill health for female staff. Finally, Holgate and Clegg (1991) showed that the process of burnout differs between age groups; for younger COs role conflict contributed to increased emotional exhaustion and to increased contact with inmates, whereas for older COs emotional exhaustion contributed to decreased contact with inmates. The results of these three studies suggest complex patterns of interactions rather than direct effects of gender, ethnicity, and age on stress reactions.

In sum: COs are under stress. This is illustrated by relatively high turnover, absenteeism, and disablement rates compared to other occupations. Moreover, they suffer more than other professionals from psychosomatic risk factors such as hypertension and elevated secretion of stress hormones. Additionally, stress-related cardiovascular disease is more common among COs. Finally, and probably most typically, COs experience a number of negative feelings and attitudes, including job dissatisfaction, cynicism, and burnout.

WHAT KINDS OF JOB STRESSORS ARE FOUND AMONG COS?

Based on earlier reviews of literature on job stressors (e.g., Warr, 1987; Kahn & Byosiere, 1994; Buunk, de Jonge, Ybema, & de Wolff, 1998), we distinguish between ten psychosocial risk factors for developing stress reactions. Each of these risk factors will be briefly discussed in relation to the CO's job so that a particular psychosocial risk profile emerges.

High Workload

Many studies indicate that the workload of COs is high (for reviews see Philliber, 1987; Huckabee, 1992). For instance, in several Dutch studies, between 65% and 75% of the COs report that they feel under strain because of high workload (Kommer, 1990). More particularly, they complain about high peak load (i.e., having too much to do in too short a time), brief periods of recovery (i.e., intervals between peak hours are too short), and multiple workload (having to perform different tasks simultaneously). It is quite likely that the workload of COs has increased over the past years because of financial cutbacks and reduction of staff. Furthermore, it was observed that high absenteeism rates have a negative impact on COs' workload since more overtime has to be performed (Kommer, 1990). A study among COs in the United States showed a positive relationship between workload and burnout: the higher the workload the more burnout symptoms were observed (Dignam, Barrera, & West, 1986). In a somewhat similar vein, COs who report problems with shiftwork showed more burnout symptoms (particularly emotional exhaustion) than officers who did not report such problems (Schaufeli et al., 1994). Shamir and Drory (1982) found work-overload to be a significant predictor of tedium among Israeli COs. Finally, a recent study among Australian COs not only found that those who experienced high job demands reported more psychological distress, more job dissatisfaction, and more physical health symptoms, but also that these negative effects were aggravated when high job demands were accompanied by low control and lack of social support (Dollard & Winefield, 1998). Obviously, a *combination* of high demands, poor control, and lack of social support constitutes a special risk for COs' health and well-being.

Lack of Autonomy

As noted above, a recent test of the so-called Job Demand Control Support model (Karasek & Theorell, 1990) in Australian COs was successful in that it showed both significant main effects and interaction effects of job demands, job control (or autonomy), and social support on various measures of health and well-being (e.g., psychological distress, job dissatisfaction, physical health symptoms) (Dollard & Winefield, 1998). More specifically, two aspects of job autonomy can be distinguished: skill discretion and decision authority (Karasek & Theorell, 1990). The former refers to the level of control the worker has in performing the task, whereas the latter refers to the level of social authority over making decisions. It appears that COs who report low levels of skill discretion experience fewer feelings of personal accomplishment, compared to COs who report higher levels (Schaufeli et al., 1994). In addition, COs' perceived influence on administrative supervisors (decision authority) appeared to be negatively related to cynicism (Ulmer, 1992), whereas lack of participation in decision making is positively associated with job stress (Lasky, Gordon, & Strebalus, 1986; Slate & Vogel, 1997). A possible explanation for these relationships is offered by Whitehead (1989) who showed that role problems play a mediating role between lack of participation in decision making and burnout. Because COs do not sufficiently participate in decision making (i.e., lack decision authority), their role problems are not solved and as a result of that burnout might develop. On the other hand, COs with supervisory responsibilities perceive less job-related stress and more job satisfaction than their colleagues who have less decision authority (Saylor & Wright, 1992). In the Netherlands, a small but significant proportion of COs (15%) complains about lack of decision authority (Kommer, 1990).

Underutilization of Knowledge and Skill

A job that requires the use of knowledge and skills is challenging and provides learning opportunities.

However, a large majority (69%) of Dutch COs indicate that only "every now and then" they have the opportunity to use the knowledge and skills they acquired during their training (Kommer, 1990). In other words, most COs feel underutilized, particularly in custody-oriented institutions as compared to rehabilitation-oriented institutions (so-called "half-open prisons"). In Sweden, "understimulation" of COs was associated with higher sick-leave rates and higher levels of stress hormones, like plasma Cortisol (Härenstam et al., 1988). Willett (1982) claimed that many Canadian COs feel "trapped" because they are paid a disproportionately high salary for a job that requires a low level of education and few skills. Another Canadian study showed opposite results suggesting that the stereotype of COs is incorrect (Hughes & Zamble, 1993): COs felt neither undereducated, nor did they evidence exceptional stress, in fact they were content to stay in their job. Since the authors do not present any rationale for their deviant findings, it may be speculated that these are due to sampling bias.

Lack of Variety

Typically, the CO's job is considered to be dull and routine (Philliber, 1987). In recent decades, task variety has been further reduced by the influx of other professional staff such as social workers and counselors who have taken over part of the traditional CO's job (Fry, 1989). Although this might make the CO's daily work even more tedious, in the Netherlands only a small minority (15%) experiences lack of variety to be a problem (Kommer, 1990). Moreover, skill variety was not significantly related to burnout in an Israeli study (Drory & Shamir, 1988). Hughes and Zamble (1993), however, found among Canadian COs that boredom was the second source of stress after poor management. But as noted previously, they found COs, in contrast to previous reports, to be reasonably effective and adaptive, with little evidence of job stress.

Role Problems

Perhaps the most important job stressor COs are faced with are role problems of several kinds. After a thorough review of empirical studies Philliber (1987, p. 19) concludes: "Overall, role difficulties in prisons appear to take a rather serious toll." Basically two different kinds of role problems are observed among COs: role ambiguity and role conflict. The former occurs when no adequate information is available to do the job well, whereas the latter occurs when conflicting demands have to be met. The role of the CO is problematic by its very nature since two conflicting demands have to be met simultaneously—guarding prisoners and facilitating their rehabilitation. This typical role conflict is convincingly demonstrated by the results of a Dutch survey (Kommer, 1990) in which a large majority (80%) agrees with the statement that "keeping peace and order" is a crucial task for COs. At the same time, however, a similar percentage (74%) agrees with the statement that "encouraging the inmate to understand himself better" is a crucial task as well. Clearly, to a large degree both tasks are incompatible. The former statement implies that rules are applied strictly, whereas the latter statement implies that the rules are interpreted rather smoothly. Role problems are aggravated because the objectives of rehabilitation are usually rather vaguely described so that, in addition, role ambiguity is likely to result. That is, COs hardly know what is expected of them when it comes to rehabilitating prisoners. Not surprisingly, it has been argued that the emphasis on rehabilitation and the recent influx of other professionals have increased role problems of COs (Philliber, 1987). COs feel uncertain about their role, are doubtful about which services they have to provide, and blame their superiors for the lack of standardization of policies in dealing with inmates (Poole & Regoli, 1981; Toch & Klofas, 1982). It was demonstrated that such role ambiguity resulting from poor leadership is strongly related to job stress (Rosefield, 1981; Cheek & Miller, 1983). In a somewhat similar vein, Poole and Regoli (1980a) observed that changing correctional philosophies and institutional practices concerning the handling of prisoners produced stress among COs because they are associated with role conflicts. Similar direct relationships between role conflict and stress have also been found by Cullen, Link, Wolfe, and Frank (1985), Lindquist and Whitehead (1986), and Grossi and Berg (1991). However, interestingly, in another study of Poole and Regoli (1980b), a reverse pattern was suggested—namely, that stress increases levels of role conflict as well as conflicts between professional and nonprofessional staff. Despite claims for causality, all above-mentioned studies are cross-sectional in nature, so that a causal order between variables cannot be determined.

In various studies, role problems such as role conflict and role ambiguity were found to be predictors of burnout (Shamir & Drory, 1982; Lindquist & Whitehead, 1986; Dignam, Barrera, & West, 1986; Drory & Shamir, 1988; Whitehead, 1989; Schaufeli et al., 1994). Whitehead's (1989) model of CO burnout illustrates the crucial function of role problems in the burnout process. The model is based on survey data of over two hundred Alabama COs and suggests that role problems have both a direct and an indirect effect on burnout. Indirect paths run through job dissatisfaction and job stress. In its turn, role problems are aggravated by lacking social support and by poor participation in decision making.

Demanding Social Contacts

Intensive and emotionally charged contacts with prisoners are the hallmark of the CO's job. The relationship between CO and prisoner has been characterized as a situation of structural conflict (Poole & Regoli, 1931): the role of the officer ("the keeper") fundamentally contradicts the role of the prisoner ("the kept"). Recently, several changes in the population of the prisoners have intensified the stressful social contacts between COs and inmates. For instance, more and more mentally disturbed delinquents and drug addicts are imprisoned (Harding & Zimmermann, 1989). Härenstam et al. (1988) found a high proportion of drug abuse in correctional institutions to be positively correlated with COs' symptoms of ill health, high sick-leave rates, and low work satisfaction. Moreover, prisoners are more entitled than they used to be, whereas the authority of COs has declined. The demanding nature of prisoner contact is further illustrated by the positive relationship between the intensity of prisoner contact and CO burnout. The more hours per week COs spend in direct contact with prisoners, the more burnout symptoms are reported—particularly, diminished personal accomplishment (Whitehead, 1989).

A distinction should be made between positive and negative direct contact with prisoners (Dignam, Barrera, & West, 1986). The former is positively related with COs' feelings of personal accomplishment, whereas the latter is positively related with both other dimensions of burnout (i.e., emotional exhaustion and depersonalization). Schaufeli et al. (1994) showed that the discrepancy COs experience between their investments and outcomes in relationships with prisoners is positively related to all three dimensions of burnout. That is, COs who feel that they continuously put more into relationships with prisoners than they get back from them in return tend to burn out.

Social contacts of COs are not restricted to prisoners but include colleagues and superiors as well. It has been argued that group loyalty and collegiality among COs are weakly developed because they interact only occasionally (Poole & Regoli, 1981). The main reason for this is that the organization emphasizes individual responsibility rather than team responsibility. As a result, an individualistic culture develops in which asking for social support is considered to be an expression of incompetence. Therefore, it is not surprising that the so-called *John Wayne syndrome* is often observed: the CO as a tough lonesome cowboy who is emotionally unaffected by his job, and who can solve his own problems without the help of others. As in many occupations (for overviews see Warr, 1987; Buunk et al., 1998), social support of colleagues and supervisor reduces stress among COs (Dollard & Winefield, 1995). This was particularly the case among COs with high levels of anxiety. However, results concerning social support are equivocal since other studies suggested that peer support *increases* rather than reduces COs' level of job stress (Grossi & Berg, 1991; Morrison et al., 1992). Similarly, a Dutch study showed that COs' social support does not unconditionally lead to positive affect (Peeters, Buunk, & Schaufeli, 1995): COs perceived social support as a restriction of their personal freedom, which in turn induced feelings of inferiority to the donor of the support.

COs have rather negative attitudes about their superiors. For instance, 42% of the COs in the United States believed that prisoners are treated better by their superiors than they are (Toch & Klofas, 1982). One-third of the COs fully agree with the statement: "My superiors care more about the inmates than about the officers." The poor relationship between COs and their superiors constitutes a serious problem since feedback and support from superiors are crucial for performing adequately on the job, particularly when structural role problems exist. Typically, COs attribute much of their stress to poor communication with their supervisors (Cheek & Miller, 1983). Drory and Shamir (1988) found lacking management support to be positively related to burnout.

Uncertainty

Two types of uncertainty can be distinguished among COs: the threat of losing one's job and uncertain career prospects. In many European countries such as the Netherlands, Germany, and Sweden, COs are civil servants who enjoy strong legal protection against dismissal. It has been noted that such a high level of job certainty also has a negative side in that COs tend to accept poor working conditions in exchange for a stable job (Kommer, 1990). It is quite likely that the present discussions in many countries about the privatization of prisons will enhance feelings of job insecurity among COs. There is ample evidence that the psychological effects of anticipated job loss are at least just as serious, or perhaps even more so, than actual job loss (Hartley, Jacobsen, Klandermans, & Van Vuren, 1991). In the Netherlands, the majority of the COs (54%) is quite uncertain about their future career prospects and many COs (39%) indicate that they experience a career dead-end (Kommer, 1990).

Health and Safety Risks

The situation of structural conflict between COs and prisoners may easily escalate and end up in a violent confrontation. Thus, the threat of violence is an important stressor for COs. For instance, 75% of Israeli COs considered potential violence as the most stressful aspect of their work (Shamir & Drory, 1982). Similar figures have been reported in the United States (see Philliber, 1987). Danger is reported as another major source of stress (e.g., Lombardo, 1981; Cullen et al., 1990; Triplett, Mullings, & Scarborough, 1996). Recently, the risk of AIDS or hepatitis infection has increased because many inmates are drug addicted.

A Dutch survey showed that many COs complain about the physical climate in the institution (Verhagen, 1986b), most notably dry air (41%), lack of fresh air (74%), and draught (70%). Jacobs and Crotty (1983) found specific job conditions that are associated with prison employment—such as dirt and odor—to be related to COs' level of job stress.

Inadequate Pay

Research on pay shows that the experienced fairness of the pay level is related to the worker's well-being, rather than absolute pay (Warr, 1987). Is the pay appropriate for the kind of job that is performed compared to other similar jobs? Indeed, a moderate negative relationship was observed between satisfaction with pay and burnout among Israeli COs (Shamir & Drory, 1982). Rosefield (1981) found factors as low pay, slow promotions, and insufficient fringe benefits to contribute to work-related stress.

Poor Social Status

Working in a prison has low social status. This is illustrated by the fact that for most COs their current job is their second choice (Philliber, 1987). Rather than being unemployed, COs "choose" to work in the prison. The major attraction of their job is employment security and pay. Stalgaitis et al. (1982) found that COs considered the poor social status of their job as a significant source of work-related stress. Among Israeli COs, community esteem for the incumbent's occupation was about as strongly correlated with burnout as was role conflict (Shamir & Drory, 1982). The poorer the experienced community support, the more burnout symptoms were reported. In addition, the status of the job is also poor in the eyes of the prisoners. As one prisoner notes: "We don't actually have any respect for a regular guard, he just carries the keys. It's those up there who have something to say; captain, doctor, and inspector" (Kommer, 1990, p. 36).

In sum, virtually all psychosocial risk factors that have been identified in the occupational stress literature apply more or less to the CO's job. However, the most prominent psychosocial risks that may lead to stress and burnout among COs are: (1) role problems; (2) stressful social contacts with superiors, prisoners, and colleagues; (3) work overload; and (4) poor social status. In addition, three risk factors seem to play a minor role: lack of participation in decision making, inadequate pay, and underutilization of knowledge and skills. It should be noted, however, that these conclusions are almost exclusively based on cross-sectional surveys that are conducted in relatively small and/or nonrepresentative samples....

STUDY QUESTIONS

1. How might the findings of this article be used to improve the way prisons operate?
2. Which of the reasons for correctional officer stress and burnout appear to be the most applicable to correctional officers in the United States?
3. How could each of the kinds of job stress identified by the authors (high work load, lack of autonomy, etc.) be mitigated?
4. In what ways could the findings of this selection be used in the hiring of correctional officers or for job-orientation materials once a new officer is hired?
5. What appear to be the primary differences in correctional officer burnout and stress between the United States and other countries?
6. What might be the reasons for the differences in job-related stress for correctional officers between the United States and other countries?

REFERENCES

Augestad, L. B., & Levander, S. (1992). Personality, health and job stress among employees in a Norwegian penitentiary and in a maximum security hospital. *Work & Stress, 6*, 65–79.

Bandura, A. (1986). *Social foundations of thought and action: A social cognitive theory.* Englewood Cliffs, NJ: Prentice Hall.

Britton, D. M. (1997). Perceptions of the work environment among correctional officers. Do race and sex matter? *Criminology, 35*, 85–105.

Buunk, B. P., de Jong, J., Ybema, J. F., & de Wolff, Ch.J. (1998). Psychosocial aspects of occupational stress. In P. J. Drenth, H. Theirry, & Ch.J. de Wolff (Eds.), *Handbook of work and organizational psychology* (pp. 145–182). London: Taylor & Francis.

Cheek, F. E., & Miller, M. (1983). The experience of stress for correctional officers: A double bind theory of correctional stress. *Journal of Criminal Justice, II*, 105–120.

Cherniss, C. (1980). *Professional burnout in human service organizations.* New York: Praeger.

Corrections Compendium (1996). *The National Journal for Corrections.* Published by The American Correctional Association, Lanham USA.

Cullen, F. T., Link, B. G., Wolfe, N. T., & Frank, J. (1985). The social dimensions of correctional officers' stress. *Justice Quarterly, 2*, 505–535.

Cullen, F. T., Link, B. G., Cullen, J. B„ & Wolfe, N. T. (1990). How satisfying is prison work? A comparative occupational approach. *Journal of Offender Counseling, Services and Rehabilitation, 14*, 89–108.

Dignam, J. T., Barrera, M., & West, S. G. (1986). Occupational stress, social support, and burnout among correctional officers. *American Journal of Community Psychology, 14*, 177–193.

Dignam, J. T., & West, S. G. (1988). Social support in the workplace: Tests of six theoretical models. *American Journal of Community Psychology, 16*, 701–724.

Dollard, M. F., & Winefield, A. H. (1994). Organizational response to recommendations based on a study among correctional officers. *International Journal of Stress Management, 1*, 81–101.

Dollard, M. F., & Winefield, A. H. (1995). Trait anxiety, work demands, social support and psychological distress in correctional officers. *Anxiety Stress & Coping, 8*, 25–35.

Dollard, M. F., & Winefield, A. H. (1998). A test of the demand-control/support model of work stress in correctional officers. *Journal of Occupational Health Psychology 3*, 243–264.

Drory, A., & Shamir, B. (1988). Effects of organizational and life variables on job satisfaction and burnout. *Group and Organization Studies, 13*, 441–455.

Edelwich, J., & Brodsky, A. (1980). *Burnout: States of disillusionment in the helping professions.* New York: Human Resources Press.

Farmer, J. A. (1988). Relationship between job burnout and perceived inmate exploitation of juvenile correctional workers. *International Journal of Offender Therapy and Comparative Criminology, 32*, 67–73.

Frese, M., & Zapf, D. (1988). Methodological issues in the study of work stress: Objective versus subjective measurement of work stress and the question of longitudinal studies. In C. L. Cooper & R. Payne (Eds.), *Cause, coping and consequences of stress at work* (pp. 375–411). Chichester: Wiley.

Fry, L. J. (1989). Counselor reactions to work in prison settings. *Journal of Offender Counseling, Services and Rehabilitation, 14*, 121–132.

Gerstein, L. H., Topp, C. G., & Correll, G. (1987). The role of the environment and person when predicting burnout among correctional personnel. *Criminal Justice and Behavior, 14*, 352–369.

Greuter, M. A. M., & Castelijns, M. T. (1992). *Ziekteverzuim en verloop en de relatie met het werk en de werksituatie van penintentiare inrichtingswerker* [Absenteeism and turnover and their relationship with the working environment of COs). Utrecht: PsychoTechniek.

Grossi, W. L., & Berg. B. L. (1991). Stress and job dissatisfaction among correctional officers: An unexpected finding. *International Journal of Offender Therapy and Comparative Criminology, 35*, 73–81.

Harding, T. W., & Zimmermann, E. (1989). Psychiatric symptoms, cognitive stress and vulnerability factors: A study in a remand prison. *British Journal of Psychiatry, 155*, 36–43.

Härenstam, A. (1989). *Prison personnel—Working conditions, stress and health: A study of 2,000 prison employees in Sweden.* Unpublished PhD thesis, University of Stockholm, Sweden.

Härenstam, A., Palm, U-B., & Theorell, T. (1988). Stress, health and the working environment of Swedish prison staff. *Work & Stress, 2*, 281–290.

Härenstam, A., & Theorell, T. (1990). Cortisol elevation and serum g-glutamyltranspeptidase in response to adverse job conditions: How are they interrelated? *Biological Psychology, 31*, 157–171.

Hartley, J., Jacobson, D., Klandermans, B., & Van Vuuren, T. (1991). *Job insecurity: Coping with jobs at risk.* London: Sage.

Hepburn. J. R. (1987). The prison control structure and its effects on work attitudes: The perceptions and attitudes of prison guards. *Journal of Criminal Justice, 15*, 49–64.

Holgate, A. M„ & Clegg, I. J. (1991). The path to probation officer burnout: New dogs, old tricks. *Journal of Criminal Justice, 19,* 325–337.

Houtman, I. L. D. (1997). *Trends in arbeid en gezondheid 1996* [Trends in work and health 1996]. Amsterdam: NIA'TNO.

Huckabee, R. G. (1992). Stress in corrections: An overview of the issues. *Journal of Criminal Justice, 20,* 479–486.

Hughes, G. V. (1990). *Personal disposition, coping, and adaptation in correctional workers.* Unpublished doctoral dissertation. Queen's University, Kingston: Ontario.

Hughes, G. V., & Zamble, E. (1993). A profile of Canadian correctional workers. *International Journal of Offender Therapy and Comparative Criminology, 37,* 99–113.

Hurst, T. E., & Hurst, M. M. (1997). Gender differences in mediation of severe occupational stress among correctional officers. *American Journal of Criminal Justice, 22,* 212–237.

Jacobs, J. B., & Crotty, N. (1983). The guard's world. In J. B. Jacobs (Ed.), *New perspectives on prisons and imprisonment.* Ithaca, NY: Cornell University Press.

Jurik, N. C., & Winn, R. (1987). Describing correctional-security dropouts and rejects. An individual or organizational profile? *Criminal Justice and Behavior, 14,* 5–25.

Kahn, R. L., & Boysiere, P. (1994). Stress in organizations. In M. D. Dunette, J. M. Hough, & H. C. Triandis (Eds.), *Handbook of industrial and organizational psychology* (Vol. 4, pp. 573–650). Palo Alto: Consulting Psychologist Press.

Karasek, R., & Theorell, T. (1990). *Healthy work: Stress, productivity and the reconstruction of working life.* New York: Basic Books.

Kiely, J., & Hodgson, G. (1990). Stress in the prison service: The benefits of exercise programs. *Human Relations, 43,* 551–572.

Kommer, M. M. (1990). *Werken met mensen: Een onderzoek naar de werksituatie en functioneren van penitentiaire inrichtingswerkers* [Working with people: A study on the working environment and the functioning of COs]. The Hague: Ministry of Justice.

Kommer, M. M. (1993). A Dutch prison officers work: Balancing between prison policy, organizational structure and professional autonomy. *The Netherlands Journal of Social Science, 29,* 130–143.

Klofas, J., & Toch, H. (1986). The guard subculture myth. *Journal of Research in Crime & Delinquency, 19,* 238–254.

Lasky, G. L., Gordon, B., & Strebalus, D. J. (1986). Occupational stressors among federal correctional officers working in different security levels. *Criminal Justice and Behavior, 13,* 317–327.

Launay, G., & Fielding, P. J. (1989). Stress among prison officers: Some empirical evidence based on self report. *The Howard Journal, 28,* 138–147.

Lazarus, R. S. & Folkman, S. (1984). *Stress, appraisal and coping.* New York: Springer.

Leiter, M. P. (1993). Burnout as a developmental process: Consideration of models. In W. B. Schaufeli, C. Maslach, & T. Marek (Eds.), *Professional burnout: Recent developments in theory and research* (pp. 237–250). Washington: Taylor & Francis.

Levi, L. (1987). Definitions and the conceptual aspects of health in relation to work. In R. Kalimo, M. A. EI-Batawi, M., & C. L. Cooper (Eds.), *Psychosocial factors at work and their relation to health.* Geneva: World Health Organization.

Lindquist, C. A., & Whitehead, J. T. (1986). Burnout, job stress and job satisfaction among Southern correctional officers. *Journal of Offender Counseling. Services and Rehabilitation, 10,* 5–26.

Lombardo, L. X. (1981). Occupational stress in correction officers: Sources, coping strategies, and implications. In E. Zimmerman & H. I). Miller (Eds.), *Corrections at the crossroads.* Beverly Hills, CA: Sage.

Lombardo, L. X. (1989). A comparative study of correctional management. *American Journal of Sociology, 94,* 902–904.

Maslach, C. (1993). Burnout: A multidimensional perspective. In W. Schaufeli, C. Maslach, & T. Marek (Eds.), *Professional burnout: Recent developments in theory and research* (pp. 19–32). Washington: Taylor & Francis.

Maslach, C., & Leiter, M. P. (1997). *The truth about burnout. How organizations cause personal stress and what to do about it.* San Francisco: Jossey-Bass.

Maslach, C., Letter, M. P., & Jackson, S. E. (1996). *MBI: Maslach Burnout Inventory: Manual research edition.* Palo Alto: University of California, Consulting Psychologists Press (1st ed. 1981; 2nd ed. 1986).

Maslach, C. & Schaufeli, W. B. (1993). Historical and conceptual development of burn-out. In W. B. Schaufeli, C. Maslach, & T. Marck (Eds.), *Professional burnout: Recent developments in theory and research* (pp. 1–16). Washington: Taylor & Francis.

Morrison, D. L. Dunne, M. P., Fitzgerald, R., & Cloghan, D. (1992). Job design and levels of physical and mental strain among Australian prison officers. *Work & Stress, 6,* 13–31.

Patterson, B. L. (1992). Job experience and perceived job stress among police, correctional and probation/parole officers. *Criminal Justice and Behavior, 19,* 260–285.

Peeters, M. C. W., Buunk, A. P., & Schaufeli, W. B. (1995). Social interaction processes and negative affect among correctional officers: A daily event-recording approach. *Journal of Applied Social Psychology, 25,* 1073–1089.

Philliber, S. (1987). Thy brothers keeper: A review of the literature on correctional officers. *Justice Quarterly, 4,* 9–37.

Pollack, C., & Sigler, R. (1998). Low levels of stress among Canadian correctional officers in the northern region of Ontario. *Journal of Criminal Justice, 26,* 117–128.

Poole, E. D., & Regoli, R. M. (1980a). Work relations and cynicism among prison guards. *Criminal Justice and Behavior, 7,* 303–314.

Poole, E. D., & Regoli, R. M. (1980b). Role stress, custody orientation and disciplinary actions. *Criminology, 18,* 215–226.

Poole, E. D., & Regoli, R. M. (1981). Alienation in prison; An examination of the work relations of prison guards. *Criminology, 9,* 251–270.

Rosefield, H. A., Jr. (1981). *Self-identified stressors among correctional officers.* Unpublished PhD thesis, North Carolina State University, Raleigh, NC.

Quick, J. C., Quick, J. D., Nelson, D., & Hurell, J. J. (1997). *Preventive stress management in organizations.* Washington, DC: American Psychological Association.

Saylor, W. G., & Wright, K. N. (1992). Status, longevity, and perceptions of the work environment among Federal prison employees. *Journal of Offender Rehabilitation, 17,* 133–160.

Schaufeli, W. B., & Enzmann, D. (1998). *The burnout companion for research and practice: A critical analysis.* London: Taylor & Francis.

Schaufeli, W. B., Van den Eijnde, R. J. J. M., & Brouwers, H. M. G. (1994). Stress en burnout bij penitentiairc inrichtingswerkers [Stress and burnout among COs]. *Gedrag & Organisatie, 7,* 216–224.

Shamir, B., & Drory, A. (1981). A study of cross-cultural differences in work attitudes among three groups of Israeli prison employees. *Journal of Occupational Behavior, 2,* 267–282.

Shamir, B., & Drory, A. (1982). Occupational tedium among prison officers. *Criminal Justice and Behavior, 9,* 79–99.

Slate, R. N., & Vogel, R. E. (1997). Participative management and correctional personnel: A study of the perceived atmosphere for participation in correctional decision making and its impact on employee stress and thoughts about quitting. *Journal of Criminal Justice, 25* , 397–408.

Stalgaitis, S. J., Meyers, A. W., & Krisak, J. (1982). A social learning theory model for reduction of correctional officer stress. *Federal Probation, 46,* 33–41.

Toch, H., & Klofas, J. (1982). Alienation and the desire for job enrichment among correctional officers. *Federal Probation, 46,* 35–44.

Triplett, R., Mullings, J. L., & Scarborough. (1996). Work-related stress and coping among correctional officers: Implications from organizational literature. *Journal of Criminal Justice, 24,* 291–308.

Ulmer, J. T. (1992). Occupational socialization and cynicism toward prison administration. *Social Science Journal, 19,* 423–443.

Van der Klink, J. J. L., Blonk, R. W. B., Schene, A. H., & van Dijk, F. J. H. (1999). *The benefits of interventions for work related stress.* Manuscript submitted for publication.

Verhaeghe, P. (1993). *Werktevredenheid bij gevangenisbewaarders [Job satisfaction among COs].* Unpublished PhD thesis, Vrije Universiteit Brussel, Belgium.

Verhagen, J. (1986a). Stress in de werksituatie van bewaarders [Job stress among COs]. *Balans, 9,* 20–22.

Verhagen, J. (1986b). Persoonskenmerken van de bewaarder [COs' personality characteristics]. *Balans, 9,* 3–5.

Voorhis, P. van, Cullen, F. T., Link, B. G., & Wolfe, N. T. (1991). The impact of race and gender on correctional officers' orientation to the integrated environment. *Journal of Research in Crime and Delinquency, 28,* 472–500.

Warr, P. (1987). *Work, unemployment and mental health.* Oxford: Clarendon Press.

Whitehead, J. T. (1989). *Burnout in probation and corrections.* New York: Praeger.

Whitehead, J. T., Linquist, C., & Klofas, J. (1987). Correctional officer professional orientation. *Criminal Justice and Behavior, 14,* 468–486.

Wicks, R. J. (1980). *Guard! Society's professional prisoner.* Houston: Gulf Publications.

Willett, T. C. (1982). *Follow-up study of correctional officers and their partners in 1981.* Unpublished communications branch report, Canada Solicitor General, Ottawa.

Wright, T. A. (1993). Correctional employee turnover: A longitudinal study. *Journal of Criminal Justice, 21,* 131–142.

PART

IV

CORRECTIONAL POLICY AND OFFENDER RIGHTS

Until the beginning of the 1960s, the rights (constitutional or otherwise) afforded to prison inmates were largely at the discretion of institutional administration. In early America, *Ruffin v. Commonwealth* had established that prison inmates were to be regarded as "slaves of the state." The concept of slavery denotes unpaid, forced labor. In effect, history translated into exactly that for many inmates throughout the United States for much of the nineteenth and twentieth centuries.

Prior to the 1960s, the courts maintained a "hands-off" doctrine regarding the administration of prisons. This approach was fueled by a desire to keep executive-level powers separate, in addition to a deference of the court system toward correctional professionals. The institutions themselves were physically out of sight of the general public and conceptually out of sight of litigation. With very little sympathy for the plight of prisoners, conditions inside institutions were ignored. Prison was intended to be a "punishment" in and of itself, which stymied motivation to improve conditions or policies. The movement toward humane punishment had ended with the retirement of the stocks and the implementation of mass warehousing for offenders. Not surprisingly, however, because of an apparent lack of executive oversight, institutions were often allowed to deteriorate both in physical condition and in the interaction between inmates and correctional officers.

In large-scale penal institutions, efforts are placed toward making life as uniform as possible. In essence, it is advantageous to allow for very few, if any, exceptions in the daily lives of inmates. This is readily apparent when the history and development of the U.S. prison is examined. The hands-off doctrine reinforced this concept because prison inmates were believed to have experienced a complete civil death. That is, because of their crimes against society, offenders were no longer entitled to many of the "basic" human rights enjoyed by free citizens. Most significantly, however, the concept of civil death was perceived to include deprivation of many of the rights outlined in the Bill of Rights of the U.S. Constitution. In addition, and perhaps most importantly, inmates were not afforded access to the very court system that had committed them in the first place.

Although many of the societal and legal changes that marked the beginning of the prisoners' rights movement are widely believed to have occurred throughout the 1960s, the seeds of this movement were undoubtedly planted during the 1940s. Perhaps the first effort toward breaking through the hands-off doctrine was held by *Ex Parte Hull* (1941). Through the review of this court case, the Supreme Court declared that prisoners have the unrestricted right of access to the federal court system. Similarly, three years later, *Coffin v. Reichard* (1944) established that inmates had the right of court review when challenging the conditions of confinement. Both of these court cases, while significant in what they later came to symbolize, applied only to federal prisoners. Regardless, precedent had been set for similar cases that would apply to state-level prisons and other institutions designed to house offenders.

Many of the initial challenges to the conditions of confinement occurred in the area of freedom to practice individual religion. Several religions (both Eastern and Western) require access to materials that may be considered contraband by a prison system. Similarly, many religions require certain facilities, clothing, movement, and celebrations that may disrupt the desired uniformity that make prisons easier to manage. In *Cooper v. Pate* (1964) the U.S. Supreme Court maintained that denial of the inmates' right to practice their religion was indeed a violation of their First Amendment rights of expression. *Cooper v. Pate* was brought to the Supreme Court under Section 1983 of the Federal Civil Rights Act and later became the primary avenue through which conditions of confinement would be challenged.

Although attention to freedom of religion was seen by many as a major victory in prisoner rights, this did not address the physical conditions of confinement. The 1970s and 1980s brought numerous cases before the Supreme Court under the Eighth Amendment, claiming that the current state of many prisons constituted cruel and unusual punishment. Judges often determined that finding grotesque filth, vermin infestations, inadequate heating and ventilation, fire hazards, and noise levels prohibited anything that resembled a peaceful environment. A number of these court cases did result in the improvement of physical conditions inside prison walls. Currently, prisoners' rights and protections generally include religious freedom, freedom of speech, rights to medical treatment, physical protection from attack and assault, due process prior to additional institutional punishment (such as isolation or labor), and equal treatment regarding institutional jobs and educational opportunities.

It is important to note that although conditions inside prisons have greatly improved since the 1960s, the rights outlined here (as well as others not mentioned) are still considered to be provisional. Because prison administrators are responsible first and foremost to confine the convicted offender, the Supreme Court in most cases has ruled that rights be upheld only as much as possible without compromising the security of the prisons' charges. This is not to say that the advances and changes brought about by prison litigation have been meaningless—far from it. However, a significant amount of discretion naturally lies within official hands.

While the rights of inmates and conditions within the walls have been the subject of many court cases, more recently there has been increased attention on offenders who are in the community, specifically sex offenders. As policy makers have sought to restrict the movement and rights of the convicted sex offender, new issues have arisen. Civil commitment, registration, GPS tracking, and other forms of control have been increasingly placed on one of the most feared offenders of all, the sex offender.

The selections in this part were included in this volume to serve three functions—to offer an in-depth exploration of prison conditions both in general policy and specific inmate rights, to provide an example of what yet can happen within institutional settings despite advances that have occurred, and to examine the limits and restrictions that have been imposed on sex offenders.

A broad and detailed account of how prison policy has changed in the years since the "Stanford Prison Experiments" is included in order to examine important issues in light of the prisoners' rights movement, as well as other general conditions and trends. Also included is an in-depth account and analysis of the Supreme Court's position regarding prisoners' rights and the landmark cases that have influenced those rights. An article about sex offender laws has been added to examine some of the justifications, policies, and approaches that have been taken with this population. Every year, women constitute a larger portion of the total prison population. Because the vast majority of major cases before the courts have concerned male inmates, many of the old issues may need to be revisited to apply to females in custody. Moreover, new issues regarding women prisoners may bring about other conditions not previously reviewed. In the final reading in this part the experiences of registered female sex offenders are reviewed. While a distinct minority of offenders, this unique and understudied slice of the correctional population allows us to consider some of the ramifications of the laws enacted in the name of public safety.

Without question, prisoners' rights litigation and advances in research regarding what the best prison policies may be have settled many critical issues. The general issue of inmate rights is far from settled, however. The burgeoning prison population that spurred many of the initial legal inquiries is still increasing at dramatic rates in many states. In addition, the population of the prison system is changing.

13
THE PAST AND FUTURE OF U.S. PRISON POLICY

TWENTY-FIVE YEARS AFTER THE STANFORD PRISON EXPERIMENT

CRAIG HANEY
PHILIP ZIMBARDO

The Stanford Prison Experiment, conducted by Philip Zimbardo, W. Curtis Banks, and Craig Haney in 1973, is perhaps one of the best-known studies of the custodial institutional environment. Few, if any, other studies have gained as much notoriety or brought such a large number of issues regarding prisons and how they are run into the academic and public discourse. In this article from 1998, Haney and Zimbardo reflect on the 25 years of prison policy in the United States that followed their initial experiment. The authors begin by reviewing the "state" of crime and punishment at the time they conducted the experiment, and then present what they believe have been the most critical changes in U.S. prison policy that have occurred since. Of particular import are discourses regarding the prisoners' rights movement, what the authors term the "death of rehabilitation," changes in sentencing patterns and policies, and, most important, the U.S. tendency to "binge" on incarceration and punishment in general, which includes three-strikes legislation and the development of the supermax prison. Haney and Zimbardo reflect in detail on the Stanford Prison Experiment and reveal how what they discovered via the methodologies used may have been a harbinger of what was to come in the U.S. penal system. Readers of this article will receive the best of two very important components—exposure to what is arguably one of the most notable studies in correctional research and the authors' reflection and insight into prison policy over the 25 years that followed it.

Twenty-five years ago, a group of psychologically healthy, normal college students (and several presumably mentally sound experimenters) were temporarily but dramatically transformed in the course of six days spent in a prison-like environment, in research that came to be known as the Stanford Prison Experiment (SPE; Haney, Banks, & Zimbardo, 1973). The outcome of our study was shocking and unexpected to us, our professional colleagues, and the general public. Otherwise emotionally strong college students who were randomly assigned to be mock-prisoners suffered acute psychological trauma and breakdowns. Some of the students begged to be released from the intense pains of less than a week of merely simulated imprisonment, whereas others adapted by becoming blindly obedient to the unjust authority of the guards. The guards, too—who also had been carefully chosen on the basis of their normal-average scores on a variety of personality measures—quickly internalized their randomly assigned role. Many of these seemingly gentle and caring young men, some of whom had described themselves as pacifists or Vietnam War "doves," soon began mistreating their peers and were indifferent to the obvious suffering that their actions produced. Several of them devised sadistically inventive ways to harass and degrade the prisoners, and none of the less actively cruel mock-guards ever intervened or complained about the abuses they witnessed. Most of the worst prisoner treatment came on the night shifts and other occasions when the guards thought they could avoid the surveillance and interference of the research team. Our planned two-week experiment had to be aborted after only six days because the experience dramatically and painfully transformed most of the participants in ways we did not anticipate, prepare for, or predict.

These shocking results attracted an enormous amount of public and media attention and became the focus of much academic writing and commentary. For example, in addition to our own analyses of the outcome of the study itself (e.g., Haney et al., 1973; Haney & Zimbardo, 1977; Zimbardo, 1975; Zimbardo, Haney, Banks, & Jaffe, 1974) and the various methodological and ethical issues that it raised (e.g., Haney, 1976; Zimbardo, 1973), the SPE was hailed by former American Psychological Association president George Miller (1980) as an exemplar of the way in which psychological research could and should be "given away" to the public because its important lessons could be readily understood and appreciated by nonprofessionals. On the 25th anniversary of this study, we reflect on its continuing message for contemporary prison policy in light of the quarter century of criminal justice history that has transpired since we concluded the experiment.

When we conceived of the SPE, the discipline of psychology was in the midst of what has been called a "situational revolution." Our study was one of the "host of celebrated laboratory and field studies" that Ross and Nisbett (1991) referred to as having demonstrated the ways in which "the immediate social situation can overwhelm in importance the type of individual differences in personal traits or dispositions that people normally think of as being determinative of social behavior" (p. xiv). Along with much other research conducted over the past two and one-half decades illustrating the enormous power of situations, the SPE is often cited in textbooks and journal articles as a demonstration of the way in which social contexts can influence, alter, shape, and transform human behavior.

Our goal in conducting the SPE was to extend that basic perspective—one emphasizing the potency of social situations—into a relatively unexplored area of social psychology. Specifically, our study represented an experimental demonstration of the extraordinary power of *institutional* environments to influence those who passed through them. In contrast to the companion research of Stanley Milgram (1974) that focused on individual compliance in the face of an authority figures increasingly extreme and unjust demands, the SPE examined the conformity pressures brought to bear on groups of people functioning within the same institutional setting (see Carr, 1995). Our "institution" rapidly developed sufficient power to bend and twist human behavior in ways that confounded expert predictions and violated the expectations of those who created and participated in it. And, because the unique design of the study allowed us to minimize the role of personality or dispositional variables, the SPE yielded especially clear psychological insights about the nature and dynamics of social and institutional control.

The behavior of prisoners and guards in our simulated environment bore a remarkable similarity to patterns found in actual prisons. As we wrote, "Despite the fact that guards and prisoners were essentially free to engage in any form of interaction . . . the characteristic nature of their encounters tended to be negative, hostile, affrontive and dehumanizing" (Haney et al., 1973, p. 80). Specifically, verbal interactions were pervaded by threats, insults, and deindividuating references that were most commonly directed by guards against prisoners. The environment we had fashioned in the basement hallway of Stanford University's Department of Psychology became so real for the participants that it completely dominated their day-to-day existence (e.g., 90 percent of prisoners' in cell conversations focused on "prison"-related topics), dramatically affected their moods and emotional states (e.g., prisoners expressed three times as much negative affect as did guards), and at least temporarily undermined their sense of self (e.g., both groups expressed increasingly more deprecating self-evaluations over time). Behaviorally, guards most often gave commands and engaged in confrontive or aggressive acts toward prisoners, whereas the prisoners initiated increasingly less behavior; failed to support each other more often than not; negatively evaluated each other in ways that were consistent with the guards' views of them; and as the experiment progressed, more frequently expressed intentions to do harm to others (even as they became increasingly more docile and conforming to the whims of the guards). We concluded,

> The negative, anti-social reactions observed were not the product of an environment created by combining a collection of deviant personalities, but rather the result of an intrinsically pathological situation which could distort and rechannel the behaviour of essentially normal individuals. The abnormality here resided in the psychological nature of the situation and not in those who passed through it. (Haney et al., 1973, p. 90)

In much of the research and writing we have done since then, the SPE has served as an inspiration and intellectual platform from which to extend the conceptual relevance of situational variables into two very different domains. One of us examined the coercive power of legal institutions in general and prisons in particular (e.g., Haney, 1993a, 1997b, 1997c, 1997d, 1998; Haney & Lynch, 1997), as well as the importance of situational factors in explaining and reducing crime (e.g., Haney, 1983, 1994, 1995, 1997a). The other of us explored the dimensions of intrapsychic "psychological prisons" that constrict human experience and undermine human potential (e.g., Brodt & Zimbardo, 1981; Zimbardo, 1977; Zimbardo, Pilkonis, & Norwood, 1975) and the ways in which "mind-altering" social psychological dynamics can distort individual judgment and negatively influence behavior (e.g., Zimbardo, 1979a; Zimbardo & Andersen, 1993). Because the SPE was intended as a critical demonstration of the negative effects of extreme institutional environments, much of the work that grew out of this original study was change-oriented and explored the ways in which social and legal institutions and practices might be transformed to make them more responsive to humane psychological imperatives (e.g., Haney, 1993b; Haney & Pettigrew, 1986; Haney & Zimbardo, 1977; Zimbardo, 1975; Zimbardo et al., 1974).

In this article, we return to the core issue that guided the original study (Haney et al., 1973)—the implications of situational models of behavior for criminal justice institutions. We use the SPE as a point of historical departure to briefly examine the ways in which policies concerning crime and punishment have been transformed over the intervening 25 years. We argue that a series of psychological insights derived from the SPE and related studies, and the broad perspective that they advanced, still can contribute to the resolution of many of the critical problems that currently plague correctional policy in the United States.

CRIME AND PUNISHMENT A QUARTER CENTURY AGO

The story of how the nature and purpose of imprisonment have been transformed over the past 25 years is very different from the one that we once hoped and expected we would be able to tell. At the time we conducted the SPE—in 1971—there was widespread concern about the fairness and the efficacy of the criminal justice system. Scholars, politicians, and members of the public wondered aloud whether prisons were too harsh, whether they adequately rehabilitated prisoners, and whether there were alternatives to incarceration that would better serve correctional needs and interests. Many states were already alarmed about increased levels of overcrowding. Indeed, in those days, prisons that operated at close to 90 percent of capacity were thought to be dangerously overcrowded. It was widely understood by legislators and penologists alike that under such conditions, programming resources were stretched too thin, and prison administrators were left with increasingly fewer degrees of freedom with which to respond to interpersonal conflicts and a range of other inmate problems.

Despite these concerns about overcrowding, there was a functional moratorium on prison construction in place in most parts of the country. Whatever else it represented, the moratorium reflected a genuine skepticism at some of the very highest levels of government about the viability of prison as a solution to the crime problem. Indeed, the report of the National Advisory Commission on Criminal Justice Standards and Goals (1973), published at around the same time we published the results of the SPE, concluded that prisons, juvenile reformatories, and jails had achieved what it characterized as a "shocking record of failure" (p. 597), suggested that these institutions may have been responsible for creating more crime than they prevented, and recommended that the moratorium on prison construction last at least another 10 years.

To be sure, there was a fiscal undercurrent to otherwise humanitarian attempts to avoid the overuse of imprisonment. Prisons are expensive, and without clear evidence that they worked very well, it was difficult to justify building and running more of them (cf. Scull, 1977). But there was also a fair amount of genuine concern among the general public about what was being done to prisoners behind prison walls and what the long-term effects would be (e.g., Mitford, 1973; Yee, 1973). The SPE and its attendant publicity added to that skepticism, but the real challenge came from other deeper currents in the larger society.

The late 1960s saw the beginning of a prisoners' rights movement that eventually raised the political consciousness of large numbers of prisoners, some of whom became effective spokespersons for their cause (e.g., American Friends Service Committee. 1971; Jackson, 1970; Smith, 1993). Widely publicized, tragic events in several prisons in different parts of the country vividly illustrated how prisoners could be badly mistreated by prison authorities and underscored the potentially serious drawbacks of relying on prisons as the centerpiece in a national strategy of crime control. For example, just a few weeks after the SPE was concluded, prisoners in Attica, New York, held a number of correctional officers hostage in a vain effort to secure more humane treatment. Although national celebrities attempted to peaceably mediate the standoff, an armed assault to retake the prison ended tragically with the deaths of many hostages and prisoners. Subsequent revelations about the use of excessive force and an official cover-up contributed to public skepticism about prisons and doubts about the wisdom and integrity of some of their administrators (e.g., Wicker, 1975).

Legal developments also helped to shape the prevailing national Zeitgeist on crime and punishment. More than a decade before we conducted the

SPE, the U.S. Supreme Court had defined the Eighth Amendment's ban on cruel and unusual punishment as one that drew its meaning from what Chief Justice Warren called "the evolving standards of decency that mark the progress of a maturing society" (*Trop v. Dulles,* 1958, p. 101). It is probably fair to say that most academics and other informed citizens anticipated that these standards *were* evolving and in such a way that the institution of prison—as the major organ of state-sanctioned punishment in American society—would be scrutinized carefully and honestly in an effort to apply contemporary humane views, including those that were emerging from the discipline of psychology.

Psychologists Stanley Brodsky, Carl Clements, and Raymond Fowler were engaged in just such a legal effort to reform the Alabama prison system in the early 1970s (*Pugh v. Locke,* 1976; Yackle, 1989). The optimism with which Fowler (1976) wrote about the results of that litigation was characteristic of the time: "The practice of psychology in the nation's correctional systems, long a neglected byway, could gain new significance and visibility as a result [of the courts ruling]" (p. 15). The same sentiments prevailed in a similar effort in which we participated along with psychologist Thomas Hilliard (1976) in litigation that was designed to improve conditions in a special solitary confinement unit at San Quentin (*Spain v. Procunier,* 1976). Along with other psychologists interested in correctional and legal reform, we were confident that psychology and other social scientific disciplines could be put to effective use in the creation and application of evolving standards inside the nation's prisons (see Haney & Zimbardo, 1977).

And then, almost without warning, all of this critical reappraisal and constructive optimism about humane standards and alternatives to incarceration was replaced with something else. The counterrevolution in crime and punishment began slowly and imperceptibly at first and then pushed forward with a consistency of direction and effect that could not be overlooked. It moved so forcefully and seemingly inexorably during the 1980s that it resembled nothing so much as a runaway punishment train, driven by political steam and fueled by media-induced fears of crime. Now, many years after the SPE and that early optimism about psychologically based prison reform, our nation finds itself in the midst of arguably the worst corrections crisis in U.S. history, with every indication that it will get worse before it can possibly get better. For the first time in the 200-year history of imprisonment in the United States, there appear to be no limits on the amount of prison pain the public is willing to inflict in the name of crime control (cf. Haney, 1997b, 1998). Retired judge Lois Forer (1994), in her denunciation of some of these recent trends, warned of the dire consequences of what she called the "rage to punish." But this rage has been indulged so completely that it threatens to override any of the competing concerns for humane justice that once served to make this system more compassionate and fair. The United States has entered what another commentator called the "mean season" of corrections, one in which penal philosophy amounts to little more than devising "creative strategies to make offenders suffer" (Cullen, 1995, p. 340).

THE RADICAL TRANSFORMATION OF "CORRECTIONS"

We briefly recount the series of wrenching transformations that laid the groundwork for the mean season of corrections that the nation has now entered—the some 25 years of correctional policy that have transpired since the SPE was conducted. Whatever the social and political forces that caused these transformations, they collectively altered the correctional landscape of the country. The criminal justice system not only has become increasingly harsh and punitive but also has obscured many of the psychological insights on which the SPE and numerous other empirical studies were based—insights about the power of social situations and contexts to influence and control behavior. Specifically, over a very short period of time, the following series of transformations occurred to radically change the shape and direction of corrections in the United States.

THE DEATH OF REHABILITATION

A dramatic shift in correctional philosophy was pivotal to the series of changes that followed. Almost overnight, the concept that had served as the intellectual cornerstone of corrections policy far nearly a century—rehabilitation—was publicly and politically discredited. The country moved abruptly in the mid-1970s from a society that justified putting people in prison on the basis of the belief that their incarceration would somehow facilitate their productive reentry into the free world to one that used imprisonment merely to disable criminal offenders ("incapacitation") or to keep them far away from the rest of society ("containment"). At a more philosophical level, imprisonment was now said to further something called "just deserts"—locking people up for no other reason than they deserved it and for no other purpose than to punish them (e.g., von Hirsch, 1976). In fact, prison punishment soon came to be thought of as its own reward, serving only the goal of inflicting pain.

DETERMINATE SENTENCING AND THE POLITICIZING OF PRISON PAIN

Almost simultaneously—and, in essence, as a consequence of the abandonment of rehabilitation—many states moved from indeterminate to determinate models of prison sentencing. Because indeterminate sentencing had been devised as a mechanism to allow for the release of prisoners who were rehabilitated early—and the retention of those whose in-prison change took longer—it simply did not fit with the new goals of incarceration. This shift to determinate sentencing did have the intended consequence of removing discretion from the hands of prison administrators and even judges who, studies showed, from time to time abused it (e.g., American Friends Service Committee, 1971). However, it also had the likely unintended consequence of bringing prison sentencing into an openly political arena. Once largely the province of presumably expert judicial decision makers, prison administrators, or parole authorities who operated largely out of the public view, prison sentencing had remained relatively free from at least the most obvious and explicit forms of political influence. They no longer were. Moreover, determinate sentencing and the use of rigid sentencing guidelines or "grids" undermined the role of situation and context in the allocation of punishment (cf. Freed, 1992).

THE IMPRISONING OF AMERICA

The moratorium on new prison construction that was in place at the time of the SPE was ended by the confluence of several separate, powerful forces. For one, legislators continued to vie for the mantle of "toughest on crime" by regularly increasing the lengths of prison sentences. Of course, this meant that prisoners were incarcerated for progressively longer periods of time. In addition, the sentencing discretion of judges was almost completely subjugated to the various aforementioned legislative grids, formulas, and guidelines. Moreover, the advent of determinate sentencing meant that prison administrators had no outlets at the other end of this flow of prisoners to relieve population pressures (which, under indeterminate sentencing, had been discretionary). Finally, federal district court judges began to enter judicial orders that prohibited states from, among other things, cramming two and three or more prisoners into one-person (typically six feet by nine feet) cells (e.g., *Burks* v. *Walsh*, 1978; *Capps v. Atiyeh*, 1980). Eventually even long-time opponents of new prisons agreed that prisoners could no longer be housed in these shockingly inadequate spaces and reluctantly faced the inevitable: Prison construction began on an unprecedented scale across the country.

Although this rapid prison construction briefly eased the overcrowding problem, prisoner populations continued to grow at unprecedented rates (see Table 13.1). It soon became clear that even dramatic increases in the number of new prisons could not keep pace. In fact, almost continuously over

TABLE 13.1 CHANGE IN ESTIMATED NUMBER OF SENTENCED PRISONERS, BY MOST SERIOUS OFFENSE AND RACE, BETWEEN 1985 AND 1995

Most Serious Offense	Total % change, 1985–1995	White % change, 1985–1995	Black % change, 1985–1995
Total	119	109	132
Violent offenses	86	92	83
Property offenses	69	74	65
Drug offenses	478	306	707
Public-order offenses[a]	187	162	229
Other/unspecified[b]	–6	–72	64

Note: Adapted from *Prisoners in 1996* (Bureau of Justice Statistics Bulletin NCJ 164619, p. 10), by C. J. Mumola and A. J. Beck, 1997, Rockville, MD: Bureau of Justice Statistics. In the Public domain.

[a] Includes weapons, drunk driving, escape, court offenses, obstruction, commercialized vice, morals and decency charges, liquor law violations, and other public-order offenses.
[b] Includes juvenile offenses and unspecified felonies.

the past 25 years, penologists have described U.S. prisons as "in crisis" and have characterized each new level of overcrowding as "unprecedented." As the decade of the 1980s came to a close, the United States was imprisoning more people for longer periods of time than ever before in our history, far surpassing other industrialized democracies in the use of incarceration as a crime control measure (Mauer, 1992, 1995). As of June 1997, the most recent date for which figures are available, the total number of persons incarcerated in the United States exceeded 1.7 million (Bureau of Justice Statistics, 1998), which continues the upward trend of the previous 11 years, from 1985 to 1996, when the number rose from 744,208 to 1,630,940. Indeed, 10 years ago, long before today's record rates were attained, one scholar concluded, "It is easily demonstrable that America's use of prison is excessive to the point of barbarity, with a prison rate several times higher than that of other similarly developed Western countries" (Newman, 1988, p. 346). A year later, a reviewer wrote in the pages of *Contemporary Psychology:*

> American prison and jail populations have reached historically high levels.... It is noteworthy that, although in several recent years the levels of reported crime declined, the prison and jail populations continued to rise. The desire for punishment seems to have taken on a life of its own. (McConville, 1989, p. 928)

The push to higher rates and lengths of incarceration has only intensified since then. Most state and federal prisons now operate well above their rated capacities, with many overcrowded to nearly twice their design limits. At the start of the 1990s, the United States incarcerated more persons per capita than any other modern nation in the world. The international disparities are most striking when the U.S. incarceration rate is contrasted to those of other nations with which the United States is often compared, such as Japan, The Netherlands, Australia, and the United Kingdom; throughout most of the present decade, the U.S. rates have consistently been between four and eight times as high as those of these other nations (e.g., Christie, 1994; Mauer, 1992, 1995). In fact, rates of incarceration have continued to climb in the United States, reaching the unprecedented levels of more than 500 per 100,000 in 1992 and then 600 per 100,000 in 1996. Although in 1990 the United States incarcerated a higher proportion of its population than any other nation on earth (Mauer, 1992), as of 1995, political and economic upheaval in Russia was associated with an abrupt increase in rate of incarceration, and Russia surpassed the United States....

The increase in U.S. prison populations during these years was not produced by a disproportionate increase in he incarceration of violent offenders. In 1995, only one quarter of persons sentenced to state prisons were convicted of a violent offense, whereas three quarters were sent for property or drug offenses or other nonviolent crimes such as receiving stolen property or immigration violations (Bureau of Justice Statistics, 1996). Nor was the increased use of imprisonment related to increased levels of crime. In fact, according to the National Crime Victimization Survey, conducted by the Bureau of the Census, a survey of 94,000 U.S. residents found that many fewer of them were the victims of crime during the calendar year 1995–1996, the year our incarceration rate reached an all-time high (Bureau of Justice Statistics, 1997b).

THE RACIALIZATION OF PRISON PAIN

The aggregate statistics describing the extraordinary punitiveness of the U.S. criminal justice system mask an important fact: The pains of imprisonment have been inflicted disproportionately on minorities, especially Black men. Indeed, for many years, the rate of incarceration of White men in the United States compared favorably with those in most Western European nations, including countries regarded as the most progressive and least punitive (e.g., Dunbaugh, 1979). Although in recent years the rate of incarceration for Whites in the United States has also increased and no longer compares favorably with other Western European nations, it still does not begin to approximate the rate for African Americans. Thus, although they represent less than 6 percent of the general U.S. population, African American men constitute 48 percent of those confined to state prisons. Statistics collected at the beginning of this decade indicated that Blacks were more than six times more likely to be imprisoned than their White counterparts (Mauer, 1992). By 1995, that disproportion had grown to seven and one-half times (Bureau of Justice Statistics, 1996). In fact, the United States incarcerates African American men at a rate that is approximately four times the rate of incarceration of Black men in South Africa (King, 1993).

All races and ethnic groups and both sexes are being negatively affected by the increases in the incarcerated population, but the racial comparisons are most telling. The rate of incarceration for White men almost doubled between 1985 and 1995, growing from a rate of 528 per 100,000 in 1985 to a rate of 919 per 100,000 in 1995. The impact of incarceration on African American men, Hispanics, and women of all racial and ethnic groups is greater than that for White men, with African American men being the most profoundly affected. The number of African American men who are incarcerated rose from a rate of 3,544 per 100,000 in 1985 to an astonishing rate of 6,926 per 100,000 in 1995. Also, between 1985 and 1995, the number of Hispanic prisoners rose by an average of 12 percent annually (Mumola & Beck, 1997)....

THE OVERINCARCERATION OF DRUG OFFENDERS

The increasingly disproportionate number of African American men who are being sent to prison seems to be related to the dramatic increase in the number of persons incarcerated for drug-related offenses, combined with the greater tendency to imprison Black drug offenders as compared with their White counterparts. Thus, although Blacks and Whites use drugs at approximately the same rate (Bureau of Justice Statistics, 1991), African Americans were arrested for drug offenses during the so-called war on drugs at a much higher rate than were Whites (Blumstein, 1993). The most recent data show that between 1985 and 1995, the number of African Americans incarcerated in state prisons due to drug violations (which were their only or their most serious offense) rose 707 percent (see Table 13.1b). In contrast, the number of Whites incarcerated in state prisons for drug offenses (as their only or most serious offense) underwent a 306 percent change. In 1986, for example, only 7 percent of Black prison inmates in the United States had been convicted of drug crimes, compared with 8 percent of Whites. By 1991, however, the Black percentage had more than tripled to 25 percent, whereas the percentage of White inmates incarcerated for drug crimes had increased by only half to 12 percent (Tonry, 1995). In the federal prison system, the numbers of African Americans incarcerated for drug violations are shockingly high: Fully 64 percent of male and 71 percent of female Black prisoners incarcerated in federal institutions in 1995 had been sent there for drug offenses (Bureau of Justice Statistics, 1996).

According to a historical report done for the Bureau of Justice Statistics (Cahalan, 1986), the offense distribution of federal and state prisoners—a measure of the types of crimes for which people are incarcerated—remained stable from 1910 to 1984. The classification of some offenses changed. For example, robbery is now included in the category of violent crime rather than being classified with property crimes, as it was in the past. Public order offenses, also called morals charges, used to include vagrancy, liquor law violations, and drug offenses. Drug offenses are no longer classified with public order crimes. Of course, not only contexts and communities from which minority citizens come. Remarkably, as the present decade began, there were more young Black men (between the ages of 20 and 29) under the control of the nation's criminal justice system (including probation and parole supervision) than the total number in college (Mauer, 1990). Thus, one scholar has predicted that "imprisonment will become the most significant factor contributing to the dissolution and breakdown of African American families during the decade of the 1990s" (King, 1993, p. 145), and another has concluded that "crime control policies are a major contributor to the disruption of the family, the prevalence of single parent families, and children raised without a father in the ghetto, and the 'inability of people to get the jobs still available'" (Chambliss, 1994, p. 183).

THE RISE OF THE "SUPERMAX" PRISON

In addition to becoming dangerously overcrowded and populated by a disproportionate number of minority citizens and drug offenders over the past 25 years, many U.S. prisons also now lack meaningful work, training, education, treatment, and counseling programs for the prisoners who are confined in them. Plagued by increasingly intolerable living conditions where prisoners serve long sentences that they now have no hope of having reduced through "good time" credits, due to laws imposed by state legislatures, many prison officials have turned to punitive policies of within-prison segregation in the hope of maintaining institutional control (e.g., Christie, 1994; Haney, 1993a; Haney & Lynch, 1997; Perkinson, 1994). Indeed, a penal philosophy of sorts has emerged in which prison systems use long-term solitary confinement in so-called supermax prisons as a proactive policy of inmate management. Criticized as the "Marionization" of U.S. prisons, after the notorious federal penitentiary in Marion, Illinois, where the policy seems to have originated (Amnesty International, 1987; Olivero & Roberts, 1990), one commentator referred to the "accelerating movement toward housing prisoners officially categorized as violent or disruptive in separate, free-standing facilities where they are locked in their cells approximately 23 hours per day" (Immarigeon, 1992, p. 1). They are ineligible for prison jobs, vocational training programs, and, in many states, education.

Thus, in the 25 years since the SPE was conducted, the country has witnessed the emergence of a genuinely new penal form—supermax prisons that feature state-of-the-art, ultra secure, long-term segregated confinement supposedly reserved for the criminal justice system's most troublesome or incorrigible offenders. Human Rights Watch (1997) described the basic routine imposed in such units: Prisoners "are removed from general population and housed in conditions of extreme social isolation, limited environmental stimulation, reduced privileges and service, scant recreational, vocational or educational opportunities, and extraordinary control over their every movement" (p. 14). (See also Haney, 1993a, 1997d, and Haney and Lynch, 1997, for discussions of the psychological effects of these special conditions of confinement.) By 1991, these prisons imposing extreme segregation and isolation were functioning in some 36 states, with many others in the planning stages (e.g., "Editorial," 1991). A newly opened, highly restrictive, modern "control unit" apparently committed the federal penitentiary system to the use of this penal form for some time to come (Dowker & Good, 1992; Perkinson, 1994). Thus, by 1997 Human Rights Watch expressed concern over what it called "the national trend toward supermaximum security prisons" (p. 13), noting that in addition to the 57 units currently in operation, construction programs already underway "would increase the nationwide supermax capacity by nearly 25 percent" (p. 14).

A constitutional challenge to conditions in California's supermax—one that many legal observers viewed as a test case on the constitutionality of these "prisons of the future"—resulted in a strongly worded opinion in which the federal court condemned certain of its features, suggesting that the prison, in the judge's words, inflicted "stark sterility and unremitting monotony" (*Madrid v. Gomez*, 1995, p. 1229) on prisoners and exposed them to overall conditions that "may press the outer bounds of what most humans can psychologically tolerate" (p. 1267) but left the basic regimen of segregation and isolation largely intact.

Here, too, the importance of context and situation has been ignored. Widespread prison management problems and gang-related infractions are best understood in systematic terms, as at least in large part the products of worsening overall institutional conditions. Viewing them instead as caused exclusively by "problem prisoners" who require nothing more than isolated and segregated confinement ignores the role of compelling situational forces that help to account for their behavior. It also overlooks the capacity of deteriorated prison conditions to continue to generate new replacements who will assume the roles of those prisoners who have been taken to segregation. Finally, the continued use of high levels of punitive isolation, despite evidence of significant psychological trauma and psychiatric risk (e.g., Grassian, 1983; Haney, 1997d; Haney & Lynch, 1997), reflects a legal failure to fully appreciate the costs of these potentially harmful social contexts—both in terms of immediate pain and emotional damage as well as their long-term effects on post-segregation and even post-release behavior.

THE RETREAT OF THE SUPREME COURT

The final component in the transformation of U.S. prison policy during this 25-year period came from the U.S. Supreme Court, as the Justices significantly narrowed their role in examining and correcting unconstitutionally cruel prison conditions as well as drastically redefining the legal standards that they applied in such cases. Ironically, the early constitutional review of conditions of confinement at the start of this historical period had begun on an encouraging note. Indeed, it was one of the things that helped fuel the early optimism about "evolving standards" to which we earlier referred. For example, in 1974, just three years after the SPE, the Supreme Court announced that "there is no iron curtain drawn between the Constitution and the prisons of this country" (*Wolff v. McDonnell*, 1974, pp. 556–567). Given the Warren Court's legacy of protecting powerless persons who confronted potent situations and adverse structural conditions, and the Court's legal realist tendencies to look carefully at the specific circumstances under which abuses occurred (e.g., Haney, 1991), hopes were raised in many quarters that a majority of the Justices would carefully evaluate the nation's worst prison environments, acknowledge their harmful psychological effects, and order badly needed reform.

However, a sharp right turn away from the possibility and promise of the Warren Court's view became evident at the start of the 1980s. The first time the Court fully evaluated the totality of conditions in a particular prison, it reached a very discouraging result. Justice Powell's majority opinion proclaimed that "the Constitution does not mandate comfortable prisons, and prisons...which house persons convicted of serious crimes cannot be free of discomfort" (*Rhodes v. Chapman,* 1981, p. 349). None of the Justices attempted to define the degree of acceptable discomfort that could be inflicted under the Constitution. However, Powell used several phrases that were actually taken from death penalty cases to provide a sense of just how painful imprisonment could become before beginning to qualify as "cruel and unusual": Punishment that stopped just short of involving "the *unnecessary* and *wanton* infliction of pain" (p. 345, citing *Gregg v. Georgia,* 1976, p. 173) would not be prohibited, pains of imprisonment that were not *"grossly* disproportionate to the severity of the crime" (p. 345. citing *Coker v. Georgia,* 1977, p. 592) would be allowed, and harm that was not *"totally* without penological justification" (p. 345, citing *Gregg v. Georgia,* p. 183) also would be acceptable (italics added).

The Supreme Court thus set a largely unsympathetic tone for Eighth Amendment prison cases and established a noninterventionist stance from which it has rarely ever wavered. Often turning a blind eye to the realities of prison life and the potentially debilitating psychological effects on persons housed in badly overcrowded, poorly run, and increasingly dangerous prisons, the Court developed several constitutional doctrines that both limited the liability of prison officials and further undermined the legal relevance of a careful situational analysis of imprisonment. For example, in one pivotal case, the Court decided that the notion that "overall prison conditions" somehow could produce a cruel and unusual living environment—a view that not only was psychologically straightforward but also had guided numerous lower court decisions in which overall conditions of confinement in particular prisons were found unconstitutional was simply "too amorphous" to abide any longer (*Wilson* v. *Seiter,* 1991, p. 304).

In the same case, the Court decisively shifted its Eighth Amendment inquiry from the conditions themselves to the thought processes of the officials responsible for creating and maintaining them. Justice Scalia wrote for the majority that Eighth Amendment claims concerning conduct that did not purport to be punishment required an inquiry into prison officials' state of mind in this case, their "deliberate indifference" (*Wilson v. Seiter,* 1991). Justice Scalia also had rejected a distinction between short-term deprivations and "continuing" or "systemic" problems of the sort that might have made state of mind less relevant. The argument here had been that evidence of systemic problems would obviate the need to demonstrate state of mind on the part of officials who had presumably known about and tolerated them as part of the correctional status quo. Scalia said instead that although the long duration of a cruel condition might make it easier to establish knowledge and, hence, intent, it would not eliminate the intent requirement.

Prison litigators and legal commentators criticized the decision as having established a constitutional hurdle for conditions of confinement claims that was "virtually insurmountable" and speculated that the impossibly high threshold "reflects recent changes in public attitudes towards crime and allocation of scarce public resources" (Hall, 1993, p. 208). Finally, in 1994, the Court seemed to raise the hurdle to a literally insurmountable level by explicitly embracing the criminal law concept of "subjective recklessness" as the Eighth Amendment test for deliberate indifference (*Farmer v. Brennan,* 1994). In so doing, the Court shunned the federal government's concern that the new standard meant that that triers of fact would first have to find that "prison officials acted like criminals" before finding them liable (*Farmer v. Brennan,* 1994, p. 1980).

This series of most recent cases has prompted commentators to speculate that the Supreme Court is "headed toward a new hands-off doctrine in correctional law" (Robbins, 1993, p. 169) that would require lower courts "to defer to the internal actions and decisions of prison officials" (Hall, 1993, p. 223). Yet, the narrow logic of these opinions suggests that the Justices intend to keep not only their hands off the faltering prison system but their eyes averted from the realities of prison life as well. It is difficult to avoid the conclusion that the Court's refusal to examine the intricacies of day-to-day existence in those maximum security prisons whose deteriorated and potentially harmful conditions are placed at issue is designed to limit the liability of those who create and run them.

Unfortunately, the U.S. Supreme Court was not the only federal governmental agency contributing to this retreat from the meaningful analysis of conditions of confinement inside the nation's prisons and jails. In April 1996, the U.S. Congress passed legislation titled the Prison Litigation Reform Act (PLRA) that significantly limited the ability of the federal courts to monitor and remedy constitutional violations in detention facilities throughout the country. Among other things, it placed substantive and procedural limits on injunctions and consent decrees (where both parties reach binding agreements to fix existing problems in advance of trial) to improve prison conditions. The PLRA also impeded the appointment of "special masters" to oversee prison systems' compliance with court orders and appeared to forbid the filing of legal actions by prisoners for mental or emotional injury without a prior showing of physical injury. Although the full impact of this remarkable legislation cannot yet be measured, it seems to have been designed to prevent many of the problems that have befallen U.S. prisons from ever being effectively addressed. Combined with the Supreme Court's stance concerning prison conditions, the PLRA will likely contribute to the growing tendency to avoid any meaningful contextual analysis of the conditions under which many prisoners are now confined and also to a growing ignorance among the public about the questionable utility of prison as a solution to the nation's crime problem.

RESPONDING TO THE CURRENT CRISIS: SOME LESSONS FROM THE STANFORD PRISON EXPERIMENT

Where has this series of transformations left the U.S. criminal justice system? With startling speed, national prison policy has become remarkably punitive, and correspondingly, conditions of confinement have dramatically deteriorated in many parts of the country. These transformations have been costly in economic, social, and human terms. At the beginning of the present decade, a stark fact about governmental priorities was reported: "For the first time in history, state and municipal governments are spending more money on criminal justice than education" (Chambliss, 1994, p. 183). In California, the corrections budget alone has now surpassed the state's fiscal outlays for higher education (e.g., Butterfield, 1995; Jordan, 1995). Despite this historic shift in expenditures and the unprecedented prison construction that took place during the past 25 years, many commentators still lament what has been referred to as the "national scandal of living conditions in American prisons" (Gutterman, 1995, p. 373). As we have noted and one reviewer recently observed, "For over a decade, virtually every contemporary commentary on corrections in the United States has reminded us that the system [is] in crisis" (Cullen, 1995, p. 338).

The dimensions of this crisis continue to expand and do not yet reflect what promises to be an even more significant boost in prison numbers—the effects of recently passed, so-called three-strikes legislation that not only mandates a life sentence on a third criminal conviction but, in some states, also doubles the prison sentence for a second criminal conviction and reduces existing good-time provisions for every term (so that all prisoners actually are incarcerated for a longer period of time). This three-strikes legislation was written and rapidly passed into law to capitalize on the public's fear of violent crime (Haney, 1994, 1997b). Despite the fact that the crime rate in the United States has been declining for some time in small but steady increments, many of these bills were written in such a way as to cast the widest possible net—beyond violent career criminals (whom most members of the public had in mind)—to include nonviolent crimes like felony drug convictions and minor property offenses. As a consequence, a disproportionate number of young Black and Hispanic men are likely to be imprisoned for life under scenarios in which they are guilty of little more than a history of untreated addiction and several prior drug-related offenses. The mandate to create lifetime incarceration for so many inmates under circumstances where overcrowding precludes their participation in meaningful programs, treatment, and other activities is likely to raise the overall level of prisoners' frustration, despair, and violence. States will absorb the staggering cost of not only constructing additional prisons to accommodate increasing numbers of prisoners who will never be released but also warehousing them into old age (Zimbardo, 1994).

Remarkably, the radical transformations we have described in the nation's penal policy occurred with almost no input from the discipline of psychology. Correctional administrators, politicians, policymakers, and judicial decision makers not only ignored most of the lessons that emerged from the SPE but also disregarded the insights of a number of psychologists who preceded us and the scores of others who wrote about, extended, and elaborated on the same lessons in empirical studies and theoretical pieces published over the past several decades. Indeed, there is now a vast social science literature that underscores, in various ways, the critical importance of situation and context in influencing social behavior, especially in psychologically powerful situations like prisons. These lessons, insights, and literature deserve to be taken into account as the nation's prison system moves into the next century.

Here then is a series of propositions derived or closely extrapolated from the SPE and the large body of related research that underscores the power of situations and social context to shape and transform human behavior. Each proposition argues for the creation of a new corrections agenda that would take us in a fundamentally different direction from the one in which we have been moving over the past quarter century.

First, the SPE underscored the degree to which prison environments are themselves powerful, potentially damaging situations whose negative psychological effects must be taken seriously, carefully evaluated, and purposefully regulated and controlled. When appropriate, these environments must be changed or (in extreme cases) eliminated. Of course, the SPE demonstrated the power of situations to overwhelm psychologically normal, healthy people and to elicit from them unexpectedly cruel, yet "situationally appropriate" behavior. In many instances during our study, the participants' behavior (and our own) directly contravened personal value systems and deviated dramatically from past records of conduct. This behavior was elicited by the social context and roles we created, and it had painful, even traumatic consequences for the prisoners against whom it was directed.

The policy implications of these observations seem clear. For one, because of their harmful potential, prisons should be deployed very sparingly in the war on crime. Recognition of the tendency of prison environments to become psychologically damaging also provides a strong argument for increased and more realistic legal and governmental oversight of penal institutions in ways that are sensitive to and designed to limit their potentially destructive impact. In addition, it argues in favor of significantly revising the allocation of criminal justice resources to more seriously explore, create, and evaluate: humane alternatives to traditional correctional environments.

Second, the SPE also revealed how easily even a minimalist prison could become painful and powerful. By almost any comparative standard, ours was an extraordinarily benign prison. None of the guards at the "Stanford Prison" were armed, and there were obvious limits to the ways in which they could or would react to prisoners' disobedience, rebellion, or even escape. Yet, even in this minimalist prison setting, all of our "guards" participated in one way or another in the pattern of mistreatment that quickly developed. Indeed, some escalated their definition of "role-appropriate" behavior to become highly feared, sadistic tormentors. Although the prisoners' terms of incarceration were extremely abbreviated (corresponding, really, to very short-term pretrial detention in a county jail), half of our prisoner-participants left before the study was terminated because they could not tolerate the pains of this merely simulated imprisonment. The pains were as much psychological feelings of powerlessness, degradation, frustration, and emotional distress—as physical—sleep deprivation, poor diet, and unhealthy living conditions. Unlike our participants, of course, many experienced prisoners have learned to suppress such outward signs of psychological vulnerability lest they be interpreted as weakness, inviting exploitation by others.

Thus, the SPE and other related studies demonstrating the power of social contexts teach a lesson about the way in which certain situational conditions can interact and work in combination to produce a dehumanizing whole that is more damaging than the sum of its individual institutional parts. Legal doctrines that fail to explicitly take into account and formally consider the totality of these situational conditions miss this psychological point. The effects of situations and social contexts must be assessed from the perspective of those within them. The experiential perspective of prison inmates—the meaning of the prison experience and its effects on them—is the most useful starting point for determining whether a particular set of prison conditions is cruel and unusual. But a macroexperiential perspective does not allow for the parsing of individual factors or aspects of a situation whose psychological consequences can then be separately assessed. Thus, legal regulators and the psychological experts who assist them also must be sensitive to the ways in which different aspects of a particular situation interact and aggregate in the lives of the persons who inhabit total institutions like prisons as well as their capacity to produce significant effects on the basis of seemingly subtle changes and modifications that build up over time. In contexts such as these, there is much more to the "basic necessities of life" than "single, identifiable human need[s] such as food, warmth or exercise" (*Wilson v. Seiter,* 1991, p. 304). Even if this view is "too amorphous" for members of the current Supreme Court to appreciate or apply, it is the only psychologically defensible approach to assessing the effects of a particular prison and gauging its overall impact on those who live within its walls.

In a related vein, recent research has shown how school children can develop maladjusted, aggressive behavior patterns based on initially marginal deviations from other children that get amplified in classroom interactions and aggregated over time until they become manifested as "problem children" (Caprara & Zimbardo, 1996). Evidence of the same processes at work can be found in the life histories of persons accused and convicted of capital crime (Haney, 1995). In similar ways, initially small behavioral problems and dysfunctional social adaptations by individual prisoners may become amplified and aggravated over time in prison settings that require daily interaction with other prisoners and guards.

Recall also that the SPE was purposely populated with young men who were selected on the basis of their initial mental and physical health and normality, both of which, less than a week later, had badly deteriorated. Real prisons use no such selection procedures. Indeed, one of the casualties of severe overcrowding in many prison systems has been that even rudimentary classification decisions based on the psychological makeup of entering cohorts of prisoners are forgone (see Clements, 1979, 1985). Pathology that is inherent in the structure of the prison situation is likely given a boost by the pathology that some prisoners and guards bring with them into the institutions themselves. Thus, although ours was clearly a study of the power of situational characteristics, we certainly acknowledge the value of interactional models of social and institutional behavior. Prison systems should not ignore individual vulnerabilities in attempting to optimize institutional adjustment, minimize behavioral and psychological problems, understand differences in institutional adaptations and capacities to survive, and intelligently allocate treatment and other resources (e.g., Haney & Specter, in press).

Third, if situations matter and people can be transformed by them when they go into prisons, they matter equally, if not more, when they come out of prison. This suggests very clearly that programs of prisoner change cannot ignore situations and social conditions that prevail after release if they are to have any hope of sustaining whatever positive gains are achieved during periods of imprisonment and lowering distressingly high recidivism rates. Several implications can be drawn from this observation. The first is that prisons must more routinely use transitional or "decompression" programs that gradually reverse the effects of the extreme environments in which convicts have been confined. These programs must be aimed at preparing prisoners for the radically different situations that they will enter in the free world. Otherwise, prisoners who were ill-prepared for job and social situations before they entered prison become more so over time, and the longer they have been imprisoned, the more likely it is that rapid technological and social change will have dramatically transformed the world to which they return.

The SPE and related studies also imply that exclusively individual-centered approaches to crime control (like imprisonment) are self-limiting and doomed to failure in the absence of other approaches that simultaneously and systematically address criminogenic situational and contextual factors. Because traditional models of rehabilitation are person-centered and dispositional in nature (focusing entirely on individual-level change), they typically have ignored the post-release situational factors that help to account for discouraging rates of recidivism. Yet, the recognition that people can be significantly changed and transformed by immediate situational conditions also implies that certain kinds of situations in the free world can override and negate positive prison change. Thus, correctional and parole resources must be shifted to the transformation of certain criminogenic situations in the larger society if ex-convicts are to meaningfully and effectively adapt. Successful post-release adjustment may depend as much on the criminal justice system's ability to change certain components of an ex-convict's situation *after* imprisonment—helping to get housing, employment, and drug or alcohol counseling for starters—as it does on any of the positive rehabilitative changes made by individual prisoners during confinement itself.

This perspective also underscores the way in which long-term legacies of exposure to powerful and destructive situations, contexts, and structures means that prisons themselves can act as criminogenic agents—in both their primary effects on prisoners and secondary effects on the lives of persons connected to them—thereby serving to increase rather than decrease the amount of crime that occurs within a society. Department of corrections data show that about a fourth of those initially imprisoned for nonviolent crimes are sentenced a second time for committing a violent offense. Whatever else it reflects, this pattern highlights the possibility that prison serves to transmit violent habits and values rather than to reduce them. Moreover, like many of these lessons, this one counsels policymakers to take the full range of the social and economic costs of imprisonment into account in calculations that guide long-term crime control strategies. It also argues in favor of incorporating the deleterious effects of prior terms of incarceration into at least certain models of legal responsibility (e.g., Haney, 1995).

Fourth, despite using several valid personality tests in the SPE, we found that we were unable to predict (or even postdict) who would behave in what ways and why (Haney et al., 1973). This kind of failure underscores the possibility that behavioral prediction and explanation in extreme situations like prisons will be successful only if they are approached with more situationally sensitive models than are typically used. For example, most current personality trait measures ask respondents to report on characteristic ways of responding in familiar situations or scenarios. They do not and cannot tap into reactions that might occur in novel, extreme, or especially potent situations—like the SPE or Milgram's (1974) obedience paradigm—and thus have little predictive value when extrapolated to such extreme cases. More situationally sensitive models would attend less to characteristic ways of behaving in typical situations and more to the characteristics of the particular situations in which behavior occurs. In prison, explanations of disciplinary infractions and violence would focus more on the context in which they transpired and less on the prisoners who engaged in them (e.g., Wenk & Emrich, 1972; Wright, 1991). Similarly, the ability to predict the likelihood of reoffending and the probability of repeated violent behavior should be enhanced by conceptualizing persons as embedded in a social context and rich interpersonal environment, rather than as abstract bundles of traits and proclivities (e.g., Monahan & Klassen, 1982).

This perspective has implications for policies of crime control as well as psychological prediction. Virtually all sophisticated, contemporary accounts of social behavior now acknowledge the empirical and theoretical significance of situation, context, and structure (e.g., Bandura, 1978, 1991; Duke, 1987; Ekehammar, 1974; Georgoudi & Rosnow, 1985; Mischel, 1979; Veroff, 1983). In academic circles at least, the problems of crime and violence—formerly viewed in almost exclusively individualistic terms—are now understood through multilevel analyses that grant equal if not primary significance to situational, community, and structural variables (e.g., Hepburn, 1973; McEwan & Knowles, 1984; Sampson & Lauritsen, 1994; Toch, 1985). Yet, little of this knowledge has made its way into prevailing criminal justice policies. Lessons about the power of extreme situations to shape and transform behavior—independent or in spite of preexisting dispositions—can be applied to contemporary strategies of crime control that invest more substantial resources in transforming destructive familial and social contexts rather than concentrating exclusively on reactive; policies that target only individual lawbreakers (cf. Masten & Garmezy, 1985; Patterson, DeBaryshe, & Ramsey, 1989).

Fifth, genuine and meaningful prison and criminal justice reform is unlikely to be advanced by persons who are themselves "captives" of powerful correctional environments. We learned this lesson in a modest but direct way when in the span of six short days in the SPE, our own perspectives were radically altered, our sense of ethics, propriety, and humanity temporarily suspended. Our experience with the SPE underscored the degree to which institutional settings can develop a life of their own, independent of the wishes, intentions, and purposes of those who run them (Haney & Zimbardo, 1977). Like all powerful situations, real prisons transform the worldviews of those who inhabit them, on both sides of the bars. Thus, the SPE also contained the seeds of a basic but important message about prison reform—that good people with good intentions are not enough to create good prisons. Institutional structures themselves must be changed to meaningfully improve the quality of prison life (Haney & Pettigrew, 1986).

Indeed, the SPE was an "irrational" prison whose staff had no legal mandate to punish prisoners who, in turn, had done nothing to deserve their mistreatment. Yet, the "psychologic" of the environment was more powerful than the benign intentions or predispositions of the participants. Routines develop; rules are made and applied, altered and followed without question; policies enacted for short-term convenience become part of the institutional status quo and difficult to alter; and unexpected events and emergencies challenge existing resources and compromise treatment in ways that persist long after the crisis has passed. Prisons are especially vulnerable to these common institutional dynamics because they are so resistant to external pressures for change and even rebuff outside attempts at scrutinizing their daily operating procedures.

These observations certainly imply that the legal mechanisms supposedly designed to control prison excesses should not focus exclusively on the intentions of the staff and administrators who run the institution but would do well to look instead at the effects of the situation or context itself in shaping their behavior (cf. *Farmer v. Brennan*, 1994). Harmful structures do not require ill-intentioned persons to inflict psychological damage on those in their charge and can induce good people with the best of intentions to engage in evil deeds (Haney & Zimbardo, 1977; Zimbardo, 1979a). "Mechanisms of moral disengagement" distance people from the ethical ambiguity of their actions and the painful consequences of their deeds, and they may operate with destructive force in many legal and institutional contexts, facilitating cruel and unusual treatment by otherwise caring and law-abiding persons (e.g., Bandura, 1989; Browning, 1993; Gibson, 1991; Haney, 1997c).

In addition, the SPE and the perspective it advanced also suggest that prison change will come about only when those who are outside of this powerful situation are empowered to act on it. A society may be forced to presume the categorical expertise of prison officials to run the institutions with which they have been entrusted, but this presumption is a rebuttable one. Moreover, to depend exclusively on those whose perspectives have been created and maintained by these powerful situations to, in turn, transform or control them is shortsighted and psychologically naive. This task must fall to those with a different logic and point of view, independent of and free from the forces of the situation itself. To be sure, the current legal retreat to hands-off policies in which the courts defer to the presumably greater expertise of correctional officials ignores the potency of prison settings to alter the judgments of those charged with the responsibility of running them. The SPE and much other research on these powerful environments teach that this retreat is terribly ill-advised.

Finally, the SPE implicitly argued for a more activist scholarship in which psychologists engage with the important social and policy questions of the day. The implications we have drawn from the SPE argue in favor of more critically and more realistically evaluating the nature and effect of imprisonment and developing psychologically informed limits to the amount of prison pain one is willing to inflict in the name of social control (Haney, 1997b, 1998). Yet, this would require the participation of social scientists willing to examine these issues, confront the outmoded models and concepts that guide criminal justice practices, and develop meaningful and effective alternatives. Historically, psychologists once contributed significantly to the intellectual framework on which modern corrections was built (Haney, 1982). In the course of the past 25 years, they have relinquished voice and authority in the debates that surround prison policy. Their absence has created an ethical and intellectual void that has undermined both the quality and the legitimacy of correctional practices. It has helped compromise the amount of social justice our society now dispenses.

CONCLUSION

When we conducted the SPE 25 years ago, we were, in a sense, on the cutting edge of new and developing situational and contextual models of behavior. Mischel's (1968) pathbreaking review of the inadequacy of conventional measures of personality traits to predict behavior was only a few years old, Ross and Nisbett (1991) were assistant professors who had not yet written about situational control as perhaps the most important leg in the tripod of social psychology, and no one had yet systematically applied the methods and theories of modern psychology to the task of understanding social contextual origins [of] crime and the psychological pains of imprisonment. Intellectually, much has changed since then. However, without the renewed participation of psychologists in debates over how best to apply the lessons and insights of their discipline to the problems of crime and punishment, the benefits from these important intellectual advances will be self-limiting. It is hard to imagine a more pressing and important task for which psychologists have so much expertise but from which they have been so distanced and uninvolved than the creation of more effective and humane criminal justice policies. Indeed, politicians and policymakers now seem to worship the very kind of institutional power whose adverse effects were so critically evaluated over the past 25 years. They have premised a vast and enormously expensive national policy of crime control on models of human nature that are significantly outmoded. In so doing, they have faced little intellectual challenge, debate, or input from those who should know better.

So, perhaps it is this one last thing that the SPE stood for that will serve the discipline best over the next 25 years. That is, the interrelated notions that psychology can be made relevant to the broad and pressing national problems of crime and justice, that the discipline can assist in stimulating badly needed social and legal change, and that scholars and practitioners can improve these policies with sound data and creative ideas. These notions are as germane now, and needed more, than they were in the days of the SPE. If they can be renewed, in the spirit of those more optimistic times, despite having lost many battles over the past 25 years, the profession still may help win the more important war. There has never been a more critical time at which to begin the intellectual struggle with those who would demean human nature by using prisons exclusively as agencies of social control that punish without attempting to rehabilitate, that isolate and oppress instead of educating and elevating, and that tear down minority communities rather than protecting and strengthening them.

STUDY QUESTIONS

1. Did the Supreme Court's stance change regarding prison policy over the 25-year period covered by this article? If yes, in what ways?
2. What appear to have been the main differences between the Stanford Prison Experiment "prison" and a real prison? In what ways might these differences be beneficial regarding what was revealed by the research?
3. Of all the changes in prison and/or sentencing policy that have occurred over the 25-year period that is covered by this article, which do you think have affected the prison system the most? Why?
4. For what reasons did the prison system see a huge influx of drug offenders?
5. For what reasons do you think the American prison system gave rise to the "supermax" facility? What do you see as the major benefits of the supermax facility, if any? What do you see as the major detriments of the supermax facility?

Editor's note. Melissa G. Warren served as action editor for this article.

Author's note. Craig Haney, Department of Psychology, University of California, Santa Cruz; Philip Zimbardo, Department of Psychology, Stanford University. We would like to acknowledge our colleague and coinvestigator in the original Stanford Prison Experiment, W. Curtis Banks, who died last year. We also acknowledge the assistance of Marc Mauer and The Sentencing Project... [who] helped us locate other sources of information, and Sandy Pisano, librarian at the Arthur W. Melton Library, who helped compile some of the data that appear in the table.

Correspondence concerning this article should be addressed to Craig Haney, Department of Psychology, University of California, Santa Cruz, CA 95064. Electronic mail may be sent to psylaw@cats.ucsc.edu. Readers interested in the corrections system may contact the American Psychology-Law Society or Psychologists in Public Service, Divisions 41 and 18, respectively, of the American Psychological Association.

REFERENCES

American Friends Service Committee. (1971). *Struggle for justice: A report on crime and punishment.* New York: Hill & Wang.

Amnesty International. (1987). *Allegations of mistreatment in Marion Prison, Illinois, USA.* New York: Author.

Bandura, A. (1978). The self system in reciprocal determinism. *American Psychologist, 33,* 344–358.

Bandura, A. (1989). Mechanisms of moral disengagement In W. Reich (Ed.), *Origins of terrorism: Psychologies, ideologies, theologies, states of mind* (pp. 161–191). New York: Cambridge University Press.

Bandura, A. (1991). Social cognitive theory of moral thought and action. In W. Kurtines & J. Gewirtz (Eds.), *Handbook of moral behavior and development: Vol 1. Theory* (pp. 45–102). Hillsdale, NJ: Erlbaum.

Blumstein, A. (1993). Making rationality relevant—The American Society of Criminology 1992 Presidential Address. *Criminology, 31,* 1–16.

Brodt, S., & Zimbardo, P. (1981). Modifying shyness-related social behavior through symptom misattribution. *Journal of Personality and Social Psychology, 41,* 437–449.

Browning, C. (1993). *Ordinary men: Reserve Police Battalion 101 and the final solution in Poland.* New York: Harper Perennial.

Bureau of Justice Statistics. (1991). *Sourcebook of criminal justice statistics.* Washington, DC: U.S. Department of Justice.

Bureau of Justice Statistics. (1996). *Sourcebook of criminal justice statistics, 1996.* Washington, DC: U.S. Department of Justice.

Bureau of Justice Statistics. (1997a, May). *Correctional populations in the United States, 1995* (NCJ 163916). Rockville, MD: Author.

Bureau of Justice Statistics. (1997b, November). *Criminal victimization 1996: Changes 1995–96 with trends 1993–96* (Bureau of Justice Statistics Bulletin NCJ 165812). Rockville, MD.

Bureau of Justice Statistics. (1998, January 18). *Nation's prisons and jails hold more than 1.7 million: Up almost 100,000 in a year* [Press release]. Washington, DC: U.S. Department of Justice.

Burks v. Walsh, 461 F. Supp. 934 (W.D. Missouri 1978).

Butterfield, F. (1995, April 12). New prisons cast shadow over higher education. *'The New York Times,* p. A21.

Cahalan, M. W. (1986, December). *Historical corrections statistics in the United States, 1850–1984* (Bureau of Justice Statistics Bulletin NCJ 102529). Rockville, MD: Bureau of Justice Statistics.

Capps v. Atiyeh, 495 F. Supp. 802 (D. Ore. 1980).

Caprara, G., & Zimbardo, P. (1996). Aggregation and amplification of marginal deviations in the social construction of personality arid maladjustment. *European Journal of Personality, 10,* 79–110.

Carr, S. (1995). Demystifying the Stanford Prison Study. *The British Psychological Society Social Psychology Section Newsletter, 33,* 31–34.

Chambliss, W. (1994). Policing the ghetto underclass: The politics of law and law enforcement. *Social Problems, 41,* 177–194.

Christie, N. (1994). *Crime control as industry: Towards gulags, Western style?* (2nd ed.). London: Routledge.

Clements, C. (1979). Crowded prisons: A review of psychological and environmental effects. *Law and Human Behavior, 3,* 217–225.

Clements, C. (1985). Towards an objective approach to offender classification. *Law & Psychology Review, 9,* 45–55.

Coker v. Georgia, 433 U.S. 584, 592 (1977).

Cullen, F. (1995). Assessing the penal harm movement. *Journal of Research in Crime and Delinquency 32,* 338–358.

Dowker, F., & Good, G. (1992). From Alcatraz to Marion to Florence, In W. Churchill & J. J. Vander Wall (Eds.) *Cages of steel: The politics of imprisonment in the United, States* (pp. 131–151). Washington, DC: Maisonneuve Press.

Duke, M. (1987). The situational stream hypothesis: A unifying view of behavior with special emphasis on adaptive and maladaptive personality patterns. *Journal of Research in Personality, 21,* 239– 263.

Dunbaugh, F. (1979). Racially disproportionate rates of incarceration in the United States. *Prison Law Monitor, 1,* 205–225.

Editorial: Inside the super-maximum prisons. (1991, November 24). *The Washington Post,* p. C6.

Ekehammar, B. (1974). Interactionism in personality from a historical perspective. *Psychological Bulletin, 81,* 1026–1048.

Farmer v. Brennan, 114 S. Ct. 1970 (1994).

Forer, L. (1994). *A rage to punish: The unintended consequences of mandatory sentencing.* New York: Norton.

Fowler, R. (1976). Sweeping reforms ordered in Alabama prisons. *APA Monitor, 7,* pp. 1, 15.

Freed, D. (1992). Federal sentencing in the wake of guidelines: Unacceptable limits on the discretion of sentences. *Yale Law Journal, 101,* 1681–1754.

Georgoudi, M., & Rosnow, R. (1985). Notes toward a contextualist understanding of social psychology. *Personality and Social Psychology Bulletin, 11,* 5–22.

Gibson, J. (1991). Training good people to inflict pain: State terror and social learning. *Journal of Humanistic Psychology, 31,* 72–87.

Grassian, S. (1983). Psychopathological effects of solitary confinement. *American Journal of Psychiatry, 140,* 1450–1454.

Gregg v. Georgia, 428 U.S. 153, 173 (1976) (joint opinion).

Gutterman, M. (1995). The contours of Eighth Amendment prison jurisprudence: Conditions of confinement. *Southern Methodist University Law Review, 48,* 373–407.

Hall, D. (1993). The Eighth Amendment, prison conditions, and social context. *Missouri Law Review, 58,* 207–236.

Haney, C. (1976). The play's the thing: Methodological notes on social simulations. In P. Golden (Ed.), *The research experience* (pp. 177–190). Itasca, IL: Peacock.

Haney, C. (1982). Psychological theory and criminal justice policy: Law and psychology in the "Formative Era." *Law and Human Behavior, 6,* 191–235.

Haney, C. (1983). The good, the bad, and the lawful: An essay on psychological injustice. In W. Laufer & J. Day (Eds.), *Personality theory, moral development, and criminal behavior* (pp. 107–117). Lexington, MA: Lexington Books.

Haney, C. (1991). The Fourteenth Amendment and symbolic legality: Let them eat due process. *Law and Human Behavior, 15,* 183–204.

Haney, C. (1993a). Infamous punishment: The psychological effects of isolation. *National Prison Project Journal, 8,* 3–21.

Haney, C. (1993b). Psychology and legal change: The impact of a decade. *Law and Human Behavior, 77,* 371–398.

Haney, C. (1994, March 3). Three strikes for Ronnie's kids, now Bill's. *Los Angeles Times,* p. B7.

Haney, C. (1995). The social context of capital murder: Social histories and the logic of mitigation. *Santa Clara Law Review, 35,* 547–609.

Haney, C. (1997a). Psychological secrecy and the death penalty: Observations on "the mere extinguishment of life." *Studies in Law, Politics, and Society, 16,* 3–68.

Haney, C. (1997b). Psychology and the limits to prison pain: Confronting the coming crisis in Eighth Amendment law. *Psychology, Public Policy, and Law, 3,* 499–588.

Haney, C. (1997c). Violence and the capital jury: Mechanisms of moral disengagement and the impulse to condemn to death. *Stanford Law Review, 46,* 1447–1486.

Haney, C. (1997d). The worst of the worst: Psychological trauma and psychiatric symptoms in punitive segregation. Unpublished manuscript, University of California, Santa Cruz.

Haney, C. (1998). *Limits to prison pain: Modern psychological theory and rational crime control policy.* Washington, DC: American Psychological Association.

Haney, C., Banks, W., & Zimbardo, P. (1973). Interpersonal dynamics in a simulated prison.

International Journal of Criminology and Penology, 1, 69–97.

Haney, C., & Lynch, M. (1997). Regulating prisons of the future: A psychological analysis of supermax and solitary confinement. *New York Review of Law and Social Change, 23*, 101–195.

Haney, C., & Pettigrew, T (1986). Civil rights and institutional law: The role of social psychology in judicial implementation. *Journal of Community Psychology, 14*, 267–277.

Haney, C., & Specter, D. (in press). Legal considerations in treating adult and juvenile offenders with special needs. In J. Ashford, B. Sales, & W. Reid (Eds.), *Treating adult and juvenile offenders with special needs.* Washington, DC: American Psychological Association.

Haney, C., & Zimbardo, P. (1977). The socialization into criminality: On becoming a prisoner and a guard. In J. Tapp & F. Levine (Eds.), *Law, justice, and the individual in society: Psychological and legal issues* (pp. 198–223). New York: Holt, Rinehart & Winston.

Hepburn, J. (1973). Violent behavior in interpersonal relationships. *Sociological Quarterly, 14*, 419–429.

Hilliard, T. (1976). The Black psychologist in action: A psychological evaluation of the Adjustment Center environment at San Quentin Prison. *Journal of Black Psychology, 2*, 75–82.

Human Rights Watch. (1997). *Cold storage: Super-maximum security confinement in Indiana.* New York: Author.

Immarigeon, R. (1992). The Marionization of American prisons. *National Prison Project Journal, 7(4)*, 1–5.

Jackson, G. (1970). *Soledad brother: The prison letters of George Jackson.* New York: Coward-McCann.

Jordan, H. (1995, July 8). '96 budget favors prison over college; "3 strikes" to eat into education funds. *San Jose Mercury News*, p. 1A.

King, A. (1993). The impact of incarceration on African American families: Implications for practice. Families in Society. *The Journal of Contemporary Human Services, 74*, 145–153.

Madrid v. Gomez, 889 F. Supp. 1146 (N.D. Cal. 1995).

Maguire, K, & Pastore, A. (Eds.). (1997). *Sourcebook of criminal justice statistics 1996* (NCJ 165361). Washington, DC: U.S. Government Printing Office.

Masten, A., & Garmezy, N. (1985). Risk, vulnerability and protective factors in developmental psychopathology. In F. Lahey & A. Kazdin (Eds.), *Advances in clinical child psychology* (pp. 1–52). New York: Plenum.

Mauer, M. (1990). *More young Black males under correctional control in US than in college.* Washington, DC: The Sentencing Project.

Mauer, M. (1992). Americans behind bars: A comparison of international rates of incarceration. In W. Churchill & J. J. Vander Wall (Eds.), *Cages of steel: The politics of imprisonment in the United States* (pp. 22–37). Washington, DC: Maisonneuve Press.

Mauer, M. (1995). The international use of incarceration. *Prison Journal, 75*, 113–123.

Mauer, M. (1997, June). *Americans behind bars: U.S. and international use of incarceration, 1995.* Washington, DC: The Sentencing Project.

McConville, S. (1989). Prisons held captive. *Contemporary Psychology, 34*, 928–929.

McEwan, A., & Knowles, C. (1984). Delinquent personality types and the situational contexts of their crimes. *Personality & Individual Differences, 5*, 339–344.

Milgram, S. (1974). *Obedience to authority: An experimental view.* New York: Harper & Row.

Miller, G. (1980). Giving psychology away in the '80s. *Psychology Today, 13*, 38ff.

Mischel, W. (1968). *Personality and assessment.* New York: Wiley.

Mischel, W. (1979). On the interface of cognition and personality: Beyond the person-situation debate. *American Psychologist, 34*, 740–754.

Mitford, J. (1973). *Kind and usual punishment: The prison business.* New York: Knopf.

Monahan, J., & Klassen, D. (1982). Situational approaches to understanding and predicting individual violent behavior. In M. Wolfgang & G. Weiner (Eds.), *Criminal violence* (pp. 292–319). Beverly Hills, CA: Sage.

Mumola, C. J., & Beck, A. J. (1997, June). *Prisoners in 1996* (Bureau of Justice Statistics Bulletin NCJ 164619). Rockville, MD: Bureau of Justice Statistics.

National Advisory Commission on Criminal Justice Standards and Goals. (1973). *Task force report on corrections.* Washington, DC: U.S. Government Printing Office.

Newman, G. (1988). Punishment and social practice: On Hughes's The Fatal Shore. *Law and Social Inquiry, 13,* 337–357.

Olivero, M., & Roberts, J. (1990). The United States Federal Penitentiary at Marion, Illinois: Alcatraz revisited. *New England Journal of Criminal and Civil Confinement, 16,* 21–51.

Patterson, G., DeBaryshe, B., & Ramsey, E. (1989). A developmental perspective on antisocial behavior. *American Psychologist, 44,* 329–335.

Perkinson, R. (1994). Shackled justice: Florence Federal Penitentiary and the new politics of punishment. *Social Justice, 21,* 117–132.

Pugh v. Locke, 406 F. Supp. 318 (1976).

Rhodes v. Chapman, 452 U.S. 337 (1981).

Robbins, I. (1993). The prisoners' mail box and the evolution of federal inmate rights. *Federal Rules Decisions, 114,* 127–169.

Ross, L., & Nisbett, R. (1991). *The person and the situation: Perspectives of social psychology.* New York: McGraw-Hill.

Sampson, R., & Lauritsen, J. (1994). Violent victimization and offending: Individual-, situational-, and community-level risk factors. In A. Reiss, Jr. & J. Roth (Eds.), *Understanding and preventing violence: Vol. 3. Social influences* (pp. 1–114). Washington, DC: National Research Council, National Academy Press.

Sandin v. Conner, 115 S. Ct. 2293 (1995).

Scull, A. (1977). *Decarceration: Community treatment and the deviant: A radical view.* Englewood Cliffs, NJ: Prentice Hall.

Smith, C. (1993). Black Muslims and the development of prisoners' rights. *Journal of Black Studies, 24,* 131–143.

Spain v. Procunier, 408 F. Supp. 534 (1976), affd in part, rev'd in part, 600 F.2d 189 (9th Cir. 1979).

Toch, H. (1985). The catalytic situation in the violence equation. *Journal of Applied Social Psychology, 15,* 105–123.

Tonry, M. (1995). *Malign neglect: Race, crime, and punishment in America.* New York: Oxford University Press.

Trop v. Dulles, 356 U.S. 86 (1958).

Veroff, J. (1983). Contextual determinants of personality. *Personality and Social Psychology Bulletin, 9,* 331–343.

von Hirsch, A. (1976). *Doing justice: The choice of punishment.* New York: Hill & Wang.

Wenk, E., & Emrich, R (1972). Assaultive youth: An exploratory study of the assaultive experience and assaultive potential of California Youth Authority wards. *Journal of Research in Crime & Delinquency, 9,* 171–196.

Wicker, T. (1975). *A time to die.* New York: New York Times Books.

Wilson v. Seiter, 501 U.S. 294 (1991).

Wolff v. McDonnell, 418 U.S. 554, 556—557 (1974).

Wright, K. (1991). The violent and victimized in the male prison. *Journal of Offender Rehabilitation, 16,* 1–25.

Yackle, L. (1989). Reform and regret: The story of federal judicial involvement in the Alabama prison system. New York: Oxford University Press.

Yee, M. (1973). *The melancholy history of Soledad Prison.* New York: Harper's Magazine Press.

Zimbardo, P. (1973). On the ethics of intervention in human psychological research: With special reference to the Stanford Prison Experiment. *Cognition, 2,* 243–256.

Zimbardo, P. (1975). On transforming experimental research into advocacy for social change. In M. Deutsch & H. Hornstein (Eds.), *Applying social psychology: Implications for research, practice, and training* (pp. 33–66). Hillsdale, NJ: Erlbaum.

Zimbardo, P. G. (1977). *Shyness: What it is and what to do about it.* Reading, MA: Addison-Wesley.

Zimbardo, P. G. (1979a). The psychology of evil: On the perversion of human potential. In T. R. Sarbin (Ed.), *Challenges to the criminal justice system: The perspective of community psychology* (pp. 142–161). New York: Human Sciences Press.

Zimbardo, P. G. (1979b). Testimony of Dr. Philip Zimbardo to U.S. House of Representatives Committee on the Judiciary. In J. J. Bonsignore et al. (Eds.), *Before the law: An introduction to the legal process* (2nd ed., pp. 396–399). Boston: Houghton Mifflin.

Zimbardo, P. G. (1994). *Transforming California's prisons into expensive old age homes for felons: Enormous hidden costs and consequences for California's taxpayers*. San Francisco: Center on Juvenile and Criminal Justice.

Zimbardo, P. G., & Andersen, S. (1993). Understanding mind control: Exotic and mundane mental manipulations. In M. Langone (Ed.), *Recover from cults: Help for victims of psychological and spiritual abuse* (pp. 104–125). New York: Norton.

Zimbardo, P. G., Haney, C., Banks, C., & Jaffe, D. (1974). The psychology of imprisonment: Privation, power, and pathology. In Z. Rubin (Ed.), *Doing unto others: Explorations in social behavior* (pp. 61–73). Englewood Cliffs, NJ: Prentice Hall.

Zimbardo, P. G., Pilkonis, P. A., & Norwood, R. M. (1975, May). The social disease called shyness. *Psychology Today, 72*, 69–70.

14
THE SUPREME COURT AND PRISONERS' RIGHTS

JACK E. CALL

The highest court in the United States, through the rendering of various decisions (or by choosing not to intervene), has set the tone for many aspects of prison operations. The relationship between the U.S. Supreme Court and the conditions within prisons has been dynamic, particularly over the past 40 years. The author presents a comprehensive summary of numerous landmark cases within prisoner litigation that have been argued before the Supreme Court. Three periods are identified, each of which is characterized by the overall position that the Court appeared to take when confronted with prisoners' rights and the constitutionality of prison conditions. In broad terms, the Supreme Court adhered to a hands-off doctrine prior to the mid-1960s, followed by a prisoners' rights period until 1978, during which a propensity to intervene on several fronts occurred. This prisoners' rights period was followed by a deference period, indicating the Court's desire to place more power and discretion, and the administration of the prisons themselves, into the hands of the lower courts. In addition to detailing these three eras of Supreme Court decision making, the author also highlights many additional cases classified into several areas concerning specific rights. For example, important cases pertaining to access to the court itself, individual rights, due process, and cruel and unusual punishment are reviewed. This chapter offers the reader the opportunity to gain a broad understanding of the most important cases in prisoner litigation, as well as a chance to glean a historical perspective.

As substantive areas of the law go, the law of prisoners' rights is still in its infancy. Until the 1960's, the courts largely stayed out of this area. The movement away from this abstention was led by the lower Federal courts. In the late 1960's, however, the United States Supreme Court began to involve itself as well. Since then, the Supreme Court has decided more than 30 cases dealing with the rights of the incarcerated. Surprisingly, there has been very little scholarly attention paid to the efforts of the Supreme Court *as a whole* in this area. This article attempts to fill in some of this gap in the literature on prisoners' rights. It examines the Supreme Court case law from two perspectives: chronologically and by major subject area.

A CHRONOLOGICAL PERSPECTIVE

Historically, the Supreme Court case law on prisoners' rights can be divided into three periods: (1) the Hands-Off Period (before 1964), (2) the Rights Period (1964–78), and (3) the Deference Period (1979–present).

THE HANDS-OFF PERIOD (BEFORE 1964)

Before the 1960s, courts (including the Supreme Court) did not involve themselves in the issue of prisoners' rights. Initially, this stance was the result of a legal approach that held that prisoners were slaves of the state. Upon conviction, criminals lost virtually all legal rights. Any rights they had were not the rights shared with other citizens, but those rights which the state chose to extend to them.

Ruffin v. Commonwealth[1] illustrates this approach. In rejecting Ruffin's contention that the Virginia Constitution required that he be tried in his home county for a crime he committed while in prison, the Virginia Court of Appeals indicated that

> [t]he bill of rights is a declaration of general principles to govern a society of free men, and not of convicted felons and men civilly dead. Such men have some rights it is true, such as the law in its benignity accords to them, but not the rights of free men. They are the slaves of the State undergoing punishment for heinous crimes committed against the laws of the land.

In time, this convict-as-slave approach gave way to an abstention approach. The courts during this period recognized that prisoners did retain constitutional rights, but it was not the role of the courts to intervene to protect those rights. Instead, courts saw the legislative and executive branches as having responsibility for identifying and honoring the constitutional rights of inmates.

There are several reasons given typically to explain this abstention approach by the courts.[2] First, the courts perceived that to intervene in these matters would be to usurp the proper functions of the legislative and executive branches of government. Second, and somewhat related to the separation of powers concern just mentioned, was a belief by the courts that they lacked the expertise to become involved in these matters. Because of their lack of understanding of the operation of prisons, if courts took steps to protect prisoners' rights, they ran a great risk of interfering with the proper functioning of the institutions.

Third, most prisoners are housed in state prisons. If they sought protection of their rights in Federal courts, these courts felt that their intervention intruded upon the proper functioning of a Federal system of government. And last, most courts, although they seldom said so explicitly, seemed to fear that if they acted to protect prisoners' rights the courts would experience a flood of frivolous lawsuits from prisoners.

As with most of the generalizations that will be made about these historic periods in prisoners' rights, there are exceptions to the generalization that courts declined to intervene on behalf of prisoners during the hands-off period. For example, the Supreme Court held in 1941 that the states could not require inmates to submit formal legal documents to state officials for review and approval before filing those papers with the courts.[3] Nevertheless, such instances of judicial recognition of rights held by prisoners were isolated.

THE RIGHTS PERIOD (1964–78)

In the early 1960s, lower Federal courts began moving away from the hands-off approach. They demonstrated an increasing willingness to identify rights of prisoners found in the Constitution and to protect those rights. This change in approach is attributed to several factors.[4]

First, prisoners, perhaps reflecting society as a whole at the time, became more militant and aggressive in asserting their rights. Second, the legal profession developed a cadre of "public interest lawyers" who were willing to take on these cases, either pro bono or with financial support from government and private foundation grants. Third, the judiciary as a whole seemed to become more responsive to the legal arguments advanced by politically disadvantaged groups. Fourth, judges were often presented with cases that involved such horrible conditions of confinement that they cried out for some sort of remedial action.

And last, two developments in Federal law created a more favorable environment for prisoners' rights cases in the Federal courts. The first development involved interpretation of the Civil Rights Statute (42 U.S.C. Section 1983), a post-Civil War law. Lawsuits brought under this statute are commonly referred to as Section 1983 suits. Section 1983 permits a person whose rights under

Federal law are violated by a person acting "under color of state law" to sue for damages or some sort of remedial order.

Before 1961, the accepted interpretation of Section 1983 was that a state official who acted in violation of state law was not acting "under color" of state law. In *Monroe v. Pape,*[5] the Supreme Court rejected this prior interpretation as being inconsistent with the desire of Congress to provide relief for persons whose constitutional rights were violated by state and local government officials, even when their actions were not officially approved. This change in the interpretation of Section 1983 enabled prisoners to file their suits complaining of rights violations in Federal courts, where it was generally thought that they would receive a more sympathetic hearing than in state courts.

The second development in Federal law concerned the Supreme Court's interpretation of the Due Process Clause of the 14th amendment, another post-Civil War provision. The Due Process Clause prohibits a *state* from depriving persons of life, liberty, or property without due process of law. Through a long process called Selective Incorporation that began in the 1920's and picked up a full head of steam in the 1960's, the Supreme Court ruled that the Due Process Clause "incorporated" most of the rights contained in the Bill of Rights into the 14th amendment.

This meant that state and local governments had to extend to persons under their jurisdiction most of the rights in the first 10 amendments to the Constitution, such as free speech, freedom of religion, right to counsel, right against self-incrimination, right against unreasonable searches and seizures, and many others. Thus, one's constitutional rights, the violation of which by state and local officials could result in a Section 1983 lawsuit, became more extensive.

In due course, the Supreme Court itself jumped on the prisoners' rights bandwagon, although somewhat inconspicuously at first. In three of its first four prisoners' rights cases, the Court issued per curiam decisions. These are unsigned decisions (i.e., no particular Justice is identified as the opinion's author) usually affirming the decision of the lower court without hearing oral argument and without explaining the Court's reasons for affirming.

In the first of these cases, *Cooper v. Pate,*[6] the Court held unanimously that a state prison inmate could bring a Section 1983 suit alleging that his freedom of religion was violated by the prison's refusal to permit him to purchase certain religious material. Four years later, in *Lee v. Washington,*[7] the Court again unanimously upheld a lower court's order to Alabama to desegregate its prisons and jails, although three Justices concurred in a brief opinion expressing their belief that the Court's decision should not be viewed as prohibiting corrections officials from taking racial tensions into account in their decisionmaking. Then in 1971, in *Younger v. Gilmore,*[8] the Court again unanimously upheld a lower court decision that required a prison to provide inmates an adequate law library.

Sandwiched in between *Lee* and *Younger* in 1969 was the Court's first full opinion venture into prisoners' rights, *Johnson v. Avery.*[9] Johnson was a "writ writer," an inmate who assisted other inmates in preparing legal papers challenging their convictions. He was disciplined by prison authorities for engaging in this activity. The Court held that, "unless and until the State provides some reasonable alternative to assist inmates in the preparation of petitions for post-conviction relief,"[10] it could not constitutionally prohibit inmates from functioning as jailhouse lawyers. This case is important, not only because it was the Court's first prisoners' rights case in over 25 years with a full written opinion, but also because it ruled in favor of the inmate and thereby established the general tone of its cases during the Rights Period.

In two cases the Court upheld the first amendment rights of a prisoner. In *Cruz v. Beto* (1972),[11] the Court held that a prison could not prevent a Buddhist inmate from using the prison chapel, from corresponding with religious advisors, and from distributing religious materials to other inmates, if the prison permitted inmates of other faiths to engage in these same activities.

In *Procunier v. Martinez* (1974),[12] the Court found that prisons could not censor outgoing mail that was viewed by prison authorities as expressing "inflammatory" views, unduly complaining, or "otherwise inappropriate." These standards were too broad and failed to exclude only material that posed a legitimate threat to institutional interests.

If mail was censored (under constitutionally acceptable standards), the inmate sending the mail has to be notified and given an opportunity to object to some official who was not involved in the original censorship decision. Although the Court based this holding on the first amendment rights of the correspondent outside the prison, its effect, of course, was to protect inmates as well.

In a Due Process case, the Court ruled in *Wolff v. McDonnell* (1974)[13] that inmates had a liberty interest in good time credits.[14] Good time credits could not be denied without holding a hearing before which an accused inmate was given notice of the alleged infraction, at which the inmate was given the opportunity to call witnesses and present documentary evidence (unless allowing either would be "unduly hazardous to institutional safety or correctional goals"), and after which the prison would issue a written statement of the reasons for its action and the evidence relied upon in coming to its decision.

The Court issued several rulings upholding the right of inmates to access the courts. The Court ruled in *Wolff* that the *Avery* rule, protecting the status of writ writers when other provisions for legal assistance have not been made, applied to writ writers who were assisting other inmates in the preparation of Section 1983 suits (and was not limited to assisting with habeas corpus petitions).

In *Martinez*, the Court also struck down a prison rule that prohibited visits from employees (other than two licensed investigators) of lawyers who were representing inmates. The clear effect of this rule was to inhibit inmates' ability to access the courts because the rule made it more difficult for attorneys to communicate in person with their clients.

In 1977, in *Bounds v. Smith*,[15] the Court examined the adequacy of the law libraries established by North Carolina for its inmates. Although the Court upheld the adequacy of the libraries, it made it clear that the state was indeed required by the Constitution to establish law libraries to assist inmates in their efforts to petition the courts unless the state provided inmates with adequate assistance from persons trained in the law. And finally, in an eighth amendment case, *Hutto v. Finney* (1978),[16] the Court held that, given the harsh conditions of punitive isolation cells in the Arkansas prison system, inmates could not be placed constitutionally in those cells for more than 30 days.

While these cases demonstrated a willingness by the Court to support the rights of prisoners, there were issues during the Rights Period on which inmates did not receive favorable rulings from the Court. In *Wolff*, the Court refused to extend the rights of counsel, confrontation, and cross-examination to the good time hearings that it required in that case. The Court also indicated that in adopting a rule that mail from attorneys could be opened by the prison in the presence of the inmate receiving the mail, the prison "had done all, and perhaps even more" than the Constitution requires.

In *Pell v. Procunier* (1974),[17] the Court upheld a California prison regulation which prohibited the press from interviewing *individual* inmates. However, it seemed important to the Court's decision that the press was permitted to visit and observe conditions in the prisons and to interview inmates at random.

In *Meachum v. Fano* (1976),[18] the Court held that inmates had no liberty interest under the Due Process Clause in avoiding transfer to another prison where conditions were harsher because such a transfer was "within the normal limits or range of custody" which the conviction authorizes the state to impose. What's more, it makes no difference whether the transfer is simply for administrative reasons, as in *Meachum*, or is for disciplinary reasons, as was the case in *Montanye v. Haymes*.[19]

In *Baxter v. Palmigiano*,[20] decided the same year as *Meachum* and *Montanye*, the Court held that an inmate's right against self-incrimination is not violated if the inmate's refusal to answer questions at a disciplinary hearing is held against him at the hearing. (Note, however, that inmates *do* have a constitutional right not to answer questions at the hearing that would tend to incriminate them, unless they are granted immunity for the statements they are compelled to give.) In *Baxter*, the Court also held that prisons do not have to give reasons for denying an inmate's request to call a witness at the disciplinary hearing, do not have to permit cross-examination of witnesses, and in making their disciplinary decisions may rely upon evidence not presented at the hearing.

Also in 1976, in *Estelle v. Gamble*,[21] the Court held that an inmate cannot prove that inadequate medical care by the prison is cruel and unusual punishment unless he can also prove that prison officials were deliberately indifferent to a serious medical need of the inmate. The next year, in *Jones v. N.C. Prisoners' Labor Union*,[22] the Court concluded that prisons may ban meetings of prisoners' unions, as well as prohibit the unions from soliciting members and from making bulk mailings to members.

It should be clear from a careful consideration of these cases decided during the Rights Period that the Court was not engaged in a prisoners' rights revolution. In many instances it decided that the rights of inmates had to give way to the legitimate needs of the prisons to maintain security, control inmate behavior, and attempt to rehabilitate inmates. Nevertheless, what is most remarkable about the Rights Period is the Court's willingness, first, to recognize that inmates retain constitutional rights and, second, to view those rights as being nearly as important as the legitimate needs of the prisons.

THE DEFERENCE PERIOD (1979–PRESENT)

The year 1979 was chosen to begin the period that I have labeled the Deference Period because that was the year the Supreme Court decided *Bell v. Wolfish*.[23] The *Court* resolved five issues in that case and ruled against the inmates on all of them. It held that cells of 75 square feet that had been double-bunked were not so overcrowded as to constitute punishment under the Due Process Clause. It also upheld jail rules that: (1) permitted inmates to receive hardback books only if they came directly from the publisher, a bookstore, or a book club (publishers' only rule), (2) prohibited inmates from receiving packages from outside the jail, (3) prohibited inmates from observing shakedown searches of their cells, and (4) subjected inmates to visual body cavity searches after contact visits.

In ruling against the inmates, the Court set the tone for the Deference Period. During this period, inmates would lose on most prisoners' rights issues before the Court, which would stress the need to give deference to the expertise of corrections officials. The Court applauded the judicial trend away from the traditional hands-off approach and the willingness of courts to intervene where institutions were characterized by "deplorable conditions and draconian restrictions." However, the Court followed with this caution:

> But many of these same courts have, in the name of the Constitution, become increasingly enmeshed in the minutiae of prison operations. Judges, after all, are human. They, no less than others in our society, have a natural tendency to believe that their individual solutions to often intractable problems arc better and more workable than those of the persons who are actually charged with and trained in the running of the particular institution under examination. But under the Constitution, the first question to be answered is not whose plan is best, but in what branch of the Government is lodged the authority to initially devise the plan. This does not mean that constitutional rights are not to be scrupulously

> observed. It does mean, however, that the inquiry of federal courts into prison management must be limited to the issue of whether a particular system violates any prohibition of the Constitution.... The wide range of "judgment calls" that meet constitutional... requirements are confined to officials outside of the Judicial Branch of Government.[24]

In another overcrowding case in 1981, *Rhodes v. Chapman*,[25] the Court held that double-bunking was not unconstitutional per se and that double-bunking of cells of 63 square feet without a showing of specific harmful effects on inmates was not cruel and unusual punishment.[26] As in *Wolfish*, the Court admonished judges that they "cannot assume that state legislatures and prison officials are insensitive to the requirements of the Constitution...."

Several times during this period, the Court held that actions taken against inmates by corrections officials did not affect a liberty interest of inmates and were therefore not subject to the protections of the Due Process Clause. The Court held that an inmate had no liberty interest in: (1) a decision by the Board of Commutation as to whether to commute a life sentence, even though the Board granted 75 percent of all petitions for commutation from lifers and those lifers receiving commutation nearly always were paroled earlier than they would have been otherwise (*Connecticut Board of Pardons v. Dumschat*, 1981[27]); (2) the overturning of an early parole decision, even though the parole board changed its mind because of information it received about dishonesty on the part of the inmate (*Jago v. Van Curen*, 1981[28]); (3) a decision to transfer an inmate to a prison in another state (*Olim v. Wakinekona*, 1983[29]); and (4) a decision to exclude visitors because of alleged misconduct on their part (*Kentucky v. Thompson*, 1989[30]).

Even in two cases where the Court held that inmates had a liberty interest (*Greenholtz v. Nebraska Penal Inmates*, 1979,[31] and *Hewitt v. Helms*, 1983[32]), it was only because state law had specified conditions under which adverse action could be taken against inmates and provided that this action could be taken only when the specified conditions were found to exist. *Greenholtz* involved the decision whether to grant parole, and *Hewitt* involved whether to place an inmate in administrative segregation. In another important due process decision, the Court ruled in *Superintendent v. Hill* that a decision of a prison administrative body should be upheld when challenged in court if there is "some evidence" in the record to support the decision.[33]

The Court also ruled against inmates in two search cases during this period. In *Hudson v. Palmer*,[34] the Court held that the fourth amendment does not apply to cell searches (even a shakedown search with no reason to think contraband will be found) because inmates have no reasonable expectation of privacy in their cells. The Court also concluded that inmates have no due process right to observe shakedown searches of their cells (*Block v. Rutherford*, 1984[35]).

Inmates also lost several first amendment issues during the Deference Period. In *Block*, the Court rejected an argument that pretrial detainees who were judged by jail officials to be low security risks and who had been in jail more than a month had a constitutional right to *contact* visits. The Court held that it was reasonable for the jail to ban contact visits to prevent contraband from being smuggled in.

In *Turner v. Safley* (1987),[36] the Court held that a prison rule which prohibited inmates from corresponding with inmates in other prisons was constitutional. The Court viewed this regulation as a reasonable way to protect prison security, since the correspondence that was banned could have been used to communicate escape plans or to encourage assaults on other inmates.

O'Lone v. Shabazz (1987)[37] dealt with the right of inmates to practice their religion. Shabazz was a Muslim who was not permitted to observe Jumu'ah services in the prison on Friday afternoons (the only lime that Jumu'ah may be observed) because his security classification required him to be on a work detail outside the prison. The Court held that the prison did not have to permit Shabazz to return to the prison for the service because that would have created a security risk. Nor did the prison have to allow Shabazz to stay in the prison all day Friday and then let him make up the work on Saturday because that would require additional prison resources. Thus, the prison's actions in denying Shabazz the opportunity to observe Jumu'ah were reasonable in light of the security and resources needs of the prison.

In *Thornburgh v. Abbott* (1989),[38] the Court dealt with the authority of prisons to exclude publications that are mailed to inmates. The rule at issue permitted wardens in Federal prisons to exclude publications (although only on an issue-by-issue basis) that they deemed to be "detrimental to the security, good order, or discipline of the institution, or... [that] might facilitate criminal activity." Publications could not be excluded because they expressed unpopular views or were religious, political, social, or sexual in nature.

The Court found that this regulation was reasonable in light of the prisons' need to maintain security. It distinguished this case from *Procunier v. Martinez,* where the Court had struck down a prison censorship regulation as too broad, on the basis that *Martinez* dealt with incoming mail and this case dealt with outgoing mail. The Court believed that outgoing mail posed greater threats to prison security.

In another case involving an individual right, the Court concluded in *Washington v. Harper* that a mentally ill inmate could, after a hearing, be treated with antipsychotic drugs against his will.[39] Although the Court found that the inmate did have a liberty interest in not being administered the drug, it also found that the policy of involuntary treatment is permissible because it is reasonably related to the prison's interest in controlling the violent behavior of such an inmate.

Inmates also lost three important eighth amendment issues. In *Whitley v. Albers* (1986),[40] an inmate sued a prison guard who had wounded him in the knee during an inmate uprising, alleging that the shooting was cruel and unusual punishment. The inmate alleged that he had not been involved in the uprising, had assured the prison security chief that he would protect from harm a guard that other inmates had taken hostage, and had made no threatening moves just before being shot.

The Court ruled that, in cruel and unusual punishment cases where the government action at issue is not part of the sentence awarded the prisoner, the prisoner must prove that prison officials acted wantonly. In the context of a prison disturbance, that means the inmate must show that officials acted "maliciously and sadistically for the very purpose of causing harm." In this case, according to the Court, the inmate had failed to allege facts from which such a state of mind could be inferred.

In *Wilson v. Seiter* (1991),[41] the Court again addressed the issue of the state of mind necessary to prove a violation of the Cruel and Unusual Punishment Clause in the prison context. This time, rather than dealing with a discreet act against an individual inmate, as had been the case in *Estelle* and *Whitley,* the Court dealt with allegations that the general conditions of confinement in an overcrowded prison were cruel and unusual punishment.

The Court concluded that general conditions of confinement are not part of the sentence awarded a convicted defendant. Therefore, it is necessary to prove that, in permitting overcrowded conditions to persist, prison officials acted wantonly, otherwise officials have not acted with intent to punish inmates. Where general conditions of confinement are at issue, inmates must show that prison officials acted with deliberate [in]difference to some basic human need of the inmates.

The Court also clarified a point that lower courts had dealt with for some [time]. Lower courts had frequently held that the totality of adverse conditions in an institution violated the eighth amendment. The Court rejected this approach. While it conceded that two or more conditions might have a "mutually enforcing effect," the eighth amendment has not been violated unless there is evidence that the effect has been to deprive inmates "of a single, identifiable human need such as food, warmth, or exercise." The Court indicated that interaction of conditions in this way "is a far cry from saying that all prison conditions are a seamless web for Eighth Amendment purposes."

Then in *Farmer v. Brennan* (1994),[42] the Court gave some definition to what it meant by deliberate indifference. After stating the fairly obvious, that deliberate indifference is something more than mere negligence but something less than a specific intent to cause harm to a particular inmate or inmates, the Court concluded that deliberate indifference means recklessness. The Court also recognized that while both civil (tort) law and criminal law utilize the concept of recklessness, their definitions are somewhat different. Tort law usually views recklessness as action "in the face of an unjustifiably high risk of harm that is either known or so obvious that it should be known." This is sometimes referred to as an objective approach to recklessness.

The criminal law, on the other hand, usually takes a subjective approach, requiring that an actor be aware of a disregarded risk. Thus, the difference between the two definitions is that tort law recklessness includes disregard of a risk of which an actor was unaware but should have been aware, while criminal law recklessness does not.

The Court decided that the subjective criminal law approach to recklessness is the one required by the eighth amendment. Although the Court went to some length to explain its reasoning for adopting this approach, in the final analysis it appears that the majority felt that it was simply fairer to hold prison officials responsible only for those risks of which they are actually aware.

In these Deference Period cases discussed so far, the inmates not only lost the case, but often the Court articulated a rule that seems to make it likely that inmates will have a difficult time winning prisoners' rights suits in the future as well.[43] Nevertheless, prisoners experienced a few successes during this period. For example, in the Due Process area, the Court concluded in *Vitek v. Jones* (1980)[44] that inmates have a liberty interest in the decision as to whether to transfer a prisoner to a mental hospital. Even if the state had not used mandatory language that prohibited such a transfer unless there is a finding that the inmate suffers from a mental illness which cannot be treated adequately in the prison, the Court found that the stigmatization of transfer to a mental hospital, coupled with the prospect of subjection to mandatory behavior modification, constitutes the kind of liberty deprivation that is protected by the Due Process Clause itself. We also saw earlier that the Court ruled that mentally ill inmates have a liberty interest in avoiding, involuntary treatment with antipsychotic drugs.[45]

Inmates also won two cases involving eighth amendment issues. In *Hudson v. McMillian* (1992), an inmate sued a guard who had beaten him and caused facial swelling, loosened teeth, a cracked dental plate, and minor bruises, but no permanent injury. The government argued that in order for a harm experienced from the use of excessive force to be sufficient to constitute cruel and unusual punishment, the force had to cause significant injury. The Court rejected this argument, finding that excessive use of force on inmates always violates contemporary standards of decency and therefore violates the eighth amendment.

The Court also concluded that the state of mind standard in all excessive force cases (and not just cases involving prison disturbances, as in *Whitley*) is the malice standard established in *Whitley*. While this can be seen as a loss for inmates, the Court did rule that the guard's use of force in this case was malicious.[46]

In *Helling v. McKinney* (1993),[47] McKinney complained that he had been placed involuntarily in a cell with another inmate who smoked five packs of cigarettes a day. McKinney contended that exposure to this smoke demonstrated deliberate indifference to his health. The prison argued that McKinney failed to meet the objective aspect of his eighth amendment claim because he failed to allege that he had suffered any harm. The Court held that cruel and unusual punishment could be demonstrated by proof of exposure to conditions that "pose an unreasonable risk of serious damage to [plaintiff's] future health." Thus, the harm that must be shown in an eighth amendment case can be either a present harm or an unreasonable risk of a future harm.

The final inmate victory during the Deference Period involved a first amendment issue. We saw earlier that the Court, in applying its rational basis test in *Safley*, upheld a prohibition on inmate correspondence with inmates in other prisons. However, it also concluded in that case that the prison's ban on inmate marriages was not reasonably related to penological interests. It viewed the marriage ban as an exaggerated response to the prison's concern for security and rehabilitation of inmates. This ruling was especially significant in light of the fact that a prison survey taken in 1978 indicated that most prisons did not permit inmate marriages.[48]

The Deference Period witnessed many triumphs for prisons. The common denominator in these cases is the Court's concern that prison officials be permitted to do their difficult jobs without undue interference from the courts. In other words, courts should generally defer to the judgment of corrections officials.

A SUBSTANTIVE ASSESSMENT OF SUPREME COURT LAW ON PRISONERS' RIGHTS

How can we assess the current state of this expanding body of Supreme Court case law? The following discussion examines the four major substantive areas that have been addressed most frequently by the Court's cases: (1) right to access the courts, (2) individual rights, (3) due process issues, and (4) cruel and unusual punishment. The overall conclusion is that Supreme Court cases tend to favor inmates with respect to their right to access the courts and tend to favor the prisons in the other three areas.

RIGHT TO ACCESS THE COURTS

It is in this area that the Court has been most protective of prisoners. The Court has made it clear that prisons must either provide inmates with an adequate law library or provide them adequate assistance from persons who have been legally trained.[49] If they opt to provide a law library, they must permit inmates to assist other inmates in the preparation of legal papers.[50] This assistance extends not only to preparation of writs of habeas corpus (attacking the legality of an inmate's conviction), but also includes preparation of civil rights actions (which would typically challenge some aspect of the inmate's conditions of confinement).[51]

If the prison opts to provide legal assistance to inmates rather than a law library, or if an inmate has engaged a lawyer, the institution must have reasonable regulations concerning visitation by employees of the lawyer. A rule that prohibits anyone employed by a lawyer (such as paralegals), other than two licensed investigators, from visiting the prisoner who has engaged the lawyer places an unconstitutional burden on a prisoner's right to access the courts.[52]

Of course, there are many unanswered questions about the right of inmates to access the courts. What restrictions can a prison place on inmates desiring to use a prison law library? What restrictions may be placed on opportunities for a writ writer to consult with the inmate that he is assisting? What is an *adequate* law library? Must institutions provide inmates with paper supplies and notary services?

These unanswered questions and dozens of others like them give the Court ample opportunity to limit the scope of the right of access to the courts. It is worth noting that the Court has not decided an issue in this area since 1977. It may be that the reason why the Court appears to be rather supportive of inmates' rights of access is because it did not address any issues in this area during the present Deference Period.

INDIVIDUAL RIGHTS

The Court's initial efforts in this area suggested that it was going to be rather protective of inmates. In two of its first individual prisoners' rights cases, the Court indicated that members of "minority" religious groups, at least if the number of members is significant, must be permitted to engage in the same kinds of religious activities as members of other, more common religious groups[53] and that rules governing the censorship and withholding of mail from inmates to persons outside the prison would be subjected to close scrutiny by the Court.[54]

It is this latter holding and the Court's subsequent treatment of it that is of greatest significance in this area. Generally, when the Court identifies an individual right as particularly important (or "fundamental"), any actions taken by government which impinge upon that right are subjected to heightened scrutiny by the courts. This means that in deciding whether the government action is constitutional, the government will have to demonstrate that it had a compelling reason for doing what it did, that what it did was necessary in light of this compelling government need, and that government had available to it no means of carrying out its purpose that would have had less impact on the rights of individuals.

It appeared from the Court's opinion in *Procunier v. Martinez* that it intended to take this approach, or one similar to it, in assessing the actions of prisons that adversely affected the individual rights of prisoners. In several later cases involving individual rights of prisoners, the Court ruled against the inmates without a very clear discussion of whether it was using a heightened scrutiny approach.

Then in 1987 in *Turner v. Safley,* the Court made it clear that it was *not* going to use a heightened scrutiny approach in individual rights cases. In its review of prison regulations prohibiting inmate marriages and inmate correspondence with inmates in other prisons, the Court reviewed all its prisoners' rights cases and concluded that these cases had used a rational basis test. The Court stated emphatically that "when a prison regulation impinges on inmates' constitutional rights, the regulation is valid if it is reasonably related to legitimate penological interests."[55]

This approach is usually referred to as the rational basis test. It is a much easier standard for the government to satisfy than the heightened scrutiny approach. Under the rational basis test, the burden is shifted to the party whose rights have allegedly been violated to demonstrate that the government had no rational reason for doing what it did or that, if it did have a rational reason, what it did was not reasonably related to it.

In *Safley,* the Court also established four factors that should be considered in assessing the reasonableness of a prison regulation that impinges upon an individual right of an inmate: (1) whether there is a rational connection between the prison regulation and the legitimate governmental interest put forward to justify it, (2) whether an alternative means of exercising the right exists in spite of what the prison has done, (3) whether striking down the prison's action would have a significant ripple effect on fellow inmates or staff, and (4) whether there are ready alternatives available to the prison or whether the regulation appears instead to be [an] "exaggerated response" to the problem it is intended to address.

The Court has utilized these four factors in determining the constitutionality of the two regulations at issue in *Safley,* the regulation in *Shabazz* that prevented Muslim inmates from participating in Jumu'ah, and the publishers-only regulation in *Thornburgh.* Although the Court did strike down the ban on inmate marriages, it upheld the other three regulations. More importantly, its application of the four *Safley* factors suggests that prisons should not experience great difficulty in satisfying them.

The right of inmates to be free from unreasonable searches and seizures is an individual right that is not affected directly by the rational basis test. However, the Court has engaged in a somewhat similar analysis by comparing the needs of prisons to maintain discipline and security with the interest of prisoners in privacy and finding consistently that the prisoners' interests are outweighed by the prisons' interests. Thus, inmates have no reasonable expectation of privacy in their cells,[56] inmates who have had contact visits may be subjected to visual body cavity inspections even in the absence of any reason to think that the inspections will turn up evidence,[57] and inmates have no right to observe shakedown searches of their cells.[58] It seems apparent that when prisons take actions that adversely affect the individual rights of inmates, those actions will be upheld by the Court unless they are clearly unreasonable.

DUE PROCESS ISSUES

Of the four substantive areas with which Supreme Court prisoners' rights [cases] have dealt most frequently, it is in the area of Due Process rights that the Court has spoken with least clarity. The Due Process Clauses (in the 5th and 14th amendments) raise two basic questions: (1) When is a person entitled to due process of law? (2) When a person is so entitled, what process is due?

In the prison context, the answer to the first question has arisen in the context of actions taken against an inmate. Such actions include (but are certainly not limited to) loss of good time credits, a decision not to grant parole, transfer to a mental hospital, transfer to a less desirable prison, removal to solitary confinement, and denial of a visitor. Since these actions do not deprive an inmate of life or property, the question is whether the inmate has been deprived of a liberty interest in these situations.

The Court has indicated that prisoners acquire liberty interests from one of two sources: (1) the Constitution itself and (2) by creation of state law. The Court has been far from clear as to what kind of interest is a liberty interest protected by the Constitution itself. The Court has indicated that not every "change in the conditions of confinement having a substantial adverse impact on the prisoner involved is sufficient...."[59] Instead, a liberty interest arises when the action taken by the prison is not "within the terms of confinement ordinarily contemplated by a prison sentence."[60]

Unfortunately, this phrase does not carry us very far toward a clear conception of when an inmate has a constitutionally protected liberty interest. What *is* clear is that there are very few such liberty interests. The Court has indicated that denial of a visit from a particular person,[61] granting of parole,[62] commutation of a life sentence,[63] transfer to a prison with less favorable conditions of confinement,[64] transfer to a prison in another state,[65] and transfer to administrative segregation[66] are not such liberty interests. The only liberty interest protected by the Due Process Clause and arising directly under the Constitution which the Court has found that inmates possess is an interest in not being transferred to a mental hospital.[67]

The second source of a liberty interest is by creation of state law. This kind of liberty interest is created when state law provides that a particular action may not be taken against an inmate (what the Court has called "mandatory language") unless certain conditions exist (what the Court has called "specific substantive predicates"). For example, if state law indicates that an inmate may not be placed in administrative segregation unless there is a demonstrated "need for control" or "the threat of a serious disturbance," then it has specified the conditions under which the transfer may occur and prohibited transfer for any other reasons.[68] Consequently, it has created a liberty interest. Determination of the existence of this kind of liberty interest will be very case specific, turning on the particular language used in a particular law or regulation.

In these Due Process cases, the inmate cannot argue that the Due Process Clause prohibits the prison from taking the action it took. Instead, his contention is that in taking this action, the prison failed to extend to him the procedural protections to which he was entitled. Consequently, if it is determined that a prison's action did intrude upon a liberty interest of an inmate, the next question concerns the procedural protections that an inmate is entitled to before this action may be taken. This is a very difficult question to answer because it depends on the severity of the possible consequences to the inmate. Generally, the more severe the action that is being contemplated by the prison, the greater protections that must be extended to the inmate.

The most basic protections are the right to be informed of the alleged basis for the contemplated action (e.g., the prison is considering depriving an inmate of good time credits for allegedly assaulting another inmate in the dining hall) and the right to be heard (i.e., present evidence on one's own behalf). Other possible protections include the rights to an administrative hearing, to be confronted by and cross-examine witnesses for the other side, to a written statement of the reasons for the action decided upon and the evidence relied upon in coming to that decision, and to be represented by counsel.

Limited space here does not permit a thorough treatment of this subject. However, three important generalizations should be noted. First, the Court seems to feel generally that if a liberty interest has been affected, an inmate should have written notice, an opportunity to be heard, and a written statement of the action taken, the reasons for it, and the evidence relied upon.[69] Second, the prison has considerable discretion (in the interests of security) to prohibit confrontation of the witnesses against the inmate.[70] Third, seldom will it be necessary to permit representation by legal counsel. However, the Court has displayed some sensitivity to the fact that many inmates may lack the intellectual and educational tools necessary to ensure that their side of an issue has been presented adequately. Therefore, it sometimes may be necessary to provide an educated, nonlawyer (probably a prison staff member) to assist the inmate in preparing his "case."[71]

The standards established by the Court in Due Process cases are unusually ambiguous and difficult to understand. Nevertheless, the Court has decided enough of these cases to allow a conclusion that the Court does not think inmates should win many of these cases.

CRUEL AND UNUSUAL PUNISHMENT

The eighth amendment prohibits cruel and unusual punishments. The Court has decided three kinds of prisoners' rights cases involving this provision: (1) medical treatment cases, (2) use of force cases, and (3) conditions of confinement cases.

In medical treatment cases, the Court has held that an inmate complaining about inadequate medical treatment must prove that prison officials were deliberately indifferent to a serious medical need of the inmate.[72] This increases the burden on the inmate in that he must prove more than mere negligence, but, as we will see in the next case to be discussed, the Court could have required proof of an even more difficult standard.

In dealing with the use of force issue, the Court decided that in cases where prison officials are dealing with a prison disturbance, they often must make quick, life-or-death decisions and must be concerned not only about the safety of inmates but the safety of their own staff as well. Given the volatility of this kind of situation, the Court concluded that inmates alleging excessive force on the part of prison officials in this situation must prove that officials acted maliciously and sadistically with an intent to cause harm to the inmate.[73] Of course, this is (and was undoubtedly intended by the Court to be) a very difficult standard to meet.

The Court has also decided that this malice standard will apply in *all* use of force cases.[74] However, in also concluding that the malicious infliction of harm violates the eighth amendment regardless of the extent of the harm caused, the Court clearly came down on the side of inmates.[75] Thus, in medical treatment and use of force cases, the Court has straddled the fence between inmate and institutional interests. However, there has been no such equivocation in conditions cases. Here, the Court, with one exception, has developed a body of law that clearly favors prisons.

In two of its earliest conditions cases, the Court took the first important step in favor of prisons by holding that double-bunking cells that were intended to house one inmate is not always unconstitutional.[76] In both cases, it found that double-bunked cells which provided less square footage per inmate than called for by any of the correctional standards were nevertheless constitutional. Of course, in both cases, the institutions at issue were new, inmates were permitted considerable time out of their cells, and no specific harmful effects were shown to have been caused by the double- bunking.

The Court also decided in a later conditions case that inmates not only had to show that prison conditions had caused inmates to be deprived of some specific necessity of life, but also that prison officials had allowed these conditions to occur through deliberate indifference to their effects on inmates.[77] This case came as a surprise to many students of prisoners' rights law who thought that the requirement that inmates prove a particular state of mind on the part of prison officials in cruel and unusual punishment cases was limited to situations involving a specific act against a particular inmate or group of inmates.

There was also concern on the part of those who generally espoused greater legal protections for inmates that this decision made it virtually impossible for inmates to win most conditions cases because prison officials could argue successfully that they had tried to improve conditions, but the legislature failed to give them the money they needed to do it. Thus, they were not deliberately indifferent to the inmates' needs.[78]

The Court has provided inmates one significant victory in this area. It has held that inmates do not have to wait until they have actually suffered harm before they can prove that they have been subjected to cruel and unusual punishment. It is sufficient if inmates can show that actions or conditions expose them to an unreasonable risk of deprivation of one of life's necessities.[79]

CONCLUSION

Given the recent trend in the Supreme Court toward resolution of fewer cases each term of court, the Court has provided in the last 25 years a surprisingly large body of case law on prisoners' rights. This may be due to the fact that the legal foundation for such interpretation was not laid before the process of Selective Incorporation of the Bill of Rights, and most of that foundation was not in place until the 1960s. Thus, there is some irony in the fact that the liberal Due Process Revolution of the 1960s may have provided the legal foundation for the conservative prisoners' rights decisions of the 1980s and '90s.

Will this conservative trend continue? Although I tend to think that it will, the evidence in favor of this conclusion is far from conclusive. Justices Scalia and Thomas provide two very consistent votes in favor of prisons. Even though he has not been on the Court long, Justice Thomas has voted very frequently with Justice Scalia on all issues before the Court, and Justice Scalia has never taken a pro-inmate position in a prisoners' rights case. Furthermore, the position taken in the opinions he has written or joined suggest that Justice Thomas is not likely to find a constitutional basis for providing significant protections to prisoners.

Chief Justice Rehnquist's opinion in *Wolfish* provided the rhetorical foundation for the Court's recent emphasis on deference to corrections officials, but he voted with the majority in the pro-inmate decisions in *McMillian* and *Helling*. Nevertheless, he has generally sided with prisons, and there is not much reason to think that this stance will change.

Justice O'Connor authored two of the most important pro-prison opinions, *Whitley* and *Safley*, but she also wrote the pro-inmate *McMillian* opinion. Overall, however, she has rather consistently voted in favor of the prison position. Thus, there appear to be four relatively solid pro-prison Justices on the present Court.

Justice Stevens has established an extensive track record in favor of inmates, but he is the only Justice on the present Court that can be counted on to take a pro-inmate position regularly. Justices Brennan and Marshall joined him consistently and Justice Blackmun often joined him as well, but they have all retired from the Court.

The remaining Justices—Kennedy, Souter, Ginsburg, and Breyer—have not been on the Court long enough to permit a confident prediction about which side they are likely to support. On criminal justice issues in general, Justice Kennedy has been conservative, and the best bet is that he will vote that way in prisoners' rights cases as well.

Justice Souter, on the other hand, is showing some signs of developing into a moderate, at least, and his few votes in prisoners' rights cases are consistent with that label. If Justices Ginsburg and Breyer live up to most expectations (based on their track record as Federal appellate court judges), they will likely be somewhat supportive of pro-inmate positions.

If all this speculation turns out to be accurate, we can expect to see many 5-4 prisoners' rights decisions decided in favor of prisons in the next several years. The Deference Period may be far from over.

STUDY QUESTIONS

1. In what ways has greater society (i.e., society outside of the prison environment) mirrored the three phases of Supreme Court litigation identified by the author?
2. Which of the issues brought up during the Rights Period was the most important issue, in your opinion? Why did you choose this issue (or case)?
3. Have inmates' rights eroded as a result of the Deference Period? In other words, has the Court's apparent unwillingness to become involved after the Rights Period caused inmates as a whole to "lose ground" or enjoy fewer rights?
4. From a systemic perspective, what are the pros and cons of allowing inmates easier access to the court system?
5. Of all the individual rights highlighted by the cases reviewed by the author, which do you consider to be the most important? Why did you choose that right?

NOTES

1. 62 Va. 790.
2. See generally, Sheldon Krantz and Lynn Branham, *The Law of Sentencing, Corrections, and Prisoners' Rights* (West Publishing, 1991, 4th ed.), pp. 264–66.
3. *Ex Parte Hull*, 61 S.Ct. 640.
4. See generally, Krantz and Branham, pp. 266–69, and Michael Mushlin, *Rights of Prisoners* (Shepard's/McGraw-Hill, 1994, 2nd ed.), pp. 9–11.
5. 365 U.S. 167.
6. 84 S.Ct. 1733.
7. 88 S.Ct. 994.
8. 92 S.Ct. 250.
9. 89 S.Ct. 747.
10. *Id.*, p. 751.
11. 92 S.Ct. 1079.
12. 94 S.Ct. 1800.
13. 94 S.Ct. 2963.
14. The significance of the "liberty interest" issue is that if the Court finds that action taken by corrections authorities impinges upon a liberty interest, then the action must be preceded by a hearing, as well as some other procedural protections related to the hearing. These additional procedural protections vary with the nature of the liberty interest at issue.
15. 97 S.Ct. 1491.
16. 98 S.Ct. 2565.
17. 94 S.Ct. 2800.
18. 96 S.Ct. 2532.

19. 96 S.Ct. 2543(1976).
20. 96 S.Ct. 1551.
21. 97 S.Ct. 285.
22. 97 S.Ct. 2532.
23. 99 S.Ct. 1861.
24. *Id*, p. 562.
25. 101 S.Ct. 2392.
26. *Wolfish* also involved an overcrowding claim, but there the issue was raised by pretrial detainees. Pretrial detainees are not protected by the Cruel and Unusual Punishment Clause, which extends only to those persons convicted of a crime.
27. 101 S.Ct. 2460.
28. 102 S.Ct. 31.
29. 103 S.Ct. 1741.
30. 109 S.Ct. 1904.
31. 99 S.Ct. 2100.
32. 103 S.Ct. 864.
33. 105 S.Ct. 2768 (1985).
34. 104 S.Ct. 3194(1984).
35. 104 S.Ct. 3227. The same argument was made and ruled on in *Wolfish*, but the argument had been based on the fourth amendment, not the Due Process Clause.
36. 107 S.Ct. 2254.
37. 107 S.Ct. 2400.
38. 109 S.Ct. 1874.
39. 110 S.Ct. 1028 (1990).
40. 106 S.Ct. 1078.
41. 111 S.Ct. 2821.
42. 55 CrL 2156.
43. Some commentators contend that there are some "victories" for inmates contained within these apparent losses. For example, John Boston, of the ACLU National Prison Project, argues that in *Seiter* the inmates won because the Court rejected the lower appellate court's conclusion that the state of mind required in conditions cases was the malice standard articulated by the Court in *Whitley*. Boston, "Highlights of Most Important Cases," *The National Prison Project Journal*, vol. 6, no. 3, Summer 1991, p. 4 (includes an extensive analysis of *Seiter*).
44. 100 S.Ct. 1254.
45. *Washington* v. *Harper* (1990).
46. In fact, it would seem that in any case where it is concluded that a guards use of force was excessive, it would follow logically that the guard acted maliciously as well.
47. 113 S.Ct. 2475.
48. Comment, "Prison Inmate Marriages: A Survey and a Proposal," 12 *University of Richmond Law Review* 443 (1978).
49. *Johnson v. Avery; Bounds v. Smith.*
50. *Johnson v. Avery.*
51. *Wolff v. McDonnell.*
52. *Procunier v. Martinez.*
53. *Cruz v. Beto.*
54. *Procunier v. Martinez.*
55. *Turner v. Safley*, 107 S.Ct. 2254, p. 2261.
56. *Hudson v. Palmer.*
57. *Bell v. Wolfish.*
58. *Block v. Rutherford.*
59. *Meachum v. Fano*, 96 S.Ct. 2632, p. 2538.
60. *Hewitt v. Helms*, 103 S.Ct. 864, p. 869.
61. *Kentucky v. Thompson.*
62. *Greenholtz v. Nebraska Penal Inmates.*
63. *Connecticut Board of Pardons v. Dumschat.*
64. *Meachum v. Fano.*
65. *Olim v. Wakinekona.*
66. *Hewitt v. Helms.*
67. *Vitek v. Jones.*
68. *Hewitt v. Helms.*
69. See, for example, *Wolff v. McDonnell, Yitek v. Jones*, and *Hewitt v. Helms*.
70. See, for example, *Wolff v. McDonnell.*
71. *Id.*
72. *Estelle v. Gamble.*
73. *Whitley v. Albers.*
74. *Hudson v. McMillian.*
75. *Id.*
76. *Bell v. Wolfish and Rhodes v. Chapman.*
77. *Wilson v. Seiter.*
78. See J. White's concurring opinion in *Wilson*, which for all intents and purposes is really a dissenting opinion.
79. *Helling v. McKinney.*

15
SEX OFFENDER LAWS

CAN TREATMENT, PUNISHMENT, INCAPACITATION, AND PUBLIC SAFETY BE RECONCILED?

MARY ANN FARKAS
AMY STICHMAN

Sex offenders evoke fear and other emotions that often lead us to policies that are not based on evidence. Sex offenders are often viewed as less treatable, more dangerous, and more likely to recidivate than other types of offenders. In recent years sex offenders have come under intense scrutiny, which has in turn led to specific laws that target them as a "special" group of offenders. In some states sex offenders who have completed their sentence are held indefinitely through civil commitments. Sex offender registration and community notifications, made more readily available through the Internet, only heighten our fear and anxiety. This article examines some of these and other issues surrounding sex offenders and questions the constitutionality and rationality of sex offender laws and policies.

Sex offenders are viewed as a unique type of criminal offender, particularly as more "objectionable," treatable, more dangerous, and more likely to recidivate. In recent years, these offenders have once again become the focus of intense legal scrutiny, primarily through laws specifically targeting them for indefinite confinement, registration and community notification, polygraph testing. and chemical castration. This article examines the underlying assumptions and justifications for these sex offender laws. We ask whether treatment, punishment, and public safety can be reconciled as justifications for the laws. We conclude that, even though treatment is an implicit rationale in the laws' provisions, punishment, incapacitation, and public safety are the ostensive purposes of these special laws and policies directed toward sex offenders. Moreover, this article questions the constitutionality and rationality of sex offender laws and policies and their consequences for sex offenders, treatment professionals, the mental health and criminal justice systems, and society in general.

The current political climate is one of increased public awareness of and outcry against sex offenders (Meyer & Cole, 1997). The processing of sex offenders and their return to society is the subject for media and legislative frenzy, largely as a result of some particularly heinous crimes involving sex offenders raping and murdering children.

Excerpts from "Sex Offender Laws: Can Treatment, Punishment, Incapacitation, and Public Safety Be Reconciled?" by Mary Ann Farkas and Amy Stichman (2002). *Criminal Justice Review,* 2(2):256–280.

It often appears that many of these laws fit into a "culture of fear," particularly when any violence or perceived violence threatens children (Brito, 2000). It is no coincidence that many sex offender laws are named after child victims, including the Jacob Wetterling Act (42 USCS § 14071) and Megan's Law (New Jersey Stat. Ann. §§ 2C: 7–1 to 2C: 7–11).

Schwartz (1988) contends that the politicization of sex offenses has resulted in revised rape and sexual assault statutes, increased reporting rates, and increased prosecution and conviction. The Bureau of Justice Statistics (BJS, 1997) reports that since 1980 the average annual growth in the number of prisoners has been about 7.6 percent; the number of prisoners sentenced for violent sexual assault has increased by an annual average of 15 percent—faster than any other category of violent crime, and faster than all other crime categories except drug trafficking. In 1994, there were approximately 906,000 offenders convicted of rape and sexual assault confined in state prisons, of whom 88,000 or 9.7 percent were violent sex offenders (BJS, 1997). It is this small percentage of violent offenders that evokes the fear and condemnation of society and drives legislative and correctional efforts to incapacitate and control sex offenders.

Legislators have elevated sex offending to a major public policy priority, and the criminal justice system is responding with selective prosecution and processing of sex offenders (L. Simon, 1997). A flurry of sex offender–specific laws have been passed, including those mandating indeterminate confinement, sex offender registration and community notification, chemical castration, and polygraph testing. The recent spate of sex offender laws, policies, and practices reflects a "new penology" that focuses on managing or controlling high-risk categories of offenders rather than on transforming or rehabilitating the individual offender (J. Simon, 1998). Many of these laws were created because of the public's growing frustration with the criminal justice system in dealing with offenders and recidivists in general and sex offenders in particular. "The emotionally charged nature of the problem of sexual victimization, combined with what is often extreme pressure from interest groups and the general public to 'do something,' limits and narrows the discourse on this issue within the legislative process" (Edwards & Hensley, 2001, p. 84).

With many of these laws pertaining to sex offenders, the courts have granted states wide latitude and have been reluctant to uphold constitutional challenges (Logan, 1999). Pratt (2000, p. 143) asserts that society is more willing to remove "basic civil liberties" regarding sex offenders because of their perceived risk to the community, and because of their repugnance to society few citizens are willing to oppose this trend.

The manifest intent of these laws is to protect society by incapacitating sex offenders in some fashion, whether it be through confinement in a mental or correctional institution or through specialized correctional mechanisms to control their behavior and movements in the community (Palermo & Farkas, 2001). Many of these laws suggest a treatment goal, although this "treatment" more fittingly resembles social control. This perception of "treatment" is common in corrections, however; what is often done under the guise of treatment is punitive or incapacitative in nature. The attempt to reconcile treatment and punishment in corrections has been a dilemma for decades. Whereas there is little agreement on the purposes, effects, and constitutionality of these sex offender laws and policies, this article focuses on their design to treat or rehabilitate, to punish, to incapacitate, and to protect the public. With this in mind, several of these laws are analyzed for their intent and their implications for sex offenders, sex offender treatment providers, the justice system, and society.

RESEARCH QUESTIONS AND DESIGN

We approached this study with the following questions in mind. First, what are the assumptions inherent in these sex offender laws, policies, and practices with regard to sex offenders? Is there evidence of a reasoned, critical analysis of the theoretical and empirical research on sex offenders to provide a sound basis for these assumptions?

Next, what are the justifications underlying these sex offender laws, policies, and practices? Are these laws designed with the justification of punishment or treatment for the individual offender or for an over-inclusive category of "sex offenders"? Are these laws, policies, and practices meant to offer the public a measure of safety as well? If they are intended to fulfill punishment, treatment, and public safety objectives simultaneously, will the goal of treatment be overlooked or undermined? Finally, is there evidence of policy analysis prior to the passage of these laws? In other words, was there a consideration of the potential impact on sex offenders, treatment providers, the criminal justice and mental health systems, and society overall?

These research questions were explored through a comprehensive review of the legal, health science, and social science literature.[1] We considered relevant court cases, legal analyses, and law reviews concerning the intent and goals of the laws, as well as their constitutional and practical limitations. We also examined the theoretical and research literature on the types, behaviors, and motivations of sex offenders and therapeutic approaches for the various kinds of sex offenders.

SEXUAL PREDATOR LAWS AND CIVIL COMMITMENT STATUTES

HISTORY

Different forms of laws directly pertaining to sex offenders have been around for decades.[2] The first sexual psychopath laws were passed in the 1930s as a response to high-profile sex crimes (La Fond, 1992; Wettstein, 1992; Zonana & Norko, 1999). These statutes often had the explicit purposes of treatment and incapacitation for this group of offenders as well as protection for the community. Variously referred to as sexual psychopath laws, sexually dangerous persons acts, and mentally disordered sex offender acts, these laws commonly called for the civil commitment to a state mental hospital of those persons fitting these descriptions (Falk, 1999; Gillespie, 1998; Jacobson, 1999; La Fond, 1992; Wells & Motley, 2001; Zonana & Norko, 1999). The laws were premised on the ability of psychiatry to identify, predict dangerousness and risk for, isolate, and treat sexual psychopaths (La Fond, 1992).

Although they were popular, these laws were also criticized. Often the adjudicated person was committed indefinitely with few procedural safeguards. Furthermore, there is some indication that these laws often targeted not just the habitual violent sex offender but also voyeurs, exhibitionists, and homosexuals (Falk, 1999; Gillespie, 1998; Jacobson, 1999; La Fond, 1992; Wells & Motley, 2001). There were also disillusionment with rehabilitation and doubts about the capability of rehabilitating sexual psychopaths. By the late 1960s, many states were beginning to either repeal or ignore these statutes because of definitional, constitutional, and rehabilitational concerns, while other used these statutes sparingly (Falk, 1999; Gillespie, 1998; Glovan, 1999; La Fond, 1992; Wells & Motley, 2001).

The resurgence of interest in these statutes began in the early 1990s, again as the result of the sensationalization of certain violent sex crimes. The current laws are often labeled as sexually violent predator laws and they allow the civil commitment of these individuals upon release from their state-mandated punishment or after they have been acquitted or found incompetent to stand trial on the basis of insanity or mental disease or defect (Friedland, 1999). In place of the therapeutic appeal of the earlier sexual psychopath laws, the appeal of current sexual predator laws is in their social control function (La Fond, 1992). The earlier sexual psychopath laws contained a stronger therapeutic component, coinciding with other forms of civil commitment, whereas current laws, although they contain elements of treatment, exhibit incapacitation and control as their key foci (Cornwell, 1998; Pallone, 1991).

Civil commitment statutes for mentally ill persons were on the books in most states, but the sexual predator laws expanded the range of persons who may be committed to include those with a "mental abnormality or personality disorder" predisposing them to perpetrate another sexually violent crime (Falk, 1999, p. 129; Glovan, 1999). After commitment, clinical experts periodically evaluate the committed offender medically and psychologically for signs of improvement in mental status (Matson & Lieb, 1997b).[3] The offender may subsequently petition for release, return to court, and have the court again try to determine whether the offender is a danger to society. Confinement continues until such time that the psychologists and the court agree that the offender's mental abnormality or personality disorder has so changed that the individual is deemed safe to be released. Janus (2000) contends that in practice committed sex offenders are almost never discharged. "For example, in the two states with the longest contemporary commitment programs (both operating since 1990), Washington and Minnesota, no individuals have been discharged from commitment, and only a handful are in transitional placements" (Janus, 2000, p. 10).

TREATMENT AND PUNISHMENT IN CIVIL COMMITMENT STATUTES

Since these current laws were developed, numerous constitutional questions have arisen pertaining to their use, and the courts have varied in their rulings. Again, treatment, punishment, and public safety are the stated or implicit goals of these laws. The focus on punishment has been a key to many of the court rulings, the most notable of which is the *Kansas v. Hendricks* ruling in 1997 by the U.S. Supreme Court. In this case, Leroy Hendricks was convicted multiple times for child molestation. As his latest prison term neared expiration, Hendricks found himself the target of the new Kansas sexually violent predator statute (Kan. Stat. Ann. § 59–29 a01). As a result, it was determined that he was a violent predator who would likely recidivate and he was committed to a state mental hospital. Hendricks subsequently challenged the Kansas statute, stating that it violated due process and prohibitions against double jeopardy and ex post facto laws; the U.S. Supreme Court upheld the act and Hendricks' commitment as constitutional (Falk, 1999; Gillespie, 1998; Glovan, 1999; Logan, 1999).

Interestingly, the Court rejected Hendricks' double jeopardy and ex post facto arguments mainly because, in their opinion, the civil commitment statute does not amount to punishment. Hendricks argued that because he had not received any treatment, his commitment amounted to thinly disguised punishment. The Court disagreed. First, they believed that there were no additional criminal proceedings, and the act did not seek retribution or deterrence (Glovan, 1999). They interpreted the goal of this statute to be that of incapacitation as Hendricks was untreatable. Second, they deferred to the legislature's intent. Because the law was housed within the state probate code and the law labeled "civil," the Court reasoned that the legislature's intent was not punitive. As the Court often submits to the findings of state and lower federal courts to reveal the intent of the legislature (Friedland, 1999), it pointed to the provision in the statute that called for necessary long-term care and treatment of sexually violent predators. Thus, in *Hendricks*, the Court rejected the Kansas Supreme Court's argument that the statute was indeed punitive. Third, the lack of any treatment did not presume that the law was punitive, because "it must be remembered that he was the first person committed under the Act" (*Kansas v. Hendricks*, 1997, p. 367). Furthermore, the Court stated that the liberty interests of these offenders must take second place to the goal of protection of the community.

In dissent, Justice Breyer observed that there were several similarities between the Kansas act and criminal law, such as the act's provision for involuntary detention, the use of criminal background as a determining factor, and the focus on incapacitation (Friedland, 1999; Glovan, 1999). Breyer also argued that the act was in error: There was no provision for treatment while the offender was imprisoned, yet the necessity of treating the individual was used as a partial justification for further confinement. Breyer said that, if treatment were necessary and available for this difficult-to-treat population, it should begin as soon after incarceration as possible.[4]

In accordance with Justice Breyer, Friedland (1999) writes that the detention of this specific type of offender appears to be based on the desire to further punish and incapacitate. This intent is revealed in many ways. First, the law includes people with personality disorders or mental abnormalities that may not be treatable and those who would not benefit from involuntary hospitalization, although the law seems to imply that favorable treatment is possible (Friedland, 1999; Glovan, 1999). Some sex offenders' risk level is high enough that "no treatment could reasonably be expected to lower it to a level where release to the community" would be possible (Harris, Rice, & Quinsey, 1998, p. 106), and other psychologists caution that certain types of sex offenders (e.g., pedophiles) can be extremely difficult to treat successfully (Prendergast, 1991).

Second, treatment is only given *after* the offender has been criminally incarcerated and appears to be a "pretext for extended confinement" (Friedland, 1999, p. 110). It is possible and even likely that detention may last long after efforts at treatment have occurred. Wettstein (1992) further notes that these laws misuse the mental health profession. Many of these sex offenders, committed through having a mental defect or personality disorder, may not be "authentically mentally ill" (Friedland, 1999, p. 132), inasmuch as neither term corresponds to diagnostic categories in the American Psychiatric Association's *Diagnostic and Statistical Manual of Mental Disorders* (DSM-IV) (American Psychiatric Association, 1994) or any other psychiatric classification (Vatz & Weinberg, 2001). Indefinite, preventive detention underlies the pretext of fender treatment and "allows clinicians to collude with a nonclinical social agenda, with substantial likely harm to the offender through excessive false positive predictions of sexual violence" (Wettstein, 1992, p. 624).

The Court revisited the Kansas Act in *Kansas v. Crane* (2002). The Court ruled in *Crane* that, in addition to the demonstrated likelihood that the person would commit sex crimes if released, there must be a determination of a "serious difficulty in controlling the behavior," and the mental abnormality must distinguish the person from an ordinary recidivist (*Kansas v. Crane,* 2002, p. 409). This distinction is important, as the Court acknowledged the potential for the act to become too far- reaching (Cornwell, 1998; Friedland, 1999). If a simple judgment of the existence of a mental abnormality is sufficient to commit the offender civilly, what prohibitions are there to prevent the civil commitment of other recidivists? Although many scholars would still be wary of a slippery slope (e.g., a pyromaniac or kleptomaniac could fit the identical criteria), this distinction is a movement to limit those who may be committed.

Ironically, these statutes may be seen to decrease public safety if examined on a larger scale. Finances for the mental health profession would be consumed by the increasing number of sex offenders and the need to incapacitate them (Friedland, 1999; Glovan, 1999; La Fond, 1992; Wettstein, 1992). Janus (2000) questions whether these expensive commitment policies are the most effective use of scarce mental health resources. The reliance on the treatment community to house these offenders would divert necessary and already scarce money from treatment for both these offenders and other offenders who are in need of mental health services. Without this treatment, it is possible that many others who may be more amenable to treatment—not just sex offenders—may turn to crime.

In sum, the sexual predator statutes are designed to control a category of sexual offenders deemed incurable or, at best, resistive to therapy. Indefinite confinement of the sex offender is simply justification for lifetime preventive detention and continued state control (La Fond, 1992). Although these laws have withstood a myriad of legal challenges, their intention and their use warrant closer examination. The laws should more clearly specify exactly who should be targeted, and treatment should begin prior to release from incarceration. Measurable goals and objectives should be used to determine progress in treatment and to decide whether further commitment is necessary. Assessment tools, standards of commitment and release, conditions of confinement, and the actual application of the law need to be scrutinized to ensure that the law is not abused or used solely for punishment objectives.

REGISTRATION AND COMMUNITY NOTIFICATION FOR SEX OFFENDERS

HISTORY

Registration of people who have been charged or convicted of various offenses has been used for decades, particularly for sex offenders. Probably the most important development in registration and community notification of sex offenders occurred in 1994 when Congress passed the Jacob Wetterling Crimes Against Children and Sexually Violent Offender Registration Act (42 USCS § 14071). This act required states without registration laws to create them within three years and targeted those offenders who committed a sexual act against a minor or a sexually violent offense. Registration of the sex offender is justified as necessary so that police can know the whereabouts of sex offenders in their jurisdictions.[5] This information can then be used in subsequent investigations of sex offenses. In 1996, the law was amended to require the disclosure of information about registered sex offenders to the public (Scholle, 2000). For both forms, the federal government threatened to withhold part of the states' federal law enforcement funding if they did not comply with the act. New Jersey in 1994 passed one of the most well-known notification statutes, referred to as "Megan's Law" (New Jersey Stat. Ann. §§ 2C: 7-1 to 2C: 7-11), after Megan Kanka was sexually assaulted and murdered by a neighbor who had been previously convicted of violent sex crimes (Logan, 1999; Scholle, 2000).

The rationale for community notification is that protection of children will be more meaningful if the community has knowledge about the presence of a convicted sex offender in the neighborhood. Protecting the public is the crux of the argument, with punishment underlying this rhetoric (Billings & Bulges, 2000; Edwards & Hensley, 2001; Prentky, 1996; J. Simon, 2000). There is little attempt to integrate treatment into these laws, although offender reintegration into the community remains a focus in corrections (Zevitz & Farkas, 2000a). These laws are very popular politically and publicly; many legislatures have passed them unanimously because they give the public the perception of control and safety in their communities (Edwards & Hensley, 2001; Lieb, 1996; Parks, 2000; Scholle, 2000).

Many states that use community notification have a three-tiered system that determines how much proactive notification will occur based on the dangerousness of the offender (Matson & Lieb, 1997a). For offenders classified as the lowest risk (Level I) for endangering public safety, notification is limited to law enforcement personnel. Level II offenders are at medium risk for reoffending, so notification is expanded to include schools, day care centers, or other community organizations that serve primarily women and children. Level III offenders are seen as posing the highest risk; therefore, the highest degree of notification is implemented whereby the general public is notified. Some states use formal assessment instruments to systematically classify an offender's level of risk to reoffend, while others use an advisory committee to assess risk on a case-by-case basis. Registration and community notification provisions can be lengthy; more than half of the states require offenders to be registered and the community notified of their presence for at least 10 years to a lifetime after the expiration of their sentences (Kabat, 1998; Matson & Lieb, 1997a).

BENEFITS AND PROBLEMS WITH REGISTRATION/NOTIFICATION LAWS

As with the civil commitment statutes, the courts are mixed in their determination of the constitutionality of these registration and notification statutes but generally tend to support them. Constitutional challenges have centered on allegations of ex post facto and cruel and unusual punishment. Courts frequently reject the constitutional challenges by reiterating that punishment is not being given and by supporting the liberty and protection of the community over that of the individual sex offender (Logan, 1999). Proponents of the laws argue that whatever punitiveness occurs is only incidental to the public protection function and is not intended to be punishment (Brooks, 1995). There is some indication that community mobilization is occurring and that probation and parole officers and the community are taking a more proactive approach to supervising these offenders (Johnson, 1998; Lieb, 1996; Parks, 2000; Zevitz & Farkas, 2000b). For example, in California local police initiated surveillance of one child molester. They caught him driving slowly past a school yard, which was a violation of his parole, and reincarcerated him (Parks, 2000). Penalties for failing to register have also been increased to a major misdemeanor or low-level felony (Johnson, 1998; Lieb, 1996; Parks, 2000).

The current degree and public perception of community protection are debated, however. Zevitz and Farkas (2000a) found that increases in community protection strained probation and parole agent resources because of the requisite increases for supervision. Scholars (Berliner, 1996; Edwards & Hensley, 2001; Federoff & Moran, 1997; Freeman-Longo, 1996; Loe & Porter, 2000; Prentky, 1996; J. Simon, 2000) caution that community protection is often lower than it is perceived to be. While these laws often frame the risk of victimization as that of assault by strangers, studies show that children are more likely to be abused by someone known to them, such as a family member or friend (Freeman-Longo, 1996; J. Simon, 2000). The possibility of community notification may actually discourage reporting if the offender is a family member. Victims may either fear being found out themselves or fear for their loved ones, even the abusers (Edwards & Hensley, 2001; Freeman-Longo, 1996). Notification also does little to prevent the undetected sex abusers, who constitute the majority of sex offenders, from victimizing others or from venturing into nearby communities (Freeman-Longo, 1996). Offenders may also threaten victims more seriously in order to lessen the chance of being reported. Furthermore, these laws are criticized as being overreaching: Even when risk instruments and knowledge of likelihood of reoffending are used, there tend to be false positives. In other words, police may err on the side of caution in targeting these offenders.

Additionally, as with many policies, what the legislature desires and what the criminal justice system can provide are divergent. Registration and notification bills were quickly introduced and passed in most states; however, implementation of these laws has its difficulties. Many jurisdictions have had to come up with innovative ways to disseminate the information, especially when little or no money was given to aid in this notification. Often community notification takes the form of community meetings, door-to-door visits by the police, Internet notices, newspaper articles and ads, and flyers placed in the area (Adams, 1999; Farkas & Zevitz, 2000; Kabat, 1998). In Wisconsin, Farkas and Zevitz (2000) noted that resources were not made available to carry out the law as intended. There were no additional funds for officer training on the notification procedures or for the creation of community meetings. Smaller communities were unable to spare enough officers to meet with citizens, and police in larger cities noted that their workload was increased by having to check up on these offenders more and to field the public's questions, complaints, and concerns. Probation and parole agents noted further difficulties. Because these cases were high-profile, agents described having to invest more time and energy into community notification cases, thereby spending less time on other cases (Zevitz & Farkas, 2000a). Both police and probation and parole agents also described lags in obtaining information to aid in determining notification level and supervision considerations (Farkas & Zevitz, 2000; Zevitz & Farkas, 2000a).

Further difficulties are evident in any attempt to balance treatment with punishment and public safety. Not all sex offenders are incurable, and some respond well to therapy. "Community notification laws fail to discriminate between those capable of rehabilitation and those whose deviancy may be permanent" (Bedarf, 1995, p. 910). Unfortunately, this trend is common in correctional policy making and practice; practices are often "one size fits all" and offenders are treated identically regardless of wide individual differences (Clear & Cole, 2000). Rather than help sex offenders reintegrate into their neighborhoods, notification excludes, labels, and stigmatizes them. A commonly cited problem is the inability of many of these offenders to get on with their lives (Zevitz & Farkas, 2000b). Being subject to decades of registration and community notification could result in a perpetual burden on the offender's privacy interests (Kabat, 1998), thereby impeding successful reintegration into the community.

Zevitz and Farkas (2000a) describe the problems that many probation and parole agents had in locating adequate housing for sex offenders and the problems that offenders experienced in finding meaningful employment. The laws assume that neighbors will act responsibly, provide adequate supervision for their children, and act within the law toward the offender. "Reintegration requires effort from both parties: the offender must abide by the rules of society, and the community must allow the offender to enter community life" (Bedarf, 1995, p. 910). In another study by Zevitz and Farkas (2000b), sex offenders described the humiliation in their daily lives and the negative effects on the lives of their family members, and they reported being ostracized by neighbors and lifetime acquaintances and being harassed or threatened by nearby residents or strangers. The evidence suggests that occasional vigilantism occurs in the community in efforts to remove offenders from neighborhoods or to further punish offenders (Edwards & Hensley, 2001; Freeman- Longo, 1996; Lieb, 1996; Prentky, 1996).

Psychologists are concerned that community reaction may increase an offender's anxiety, which may lead to poor decision making and ultimately a relapse event (Billings & Bulges, 2000; Edwards & Hensley, 2001; Freeman-Longo, 1996; Prentky, 1996). These laws may also inhibit willingness to accept responsibility for one's crime. Ironically, under these laws, if an offender commits another sex crime, the blame may not rest solely on the offender. With the impetus placed on the community to track and monitor, these offenders can conceivably blame the community for not adequately supervising them. This transfer of blame is contrary to the law's purpose and is contraindicated in treatment. Many sex offender treatment programs require that the offenders admit to wrongdoing and develop appropriate self-control techniques to regulate their own behavior (Billings & Bulges, 2000; Edwards & Hensley, 2001; J. Simon, 2000). Other criticisms include the potential of the laws to decrease offender self-reporting and desire for treatment and to serve as a disincentive for sex offenders to plead guilty and get treatment (Freeman-Longo, 1996; Prentky, 1996).

In reality, community notification and registration laws are predicated on the failure of treatment and rehabilitation programs in prison (J. Simon, 1998). These laws are intended to provide a long-term, protective strategy to incapacitate or control what is labeled as a permanently dangerous and contemptible class of offenders. However, in this legislative rush to enact another "get tough on sex offenders" law, a meaningful balance between the constitutional and civil rights of sex offenders and the interests of victims and the general public has been overlooked. Creating rational and thoughtful levels of risk and carefully controlled means of public disclosure will ideally lead to notification systems that lessen public fear and that do not impede the rehabilitation or reintegration of sex offenders (Kabat, 1998). To accomplish this objective, states can learn from one another. Information sharing about the difficulties experienced in the development and implementation of sex offender registration and notification laws is recommended. States could share solutions as well as problems encountered. More research is also advised to better inform policy makers about the impact of such laws on corrections, law enforcement, sex offenders, and the community.

CHEMICAL CASTRATION LAWS

HISTORY AND USE

Physical castration or orchiectomy has a long history dating back to biblical times. Under the "eye for an eye," *lex talionis* principle, for centuries rapists were castrated as punishment for their crimes (Miller, 1998). During the colonial period, slaves were castrated if they were suspected of having sexual relations with white women (Druhm, 1997). The eugenics movement in early nineteenth-century America endorsed both castration and sterilization for criminals and the mentally ill (Spalding, 1998). Countries including Denmark, Germany, and Switzerland have used physical castration for years as an effective way of dealing with individuals who display unacceptable sexual behavior. Experimental data for physical castration indicates a low incidence of serious morbidity, an immediate reduction in sex drive, and significantly low recidivism rates, as low as 2.2 percent (Meyer & Cole, 1997, p. 7). At present, physical castration is still legally permissible in these countries, but it is by no means commonly used with sex offenders (Winslade, Stone, Smith-Bell, & Webb, 1998, p. 374). Voluntary chemical castration combined with therapy has largely replaced physical castration because physicians believe that similarly effective results can be obtained through pharmacological treatment (Winslade et al., 1998, p. 374).

The use of physical castration in the United States has also not been widely embraced because of qualms about physical mutilation, invasiveness, the permanency and irreversibleness of the surgery, and the availability of medications as an alternative. Some sex offender laws do provide surgical or chemical castration as an alternative to punishment, such as Florida's law, yet chemical castration seems to be the more socially and morally acceptable solution, at least for the short term.

Although medication has been used on a case-by-case basis by clinicians for more than 30 years, renewed interest and focus on drugs as a means of controlling the behavior of sex offenders has occurred in the past decade (Miller, 1998). Studies have shown that sex offenders treated with a pharmacological agent, such as Depo-Provera, plus counseling have gained better self-regulation of sexual behavior (Melella, Travin, & Cullen, 1989, p. 224); they were much less likely to reoffend than those who refused the medication or stopped the injections (Meyer, Cole, & Emory, 1992; Money, 1987). The promising results occurred only as long as the offenders continued the injections (Bradford, 1990).

Chemical castration essentially involves the injection of the synthetic hormone medroxyprogesterone acetate (Depo-Provera), which lowers the blood serum testosterone levels in males. When taken on a regular basis, the result is a reduction in sexual impulses, the frequency of erotic fantasy, erections, and ejaculations. Depo-Provera does not cause impotence but produces a period of "erotic apathy" in which the feeling of sex drive is at rest (Fitzgerald, 1990; Money, 1987). Upon cessation of the injections, erectile and ejaculatory capacity returns within 7 to 10 days (Money, 1987). The side effects of Depo-Provera include migraines, hypertension, hyperglycemia, nausea, weight gain, insomnia, fatigue or lethargy, leg cramps, loss of body hair, and thrombosis (Meyer et al., 1992). Most of the side effects are rare and are thought to be reversible once the treatment is discontinued; nevertheless, the long-term effects of Depo-Provera are unknown. Antipsychotic medication has also been known to reduce the frequency or intensity of sexual arousal and thoughts (Miller, 1998) and is currently under experimentation.

PROBLEMS WITH CURRENT USE OF CHEMICAL CASTRATION AS TREATMENT

Although chemical castration has been in use in the treatment of sex offenders since 1944, it was then administered with the informed consent of the individual and on an individual basis. Equally important was the desire expressed by sex offenders to be rehabilitated (Keene, 1997). The current chemical castration statutes are much different. First of all, the state statutes may stipulate forced administration of the pharmacological agent if the sex offender is a recidivist. In 1997, California became the first state to enact such a law mandating chemical castration for twice-convicted sex offenders whose victims were under the age of 13. The sentencing judge has no discretion when dealing with these repeat sex offenders (Druhm, 1997). Chemical injections are mandated prior to release on parole and are continued while the offender is under community supervision. If the offender refuses, parole is denied. Other states have followed suit, including Colorado, Florida, Georgia, Louisiana, Montana, Texas, and Wisconsin, with many of these states' statutes granting judicial discretion to impose a sentence of Depo-Provera administration. Critics contend that the judge may not be the most informed individual to make that determination and question the ability of medical staff within the Department of Corrections to make an impartial decision:

> Although no bill authorizes the judge to order physicians to prescribe the medication per se, all the bills require that the medication be started while the offender is still in the state's Department of Corrections. Correctional physicians typically have much less professional freedom than their colleagues and may be subject to considerable pressure to provide the treatment, regardless of their competency to administer it or any ethical objections that they may have. (J. Simon, 1998, p. 196)

Accordingly, the role of the physician as a healer and his or her code of ethics have also been challenged. Does the physician become an agent of social control with the best interests of the patient subordinate to the societal protection interest of the state? Nassi (1980) explored this issue in her study of treatment providers in California prisons for men. She found that prison psychiatrists and psychologists experienced "dissonance" or conflict between their role as a helping agent for the offender and as an employee of the state. As a helping agent, caring for the individual and his mental health and growth were central concerns. As a state employee, the goals of prisoner control and societal protection became the major foci.

Nassi discovered that psychiatrists and psychologists reacted to this role dissonance in a variety of ways. Those treatment professionals who were unable to resolve the conflict terminated their employment for practice elsewhere. Those who remained were compelled to alter, and even relinquish, their professional standards and ethics in order to conform to the punitive function of the prison. Some treatment providers assumed a role equivalent to that of a custody officer and ceased any pretense of treatment. Their purpose became one of ensuring that the punishment and control process moved along more smoothly. Other psychiatrists and psychologists chose to simply withdraw from the therapeutic process and merely go through the motions of therapy. Both of these last two approaches could be perceived as practicing "penal harm medicine," the treatment providers abdicating their healing and caring mission so that custodial interests could be accommodated (Maeve & Vaughn, 2001). Finally, there were some treatment providers who reduced their dissonance by forcing the system to be more consonant with their belief systems. They resisted the system in an active manner, by confronting correctional officers about inmate complaints, or passively, by honoring confidentiality or by quietly helping their patients (Nassi, 1980, p. 331).

Another study shows that working with sex offenders in particular may create conflict or dissonance between a therapeutic role and function and a custodial role and control. Sex offender behaviors, including a propensity to manipulate and to persistently deny or minimize their crimes, affect the perceptions and attitudes of therapists and their work with these offenders (Lea, Auburn, &. Kibblewhite, 1999). Farrenkopf (1992) found that more than half (54 percent) of sex offender therapists reported a shift in their work perspective with their hopes and expectations for effective treatment diminishing over time. A hardening or dulling of emotions was also evident in almost half (42 percent) of therapists. Thirty-eight percent were frustrated with the correctional system, complaining of punitive correctional staff and a pronounced lack of support for services. "Impact from this work appears to progress from a period of professional zeal to emotional hardening and decreased hope for effectiveness" (Farrenkopf, 1992, p. 222).

These studies illustrate the difficulties of working with sex offenders and the dissonance between the roles and functions of therapeutic agent and social control agent experienced by many sex offender treatment providers in corrections. Often, they may be forced to compromise their role as therapeutic agents to be more consonant with prison goals.

Chemical castration laws have also been faulted in several other ways. Some of the laws, most notably California's statute, 1996 Cal. Stats. 596 § 2 (A.B 3339), have no requirement for counseling along with the chemical injections; rather, the injections are considered the treatment. Without some form of sex offender-focused therapy, there is a question of whether chemical castration can even be called "treatment" (Palermo & Farkas, 2001). Research has shown that the use of chemical agents is widely thought to be effective only when used with sex offender-specific psychotherapy (Meyer & Cole, 1997). Several states, e.g., Florida, Georgia, and Wisconsin, have added a provision for sex offender treatment to correspond with the injections of Depo-Provera.

A complete medical or psychiatric evaluation prior to the injections of the chemical agent is typically not required in the statutes. Without an evaluation, there is no clinical determination of whether the medication is indicated for a particular offender. Lumping all sex offenders into one broad category hinders their effective management and treatment (Peters-Baker, 1998). Not all sex offenders are suitable candidates. "The legislature, in enacting the chemical castration statute, has proceeded on the belief, or perhaps more accurately, on the hope, that administering a single drug—even involuntarily—can effectively alter abusive behavior in all categories of sexual offenders" (Spalding, 1998, p. 126). There is no differentiation between types of sex offenders suitable for chemical castration in the statutes. Injections of Depo-Provera will not have any meaningful effect on sex offenders who deny perpetrating the offense or the criminal nature of the act, those who admit the offense but blame their behavior on nonsexual or nonpersonal factors such as drugs, alcohol, and job stress, and those who are violent and appear to be motivated by nonsexual gain, anger, power, and violence (Fitzgerald, 1990). For example, chemical castration will not work for a sex offender motivated by anger, violence, or power. With this group of offenders, even if rendered impotent, they would find some other means to violate their victims (Hicks, 1993, p. 648).

Evaluation of sex offenders for possible use of Depo-Provera should be conducted by an experienced psychiatrist. The psychiatrist must be able to assess the frequency and intensity of sexual fantasy, evaluate the offender's professed desire for treatment (Miller, 1998), and characterize the type of sex offender according to a psychiatric typology as opposed to a crime-based classification. A crime-based classification of sex offenders is predicated on the crime committed and not the underlying motivation or disorder of the perpetrator. A psychiatric typology of sex offenders has psychiatric meaning relating to sexual disorders as defined in the DSM-IV. A medical evaluation of the sex offender would be necessary in order to determine the type of sexual disorder, the appropriate treatment for this disorder, and the medications that would work for this type of disorder. "The majority of jurisdictions lack any knowledgeable and experienced psychiatrists who are capable of evaluating offenders for appropriateness of treatment, prescribing it correctly and monitoring the effects of the treatment" (Miller, 1998, p. 193).

Fundamental rights of privacy and procreation may also be contravened with the imposition of Depo-Provera injections. Privacy concerns arise when an individual's right to bodily autonomy, to the control of his own person and the right to refuse treatment, is compromised. In *Washington v. Harper* (1990), the U.S. Supreme Court held that the state could override a prisoner's refusal to take antipsychotic medication if the administration of the medication was in the inmate's best medical interest and the inmate was dangerous to himself or others: "Where an inmate's mental disability is the root cause of the threat he poses to the inmate population, the state's interest in decreasing the danger to others necessarily encompasses an interest in providing him with medical treatment for his illness" (p. 226). Before a prisoner could be treated with antipsychotic drugs involuntarily, the Washington Department of Corrections policy required a hearing before a committee consisting of a psychiatrist, a psychologist, and the associate superintendent of the prison.[6] The committee must find by a majority that the prisoner suffered from a mental disability, was gravely disabled, and posed a likelihood of serious harm to himself or others (p. 1028).[7] However, Justice Stevens dissented, asserting that a prisoner's liberty interest was seriously contravened by the administration of antipsychotic drugs that caused severe and often permanent side effects and that altered the will and mind of the subject. He also expressed concerns that institutional and administrative pressures would subvert the use of medication in the best medical interest of the prisoner.

Antipsychotic drugs can be used to simultaneously medically treat and control psychotic inmates; however, it is precisely this duality of purpose that makes them subject to misuse and abuse. The use of psychotropic drugs on prisoners is widespread,[8] and this also presents a correspondingly high opportunity for state-sanctioned abuse in the administration of the drugs (Floyd, 1990, p. 254). Furthermore, Ryan (1990) contends that the administrative procedures for involuntary medication outlined in *Harper* may be insufficient to protect prisoners from arbitrary and unfair decisions by prison psychiatrists. In particular, the objectivity and independence of a committee composed of prison employees and the nonadversarial nature of the hearing afford little protection from erroneous and misguided psychiatric diagnosis (Ryan, 1990, p. 1414). Moreover, the only administrative recourse for the prisoner after the committee's decision to involuntarily medicate is to appeal to another prison employee, the superintendent (Alexander, 1991, p. 1235).

The right to privacy and bodily autonomy also encompasses the right of an individual to make procreative decisions (*Griswold v. Connecticut,* 1965). Proponents argue that the use of chemical castration does not violate the fundamental right of an individual to procreate. The effects of Depo-Provera, the diminution of penile erections and ejaculations and decrease in sperm production, are believed to be only temporary and to be fully reversible with cessation of the injections (Melella et al., 1989, p. 227). The sex offender still has the ability to engage in sex and to procreate (Fitzgerald, 1990, p. 58). Nevertheless, Spalding (1998) argues that, even though it is only a temporary interference, the sex offender's ability to procreate is still infringed upon during the period of treatment, which may last for years. Some chemical castration statutes, e.g., Florida's law (1997 Fla. Stat.§ 794.0235(2)(a)), provide the courts with the authority to order weekly injections of Depo-Provera for life (Spalding, 1998, p. 130). For those sex offenders who are sentenced to lifetime injections, the right to procreate may be interfered with on a more permanent basis. Moreover, the long-term effects of Depo-Provera on sexual performance and potency are still very much in question (Meyer & Cole, 1997).

The issues of informed consent and the voluntariness of that consent have also been raised. Under the law, the treating physician must inform the patient of the potential risks and side effects, as well as the benefits of the drug or medical procedure, in order for informed consent to be established (Druhm, 1997). A few states do require the consent of the sex offender to be chemically castrated; nevertheless, it is arguable whether that consent is truly voluntary when the alternative is loss of liberty (Meyer & Cole, 1997, p. 13). The therapist wields the threat of imprisonment as a consequence of noncompliance with treatment objectives. The lack of research concerning the long-term risks of chemical castration may also preclude informed consent (Druhm, 1997).

The legally mandated use of chemical castration brings to the fore the constitutionality and ethics of using medication for purposes other than treatment (Palermo & Farkas, 2001). "By using psychiatrists and their medications, the criminal justice system is attempting to legitimize and sanitize what are, at heart, punitive programs" (Miller, 1998, p. 199). Does chemical castration constitute cruel and unusual punishment in violation of the Eighth Amendment? In *People v. Gauntlett* (1986), Gauntlett challenged as cruel and unusual punishment a condition of probation that required him to be injected with Depo-Provera for five years. The Michigan Supreme Court found that treatment with the medication was not a lawful condition of probation because it had not found acceptance as a safe and reliable medical practice.

To pass constitutional muster, chemical castration must have some therapeutic value and must be considered a legitimate treatment used in good faith as a preventative or curative measure (Fitzgerald, 1990, pp. 31–33). In *Rennie v. Klein* (1978, p. 1143), the U.S. District Court for New Jersey utilized a four-part test to distinguish between treatment and punishment: (a) Does the drug treatment have a therapeutic value? (b) Is the drug recognized as accepted medical practice? (c) Are the effects of the drug unduly harsh in relation to its benefits? (d) Is the drug part of an ongoing treatment program?

In the *Rennie* case, the court held that there was no violation of the Eighth Amendment because the drug prolixin was justifiably administered as treatment, not punishment (Fitzgerald, 1990, p. 31). Applying the *Rennie* test, Druhm (1997) and Fitzgerald (1990) contend that chemical castration would be considered therapeutic based on the following rationales. First, usage of Depo-Provera reduces the individual's sex drive, allows a measure of sexual self-control over obsessive sexual fantasies, and makes the sex offender more amenable to treatment. Depo-Provera itself is not considered experimental[9] and chemical castration has been an accepted treatment of sex offenders since the 1960s, making the side effects of the drug not so unduly harsh as to outweigh its benefits. To meet the final criterion, injections of Depo-Provera would have to be administered as part of an ongoing treatment program under medical supervision.

Critics point to the lack of any clearly defined treatment effort in chemical castration laws (Keene, 1997; Smith, 1999). As previously mentioned, counseling must accompany the chemical injections. Depo-Provera stabilizes the sex offender's fantasies, compulsions, and arousal; however, the offender and the treatment provider still need to work on identifying the underlying causes and precursors of the behavior (Marsh & Walsh, 1995). The question is whether the underlying aim of forced injections of medication without corresponding therapy is really punishment or social control of individuals whom society finds morally reprehensible.

Even with treatment as the expressed focus of the law, punishment may be inherent either by design or by incidental consequence. The case of *Arizona v. Christopher* (1982) illustrates this dilemma between the purposes of treatment and punishment. The defendant Christopher asserted that being placed on probation constitutionally entitled him to be effectively treated and rehabilitated. He further argued that the state denied him this right when his treatment did not include chemical castration and behavior modification. The Arizona Supreme Court rejected the defendant's argument, stating that rehabilitation is only one goal alongside retribution, restraint, and deterrence when penalties are imposed on offenders. The court also stated that "at this stage of human and scientific development, no society should be forced to guarantee rehabilitation to all offenders and ignore the other purposes of punishment. To maintain order and prevent vigilante justice, society needs to consider retribution in its disposition of convicted criminals. Also, it cannot be guaranteed that effective rehabilitation will be successful even if the convicted criminal participates in a treatment program" (*Arizona v. Christopher*, 1982, p. 1034).

In summary, the goals of rehabilitation and reduction in recidivism can be met with chemical castration only when the drug can effectively treat the sexual disorder of the individual, administration of the drug is voluntary and with informed consent, and the individual is motivated to address his aberrant behavior. Thus, the most appropriate candidates for the procedure (e.g., paraphiliacs) must be identified based on research findings. The laws should also incorporate a counseling component to address the root causes of the sexual behavior.

POLYGRAPH TESTING

HISTORY AND USE OF POLYGRAPH TESTING FOR SEX OFFENDERS

In the past decade, the polygraph has also been introduced as another tool to manage, supervise, and treat sex offenders under community supervision. Laws have been passed in several states, including Arizona, Colorado, Florida, Tennessee, Texas, and Wisconsin, requiring anyone convicted of two sexual offenses to undergo periodic mandatory polygraph supervision (Wilcox, 2000). Thirty states have at least some local jurisdictions using polygraphs to supervise sex offenders (Marshall, 2001).

The polygraph is used in three basic ways: a disclosure polygraph administered after sentencing, a denial and specific issues exam, and a maintenance polygraph administered while in treatment (English, Jones, Pasini-Hill, Patrick, & Cooley-Towell, 2000; Scott, 1997). The disclosure polygraph requires sex offenders to answer questions in detail about their sex offense history and history of sexually deviant behavior. The denial exam is administered when there is a conflict between the sex offender's and the victim's versions of the crime or when the offender denies culpability, and a specific issues examination focuses on a specific crime, accusation, or suspicion (English et al., 2000). The maintenance polygraph monitors the offender's management of inappropriate thoughts and fantasies, reduces denial, and measures compliance with supervisory conditions. A diagnosis of deception is an inference based on increased physiological arousal (increased heart activity, rate and depth of breathing, and palmar sweating) in response to relevant questions (Cross & Saxe, 1992, p. 22).

ADMISSIBILITY OF POLYGRAPH RESULTS

The admissibility of polygraph results and other scientific evidence in court was governed for more than half a century by the 1923 case *Frye v. United States* (Baranowski, 1998). State and federal courts almost unanimously refused to admit polygraph test results based on the *Frye* criteria[10] (Henseler, 1997). More recently, in *Daubert v. Merrell Dow Pharmaceuticals* (1993), the U.S. Supreme Court decided that the Federal Rules of Evidence should provide the standard for admitting expert scientific testimony.[11] "At present, most states consider polygraph evidence *per se* inadmissible in courts of law, although a few states admit polygraph evidence in some limited circumstances by stipulation of both parties" (English et al, 2000, p. 23).

With regard to sex offenders under community supervision, the appellate courts have ruled that polygraph evidence is admissible and is sufficiently reliable for use at revocation hearings (*Himes v. Thompson*, 2000; *Kansas v. Lumley*, 1999). Relatedly, the courts have held that polygraph testing as a condition of community placement is allowable as long as the testing is limited to topics related to the sex offender's crime (*State v. Flores-Moreno*, 1994; *State v. Riles*, 1997). In *State v. Eaton* (1996), the Washington Court of Appeals further opined that requiring polygraph testing is not itself a sentencing condition but, rather, a necessary and effective method to monitor an offender's compliance with crime-related conditions of supervision.

BENEFITS OF USING POLYGRAPHS WITH SEX OFFENDERS

Sex offenders can be highly manipulative, deceitful, and evasive during questioning. They can minimize their culpability and deny any deviant sexual fantasies and preoccupations. They can be extremely reluctant to disclose their offending histories for a variety of psychosocial and legal reasons (Ahlmeyer, Heil, McKee, & English, 2000, p. 123). "Some individuals are extremely adept at disguising their sexual pathology, while others exaggerate their symptoms in a histrionic fashion. In many cases, the sexual offender will simply not provide accurate information" (Maletsky, 1991, p. 37). In order for sex offenders to "get past" their denial mechanisms and deception, they need to be open and to divulge their sex offense history and their deviant fantasies and external behaviors (English, Pullen, & Jones, 1997).

The polygraph has been touted as an effective intervention in reducing denial, eliciting admissions of past and present sexual offending, improving treatment outcomes, and improving the supervision of sex offenders (Ahlmeyer et al., 2000; Blasingame, 1998; Wilcox, 2000). Therapists and supervising agents who work with sex offenders point to the tremendous value of the polygraph, and even the threat of a polygraph, in compelling sex offenders to be truthful in therapy.

DIFFICULTIES WITH THE IMPLEMENTATION OF THE POLYGRAPH

Despite the advantages associated with this instrument, there are also problems surrounding the validity of polygraph results, the lack of standardization in its use, and the potential for overreliance on the results. The admissibility, validity, and accuracy of polygraph data are much debated issues. Validity refers to the likelihood that the test procedure will correctly differentiate truthfulness from untruthful responses (Holden, 2000). In their review of field studies, Iacono and Lykken (1997) found no evidence for the validity of polygraph results and raised concerns about the risk of false positives and negatives even with the use of control questions. "The fear of being falsely accused and of being falsely judged guilty may cause innocent subjects to have physiological reactions while the lack of concern or acceptance of responsibility of guilty parties may result in an innocent test outcome" (Cross & Saxe, 1992, p. 23).

In addition, repeated polygraph testing may lead to subjects becoming desensitized to the relevant questions or learning countermeasures, resulting in inaccurate conclusions. Accuracy rates vary depending on the study. Although proponents (Ansley, 1997; Raskin, Honts, & Kircher, 1997) have reported accuracy rates exceeding 90 percent, skeptics argue that these studies lack adequate peer review and have fatal methodological flaws (Iacono & Lykken, 1997). With no agreement among scientists as to the accuracy of the polygraph, ethical concerns are raised about using an unvalidated test in sex offender treatment (Cross & Saxe, 2001; Iacono & Lykken, 1997; Saxe & Ben-Shakkar, 1999). Empirically based standards for the use and interpretation of the polygraph results have also been found to be lacking in many treatment programs (Blasingame, 1998).

DIFFICULTIES IN MIXING PUNITIVENESS AND TREATMENT IN POLYGRAPH USE

Treatment is assumed to be more effective if the sex offender fully discloses prior deviant acts and if the therapist is aware of the extent and nature of the deviant behavior (Abrams, 1989, p. 33). Amenability to treatment and successful rehabilitation are believed to hinge upon eliminating denial and replacing it with an admission of responsibility for past sexual deviancy (Kaden, 1998). Previous offenses that are disclosed for treatment purposes are typically not reported, because there may be insufficient information to consider formal charges (Wilcox, 2000).[12]

Another problem with the use of the polygraph is that it changes the nature of the sex offender patient–therapist relationship. The social control aspect may overpower the support and advocacy role of the therapist. The polygraph has placed treatment providers in a double bind. If the sex offender discloses deviant thoughts, the therapist may feel obligated to inform the offender's probation or parole agent. The technique to motivate or effect behavioral change in therapy becomes the threat of criminal justice consequences, such as electronic monitoring, more frequent monitoring by the agent, or even incarceration (English, 1998). The therapist may feel tempted to contact the police if the sex offender discloses a previous offense. Yet the honesty of the sex offender may be an indication of a trust relationship building between therapist and patient and a sign of progress in treatment. The therapist may jeopardize that fragile trust in the interest of cooperating with the criminal justice system.

Finally, the therapist may become overly dependent on the polygraph in working with sex offenders. Instead of reading behavioral cues and learning additional techniques to elicit information, the therapist may come to rely solely on information from the polygraph as authority to make case management or legal decisions regarding sex offenders (Blasingame, 1998). The integrity of the therapeutic relationship may be compromised when an honest offender is misidentified as "deceptive" and a dishonest offender "beats" the polygraph (Cross & Saxe, 2001).

In summation, polygraphs may elicit important information about sex offenders that may advance treatment goals, but the potential costs due to errors introduce genuine concerns. Erroneous conclusions with deceptive individuals can lead to a new sex offense, and faulty conclusions with truthful offenders can result in more stringent conditions of supervision and even revocation (Cross & Saxe, 2001). Although polygraphs can be useful intimidation devices, further study is recommended to establish their validity. Until that time, failed polygraph tests or refusals to take the tests should not be used as primary evidence for revocation. Wisely, Hagler (1995) cautions that polygraph tests should be used as only one component of a comprehensive treatment and management program and as one source of information with regard to decision making.

CONCLUSION

History has shown the intense focus on sex crimes and sex offenders and the rush to respond to the will of the people on the part of legislators and politicians. Public policy, especially concerning sex offenders, is often tainted by emotion and political rhetoric rather than grounded in factual information or empirical data. "The phenomenon of sexual abuse is intertwined with a strong emotionalism that exacts an almost visceral response in nearly everyone, and this emotionalism has confounded our lawmakers' collective abilities to separate legislative proposals that are functionally efficacious from those that are certainly well-intentioned but are nonetheless unsuccessful" (Edwards & Hensley, 2001, p. 84). As we have discussed in this article, this emotionalism and lack of foresight in the passage of sex offender laws has had many consequences for sex offenders, treatment providers, the criminal justice and mental health systems, and society in general.

How sex offenders are viewed by society is critical to our notion of how to treat, manage, and control these offenders (Mellela et al., 1989). If the sex offender is portrayed as an evil monster deserving of punishment, punitive and incapacitative measures become the primary management strategy. Any sort of treatment effort may be co-opted by punishment. The past provides evidence of the cruelty of state- imposed "treatment" to repugnant groups—lobotomies for the mentally ill and eugenic sterilization of the mentally retarded and habitual criminals (Smith, 1999). Individual offender rights are abrogated by public safety concerns.

Furthermore, there is a pronounced tendency in policy making to characterize all sex offenders as being comparable, when in reality there is a wide range of differences in behavior represented by sex offenders (Tancredi, 1981). "Clinical experience suggests that sexual offenders can be as diverse in personality patterns and behavior habits as many other large diagnostic groups" (Maletsky, 1991, p. 141). This unitary view of sex offenders has resulted in a "one size fits all" approach to policy making. In reality, there is no single treatment modality, or for that matter law, policy, or practice, that will apply to all sex offenders. As an example, research on the use of chemical castration has found it to be an effective strategy for paraphiliacs when combined with treatment. Yet chemical castration is mandated for rapists in California's law. As was discussed earlier, rapists are not good candidates for chemical castration because their underlying motivation to rape is anger, power, and control, not sexual desire alone. Depo-Provera inhibits the sex drive but it does not impact violent tendencies. As an added note, the goal of public safety is certainly not met if Depo-Provera is legally mandated for all sex offenders without a consideration of the clinical research on the drug.

In addition, the goals of the mental health system may become subverted by the goals of the criminal justice system. For psychiatrists, psychologists, and other treatment providers, this punitive attitude toward the management of sex offenders has produced a dissonance between their therapeutic, "helping;" ethic and the reality of a custodial work environment They are forced to compromise their professional values and ethics to incorporate a punitive, control function. Treatment providers may be called upon to sit on disciplinary boards, to participate in institutional security practices (e.g., application of fixed restraints or performance of body cavity searches), and to prescribe medication for behavioral control (Reams, Smith, Fletcher, & Spencer, 1998). They may need to continually evaluate their participation in institutional procedures for its therapeutic foundation or value (Nassi, 1980, pp. 332–333).

It appears that most of these laws, policies, and practices have been enacted, implemented, and upheld publicly, politically, and legally because of the population that they are targeting. "Legislative actions regarding sex offenders have grown out of core assumptions that have yielded a legislative paradigm of punitiveness" (Edwards & Hensley, 2001, p. 85). The legislative actions are based on age-old assumptions about the dangerousness of sex offenders as a "group" and the efficacy of treatment for that group.

The suppositions that a sex offender (of any variety) cannot be truly rehabilitated, will continue to pose a danger to society, and warrants a long-term management and control strategy affect our policies and practices in the criminal justice and mental health systems. Law enforcement confronts a high cost in terms of time, effort, and resources for surveillance and enforcement of "dangerous" sex offenders in the community (Farkas & Zevitz, 2000), and corrections must manage and supervise large caseloads of sex offenders in an intensive manner (Zevitz & Farkas, 2000a). These assumptions about sex offenders have never been reexamined or tested, and most of these laws, policies, and practices have been implemented without any form of analysis or evaluation of their intended outcome and of their social, psychological, economic, and legal consequences. This analysis is critical before one rushes to pass a law or initiate a policy in any area, but it is especially critical when the initiatives are already in place. Research and evaluation are necessary regarding both the process and the outcomes of sex offender-specific laws, policies, and practices.

In conclusion, anticipatory social control is at the core of our laws and policies; sex offenders are punished and incapacitated for fear of what they might do in the future rather than for their crimes of conviction. Civil commitment laws provide a process to indefinitely confine a sex offender. Community notification, chemical castration, and polygraph statutes extend social control over the sex offender released to the community. The controls are justified as necessary to help sex offenders to change or to manage their behavior and to be reintegrated into society. The practical emphases of the laws are usually punitive and incapacitative, overshadowing or subverting any genuine attempt at treatment. "Our laws must provide treatment options for those who will respond to treatment in addition to protection for society from those who will not respond to treatment or do not want treatment" (Freeman-Longo, 1996, p. 317). Yet the courts have never held that the criminal justice system must subscribe to a rehabilitation model or even have rehabilitation as one of its goals (Fitzgerald, 1990, pp. 53–57). The inclusion of treatment terminology, however, is often used to pass constitutional scrutiny. Unfortunately, with the lack of differentiation among sex offenders and the lack of meaningful treatment or emphasis on long-term behavioral change, it is unlikely that these laws will truly provide community protection.

STUDY QUESTIONS

1. After reading this article, write a brief paragraph summarizing what in your opinion has led to laws restricting sex offenders.
2. Trace the history of sex predator laws and civil commitment statutes.
3. What have been some of the major court cases and findings involving sex offenders?
4. What is the history of registration and community notification laws for sex offenders, and what are some of the benefits and problems?
5. While chemical castration has been touted as a treatment for sex offenders, what do we know about its use and effectiveness?
6. What is the history of polygraph use with sex offenders, and what do we know about its effectiveness?

NOTES

1. The research and legal information were extracted from the following databases: Legal Trac, Lexis-Nexis Academic Universe, Health Sciences in EBSCO, Health Sciences in ProQuest, Social Sciences in ProQuest, Criminal Justice Abstracts (via Silver Platter 5.0). and the National Criminal Justice Reference Service (NCJRS). Approximately 14 cases were considered as the most important concerning the issue at hand; however, at least 80 court cases were analyzed, as reviewing some cases led to the review of several other related cases. The deciding factor in our inclusion of these specific cases was the highest court's decision regarding the issue. In examining the legal research in these areas, we selected the years 1994–1999 in Lexis-Nexis and Legal Trac. These years were chosen because most of these laws were passed during this time frame or their use became more prevalent. Because of the multitude of articles written in these areas, we chose those that specifically

focused on the purposes of the laws and on their treatment and punishment aspects. With regard to the health and social science literature on sex offenders, more than 200 articles were compiled that addressed treatment and legal concerns. These articles were then further analyzed for their significance for our research topic.

2. Involuntary civil commitment has been used since colonial times in the U.S. to place in mental institutions those individuals who are considered a threat to themselves or to others. These commitments are typically based on the individuals' mental illness and a determination of their dangerousness, although commitment can be used for other purposes as well, such as controlling the spread of contagious diseases (Barnickol, 2000; Cornwell, 1998; Friedland, 1999). Many states have decided that these existing statutes did not adequately cover the problem of sexual offenders because of the "mental illness" requirement, so they have begun to create laws designed specifically for this group (Barnickol, 2000; Cornwell, 1998).
3. The states are fairly consistent in how often they require these committed offenders to be evaluated and reports submitted to the court regarding their mental condition. For example, states such as Arizona, California, Kansas, and Washington require that the offender be examined annually with reports to the court. Other states such as Wisconsin and Illinois add an examination within six months of commitment (Matson & Lieb, 1997b). States such as Arizona also allow the superintendent of the institution to petition the court for placing the offender into a less restrictive alternative such as a halfway house (Matson & Lieb, 1997b).
4. There are, however, practical concerns regarding when treatment should be delivered to these offenders. With treatment for long-term offenders delayed until just before their release, the offenders can lose interest in changing their behavior, or they can continue to reinforce their deviant attitudes, self-perceptions, fantasies, and distorted values (Schwartz, 1995; Spencer, 1999). Once treatment is finally given, these attitudes may also be supported by other inappropriate values obtained while incarcerated (Spencer, 1999). On the other hand, if treatment is completed long before the sentence is over, any treatment benefits may deteriorate because of the nature of imprisonment (Spencer, 1999). Nonetheless, for Breyer, if long-term incarcerative treatment is deemed necessary in order to reduce recidivism for these offenders, efforts at treatment should begin during imprisonment and should not be delayed until after the sentence has been completed. The Association for the Treatment of Sexual Abuse (ATSA) recommends that offenders should have at least the opportunity to participate in sex offender treatment while in prison.
5. The sex offender is typically required to provide police with name, address, birth date, Social Security number, fingerprints, photograph, offense history, and date and place of convictions (Bedarf, 1995). The duration of sex offender registration may vary from 10 years to life, depending on the state statute.
6. None of the individuals on the committee could, at the time of the hearing, be involved in the prisoner's treatment or diagnosis (*Washington v. Harper*, 1990, p. 210).
7. The Court concluded that this administrative procedure comported with the procedural due process requirements of the Fourteenth Amendment. The Court noted that under state law in inmate could obtain judicial review of the committee's decision through the use of a personal restraint petition or an extraordinary writ (*Washington v. Harper*, 1990, pp. 228–236).
8. According to a National Institute of Justice (NIJ) survey of mental health treatment in 2000, one of the most common forms of treatment was the distribution of psychotropic medication

in correctional confinement facilities. The NIJ study reported that 1 in 10 state inmates was receiving psychotropic medications (Beck & Maruschak, 2000).

9. It is debatable whether Depo-Provera would be considered experimental for use with male sex offenders because the FDA only approved it for use as a contraceptive for women.
10. In *Frye v. United States* the court established the "general acceptance" rule. "When the question involved does not lie within the range of common experience or common knowledge, but requires special experience or special knowledge, then the opinions of witnesses skilled in that particular science, art, or trade to which the question relates are admissible in evidence" (*Frye v. United States,* 1923, p. 1014).
11. The Court referenced numerous criteria, now known as the *Daubert* test, to assist the trial court in its determination. Courts were compelled to consider such factors as whether the theory or technique has been scientifically tested and subjected to peer review and publication, the known or potential rate of error of the scientific technique, explicit identification of a relevant scientific community, and the degree of acceptance of the theory or technique within that scientific community (*Daubert v. Merrell Dow Pharmaceuticals,* 1993, p. 483).
12. Blasingame (1998) recommends that a non-prosecution agreement be in place through the district attorney's office or the corrections department to protect the constitutional rights of sex offenders and to avoid challenges of self-incrimination.

REFERENCES

Abrams, S. (1989). Probation, polygraph surveillance of child abusers. *The Prosecutor, 22,* 29–38.

Adams, D. B. (1999). *Summary of state sex offender registry dissemination procedures.* Washington, DC: U.S. Department of Justice, National Institute of Justice.

Ahlmeyer, S., Heil, P., McKee, B., & English, K. (2000). The impact of polygraphy on admission of victims and offenses in adult sex offenders. *Sexual Abuse: A Journal of Research and Treatment, 12*(2), 123–138.

Alexander, R. (1991). The United States Supreme Court and an inmate's right to refuse mental health treatment. *Criminal Justice Policy Review, 5*(3), 225–240.

American Psychiatric Association. (1994). *Diagnostic and statistical manual of mental disorders* (4th ed.). *Washington, DC: American Psychiatric Association.*

Ansley N. (1997). The validity and reliability of polygraph testing. *Polygraph, 26*(4), 215–239.

Arizona v. Christopher, 652 P.2d 1031 (Ariz. 1982).

Baranowski, G. (1998). Managing sex offenders in the community with the assistance of polygraph testing. *Polygraph, 27*(2), 75–85.

Barnickol, L. (2000). Access to justice: The social responsibility of lawyers. Recent development: Missouri's sexually violent predator law. Treatment or punishment? *Washington University Journal of Law and Policy, 4,* 321–339.

Beck, A. J., & Maruschak, L. M. (2000). *Mental health treatment in stale prisons, 2000* (Bureau of Justice Statistics Publication No. NCJ-188215). Washington, DC: U.S. Department of Justice.

Bedarf, A. (1995). Examining sex offender community notification laws. *California Law Review, 83,* 885–937.

Berliner, L. (1996). Commentary: Community notification of sex offenders: A new tool or false promise. *Journal of Interpersonal Violence. 11*(2), 294–295.

Billings, J., & Bulges, C. (2000). Comment: Maine's sex offender registration ;and notification act. Wise or wicked? *Maine Law Review, 52,* 175–259.

Blasingame, G. D. (1998). Suggested clinical uses of polygraphy in community-based sexual offender treatment programs. *Sexual Abuse: A Journal of Research and Treatment, 10*(1), 37–45.

Bradford, J. M. (1990). The antiandrogen and hormonal treatment of sex offenders. In W. L. Marshall, D. R. Laws, & H. E. Barbaree (Eds.), *Handbook of sexual assault: Issues, theories, and treatment of the offender* (pp. 297–310). New York: Plenum Press.

Brito, T. (2000). Paranoid parents, phantom menaces, and the culture of fear. *Wisconsin Law Review*, 2000, 519–529.

Brooks, A D. (1995). Megan's Law: The legal issues. *Criminal Justice Ethics 14*(2), 12–16.

Bureau of Justice Statistics. (1997). Sex *offenses and offenders: An analysis of data on rape and sexual assault. Washington DC: U.S. Department of Justice.*

Clear, T., & Cole, G. (2000). *American corrections* (5th ed.). Belmont, CA, Wadsworth.

Cornwell, J. K. (1998). Understanding the role of the police and *parens patriae* powers in involuntary civil commitment before and after *Hendricks. Psychology, Public Policy, and Law, 4*(1/2), 377–413.

Cross, T. P., & Saxe, L. (1992). A critique of the validity of polygraph testing in child sexual abuse cases. *Journal of Child Sexual Abuse, 1*(4), 19–33.

Cross, T. P., & Saxe, L. (2001). Polygraph testing and sexual abuse: The lure of the magic lasso. *Child Maltreatment 6*(3), 195–206.

Daubert v. Merrell Dow Pharmaceuticals, 509 U.S. 579 (1993).

Druhm, K. A. (1997). A welcome reaction to draconia: California's penal law section 645. The castration of sex offenders and the Constitution. *Albany Law Review. 61*(1), 285–343.

Edwards, W., & Hensley, C. (2001). Contextualizing sex offender management legislation and policy: Evaluating the problem of latent consequences in community notification laws. *International Journal of Offender Therapy and Comparative Criminology. 45*(1), 83–101.

English, K. (1998). The containment approach: An aggressive strategy for the community management of adult sex offenders. *Psychology, Public Policy, and Law, 4*(1/2), 218–235.

English, K., Jones, L., Pasini-Hill, D., Patrick, D., & Cooley-Towell, S. (2000). *The value of polygraph testing in sex offender management*, Washington, DC: U.S. Department of Justice, National Institute of Justice.

English, K., Pullen, S., & Jones, L. (1997). *Managing adult sex offenders in the community—A containment approach.* Washington, DC: U.S. Department of Justice, National Institute of Justice.

Falk, A. (1999). Sex offenders, mental illness, and criminal responsibility: The constitutional boundaries of civil commitment after *Kansas v. Hendricks. American Journal of Law and Medicine, 25*(1), 117–147.

Farkas, M. A., & Zevitz, R. G. (2000). The law enforcement role in sex offender community notification: A research note. *Journal of Crime and Justice, 23*(1), 125–139.

Farrenkopf, T. (1992). What happens to therapists who work with sex offenders? *Journal of Offender Rehabilitation, 18* (3/4), 217–223.

Federoff, J. P., & Moran, B. (1997). Myths and misconceptions about sex offenders. *Canadian Journal of Human Sexuality 6*(4), 263–277.

Fitzgerald, E. A. (1990). Chemical castration: MPA treatment of the sexual offender. *American Journal of Criminal Law 18*(1), 1–60.

Floyd, J. (1990). The administration of antipsychotic drugs to prisoners: State of the law and beyond. *California Law Review, 78*, 1243–1285.

Freeman-Longo, R. (1996). Feel good legislation: Prevention or calamity. *Child Abuse and Neglect, 20*, 95–101.

Friedland, S. (1999). On treatment, punishment, and the civil commitment of sex offenders. *University of Colorado Law Review, 70*(1), 73–154.

Frye v. United States, 293 F. 1013 (D.C. Cir. 1923).

Gillespie, A. (1998). Note: Constitutional challenges to civil commitment laws: An uphill battle for sexual predators after *Kansas v. Hendricks. Catholic University Law Review, 47*, 1145.

Glovan, J. (1999). 1 don't think we're in Kansas anymore, Leroy: *Kansas v. Hendricks* and the tragedy of judicial restraint. *McGeorge Law Review, 30,* 329–366.

Griswold v. Connecticut, 381 U.S. 479(1965).

Hagler, H. L. (1995). Polygraph as a measure of progress in the assessment, treatment, and surveillance of sex offenders. *Sexual Addiction and Compulsion, 2*(2), 98–111.

Harris, G. T., Rice, M. E., & Quinsey, V. L. (1998). Appraisal and management of risk in sexual aggressors: Implications for criminal justice policy. *Psychology, Public Policy, and Law, 4*(1/2), 73–115.

Henseler, T. B. (1997). Comment: A critical look at the admissibility of polygraph evidence in the wake of *Daubert.* The lie detector fails the test. *Catholic University Law Review, 46,* 1247–1297.

Hicks, P. K. (1993). Castration of sexual offenders: Legal and ethical issues. *Journal of Legal Medicine, 14,* 641–667.

Himes v. Thompson, 225 F.3d 662 (9th Cir. 2000).

Holden, E.J. (2000). Pre-and post-conviction polygraphs: Building blocks for the future. Procedures, principles and policies. *Polygraph, 29*(1), 69–98.

Iacono, W. G., & Lykken, D. T. (1997). The validity of the lie-detector: Two surveys of scientific opinion. *Journal of Applied Psychology, 82,* 426–433.

Jacobson, R, (1999). "Megan's Laws": Reinforcing old patterns of anti-gay police harassment. *Georgetown Law Journal, 87*(7), 2431–2473.

Janus, E. (2000). Sexual predator commitment laws: Lessons for law and the behavioral sciences. *Behavioral Science and the Law, 18,* 5–21.

Johnson, M. (1998). Notification dilemmas: Megan's Law spawned flurry of state acts, but implementation proves problematic for all. *The Quill, 86*(7), 9–12.

Kabat, A. R. (1998). Scarlet letter sex offender databases and community notification: Sacrificing personal privacy for a symbol's sake. *American Criminal Law Review, 35*(2), 333–370.

Kaden, J. (1998). Therapy for convicted sex offenders: Pursuing rehabilitation without incrimination. *Journal of Criminal Law and Criminology, 89*(1), 347–392.

Kansas v. Crane, 534 U.S. 407 (2002).

Kansas v. Hendricks, 521 U.S. 346 (1997).

Kansas v. Lumley, 977 P.2d 914 (Kan. 1999).

Keene, B. (1997). Chemical castration: An analysis of Florida's "cutting edge" policy towards sex criminals. *Florida Law Review, 49,* 803–820.

La Fond, J. (1992). Washington's sexually violent predator law: A deliberate misuse of the therapeutic state for social control. *University of Puget Sound Law Review, 15,* 655–702.

Lea, S., Auburn, T., & Kibblewhite, K. (1999). Working with sex offenders: The perceptions and experiences of professionals and paraprofessionals. *International Journal of Offender Therapy and Comparative Criminology, 43*(1), 103–119.

Lieb, R. (1996). Commentary: Community notification laws. A step toward more effective solutions. *Journal of Interpersonal Violence, 11*(2), 298–300.

Loe, M., & Porter, M. (2000). Case note: Arkansas sexual offender registration and notification laws. An ex post facto violation? *Arkansas Law Review, 53,* 175–195.

Logan, W. (1999). Liberty interests in the preventive state: Procedural due process and sex offender community notification laws. *Journal of Criminal Law and Criminology, 89*(4), 1167–1231.

Maeve, M. K., & Vaughn, M. S. (2001). Nursing with prisoners: The practice of caring, forensic nursing, or penal harm. *Advances in Nursing Science, 24*(2), 47–64.

Maletsky, B. M. (1991). *Treating the sexual offender.* Newbury Park, CA: Sage Publications.

Marsh, R. L., & Walsh, A. (1995). Physiological and psychosocial assessment and treatment of sex offenders: A comprehensive victim-oriented approach. *Journal of Offender Rehabilitation, 22*(1/2), 77–96.

Marshall, S. (2001, July 9). County uses lie detectors to supervise sex offenders. *North County Times,* pp. Al, A4.

Matson, S., & Lieb, R. (1997a). *Megan's Law: A review of state and federal legislation.* Olympia: Washington State Institute for Public Policy.

Matson, S., & Lieb, R. (1997b). *Sexual predator commitment laws.* Olympia: Washington State Institute for Public Policy.

Melella, J. T., Travin, S., & Cullen, K. (1989). Legal and ethical issues in the use of antiandrogens in treating sex offenders. *Bulletin of the American Academy of Psychiatry and Law, 17*(3), 223–232.

Meyer, W. J., & Cole, C. (1997). Physical and chemical castration of sex offenders: A review. *Journal of Offender Rehabilitation, 25*(3/4), 1–16.

Meyer, W. J., Cole, C., & Emory, E. (1992). Depo-Provera treatment for sex offending behavior: An evaluation of outcome. *Bulletin of the American Academy of Psychiatry and Law, 20*(3), 249–259.

Miller, R. D. (1998). Forced administration of sex drive reducing medications to sex offenders: Treatment or punishment? *Psychology, Public Policy, and Law, 4*(1/2), 175–199.

Money, J. (1987). Treatment guidelines: Antiandrogen and counseling of paraphiliac sex offenders. *Journal of Sex and Marital Therapy, 13*(3), 219–223.

Nassi, A. J. (1980). Therapy of the absurd: A study of punishment and treatment in California prisons and the roles of psychiatrists and psychologists. In H. J. Vetter & R. W. Rieber (Eds.), *The psychological foundations of criminal justice: Contemporary perspectives on forensic psychiatry and psychology* (Vol. 2, pp. 322–334). New York: John Jay Press.

Palermo, G., & Farkas, M. A. (2001). *The dilemma of the sexual offender.* Springfield, IL: Charles C Thomas Publisher.

Pallone, N. (1991). The American Bar Association and legislatively mandated treatment for sex offenders. *Journal of Offender Rehabilitation, 17*(1/2), 105–117.

Parks, B. (2000). Sex offender registration enforcement: A proactive stance to monitoring convicted sex offenders. *FBI Law Enforcement Bulletin, 69*(10), 6–9.

People v. Gauntlett, 353 N.W. 2d 463 (Mich. 1986).

Peters-Baker, J. (1998). Comment: Challenging traditional notions of managing sex offenders. Prognosis is lifetime management. *University of Missouri Kansas City Law Review, 66,* 629.

Pratt, J. (2000). Sex crimes and the new punitiveness. *Behavioral Sciences and the Law, 18,* 135–151.

Prendergast, W. E. (1991). *Treating sex offenders in correctional institutions and outpatient clinics: A guide to clinical practice.* Binghamton, NY: Haworth Press.

Prentky, R. (1996). Commentary: Community notification laws and constructive risk reduction. *Journal of Interpersonal Violence, 11*(2), 295–298.

Raskin, D. C., Honts, C. R., & Kircher, J. C. (1997). The scientific status of research on polygraph tests. In D. L. Faigman, D. Kaye, M. J. Saks, & J. Sanders (Eds.), *The West companion to scientific evidence* (pp. 565–582). St. Paul, MN: West Publishing.

Reams, P. N., Smith, M. N., Fletcher, J., & Spencer, E. (1998). Making the case for bioethics in corrections. *Corrections Today, 60*(2), 112–117.

Rennie v. Klein, 462 F. Supp. 1131 (D. NJ. 1978).

Ryan, L. (1990). Washington State Prison procedure for the forcible administration of antipsychotic medication to prison inmates does not violate due process: *Washington v. Harper. University of Cincinnati Law Review, 59,*1373–1415.

Saxe, L., & Ben-Shakkar, G. (1999). Admissibility of polygraph tests: The application of scientific standards post- *Daubert. Psychology, Public Policy, and Law, 5,* 203–223.

Scholle, A (2000). Sex offender registration. *FBI Law Enforcement Bulletin, 69*(7), 17–24.

Schwartz, B. (1988). *A practitioner's guide to treating the incarcerated male sex offender.* Washington, DC: National Institute of Corrections.

Schwartz, B. (1995). Decision making with incarcerated sex offenders. In B. K. Schwartz & H. R. Cellini (Eds.), *The sex offender: Corrections, treatment, and legal practice* (pp. 8-1–8-18). Kingston, NJ: Civic Research Institute.

Scott, L. K. (1997). Community management of sex offenders. In B. K. Schwartz & H. R. Cellini (Eds), *The sex offender: New insights, treatment innovations, and legal developments* (pp. 15-1–15-12). Kingston, NJ: Civic Research Institute.

Simon, J. (1998). Managing the monsters: Sex offenders in the "new penology." *Psychology, Public Policy, and Law.* 4(1/2), 452–467.

Simon, J. (2000). Megan's Law: Crime and democracy in late modern America. *Law and Social Inquiry, 25,* 1111–1150.

Simon, L. (1997). An examination of the assumptions of specialization, mental disorder, and dangerousness in sex offenders. *Behavioral Sciences and the Law, 23*(2/3), 275–308.

Smith, K. L. (1999). Making pedophiles take their medicine: California's chemical castration law. *Buffalo Public Interest Law Journal, 17,* 123.

Spalding, L. H. (1998). Article: Florida's 1997 chemical castration law. A return to the dark ages. *Florida State University Law Review, 25,* 117–139.

Spencer, A. (1999). *Working with sex offenders in prisons and through release to the community: A handbook.* Philadelphia: Jessica Kingsley Publishers.

State v. Eaton, 919 P. 2d 116 (Wash. App. 1996).

State v. Flores-Moreno, 879 P. 2d 292 (Wash. 1994).

State v. Riles, 936 P.2d 11 (Wash. App. 1997).

Tancredi, L. (1981). Informed consent: The dilemma. In E. B. Roberts, R. J. Levy, & S. W. Finkelstein (Eds.), *Biomedical innovation* (pp. 301–323). Cambridge, MA: M.I.T. Press.

Vatz, R. E., & Weinberg, L. S. (2001). Sex offender statutes and psychiatric confusion. *USA Today Magazine, 130,* 61–62.

Washington v. Harper, 494 U.S. 210 (1990).

Wells, C., & Motley, E. (2001). Article: Reinforcing the myth of the crazed rapist: A feminist critique of recent rape legislation. *Boston University Law Review, 81,* 127–198.

Wettstein, W. M. (1992). A psychiatric perspective of Washington's sexually violent predator statute. *University of Puget Sound Law Review, 15,* 597–633.

Wilcox, D. T. (2000). Application of the clinical polygraph examination to the assessment, treatment, and monitoring of sex offenders. *Journal of Sexual Aggression, 5*(2), 134–152.

Winslade, W., Stone, T. H., Smith-Bell, M., & Webb, D. M. (1998). Castrating pedophiles convicted of sex offenses against children: New treatment or old punishment? *Southern Methodist University Law Review, 51.* 349–412.

Zevitz, R., & Farkas, M. A. (2000a). The impact of sex-offender community notification on probation/parole in Wisconsin. *International Journal of Offender Therapy and Comparative Criminology, 44*(1), 8–21.

Zevitz, R., & Farkas, M. A. (2000b). Sex offender community notification: Managing high-risk criminals or exacting further vengeance? *Behavioral Science & the Law, 18*(2/3), 375–391.

Zonana, H., & Norko, M. (1999). Sexual predators. *Forensic Psychiatry. 22*(1), 109–127.

16

EXPERIENCES AND ATTITUDES OF REGISTERED FEMALE SEX OFFENDERS

RICHARD TEWKSBURY

When we think of sex offenders most of us think of male offenders, yet increasingly females are being caught up in the wide net of the criminal justice system. While only a small percentage of all sex offenders, this unique and understudied group piques our interest and curiosity. Who are these offenders, and what do they think about what they have done and what has been done to them? In this article, Tewksbury reports on the findings from a survey he conducted on female sex offenders. The results of this study clearly show that registered female sex offenders often experience collateral consequences that have detrimental effects on their lives.

Recently changes and innovations in public policies and sentencing structures have extended criminal sanctions beyond the immediate needs of offenders, victims, and society in general. One clear example of reaching beyond immediate needs and extending the form, length, and consequences of sentencing is the use of community notification and registration of sex offenders. The present research identifies how such practices have created unintended and potentially serious collateral consequences for convicted sex offenders, with a special focus on female sex offenders.

Research on sex offenders has historically focused, almost exclusively, on male offenders. Studies of female sex offenders are relatively rare, at least in part because most known sex offenders are male. Females comprise only 1.2 percent of arrests for rape and 8.0 percent of arrests for all other sex offenses (U.S. Department of Justice, 2002). Women who are sex offenders are most often convicted of offenses against children (Faller, 1987; Lewis and Stanley, 2000; Rosencrans, 1997; Vandiver and Walker, 2002) or low level felonies (other than rape); because of the latter, female sex offenders are often considered "less serious" sex offenders (Hetherton, 1999).

In the criminological literature, attention to female sex offenders is rare, with the first articles appearing in the 1980s. Although recognized, female sex offending is not only often considered less serious than that of males (Hetherton, 1999), but is also acknowledged as possibly less likely to be detected or reported (Berliner and Barbieri, 1984; Johnson and Shrier, 1987).

Recently, much attention has been focused on community notification and registration of (male and female) sex offenders. To date, there are few studies of sex offender registries. The existing assessments are of four varieties: overviews and "profiles" of the population of registered sex offenders, evaluations of recidivism rates for registered sex offenders, examinations of the accuracy of information

Excerpts from "Experiences and Attitudes of Registered Female Sex Offenders" by Richard Tewksbury (2004). *Federal Probation* 68(3):30–33.

in the registries, and assessments of the experience of registration from the point of view of offenders. However, only one study to date has focused on female registered sex offenders.

The Bureau of Justice Statistics (Adams, 2002) reports that a total of 386,000 convicted sex offenders were registered in 49 states[1] and the District of Columbia in 2001. The use of sex offender registries has grown rapidly; the 2001 total represents a 46.2 percent increase over the registered offender population in 1998. However, statistics on the sex of registered sex offenders is not available. Individual studies have reported that females comprise 0.8 percent of registered sex offenders in Hawaii (Szymkowiak and Fraser, 2002), 3 percent of sex offenders in Iowa, 2.4 percent of registered sex offenders in Arkansas, and in the present research, 2.7 percent and 2 percent of registered sex offenders in Kentucky and Indiana respectively.

The most comprehensive assessment of registered sex offenders to date is the overview of 1,458 offenders on the Hawaii registry (Szymkowiak and Fraser, 2002). The demographic assessment shows that the "average" registered sex offender in Hawaii is between the ages of 40 and 49, lives in the greater Honolulu metropolitan area, has a criminal record of between one and five (typically non-violent) felonies (and a similar number of misdemeanor convictions), and has only one sex offense conviction. In Iowa, the "typical" registered sex offender was a white male with a median age of 31.1 at time of conviction; a majority (57.9 percent) have a previous criminal (but not necessarily sexual) conviction (Adkins, Huff, and Stageberg, 2000).

The only assessment to date of female registered sex offenders (Vandiver and Walker, 2002) focused on identifying a typology of offending patterns, including victim and offender characteristics. This review of official records revealed that these offenders were almost all white, with a mean age of 31 at the time of their first sex offense. Females comprised a slight majority (55 percent) of the victims of these female sex offenders. All had juvenile victims and less serious (if any) criminal records than their male counterparts. Vandiver and Walker (2002) were not able to gather complete data on how many of their sample of female sex offenders were related to their victims; from the data available, though, 94 percent of the victims were related to the offender.

The Iowa study also assessed recidivism of registered sex offenders over a 4.3 year period and showed "mixed effects on recidivism rates" when comparing sex offenders that were and were not (due to a different time period in question) required to register (Adkins, et al., 2000: 19). Registered sex offenders had a sex-offense recidivism rate of 3.0 percent; the comparison group had a recidivism rate of 3.5 percent; total recidivism (for all offenses) was 24.5 percent for the registered offenders and 33.3 percent for the comparison group.

All of the examples of research focused on identifying the characteristics and recidivism of offenders listed on sex offender registries is superficial and macro in nature.

As a third focus, Tewksbury (2002) examined a sample of 537 sex offender listings on the Kentucky Sex Offender Registry in 2001, examining whether offenders' listed information was complete and accurate. Results showed that while most offenders' information was provided, the registry showed a significant degree of missing data. One in twelve (8.2 percent) registrants had "unknown" addresses listed. The problem of accuracy was most acute for sex offenders listed as residing in an urban county: 10.5 percent had "unknown" addresses, 10.5 percent listed addresses that turned out to be commercial locations and 5.4 percent had addresses that did not exist.

Finally, a fourth focus of research on sex offender registries has examined the experiences of registered sex offenders, examining the collateral consequences of registration. Focusing on registered sex offenders in Kentucky, Tewksbury (in press) found that serious social consequences were reported by more than one in four registrants. Specifically, at least one-quarter of registrants reported having received harassing/threatening mail and telephone calls, losing a job, being denied a promotion at work, losing (or being unable to obtain) a place to live, being treated rudely in public, being harassed/threatened in person, and losing at least one friend. These experiences were more common for registrants from non-metropolitan communities, and (surprisingly) less common for offenders with child victims. Tewksbury (in press) further suggested that child-victimizing sex offenders were able to more closely control information about their status as a sex offender, and consequently limit the collateral consequences experienced. One shortcoming of this research, however, is that females comprised only 7.5 percent of the sample, rendering an assessment of female registered sex offenders impossible.

This shortcoming provides the impetus for the current research. With an exclusive focus on female registered sex offenders, the present study examines if and to what degree female registered sex offenders perceive they are known in their community as sex offenders; what consequences are experienced as a result of being listed on the publicly accessible sex offender registry; and registrants' attitudes regarding the registration process.

METHOD

Data for this study were collected through a mailed, anonymous questionnaire sent to all female offenders listed on the Kentucky Sex Offender Registry (http://kspsor.state.ky.us) and Indiana Sex and Violent Offender Registry (http://www.indianasheriffs.org/default.asp). Once identified, sample members' addresses were recorded from their individual registry pages. All sample members were mailed a cover letter, informed consent explanation, survey, and postage-paid return envelope. The Human Studies Protection Program office at the author's university reviewed all materials. Data collection was conducted in May 2004.

SAMPLE

A review of all entries on the Indiana and Kentucky registries reveals a total of 227 females. The Kentucky registry had 97 females listed among the total of 3,586 individuals. Females accounted for 130 of 6,407 registrations on the Indiana registry. This means that 2.7 percent of the registrants in Kentucky and 2.0 percent in Indiana are female.

A total of 40 completed and usable surveys were obtained,[2] for a response rate of 20.5 percent. While this is not a very high response rate,[3] this needs to be understood as a difficult to access population. Previous research looking at registrants has relied on small samples (2.4 percent, Vandiver and Walker, 2002; 14.3 percent, Tewksbury, in press) or has used only officially recorded data, avoiding collection of data directly from registrants (Adkins, et al., 2000; Szymkowiak and Fraser, 2002; Tewksbury, 2002). And, as Vandiver and Walker (2002:286) state, "the number of subjects in female sex offender research has consistently remained low.... The number of subjects in female sex offender literature has been as low as 2 (Peluso and Putnam, 1996) and as high as 93 (Rosencrans, 1997)." Additionally, studies of sex offenders in general have almost always collected data either from offenders who are incarcerated or in treatment, or researchers have collected data from professionals working with sex offenders (treatment providers, probation officers, etc.). Only two studies have gathered data directly from sex offenders in the community (Sack and Mason, 1980; Tewksbury, in press), and both have samples of 112.

Table 16.1 presents the demographic and registration information for the respondents.

INSTRUMENT

The data collection instrument was designed specifically for this study. The instrument is a four-page questionnaire containing 35 closed-ended

TABLE 16.1 DESCRIPTION OF SAMPLE

Number of Offenders	40
Registration Period	
10 Years	75.7%
Lifetime	24.3%
Mean length of time on registry	38.5
Mean Age	37.3
Race	
White	92.3%
Black	5.1%
Other	2.6%
Victims*	
Male	41.0%
Female	43.6%
Children	71.8%
Multiple Victims	2.6%
A Relative as Victim	15.4%

* Percentages total more than 100 percent due to multiple responses permitted.

items. The items assess demographics, offenses characteristics, questions about whether, by whom, and how often the offender is recognized as a registered sex offender, and attitudes regarding registries in general and the registration experience specifically.

The dependent variables for this analysis are self-reports by registered sex offenders regarding ten different negative consequences they may have experienced (loss of a job, denial of promotion, loss/denial of a place to live, being treated "rudely" in a public place, being asked to leave a business, loss of a friend, harassment or assault and receipt of harassing/threatening telephone calls or mail). Also used as dependent variables are items assessing registrants' perceptions of shame, being unfairly punished by registration, understanding the purpose/goal for the registry and perceiving social stigmatization, all as a result of registration.

RESULTS

Analysis focused on identifying the distribution of negative consequences reported by registrants as arising from registration, as well as perceptions and attitudes of registrants toward registries and the activities of officials charged with maintaining the registries.

In order to understand the negative consequences that may come from a sex offender being placed on the registry, it is important to assess the degree to which others in a registrant's social milieu know of the registrant's status and offenses. When asked to indicate what portion of their "family, friends, coworkers, and other people you consider a part of your life know about your sexual offense conviction(s)," responses indicated that for almost all offenders, at least a sizable minority if not all or nearly all of these persons know of the offender's offenses. Only 5.0 percent of registrants report that fewer than 10 percent of others in their lives know about their offenses. However, fully 45.0 percent report that 90 percent or more of others know of their offenses, with 25.0 percent saying everyone they know has knowledge of their offenses. Whether this knowledge is attributable to the registration process and site is not known; however, the important point is that for most registered sex offenders, others know their status as sexual offenders.

PERCEIVED COLLATERAL CONSEQUENCES OF REGISTRATION

As shown in Table 16.2, a number of negative experiences stemming from sex offender registration are commonly reported by registrants. More than 30 percent of registrants report having lost a job, losing or being denied a place to live, being treated rudely in public, losing friends, and being personally harassed as a result of public knowledge of one's offenses.

Table 16.3 presents the distribution of negative experiences resulting from registration for registrants based on length of time on the sex offender registry. It is apparent that for all ten collateral consequences, a greater percentage of women who have been on the registry for longer than the sample

TABLE 16.2 NEGATIVE EXPERIENCES RESULTING FROM REGISTRATION

Experience	Percent
Loss of job	42.1
Denial of promotion at work	10.5
Loss/Denial of place to live	31.6
Treated rudely in a public place	31.6
Asked to leave a business	2.6
Lost a friend who found out about registration	39.5
Harassed in person	34.2
Assaulted	10.5
Received harassing/threatening telephone calls	10.5
Received harassing/threatening mail	15.8

TABLE 16.3 NEGATIVE EXPERIENCES RESULTING FROM REGISTRATION, ABOVE AND BELOW MEDIAN SAMPLE TIME ON REGISTRY

Experience	32 Months or Less Time on Registry (Percent)	More than 32 Months on Registry (Percent)
Loss of job	38.9	45.0
Denial of promotion at work	–	20.0
Loss/Denial of place to live	27.8	35.0
Treated rudely in a public place	22.2	40.0
Asked to leave a business	–	5.0
Lost a friend who found out about registration	27.8	50.0
Harassed in person	22.2	45.0
Assaulted	5.6	15.0
Received harassing/ threatening telephone calls	5.6	15.0
Received harassing/ threatening mail	5.6	25.0

median of 32 months report having had such a negative experience.

ATTITUDES TOWARD REGISTRATION

In addition, to assess registered female sex offenders' perceptions and reports of negative consequences arising from their listing on the registry, analysis also examined registrants' responses to five attitudinal items. Women were asked to report their level of agreement with each of 5 statements (1= strongly disagree, 10 = strongly agree), as shown in Table 16.4. Registrants report a high level of shame about their registration and largely believe that registration is an unfair form of punishment; yet typically say they understand why society desires a sex offender registry.

There are no statistically significant mean differences in responses to the five attitudinal items across registered female sex offenders based on the length of time they have been on the sex offender registry.

All registrants were also asked whether they believed that "because my name and personal information is listed on the Sex Offender Registry I am less likely to commit another sexual offense in the future." The mean response to this item is 7.42. Nearly two-thirds (61.1 percent) of registrants report complete agreement with the statement, although the actual effect of registration on recidivism cannot be determined. No statistically significant differences are seen for registrants based on length of time on the registry.

TABLE 16.4 MEAN RESPONSES TO ATTITUDINAL ITEMS

Item	Total Sample	Shorter Than Median Time	Longer Than Median Time
"I feel ashamed that I am on the Kentucky Sex Offender Registry"	8.20	7.74	8.62
"I feel I am being unfairly punished by being on the Sex Offender Registry"	7.50	7.74	7.29
"I understand why people want there to be a Sex Offender Registry"	7.53	8.16	6.95
"People avoid being around or talking with me if they know I am on the Sex Offender Registry"	5.28	4.95	5.57
"I think that the Sex Offender Registry is a good thing"	6.45	6.21	6.67

DISCUSSION

As one of the more recent responses to sexual offending, the use of sex offender registries clearly has far-reaching implications for society as well as for individuals listed on registries. However, little previous research has examined these implications. The present research is one of the first attempts to examine both the consequences of sex offender registration for offenders and one of the few assessments of female sex offenders outside of clinical settings.

The results of this research make clear that registered female sex offenders frequently experience collateral consequences that may have serious deleterious effects on their social, economic, and physical well-being. While the goal of shaming sex offenders seems to be achieved through registration, and registered female sex offenders report an understanding of why society would want to have such registries, there are also obvious indications of registration having lasting negative consequences for individual offenders. Approximately one in three (or more) registered female sex offenders report that as a result of their listing on a sex offender registry they have lost a job, lost or been denied a place to live, lost friends, and been personally harassed. Such experiences arc directly contradictory with the goals and resources known to be critical to successful community reentry and the reduction of recidivism. And, as women remain on a sex offender registry for longer periods of time, these (and other) collateral consequences become more common.

In light of these findings, the importance of sex offender registration as a tool for promoting public safety needs to be questioned. While the present research does not definitively conclude that sex offender registration leads to recidivism or poor community adjustment following conviction, it does suggest that the very resources identified as centrally important for successful reentry are diminished and weakened by registration. As such, it is important to continue to assess the consequences of sex offender registration on recidivism, and on accompanying costs (both financial and social) experienced by offenders and communities. If registration cannot be shown to be associated with significantly lower rates of recidivism (see Adkins et al., 2000), the costs may well outweigh the benefits of registration. And, if registration in fact is associated with lower rates of sexual offending recidivism, it may be useful to examine whether the current method for registering (and publicizing information about registrants) can be modified in a way that maintains the positive outcomes while reducing the costly collateral consequences.

The present study is a first step toward evaluating these costs and benefits. Future research needs to look more closely at the costs of sex offender registration and the benefits. At present it appears that registration of sex offenders—or at least the female sex offenders questioned in this study—may generate more societal costs and negative consequences for individuals than intended, necessary, and appropriate.

STUDY QUESTIONS

1. How do female sex offenders differ from their male counterparts?
2. What are some of the perceived collateral consequences of registration for female sex offenders?
3. Describe the respondents' attitudes toward registration. Do you agree that their conclusions are warranted?
4. Do you think that requiring female sex offenders to register improves public safety?
5. Given the need for the criminal justice system to have "equal" justice, how might we develop a system of registration that is perceived as both fair and effective?

NOTES

1. Massachusetts data was not included due to a court injunction prohibiting registration without first providing a hearing to the offender.

2. Twenty-three (23) surveys were returned as undeliverable, invalid, or non-existent addresses. Nineteen (19) (14.6 percent) of the 130 female registrants in Indiana had mail returned as an incorrect address or undeliverable and 4 (4.1 percent) of those in Kentucky were returned. The final sample of contacted female registered sex offenders, therefore, is 204.
3. It should be noted that response rates for mailed surveys with no sponsorship or follow-ups may run as low as 20 percent (Monette, Sullivan and DeJong, 2005; Hagan, 2003; Miller, 1991).

REFERENCES

Adams, D. B. (2002). *Summary of State Sex Offender Registries, 2001.* Washington, D.C.: U.S. Department of Justice.

Adkins, G., Huff, D., & Stageberg, P. (2000). *The Iowa Sex Offender Registry and Recidivism.* Des Moines, Iowa: Iowa Department of Human Rights.

Berliner, L. and Barbieri, M.K. (1984). The testimony of the child victim of sexual assault. *Journal of Social Issues,* 40(2), 125–137.

Faller, K. C. (1987). Women who sexually abase children. *Violence and Victims,* 2(4), 263–276.

Hagan, F. E. 2003. *Research Methods in Criminal Justice and Criminology* (6th ed.). Boston: Allyn & Bacon.

Hetherton, J. (1999). The idealization of women: its role in the minimization of child sexual abuse by females. *Child Abuse and Neglect,* 23(2), 161–174.

Johnson, R.L. and D. Shrier. (1987). Past sexual victimization by females of male patients in an adolescent medicine clinic population. *American Journal of Psychiatry,* 144(5), 650–652.

Lewis, C.F. and C.R. Stanley. (2000). Women accused of sexual offenses. *Behavioral Sciences and the Law,* 18(1), 73–81.

Miller, Delbert C. (1991). *Handbook of Research Design and Social Measurement* (5th ed.). New York: McKay.

Monette, DR., T.J. Sullivan, and C.R. DeJong. 2005. *Applied Social Research* (6th ed.). Belmont, CA: Brooks-Cole, Thomson.

Peluso, E. and N. Putnam. (1996). Case study: Sexual abuse of boys by females. *Journal of the American Academy of Adolescent Psychiatry,* 35(1), 51–54.

Rosencrans, 15. (1997). *The Last Secret: Daughters Sexually Abused by Mothers.* Orwell, VT: Safer Society Press.

Sack, William H. and Robert Mason. 1980. Child abuse and conviction of sexual crimes: A preliminary finding. *Law and Human Behavior,* 4(3): 211–215.

Szymkowiak, K., &. Fraser, T. (2002). *Registered Sex Offenders in Hawaii.* Honolulu: Department of the Hawaii Attorney General.

Tewksbury, R. (2002). Validity and utility of the Kentucky sex offender registry. *Federal Probation,* 66(1): 21–26.

Tewksbury, R. (in press). Collateral consequences of sex offender registration. *Journal of Contemporary Criminal Justice.*

U.S. Department of Justice, 2002. *Crime in the United States, 2001.* Washington, D.C.: Federal Bureau of Investigation.

Vandiver, D. M., & Walker, J. T. (2002). Female sex offenders: An overview and analysis of 40 cases. *Criminal Justice Review,* 27(2):284–300.

PART

V

OFFENDER PROGRAMMING AND TREATMENT

"With few and isolated exceptions, the rehabilitative efforts that have been reported so far have not had an appreciable effect on recidivism."

—Robert Martinson

After examining more than two decades of correctional research, Martinson's now famous study had a tremendous impact on the field of corrections. Whatever the limitations of the Martinson study, and there were many, the conclusion drawn by many was that treatment or rehabilitation is not effective. Thus, what became known as the "nothing works" doctrine led to renewed efforts to demonstrate the effectiveness of correctional programs. The effectiveness of correctional programs has been debated and studied for many years. Evaluating the effectiveness of correctional programs is not easy even under the best circumstances. Political, ethical, and programmatic reasons may not permit the researcher to develop adequate control groups or measures. Furthermore, tracking offenders once they have been released from prison is time consuming and difficult at best. Despite these constraints, there have been many studies conducted on the effectiveness of correctional programming and treatment.

As you shall learn, there is a large body of knowledge based on over 30 years of research conducted by numerous scholars that has demonstrated that correctional programs can indeed reduce recidivism. Also referred to as evidence-based practice, the "what works" movement demonstrates empirically that theoretically sound, well-designed programs that meet certain conditions can appreciably reduce recidivism rates for offenders. Through the review and analysis of hundreds of studies, researchers have identified a set of principles that should guide correctional programs.

The first is the risk principle, or the "who" to target—those offenders who pose the higher risk of continued criminal conduct. This principle states that our most intensive correctional treatment and intervention programs should be reserved for higher risk offenders. Risk in this context refers to those offenders with a higher probability of recidivism. Why waste our programs on offenders who do not need them? This is a waste of resources, and, more importantly, research has clearly demonstrated that when we place lower risk offenders in more structured programs, we often increase their failure rates (and thus reduce the overall effectiveness of the program).

The second principle is referred to as the need principle, or the "what" to target—criminogenic factors that are highly correlated with criminal conduct. The need principle states that programs should target crime-producing needs, such as antisocial attitudes, values, and beliefs; antisocial peer associations; substance abuse; lack of problem-solving and self-control skills; and other factors that are highly correlated with criminal conduct. Furthermore, programs need to ensure that the vast majority of their interventions are focused on these factors. Noncriminogenic factors such as self-esteem, physical conditioning, understanding one's culture or history, and creative abilities will not have much effect on recidivism rates.

The third principle is the responsivity principle, or the "how"—the ways in which correctional programs should target risk and need factors. This principle states that the most effective programs are behavioral in nature. Behavioral programs have several attributes. First, they are centered on the *present* circumstances and risk factors that are responsible for the offender's behavior. Second, they are *action* oriented rather than talk oriented. In other words, offenders do something about their difficulties rather than just talk about them. Third, they teach offenders new, prosocial skills to replace the antisocial ones (e.g., stealing, cheating, lying) through modeling, practice, and reinforcement. Examples of behavioral programs would include structured social learning programs where new skills are taught and behaviors and attitudes are consistently reinforced; cognitive behavioral programs that target attitudes, values, peers, substance abuse, anger, and so on; and family-based interventions that train family members in appropriate behavioral techniques. Interventions based on these approaches are very structured and emphasize the importance of modeling and behavioral rehearsal techniques that engender self-efficacy, challenge cognitive distortions, and assist offenders in developing good problem-solving and self-control skills. These strategies have been demonstrated to be effective in reducing recidivism. Nonbehavioral interventions that are often used in programs would include drug and alcohol education, fear tactics and other emotional appeals, talk therapy, nondirective client-centered approaches, books, lectures, milieu therapy, and self-help. There is little empirical evidence that these approaches will lead to long-term reductions in recidivism. If we put it all together, we have the "who, what, and how" of correctional intervention, also known as "what works."

We have come a long way since Martinson's early attempt at reviewing the research on correctional treatment effectiveness. Most contemporary scholars who study correctional treatment have concluded that we can indeed develop programs that are effective in reducing recidivism. That does not mean that challenges do not remain. Designing and implementing effective correctional programs remain daunting tasks. Many still practice "correctional quackery," but increasingly we find correctional officials paying attention to the research.

The articles in Part V provide a good overview of how far we have come in learning about the effectiveness of correctional programs. In some ways they also illustrate the debate over rehabilitation, some of which centers around institutional programming. We know that programs are an important part of a correctional institution. What we want is for the most effective programs to be operated and supported.

17

WHAT WORKS?

QUESTIONS AND ANSWERS ABOUT PRISON REFORM

ROBERT MARTINSON

The tremendous increase of crime during the 1960s heralded a shift in the way Americans would come to view criminals in the next decade, leading to a law-and-order movement in the early 1970s. The Martinson Report, a massive study undertaken at that time to determine the most effective means of rehabilitating prisoners, concluded that, "with few and isolated exceptions, the rehabilitative efforts that have been reported so far have had no appreciable effect on recidivism." These words were interpreted to mean that "nothing works" as far as rehabilitating prisoners was concerned and that a new direction needed to be found. In 1974, a summary of the study's findings was presented by Robert Martinson in *The Public Interest.* Other research studies supported Martinson's conclusion and, by the end of the decade, a paradigm shift had occurred in corrections from rehabilitation to deterrence and just deserts. The influence of Martinson's article, the first published account of the aforementioned survey, cannot be underestimated—it was "the straw that broke the camel's back." Support for the rehabilitative ideal and the medical model of corrections decreased substantially after its publication.

In the past several years, American prisons have gone through one of their recurrent periods of strikes, riots, and other disturbances. Simultaneously, and in consequence, the articulate public has entered another one of its sporadic fits of attentiveness to the condition of our prisons and to the perennial questions they pose about the nature of crime and the uses of punishment. The result has been a widespread call for "prison reform," i.e., for "reformed" prisons which will produce "reformed" convicts. Such calls are a familiar feature of American prison history. American prisons, perhaps more than those of any other country, have stood or fallen in public esteem according to their ability to fulfill their promise of rehabilitation.

One of the problems in the constant debate over "prison reform" is that we have been able to draw very little on any systematic empirical knowledge about the success or failure that we have met when we *have* tried to rehabilitate offenders, with various treatments and in various institutional and noninstitutional settings. The field of penology has produced a voluminous research literature on this

Excerpts from "What Works? Questions and Answers About Prison Reform" by Robert Martinson. *The Public Interest* 35:22–54.

subject, but until recently there has been no comprehensive review of this literature and no attempt to bring its findings to bear, in a useful way, on the general question of "What works?" My purpose in this [chapter] is to sketch an answer to that question.

THE TRAVAILS OF A STUDY

In 1966, the New York State Governor's Special Committee on Criminal Offenders recognized their need for such an answer. The Committee was organized on the premise that prisons could rehabilitate, that the prisons of New York were not in fact making a serious effort at rehabilitation, and that New York's prisons should be converted from their existing custodial basis to a new rehabilitative one. The problem for the Committee was that there was no available guidance on the question of what had been shown to be the most effective means of rehabilitation. My colleagues and I were hired by the committee to remedy this defect in our knowledge; our job was to undertake a comprehensive survey of what was known about rehabilitation.

In 1968, in order to qualify for federal funds under the Omnibus Crime Control and Safe Streets Act, the state established a planning organization, which acquired from the Governor's Committee the responsibility for our report. But by 1970, when the project was formally completed, the state had changed its mind about the worth and proper use of the information we had gathered. The Governor's Committee had begun by thinking that such information was a necessary basis for any reforms that might be undertaken; the state planning agency ended by viewing the study as a document whose disturbing conclusions posed a serious threat to the programs which, in the meantime, they had determined to carry forward. By the spring of 1972—fully a year after I had re-edited the study for final publication—the state had not only failed to publish it, but had also refused to give me permission to publish it on my own. The document itself would still not be available to me or to the public today had not Joseph Alan Kaplon, an attorney, subpoenaed it from the state for use as evidence in a case before the Bronx Supreme Court.[1]

During the time of my efforts to get the study released, reports of it began to be widely circulated, and it acquired something of an underground reputation. But this article is the first published account, albeit a brief one, of the findings contained in that 1,400-page manuscript.

What we set out to do in this study was fairly simple, though it turned into a massive task. First we undertook a six-month search of the literature for any available reports published in the English language on attempts at rehabilitation that had been made in our corrections systems and those of other countries from 1945 through 1967. We then picked from that literature all those studies whose findings were interpretable—that is, whose design and execution met the conventional standards of social science research. Our criteria were rigorous but hardly esoteric: A study had to be an evaluation of a treatment method, it had to employ an independent measure of the improvement secured by that method, and it had to use some control group, some untreated individuals with whom the treated ones could be compared. We excluded studies only for methodological reasons: They presented insufficient data, they were only preliminary, they presented only a summary of findings and did not allow a reader to evaluate those findings, their results were confounded by extraneous factors, they used unreliable measures, one could not understand their descriptions of the treatment in question, they drew spurious conclusions from their data, their samples were undescribed or too small or provided no true comparability between treated and untreated groups, or they had used inappropriate statistical tests and did not provide enough information for the reader to recompute the data. Using these standards, we drew from the total number of studies 231 acceptable ones, which we not only analyzed ourselves but summarized in detail so that a reader of our analysis would be able to compare it with his independent conclusions.

These treatment studies use various measures of offender improvement: recidivism rates (that is, the rates at which offenders return to crime), adjustment to prison life, vocational success, educational achievement, personality and attitude change, and general adjustment to the outside community. We included all of these in our study; but in these pages I will deal only with the effects of rehabilitative treatment on recidivism, the phenomenon which reflects most directly how well our present treatment programs are performing the task of rehabilitation. The use of even this one measure brings with it enough methodological complications to make a clear reporting of the findings most difficult. The groups that are studied, for instance, are exceedingly disparate, so that it is hard to tell whether what "works" for one kind of offender also works for others. In addition, there has been little attempt to replicate studies; therefore one cannot be certain how stable and reliable the various findings are. Just as important, when the various studies use the term "recidivism rate," they may in fact be talking about somewhat different measures of offender behavior—i.e., "failure" measures such as arrest rates or parole violation rates, or "success" measures such as favorable discharge from parole or probation. And not all of these measures correlate very highly with one another. These difficulties will become apparent again and again in the course of this discussion.

With these caveats, it is possible to give a rather bald summary of our findings: *With few and isolated exceptions, the rehabilitative efforts that have been reported so far have had no appreciable effect on recidivism.* Studies that have been done since our survey was completed do not present any major grounds for altering that original conclusion. What follows is an attempt to answer the questions and challenges that might be posed to such an unqualified statement.

EDUCATION AND VOCATIONAL TRAINING

1. *Isn't it true that a correctional facility running a truly rehabilitative program—one that prepares inmates for life on the outside through education and vocational training—will turn out more successful individuals than will a prison which merely leaves its inmates to rot?*

If this *is* true, the fact remains that there is very little empirical evidence to support it. Skill development and education programs are in fact quite common in correctional facilities, and one might begin by examining their effects on young males, those who might be thought most amenable to such efforts. A study by New York State (1964)[2] found that for young males as a whole, the degree of success achieved in the regular prison academic education program, as measured by changes in grade achievement levels, made no significant difference in recidivism rates. The only exception was the relative improvement, compared with the sample as a whole, that greater progress made in the top 7 percent of the participating population—those who had high I.Q.'s, had made good records in previous schooling, and who also made good records of academic progress in the institution. And a study by Glaser (1964) found that while it was true that, when one controlled for sentence length, more attendance in regular prison academic programs slightly decreased the subsequent chances of parole violation, this improvement was not large enough to outweigh the associated disadvantage for the "long-attenders": Those who attended prison school the longest also turned out to be those who were in prison the longest. Presumably, those getting the most education were also the worst parole risks in the first place.[3]

Studies of special education programs aimed at vocational or social skill development, as opposed to conventional academic education programs, report similarly discouraging results and reveal additional problems in the field of correctional research. Jacobson (1965) studied a program of "skill re-education" for institutionalized young males, consisting of 10 weeks of daily discussions aimed at developing problem-solving skills. The discussions were led by an adult who was thought capable of serving as a role model for the boys, and they were encouraged to follow the example that he set. Jacobson found that over all, the program produced no improvement in recidivism rates. There was only one special subgroup which provided an exception to this pessimistic finding: If boys in the experimental program decided afterwards to go on to take three or more regular prison courses, they did better upon release than "control" boys who had done the same. (Of course, it also seems likely that experimental boys who did *not* take these extra courses did worse than their controls.)

Zivan (1966) also reported negative results from a much more ambitious vocational training program at the Children's Village in Dobbs Ferry, New York. Boys in his special program were prepared for their return to the community in a wide variety of ways. First of all, they were given, in sequence, three types of vocational guidance: "assessment counseling," "development counseling," and "pre-placement counseling." In addition, they participated in an "occupational orientation," consisting of role-playing, presentations via audiovisual aids, field trips, and talks by practitioners in various fields of work. Furthermore, the boys were prepared for work by participating in the Auxiliary Maintenance Corps, which performed various chores in the institution; a boy might be promoted from the Corps to the Work Activity Program, which "hired" him, for a small fee, to perform various artisans' tasks. And finally, after release from Children's Village, a boy in the special program received supportive after-care and job placement aid.

None of this made any difference in recidivism rates. Nevertheless, one must add that it is impossible to tell whether this failure lay in the program itself or in the conditions under which it was administered. For one thing, the education department of the institution itself was hostile to the program; they believed instead in the efficacy of academic education. This staff therefore tended to place in the pool from which experimental subjects were randomly selected mainly "multi-problem" boys. This by itself would not have invalidated the experiment as a test of vocational training for this particular type of youth, but staff hostility did not end there; it exerted subtle pressures of disapproval throughout the life of the program. Moreover, the program's "after-care" phase also ran into difficulties; boys who were sent back to school before getting a job often received advice that conflicted with the program's counseling, and boys actually looking for jobs met with the frustrating fact that the program's personnel, despite concerted efforts, simply could not get businesses to hire the boys.

We do not know whether these constraints, so often found in penal institutions, were responsible for the program's failure; it might have failed anyway. All one can say is that this research failed to show the effectiveness of special vocational training for young males.

The only clearly positive report in this area comes from a study by Sullivan (1967) of a program that combined academic education with special training in the use of IBM equipment. Recidivism rates after one year were only 48 percent for experimentals, as compared with 66 percent for controls. But when one examines the data, it appears that this difference emerged only between the controls and those who had successfully *completed* the training. When one compares the control group with all those who had been *enrolled* in the program, the difference disappears. Moreover, during this study the random assignment procedure between experimental and control groups seems to have broken down, so that towards the end, better risks had a greater chance of being assigned to the special program.

In sum, many of these studies of young males are extremely hard to interpret because of flaws in research design. But it can safely be said that they provide us with no clear evidence that education or skill development programs have been successful.

TRAINING ADULT INMATES

When one turns to adult male inmates, as opposed to young ones, the results are even more discouraging. There have been six studies of this type; three of them report that their programs, which ranged from academic to prison work experience, produced no significant differences in recidivism rates, and one—by Glaser (1964)—is almost impossible to interpret because of the risk differentials of the prisoners participating in the various programs.

Two studies—by Schnur (1948) and by Saden (1962)—*do* report a positive difference from skill development programs. In one of them, the Saden study, it is questionable whether the experimental and control groups were truly comparable. But what is more interesting is that both these "positive" studies dealt with inmates incarcerated prior to or during World War II. Perhaps the rise in our educational standards as a whole since then has lessened the differences that prison education or training can make. The only other interesting possibility emerges from a study by Gearhart (1967). His study was as one of those that reported vocational education to be nonsignificant in effecting recidivism rates. He did note, however, that when a trainee succeeded in finding a job related to his area of training, he had a slightly higher chance of becoming a successful parolee. It is possible, then, that skill development programs fail because what they teach bears so little relationship to an offender's subsequent life outside the prison.

One other study of adults, this one with fairly clear implications, has been performed with women rather than men. An experimental group of institutionalized women in Milwaukee was given an extremely comprehensive special education program, accompanied by group counseling. Their training was both academic and practical; it included reading, writing, spelling, business filing, child care, and grooming. Kettering (1965) found that the program made no difference in the women's rates of recidivism.

Two things should be noted about these studies. One is the difficulty of interpreting them as a whole. The disparity in the programs that were tried, in the populations that were affected, and in the institutional settings that surrounded these projects make it hard to be sure that one is observing the same category of treatment in each case. But the second point is that despite this difficulty, one can be reasonably sure that, so far, educational and vocational programs have not worked. We don't know why they have failed. We don't know whether the programs themselves are flawed, or whether they arc incapable of overcoming the effects of prison life in general. The difficulty may be that they lack applicability to the world the inmate will face outside of prison. Or perhaps the type of educational and skill improvement they produce simply doesn't have very much to do with an individual's propensity to commit a crime. What we do know is that, to date, education and skill development have not reduced recidivism by rehabilitating criminals.

THE EFFECTS OF INDIVIDUAL COUNSELING

2. *But when we speak of a rehabilitative prison, aren't we referring to more than education and skill development alone? Isn't what's needed [is] some way of counseling inmates or helping them with the deeper problems that have caused their maladjustment?*

This, too, is a reasonable hypothesis; but when one examines the programs of this type that have been tried, it's hard to find any more grounds for enthusiasm than we found with skill development and education. One method that's been tried—though so far, there have been acceptable reports only of its application to young offenders—has been individual psychotherapy. For young males, we found seven such reported studies. One study, by Guttman (1963) at the Nelles School, found such treatment to be ineffective in reducing recidivism rates; another, by Rudoff (1960), found it unrelated to *institutional* violation rates, which were themselves related to parole success. It must be pointed out that Rudoff used only this indirect measure of association, and the study therefore cannot rule out the possibility of a treatment effect. A third, also by Guttman (1963) but at another institution, found that such treatment was actually related to a slightly *higher* parole violation rate; and a study by Adams (1959b and 1961b) also found a lack of improvement in parole revocation and first suspension rates.

There were two studies at variance with this pattern. One by Persons (1966) said that if a boy was judged to be "successfully" treated—as opposed to simply being subjected to the treatment experience—he did tend to do better. And there was one finding both hopeful and cautionary: At the Deuel School (Adams, 1961a), the experimental boys were first divided into two groups, those rated as "amenable" to treatment and those rated "non-amenable." Amenable boys who got the treatment did better than non-treated boys. On the other hand, "non-amenable" boys who were treated actually did worse than they would have done if they had received no treatment at all. It must be pointed out that Guttman (1963), dealing with younger boys in his Nelles School study, did not find such an "amenability" effect, either to the detriment of the non-amenables who were treated *or* to the benefit of the amenables who were treated. But the Deuel School study (Adams, 1961a) suggests both that there is something to be hoped for in treating properly selected amenable subjects and that if these subjects are not properly selected, one may not only wind up doing no good but may actually produce harm. There have been two studies of the effects of individual psychotherapy on young incarcerated *female* offenders, and both of them (Adams, 1959a; Adams, 1961b) report no significant effects from the therapy. But one of the Adams studies (1959a) does contain a suggestive, although not clearly interpretable, finding: If this individual therapy was administered by a psychiatrist or a psychologist, the resulting parole suspension rate was almost two-and-a-half times *higher* than if it was administered by a social worker without this specialized training.

There has also been a much smaller number of studies of two other types of individual therapy: counseling, which is directed towards a prisoner's gaining new insight into his own problems, and casework, which aims at helping a prisoner cope with his more pragmatic immediate needs. These types of therapy both rely heavily on the empathetic relationship that is to be developed between the professional and the client. It was noted above that the Adams study (1961b) of therapy administered to girls, referred to in the discussion of individual psychotherapy, found that social workers seemed better at the job than psychologists or psychiatrists. This difference seems to suggest a favorable outlook for these alternative forms of individual therapy. But other studies of such therapy have produced ambiguous results. Bernsten (1965) reported a Danish experiment that showed that socio-psychological counseling combined with comprehensive welfare measures—job and residence placement, clothing, union and health insurance membership, and financial aid—produced an improvement among some short-term male offenders, though not those in either the highest-risk or the lowest-risk categories. On the other hand, Hood, in Britain (1966), reported generally non-significant results with a program of counseling for young males. (Interestingly enough, this experiment *did* point to a mechanism capable of changing recidivism rates. When boys were released from institutional care and entered the army directly, "poor risk" boys among both experimentals *and* controls did better than expected. "Good risks" did worse.)

So these foreign data are sparse and not in agreement; the American data are just as sparse. The only American study which provides a direct measure of the effects of individual counseling—a study of California's Intensive Treatment Program (California, 1958a), which was "psychodynamically" oriented—found no improvement in recidivism rates.

It was this finding of the failure of the Intensive Treatment Program which contributed to the decision in California to de-emphasize individual counseling in its penal system in favor of group methods. And indeed one might suspect that the preceding reports reveal not the inadequacy of counseling as a whole but only the failure of one *type* of counseling, the individual type. Group counseling methods, in which offenders are permitted to aid and compare experiences with one another, might be thought to have a better chance of success. So it is important to ask what results these alternative methods have actually produced.

GROUP COUNSELING

Group counseling has indeed been tried in correctional institutions both with and without a specifically psychotherapeutic orientation. There has been one study of "pragmatic," problem-oriented counseling on *young* institutionalized males by Seckel (1965). This type of counseling had no significant effect. For adult males, there have been three such studies of the "pragmatic" and "insight" methods. Two (Kassebaum, 1971; Harrison, 1964) report no long-lasting significant effects. (One of these two did report a real but short-term effect that wore off as the program became institutionalized and as offenders were at liberty longer.) The third study of adults, by Shelley (1961), dealt with a "pragmatic" casework program, directed towards the educational and vocational needs of institutionalized young adult males in a Michigan prison camp. The treatment lasted for six months and at the end of that time Shelley found an improvement in attitudes; the possession of "good" attitudes was independently found by Shelley to correlate with parole success. Unfortunately, though, Shelley was not able to measure the *direct* impact of the counseling on recidivism rates. His two separate correlations are suggestive, but they fall short of being able to tell us that it really is the counseling that has a direct effect on recidivism.

With regard to more professional group *psychotherapy*, the reports are also conflicting. We have two studies of group psychotherapy on young males. One, by Persons (1966), says that this treatment did in fact reduce recidivism. The improved recidivism rate stems from the improved performance only of those who were clinically judged to have been "successfully" treated; still, the overall result of the treatment was to improve recidivism rates for the experimental group as a whole. On the other hand, a study by Craft (1964) of young males designated "psychopaths," comparing "self-government" group psychotherapy with "authoritarian" individual counseling, found that the "group therapy" boys afterwards committed twice as many new offenses as the individually treated ones. Perhaps some forms of group psychotherapy work for some types of offenders but not others; a reader must draw his own conclusions on the basis of sparse evidence.

With regard to young females, the results are just as equivocal. Adams, in his study of females (1959a), found that there was no improvement to be gained from treating girls by group rather than individual methods. A study by Taylor of borstal (reformatory) girls in New Zealand (1967) found a similar lack of any great improvement for group therapy as opposed to individual therapy or even to no therapy at all. But the Taylor study does offer one real, positive finding: When the "group therapy" girls *did* commit new offenses, these offenses were less serious than the ones for which they had originally been incarcerated.

There is a third study that does report an overall positive finding as opposed to a partial one. Truax (1966) found that girls subjected to group psychotherapy and then released were likely to spend less time reincarcerated in the future. But what is most interesting about this improvement is the very special and important circumstance under which it occurred. The therapists chosen for this program did not merely have to have the proper analytic training; they were specially chosen for their "empathy" and "non-possessive warmth." In other words, it may well have been the therapists' special personal gifts rather than the fact of treatment itself which produced the favorable result. This possibility will emerge again when we examine the effects of other types of rehabilitative treatment later in this article.

As with the question of skill development, it is hard to summarize these results. The programs administered were various; the groups to which they were administered varied not only by sex but by age as well; there were also variations in the length of time for which the programs were carried on, the frequency of contact during that time, and the period for which the subjects were followed up. Still, one must say that the burden of the evidence is not encouraging. These programs seem to work best when they are new, when their subjects are amenable to treatment in the first place, and when the counselors are not only trained people but "good" people as well. Such findings, which would not be much of a surprise to a student of organization or personality, are hardly encouraging for a policy planner, who must adopt measures that are generally applicable, that are capable of being successfully institutionalized, and that must rely for personnel on something other than the exceptional individual.

TRANSFORMING THE INSTITUTIONAL ENVIRONMENT

3. *But maybe the reason these counseling programs don't seem to work is not that they are ineffective per se, but that the institutional environment outside the program is unwholesome enough to undo any good work that the counseling does. Isn't a truly successful rehabilitative institution the one where the inmate's whole environment is directed towards true correction rather than towards custody or punishment?*

This argument has not only been made, it has been embodied in several institutional programs that go by the name of "milieu therapy." They are designed to make every element of the inmates environment a part of his treatment, to reduce the distinctions between the custodial staff and the treatment staff, to create a supportive, non-authoritarian, and non-regimented atmosphere, and to enlist peer influence in the formation of constructive values. These programs are especially hard to summarize because of their variety. They differ, for example, in how "supportive" or "permissive" they are designed to be, in the extent to which they are combined with other treatment methods such as individual therapy, group counseling, or skill development, and in how completely the program is able to control all the relevant aspects of the institutional environment.

One might well begin with two studies that have been done of institutionalized adults, in regular prisons, who have been subjected to such treatment; this is the category whose results are the most clearly discouraging. One study of such a program, by Robison (1967), found that the therapy did seem to reduce recidivism after one year. After two years, however, this effect disappeared, and the treated convicts did no better than the untreated. Another study by Kassebaum, Ward, and Wilnet (1971), dealt with a program which had been able to effect an exceptionally extensive and experimentally rigorous transformation of the institutional environment. This sophisticated study had a follow-up period of 36 months, and it found that the program had no significant effect on parole failure or success rates.

The results of the studies of youth are more equivocal. As for young females, one study by Adams (1966) of such a program found that it had no significant effect on recidivism; another study, by Goldberg and Adams (1964), found that such a program did have a positive effect. This effect declined when the program began to deal with girls who were judged beforehand to be worse risks.

As for young males, the studies may conveniently be divided into those dealing with juveniles (under 18) and those dealing with youths. There have been five studies of milieu therapy administered to juveniles. Two of them—by Lavlicht (1962) and by Jesness (1965)—report clearly that the program in question either had no significant effect or had a short-term effect that wore off with passing time. Jesness does report that when his experimental juveniles did commit new offenses, the offenses were less serious than those committed by controls. A third study of juveniles, by McCord (1953) at the Wiltwyck School, reports mixed results. Using two measures of performance, a "success" rate and a "failure" rate, McCord found that his experimental group achieved both less failure *and* less success than the controls did. There have been two positive reports on milieu therapy programs for male juveniles; both of them have come out of the Highfields program, the milieu therapy experiment which has become the most famous and widely quoted example of "success" via this method. A group of boys was confined for a relatively short time to the unrestrictive, supportive environment of Highfields; and at a follow-up of six months, Freeman (1956) found that the group did indeed show a lower recidivism rate (as measured by parole revocation) than a similar group spending a longer time in the regular reformatory. McCorkle (1958) also reported positive findings from High-fields. But in fact, [as] the McCorkle data show[s], this improvement was not so clear: The Highfields boys had lower recidivism rates at 12 and 36 months in the follow-up period, but not at 24 and 60 months. The length of follow-up, these data remind us, may have large implications for a study's conclusions. But more important were other flaws in the Highfields experiment: The populations were not fully comparable (they differed according to risk level and time of admission); different organizations—the probation agency for the Highfield boys, the parole agency for the others—were making the revocation decisions for each group; more of the Highfields boys were discharged early from supervision, and thus removed from any risk of revocation. In short, not even from the celebrated Highfields case may we take clear assurance that milieu therapy works.

In the case of male youths, as opposed to male juveniles, the findings are just as equivocal, and hardly more encouraging. One such study by Empey (1966) in a residential context did not produce significant results. A study by Seckel (1967) described California's Fremont Program, in which institutionalized youths participated in a combination of therapy, work projects, field trips, and community meetings. Seckel found that the youths subjected to this treatment committed more violations of law than did their non-treated counterparts. This difference could have occurred by chance; still, there was certainly no evidence of relative improvement. Another study, by Levinson (1962–1964), also found a lack of improvement in recidivism rates—but Levinson noted the encouraging fact that the treated group spent somewhat more time in the community before recidivating, and committed less serious offenses. And a study by the State of California (1967) also shows a partially positive finding. This was a study of the Marshall Program, similar to California's Fremont Program but different in several ways. The Marshall Program was shorter and more tightly organized than its Fremont counterpart. In the Marshall Program, as opposed to the Fremont Program, a youth could be ejected from the group and sent back to regular institutions before the completion of the program. Also, the Marshall Program offered some additional benefits: the teaching of "social survival skills" (i.e., getting and holding a job), group counseling of parents, and an occasional opportunity for boys to visit home. When youthful offenders were released to the Marshall Program, either directly or after spending some time in a regular institution, they did no better than a comparable regularly institutionalized population, though both Marshall youth and youth in regular institutions did better than those who were directly released by the court and given no special treatment.

So the youth in these milieu therapy programs at least do no worse than their counterparts in regular institutions and the special programs may cost less. One may therefore be encouraged—not on grounds of rehabilitation but on grounds of cost effectiveness.

WHAT ABOUT MEDICAL TREATMENT?

4. *Isn't there anything you can do in an institutional setting that will reduce recidivism, for instance, through strictly medical treatment?*

A number of studies deal with the results of efforts to change the behavior of offenders through drugs and surgery. As for surgery, the one experimental study of a plastic surgery program—by Mandell (1967)—had negative results. For non-addicts who received plastic surgery, Mandell purported to find improvement in performance on parole; but when one reanalyzes his data, it appears that surgery alone did not in fact make a significant difference.

One type of surgery does seem to be highly successful in reducing recidivism. A twenty-year Danish study of sex offenders, by Stuerup (1960), found that while those who had been treated with hormones and therapy continued to commit both sex crimes (29.6 percent of them did so) and non-sex crimes (21.0 percent), those who had been castrated had rates of only 3.5 percent (not, interestingly enough, a rate of zero; where there's a will, apparently there's a way) and 9.2 percent. One hopes that the policy implications of this study will be found to be distinctly limited.

As for drugs, the major report on such a program—involving tranquilization—was made by Adams (1961b). The tranquilizers were administered to male and female institutionalized youths. With boys, there was only a slight improvement in their subsequent behavior; this improvement disappeared within a year. With girls, the tranquilization produced worse results than when the girls were given no treatment at all.

THE EFFECTS OF SENTENCING

5. *Well, at least it may be possible to manipulate certain gross features of the existing, conceptional prison system—such as length of sentence and degree of security—in order to affect these recidivism rates. Isn't this the case?*

At this point, it's still impossible to say that this is the case. As for the degree of security in an institution, Glaser's (1964) work reported that, for both youth and adults, a less restrictive "custody grading" in American federal prisons was related to success on parole; but this is hardly surprising, since those assigned to more restrictive custody are likely to be worse risks in the first place. More to the point, an American study by Fox (1950) discovered that for "older youths" who were deemed to be good risks for the future, a minimum security institution produced better results than a maximum security one. On the other hand, the data we have on youths under 16—from a study by McClintock (1961), done in Great Britain—indicate that so-called Borstals, in which boys are totally confined, are more effective than a less restrictive regime of partial physical custody. In short, we know very little about the recidivism effects of various degrees of security in existing institutions; and our problems in finding out will be compounded by the probability that these effects will vary widely according to the particular *type* of offender that we're dealing with.

The same problems of mixed results and lack of comparable populations have plagued attempts to study the effects of sentence length. A number of studies—by Narloch (1959), by Bernsten (1965), and by the State of California (1956)—suggest that those who are released earlier from institutions than their scheduled parole date, or those who serve short sentences of under three months rather than longer sentences of eight months or more, either do better on parole or at least do no worse.[4] The implication here is quite clear and important: Even if early releases and short sentences produce no improvement in recidivism rates, one could at least maintain the same rates while lowering the cost of maintaining the offender and lessening his own burden of imprisonment. Of course, this implication carries with it its concomitant danger: the danger that though shorter sentences cause no worsening of the recidivism rate, they may increase the total amount of crime in the community by increasing the absolute number of potential recidivists at large.

On the other hand, Glaser's (1964) data show not a consistent linear relationship between the shortness of the sentence and the rate of parole success, but a curvilinear one. Of his subjects, those who served less than a year had a 73 percent success rate, those who served up to two years were only 65 percent successful, and those who served up to three years fell to a rate of 56 percent. But among those who served sentences of *more* than three years, the success rate rose again—to 60 percent. These findings should be viewed with some caution since Glaser did not control for the pre-existing degree of risk associated with each of his categories of offenders. But the data do suggest that the relationship between sentence length and recidivism may not be a simple linear one.

More important, the effect of sentence length seems to vary widely according to type of offender. In a British study (1963), for instance, Hammond found that for a group of "hard-core recidivists," shortening the sentence caused no improvement in the recidivism rate. In Denmark, Bernsten (1965) discovered a similar phenomenon: That the beneficial effect of three-month sentences as against eight-month ones disappeared in the case of these "hard-core recidivists." Garrity found an other such distinction in his 1956 study. He divided his offenders into three categories: "pro-social," "anti-social," and "manipulative." "Pro-social" offenders he found to have low recidivism rates regardless of the length of their sentence; "anti-social" offenders did better with short sentences; the "manipulative" did better with long ones. Two studies from Britain made yet another division of the offender population, and found yet other variations. One (Great Britain, 1964) found that previous offenders—but not first offenders—did better with *longer* sentences, while the other (Cambridge, 1952) found the *reverse* to be true with juveniles.

To add to the problem of interpretation, these studies deal not only with different types and categorizations of offenders but with different types of institutions as well. No more than in the case of institution type can we say that length of sentence has a clear relationship to recidivism.

DECARCERATING THE CONVICT

6. *All of this seems to suggest that there's not much we know how to do to rehabilitate an offender when he's in an institution. Doesn't this lead to the clear possibility that the way to rehabilitate offenders is to deal with them outside an institutional setting?*

This is indeed an important possibility, and it is suggested by other pieces of information as well. For instance, Minet (1967) reported on a milieu therapy program in Massachusetts called Outward Bound. It took youths $15\frac{1}{2}$ and over; it was oriented toward the development of skills in the out-of-doors and conducted in a wilderness atmosphere very different from that of most existing institutions. The culmination of the 26-day program was a final 24 hours in which each youth had to survive alone in the wilderness. And Miner found that the program did indeed work in reducing recidivism rates.

But by and large, when one takes the programs that have been administered in institutions and applies them in a non-institutional setting, the results do not grow to encouraging proportions. With casework and individual counseling in the community, for instance, there have been three studies; they dealt with counseling methods from psycho-social and vocational counseling to "operant conditioning," in which an offender was rewarded first simply for coming to counseling sessions and then, gradually, for performing other types of approved sets. Two of them report that the community-counseled offenders did no better than their institutional controls, while the third notes that although community counseling produced fewer arrests per person, it did not ultimately reduce the offenders chance of resuming to a reformatory.

The one study of a non-institutional skill development program, by Kovacs (1967), described the New Start Program in Denver, in which offenders participated in vocational training, role playing, programmed instruction, group counseling, college class attendance, and trips to art galleries and museums. After all this, Kovacs found no significant improvement over incarceration.

There have also been studies of milieu therapy programs conducted with youthful male probationers not in actual physical custody. One of them found no significant improvement at all. One, by Empey (1966), did say that after a follow-up of six months, a boy who was judged to have "successfully" completed the milieu program was less likely to recidivate afterwards than was a "successful," regular probationer. Empey's "successes" came out of an extraordinary program in Provo, Utah, which aimed to rehabilitate by subjecting offenders to a non-supportive milieu. The staff of this program operated on the principle that they were not to go out of their way to interact and be empathetic with the boys. Indeed, a boy who misbehaved was to be met with "role dispossession": He was to be excluded from meetings of his peer group, and he was not to be given answers to his questions as to why he had been excluded or what his ultimate fate might be. This peer group and its meetings were designed to be the major force for reform at Provo; they were intended to develop, and indeed did develop, strong and controlling norms for the behavior of individual members. For one thing, group members were not to associate with delinquent boys outside the program; for another, individuals were to submit to a group review of all their actions and problems; and they were to be completely honest and open with the group about their attitudes, their thinking patterns, their states of mind, and their personal failings. The group was granted quite a few sanctions with which to enforce these norms: They could practice derision or temporary ostracism, or they could lock up an aberrant member for the weekend, refuse to release him from the program, or send him away to the regular reformatory.

One might be tempted to forgive these methods because of the success that Empey reports, except for one thing. If one judges the program not only by its "successful" boys but by all the boys who were subjected to it—those who succeeded and those who, not surprisingly, failed—the totals show *no* significant improvement in recidivism rates compared with boys on regular probation. Empey did find that both the Provo boys and those on regular probation did better than those in regular reformatories—in contradiction, it may be recalled, to the finding from the residential Marshall Program, in which the direct releases given no special treatment did *worse* than boys in regular institutions.

The third such study of non-residential milieu therapy, by McCravy (1967), found not only that there was no significant improvement, but that the longer a boy participated in the treatment, the worse he was likely to do afterwards.

PSYCHOTHERAPY IN COMMUNITY SETTINGS

There is some indication that individual psychotherapy may "work" in a community setting. Massimo (1963) reported on one such program, using what might be termed a "pragmatic" psychotherapeutic approach, including "insight" therapy and a focus on vocational problems. The program was marked by its small size and by its use of therapists who were personally enthusiastic about the project; Massimo found that there was indeed a decline in recidivism rates. Adamson (1956), on the other hand, found no significant difference produced by another program of individual therapy (though he did note that arrest rates among the experimental boys declined with what he called "intensity of treatment"). And Schwitzgebel (1963, 1964), studying other, different kinds of therapy programs, found that the programs *did* produce improvements in the attitudes of his boys—but, unfortunately, not in their rates of recidivism.

And with *group* therapy administered in the community, we find yet another set of equivocal results. The results from studies of pragmatic group counseling are only mildly optimistic. Adams (1965) did report that a form of group therapy, "guided group interaction," when administered to juvenile gangs, did somewhat reduce the percentage that were to be found in custody six years later. On the other hand, in a study of juveniles, Adams (1964) found that while such a program did reduce the number of contacts that an experimental youth had with police, it made no ultimate difference in the detention rate. And the attitudes of the counseled youth showed no improvement. Finally, when O'Brien (1961) examined a community-based program of group psychotherapy, he found not only that the program produced no improvement in the recidivism rate, but that the experimental boys actually did worse than their controls on a series of psychological tests.

PROBATION OR PAROLE VERSUS PRISON

But by far the most extensive and important work that has been done on the effect of community-based treatments has been done in the areas of probation and parole. This work sets out to answer the question of whether it makes any difference how you supervise and treat an offender once he has been released from prison or has come under state surveillance in lieu of prison. This is the work that has provided the main basis to date for the claim that we do indeed have the means at our disposal for rehabilitating the offender or at least decarcerating him safely.

One group of these studies has compared the use of probation with other dispositions for offenders; these provide some slight evidence that, at least under some circumstances, probation may mate an offender's future chances better than if he had been sent to prison. Or, at least, probation may not worsen those chances.[5] A British study, by Wilkins (1958), reported that when probation was granted more frequently, recidivism rates among probationers did not increase significantly. And another such study by the state of Michigan in 1963 reported that an expansion in the use of probation actually improved recidivism rates—though there are serious problems of comparability in the groups and systems that were studied.

One experiment—by Babst (1965)—compared a group of parolees, drawn from adult male felony offenders in Wisconsin, and excluding murderers and sex criminals, with a similar group that had been put on probation; it found that the probationers committed fewer violations if they had been first offenders, and did no worse if they were recidivists. The problem in interpreting this experiment, though, is that the behavior of those groups was being measured by separate organizations, by probation officers for the probationers, and by parole officers for the parolees; it is not clear that the definition of "violation" was the same in each case, or that other types of uniform standards were being applied. Also, it is not clear what the results would have been if subjects had been released directly to the parole organization without having experienced prison first. Another such study, done in Israel by Shoham (1964), must be interpreted cautiously because his experimental and control groups had slightly different characteristics. But Shoham found that when one compared a suspended sentence plus probation for first offenders with a one-year prison sentence, only first offenders under 20 years of age did better on probation; those from 21 to 45 actually did *worse*. And Shoham's findings also differ from Babst's in another way. Babst had found that parole rather than prison brought no improvement for recidivists, but Shoham reported that for recidivists with four or more prior offenses, a suspended sentence was actually *better*—though the improvement was much less when the recidivist had committed a crime of violence.

But both the Babst and the Shoham studies, even while they suggest the possible value of suspended sentences, probation, or parole for some offenders (though they contradict each other in telling us *which* offenders), also indicate a pessimistic general conclusion concerning the limits of the effectiveness of treatment programs. For they found that the personal characteristics of offenders—"first offender status, or age, or type of offense"—were more important than the form of treatment in determining future recidivism. An offender with a "favorable" prognosis will do better than one without, it seems, no matter how you distribute "good" or "bad," "enlightened" or "regressive" treatments among them.

Quite a large group of studies deals not with probation as compared to other dispositions, but instead with the type of treatment that an offender receives once he is on probation or parole. These are the studies that have provided the most encouraging reports on rehabilitative treatment and that have also raised the most serious questions about the nature of the research that has been going on in the corrections field.

Five of these studies have dealt with youthful probationers from 13 to 18 who were assigned to probation officers with small caseloads or provided with other ways of receiving more intensive supervision (Adams, 1966 [two reports]; Feistman, 1966; Kawaguchi, 1967; Pilnick, 1967). These studies report that, by and large, intensive supervision does work—that the specially treated youngsters do better according to some measure of recidivism. Yet these studies left some important questions unanswered. For instance, was this improved performance a function merely of the number of contacts a youngster had with his probation officer? Did it also depend on the length of time in treatment? Or was it the quality of supervision that was making the difference, rather than the quantity?

INTENSIVE SUPERVISION: THE WARREN STUDIES

The widely reported Warren studies (1966a, 1966b, 1967) in California constitute an extremely ambitious attempt to answer these questions. In this project, a control group of youths, drawn from a pool of candidates ready for first admission to a California Youth Authority institution, was assigned to regular detention, usually for eight to nine months, and then released to regular supervision. The experimental group received considerably more elaborate treatment. They were released directly to probation status and assigned to 12-man caseloads. To decide what special treatment was appropriate within these caseloads, the youths were divided according to their "interpersonal maturity level classification," by use of a scale developed by Grant and Grant. And each level dictated its own special type of therapy. For instance, a youth might be judged to occupy the lowest maturity level; this would be a youth, according to the scale, primarily concerned with "demands that the world take care of him.... He behaves impulsively, unaware of anything except the grossest effects of his behavior on others." A youth like this would be placed in a supportive environment such as a foster home; the goals of his therapy would be to meet his dependency needs and help him gain more accurate perceptions about his relationship to others. At the other end of the three-tier classification a youth might exhibit high maturity. This would be a youth who had internalized "a set of standards by which he judges his and others' behavior. ... He shows some ability to understand reasons for behavior, some ability to relate to people emotionally and on a long-term basis." These high-maturity youths could come in several varieties—a "neurotic acting out," for instance, a "neurotic anxious," a "situational emotional reactor," or a "cultural identifier." But the appropriate treatment for these youths was individual psychotherapy, or family or group therapy for the purpose of reducing internal conflicts and increasing the youths' awareness of personal and family dynamics.

"Success" in this experiment was defined as favorable discharge by the Youth Authority; "failure" was unfavorable discharge, revocation, or recommitment by a court. Warren reported an encouraging finding: Among all but one of the "subtypes," the experimentals had a significantly lower failure rate than the controls. The experiment did have certain problems: The experimentals might have been performing better because of the enthusiasm of the staff and the attention lavished on them; none of the controls had been *directly* released to their regular supervision programs instead of being detained first; and it was impossible to separate the effects of the experimentals' small caseloads from their specially designed treatments, since no experimental youths had been assigned to a small caseload with "inappropriate" treatment, or with no treatment at all. Still, none of these problems were serious enough to vitiate the encouraging prospect that this finding presented for successful treatment of probationers.

This encouraging finding was, however, accompanied by a rather more disturbing clue. As has been mentioned before, the experimental subjects, when measured, had a lower *failure* rate than the controls. But the experimentals also had a lower *success* rate. That is, fewer of the experimentals as compared with the controls had been judged to have successfully completed their program of supervision and to be suitable for favorable release. When my colleagues and I undertook a rather laborious reanalysis of the Warren data, it became clear why this discrepancy had appeared. It turned out that fewer experimentals were "successful" because the experimentals were actually committing more offenses than their controls. The reason that the experimentals' relatively large number of offenses was not being reflected in their failure rates was simply that the experimentals' probation officers were using a more lenient revocation policy. In other words, the controls had a higher failure rate because the controls were being revoked for less serious offenses.

So it seems that what Warren was reporting in her "failure" rates was not merely the treatment effect of her small caseloads and special programs. Instead, what Warren was finding was not so much a change in the behavior of the experimental youths as a change in the behavior of the experimental *probation officers*, who knew the "special" status of their charges and who had evidently decided to revoke probation status at a lower than normal rate. The experimentals continued to commit offenses; what was different was that when they committed these offenses, they were permitted to remain on probation.

The experimenters claimed that this low revocation policy, and the greater number of offenses committed by the special treatment youth, were *not* an indication that these youth were behaving specially badly and that policy makers were simply letting them get away with it. Instead it was claimed, the higher reported offense rate was primarily an artifact of the more intense surveillance that the experimental youth received. But the data show that this is not a sufficient explanation of the low failure rate among experimental youth; the difference in "tolerance" of offenses between experimental officials and control officials was much greater than the difference in the rates at which these two systems detected youths committing new offenses. Needless to say, this reinterpretation of the data presents a much bleaker picture of the possibilities of intensive supervision with special treatment.

"TREATMENT EFFECT" VERSUS "POLICY EFFECTS"

This same problem of experimenter bias may also be present in the predecessors of the Warren study, the ones which had also found positive results from intensive supervision on probation; indeed, this disturbing question can be raised about many of the previously discussed reports of positive "treatment effects."

This possibility of a "policy effect" rather than a "treatment effect" applies, for instance, to the previously discussed studies of the effects of intensive supervision on juvenile and youthful probationers. These were the studies, it will be recalled, which found lower recidivism rates for the intensively supervised.[6]

One opportunity to make a further check on the effects of this problem is provided, in a slightly different context, by Johnson (1962a). Johnson was measuring the effects of intensive supervision on youthful *parolees* (as distinct from probationers). There have been several such studies of the effects on youths of intensive parole supervision plus special counseling and their findings are on the whole less encouraging than the probation studies; they are difficult to interpret because of experimental problems, but studies by Boston University in 1966, and by Van Couvering in 1966, report no significant effects and possibly some bad effects from such special programs. But Johnson's studies were unique for the chance they provide to measure both treatment effects and the effect of agency policy.

Johnson, like Warren, assigned experimental subjects to small caseloads and his experiment had the virtue of being performed with two separate populations and at two different times. But in contrast with the Warren case, the Johnson experiment did not engage in a large continuing attempt to choose the experimental counselors specially, to train them specially, and to keep them informed about the progress and importance of the experiment. The first time the experiment was performed, the experimental youths had a slightly lower revocation rate than the controls at six months. But the second time, the experimentals did *not* do better than their controls; indeed, they did slightly worse. And with the experimentals from the first group—those who *had* shown an improvement after six months—this effect wore off at 18 months. In the Johnson study, my colleagues and I found, "intensive" supervision did not increase the experimental youths' risk of detection. Instead, what was happening in the Johnson experiment was that the first time it had been performed—just as in the Warren study—the experimentals were simply revoked less often per number of offenses committed, and they were revoked for offenses more serious than those which prompted revocation among the controls. The second time around, this "policy" discrepancy disappeared; and when it did, the "improved" performance of the experimentals disappeared as well. The enthusiasm guiding the project had simply worn off in the absence of reinforcement.

One must conclude that the "benefits" of intensive supervision for youthful offenders may stem not so much from a "treatment" effect as from a "policy" effect—that such supervision, so far as we now know, results not in rehabilitation but in a decision to look the other way when an offense is committed. But there is one major modification to be added to this conclusion. Johnson performed a further measurement (1962b) in his parole experiment: He rated all the supervising agents according to the "adequacy" of the supervision they gave. And he found that an "adequate" agent, whether he was working in a small *or* a large caseload produced a relative improvement in his charges. The converse was not true: An inadequate agent was more likely to produce youthful "failures" when he was given a *small* caseload to supervise. One can't much help a "good" agent, it seems, by reducing his caseload size; such reduction can only do further harm to those youths who fall into the hands of "bad" agents.

So with youthful offenders, Johnson found, intensive supervision does not seem to provide the rehabilitative benefits claimed for it; the only such benefits may flow not from intensive supervision itself but from contact with one of the "good people" who are frequently in such short supply.

INTENSIVE SUPERVISION OF ADULTS

The results are similarly ambiguous when one applies this intensive supervision to adult offenders. There have been several studies of the effects of intensive supervision on adult parolees. Some of these are hard to interpret because of problems of comparability between experimental and control groups (general risk ratings, for instance, or distribution of narcotics offenders, or policy changes that took place between various phases of the experiments), but two of them (California, 1966; Stanton, 1964) do not seem to give evidence of the benefits of intensive supervision. By far the most extensive work, though, on the effects of intensive supervision of adult parolees has been a series of studies of California's Special Intensive Parole Unit (SIPU), a 10-year-long experiment designed to test the treatment possibilities of various special parole programs. Three of the four "phases" of this experiment produced "negative results." The first phase tested the effect of a reduced caseload size; no lasting effect was found. The second phase slightly increased the size of the small caseloads and provided for a longer time in treatment; again there was no evidence of a treatment effect. In the fourth phase, caseload sizes and time in treatment were again varied, and treatments were simultaneously varied in a sophisticated way according to personality characteristics of the parolees; once again, significant results did not appear.

The only phase of this experiment for which positive results were reported was Phase Three. Here, it was indeed found that a smaller caseload improved one's chances of parole success. There is, however, an important caveat that attaches to this finding: When my colleagues and I divided the whole population of subjects into two groups—those receiving supervision in the North of the state and those in the South— we found that the "improvement" of the experimentals' success rates was taking place primarily in the North. The North differed from the South in one important aspect: Its agents practiced a policy of resuming both "experimental" and "control" violators to prison at relatively high rates. And it was the North that produced the higher success rate among its experimentals. So this improvement in experimentals' performance was taking place only when accompanied by a "realistic threat" of severe sanctions. It is interesting to compare this situation with that of the Warren studies. In the Warren studies, experimental subjects were being revoked at a relatively *low* rate. These experimentals "failed" less, but they also committed more new offenses than their controls. By contrast, in the Northern region of the SIPU experiment, there was a policy of *high* rate of return to prison for experimentals; and here, the special program *did* seem to produce a real improvement in the behavior of offenders. What this suggests is that when intensive supervision *does* produce an improvement in offenders' behavior, it does so not through the mechanism of "treatment" or "rehabilitation," but instead through a mechanism that our studies have almost totally ignored; the mechanism of *deterrence.* And a similar mechanism is suggested by Lohman's study (1967) of intensive supervision of probationers. In this study intensive supervision led to higher total violation rates. But one also notes that intensive supervision combined the highest rate of technical violations with the lowest rate for *new* offenses.

THE EFFECTS OF COMMUNITY TREATMENT

In sum, even in the case of treatment programs administered outside penal institutions, we simply cannot say that this treatment in itself has an appreciable effect on offender behavior. On the other hand, there is one encouraging set of findings that emerges from these studies. For from many of them there flows the strong suggestion that even if we can't "treat" offenders so as to make them do better, a great many of the programs designed to rehabilitate them at least did not make them do *worse*. And if these programs did not show the advantages of actually rehabilitating, some of them did have the advantage of being less onerous to the offender himself without seeming to pose increased danger to the community. And some of these programs—especially those involving less restrictive custody, minimal supervision, and early release—simply cost fewer dollars to administer. The information on the dollar costs of these programs is just beginning to be developed but the implication is clear: *that if we can't do more for (and to) offenders, at least we can safely do less.*

There is, however, one important caveat even to this note of optimism: In order to calculate the true costs of these programs, one must in each case include not only their administrative cost but also the cost of maintaining in the community an offender population increased in size. This population might well not be committing new offenses at any greater rate; but the offender population might, under some of these plans, be larger in absolute *numbers*. So the total number of offenses committed might rise, and our chances of victimization might therefore rise too. We need to be able to make a judgment about the size and probable duration of this effect; as of now, we simply do not know.

DOES NOTHING WORK?

7. *Do all of these studies lead us irrevocably to the conclusion that nothing works, that we haven't the faintest clue about how to rehabilitate offenders and reduce recidivism? And if so, what shall we do?*

We tried to exclude from our survey those studies which were so poorly done that they simply could not be interpreted. But despite our efforts, a pattern has run through much of this discussion—of studies which "found" effects without making any truly rigorous attempt to exclude competing hypotheses, of extraneous factors permitted to intrude upon the measurements, of recidivism measures which are not all measuring the same thing, of "follow-up" periods which vary enormously and rarely extend beyond the period of legal supervision, of experiments never replicated, of "system effects" not taken into account, of categories drawn up without any theory to guide the enterprise. It is just possible that some of our treatment programs *are* working to some extent, but that our research is so bad that it is incapable of telling.

Having entered this very serious caveat, I am bound to say that these data, involving over two hundred studies and hundreds of thousands of individuals as they do, are the best available and give us very little reason to hope that we have in fact found a sure way of reducing recidivism through rehabilitation. This is not to say that we found no instances of success or partial success; it is only to say that these instances have been isolated, producing no clear pattern to indicate the efficacy of any particular method of treatment. And neither is this to say that factors *outside* the realm of rehabilitation may not be working to reduce recidivism—factors such as the tendency for recidivism to be lower in offenders over the age of 30; it is only to say that such factors seem to have little connection with any of the treatment methods now at our disposal.

From this probability, one may draw any of several conclusions. It may be simply that our programs aren't yet good enough—that the education we provide to inmates is still poor education, that the therapy we administer is not administered skillfully enough, that our intensive supervision and counseling do not yet provide enough personal support for the offenders who are subjected to them. If one wishes to believe this, then what our correctional system needs is simply a more full-hearted commitment to the strategy of treatment.

It may be, on the other hand, that there is a more radical flaw in our present strategies—that education at its best, or that psychotherapy at its best, cannot overcome, or even appreciably reduce, the powerful tendency for offenders to continue in criminal behavior. Our present treatment programs are based on a theory of crime as a "disease"—that is to say, as something foreign and abnormal in the individual which can presumably be cured. This theory may well be flawed, in that it overlooks—indeed, denies—both the normality of crime in society and the personal normality of a very large proportion of offenders, criminals who are merely responding to the facts and conditions of our society.

This opposing theory of "crime as a social phenomenon" directs our attention away from a "rehabilitative" strategy, away from the notion that we may best insure public safety through a series of "treatments" to be imposed forcibly on convicted offenders. These treatments have on occasion become, and have the potential for becoming, so draconian as to offend the moral order of a democratic society; and the theory of crime as a social phenomenon suggests that such treatments may be not only offensive but ineffective as well. This theory points, instead, to decarceration for low-risk offenders—and, presumably, to keeping high-risk offenders in prisons which are nothing more (and aim to be nothing more) than custodial institutions.

But this approach has its own problems. To begin with, there is the moral dimension of crime and punishment. Many low-risk offenders have committed serious crimes (murder, sometimes) and even if one is reasonably sure they will never commit another crime, it violates our sense of justice that they should experience no significant retribution for their actions. A middle-class banker who kills his adulterous wife in a moment of passion is a "low-risk" criminal; a juvenile delinquent in the ghetto who commits armed robbery has, statistically, a much higher probability of committing another crime. Are we going to put the first on probation and sentence the latter to a long term in prison?

Besides, one cannot ignore the fact that the punishment of offenders is the major means we have for *deterring* incipient offenders. We know almost nothing about the "deterrent effect," largely because "treatment" theories have so dominated our research, and "deterrence" theories have been relegated to the status of a historical curiosity. Since we have almost no idea of the deterrent functions that our present system performs or that future strategies might be made to perform, it is possible that there is indeed something that works—that to some extent is working right now in front of our noses, and that might be made to work better—something that deters rather than cures, something that does not so much reform convicted offenders as prevent criminal behavior in the first place. But whether that is the case and, if it is, what strategies will be found to make our deterrence system work better than it does now, are questions we will not be able to answer with data until a new family of studies has been brought into existence. As we begin to learn the facts, we will be in a better position than we are now to judge to what degree the prison has become an anachronism and can be replaced by more effective means of social control.

STUDY QUESTIONS

1. What was the original impetus for Martinson's study of the effectiveness of rehabilitation programs?
2. Discuss the methodology (research design, data collection methods, sample, and measures) used by the author.
3. Many times, authors citing the Martinson Report erroneously state that his conclusion was that "nothing works." What was his actual conclusion? Does this differ from the one just stated?
4. What exactly were the author's conclusions about community treatment programs?

NOTES

1. Following this case, the state finally did give its permission to have the work published; it will

appear in its complete form in a forthcoming book by Praeger.

2. All studies cited in the text are referenced in the bibliography which appears at the conclusion of the article.
3. The net result was that those who received less prison education—because their sentences were shorter or because they were probably better risks—ended up having better chances than those who received more prison education.
4. A similar phenomenon has been measured indirectly by studies that have dealt with the effect of various parole policies on recidivism rates. Where parole decisions have been liberalized so that an offender could be released with only the "reasonable assurance" of a job rather than with a definite job already developed by a parole officer (Stanton, 1963), this liberal release policy has produced no worsening of recidivism rates.
5. It will be recalled that Empey's report on the Provo program made such a finding.
6. But one of these reports, by Kawaguchi (1967), also found that an intensively supervised juvenile, by the time he finally "failed," had had more previous detentions while under supervision than a control juvenile had experienced.

REFERENCES

Adams, Stuart. "Effectiveness of the Youth Authority Special Treatment Program: First Interim Report." Research Report No. 5. California Youth Authority, March 6, 1959. (Mimeographed.)

Adams, Stuart. "Assessment of the Psychiatric Treatment Program: Second Interim Report." Research Report No. 15. California Youth Authority, December 13, 1959. (Mimeographed.)

Adams, Stuart. "Effectiveness of Interview Therapy with Older Youth Authority Wards: An Interim Evaluation of the PICO Project." Research Report No. 20. California Youth Authority, January 20, 1961. (Mimeographed.)

Adams, Stuart. "Assessment of the Psychiatric Treatment Program, Phase I: Third Interim Report." Research Report No. 21. California Youth Authority, January 31, 1961. (Mimeographed.)

Adams, Stuart. "An Experimental Assessment of Group Counseling with Juvenile Probationers." Paper presented at the 18th Convention of the California State Psychological Association, Los Angeles, December 12, 1964. (Mimeographed.)

Adams, Stuart, Rice, Rogert E., and Olive, Borden. "A Cost Analysis of the Effectiveness of the Group Guidance Program." Research Memorandum 65-3. Los Angeles County Probation Department, January 1965. (Mimeographed.)

Adams, Stuart. "Development of a Program Research Service in Probation." Research Report No. 27 (Final Report, NIMH Project MH007 18.) Los Angeles County Probation Department, January 1966. (Processed.)

Adamson, LeMay, and Dunham, H. Warren. "Clinical Treatment of Male Delinquents. A Case Study in Effort and Result," *American Sociological Review*, XXI, 3 (1956), 312–320.

Babst, Dean V., and Mannering, John W. "Probation versus Imprisonment for Similar Types of Offenders: A Comparison by Subsequent Violations," *Journal of Research in Crime and Delinquency*, II, 2 (1965), 60–71.

Bernsten, Karen, and Christiansen, Karl O. "A Resocialization Experiment with Short-term Offenders," *Scandinavian Studies in Criminology*, I (1965), 35–54.

California Adult Authority, Division of Adult Paroles. "Special Intensive Parole Unit, Phase I: Fifteen Man Caseload Study." Prepared by Walter I. Stone. Sacramento, CA, November 1956. (Mimeographed.)

California, Department of Corrections. "Intensive Treatment Program: Second Annual Report." Prepared by Harold B. Bradley and Jack D. Williams. Sacramento, CA, December 1, 1958. (Mimeographed.)

California, Department of Corrections. "Special Intensive Parole Unit, Phase II: Thirty Man Caseload Study." Prepared by Ernest Reimer and Martin Warren. Sacramento, CA, December 1958. (Mimeographed.)

California, Department of Corrections. "Parole Work Unit Program: An Evaluative Report." A memorandum to the California Joint Legislative Budget Committee, December 30, 1966. (Mimeographed.)

California, Department of the Youth Authority. "James Marshall Treatment Program: Progress Report." January 1967. (Processed.)

Cambridge University, Department of Criminal Science. *Detention in Remard Homes*. London: Macmillan, 1952.

Craft, Michael, Stephenson, Geoffrey, and Granger, Clive. "A Controlled Trial of Authoritarian and Self-Governing Regimes with Adolescent Psychopaths," *American Journal of Orthopsychiatry*, XXXIV, 3 (1964), 543–554.

Empey, LeMar T. "The Provo Experiment: A Brief Review." Los Angeles: Youth Studies Center, University of Southern California. 1966. (Processed.)

Feistman, Eugene G. "Comparative Analysis of the Willow-Brook-Harbor Intensive Services Program, March 1, 1965 through February 28, 1966." Research Report No. 28. Los Angeles County Probation Department, June 1966. (Processed.)

Forman, B. "The Effects of Differential Treatment on Attitudes, Personality Traits, and Behavior of Adult Parolees." Unpublished Ph.D. dissertation, University of Southern California, 1960.

Fox, Vernon. "Michigan's Experiment in Minimum Security Penology," *Journal of Criminal Law, Criminology, and Police Science*, XLI, 2 (1950), 150–166.

Freeman, Howard E., and Weeks, H. Ashley. "Analysis of a Program of Treatment of Delinquent Boys," *American Journal of Sociology*, LXII, 1 (1956), 56–61.

Garrity, Donald Lee. "The Effects of Length of Incarceration upon Parole Adjustment and Estimation of Optimum Sentence: Washington State Correctional Institutions." Unpublished Ph.D. dissertation, University of Washington, 1956.

Gearhart, J. Walter, Keith, Harold L., and Clemmons, Gloria. "An Analysis of the Vocational Training Program in the Washington State Adult Correctional Institutions." Research Review No. 23. State of Washington, Department of Institutions, May 1967. (Processed.)

Glaser, Daniel. *The Effectiveness of a Prison and Parole System*. New York: Bobbs-Merrill, 1964.

Goldberg, Lisbeth, and Adams, Stuart. "An Experimental Evaluation of the Lathrop Hall Program." Los Angeles County Probation Department, December 1964. (Summarized in Adams, Stuart. "Development of a Program Research Service in Probation," pp. 19–22.)

Great Britain. Home Office. *The Sentence of the Court: A Handbook for Courts on the Treatment of Offenders*. London: Her Majesty's Stationery Office, 1964.

Guttman, Evelyn S. "Effects of Short-Term Psychiatric Treatment on Boys in Two California Youth Authority Institutions." Research Report No. 36. California Youth Authority, December 1963. (Processed.)

Hammond, W. H., and Chayen, E. *Persistent Criminals: A Home Office Research Unit Report*. London: Her Majesty's Stationery Office, 1963.

Harrison, Robert M., and Mueller, Paul F. C. "Clue Hunting About Group Counseling and Parole Outcome." Research Report No. 11. California Department of Corrections, May 1964. (Mimeographed.)

Havel, Joan, and Sulka, Elaine. "Special Intensive Parole Unit: Phase Three." Research Report No. 3. California Department of Corrections, March 1962. (Processed.)

Havel, Joan. "A Synopsis of Research Report No. 10, SIPU Phase IV—The High Base Expectancy Study." Administrative Abstract No. 10. California Department of Corrections, June 1963. (Processed.)

Havel, Joan. "Special Intensive Parole Unit—Phase Four: 'The Parole Outcome Study.'" Research Report No. 13. California Department of Corrections, September 1965. (Processed.)

Hood, Roger. *Homeless Borstal Boys: A Study of Their After-Care and After Conduct.* Occasional Papers on Social Administration No. 18. London: G. Bell & Sons, 1966.

Jacobson, Frank, and McGee, Eugene. "Englewood Project: Re-education: A Radical Correction of Incarcerated Delinquents." Englewood, CO: July 1965. (Mimeographed.)

Jesness, Carl F. "The Fricot Ranch Study: Outcomes with Small versus Large Living Groups in the Rehabilitation of Delinquents." Research Report No. 47. California Youth Authority, October 1, 1965. (Processed.)

Johnson, Bertram. "Parole Performance of the First Year's Releases, Parole Research Project: Evaluation of Reduced Caseloads." Research Report No. 27. California Youth Authority, January 31, 1962. (Mimeographed.)

Johnson, Bertram. "An Analysis of Predictions of Parole Performance and of Judgements of Supervision in the Parole Research Project," Research Report No. 32. California Youth Authority, December 31, 1962. (Mimeographed.)

Kassebaum, Gene, Ward, David, and Wilnet, Daniel. *Prison Treatment and Parole Survival: An Empirical Assessment.* New York: Wiley, 1971.

Kawaguchi, Ray M., and Siff, Leon, M. "An Analysis of Intensive Probation Services—Phase II." Research Report No. 29. Los Angeles County Probation Department, April 1967. (Processed.)

Kettering, Marvin E. "Rehabilitation of Women in the Milwaukee County Jail: An Exploration Experiment." Unpublished Master's Thesis, Colorado State College, 1965.

Kovacs, Frank W. "Evaluation and Final Report of the New Start Demonstration Project." Colorado Department of Employment, October 1967. (Processed.)

Lavlicht, Jerome, et al., in Berkshire Farms Monographs, I, 1 (1962), 11–48.

Levinson, Robert B., and Kitchenet, Howard L. "Demonstration Counseling Project." 2 vols. Washington, DC: National Training School for Boys, 1962–1964. (Mimeographed.)

Lohman, Joseph D. et al., "The Intensive Supervision Caseloads: A Preliminary Evaluation." The San Francisco Project: A Study of Federal Probation and Parole. Research Report No. 11. School of Criminology, University of California, March 1967. (Processed.)

McClintock, F. H. *Attendance Centres.* London. Macmillan, 1961.

McCord, William and Joan. "Two Approaches to the Cure of Delinquents," *Journal of Criminal Law, Criminology and Police Science,* XL IV, 4 (1953), 442–467.

McCorkle, Lloyd W., Elias, Albert, and Bixby, F. Lovell. *The Highfields Story: An Experimental Treatment Project for Youthful Offenders.* New York: Holt, 1958.

McCravy, Newton, Jr., and Delehanty, Dolores S. "Community Rehabilitation of the Younger Delinquent Boy, Parkland Non-Residential Group Center." Final Report, Kentucky Child Welfare Research Foundation, Inc., September 1, 1967. (Mimeographed.)

Mandell, Wallace, et al. "Surgical and Social Rehabilitation of Adult Offenders." Final Report. Montefiore Hospital and Medical Center, With Staten Island Mental Health Society. New York City Department of Correction, 1967. (Processed.)

Massimo, Joseph L., and Shore, Milton F. "The Effectiveness of a Comprehensive Vocationally

Oriented Psychotherapeutic Program for Adolescent Delinquent Boys," *American Journal of Orthopsychiatry,* XXXIII, 4 (1963), 634–642.

Minet, Joshua, III, Kelly, Francis J., and Hatch, M. Charles. "Outward Bound, Inc.: Juvenile Delinquency Demonstration Project, Year End Report." Massachusetts Division of Youth Service, May 31, 1967.

Narloch, R. P., Adams, Stuart, and Jenkins, Kendall J. "Characteristics and Parole Performance of California Youth Authority Early Release." Research Report No. 7. California Youth Authority, June 22, 1959. (Mimeographed.)

New York State Division of Parole Department of Correction. "Parole Adjustment and Prior Educational Achievement of Male Adolescent Offenders, June 1957–June 1961." September 1964. (Mimeographed.)

O'Brien, William J. "Personality Assessment as a Measure of Change Resulting from Group Psychotherapy with Male Juvenile Delinquents." The Institute for the Study of Crime and Delinquency, and the California Youth Authority, December 1961. (Processed.)

Persons, Roy W. "Psychological and Behavioral Change in Delinquents Following Psychotherapy," *Journal of Clinical Psychology,* XXII, 3 (1966), 337–340.

Pilnick, Saul, et al. "Collegefields: From Delinquency to Freedom." A Report... on Collegefields Group Educational Center. Laboratory for Applied Behavioral Science, Newark State College, February 1967. (Processed.)

Robison, James, and Kevotkian, Marinette. "Intensive Treatment Project: Phase II. Parole Outcome: Interim Report." Research Report No. 27. California Department of Corrections, Youth and Adult Correctional Agency, January 1967. (Mimeographed.)

Rudoff, Alvin. "The Effect of Treatment on Incarcerated Young Adult Delinquents as Measured by Disciplinary History." Unpublished Master's thesis, University of Southern California, 1960.

Saden, S. J. "Correctional Research at Jackson Prison," *Journal of Correctional Education,* XV (October 1962), 22–26.

Schnur, Alfred C. "The Educational Treatment of Prisoners and Recidivism," *American Journal of Sociology,* LIV, 2 (1948), 142–147.

Schwitzgebel, Robert and Ralph. "Therapeutic Research: A Procedure for the Reduction of Adolescent Crime." Paper presented at meetings of the American Psychological Association, Philadelphia, August 1963.

Schwitzgebel, Robert and Kolb, D. A. "Inducing Behavior Change in Adolescent Delinquents," *Behavior Research Therapy,* I (1964), 297–304.

Seckel, Joachim P. "Experiments in Group Counseling at Two Youth Authority Institutions." Research Report No. 46. California Youth Authority, September 1965. (Processed.)

Seckel, Joachim P. "The Fremont Experiment, Assessment of Residential Treatment at a Youth Authority Reception Center." Research Report No. 50. California Youth Authority, January 1967. (Mimeographed.)

Shelley, Ernest L. V., and Johnson, Walter F., Jr. "Evaluating an Organized Counseling Service for Youthful Offenders," *Journal of Counseling Psychology,* VIII, 4 (1961), 351–354.

Shoham, Shlomo, and Sandberg, Moshe. "Suspended Sentences in Israel: An Evaluation of the Preventive Efficacy of Prospective Imprisonment," *Crime and Delinquency,* X, 1 (1964), 74–83.

Stanton, John M. "Delinquencies and Types of Parole Programs to Which Inmates Are Released." New York State Division of Parole, May 15, 1963. (Mimeographed.)

Stanton, John M. "Board Directed Extensive Supervision." New York State Division of Parole, August 3, 1964. (Mimeographed.)

Stuerup, Georg K. "The Treatment of Sexual Offenders," *Bulletin de la societe internationale de criminologie* (1960), pp. 320–329.

Sullivan, Clyde E., and Mandell, Wallace. "Restoration of Youth Through Training: A Final Report." Staten Island, NY: Wakoff Research Center, April 1967. (Processed.)

Taylor, A. J. W. "An Evaluation of Group Psychotherapy in a Girls Borstal," *International Journal of Group Psychotherapy*, XVII, 2 (1967), 168–177.

Truax, Charles B., Wargo, Donald G., and Silber, Leon D. "Effects of Group Psychotherapy with High Adequate Empathy and Nonpossessive Warmth upon Female Institutionalized Delinquents," *Journal of Abnormal Psychology*, LXXXI, 4 (1966), 267–274.

Warren, Marguerite, et al. "The Community Treatment Project after Five Years." California Youth Authority, 1966. (Processed.)

Warren, Marguerite, et al. "Community Treatment Project, An Evaluation of Community Treatment for Delinquents: A Fifth Progress Report." C.T.P. Research Report No. 7. California Youth Authority, August 1966. (Processed.)

Warren, Margeurite, et al. "Community Treatment Project, An Evaluation of Community Treatment for Delinquents: Sixth Progress Report." C.T.P. Research Report No. 8. California Youth Authority, September 1967. (Processed.)

Wilkins, Leslie T. "A Small Comparative Study of the Results of Probation," *British Journal of Criminology*, VIII, 3 (1958), 201–209.

Zivan, Morton. "Youth in Trouble: A Vocational Approach." Final Report of a Research Demonstration Project, May 31, 1961–August 31, 1966. Dobbs Ferry, NY, Children's Village, 1966. (Processed.)

18

THE PRINCIPLES OF EFFECTIVE CORRECTIONAL PROGRAMS

DON A. ANDREWS

As we have read, Martinson was actually more cautious in his conclusions than many believe. The message, however, was interpreted as "nothing works." While some have criticized Martinson for his methodology and public pronouncements, the real value of his work comes from others who answered the challenge. Scholars like Don Andrews began focusing on determining "what works" with offenders. Using a relatively new technique, meta-analysis, researchers have been able to demonstrate that correctional treatment can indeed have an appreciable effect on recidivism rates, provided that certain principles are met. The principles of effective intervention identified by Andrews include the risk principle (targeting higher-risk offenders), the need principle (targeting crime-producing needs), the responsivity principle (cognitive and behavioral treatment matched with offender need and learning styles), and the fidelity principles (attending to program integrity). These and other important principles are clearly identified and explained in this selection.

This chapter provides a brief outline of principles of effective correctional treatment. The principles recognize the importance of individual differences in criminal behaviour. A truly interdisciplinary psychology of criminal conduct (PCC; Andrews & Bonta, 1998) has matured to the extent that progress has been made with reference to the achievement of two major scientific standards of understanding. In brief, individual differences in criminal activity can be predicted and influenced at levels well above chance and to a practically significant degree. The following principles of effective treatment draw heavily upon that knowledge base. This does not imply that the research base is anywhere near complete with reference to most issues. Rather, all of the following principles are subject to further investigation, including even those principles with relatively strong research support at this time. Also, principles not even hinted at here are expected to be developed and validated in the coming months and years.

To date, PCC has advanced because it is specific about what it attempts to account for, that is, individual differences in criminal behaviour including reoffending on the part of adjudicated offenders. It has advanced also because it recognizes that the risk factors for criminal conduct may be biological, personal, interpersonal, and/or structural, cultural, political and economic; and may reflect immediate circumstances. PCC does not limit its view to the biological, the personal, or to differential levels of privilege and/or victimisation in social origin as may be indexed by age, race, class and gender. This PCC does not purport to be a psychology of criminal justice, a psychology of social justice, a sociology of aggregated crime rates, or a behavioural or social science of social inequality, of poverty, or of a host of other legitimate but different interests.

In applications of PCC, however, these many other legitimate but different interests may not only be of value but may well be paramount. For example, within criminal law and justice systems, principles of retribution and/or restoration may be considered paramount and hence any correctional treatment efforts, if offered at all, must be offered and evaluated within the retributive and/or restorative context. Similarly, the effects of human service efforts may be evaluated within the context of institutional and/or community corrections. Moreover, ideals of justice, ethicality, decency, legality, safety and cost-efficiency are operating in judicial and correctional contexts as they are operating in other contexts of human endeavour. Thus, the principles of effective human service reviewed here are presented in the context of seeking ethical, legal, decent, cost-effective, safe, just and otherwise normative human service efforts aimed at reducing reoffending.

The phrase "otherwise normative" covers a vast area and is included in recognition of the fact that under some political conditions the values and norms of some privileged groups may be dominant no matter how weak the connection between compliance with their norms and the enhancement of peace and security. For example, sentencing according to criminal law and the principle of specific deterrence continues to occur in Canada and other countries even though there is no consistent evidence that reoffending is reduced through increases in the severity of negative sanctioning. Similarly, principles of effective human service in a justice context may be applied even when the sanctions themselves have been handed down with little concern for reducing reoffending (for example, under a pure just desert sanction) or as an attempt to provide restitution for the victim (for example, under a restorative justice disposition).

The following principles have to do with clinically relevant programming and with setting, staff, implementation and integrity issues. The first set of principles, however, restate and underscore the importance of the theoretical and normative issues referred to in the opening paragraphs. The research evidence is appended along with some relevant references to earlier reviews of principles.

SOME PRINCIPLES OF THEORY, IDEOLOGY, JUSTICE, AND SETTING IN SEEKING REDUCED REOFFENDING

PRINCIPLE 1

Base your intervention efforts on a psychological theory of criminal behaviour as opposed to a biological, behavioural, psychological, sociological, humanistic, judicial or legal perspective on justice, social equality or aggregated crime rates. When the interest is reduced reoffending at the individual level, theories that focus on some other outcome are of reduced value because they are less likely to identify relevant variables and strategies. The average effects on reduced reoffending of interventions based on alternatives to a psychology of crime have been negative or negligible.... In brief, if you are interested in individual differences in criminal activity (for example, reducing reoffending) work from a theory of criminal behaviour.

PRINCIPLE 2

The recommended psychological perspective is a broad band general personality and social learning approach to understanding variation in criminal behaviour including criminal recidivism. This perspective identifies the [six] following major risk factors for criminal behaviour:

- attitudes, values, beliefs, rationalisations and cognitive emotional states specifically supportive of criminal behaviour;

- immediate interpersonal and social support for antisocial behaviour;
- fundamental personality and temperamental supports such as weak self-control, restless aggressive energy and adventurous pleasure seeking;
- a history of antisocial behaviour including early onset;
- problematic circumstances in the domains of home, school/work, and leisure/recreation; substance abuse. (Principles 5–8.)

The general personality and social learning perspectives also identify the major behavioural influence strategies such as modelling, reinforcement and cognitive restructuring in the context of a reasonably high quality interpersonal relationship (Principle 9, 16). The behavioural base of this perspective also suggests that treatment is best offered in the community-based settings in which problematic behaviour occurs (Principle 4). In addition, the behaviour of workers in correctional settings is also under the influence of cognition, social support, behavioural history and fundamental personality predisposition and hence the emphasis placed on the selection, training and supervision of workers (Principle 16, 17).

PRINCIPLE 3

Introduce human service strategies and do not rely on the principles of retribution or restorative justice and do not rely on principles of deterrence (specific and/or general) and/or on incapacitation. Moreover, seriously consider and introduce but do not rely upon other principles of justice and normative appropriateness such as professional credentials, ethicality, legality, decency, and efficiency. Rather, reductions in reoffending are to be found through the design and delivery of clinically relevant and psychologically appropriate human service under conditions and settings considered just, ethical, legal, decent, efficient, and otherwise normative. In brief, the task assigned by the human service principle of effective service is to design and deliver effective human service in a just and otherwise normative context. The principles of effective human service do not vary greatly with such considerations, although the justice and normative contexts themselves may vary tremendously. The setting factor of community versus institutional corrections, however, does lead to a separate principle.

PRINCIPLE 4

Community-based services are preferred over residential/institutional settings but, if justice or other concerns demand a residential or custodial placement, community-oriented services are recommended. Community-oriented services refer to services facilitating return to the community and facilitating appropriate service delivery in the community. The principles of relapse prevention provide guidance for clinically relevant community-oriented services. When services are community-based, a supplementary consideration is to favour home and school-based services rather than agency-based services. For example, the best of the family interventions are not delivered in agency offices but in the natural settings of home and community.

PRINCIPLES OF RISK, NEED, RESPONSIVITY, STRENGTH, MULTIMODAL SERVICE, AND SERVICE RELEVANT ASSESSMENT

PRINCIPLE 5—*RISK*

More intensive human services are best reserved for higher risk cases. Low risk cases have a low probability of recidivism even in the absence of service. With the lowest risk cases, justice may be served through just dispositions and there is no need to introduce correctional treatment services in order to reduce risk. Indeed, a concern in working with the lowest risk cases is that the pursuit of justice does not inadvertently increase risk through, for example, increased association with offenders and/or the acquisition of pro-criminal attitudes and beliefs. Additionally, recognize that well controlled outcome studies have yet to find reduced reoffending when human service is delivered to the highest risk cases such as very high risk egocentric offenders with extended histories of antisocial behaviour. There is the possibility that psychopaths may put any new skills acquired in treatment to antisocial use (see Principle 10, specific responsivity). At this time, however, there are no well-controlled outcome studies of clinically appropriate treatment with psychopaths.

PRINCIPLE 6—*TARGET CRIMINOGENIC NEED*

Treatment services best attempt to reduce major dynamic risk factors and/or to enhance major protective or strength factors. Criminogenic needs are dynamic risk factors that when reduced are followed by reduced reoffending and/or protective factors that when enhanced are followed by reduced reoffending. Following the major risk factors, the most promising targets include moving antisocial cognition and cognitive emotional states such as resentment in the less antisocial direction, reducing association with antisocial others and enhancing association with anticriminal others, and building self-management, self-regulation and problem solving skills. A history of antisocial behaviour can not be eliminated but new less risky behaviours may be acquired and practised in risky situations (as in relapse prevention programs). Rewards for non-criminal behaviour may be enhanced in the settings of home, school/work and leisure. In the home, the major intermediate targets are enhanced caring, nurturance and mutual respect in combination with monitoring, supervision and appropriate discipline. Similarly, reduced substance abuse may shift the pattern of rewards such that the non-criminal is favoured. The less promising intermediate targets of change include enhancing self-esteem and reducing personal distress without touching personal and interpersonal supports for crime, increasing fear of official punishment, and a focus on other weak risk factors. In summary, for adherence with the need principle, emphasize the reduction of criminogenic need and do not rely upon or emphasize the reduction of noncriminogenic need.

PRINCIPLE 7—*MULTIMODAL*

Target a number of criminogenic needs. The meta-analyses now make it clear that a number of the criminogenic needs of high-risk cases are best targeted.

PRINCIPLE 8—*ASSESSING RISK AND DYNAMIC FACTOR*

Adherence to the principles of risk and criminogenic need depend upon the reliable and valid assessment of risk and need. The best instruments sample the major risk factors and can provide evidence of validity with younger and older cases, men and women, and different ethnic groups in a number of justice and correctional contexts. Assessments of risk best sample the eight risk factors as well as very specific indicators when specialized outcomes are sought. The latter specific indicators, for example, would include deviant sexual arousal and cognitive and/or social support for sexual offending when reduced sex offending is the desired outcome. Similarly, attitudinal and social support for battering would be specific risk factors when reduced family violence is the desired outcome. Please do not confuse seriousness of the current offence with risk of reoffending. Seriousness of the offence is an aggravating factor at time of sentencing but not a major risk factor.

PRINCIPLE 9—*GENERAL RESPONSIVITY*

Responsivity has to do with matching the style, modes and influence strategies of service with the learning styles, motivation, aptitude and ability of cases. Generally, offenders are human beings and hence the principle suggests use of the most powerful influencing strategies that have been demonstrated with human beings. Consistent with the general personality and social learning perspective, these most powerful approaches are structured behavioural, social learning and cognitive behavioural influence strategies. These fundamentals include reinforcement, modelling, skill acquisition through reinforced practice in the context of role playing and graduated approximations, extinction, and cognitive restructuring. Reinforcement, extinction, modelling effects and the attractiveness of the setting of change are all enhanced by high quality interpersonal relationships characterized as open, warm, non-hostile, non-blaming and engaging. Structuring activities include anticriminal modeling and reinforcement, skill building through structured learning, problem solving, advocacy and brokerage, and the effective use of authority (see Principle 16, staff considerations).

PRINCIPLE 10—*SPECIFIC RESPONSIVITY AND STRENGTHS*

Specific responsivity factors include personality, ability, motivation, strengths, age, gender, ethnicity/race, language, and various barriers to successful participation in service. The personality set, for example, includes interpersonal anxiety (avoid heavy confrontation), interpersonal and cognitive immaturity (use structured approaches), psychopathy (keep very open communication among all workers) and low verbal intelligence (be concrete). Motivational considerations suggest matching treatment style and goals with level of motivation for change (from not even thinking of change though currently involved in change activities). The relationship principle noted under general responsivity is widely applicable but many feminist scholars stress in particular quality of interpersonal interactions in working with female offenders. Aboriginal writers support the introduction of a spiritual component when working with Aboriginal offenders. When working with reluctant cases the general rule of high quality interpersonal interactions is underscored as is the removal of concrete barriers such as inconvenient timing and location of service. Make use of personal, interpersonal and circumstantial strengths in planning and delivering service. Some of these helpful strengths are problem-solving skills, respect for family, a particularly prosocial friend or being happily employed in delivering effective service.

PRINCIPLE 11—*ASSESS RESPONSIVITY AND STRENGTH FACTORS*

Sophisticated assessment instruments are available for assessment of some of the personality factors and a new generation of risk/need scales are introducing routine assessment of strength and other responsivity factors. Generally, however, watch for particular strengths and for particular barriers for individual cases and for particular groups such as women and minorities.

PRINCIPLE 12—*AFTER CARE, STRUCTURED FOLLOW-UP, CONTINUITY OF CARE, AND RELAPSE PREVENTION*

This is introduced as a principle on its own because of the need to stress ongoing monitoring of progress and to intervene when circumstances deteriorate or positive opportunities emerge. Generally, and particularly for residential programs, it is important that programming be community oriented and attend to family, associates and other social settings. Going beyond Principle 4, Principle 12 stresses specific and structured after care and follow-up activity and requires co-ordination of applications of all of the previous principles. At a minimum, in the tradition of relapse prevention, high-risk situations and circumstances are identified and low-risk alternative responses are practiced.

PRINCIPLE 13—*PROFESSIONAL DISCRETION*

In a few cases, with documented reasons, deviations from the general principles may be introduced. For example, for some young people and their families, it may be recommended that facilitating a move out of a particular apartment building in a particularly high crime area is a priority intermediate goal. Similarly, a major mental disorder such as schizophrenia may move from the minor risk set to the major set when specific symptoms include antisocial thoughts that others are out to get the person and should be "got" first.

PRINCIPLE 14

Create and record a service plan and any modification of plans through re-assessment of risk/need and progress. The service plan describes how the human service principles of risk, need, general responsivity, specific responsivity, multimodal service, aftercare and professional discretion will be addressed in working with a particular case.

IMPLEMENTATION AND PROGRAM INTEGRITY

PRINCIPLE 15—*INTEGRITY IN PROGRAM IMPLEMENTATION AND DELIVERY*

Integrity has to do with whether the human service activities were introduced and delivered as planned and designed, and indeed whether the delivery of services achieved intermediate objectives. Integrity is enhanced when a highly specific and concrete version of a rational and empirically sound theory is employed. Specificity enhances the opportunity for clarity in who is being served, what is being targeted, and what style, mode and strategy of service is to be used. Specificity readily yields the production of training and program manuals in printed, taped or other formats. Integrity is enhanced when workers are selected, trained, and clinically supervised with particular reference to the attitudes and skills required for effective service delivery. Integrity is enhanced when the clinical supervisor has been trained and has access to highly relevant consultation services. In addition, specificity implies an understanding of when treatment comes to an appropriate end or an understanding of the appropriate closing of the case. The latter implies that service personnel and researchers know when dosage has been adequate and/or when treatment has been delivered successfully and/or when intermediate targets have been achieved. Thus, integrity may be enhanced through the monitoring of service process and monitoring of the achievement of intermediate objectives. At the highest levels of integrity, when clinical supervision or other styles of monitoring identify problematic circumstances (or unanticipated service opportunities) actions are initiated to modify the service plan and to overcome barriers and build on strengths. Involvement of researchers in the design and/or delivery of service amplifies integrity. In summary and in checklist format, integrity depends upon all of the following:

(a) Specific version of a rational and empirically sound theory
(b) Selection of workers
(c) Training of workers
(d) Clinical supervision of workers
(e) Trained clinical supervisors
(f) Consultation services for clinical supervisors
(g) Printed/taped program manuals
(h) Monitoring of intermediate service process
(i) Monitoring of intermediate change
(j) Action to maximize adherence to service process and enhance appropriate intermediate gain
(k) Adequate dosage/duration/intensity
(l) Involve a researcher in the design, delivery and evaluation of service—in particular, involve a researcher interested in service process, intermediate outcome and ultimate outcome in the design and delivery of service
(m) Other

Implementation and integrity issues involve staff and management issues to such a degree that their importance is underscored through statements of separate principles of staff and management considerations.

PRINCIPLE 16—*ATTEND TO STAFF*

The selection, training and clinical supervision of staff each best reflect the particular attitudes, skills and circumstances that are supportive of the delivery of the service as planned. Reflecting the general social learning and general responsivity principles, staff skill and cognition supportive of effective practice fall into the five general core practice categories of relationship/interaction skills, structuring/contingency skills, personal cognitive supportive of human service, social support for the delivery of clinically appropriate service, and other considerations.

Relationship

Indicators of relationship skills include some combination of the following: being respectful, open, warm (not cold, hostile, indifferent), caring, non-blaming, flexible, reflective, self confident, mature, enthusiastic, understanding, genuine (real), bright and verbal, and other indicators including elements of motivational interviewing strategies (express empathy, avoid argumentation, roll with resistance). Recall from the general responsivity principle that the effectiveness of modelling, reinforcement and even expressions of disapproval are all enhanced in the context of high quality interpersonal relationships.

Structuring

Indicators of structuring skills include some combination of the following social learning/cognitive behavioural strategies reformulated with particular reference to core effective practices. Modelling anticriminal alternatives to procriminal attitudes, values, beliefs, rationalizations, thoughts, feelings and behavioural patterns; anticriminal differential reinforcement; cognitive restructuring; structured learning skills; the practice and training of problem solving skills; core advocacy/brokerage activity; and effective use of authority. More generally expressed, some indicators are being directive, solution focused, contingency based and, from motivational interviewing, developing discrepancy and supporting beliefs that the person can change his or [her] behaviour (supporting prosocial self efficacy).

Personal Cognitive Supports

Some specific indicators including:

- a knowledge base favouring human service activity;
- a belief that offenders can change;
- a belief that core correctional practices work;
- a belief that personally they have the skills to practice at high levels both in terms of relationship and structuring;
- a belief that important others value core practice and value; and
- a belief that reducing recidivism is a worthwhile pursuit.

Social Support for Effective Practice

The two major indicators are association with others who practice and support clinically relevant treatment, and relative isolation from anti-treatment others and from others who promote unstructured, non-directive, client-centered practice and/or isolation from others who promote intensive service for low risk cases and promote the targeting of non-criminogenic needs.

Other

Credentials and other factors will be relevant in so far as they tap into the core practices. Obviously, the area of staff considerations is a major area for future research.

A program scores high on staff considerations when:

(a) staff are selected with reference to high level functioning on the relationship, structuring, cognitive and social support dimension of effective correctional practice;
(b) staff receive preservice and inservice training that supports high levels of core practice;
(c) staff receive on-the-job clinical supervision that is concerned with high level functioning in core practice;
(d) staff are actually observed to be functioning at high levels in their exchanges with offenders.

PRINCIPLE 17—*ATTEND TO MANAGEMENT*

Effective managers are assumed to be generally good managers with, additionally, the above-noted relationship and structuring skills along with the knowledge base and their own social support system favourable to clinically relevant and psychologically informed human service. It is management that is responsible for implementing the core principles and creating the supports for creating and maintaining integrity. Effective management will take the steps required to develop program champions inside and outside of the agency. Effective management will reward high functioning staff and have programs and sites accredited.

PRINCIPLE 18—*ATTENDING TO BROADER SOCIAL ARRANGEMENTS*

The effective prevention and correctional treatment agency in a public manner will locate crime reduction efforts in the context appropriate to local and surrounding conditions. In brief, the correctional agency will be able to clearly locate treatment in locally appropriate contexts of public safety, restorative justice, etc. Similarly, the primary prevention agency will be able to locate their crime prevention efforts in the locally appropriate context of child welfare, family service, mental health, community development, etc. However, if the host agency is preoccupied with punishment, restoration or child welfare etc.—if the host agency is not understanding of or interested in clinically relevant approaches to reduced antisocial behaviour—effectiveness will be reduced.

STUDY QUESTIONS

1. According to the author, why is the psychology of criminal conduct so important in understanding what works?
2. Explain the risk, need, and responsivity principles.
3. Why is program integrity so important?
4. What are the other principles identified by the author?

REFERENCES

Akers, R. L. (1973). *Deviant behavior: A social learning approach.* Belmont, CA: Wadsworth.

Andrews, D. A. (1979). *The dimensions of correctional counseling and supervision process in probation and parole.* Toronto, ON: Ontario Ministry of Correctional Services.

Andrews, D. A. (1980). Some experimental investigations of the principles of differential association through deliberate manipulations of the structure of service systems. *American Sociological Review, 45,* 448–462.

Andrews, D. A. (1982). A *personal, interpersonal and community-reinforcement perspective on deviant behavior* (PIC-R). Toronto, ON: Ministry of Correctional Services.

Andrews, D. A. (1989). Recidivism is predictable and can be influenced: Using risk assessments to reduce recidivism. *Forum on Corrections Research, 1*(2), 11–18.

Andrews, D. A. (1995a). *Report on an expanded exploration of appropriate correctional treatment.* Paper presented at the American Society of Criminology annual meeting, Boston, MA, 1995.

Andrews, D. A. (1995b). The psychology of criminal conduct and effective treatment. In J. McGuire (Ed.), *What works: Reducing reoffending: Guidelines from research and practice* (pp. 35–62). Chichester, UK: John Wiley & Sons.

Andrews, D. A. (1995c). *Assessing program elements for risk reduction: The Correctional Program Assessment Inventory* (CPAI). Paper presented at "Research to Results," a conference of IARCA (now ICCA), Ottawa, ON. October 11–14th.

Andrews, D. A. (1996). *Behavioral, cognitive behavioral and social learning contributions to criminological theory.* Paper presented at the American Society of Criminology annual meeting, Chicago, Illinois, November.

Andrews, D. A., & Bonta, J. (1998). *The psychology of criminal conduct* (2nd edition). Cincinnati, OH: Anderson.

Andrews, D. A., & Bonta, J. (1994). *The psychology of criminal conduct.* Cincinnati, OH: Anderson.

Andrews, D. A., Bonta, J., & Hoge, R. D. (1990). Classification for effective rehabilitation: Rediscovering psychology. *Criminal Justice and Behavior, 17,* 19–52.

Andrews, D. A., & Carvell, C. (1998). *Core correctional treatment—Core correctional supervision and counseling: Theory, research, assessment and practice.* Ottawa, ON: Carleton University.

Andrews, D. A., & Dowden, C. (2005). *Managing correctional treatment for reduced recidivism: A meta-analytical review of program integrity. Legal and Criminological Psychology, 10,* 173–187.

Andrews, D. A., Dowden, C., & Gendreau, P. (1999). *Clinically relevant and psychologically informed approaches to reduced reoffending: A meta-analytic study of human service, risk, need, responsivity, and other concerns in justice contexts.* Unpublished manuscript, Ottawa, ON: Carleton University.

Andrews, D. A., Gordon, D. A., Hill, J., Kurkowski, K. P., & Hoge, R. D. (1993). *Program integrity, methodology, and treatment characteristics: A metaanalysis of effects of family intervention with young offenders.* A paper based on a presentation at the meetings of the American Society of Criminology, 1992.

Andrews, D. A., Zinger, I., Hoge, R. D., Bonta, J., Gendreau. P., & Cullen, F. T. (1990). Does correctional treatment work? A clinically relevant and psychologically informed meta-analysis. *Criminology, 28,* 369–404.

Antonowicz, D. H., & Ross, R. R. (1994). Essential components of successful rehabilitation programs for offenders. *International Journal of Offender Therapy and Comparative Criminology, 38,* 97–104.

Cleland, C. M., Pearson, F., & Lipton, D. S. (1996). *A meta-analytic approach to the link between needs-targeted treatment and reductions in criminal offending.* American Society of Criminology annual meeting, Chicago, IL, November, 1996.

Dowden, C. (1998). *A meta-analytic examination of the risk, need and responsivity principles and their importance within the rehabilitation debate.* Unpublished masters thesis. Ottawa, ON: Carleton University, Department of Psychology.

Dowden, C., & Andrews, D. A. (1999). What works for female offenders. *Crime and Delinquency, 45,* 438–452.

Garrett, C. J. (1985). Effects of residential treatment of adjudicated delinquents: A meta-analysis. *Journal of Research in Crime and Delinquency, 22,* 287–308.

Gendreau, P. (1996). The principles of effective intervention with offenders. In A. Hartland (Ed.), *Choosing correctional options that work.* Newbury Park, CA: Sage.

Gendreau, P., Little, T., & Goggin, C. (1996). A meta-analysis of the predictors of adult offender recidivism: What works! *Criminology, 34*(4), 575–607.

Gendreau, P., & Goggin, C. (1997). Correctional treatment: Accomplishments and realities. In P. Van Voorhis, M. Braswell, & D. L. Lester (Eds.), *Correctional counseling and rehabilitation.* Cincinnati, OH: Anderson.

Gendreau, P., & Ross, R. R. (1979). Effectiveness of correctional treatment: Bibliography for cynics. *Crime and Delinquency, 25,* 463–489.

Gendreau, P., & Ross, R. R. (1987). Revivification of rehabilitation: Evidence from the 1980s. *Justice Quarterly, 4,* 349–408.

Grant, J., & Grant, M. Q. (1959). A group dynamics approach to the treatment of non-conformists in the Navy. *Annals of the American Academy of Political and Social Sciences, 322,* 126–135.

Henggeler, S. W., Schoenwald, S. K., Borduin, C. ML., Rowland, M. D., & Cunningham, R. B. (1998). *Multisystemic treatment of antisocial behavior in children and adolescents.* New York, NY: The Guilford Press.

Hill, J. K., Andrews, D. A., & Hoge, R. D. (1991). Meta-analysis of treatment programs for young offenders: The effect of clinically relevant treatment on recidivism, with controls introduced for various methodological variables. *Canadian Journal of Program Evaluation, 6,* 97–109.

Izzo, R., & Ross, R. (1990). A meta-analysis of rehabilitation programs for juvenile delinquents: A brief report. *Criminal Justice and Behavior, 17,* 134–142.

Lipsey, M. W. (1989). *The efficacy of intervention for juvenile delinquency: Results from 400 studies.* Paper presented at the 41st annual meeting of the American Society of Criminology, Reno, Nevada.

Lipsey, M. W., (1992). Juvenile delinquency treatment: A meta-analytic inquiry into the variability of effects. In T. D. Cook, H. Cooper, D. S. Cordray, H. Hartmann, L. V. Hedges, R. J. Light, T. A. Louis, & F. Mosteller (Eds.), *Metaanalysis for explanation: A casebook* (pp. 83–127). New York, NY: Russell Sage Foundation.

Lipsey, M. W. (1995). What do we learn from 400 research studies on the effectiveness of treatment with juvenile delinquents? In J. McGuirc (Ed.), *What works: Reducing reoffending: Guidelines from research and practice* (pp. 63– 78). Chichester, UK: John Wiley & Sons.

Lipsey, M. W., & Wilson, D. B. (1997). *Effective intervention for serious juvenile offenders: A synthesis of research.* A paper prepared for the OJJDP Study Group on Serious and Violent Juvenile Offenders, Vanderbilt University.

Lösel. F. (1995). The efficacy of correctional treatment: A review and synthesis of meta-evaluations. In J. McGuire (Ed.), *What works: Reducing reoffending: Guidelines from research and practice* (pp. 79–111). Chichester, UK: John Wiley & Sons.

Lösel, F. (1996). Effective correctional programming: What empirical research tells us and what it doesn't. Forum on Corrections Research, 8(3), 33–36.

Lösel, F. (1998). *The importance of offender programming: German and international evaluations.* A paper presented at the International Beyond Prisons Symposium, March 15–19, 1998, Donald Gordon Centre, Queen's University, Kingston, ON.

Mayer, J. P., Gensheimer, L. K., Davidson, W. S., & Gottschalk. (1986). Social learning treatment within juvenile justice: A meta-analysis of impact in the natural environment. In S. J. Apter & A. Goldstein (Eds.), *Youth violence: Programs and prospects.* Elmsford, NY: Pergamon.

McGuire, J., & Priestley, P. (1995). Reviewing what works: Past, present and future. In J. McGuire (Ed.), *What works: Reducing reoffending—Guidelines for research and practice* (pp. 3–34). Chichester, UK: John Wiley & Sons.

Palmer, T. (1974, March). The Youth Authority's community treatment project. *Federal Probation,* 3–14.

Palmer, T. (1975). Martinson revisited. *Journal of Research in Crime and Delinquency,* 12, 133–152.

Patterson, G. R. (1982). *Coercive family process.* Eugene, OR: Cascadia.

Trotter, C. (1999). *Working with involuntary clients: A guide to practice.* London, UK: Sage Publications.

Van Voorhis, P., Braswell, M., & Lester, D. L. (1997). *Correctional counseling and rehabilitation.* Cincinnati, OH: Anderson.

Warren, M. (1971). Classification of offenders as an aid to efficient management and effective treatment. *Journal of Crime, Law, Criminology, and Police Science, 62,* 239–258.

19
RECIDIVISM OF SEX OFFENDERS

TIM BYNUM
MADELINE CARTER
SCOTT MATSON
CHARLES ONLEY

With the exception of the violent offender, no type of offender evokes more concern from the public than the sex offender. Recent laws have required sex offender registration and public notification. These strategies are designed to keep better track of sex offenders in the community. While these risk management techniques provide limited assurances that offenders will not recidivate, the more important question is whether or not risk reduction can take place through effective treatment. For many years, it was believed that treatment was ineffective in reducing recidivism among this group of offenders. However, recent studies have demonstrated that treatment can be effective in reducing recidivism for this type of offender. This reading covers all aspects of this important topic, from defining sex offenders and measuring recidivism to treatment research for both adult and juvenile sex offenders. The reading ends with a number of implications for sex offender management.

INTRODUCTION

The criminal justice system manages most convicted sex offenders with some combination of incarceration, community supervision, and specialized treatment (Knopp, Freeman-Longo, and Stevenson, 1992). While the likelihood and length of incarceration for sex offenders has increased in recent years,[1] the majority are released at some point on probation or parole (either immediately following sentencing or after a period of incarceration in prison or jail). About 60 percent of all sex offenders managed by the U.S. correctional system are under some form of conditional supervision in the community (Greenfeld, 1997).

While any offender's subsequent reoffending is of public concern, the prevention of sexual violence is particularly important given the irrefutable harm that these offenses cause victims and the fear they generate in the community. With this in mind, practitioners making decisions about how to manage sex offenders must ask themselves the following questions:

- What is the likelihood that a specific offender will commit subsequent sex crimes?
- Under what circumstances is this offender least likely to reoffend?
- What can be done to reduce the likelihood of reoffense?

The study of recidivism—the commission of a subsequent offense—is important to the criminal justice response to sexual offending. If sex offenders commit a wide variety of offenses, responses from both a public policy and treatment perspective may be no different than is appropriate for the general criminal population (Quinsey, 1984). However, a more specialized response is appropriate if sex offenders tend to commit principally sex offenses.

The purpose of this paper is to examine the critical issues in defining recidivism and provide a synthesis of the current research on the reoffense rates of sex offenders. The following sections summarize and discuss research findings on sex offenders, factors and conditions that appear to be associated with reduced sexual offending, and the implications that these findings have for sex offender management. Although studies on juvenile sex offender response to treatment exist, the vast majority of research has concentrated on adult males. Thus, this paper focuses primarily on adult male sex offenders.

ISSUES IN THE MEASUREMENT OF SEX OFFENDER RECIDIVISM

Research on recidivism can be used to inform intervention strategies with sex offenders. However, the way in which recidivism is measured can have a marked difference in study results and applicability to the day-to-day management of this criminal population. The following section explores variables such as the population(s) of sex offenders studied, the criteria used to measure recidivism, the types of offenses studied, and the length of time a study follows a sample. Practitioners must understand how these and other study variables can affect conclusions about sex offender recidivism, as well as decisions regarding individual cases.

DEFINING THE SEX OFFENDER POPULATION STUDIED

Sex offenders are a highly heterogeneous mixture of individuals who have committed violent sexual assaults on strangers, offenders who have had inappropriate sexual contact with family members, individuals who have molested children, and those who have engaged in a wide range of other inappropriate and criminal sexual behaviors. If we group various types of offenders and offenses into an ostensibly homogeneous category of "sex offenders," distinctions in the factors related to recidivism will be masked and differential results obtained from studies of reoffense patterns. Thus, one of the first issues to consider in reviewing any study of sex offender recidivism is how "sex offender" is defined; who is included in this category, and, as important, who is not.

DEFINING RECIDIVISM

Although there is common acceptance that recidivism is the commission of a subsequent offense, there are many operational definitions for this term. For example, recidivism may occur when there is a new arrest, new conviction, or new commitment to custody. Each of these criteria is a valid measure of recidivism, but each measures something different. While the differences may appear minor, they will lead to widely varied outcomes.

- *Subsequent Arrest*—Using new charges or arrests as the determining criteria for "recidivism" will result in a higher recidivism rate, because many individuals are arrested but for a variety of reasons, are not convicted.
- *Subsequent Conviction*—Measuring new convictions is a more restrictive criterion than new arrests, resulting in a lower recidivism rate. Generally, more confidence is placed in reconviction, since this involves a process through which the individual has been found guilty. However, given the process involved in reporting, prosecution, and conviction in sex offense cases, a number of researchers favor the use of more inclusive criteria (e.g., arrests or charges).
- *Subsequent Incarceration*—Some studies utilize return to prison as the criterion for determining recidivism. There are two ways in which individuals may be returned to a correctional institution. One is through the commission of a new offense and return to prison on a new sentence and the

other is through a technical violation of parole. The former is by far the more restrictive criterion, since an offender has to have been found guilty and sentenced to prison. Technical violations typically involve violations of conditions of release, such as being alone with minor children or consuming alcohol. Thus, the use of this definition will result in the inclusion of individuals who may not have committed a subsequent criminal offense as recidivists. When one encounters the use of return to prison as the criterion for recidivism, it is imperative to determine if this includes those with new convictions, technical violations, or both.

UNDERESTIMATING RECIDIVISM

Reliance on measures of recidivism as reflected through official criminal justice system data obviously omit offenses that are not cleared through an arrest or those that are never reported to the police. This distinction is critical in the measurement of recidivism of sex offenders. For a variety of reasons, sexual assault is a vastly underreported crime. The National Crime Victimization Surveys (Bureau of Justice Statistics) conducted in 1994, 1995, and 1998 indicate that only 32 percent (one out of three) of sexual assaults against persons 12 or older are reported to law enforcement. A three-year longitudinal study (Kilpatrick, Edmunds, and Seymour, 1992) of 4,008 adult women found that 84 percent of respondents who identified themselves as rape victims did not report the crime to authorities. (No current studies indicate the rate of reporting for child sexual assault, although it is generally assumed that these assaults are equally underreported.) Many victims are afraid to report sexual assault to the police. They may fear that reporting will lead to the following:

- further victimization by the offender;
- other forms of retribution by the offender or by the offender's friends or family;
- arrest, prosecution, and incarceration of an offender who may be a family member or friend and on whom the victim or others may depend;
- others finding out about the sexual assault (including friends, family members, media, and the public);
- not being believed; and
- being traumatized by the criminal justice system response.

These factors are compounded by the shame and guilt experienced by sexual assault victims, and, for many, a desire to put a tragic experience behind them. Incest victims who have experienced criminal justice involvement are particularly reluctant to report new incest crimes because of the disruption caused to their family. This complex of reasons makes it unlikely that reporting figures will change dramatically in the near future and bring recidivism rates closer to actual reoffense rates.

Several studies support the hypothesis that sexual offense recidivism rates are underreported. Marshall and Barbaree (1990) compared official records of a sample of sex offenders with "unofficial" sources of data. They found that the number of subsequent sex offenses revealed through unofficial sources was 2.4 times higher than the number that was recorded in official reports. In addition, research using information generated through polygraph examinations on a sample of imprisoned sex offenders with fewer than two known victims (on average), found that these offenders actually had an average of 110 victims and 318 offenses (Ahlmeyer, Heil, McKee, and English, 2000). Another polygraph study found a sample of imprisoned sex offenders to have extensive criminal histories, committing sex crimes for an average of 16 years before being caught (Ahlmeyer, English, and Simons, 1999).

OFFENSE TYPE

For the purpose of their studies, researchers must determine what specific behaviors qualify sex offenders as recidivists. They must decide if only sex offenses will be considered, or if the commission of any crime is sufficient to be classified as a recidivating offense. If recidivism is determined only through the commission of a subsequent sex offense, researchers must consider if this includes felonies and misdemeanors. Answers to these fundamental questions will influence the level of observed recidivism in each study.

LENGTH OF FOLLOW-UP

Studies often vary in the length of time they "follow-up" on a group of sex offenders in the community. There are two issues of concern with follow-up periods. Ideally, all individuals in any given study should have the same length of time "at risk"—time at large in the community—and, thus, equal opportunity to commit subsequent offenses. In practice, however, this almost never happens. For instance, in a 10-year follow-up study, some subjects will have been in the community for eight, nine, or 10 years while others may have been out for only two years. This problem is addressed by using survival analysis, a methodology that takes into account the amount of time every subject has been in the community, rather than a simple percentage.

Additionally, when researchers compare results across studies, similar time at risk should be used in each of the studies. Obviously, the longer the follow-up period, the more likely reoffense will occur and a higher rate of recidivism will be observed. Many researchers believe that recidivism studies should ideally include a follow-up period of five years or more.

EFFECT ON RECIDIVISM OUTCOMES

What are we to make of these caveats regarding recidivism—do they render recidivism a meaningless concept? On the contrary, from a public policy perspective, recidivism is an invaluable measure of the performance of various sanctions and interventions with criminal offenders. However, there is often much ambiguity surrounding what appears to be a simple statement of outcomes regarding recidivism. In comparing the results of various recidivism studies, one should not lose sight of the issues of comparable study samples, criteria for recidivism, the length of the follow-up period, information sources utilized to estimate risk of reoffense, and the likelihood that recidivism rates are underestimated.

FACTORS ASSOCIATED WITH SEX OFFENDER RECIDIVISM

In many instances, policies and procedures for the management of sex offenders have been driven by public outcry over highly publicized sex offenses. However, criminal justice practitioners must avoid reactionary responses that are based on public fear of this population. Instead, they must strive to make management decisions that are based on the careful assessment of the likelihood of recidivism. The identification of risk factors that may be associated with recidivism of sex offenders can aid practitioners in devising management strategies that best protect the community and reduce the likelihood of further victimization.

It is crucial to keep in mind, however, that there are no absolutes or "magic bullets" in the process of identifying these risk factors. Rather, this process is an exercise in isolating factors that *tend* to be associated with specific behaviors. While this association reflects a likelihood, it does not indicate that all individuals who possess certain characteristics will behave in a certain manner. Some sex offenders will inevitably commit subsequent sex offenses, in spite of our best efforts to identify risk factors and institute management and treatment processes aimed at minimizing these conditions. Likewise, not all sex offenders who have reoffense risk characteristics will recidivate.

This section explores several important aspects in the study of recidivism and identification of risk factors associated with sex offenders' commission of subsequent crimes.

APPLICATION OF STUDIES OF GENERAL CRIMINAL RECIDIVISM

The identification of factors associated with criminal recidivism has been an area of significant research over the past 20 years. This work has fueled the development of countless policies and instruments to guide sentencing and release decisions throughout the criminal justice system. If one assumes that sex offenders are similar to other criminal offenders, then the preponderance of research should assist practitioners in identifying risk factors in this population as well. Gottfredson and Hirschi (1990) argued that there is little specialization among criminal offenders. In this view, robbers also commit burglary and those who commit assaults also may be drug offenders. The extensive research on recidivism among the general criminal population has identified a set of factors that are consistently associated with subsequent criminal behavior. These factors include being young, having an unstable employment history, abusing alcohol and drugs, holding pro-criminal attitudes, and associating with other criminals (Gendreau, Little, and Goggin, 1996).

However, there is some evidence that suggests that sexual offending may differ from other criminal behavior (Hanson and Bussiere, 1998). Although sex offenders may commit other types of offenses, other types of offenders rarely commit sex offenses (Bonta and Hanson, 1995; Hanson, Steffy, and Gauthier, 1993). If this is the case, then a different set of factors may be associated with the recidivism of sex offenders than for the general offender population. This statement is reinforced by the finding that many persistent sex offenders receive low risk scores on instruments designed to predict recidivism among the general offender population (Bonta and Hanson, 1995).

IDENTIFICATION OF STATIC AND DYNAMIC FACTORS

Characteristics of offenders can be grouped into two general categories. First, there are historical characteristics, such as age, prior offense history, and age at first sex offense arrest or conviction. Because these items typically cannot be altered, they are often referred to as *static* factors. Second are those characteristics, circumstances, and attitudes that can change throughout one's life, generally referred to as *dynamic* factors. Examples of dynamic characteristics include drag or alcohol use, poor attitude (e.g., low remorse and victim blaming), and intimacy problems. The identification of dynamic factors that are associated with reduced recidivism holds particular promise in effectively managing sex offenders because the strengthening of these factors can be encouraged through various supervision and treatment strategies.

Dynamic factors can further be divided into *stable* and *acute* categories (Hanson and Harris, 1998). *Stable dynamic factors* are those characteristics that can change over time, but are relatively lasting qualities. Examples of these characteristics include deviant sexual preferences or alcohol or drug abuse. On the other hand, Hanson and Harris (1998) suggest that *acute dynamic factors* are conditions that can change over a short period of time. Examples include sexual arousal or intoxication that may immediately precede a reoffense.

UNDERSTANDING BASE RATES

Understanding the concept of "base rates" is also essential when studying sex offender recidivism. A base rate is simply the overall rate of recidivism of an entire group of offenders. If the base rate for an entire group is known (e.g., 40 percent), then, without other information, practitioners would predict that any individual in this group has approximately a 40 percent chance of recidivating.

If static or dynamic factors related to recidivism are identified, error rates can be improved and this information can be used to make more accurate assessments of the likelihood of rearrest or reconviction. However, if the base rate is at one extreme or the other, additional information may not significantly improve accuracy. For instance, if the base rate were 10 percent, then practitioners would predict that 90 percent of the individuals in this group would not be arrested for a new crime. The error rate would be difficult to improve, regardless of what additional information may be available about individual offenders. In other words, if we simply predicted that no one would be rearrested, we would be wrong only 10 percent of the time. It is quite difficult to make accurate individual predictions in such extreme situations.

What has come to be termed as "the low base rate problem" has traditionally plagued sex offender recidivism studies (Quinsey, 1980). As noted previously, lack of reporting, or underreporting, is higher in crimes of sexual violence than general criminal violence and may contribute to the low base rate problem. The following studies have found low base rates for sex offender populations:

- Hanson and Bussiere (1998) reported an overall recidivism rate of 13 percent.
- Grunfeld and Noreik (1986) found a 10 percent recidivism rate for rapists.
- Gibbens, Soothill, and Way (1978) reported a 4 percent recidivism rate for incest offenders.

Samples of sex offenders used in some studies may have higher base rates of reoffense than other studies. Quinsey (1984) found this to be the case in his summary of sex offender recidivism studies, as have many other authors who have attempted to synthesize this research. There is wide variation in results, in both the amount of measured recidivism and the factors associated with these outcomes. To a large degree, differences can be explained by variations in the sample of sex offenders involved in the studies. Although this is a simple and somewhat obvious point, this basic fact is "responsible for the disagreements and much of the confusion in the literature" on the recidivism of sex offenders (Quinsey, 1984).

Furthermore, results from some studies indicate that there may be higher base rates among certain categories of sex offenders (Quinsey, Lalumiere, Rice, and Harris, 1995; Quinsey, Rice, and Harris, 1995). For example, in their follow-up study of sex offenders released from a psychiatric facility, Quinsey, Rice, and Harris (1995) found that rapists had a considerably higher rate of rearrest/reconviction than did child molesters.

Conversely, Prentky, Lee, Knight, and Cerce (1997) found that over a 25-year period, child molesters had higher rates of reoffense than rapists. In this study, recidivism was operationalized as a failure rate and calculated as the proportion of individuals who were rearrested using survival analysis (which takes into account the amount of time each offender has been at risk in the community). Results show that over longer periods of time, child molesters have a higher failure rate—thus, a higher rate of rearrest—than rapists (52 percent versus 39 percent over 25 years).

MAKING SENSE OF CONTRADICTORY FINDINGS

Studies on sex offender recidivism vary widely in the quality and rigor of the research design, the sample of sex offenders and behaviors included in the study, the length of follow-up, and the criteria for success or failure. Due to these and other differences, there is often a perceived lack of consistency across studies of sex offender recidivism. For example, there have been varied results regarding whether the age of the offender at the time of institutional release is associated with subsequent criminal sexual behavior. While Beck and Shipley (1989) found that there was no relationship between these variables, Clarke and Crum (1985) and Marshall and Barbaree (1990) suggested that younger offenders were more likely to

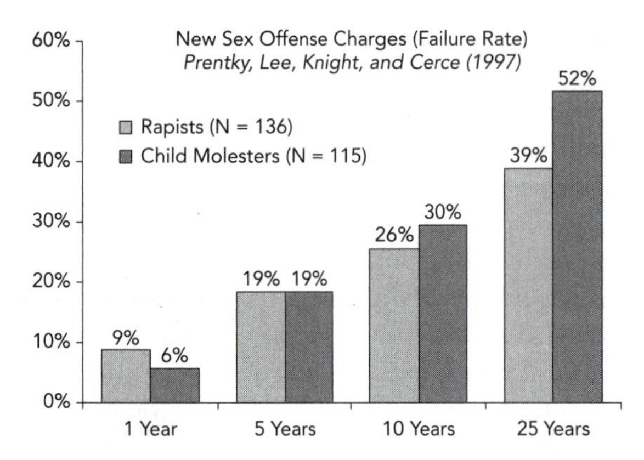

FIGURE 19.1 New Sex Offenses Charges (Failure Rates)

commit future crimes. However, Grunfeld and Noreik (1986) argued that older sex offenders are more likely to have a more developed fixation and thus are more likely to reoffend. A study by the Delaware Statistical Analysis Center (1984) found that those serving longer periods of incarceration had a lower recidivism rate—while Roundtree, Edwards, and Parker (1984) found just the opposite.

To a large degree, the variation across individual studies can be explained by the differences in study populations. Schwartz and Cellini (1997) indicated that the use of a heterogeneous group of sex offenders in the analysis of recidivism might be responsible for this confusion:

> Mixing an antisocial rapist with a socially skilled fixated pedophile with a developmentally disabled exhibitionist may indeed produce a hodgepodge of results.

Similarly, West, Roy, and Nichols (1978) noted that recidivism rates in studies of sex offenders vary by the characteristics of the offender sample. Such a situation makes the results from follow-up studies of undifferentiated sex offenders difficult to interpret (Quinsey, 1998).

One method of dealing with this problem is to examine recidivism studies of specific types of sex offenders. This approach is warranted, given the established base rate differences across types of sex offenders.[2] Marshall and Barbaree (1990) found in their review of studies that the recidivism rate for specific types of offenders varied:

- Incest offenders ranged between 4 and 10 percent.
- Rapists ranged between 7 and 35 percent.
- Child molesters with female victims ranged between 10 and 29 percent.
- Child molesters with male victims ranged between 13 and 40 percent.
- Exhibitionists ranged between 41 and 71 percent.

In summary, practitioners should recognize several key points related to research studies on sex offender recidivism. First, since sexual offending may differ from other criminal behavior, research specific to sex offender recidivism is needed to inform interventions with sex offenders. Second, researchers seek to identify static and dynamic factors associated with recidivism of sex offenders. In particular, the identification of, and support of, "positive" dynamic factors may help reduce the risk of recidivism. Third, although research studies on recidivism of sex offenders often appear to have contradictory findings, variations in outcomes can typically be explained by the differences in the study populations. Finally, since base rate differences have been identified across types of sex offenses, it makes sense to study recidivism of sex offenders by offense type.

REVIEW OF STUDIES

The following sections present findings from various studies of the recidivism of sex offenders within offense categories of rapists and child molesters.[3] Overall recidivism findings are presented, along with results concerning the factors and characteristics associated with recidivism.

RAPISTS

There has been considerable research on the recidivism of rapists across various institutional and community-based settings and with varying periods of follow-up. A follow-up study of sex offenders released from a maximum-security psychiatric institution in California found that 10 of the 57 rapists (19 percent) studied were reconvicted of a rape within five years, most of which occurred during the first year of the follow-up period (Sturgeon and Taylor, 1980). These same authors reported that among 68 sex offenders not found to be mentally disordered who were paroled in 1973, 19 (28 percent) were reconvicted for a sex offense within five years.

In a study of 231 sex offenders placed on probation in Philadelphia between 1966 and 1969, 11 percent were rearrested for a sex offense and 57 percent were rearrested for any offense (Romero and Williams, 1985). Rice, Harris, and Quinsey (1990) conducted a more recent study of 54 rapists who were released from prison before 1983. After four years, 28 percent had a reconviction for a sex offense and 43 percent had a conviction for a violent offense.

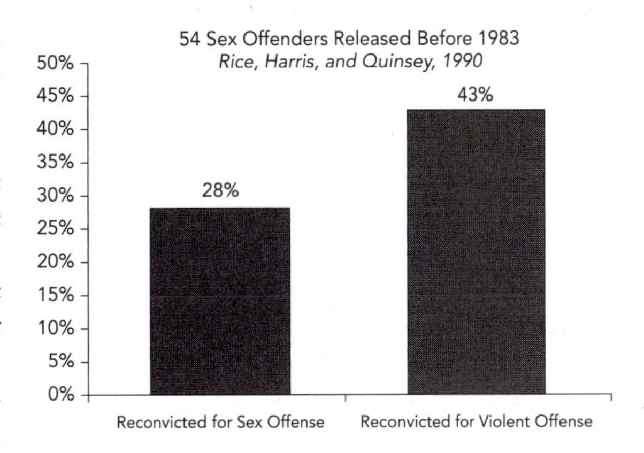

FIGURE 19.2 54 Sex Offenders Released Before 1983

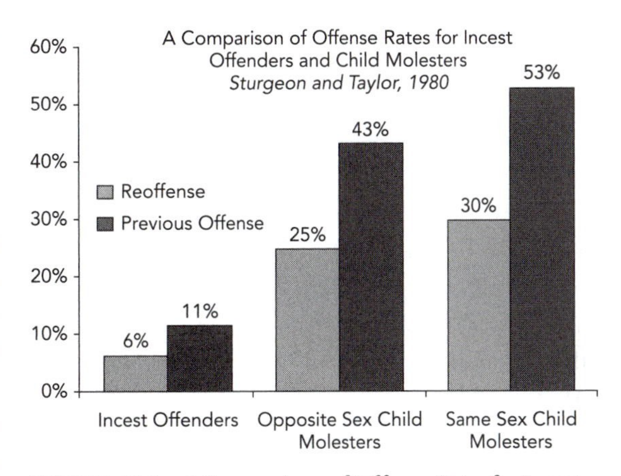

FIGURE 19.3 A Comparison of Offense Rates for Incest

In their summary of the research on the recidivism of rapists, Quinsey, Lalumiere, Rice, and Harris (1995) noted that the significant variation in recidivism across studies of rapists is likely due to differences in the types of offenders involved (e.g., institutionalized offenders, mentally disordered offenders, or probationers) or in the length of the follow-up period. They further noted that throughout these studies, the proportion of offenders who had a prior sex offense was similar to the proportion that had a subsequent sex offense. In addition, the rates of reoffending decreased with the seriousness of the offense. That is, the occurrence of officially recorded recidivism for a nonviolent nonsexual offense was the most likely and the incidence of violent sex offenses was the least likely.

CHILD MOLESTERS

Studies of the recidivism of child molesters reveal specific patterns of reoffending across victim types and offender characteristics. A study involving mentally disordered sex offenders compared same-sex and opposite-sex child molesters and incest offenders. Results of this five-year follow-up study found that same-sex child molesters had the highest rate of previous sex offenses (53 percent), as well as the highest reconviction rate for sex crimes (30 percent). In comparison, 43 percent of opposite-sex child molesters had prior sex offenses and a reconviction rate for sex crimes of 25 percent, and incest offenders had prior convictions at a rate of 11 percent and a reconviction rate of 6 percent (Sturgeon and Taylor, 1980). Interestingly, the recidivism rate for same-sex child molesters for other crimes against persons was also quite high, with 26 percent having reconvictions for these offenses. Similarly, a number of other studies have found that child molesters have relatively high rates of nonsexual offenses (Quinsey, 1984).

Several studies have involved follow-up of extra-familial child molesters. One such study (Barbaree and Marshall, 1988) included both official and unofficial measures of recidivism (reconviction, new charge, or unofficial record). Using both types of measures, researchers found that 43 percent of these offenders (convicted of sex offenses involving victims under the age of 16 years) sexually reoffended within a four-year follow-up period. Those who had a subsequent sex offense differed from those who did not by their use of force in the offense, the number of previous sexual assault victims, and their score on a sexual index that included a phallometric assessment.[4] In contrast to other studies of child molesters, this study found no difference in recidivism between opposite-sex and same-sex offenders.

In a more recent study (Rice, Quinsey, and Harris, 1991), extra-familial child molesters were followed for an average of six years. During that time, 31 percent had a reconviction for a second sexual offense. Those who committed subsequent sex offenses were more likely to have been married, have a personality disorder, and have a more serious sex offense history than those who did not recidivate sexually. In addition, recidivists were more likely to have deviant phallometrically measured sexual preferences (Quinsey, Lalumiere, Rice, and Harris, 1995).

Those who committed subsequent sex offenses were more likely to have been married, have a personality disorder, and have a more serious sex offense history than those who did not recidivate sexually.

In a study utilizing a 24-year follow-up period, victim differences (e.g., gender of the victim) were not found to be associated with the recidivism (defined as those charged with a subsequent sexual offense) of child molesters. This study of 111 extra-familial child molesters found that the number of prior sex offenses and sexual preoccupation with children were related to sex offense recidivism (Prentky, Knight, and Lee, 1997). However, the authors of this study noted that the finding of no victim differences may have been due to the fact that the offenders in this study had an average of three prior sex offenses before their prison release. Thus, this sample may have had a higher base rate of reoffense than child molesters from the general prison population.

PROBATIONERS

Research reviewed to this point has almost exclusively focused upon institutional or prison populations and therefore, presumably a more serious offender population. An important recent study concerns recidivism among a group of sex offenders placed on probation (Kruttschnitt, Uggen, and Shelton, 2000). Although the factors that were related to various types of reoffending were somewhat similar with regard to subsequent sex offenses, the only factor associated with reducing reoffending in this study was the combination of stable employment and sex offender treatment. Such findings emphasize the importance of both formal and informal social controls in holding offenders accountable for their criminal behavior. The findings also provide support for treatment services that focus on coping with inappropriate sexual impulses, fantasies, and behaviors through specific sex offender treatment.

SYNTHESIS OF RECIDIVISM STUDIES

There have been several notable efforts at conducting a qualitative or narrative synthesis of studies of the recidivism of sex offenders (Quinsey, 1984; Furby, Weinrott, and Blackshaw, 1989; Quinsey, Lalumiere, Rice, and Harris, 1995; Schwartz and Cellini, 1997). Such an approach attempts to summarize findings across various studies by comparing results and searching for patterns or trends. Another technique, known as meta-analysis, relies upon a quantitative approach to synthesizing research results from similar studies. Meta-analysis involves a statistically sophisticated approach to estimating the combined effects of various studies that meet certain methodological criteria and is far from a simple lumping together of disparate studies to obtain average effects.

Meta-analyses have certain advantages over more traditional summaries in that through the inclusion of multiple studies, a reliable estimation of effects can be obtained that is generalizable across studies and samples. As noted earlier, the results obtained from individual studies of sex offenders are heavily influenced by the sample of offenders included in the research. Therefore, there is much to be gained through the use of meta-analysis in summarizing sex offender recidivism (see Quinsey, Harris, Rice, and Lalumiere, 1993).

As has also previously been observed, it is imperative to distinguish between sex offense recidivism and the commission of other subsequent criminal behavior, as well as the type of current sex offense. One of the most widely recognized meta-analyses of sexual offender recidivism (Hanson and Bussiere, 1998) was structured around these dimensions.

META-ANALYSIS STUDIES

In Hanson and Bussiere's meta-analysis, 61 research studies met the criteria for inclusion, with all utilizing a longitudinal design and a comparison group. Across all studies, the average sex offense recidivism rate (as evidenced by rearrest or reconviction) was 18.9 percent for rapists and 12.7 percent for child molesters over a four to five year period. The rate of recidivism for nonsexual violent offenses was 22.1 percent for rapists and 9.9 percent for child molesters, while the recidivism rate for any reoffense for rapists was 46.2 percent and 36.9 percent for child molesters over a four to five year period. However, as has been noted previously and as these authors warn, one should be cautious in the interpretation of the data as these studies involved a range of methods and follow-up periods.

Perhaps the greatest advantage of the meta-analysis approach is in determining the relative importance of various factors across studies. Using this technique, one can estimate how strongly certain offender and offense characteristics are related to recidivism because they show up consistently across different studies.

In the 1998 Hanson and Bussiere study, these characteristics were grouped into demographics, criminal lifestyle, sexual criminal history, sexual deviancy, and various clinical characteristics. Regarding demographics, being young and single were consistently found to be related, albeit weakly, to subsequent sexual offending. With regard to sex offense history, sex offenders were more likely to recidivate if they had prior sex offenses, male victims, victimized strangers or extra-familial victims, begun sexually offending at an early age, and/or engaged in diverse sex crimes.

Sexual interest in children was the strongest predictor of recidivism across all studies.

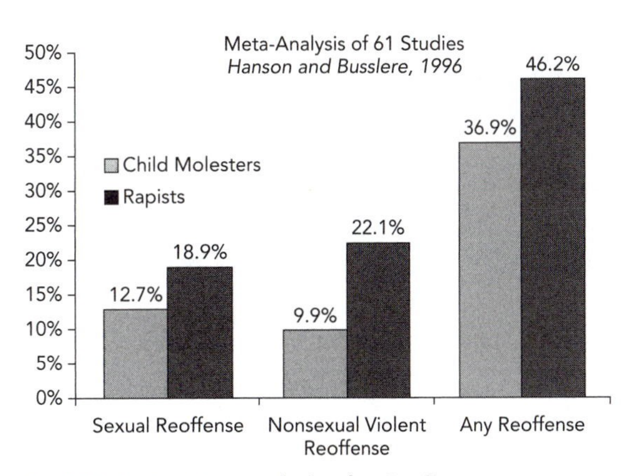

FIGURE 19.4 Meta-Analysis of 61 Studies

The factors that were found through this analysis to have the strongest relationship with sexual offense recidivism were those in the sexual deviance category: sexual interest in children, deviant sexual preferences, and sexual interest in boys. Failure to complete treatment was also found to be a moderate predictor of sexual recidivism. Having general psychological problems was not related to sexual offense recidivism, but having a personality disorder was related. Being sexually abused as a child was not related to repeat sexual offending.

STUDIES THAT FOCUS ON DYNAMIC FACTORS

As noted earlier, the detection of dynamic factors that are associated with sexual offending behavior is significant, because these characteristics can serve as the focus of intervention. However, many recidivism studies (including most of those previously discussed) have focused almost exclusively on static factors, since they are most readily available from case files. Static, or historical, factors help us to understand etiology and permit predictions of relative likelihood of reoffending. Dynamic factors take into account changes over time that adjust static risk and [inform] us about the types of interventions that are most useful in lowering risk.

In a study focused on dynamic factors, Hanson and Harris (1998) collected data on over 400 sex offenders under community supervision, approximately one-half of whom were recidivists.[5] The recidivists had committed a new sexual offense while on community supervision during a five-year period (1992–1997). A number of significant differences in stable dynamic factors were discovered between recidivists and non-recidivists. Those who committed subsequent sex offenses were more likely to be unemployed (more so for rapists) and have substance abuse problems. The nonrecidivists tended to have positive social influences and were more likely to have intimacy problems. There also were considerable attitudinal differences between the recidivists and non-recidivists. Those who committed subsequent sex offenses were less likely to show remorse or concern for the victim. In addition, recidivists tended to see themselves as being at little risk for committing new offenses, were less likely to avoid high-risk situations and were more likely to report engaging in deviant sexual activities. In general, the recidivists were described as having more chaotic, antisocial lifestyles compared to the non-recidivists (Hanson and Harris, 1998).

The researchers concluded that sex offenders are:

> ...at most risk of reoffending when they become sexually preoccupied, have access to victims, fail to acknowledge their recidivism risk, and show sharp mood increases, particularly anger.

In sum, because meta-analysis findings can be generalized across studies and samples, they offer the most reliable estimation of factors associated with the recidivism of sex offenders. Most meta-analysis studies, however, have focused on static factors. It is critical that more research be conducted to identify dynamic factors associated with sex offender recidivism. These factors will assuredly provide a foundation for developing more effective intervention strategies for sex offenders.

Characteristics* of recidivists include:

- multiple victims;
- diverse victims;
- stranger victims;
- juvenile sexual offenses;
- multiple paraphilias;
- history of abuse and neglect;
- long-term separations from parents;
- negative relationships with their mothers;
- diagnosed antisocial personality disorder;
- unemployed;

- substance abuse problems; and
- chaotic, antisocial lifestyles.

* It should be noted that these are not necessarily risk factors.

IMPACT OF INTERVENTIONS ON SEX OFFENDER RECIDIVISM

Although not the primary purpose of this document, a few words regarding sex offender treatment and supervision are in order. Factors that are linked to sex offender recidivism are of direct relevance for sex offender management. If the characteristics of offenders most likely to recidivate can be isolated, they can serve to identify those who have the highest likelihood of committing subsequent sex offenses. They can also help identify offender populations that are appropriate for participation in treatment and specialized supervision and what the components of those interventions must include.

TREATMENT

When assessing the efficacy of sex offender treatment, it is vital to recognize that the delivery of treatment occurs within different settings. Those offenders who receive treatment in a community setting are generally assumed to be a different population than those who arc treated in institutions. Thus, base rates of recidivating behavior will differ for these groups prior to treatment participation.

Sex offender treatment typically consists of three principal approaches:

- the *cognitive-behavioral approach,* which emphasizes changing patterns of thinking that are related to sexual offending and changing deviant patterns of arousal;
- the *psycho-educational approach,* which stresses increasing the offender's concern for the victim and recognition of responsibility for their offense; and
- the *pharmacological approach,* which is based upon the use of medication to reduce sexual arousal.

In practice, these approaches are not mutually exclusive and treatment programs are increasingly utilizing a combination of these techniques.

Although there has been a considerable amount of writing on the relative merits of these approaches and about sex offender treatment in general, there is a paucity of evaluative research regarding treatment outcomes. There have been very few studies of sufficient rigor (e.g., employing an experimental or quasi-experimental design) to compare the effects of various treatment approaches or comparing treated to untreated sex offenders (Quinsey, 1998).

Using less rigorous evaluation strategies, several studies have evaluated the outcomes of offenders receiving sex offender treatment, compared to a group of offenders not receiving treatment. The results of these studies are mixed. For example, Barbaree and Marshall (1988) found a substantial difference in the recidivism rates of extra-familial child molesters who participated in a community based cognitive-behavioral treatment program, compared to a group of similar offenders who did not receive treatment. Those who participated in treatment had a recidivism rate of 18 percent over a four-year follow-up period, compared to a 43 percent recidivism rate for the nonparticipating group of offenders.

However, no positive effect of treatment was found in several other quasi-experiments involving an institutional behavioral program (Rice, Quinsey, and Harris, 1991) or a milieu therapy approach in an institutional setting (Hanson, Steffy, and Gauthier, 1993).

On the other hand, an evaluation of a cognitive-behavioral program that employs an experimental design presented preliminary landings that suggest that participation in this form of treatment may have a modest (though not statistically significant) effect in reducing recidivism. After a follow-up period of

34 months, 8 percent of the offenders in the treatment program had a subsequent sex offense, compared with 13 percent of the control group, who had also volunteered for the program, but were not selected through the random assignment process (Marques, Day, Nelson, and West, 1994).

Some studies present optimistic conclusions about the effectiveness of programs that are empirically based, offense-specific, and comprehensive. A 1995 meta-analysis study on sex offender treatment outcome studies found a small, yet significant, treatment effect (Hall, 1995). This meta-analysis included 12 studies with some form of control group. Despite the small number of subjects (1,313), the results indicated an 8 percent reduction in the recidivism rate for sex offenders in the treatment group.[6]

Recently, Alexander (1999) conducted an analysis of a large group of treatment outcome studies, encompassing nearly 11,000 sex offenders. In this study, data from 79 sex offender treatment studies were combined and reviewed. Results indicated that sex offenders who participated in relapse prevention treatment programs had a combined rearrest rate of 7.2 percent, compared to 17.6 percent for untreated offenders. The overall rearrest rate for treated sex offenders in this analysis was 13.2 percent.[7]

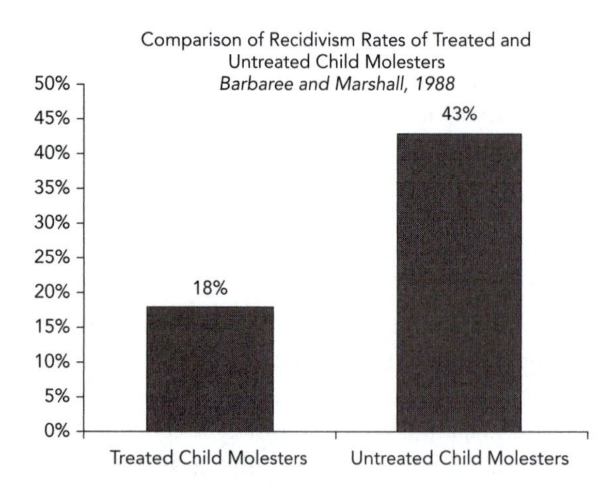

FIGURE 19.5 Comparison of Recidivism Rates of Treated and Untreated Child Molesters

The Association for the Treatment of Sexual Abusers (ATSA) has established a Collaborative Data Research Project with the goals of defining standards for research on treatment, summarizing existing research, and promoting high quality evaluations. As part of this project, researchers are conducting a meta-analysis of treatment studies. Included in the meta-analysis are studies that compare treatment groups with some form of a control group. Preliminary findings indicate that the overall effect of treatment shows reductions in both sexual recidivism, 10 percent of the treatment subjects to 17 percent of the control group subjects, and general recidivism, 32 percent of the treatment subjects to 51 percent of the control group subjects (Hanson, 2000).[8]

Just as it is difficult to arrive at definitive conclusions regarding factors that are related to sex offender recidivism, there are similarly no definitive results regarding the effect of interventions with these offenders. Sex offender treatment programs and the results of treatment outcome studies may vary not only due to their therapeutic approach, but also by the location of the treatment (e.g., community, prison, or psychiatric facility), the seriousness of the offender's criminal and sex offense history, the degree of self-selection (whether they chose to participate in treatment or were placed in a program), and the dropout rate of offenders from treatment.

JUVENILE TREATMENT RESEARCH

Research on juvenile sex offender recidivism is particularly lacking. Some studies have examined the effectiveness of treatment in reducing subsequent sexual offending behavior in youth. Key findings from these studies include the following:

- Program evaluation data suggest that the sexual recidivism rate for juveniles treated in specialized programs ranges from approximately 7 to 13 percent over follow-up periods of two to five years (Becker, 1990).

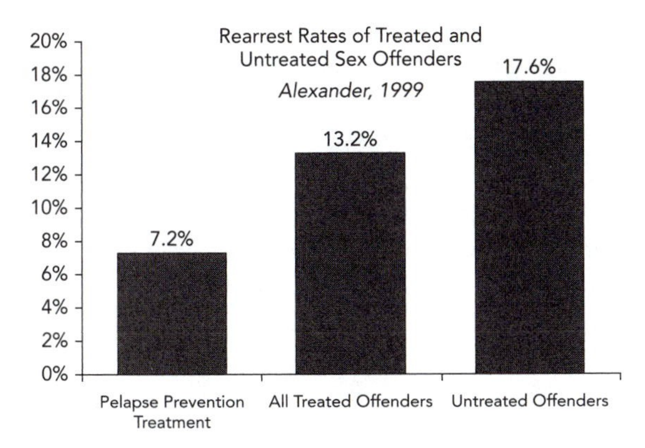

FIGURE 19.6 Rearrest Rates of Treated and Untreated Sex Offenders

- Juveniles appear to respond well to cognitive-behavioral and/or relapse prevention treatment, with rearrest rates of approximately 7 percent through follow-up periods of more than five years (Alexander, 1999).
- Studies suggest that rates of nonsexual recidivism are generally higher than sexual recidivism rates, ranging from 25 to 50 percent (Becker, 1990; Kahn and Chambers, 1991; Schram, Milloy, and Rowe, 1991).

In a recently conducted study, Hunter and Figueredo (1999) found that as many as 50 percent of youths entering a community-based treatment program were expelled during the first year of their participation. Those who failed the program had higher overall levels of sexual maladjustment, as measured on assessment instruments, and were at greater long-term risk for sexual recidivism.

SUPERVISION

There has been little research on the effectiveness of community supervision programs (exclusively) in reducing reoffense behavior in sex offenders. The majority of supervision programs for sex offenders involve treatment and other interventions to contain offenders' deviant behaviors. Therefore, it is difficult to measure the effects of supervision alone on reoffending behavior—to date, no such studies have been conducted.

EVALUATING THE EFFECTS OF INTERVENTIONS

Identification of factors associated with recidivism of sex offenders can play an important role in determining intervention strategies with this population. Yet, the effectiveness of interventions themselves on reducing recidivism must be evaluated if the criminal justice system is to control these offenders and prevent further victimization. However, not only have there been few studies of sufficient rigor on treatment outcomes, less rigorous study results thus far have been mixed. Although one study may find a substantial difference in recidivism rates for offenders who participated in a specific type of treatment, another may find only a modest positive treatment effect, and still other studies may reveal no positive effects. There has been even less research conducted to evaluate the impact of community supervision programs in reducing recidivism. More studies measuring the effects of both treatment and supervision are necessary to truly advance efforts in the field of sex offender management.

IMPLICATIONS FOR SEX OFFENDER MANAGEMENT

This paper presented a range of issues that are critical in defining the recidivism of sex offenders. Although there are certainly large gaps in criminal justice knowledge regarding the determinants of recidivism and the characteristics of effective interventions, what is known has significant implications for policy and intervention.

The Heterogeneity of Sex Offenders Must Be Acknowledged. Although sex offenders are often referred to as a "type" of offender, there are a wide variety of behaviors and offender backgrounds that fall into this classification of criminals (Knight and Prentky, 1990). As mentioned earlier, many sex offenders have histories of assaulting across sex and age groups—recent research (Ahlmeyer, Heil, McKee, and English, 2000) found that these offenders may be even more heterogeneous than previously believed.

Criminal Justice Professionals Must Continue to Expand Their Understanding of How Sex Offenders Are Different from the General Criminal Population. Although some sex offenders are unique from the general criminal population (e.g., many extra-familial child molesters), others (e.g., many rapists) possess many of the same characteristics that are associated with recidivism of general criminal behavior. As criminal justice understanding of these offenders and the factors associated with their behavior increases, more refined classification needs to be developed and treatment programs need to be redesigned to accommodate these differences.

Interventions Should Be Based on the Growing Body of Knowledge About Sex Offender and General Criminal Recidivism. Research demonstrates that while sex offenders are much more likely to commit subsequent sexual offenses than the general criminal population, they do not exclusively commit sexual offenses. Therefore, some aspects of intervention with the general criminal population may have implications for effective management of sex offenders. Quinsey (1998) has recommended that in the absence of definitive knowledge about effective sex offender treatment, the best approach would be to structure interventions around what is known about the treatment of offenders in general.

In the realm of interventions with general criminal offenders, there is a growing body of literature that suggests that the cognitive-behavioral approach holds considerable promise (Gendreau and Andrews, 1990). Cognitive-behavioral treatment involves a comprehensive, structured approach based on sexual learning theory using cognitive restructuring methods and behavioral techniques. Behavioral methods are primarily directed at reducing arousal and increasing pro-social skills. The cognitive behavioral approach employs peer groups and educational classes, and uses a variety of counseling theories. This approach suggests that interventions are most effective when they address the criminogenic needs of high-risk offenders (Andrews, 1982). The characteristics of programs that are more likely to be effective with this population include skill-based training, modeling of pro-social behaviors and attitudes, a directive but non-punitive orientation, a focus on modification of precursors to criminal behavior, and a supervised community component (Quinsey, 1998).

Although these program characteristics may be instructive in forming the basis for interventions with sex offenders, treatment approaches must incorporate what is known about this particular group of offenders. A number of characteristics that are typically associated with the recidivism of sex offenders were identified in this document, including: victim age, gender, and relationship to the offender; impulsive, anti-social behavior; the seriousness of the offense; and the number of previous sex offenses. Also, an influential factor in sex offender recidivism is the nature of the offender's sexual preferences and sexually deviant interests. The discovery and measurement of these interests can serve as a focus for treatment intervention.

Dynamic Factors Should Influence Individualized Interventions. In addition, dynamic factors associated with recidivism should inform the structure of treatment and supervision, as these are characteristics that can be altered. These factors include the formation of positive relationships with peers, stable employment, avoidance of alcohol and drugs, prevention of depression, reduction of deviant sexual arousal, and increase in appropriate sexual preferences, when they exist.

Interventions that strive to facilitate development of positive dynamic factors in sex offenders are consistent with cognitive-behavioral or social learning approaches to treatment. Such approaches determine interventions based upon an individualized planning process, utilizing standard assessment instruments to determine an appropriate intervention strategy. As Quinsey (1998: 419) noted, "with the exception of antiandrogenic medication or castration, this model is currently the only approach that enjoys any evidence of effectiveness in reducing sexual recidivism."

CONCLUSION

Although there have been many noteworthy research studies on sex offender recidivism in the last 15 to 20 years, there remains much to be learned about the factors associated with the likelihood of reoffense. Ongoing dialogue between researchers and practitioners supervising and treating sex offenders is essential to identifying research needs, gathering information about offenders and the events leading up to offenses, and ensuring that research activity can be translated into strategies to more effectively manage sex offenders in the community. Ultimately, research on sex offender recidivism must be designed and applied to practice with the goals of preventing further victimization and creating safer communities.

Practitioners must continue to look to the most up-to-date research studies on sex offender recidivism to inform their intervention strategies with individual offenders. Researchers can minimize ambiguity in study results by clearly defining measures of recidivism, comparing distinct categories of sex offenders, considering reoffense rates for both sex crimes and all other offenses, and utilizing consistent follow-up periods (preferably five years of follow-up or more). In order to reduce underestimations of the risk of recidivism, they also must strive to gather information about offenders' criminal histories from multiple sources, beyond official criminal justice data. In comparing results of various studies, practitioners should not lose sight of how these issues impact research outcomes.

Researchers must also continue to accumulate evidence about the relationship of static and dynamic factors to recidivism—such data can assist practitioners in making more accurate assessments of the likelihood of reoffending. In particular, researchers must strive to identify dynamic characteristics associated with sex offending behavior that can serve as the focus for intervention. This information can be utilized to categorize the level of risk posed by offenders, and help determine whether a particular offender is appropriate for treatment and specialized supervision. However, in order to make objective and empirically based decisions about the type of treatment and conditions of supervision that would best control the offender and protect the public, more rigorous research is needed to study the effects of various treatment approaches and community supervision on recidivism.

STUDY QUESTIONS

1. What are the various ways that *recidivism* can be defined?
2. Why is the length of follow-up important?
3. What is the difference between dynamic and static risk factors?
4. What are some of the contradictory findings from the research on sex offenders?
5. What do we know about the recidivism rates of various types of sex offenders?
6. What do the meta-analytical studies on sex offenders tell us?
7. What is the impact of interventions on sex offender recidivism?

ACKNOWLEDGMENTS

Tim Bynum, Ph.D., Michigan State University was the principal author of this paper, with contributions from Madeline Carter, Scott Matson, and Charles Onley.

This project was supported by Grant No. 1997-WT-VX-K007, awarded by the Bureau of Justice Assistance. The Bureau of Justice Assistance is a component of the Office of Justice Programs, which also includes the Bureau of Justice Statistics, the National Institute of Justice, the Office of Juvenile Justice and Delinquency Prevention, and the Office for Victims of Crime. Points of view or opinions in this document are those of the authors and do not represent the official position or policies of the United States Department of Justice.

NOTES

1. Since 1980, the number of imprisoned sex offenders has grown by more than 7 percent per year (Greenfeld, 1997). In 1994, nearly one in ten state prisoners were incarcerated for committing a sex offense (Greenfeld, 1997).
2. Recent research suggests that many offenders have histories of assaulting across genders and age groups, rather than against only one specific victim population. Researchers in a 1999 study (Ahlmeyer, English, and Simons) found that, through polygraph examinations, the number [of] offenders who "crossed over" age groups of victims is extremely high. The study revealed that before polygraph examinations, 6 percent of a sample of incarcerated sex offenders had both child and adult victims, compared to 71 percent after polygraph exams. Thus, caution must be taken in placing sex offenders in exclusive categories.
3. The studies included in this paper do not represent a comprehensive overview of the research on sex offender recidivism. The studies included represent a sampling of available research on these populations and are drawn from to highlight key points.
4. Also referred to as plethysmography: a device used to measure sexual arousal (erectile response) to both appropriate (age appropriate and consenting) and deviant sexual stimulus material.
5. For the purposes of this study, recidivism was defined as a conviction or charge for a new sexual offense, a non-sexual criminal charge that appeared to be sexually motivated, a violation of supervision conditions for sexual reasons, and self-disclosure by the offender.
6. For the purposes of this study, recidivism was measured by additional sexually aggressive behavior, including official legal charges as well as, in some studies, unofficial data such as self-report.
7. Length of follow-up in this analysis varied from less than one year to more than five years. Most studies in this analysis indicated a three to five year follow-up period.
8. Average length of follow-up in these studies was four to five years.

REFERENCES

Ahlmeyer, S., English, K., & Simons, D. (1999). *The impact of polygraphy on admissions of cross-over offending behavior in adult sexual offenders.* Presentation at the Association for the Treatment of Sexual Abusers 18th Annual Research and Treatment Conference, Lake Buena Vista, FL.

Ahlmeyer, S., Heil, P., McKee, B., & English, K. (2000). The impact of polygraphy on admissions of victims and offenses in adult sexual offenders. *Sexual Abuse: A Journal of Research and Treatment, 12 (2),* 123–138.

Alexander, M. A. (1999). Sexual offender treatment efficacy revisited. *Sexual Abuse: A Journal of Research and Treatment, 11 (2),* 101–117.

Andrews, D. A. (1982). *The supervision of offenders: Identifying and gaining control over the factors which make a difference.* Program Branch User Report. Ottawa: Solicitor General of Canada.

Barbaree, H. E. & Marshall, W. L. (1988). Deviant sexual arousal, offense history, and demographic variables as predictors of reoffense among child molesters. *Behavioral Sciences and the Law, 6 (2),* 267–280.

Beck, A. J. & Shipley, B. E. (1989). *Recidivism of prisoners released in 1983.* Washington, D.C.: U.S. Department of Justice, Bureau of Justice Statistics.

Becker, J. V. (1990). Treating adolescent sexual offenders. *Professional Psychology: Research, and Practice, 21,* 362–365.

Bonta, J. & Hanson, R. K. (1995). *Violent recidivism of men released from prison.* Paper presented at the 103rd Annual Convention of the American Psychological Association, New York.

Clarke, S. H. & Crum, L. (1985). *Returns to prison in North Carolina.* Chapel Hill, NC: Institute of Government University of North Carolina.

Delaware Statistical Analysis Center. (1984). *Recidivism in Delaware after release from incarceration.* Dover, DE: Author.

English, K., Pullen, S., & Jones, L. (Eds.) (1996). *Managing adult sex offenders: A containment approach.* Lexington, KY: American Probation and Parole Association.

Furby, L., Weinrott, M. R., & Blackshaw, L. (1989). Sex offender recidivism: A review. *Psychological Bulletin, 105 (1),* 3–30.

Gendreau, P. & Andrews, D. A. (1990). What the meta-analysis of the offender treatment literature tell us about what works. *Canadian Journal of Criminology, 32,* 173–184.

Gendreau, P., Little, T., & Goggin, C. (1996). A meta-analysis of the predictors of adult criminal recidivism: What works. *Criminology, 34,* 575–607.

Gibbens, T. C. N., Soothill, K. L., & Way, C. K. (1978). Sibling and parent-child incest offenders. *British Journal of Criminology, 18,* 40–52.

Gottfredson, M. R. & Hirschi, T. (1990). *A general theory of crime.* Stanford, CA: Stanford University Press.

Greenfeld, L.A. (1997). *Sex offenses and offenders: An analysis of data on rape and sexual assault.* Washington, D.C.: U.S. Department of Justice, Bureau of Justice Statistics.

Grunfeld, B. & Noreik, K. (1986). Recidivism among sex offenders: A follow-up study of 541 Norwegian sex offenders. *International Journal of Law and Psychiatry, 9,* 95–102.

Hall, G. C. N. (1995). Sex offender recidivism revisited: A meta-analysis of recent treatment studies. *Journal of Consulting and Clinical Psychology, 63 (5),* 802–809.

Hanson, R. K. (2000). *The effectiveness of treatment for sexual offenders: Report of the Association for the Treatment of Sexual Abusers Collaborative Data Research Committee.* Presentation at the Association for the Treatment of Sexual Abusers 19th Annual Research and Treatment Conference, San Diego, CA.

Hanson, R. K. & Bussiere, M. (1998). Predicting relapse: A meta-analysis of sexual offender recidivism studies. *Journal of Consulting and Clinical Psychology, 66 (2),* 348–362.

Hanson, R. K. & Harris, A. (1998). *Dynamic predictors of sexual recidivism.* Ottawa: Solicitor General of Canada.

Hanson, R. K., Scott, H., & Steffy, R. A. (1995). A comparison of child molesters and nonsexual criminals: Risk predictors and long-term recidivism. *Journal of Research in Crime and Delinquency, 32 (3),* 325–337.

Hanson, R. K., Steffy, R. A., & Gauthier, R. (1993). Long-term recidivism of child molesters. *Journal of Consulting and Criminal Psychology, 61 (4),* 646–652.

Hunter, J. A. & Figueredo, A. J. (1999). Factors associated with treatment compliance in a population of juvenile sexual offenders. *Sexual Abuse: A Journal of Research and Treatment, 11,* 49–68.

Kahn, T. J. & Chambers, H. J. (1991). Assessing reoffense risk with juvenile sexual offenders. *Child Welfare, 19,* 333–345.

Kilpatrick, D. G., Edmunds, C. N., & Seymour, A. (1992). *Rape in America: A report to the nation.*

Washington, D.C.: National Center for Victims of Crime and Crime Victims Research and Treatment Center.

Knight, R. A. & Prentky, R. A. (1990). Classifying sexual offenders: The development and corroboration of taxonomic models. In W. L. Marshall, D. R. Laws, and H. E. Barbaree (Eds.), *Handbook of sexual assault: Issues, theories, and treatment of the offender* (pp. 23–52). New York: Plenum.

Knopp, F. A., Freeman-Longo, R., & Stevenson, W. F. (1992). *Nationwide survey of juvenile and adult sex offender treatment programs and models.* Orwell, VT: Safer Society Press.

Kruttschnitt, C., Uggen, C., & Shelton, K. (2000). Predictors of desistance among sex offenders: The interactions of formal and informal social controls. *Justice Quarterly, 17 (1),* 61–87.

Marques, J. K., Day, D. M., Nelson, C., & West, M. A. (1994). Effects of cognitive-behavioral treatment on sex offenders' recidivism: Preliminary results of a longitudinal study. *Criminal Justice and Behavior, 21,* 28–54.

Marshall, W. L. & Barbaree, H. E. (1990). Outcomes of comprehensive cognitive-behavioral treatment programs. In W. L. Marshall, D. R. Laws, and H. E. Barbaree (Eds.), *Handbook of sexual assault: Issues, theories, and treatment of the offender* (pp. 363–385). New York: Plenum.

Prentky, R., Knight, R., & Lee, A. (1997). Risk factors associated with recidivism among extra-familial child molesters. *Journal of Consulting and Clinical Psychology. 65 (1),* 141–149.

Prentky, R., Lee, A., Knight, R., & Cerce, D. (1997). Recidivism rates among child molesters and rapists: A methodological analysis. *Law and Human Behavior, 21,* 635–659.

Quinsey, V .L. (1980). The base-rate problem and the prediction of dangerousness: A reappraisal. *Journal of Psychiatry and the Law, 8,* 329–340.

Quinsey, V. L. (1984). Sexual aggression: Studies of offenders against women. In D. N. Weisstub (Ed.), *Law and Mental Health: International Perspectives* (pp. 140–172), Vol. 2. New York: Pergamon.

Quinsey, V. L. (1998). Treatment of sex offenders. In M. Tonry (Ed.), *The handbook of crime and punishment* (pp. 403–425). New York: Oxford University Press.

Quinsey, V. L., Harris, G. T., Rice, M. E., & Lalumiere, M. (1993). Assessing treatment efficacy in outcome studies of sex offenders. *Journal of Interpersonal Violence, 8,* 512–523.

Quinsey, V. L., Lalumiere, M. L., Rice, M. E., & Harris, G. T. (1995). Predicting sexual offenses. In J. C. Campbell (Ed.), *Assessing dangerousness: Violence by sexual offenders, batterers, and child abusers* (pp. 114–137). Thousand Oaks, CA: Sage.

Quinsey, V. L., Rice, M. E., & Harris, G. T. (1995). Actuarial prediction of sexual recidivism. *Journal of Interpersonal Violence, 10 (1),* 85–105.

Rice, M. E., Harris, G. T., & Quinsey, V. L. (1990). A follow-up of rapists assessed in a maximum security psychiatric facility. *Journal of Interpersonal Violence, 5 (4),* 435–448.

Rice, M.E., Quinsey, V.L., & Harris, G.T. (1991). Sexual recidivism among child molesters released from a maximum security institution. *Journal of Consulting and Clinical Psychology, 59,* 381–386.

Romero, J. & Williams, L. (1985). Recidivism among convicted sex offenders: A 10-year follow-up study. *Federal Probation, 49,* 58–64.

Roundtree, G. A., Edwards, D. W., & Parker, J. B. (1984). A study of personal characteristics of probationers as related to recidivism. *Journal of Offender Counseling, 8,* 53–61.

Schram, D. D., Milloy, C. D., & Rowe, W. E. (1991). *Juvenile sex offenders: A follow-up study of reoffense behavior.* Olympia, WA: Washington State Institute for Public Policy.

Schwartz, B. K. & Cellini, H. R. (1997). *Sex offender recidivism and risk factors in the involuntary commitment process.* Albuquerque, NM: Training and Research Institute Inc.

Sturgeon, V. H. & Taylor, J. (1980). Report of a five-year follow-up study of mentally disordered sex offenders released from Atascadero State Hospital in 1973. *Criminal Justice Journal, 4,* 31–63.

West, D. J., Roy, C., & Nichols, F. L. (1978). *Understanding sexual attacks: A study based upon a group of rapists undergoing psychotherapy.* London: Heinemann.

20

IDENTIFYING AND TREATING THE MENTALLY DISORDERED PRISON INMATE

ELIOT S. HARTSTONE
HENRY J. STEADMAN
PAMELA CLARK ROBBINS
JOHN MONAHAN

During the 1950s, mental hospitals housed hundreds of thousands of mentally ill Americans. Today, those hospitals have given way to penal institutions. The exact number of mentally ill prisoners is unknown; however, there is little question that the mentally ill pose a significant problem for the correctional system. Providing safe and secure facilities, meeting the needs of special populations, and operating within a budget are all challenges that must be met. Eliot S. Hartstone and his associates offer a glimpse into the scope of mental health problems in prisons. By examining procedures in five states, they provide an overview of how mentally ill prisoners are handled in the United States.

"Mentally disordered offenders" can be considered as an umbrella term embracing four distinct legal categories: defendants who are incompetent to stand trial or not guilty by reason of insanity, persons adjudicated as "mentally disordered sex offenders," and convicted prisoners who are transferred to mental hospitals (Steadman et al., 1982; Monahan and Steadman, 1983a, 1983b). Public attention has focused on the first three of these categories, perhaps because of a belief that they constitute a form of "beating the system." That is, the offenders in these cases committed what would popularly be considered a crime, yet have escaped criminal conviction. Notorious cases that have raised these issues (although not always successfully), such as John Hinckley, Patricia Hearst, David Berkowitz, and Mark Chapman, no doubt contribute to this public attention.

The media, the public, and legislators, however, have yet to show comparable interest in the fourth category of mentally disordered offenders—persons first convicted of a crime, incarcerated, and later found to be in need of transfer to a mental health facility. It is likely that this lack of interest in mentally disordered inmates reflects the fact that these individuals did not "get away" with their crimes since they have already been convicted and sentenced to prison. Social scientists have also, for the most part, limited their research efforts to "incompetency" (Roesch and Golding, 1980; Mowbrey, 1979; Steadman, 1979) or "insanity" (Rogers and Bloom, 1982; Petrila, 1982; Pasewark et al., 1979;

Excerpts from "Identifying and Treating the Mentally Disordered Prison Inmate" by Eliot S. Hartstone, Henry J. Steadman, Pamela Clark Robbins, and John Monahan, in Linda A. Teplin (ed.) *Mental Health and Criminal Justice* pp. 279–296.

Pasewark and Lanthorn, 1977; Steadman, 1980; Cook and Sigorski, 1974; Morrow and Peterson, 1966) and "mentally disordered sex offender" status (Konecni et al., 1980; Sturgeon and Taylor, 1980). Researchers rarely study the less publicized situation where the prisoner's mental health problems were not manifest, or at least not identified, until after placement in prison (Gearing et al., 1990; Halleck, 1961).

Despite the meager public and research attention garnered by mentally disordered inmates, they constitute the largest category of mentally disordered offenders in the U.S.—54% of all mentally disordered offenders, and 68% of all *male* mentally disordered offenders admitted to mental health facilities in the United States in 1978 (Steadman et al., 1982). In fact, 10,831 inmates were transferred from state prisons into separate mental health units or facilities in 1978 (Steadman et al., 1982). This number does not include those inmates who were experiencing mental health problems but received care (or at least remained) in the general prison population.

It also appears that for at least two reasons, the number of mentally disordered inmates may increase in coming years. First, there is a movement in a number of states to do away with the insanity defense in favor of a "guilty but insane" verdict, which may have the effect of mandating mental health services for specified inmates who previously would have been acquitted by reason of insanity. Second, current trends in criminal sentencing seem likely to result in placing more offenders into state prisons for longer periods. In 1981, the largest annual increase in U.S. history in the number of prison inmates (41,292) was recorded (Gardner, 1982). Thus, even if the proportion of inmates who were mentally disordered remained constant, the absolute number of inmates requiring care would have skyrocketed. Using a low estimate of the proportion (15%) of inmates who are mentally disordered there would have been nearly 6200 more inmates needing mental health services in U.S. prisons in 1982 than in 1981.

The level of management problems that these mentally disordered inmates pose has been demonstrated by Uhlig (1976). Examining a group of 356 offenders throughout New England prisons who had been identified as special management problems, he found that 195 (53%) were diagnosed as having current psychiatric disturbances. Clearly, a major source of conflict in volatile prison settings are mentally disordered inmates. These inmates present problems with which prison officials usually are not prepared or trained to cope. Further, these inmates would appear to create additional management problems for prison officials by generating disruptive behavior among inmates who do not know how to respond to the unusual and inappropriate behavior displayed by the mentally disordered, and who tend to victimize these more vulnerable inmates. It is also important to note that an additional series of problems results from those inmates who are withdrawn or excessively depressed but who may not be disruptive or create management problems (Hartstone et al., 1982).

Programmatic responses to mentally disordered inmates in the United States have been cyclical: (1) responsibility for mentally disordered prison inmates repeatedly has shifted back and forth from corrections to mental health departments; and (2) the appropriateness of mixing convicted mentally disordered persons in civil mental hospitals has been viewed very differently from one era to another (Steadman and Cocozza, 1974). The experiences in New York illustrate these long-standing issues.

The first move in New York to separate civil mental patients from mentally disordered persons charged with or convicted of crimes occurred in 1782. An "Act Respecting Lunatics" was passed that prevented the overseers of the poor, who were responsible for the mentally disordered, from housing the mentally disordered in jails or "in the same room with any person charged or convicted of an offense" (N.Y. Laws 1827, Ch. 294, Sec. 2). They could be kept only in poorhouses. When the state's first asylum for the mentally disordered was opened in 1842 in Utica, however, the legislative provisions allowed for the mixing of mentally disordered convicts, those confined under indictments or criminal charge, those acquitted by reason of insanity, and patients committed under any civil process. Thus, the mental health system, rather than the more general social welfare system or corrections, came to care for mentally disordered inmates.

By 1855, there was movement again toward separating patients who were convicted or alleged criminals from civil patients. This movement culminated with the 1859 opening of an Asylum for Insane Convicts at Auburn Penitentiary, the first institution of its kind in the United States. In 1861 the state legislature directed that all mentally disordered male prisoners be transferred from Utica to Auburn. In 1869, Auburn was directed to house those persons acquitted because of insanity as well as defendants charged with murder, attempted murder, or arson who became mentally disordered prior to trial or sentencing. Thus, convicted and unconvicted patients were again confined in the same facility, separate from civil patients, as they had been before Auburn Asylum opened.

A legislative commission established in 1886 located a site in Matteawan to replace the Auburn Asylum, which would be large enough to allow for the separation, within a single facility, of unconvicted patients awaiting trial from mentally disordered convicts. As a *New York Times* article reporting the opening noted, "The two classes of patients differ widely, the criminals giving the officials much anxiety at times. They are frequently dangerous and destructive." As had happened with Auburn soon after its opening, the number of patients at Matteawan quickly increased. While the patient population continued to burgeon at Matteawan, pressure also built for the separation of the "convict insane" from the other criminally insane patients, such as insanity cases. In 1894, the State Lunacy Commission noted that separate institutions were beneficial because the presence of insane convicts "was very objectionable to the ordinary inmates" of state hospitals.

A new facility, Dannemora State Hospital, opened in northern New York in January, 1900, under the auspices of the Department of Corrections. By this time, Matteawan was overcrowded with 719 patients in a building whose capacity was 500. All inmates in the state who were determined to be mentally disordered after a felony conviction would be housed in Dannemora. All other convicted patients and pretrial cases would go to Matteawan. Between 1900 and 1966, the patient population at Matteawan and Dannemora climbed steadily, with Matteawan reaching a patient census of over 2000 in the early 1960s, At the same time, Dannemora reached a peak of about 1400 patients. However, in these 66 years little changed in either the statutes or the two facilities.

Throughout the late 1960s and early 1970s, there was a dramatic decrease in the patient census at Matteawan and Dannemora, and a gradual shift for all mental health treatment for all classes of mentally disordered offenders to the Office of Mental Health (OMH). Dannemora was closed in 1972 and Matteawan in 1977, removing the Department of Corrections (DOC) from any direct mental health care responsibilities. Instead, the OMH opened a maximum-security hospital for incompetent defendants and defendants not guilty by reason of insanity in 1972 and one for mentally disordered inmates in 1977. Thus, over this 150-year period, care of mentally disordered inmates in New York shifted from welfare, to mental health, to corrections, and back to mental health.

History appears to be again repeating itself as states continually tinker with their treatment arrangements for mentally disordered inmates, sometimes charging departments of mental health with the responsibility, either by themselves or in concert with departments of corrections, and sometimes mandating treatment by the departments of corrections themselves. Based on our 1978 national survey (Steadman et al., 1982), there appears to be little consensus on the most appropriate arrangements for mentally disordered inmates. This survey revealed that 16 states transferred most (at least 75%) of their mentally disordered inmates into mental health facilities or units administered by the DOC;[1] 28 states transferred the majority into hospitals or units run by the DMH; and six states utilized a combination of DOC and DMH units.

It may be that the lack of consensus across states on how to handle mentally disordered inmates reflects in part a lack of empirical data. There are no data on whether there is a type of arrangement that is optimal for both inmates and facilities, what such an arrangement might look like, and under what circumstances one arrangement is to be preferred over others. As prison populations climb, as the number of beds in state mental hospitals continues to be limited, and as legal rights to minimum health and mental health treatment are confirmed by the courts, more information is needed to facilitate the development of appropriate programs for mentally disordered inmates.

In an effort to provide some empirical data on the needs of these inmates and how the correctional and mental health systems respond to them, this chapter utilizes data from 67 interviews with a wide range of correctional staff in five states. Specifically, these data focus on the placement options available for mentally disordered inmates, the adequacy of procedures used to identify the inmates and transfer them to mental health facilities, and the extent to which the procedures used meet the needs of these inmates.

METHODS

Our data are drawn from a national study of the movement of offenders between prisons and mental hospitals funded by the National Institute of Justice. As part of this effort, six states—Arizona, California, Iowa, Massachusetts, New York, and Texas—were identified for an intensive examination of the confinement and criminal careers of inmates and mental patients, and of the practices and processes of transferring prison inmates to mental health facilities. Five of these six states (New York excluded) were found to use Department of Corrections (DOC) mental health settings as the main placement for mentally disordered inmates. It is these five states with their use of *intra*-agency transfers for mentally disordered inmates that are the focus of this chapter.

While approximately two-thirds of the states in the United States transfer most of their mentally disordered inmates to state departments of mental health (DMH), since the larger states tend to use DOC options, 71% of all prison inmates transferred for mental health services in 1978 were placed in

TABLE 20.1 PERCENTAGE OF INMATES IN STATE PRISONS PERCEIVED AS HAVING MENTAL HEALTH PROBLEMS (BY STAFF LOCATION)

	Mental Health Need			
	Seriously Mentally Ill		Psychological Problem Warranting Treatment	
Staff Location	Mean %	(N)	Mean %	(N)
DOC central office	4.3	(9)	30.6	(8)
Mental health facility to which inmates were transferred	6.2	(25)	42.3	(29)
Prison from which inmates were transferred	5.9	(23)	34.4	(24)
Total	5.8	(57)[a]	37.7	(61)[b]

[a] Missing data for 10 cases.
[b] Missing data for 6 cases.

DOC-operated mental health facilities. Any effort to generalize from the data reported here should be limited to those states that transfer the majority of their inmates to DOC mental health settings. The issues discussed here focus only on procedures for dealing with male inmates, since 95.8% of all inmates transferred in our 1978 study were males. Women's programs require specialized study for what are often more haphazard, less formal service arrangements.

Structured interviews were conducted with a wide range of DOC personnel in the five target states between October 1, 1980, and January 31, 1981. The interviews were primarily open-ended, with some Likert-type items, and averaged 90 minutes. A two-person interview team completed interviews with 67 persons employed by the DOC. Interviews were conducted at the DOC central office, the state prison transferring the most inmates, and the mental health setting receiving the most inmate transfers. At the DOC central office, the DOC Commissioner (or Deputy Commissioner) and the mental health treatment director were interviewed. At the prison transferring the most inmates in each state, we interviewed the warden, the treatment director, two direct clinical service providers, and a correctional officer. Hospital or Treatment Center interviews consisted of the facility or unit director, the chief of security, two clinical staff members, and a fine staff representative. In instances where there were a number of people in a particular position, we interviewed the person nominated by the facility director. Thus, the information obtained from the interviews reflects a wide range of staff locations and job responsibilities.

SCOPE OF MENTAL HEALTH PROBLEMS IN PRISONS

The first issue of interest was the perception of the various DOC staff of the scope of the problem and how their estimates compared with prior research. All respondents were asked what percentage of the DOC inmates they believed to be either seriously mentally disordered (that is, psychotic) or suffering from a psychological problem that warranted mental health treatment. The mean responses, separated by staff location, are presented in Table 20.1. It is clear that a sizeable number of state prisoners were suffering from serious mental health problems. As seen in Table 20.1, the respondents in our five target states estimated on average that 5.8% of state DOC inmates were "seriously mentally ill," and that an additional 37.7%, while not psychotic, were suffering from a psychological problem that would significantly benefit from mental health treatment. This table also shows that, when compared to central office administrators, the people actually working in the institutions (that is, prisons and DOC mental hospitals) thought considerably more DOC inmates were psychotic (6.1% versus 4.3%) or experiencing other psychological problems (38.7% versus 30.6%). While the differences may appear at first glance to be small, one must consider that given the size of the total prison populations in these five states, this translates into a difference of 6389 inmates defined as in need of mental health services.[2]

In general, the overall estimates of the respondents are similar to the best estimates of true prevalence of mental disorder that Monahan and Steadman's (1983a) literature review found:

> One is left from these studies with true prevalence rates for serious mental illness (i.e., psychoses) among offenders incarcerated in prison or jails varying from 1 percent (Guze, 1976) to 7 percent (Bolton, 1976). True prevalence rates for less severe forms of mental illness (nonpsychotic mental disorders and personality disorders) vary greatly, ranging up to 15–20 percent (Roth, 1980).

When staff were asked whether they believed there had been any change over the past ten years in the percentage of inmates suffering from a "serious mental illness," 43% of the staff said they believed the percentage of disordered inmates had gone up. In contrast, only 7% of those responding said the number had gone down. Those prison and correctional mental health facility staff persons who felt this problem was becoming increasingly severe offered a variety of explanations. Most respondents cited one of three factors: conditions in the prison, the deinstitutionalization movement in state mental hospitals, and general societal conditions. A prison guard concerned that the prisons themselves were generating the problem stated:

> The environment here in prison is changing for the worse. It is becoming more and more crowded, causing a lot of problems. There are now three to four inmates in one cell; they are in the cell for 12–14 hours at a stretch.

A clinician at a DOC-operated mental hospital blamed the problem there on DMH deinstitutionalization of mental hospitals:

> The main cause [is] deinstitutionalization by (DMH). A lot of these persons are getting criminalized. It is easier for a cop to take John Doe to a lock-up—end up here—than to send him to a state hospital.

A social worker in a state prison stated that she felt there were mental health problems in prison because of general societal conditions:

> There has been an increase in societal population, a breakdown of the families, a pressure packed society. It is a societal problem.

Due to these perceived problems, DOC staff expressed concern that there are sizeable numbers of inmates in the DOC who are experiencing serious psychiatric or psychological problems warranting some form of clinical intervention. The remainder of this chapter examines what is happening to those prison inmates who are mentally disordered—where can they receive treatment, and are they identified and placed in the designated mental health settings?

PLACEMENT OPTIONS AND PROCEDURES

While all five state DOCs treated mentally disordered inmates within the agency, these agencies did not all have the same philosophy regarding mental disorder, nor did they establish the same placement options. California had substantially more beds available and transferred more inmates than any of the other states. Within the California Department of Corrections, two major placement options were used for inmates suffering mental health problems. The California Medical Facility at Vacaville (CMF) received those inmates who were most disordered and dangerous, and the California Men's Colony (CMC) utilized one of their prison quadrants usually for less disordered and less violent mentally disordered inmates. Over 3000 inmates are transferred into either the CMF or CMC annually. Prior to 1980, some inmates were transferred to DMH's Atascadero State Hospital, but DOC staff said that since January 1980 it was practically impossible to get an inmate into Atascadero. As indicated by the number of DOC beds that were available for mental health care, the California DOC approach clearly reflects a philosophy that stresses the importance of recognizing the mentally disordered offender and placing such inmates in a separate facility or unit for treatment.

In three states (Arizona, Iowa, and Massachusetts) there was a single DOC-operated mental hospital. In these three states, the hospitals admitted all categories of "mentally disordered offenders" (transfers, insanity acquittals, and incompetency cases). The hospitals varied considerably in size and transfer admissions. There were 442 beds at Bridgewater State Hospital (Massachusetts), 80 beds at the Iowa Medical Facility, and 40 beds at Alhambra (Arizona). The Massachusetts and Iowa hospitals both admitted approximately 225–275 transfers annually, while the Arizona facility admitted fewer than 15.

The Texas Department of Corrections (TDC) operated with the philosophy that all TDC inmates are TDC's responsibility and should, whenever possible, be maintained in the general population. While a maximum security unit at Rusk State Hospital (operated by DMH) was a potential placement option, the use of this unit decreased from 65 inmates in

1978, to 37 in 1979, to 9 in 1980. Typically, when an inmate's condition caused the TDC to move an inmate out of the general population, the inmate was transferred to the Huntsville Treatment Center (HTC), located within the Huntsville prison. This unit contained 90 beds, an average census of 67, and admitted 20–25 inmates each month. The HTC was used primarily for short-term stabilization and medication, followed by the inmate's immediate transfer back to the general population. On rare and extreme occasions, inmates have been transferred from the HTC to Rusk State Hospital. The number of inmates placed in neither the HTC or Rusk State Hospital seems particularly low given the large number of inmates (approximately 30,000) residing with the Texas Department of Corrections.

In all five study states, the initial identification of the mentally disordered inmate usually resulted from observations made by a correctional officer and a referral to a prison psychologist or psychiatrist. At that point, however, considerable procedural variations occurred in the role of the prison, the mental hospital, the DOC central office, and the courts in determining which inmates were transferred. In only one state (Massachusetts) was judicial approval required. In two states (Arizona, California), transfer decisions were routinely made or approved by representatives of the DOC central office. The mental health receiving facility had an active role in the transfer decisions in two states (Iowa and Arizona), while in Texas the prison psychologist's recommendations were followed without any review. Whatever the means used to review recommendations made by the prison clinician (such as the court or DOC central office), the review appeared to be perfunctory and virtually all inmates recommended for transfer were, in fact, transferred.

An examination of available placement options and transfer procedures implemented in our five study states reveals that, although each of these states transferred most of their inmates into facilities operated within the DOC, variation occurred in the type of placements available, the extent to which they were used, and the procedures implemented for transferring an inmate to one of these facilities.

ADEQUACY OF IDENTIFICATION AND TRANSFER PROCEDURES

IDENTIFICATION

In order to ascertain which inmates were selected for transfer to mental health facilities, we asked all respondents whether transfers occurred primarily for clinical reasons (that is, mental health difficulties) or behavioral reasons (management problems),

TABLE 20.2 REASONS WHY INMATES ARE TRANSFERRED TO MENTAL HEALTH FACILITY

	Staff Work Location							
	Central Office		Mental Health Facility		Prison		Total	
Reason for Transfer	%	(N)	%	(N)	%	(N)	%	(N)
Psychotic	25.0	(6)	15.4	(10)	14.0	(8)	16.4	(24)
Other mental illness[a]	45.8	(11)	66.2	(43)	72.0	(41)	65.1	(95)
Management problem/ violent	25.0	(6)	15.4	(10)	10.5	(6)	15.1	(22)
Other	4.2	(1)	3.0	(2)	3.5	(2)	3.4	(5)
Total							100.0	(146)

[a] Other mental illness includes (1) DSM II diagnostic classification that does not fall under the heading of psychotic; (2) more general references to mental illness (for example, crazy, flaky, bizarre, mentally ill, unstable); and (3) mentally ill and dangerous.

TABLE 20.3 STAFF PERCEPTION OF THE APPROPRIATENESS OF THE NUMBER OF INMATES TRANSFERRED (BY STAFF LOCATION AND STATE)

	Number of Inmates Transferred					
	Too Few		Just Right		Too Many	
Staff Location	**%**	**(N)**	**%**	**(N)**	**%**	**(N)**
Central office	30.0	(3)	60.0	(6)	10.0	(1)
Mental hospital	41.1	(12)	48.3	(14)	10.3	(3)
Prison	62.5	(15)	33.3	(8)	4.2	(1)
			State			
A	20.0	(2)	70.0	(7)	10.0	(1)
B	62.5	(5)	25.0	(2)	12.5	(1)
C	70.0	(14)	25.0	(5)	5.0	(1)
D	30.8	(4)	69.2	(9)	0.0	(0)
E	41.7	(5)	41.7	(5)	16.7	(2)
Total	47.6	(30)	44.4	(28)	7.9	(5)

and what types of inmates were identified for referral to mental hospitals. The majority of our respondents (52.6%) reported that persons were identified for behavioral reasons, 33.3% felt that identification was usually brought about due to clinical reasons, and 14% stated that identification could occur for either reason. In only one state (California) did more respondents attribute identification to clinical reasons (52.6%) more often than to behavioral reasons (36.8%). In each of the other four states, 50% or more of the respondents said inmates were primarily identified for behavioral reasons.

When asked for specific reasons why inmates were identified for referral to mental health facilities, the respondents focused primarily on mental health problems. As presented in Table 20.2, our 67 respondents produced 146 responses: 16.4% of the responses referred to psychosis, 65.1% referred to other mental health reasons, and 15.1% focused solely on violence or management problems. The fact that behavior was felt to be a more important determinant than clinical factors in deciding whether an inmate was identified for transfer would seem to indicate that some inmates who were mentally disordered were not identified because their behavior was not particularly visible or disruptive, and that other inmates may have been identified for transfer due to behaviors which were unacceptable, but not necessarily indicators of real clinical symptomatology. However, given the high percentage of responses citing mental health problems as a reason for transfer, it appears that, while the initial identification may have been precipitated by behavior, the transfer decision typically was based on mental health problems. Thus, while it would seem that there may be some inmates transferred who are only behavior problems (not mentally disordered), the potentially more important problem is the lack of early identification of those mentally disordered inmates whose behavior does not either annoy the

TABLE 20.4 MAJOR WEAKNESSES IN IDENTIFYING INMATES FOR TRANSFER

Weakness	% of Responses	(N)
Miss some mentally ill inmates	30.0	(27)
Lack of clinical staff in prison	17.8	(16)
Seek to transfer management problems	11.1	(10)
Inadequate training of prison staff	8.9	(8)
Manipulation of staff by inmates	5.6	(5)
Lack of mental health assessment	4.5	(4)
Other	22.1	(20)
Total	100.0	(90)

DOC staff or disrupt prison operations. It seems likely that there are a number of disordered inmates who go unnoticed and, therefore, untreated.

This interpretation is supported by responses to questions about the appropriateness of the number of inmates transferred and the major weaknesses in the identification of inmates for transfer. Staff were asked how they felt about the number of inmates transferred to a mental health facility or unit. Table 20.3 shows the staff responses by staff location and state. As seen in the table, almost half of the staff members responding felt that "too few" inmates were transferred (47.6%). This compares to the small number of staff (7.9%) who felt that "too many" were transferred. Staff in three states[3] clearly were quite concerned that too few mentally disordered inmates were placed in mental health settings. When examining responses by work location of staff responding, it is interesting to note that while concern over underidentification occurred in all three locations (prisons, 62.5%; mental hospitals, 41.4%; and central office, 30.0%), the percentage of prison staff who felt that not enough inmates were transferred more than doubled the percentage of central office administrators who had that concern. While it is unclear whether this distinction reflects a lack of first-hand knowledge by the administrative staff or the lack of mental health expertise of the prison staff (or both), it is apparent that the prison staff felt they were handling inmates whom they were incapable of treating in the general prison population.

Respondents also were asked to name what they perceived to be the major strengths and weaknesses in the identification of mentally disordered inmates. While most respondents did find some strengths, frequently the strength cited was merely a reiteration of the fact that the system did exist and did identify and place mentally ill inmates. More meaningful strengths that were cited with some regularity by the corrections staff were the quality of the clinical staff, the ability of staff to work together, and the efforts made by prison guards.

Efforts to specify weaknesses in identification were more informative. As seen in Table 20.4, many of the responses dealt directly with the problem of prisons "under-identifying" mentally disordered inmates (miss some mentally disordered inmates, 30%; insufficient number of clinical staff, 17.8%; lack of mental health assessment, 4.5%). Additional responses (such as the lack of clinical training of prison staff) at least indirectly dealt with the same concern. Some examples of responses noting the "underidentification" of mentally disordered inmates were:

> There are not enough professional staff; I fear the quietly crazy are not identified. That is what concerns me [prison psychologist].
> Problems of spotting someone who needs to be there. We have only 30–40 correctional officers for 2000 inmates. Not enough of us to keep up on what's going on. Inmates usually have to show exceptional behavior before being identified. They could have problems, and not be identified [prison correctional officer].

> We primarily have a disturbance identification process rather than a patient need identification [process] [Correctional mental hospital psychiatrist].

PROCEDURES

Once an inmate was identified by the prison staff as being mentally disordered, each state had formal procedures for reviewing the transfer of the inmate to a mental health facility. All respondents were asked how well they thought the procedures were working. Almost 85% of those interviewed said the procedures were working either "very well" or "well," and in only one state was there considerable concern over how these procedures were operating (33% said "poorly" or "very poorly"). However, a significant difference was revealed in how staff at different locations (central office, mental hospital, prison) assessed the effectiveness of these procedures. Only one respondent across the five states working either at the central office or the mental health facility said the procedures were operating "poorly" or "very poorly" (2.6%). On the other hand, 36% of the prison staff interviewed viewed the operation of transfer procedures as so problematic as to define them as operating "poorly" or "very poorly." This view was found to be limited to two states. Some of the specific criticisms made by prison staff in these two states were:

> No one's going anywhere. There are a lot of mentally ill people here, but they are not housed as if they're mentally ill. Not treated any differently than other inmates [prison psychologist].
>
> Bed space problems at (the CMH) and their unwillingness to take our inmates. If they are both psychotic and management problems, they [CMH] keep them only a short period of time and say the inmate is only a management problem and send them back [prison administrator].
>
> Takes too much time! Courts' fault, always getting involved when they know nothing about it. Afraid we will put people there (the CMH) for punishment. Delay in getting hold of "shrink" and taking care of paper work. Delay is at central office...[the mental health facility] sends them back too soon, when they shouldn't be housed here at all. The inmates go back and forth [correctional officer].

While DOC staff from the other three states typically stated that procedures were operating well overall, staff in these states frequently said there were still some major weaknesses in the procedures. In one state the concerns frequently focused around the extent to which the procedures protected inmates from being transferred inappropriately:

> Procedures are not terribly tight, staff could conspire to place a person who is not mentally ill into a mental hospital. Lack of legal safeguards. Not forced to confront the man and say he is crazy [corrections administrator].
>
> [The Supreme Court] requires there should be an independent review of hospitalization. We don't have this. A good law requires judicial commitment. We don't have this [corrections administrator].

In another state, the issue involved the decision-making process. As seen below, some DOC staff (usually prison staff) felt too much decision-making control was left in the hands of hospital staff. Others (typically hospital staff) felt that too much control was given to the prison and DOC central office.

> If —— [the CMH director] doesn't want someone he doesn't have to take him. He is scared and doesn't want to be bothered by this type of person. He fears they will be disruptive to their program. His power to make this decision is the major weakness in the procedures [correctional officer].
>
> Formal decision is left in the hands of a lay person [central office]. This is a medical facility and he [DOC director] has the ultimate authority.... Not a real problem, as long as mental hospital director has right to discharge.

Despite the specific concerns noted above, the respondents were, in general, satisfied with the transfer procedures. The respondents also expressed satisfaction with the receptivity displayed by the DOC mental health facilities to mentally disordered inmates referred by the prison. Almost 90% of the staff interviewed defined the state correctional mental health facility or facilities as either "very" or "somewhat" receptive. The prison staff were considerably more likely to define the mental health facilities as "somewhat" or "very" nonreceptive (22.7%) than the staff at the mental health facilities (3.3%). Almost 75% of the staff responding in each of the five states defined the correctional mental health facility as receptive.

Thus, in general, DOC staff appear to be satisfied with the procedures for inmate transfers from the general prison population into mental health facilities and the receptivity of these facilities to mentally disordered inmates.

One area that generated little concern by the prison staff, DOC central office staff, or mental health staff was the inmate's ability to prevent transfer through procedural safeguards. When asked whether inmates prevented transfer too frequently, as often as they should, or not often enough, 92% of the DOC staff responding said "as often as should be the case." In no state did a sizable percentage of staff express concern that inmates either prevented too many transfers or were unable to prevent transfers often enough. It is not clear whether these responses reflect procedures that gave inmates an optimal amount of input into this decision or whether it more accurately reflects the frequently stated belief of DOC staff that "inmates have no control over these decisions and they shouldn't."

CONCLUSION

This chapter has used 67 interviews conducted with DOC staff in five states to describe the process of identifying state prisoners suffering from mental disorders and the transferring of these inmates into designated DOC mental health facilities. The major conclusions drawn from these interviews are:

- DOC staff perceive a sizable number of state prisoners to be suffering from a serious psychotic mental disorder (5.8% of all inmates) or psychological problems warranting treatment (37.7%).
- Different states operate with different philosophies on how to handle mentally disordered inmates and therefore identify widely divergent percentages of their inmates as warranting placement in a mental health facility.
- Once the prison psychiatrist or psychologist recommends that an inmate be transferred, it is the rare exception when a review system (prison, DOC, court) reverses that decision.
- Inmates are typically identified in the prison for behavioral management reasons, thereby making it likely that a sizable number of mentally disordered inmates remain in the general population because their behavior is insufficiently visible, annoying, or disruptive.
- A sizable percentage of staff (47.6%) stated they felt "too few" inmates were transferred to mental health settings.
- Staff typically felt that the procedures used to transfer those inmates identified as mentally disordered were working well (84.4%) and that the DOC mental health facilities were receptive to these inmates (85.5%). However, staff working at the prisons were considerably less satisfied with both the procedures and the receptivity of the mental health facilities than were the staff at either the DOC central office or the DOC mental hospitals and treatment centers.

As prison populations continue to burgeon, the problem of mentally disordered inmates will only be exacerbated. Even if the proportion of the inmate population with mental disorders remains constant, the scope of the problem within any given growing prison system will become more acute in terms of absolute human service needs (see Monahan and Steadman, 1983a). While the descriptive work discussed in this chapter is a major first step toward building knowledge in this area, it is essential that more research be devoted to studying mentally disordered inmates. Further research is needed both on inmates themselves and on the system and agencies responsible for their care and treatment.

More information is needed on the prevalence, causes, and correlates of mental disorders within the state prison inmate population. A systematic, multistate study is needed that utilizes an objective instrument across states to assess the extent to which prison inmates suffer from mental disorders. Inmates identified as mentally disordered should be studied for purposes of examining causes and correlates of both the criminal behavior and mental disturbance. Included in this assessment should be an examination of how incarceration and prison conditions contribute to inmate mental health problems and in what ways the prison experience may combine with preprison factors to generate serious inmate symptomatology.

STUDY QUESTIONS

1. What are the two reasons the authors give for the likelihood that the number of mentally ill offenders will increase in coming years?
2. Describe the research design, data collection methods, sample, and measures used by the authors in conducting this study.

3. What is the scope of mental health problems in prisons that the authors describe?
4. What are the conclusions reached by the authors of this study? Why do you think they are important for correctional officials?

ACKNOWLEDGMENTS

This work was done under partial support from the National Institute of Justice (79-NI-AX-0126). The assistance of Sharon Kantorowski Davis in the data collection phase of this project is gratefully acknowledged.

NOTES

1. According to 1978 admission data, there were 16 states in the country which transferred most (at least 75%) of their mentally disordered inmates to mental health settings within the DOC. They are California, Idaho, Illinois, Iowa, Massachusetts, Michigan, Missouri, Nevada, North Carolina, Oregon, South Carolina, Tennessee, Texas, Utah, and West Virginia. In addition, Arizona changed the agency responsible for the mental hospital treating mentally ill inmates from DMH to DOC at the end of 1978.
2. Information contained in the Bureau of Justice Statistics Bulletin (Department of Justice, 1982) showed that at the end of 1980 the state prison censuses in the five states discussed in this chapter were as follows: Arizona, 4,372; California, 24,569; Iowa, 2,513; Massachusetts, 3,191; Texas, 29,892; total: 64,537.
3. Throughout the remainder of this chapter, we do not identify any of the states by name. We felt that to do so would betray both the confidence and trust the states had in us and risk the anonymity we promised to individual respondents.

REFERENCES

Cook, G. and C. Sigorski (1974) "Factors affecting length of hospitalization in prisoners adjudicated not guilty by reason of insanity." *Bulletin of the American Academy of Psychiatry and Law* 2: 251–261.

Department of Justice (1982) Bureau of Justice Statistics Bulletin (NCJ 82262). Washington, DC: Author.

Gardner, R. (1982) "Prison population jumps to 369,725." *Corrections Magazine,* 8(4):6–11, 14, 46.

Gearing, M., R. Hecker, and W. Matthey (1990) "The screening and referral of mentally disordered inmates in a state correctional system." *Professional Psychology* 11: 849.

Halleck, S. (1961) "A critique of current psychiatric roles in the legal process." *Wisconsin Law Review* 00: 379–401.

Hartstone, E., H. J. Steadman, and J. Monahan (1982) "*Vitek* and beyond: The empirical context of prison to hospital transfers." *Law and Contemporary Problems* 45, 3.

Konecni, V., E. Mulcahy, and E. Ebbesen (1980) "Prison or mental hospital: Factors affecting the processing of persons suspected of being mentally disordered sex offenders," in P. Lipsitt and B. Sales (eds.) *New Directions in Psychological Research.* New York: Van Nostrand Reinhold.

Monahan, J. and H. J. Steadman (1983a) "Crime and mental disorder: An epidemiological analysis," in N. Morris and M. Tonrey (eds.) *Annual Review of Criminal Justice.* Chicago: University of Chicago Press.

—— [eds.] (1983b) *Mentally Disordered Offenders: Perspectives from Law and Social Science.* New York: Plenum.

Morrow, W. R. and D. B. Peterson (1966) "Follow-up on discharged offenders—'not guilty by reason of insanity' and 'criminal sexual psychopaths.'" *Journal of Criminal Law, Criminology and Police Science* 57: 31–34.

Mowbrey, C. T. (1979) "A study of patients treated as incompetent to stand trial." *Social Psychiatry* 14:31–39.

New York Laws (1827) Chapter 294, Section 2.

New York Times (1892) November 3, p. 9 col. 4.

Pasewark, R. A. and B. W. Lanthorn (1977) "Dispositions of persons utilizing the insanity defense." *Journal of Humanistics* 5:87–98.

——, M. L. Pantle, and H. J. Steadman (1982) "Detention and rearrest rates of persons found not guilty by reason of insanity and convicted felons." *American Journal of Psychiatry* 139, 7: 892–897.

—— (1979) "Characteristics and disposition of persons found not guilty by reason of insanity in New York State, 1971–76." *American Journal of Psychiatry* 136:655–660.

Petrila, J. (1982) "The insanity defense and other mental health dispositions in Missouri." *International Journal of Law and Psychiatry* 5, 1:81–102.

Roesch, R. and S. Golding (1980) *Competency to Stand Trial.* Champaign: University of Illinois Press.

Rogers, J. and J. Bloom (1982) "Characteristics of persons committed to Oregon's Psychiatric Security Review Board." *Bulletin of the American Academy of Psychiatry and the Law* 10, 3:155–164.

Steadman, H. J. (1980) "Insanity acquittals in New York State, 1965–1978." *American Journal of Psychiatry* 137:321–326.

—— (1979) Beating a Rap: Defendants Found Incompetent to Stand Trial. Chicago: University of Chicago Press.

—— and J. C. Cocozza (1974) *Careers of the Criminally Insane.* Lexington, MA: D. C. Heath.

Steadman, H. J., J. Monahan, E. Hartstone, S. K. Davis, and P.C. Robbins (1982) "Mentally disordered offenders: A national survey of patients and facilities." *Law and Human Behavior* 6, 1.

Sturgeon, V. and J. Taylor (1980) "Report of a five-year follow-up of mentally disordered sex offenders released from Atascadero State Hospital in 1973." *Criminal Justice Journal of Western State University* 4:31–64.

Uhlig, R. H. (1976) "Hospitalization experience of mentally disturbed and disruptive, incarcerated offenders." *Journal of Psychiatry and Law* 4(1):49–59.

21
PSYCHOPATHY

ETIOLOGY, DIAGNOSIS, AND TREATMENT

GARY ZAJAC

While psychopaths (also called sociopaths) are feared and loathed, they represent a small but significant portion of the offender population that poses unique challenges to corrections. What follows is a concise review of what we know about the psychopathic offender. How we identify them, what they look like, and how to deal with them are all covered in this reading.

The following provides a brief review of research on psychopathy, focusing on its core features, assessment approaches and treatment prospects.

PSYCHOPATHY—DEFINITION AND CORE FEATURES

Psychopathy can be thought of as an extreme manifestation of the antisocial, but not necessarily criminal, personality. While the term "psychopath" is widely tossed around in the popular culture—embodied in the fictional Hannibal Lecter—it is also widely misunderstood and misapplied. The concept of psychopathy has its roots in 19th century discussions of "moral insanity" and "underdeveloped superego," but the contemporary description of the psychopath was developed by Cleckley (1941). The key clinical features of the psychopath are:

- Manipulative.
- Superficial charm.
- Above-average intelligence.
- Absence of psychotic symptoms (e.g. delusions, hallucinations, etc.).
- Absence of anxiety.
- Lack of remorse.
- Failure to learn from experience.
- Egocentric.
- Lacks emotional depth (e.g. flat affect).

Other characteristics can include impulsivity, erratic and parasitic lifestyle, pathological lying and of course anti-social behavior.

Working from this basic definition, there are several key points to consider in understanding psychopathy. First, psychopaths are *not* necessarily mentally ill. Strictly speaking, psychopathy is not recognized by the Diagnostic and Statistical Manual of Mental Disorders IV (DSM-IV; more on this below). Thus, they may appear to be perfectly normal individuals during day-to-day interactions. Indeed, psychopaths may actually have a high level of social skill and may function seemingly normally in the community for many years. For example, Ted Bundy used his strong

Excerpts from "Psychopathy: Etiology, Diagnosis, and Treatment" by Gary Zajac (April 2009). *Research in Review*, Pennsylvania Department of Corrections, Vol. 12(1).

social skills to lure victims. The BTK killer (Dennis Rader) and the Green River killer (Gary Ridgway) maintained jobs, families, and a community presence for decades while committing their crimes (Rader even had a degree in Administration of Justice and worked as a codes enforcement officer).

Second, psychopaths are highly resistant to punishment or other forms of social control. They often have a suppressed fear response, which allows them to engage in high risk crimes with little anxiety. Their exaggerated egos also often make them indifferent to, or even contemptuous of, conventional incentives for pro-social behavior. This gets at the issue of possibilities for the treatment of psychopathy, discussed below.

Third, criminal behavior is not necessarily associated with psychopathy. Thus, most criminals are not psychopaths, and not all psychopaths actually engage in criminal behavior. Recent discussions of the latter type of non-criminal psychopath has coined the term "snakes in suits," referring to individuals in business, politics, and other professions who exhibit many of the personality traits of psychopaths in their quest for power and advancement (Babiak and Hare, 2006). There have even been attempts to develop instruments to assess such individuals, although this remains a controversial endeavor. In practical terms, we should understand that a theory of psychopathy does *not* necessarily suffice as a theory of crime, and vice versa.

The etiology of psychopathy is unclear. Some argue that it stems from abusive and traumatic upbringing, and is thus in some sense a survival mechanism for such individuals. Others find evidence of a biological origin (Elliot, 1999; Vien et al., 2006). Some studies have found that psychopaths have a low blink-startle response, low heart rate, suppressed fear reactions, and a high tolerance (and even desire) for risk/danger. It is likely, though, that both environment and biology play a role in the development of psychopathy (Ridenour, 2000).

Assessment research (see below) has resulted in a classification of psychopathy that breaks it into two factors (Hare et al. 1990). Factor 1, called Interpersonal/Affective, addresses the personality traits of the psychopath, such as glibness, manipulative, callousness, lack of remorse, lack of emotion, etc. Factor 1 can manifest diversely in practice, ranging from the relatively affable and manipulative example found with Ted Bundy and the relatively normal (if somewhat "peculiar") family men found with Dennis Rader and Gary Ridgway to the socially isolated, "coldblooded" example found in Richard Ramirez (California's "Nightstalker"). The common feature though is some combination of the affective deficits described above. Factor 2, called Lifestyle/Behavioral, addresses the behavioral characteristics of the psychopath, such as irresponsibility, impulsivity, parasitic lifestyle, criminal deviance, etc. More recent research has broken this further into four factors (Hare, 2003), but the original two factor model suffices for a basic understanding of the concept.

These factors are commonly referenced in research on psychopathy, leading to discussions more recently of *primary* and *secondary* psychopaths (Poythress and Skeem, 2006). A primary psychopath is one who exhibits the full range of psychopathic characteristics (Factors 1 & 2), but most especially the Factor 1 traits. Secondary psychopaths are less likely to manifest the Factor 1 traits, and have higher levels of anxiety and often more substance abuse than primary psychopaths. Psychopaths commonly portrayed in the media, such as the serial killers referenced earlier, are generally primary psychopaths.

The examples of psychopaths above were all serial killers, as these cases attract much popular attention.[1] We should note that most psychopaths do not demonstrate such extreme examples of criminal deviance. They can also be serial thieves, con artists, etc. who demonstrate little or no violent behavior, but who still exhibit the traits (especially Factor 2) of a psychopath. Thus, we should not necessarily equate psychopathy with extreme violence, or vice versa.

Due to the challenges of assessing for psychopathy (discussed below), there is no good estimate of the prevalence of psychopathy in the general or offender populations. In a study of violent offenders declared by the Canadian courts to be "dangerous offenders" (a legal category in Canada, typically resulting in long term incarceration), nearly 40% were found to be psychopaths (Bonta et al., 1996). The sample used for this study, though, was hardly representative of violent offenders in general, as it consisted of the "worst of the worst" in the Canadian penal system.

As noted earlier, the DSM-IV (American Psychiatric Association, 2000) does not specifically recognize psychopathy. Instead, it identifies the condition of Antisocial Personality Disorder (APD; ICD code 301.7). While there is a fair degree of overlap between the two concepts, APD differs from psychopathy in that APD focuses more on the behavioral aspects (i.e. Factor 2) than on the affective aspects (i.e. Factor 1). The diagnostic criteria for APD are outlined below. APD seems to have a relatively high prevalence. In a study of nearly 23,000 prisoners in 12 countries, 47% of male prisoners and 21% of females were found to have APD (Fazel and Danesh, 2002). Other studies have found prevalence rates of APD among prisoners as high as 80% (Moran, 1999). It should be noted that conditions with such a high prevalence rate are relatively less useful in discriminating between offenders (i.e. if they all have it, you cannot use it to predict who will do what). Both psychopathy and APD are diagnosed more commonly in males than females.

Having established a basic working definition of psychopathy and the related construct of APD, we turn to the assessment and measurement of these conditions.

PSYCHOPATHY—ASSESSMENT AND CLASSIFICATION

The most commonly used tool to assess for psychopathy is the Psychopathy Checklist-Revised (PCL-R) (Hare, 2003). The PCL-R has 20 items that assess core traits of the psychopath. The PCL-R can require up to three hours to administer, depending upon the quality of the agency's files and the amenability of the offender. The PCL-R produces a score of 0 to 40, with a score of 30 being the commonly accepted cut-off to diagnose someone as a psychopath.

This cut-off is itself a matter of debate surrounding whether psychopathy is a *taxon* or a *dimensional* construct. Early conceptualizations of psychopathy tended to view it as a taxon, meaning an all or nothing category (i.e. someone either was or was not a psychopath) (Hare, 1993; Harris et al., 1994). More recent research tends to support the view of psychopathy as a dimensional construct, where there are varying degrees of psychopathy, which would also imply that some psychopaths are worse than others (Hare and Neuman, 2006).

One issue that should be noted with the PCL-R is that there are fairly specific training requirements and qualifications to administer the tool. Typically, one must have advanced training in psychology, psychiatry, or a related field, with a graduate degree preferred. These training requirements may discourage some jurisdictions from the use of the PCL-R, as they lack qualified staff. Given the high level inferences required to assess an offender on the PCL-R, these training requirements seem reasonable.

Research has identified a link between psychopathy and career criminality, indicating that criminals who are assessed as psychopaths are more likely to be persistent offenders than criminals not so assessed (Vaughn and DeLisi, 2008). A number of studies have found that the score on the PCL-R is predictive of recidivism, both general and violent; in other words, the higher the score on the tool, the greater the likelihood of committing additional crimes (Gendreau et al., 1996; Hemphill et al., 1998; Salekin et al., 1996). As with any assessment tool, the PCL-R is not a perfect predictor of reoffending, and there is a certain rate of false positives and false negatives. The correlations between

PCL-R score and future violent offending are reasonably strong. Some of the research indicates that the Factor 2 (antisocial lifestyle) items may be more predictive of general criminality than the Factor 1 (affective/personality) items, but that there is no difference between the two factors in predicting violent offending. This suggests that the personality features of psychopathy may be less important than the behavioral items in predicting future crime.

Some have asserted that the PCL-R validation data support a claim that the PCL-R is the "unparalleled" measure of violent recidivism, better than other general purpose risk assessment tools such as the Level of Service Inventory-Revised (LSI-R) (Salekin et al., 1996). Other research, though, has found that tools such as the LSI-R can predict violent recidivism as well as specialized tools such as the PCL-R (Gendreau et al., 2002). Indeed, validations of the LSI-R in Pennsylvania have found that it is equally predictive for violent and non-violent offenders.

The PCL-R has contributed to the development of other, more specialized assessment tools, including the Violence Risk Appraisal Guide (VRAG). The VRAG uses a completed PCL-R as a component of the overall assessment. Interestingly, the developers of the VRAG have experimented with using another tool—called the Child and Adolescent Taxon Scale (CATS)—as a replacement for the PCL-R in the VRAG. The CATS is a much simpler tool than the PCL-R, and can be completed by staff without advanced psychological training (Quinsey et al., 2006). This research is preliminary, but may provide an avenue for the assessment of violence that does not require the assessment of the complex construct of psychopathy.

As noted above, the DSM-IV provides another approach to assessing serious criminal behavior, with the concept of Antisocial Personality Disorder (APD, ICD Code 301.7). The diagnostic criteria for APD are:

A. There is a pervasive pattern of disregard for and violation of the rights of others occurring since age 15 years, as indicated by three (or more) of the following:
   1. failure to conform to social norms with respect to lawful behaviors as indicated by repeatedly performing acts that are grounds for arrest.
   2. deceitfulness, as indicated by repeated lying, use of aliases, or conning others for personal profit or pleasure.
   3. impulsivity or failure to plan ahead.
   4. irritability or aggressiveness, as indicated by repeated physical fights or assaults.
   5. reckless disregard for safety of self or others.
   6. consistent irresponsibility, as indicated by repeated failure to sustain consistent work behavior or honor financial obligations.
   7. lack of remorse, as indicated by being indifferent to or rationalizing having hurt, mistreated, or stolen from another.

B. The individual is at least 18 years old.

C. There is evidence of Conduct Disorder with onset before age 15 years.

D. The occurrence of antisocial behavior is not exclusively during the course of Schizophrenia or a Manic Episode.

The diagnostic criteria for APD are in essence "free" (i.e. there is no instrument to purchase, other than a copy of the DSM-IV), but the understanding is that any legally valid diagnosis of the condition must be made by a properly trained and licensed clinician, such as a psychologist or psychiatrist (MD). One advantage of the APD assessment is that APD is codified in the DSM-IV, which is universally recognized as the standard for the diagnosis of mental, personality and behavioral disorders (including substance abuse).

PSYCHOPATHY—TREATMENT

The potential for rehabilitating psychopaths is a subject of much debate. The conventional wisdom has been that the typical psychopath is beyond help, and that treatment programs will be wasted on them, or may even make them worse

(Reid and Gacono, 2000). The latter is predicated on the notion that psychopaths can use the intimate setting of a treatment group to hone their skills of lying, deception, and manipulation on other offenders and even on staff (Rice et al., 1992). Indeed, the other concern is of psychopaths "hijacking" the treatment group and actually making the other participants worse through their charismatic displays of antisocial attitudes and behavior. There are certainly many clinical anecdotes of this sort of thing occurring, but it is unclear if such a pattern has been established empirically.

More recently, there is some evidence that psychopaths, particularly juveniles and young adults, can benefit from treatment (Abracen et al., 2008; Caldwell, 2006, 2007). The larger question may be not whether psychopaths can be treated, but whether programs currently in existence can work with this population. Many of the programs used to treat psychopaths (and thus the focus of existing evaluations) were poorly conceived for the challenges of this population. Thus, it may not be surprising that the literature shows little promise for the treatment of psychopaths (Hare et al., 2000).

At the moment, then, we cannot say whether treatment makes a difference for psychopaths, due to poorly designed programs and relatively few studies. Drawing from the Principles of Effective Offender Intervention, we can say that if we do offer treatment programs to psychopaths, the programs should have the following characteristics: (a) target criminogenic needs, (b) use cognitive-behavioral methods, (c) offer intensive services, (d) utilize staff who are specially trained to deal with this population, and most importantly, (e) **do not mix non-psychopaths into the treatment setting.** Efforts have been made recently to develop treatment programs specifically for psychopaths, but little to no evaluation data is available yet on them (Wong and Hare, 2005).

PSYCHOPATHY—LIMITATIONS AND SUMMARY

Psychopathy is a complex psychological construct that is widely misunderstood and even controversial. Some researchers argue that it is a poorly defined construct that is too difficult to assess and that is susceptible to bias and subjectivity in measurement (especially for the Factor 1 items). Some argue that it is better to rely upon APD and other diagnoses that are recognized by the DSM-IV. Others are concerned about the labeling effect associated with the assessment, as well as with the conclusion that those so assessed are "beyond help" (Edens et al., 2006). This concern applies especially to the assessment of psychopathy in children, adolescents and even young adults, where traits that are associated with normal adolescent development may be misinterpreted as indicators of psychopathy (Edens et al., 2001).

In spite of the concerns noted above, psychopathy, as well as APD, appear to be reasonably well established constructs that can have some value in our efforts to assess and treat offenders. It is important, though, that we acknowledge the limitations of psychopathy assessment and that we understand what it is telling us. Being assessed as a psychopath is neither a necessary nor a sufficient condition for violent offending. On a related point, the use of the PCL-R and/or the DSM-IV standards for APD should also be accompanied by a broader package of risk and needs assessment, and be reviewed by a properly trained and experienced clinician. While objective assessment tools are an absolutely *essential* part of the overall treatment process, no assessment tool is intended to stand alone or to be used as a substitute for professional decision making (American Psychiatric Association, 2000). Next, we should not unconditionally accept the conclusion that all individuals diagnosed with psychopathy or APD are beyond the reach of treatment programs. The challenge is to identify and properly implement programs that are designed for the demands of this population. Finally, applying the label of "psychopath" to an individual carries enormous implications for the disposition of that individual within the criminal justice system. Accordingly, the system has the responsibility to exercise care in this assessment and in the interpretation of the results.

STUDY QUESTIONS

1. What are the characteristics of the psychopath?
2. What are some of the assessment tools that are used to assess psychopathy?
3. What do we know about the effectiveness of treatment for psychopaths?
4. What are some of the reasons that psychopaths can be disruptive in treatment programs?

NOTE

1. It is not known if all of these individuals have been *formally* assessed as psychopaths, but given what is known of them, such a diagnosis seems plausible.

REFERENCES

Abracen, Jeffrey, Jan Looman and Calvin M. Langdon. 2008. "Treatment of Sexual Offenders with Psychopathic Traits: Recent Research Development and Clinical Implications." *Trauma, Violence & Abuse,* 9(3), 144–166.

American Psychiatric Association. 2000. *Diagnostic and Statistical Manual of Mental Disorders. 4th Edition. Text Revision.* Arlington, VA: American Psychiatric Association.

Babiak, Paul and Robert D. Hare. 2006. *Snakes in Suits: When Psychopaths Go to Work.* New York: Harper Collins.

Bonta, James, Andrew Harris, Ivan Zinger and D. Carriere. 1996. *The Crown Files Research Project: A Study of Dangerous Offenders.* Ottawa: Solicitor General Canada.

Caldwell, Michael F., David J. McCormick, Deborah Umstead and Gregory J. Van Rybroek. 2007. "Evidence of Treatment Progress and Therapeutic Outcomes Among Adolescents with Psychopathic Outcomes." *Criminal Justice and Behavior,* 34(5), 573–587.

Caldwell, Michael F., Jennifer Skeem, Randy Salekin and Gregory Van Rybroek. 2006. "Treatment Response of Adolescent Offenders with Psychopathy Features: A 2-Year Follow-up." *Criminal Justice and Behavior,* 33(5), 571–596.

Cleckley, Hervey M. 1941. *The Mask of Sanity.* St. Louis: Mosby.

Edens, John F. and John Petrila. 2006. "Legal and Ethical Issues in the Assessment and Treatment of Psychopathy." In Christopher J. Patrick (ed.). *Handbook of Psychopathy.* New York: Guilford.

Edens, John F., Jennifer L. Skeem, Keith R. Cruise and Elizabeth Cauffman. 2001. "Assessment of 'Juvenile Psychopathy' and Its Association with Violence: A Critical Review." *Behavioral Sciences and the Law,* 19(1), 53–80.

Elliot, Frank A. 1999. "A Neurological Perspective." In Michel Hersen and Vincent Van Hasselt (eds.). *Handbook of Psychological Approaches with Violent Offenders.* New York: Plenum Press.

Fazel, Seena and John Danesh. 2002. "Serious Mental Disorder in 23,000 Prisoners: A Systematic Review of 62 Surveys." *Lancet,* 359(9306), 545–550.

Gendreau, Paul, Claire Goggin and Paula Smith. 2002. "Is the PCL-R Really the "Unparalleled" Measure of Offender Risk? A Lesson in Knowledge Cumulation." *Criminal Justice and Behavior,* 29(4), 397–426.

Gendreau, Paul, Tracy Little and Claire Goggin. 1996. "A Meta-Analysis of the Predictors of Adult Offender Recidivism: What Works!" *Criminology,* 34(4), 575–607.

Hare, Robert D. 2003. *The Hare Psychopathy Checklist-Revised.* 2nd ed. Toronto: Multi-Health Systems.

Hare, Robert D. 1993. *Without Conscience: The Disturbing World of the Psychopaths Among Us.* New York: Pocket Books.

Hare, Robert D. and Craig S. Neuman. 2006. "The PCL-R Assessment of Psychopathy: Development,

Structural Properties and New Directions." In Christopher J. Patrick (ed.). *Handbook of Psychopathy.* New York: Guilford.

Hare, Robert D., Danny Clark, Martin Grann and David Thorton. 2000. "Psychopathy and the Predictive Validity of the PCL-R: An International Perspective." *Behavioral Sciences and the Law,* 18(5), 623–645.

Hare, Robert D., Timothy J. Harpur, A. R. Hakstien, Adelle E. Forth, Stephen D. Hart and Joseph P. Newman. 1990. "The Revised Psychopathy Checklist: Reliability and Factor Structure." *Psychological Assessment: A Journal of Counseling and Clinical Psychology,* 2(3), 338–341.

Harris, Grant T., Marnie E. Rice and Vernon L. Quinsey. 1994. "Psychopathy as a Taxon: Evidence That Psychopaths Are a Discrete Class." *Journal of Consulting and Clinical Psychology,* 62(2), 387–397.

Hemphill, James, Robert Hare and Stephen Wong. 1998. "Psychopathy and Recidivism: A Review." *Legal and Criminological Psychology,* 3, 139–170.

Moran, P. 1999. "The Epidemiology of Antisocial Personality Disorder." *Social Psychiatry and Psychiatric Epidemiology,* 34(5), 231–242.

Poythress, Norman and Jennifer L. Skeem. 2006. "Disaggregating Psychopathy: Where and How To Look for Subtypes." In Christopher J. Patrick (ed.). *Handbook of Psychopathy.* New York: Guilford.

Quinsey, Vernon, Grant T. Harris, Marnie E. Rice and Catherine A. Cormier. 2006. *Violent Offenders: Appraising and Managing Risk.* Washington, DC: American Psychological Association.

Reid, William H. and Carl Gacono. 2000. "Treatment of Antisocial Personality, Psychopathy and Other Characterologic Antisocial Syndromes." *Behavioral Sciences and the Law,* 18(5), 647–662.

Rice, Marnie E., Grant T. Harris and Catherine A. Cormier. 1992. "An Evaluation of a Maximum Security Therapeutic Community for Psychopaths and Other Mentally Disordered Offenders." *Law and Human Behavior,* 16(4), 399–412.

Ridenour, Ty A. 2000. "Genetic Epidemiology of Antisocial Behavior." In Diana H. Fishbein, (ed.). *The Science, Treatment and Prevention of Antisocial Behaviors.* Kingston, NJ: Civic Research Institute.

Salekin, Randall T., Richard Rogers and Kenneth W. Sewell. 1996. "A Review and Metaanalysis of the Psychopathy Checklist and Psychopathy Checklist-Revised: Predictive Validity of Dangerousness." *Clinical Psychology: Science and Practice,* 3(3), 203–215.

Vaughn, Michael G. and Matt DeLisi. 2006. "Were Wolfgang's Chronic Offenders Psychopaths? On the Convergent Validity Between Psychopaths and Career Criminality." *Journal of Criminal Justice,* 36(1), 33–42.

Vien, Anh and Anthony R. Beech. 2006. "Psychopathy: Theory, Measurement and Treatment." *Trauma, Violence and Abuse,* 7(3), 155–174.

Wong, Stephen and Robert D. Hare. 2005. *Guidelines for a Psychopathy Treatment Program.* Toronto: Multi-Health Systems.

22

EQUAL OR EQUITABLE

AN EXPLORATION OF EDUCATIONAL AND VOCATIONAL PROGRAM AVAILABILITY FOR MALE AND FEMALE OFFENDERS

KAREN F. LAHM

Traditionally, correctional programs for female inmates have been limited or restricted to stereotypical programs—what the author calls "pink collar" jobs (e.g., secretarial work, sewing, laundry). This study provides a contemporary, nationwide review of the vocational and educational programs available to male and female inmates. Over 470 state institutions were included in this review.

Female incarceration in the U.S. has been notorious for gender-stereotyped programming, inadequate medical care, and overall conditions of neglect (Rafter 1995). Specifically, past literature reveals that female inmates were offered fewer opportunities for educational and vocational training than their male counterparts (Arditi et al. 1973). Of the programs that were offered, almost all of them prepared women inmates for "typical" pink collar jobs, such as secretarial work, horticulture, sewing, and service occupations (i.e. laundry and food service). A bleak picture for the future of women inmates emerges when one combines this historical lack of programming with the continuous increase in the number of women inmates entering state and federal facilities. The Bureau of Justice Statistics estimates that as of June 1999, there were approximately 87,199 women in state and federal prisons (Bureau of Justice Statistics 1999). This is up some 5.5 percent from the previous year, and researchers indicate that the rise in the number of women inmates is outpacing the rise in the number of males entering prison (reported as a 4.3 percent increase) (Bureau of Justice Statistics 1999).

While the opportunities for these growing numbers of incarcerated women appear minimal based upon extant research, most of the research on educational and vocational programs available to female inmates is outdated for the 1990s and is based on a small sample of institutions. Most important, this previous research cannot and does not account for the changing roles of women in today's society. Not only are more women entering post-secondary education, but more women are entering the work force than ever before (U.S. Census Bureau 1997). These changes invite a re-examination of gender disparities in prison programming, because today's female inmate is entering a different economic and educational climate than that of 30 years ago.

Excerpts from "Equal or Equitable: An Exploration of Educational and Vocational Program Availability for Male and Female Offenders" by Karen F. Lahm (2002). *Federal Probation*, 64(2): 39–46.

Thus, the present study provides a much needed contemporary, nationwide examination of the educational and vocational programs available to male and female inmates from over 470 state institutions. In addition to describing program availability, I present logistic regression analysis to assess the effects of prison gender composition upon educational and vocational program availability, while controlling for other prison-level variables (i.e., age, staff size, population size, regional location, and security level). Last, I explore and discuss some of the policy and social implications of this research.

LITERATURE REVIEW

ACADEMIC EDUCATION

Academic educational programming is an area where inequalities have long flourished between male and female penal institutions. Arditi et al. (1973) found that several states in his sample lacked "proper" educational programs for women. Michigan, for example, did not provide its female inmates with even a first-through-eighth-grade education. In addition, Michigan and California did not provide any study-release programs for females, but did offer such programs to male inmates. Alabama only provided male inmates with college programs. Nebraska offered only junior college classes to its female inmates, while offering four-year college programs on the premises of all of its male institutions.

This study also revealed that female institutions had fewer teachers, but better inmate/teacher ratios. For example, Ohio had a 57:1 ratio and a 107:1 inmate teacher ratio in its female and male institutions, respectively (Arditi et al. 1973). This lower ratio provided more personal attention for female inmates, while simultaneously inhibiting the scope of training and specialization (i.e., grade level and subject matter) offered to female inmates. The findings of this study, however, are somewhat limited because the authors only examined a small sample of 15 female institutions and 47 male institutions in approximately 14 states.

More recently, Ryan (1984) conducted one of the most comprehensive studies of program availability. He examined academic education program availability across 45 states. He found that 83 percent of the female institutions offered GED and ABE (i.e. Adult Basic Education) programs, while 72 percent had college programs. These results indicated that program availability had definitely increased, but they indicated nothing about the actual participation rates in prison programs nor about the qualitative characteristics of the programming offered.

In terms of participation rates, a study by Morash et al. (1994) of more than 14,592 male inmates and 3,091 female inmates revealed that a slightly greater proportion of females (48.6 percent) than of males (45 percent) had taken part in academic programs since admission to prison. In addition, slightly more females were involved in adult basic education classes and college classes.

This involvement in educational programs is much needed, since current statistics show that many of today's female inmates are entering prison with an educational deficit. A Bureau of Justice Statistics (1994) report revealed that of the female inmates imprisoned in 1991 only 23 percent had completed high school while 33 percent had dropped out of high school. In addition, 20 percent had completed a GED and about 16 percent had some college education. This evidence supports the notion that educational programming in prisons is necessary. Leaving prison with insufficient education or job skills sets these inmates up for a life of struggle and distress.

VOCATIONAL EDUCATION

An area where female inmates seem to face particularly great disparities is vocational training. Arditi et al. (1973) revealed that males in their study were offered a greater variety of vocational programs than female inmates (males averaged 10.2 programs, while females averaged 2.7 programs).

Of the 62 facilities surveyed by the researchers, it was reported that the Department of Corrections often assigned male offenders to specific institutions based upon their rehabilitative needs, while female inmates only had the choice of going to one facility in their state (Arditi et al. 1973). Arditi et al. also showed that female inmates were only offered training in clerical skills, cosmetology, dental assistance, floral design, food service, garment manufacturing, housekeeping, IBM keypunching, and nursing assistance. Male inmates, however, were offered programs in air conditioning repair, auto mechanics, baking, cabinet making, carpentry, chemistry, driving, drafting, electronics, farming, horticulture, laundry preparation, leather work, machine shop, plumbing, printing, tailoring, welding, and many more. Not only were males offered more programs, but they were offered training in programs that could potentially earn them more income upon release.

Glick and Neto (1977) provide additional evidence for the existence of this disparity in their study, which showed that their sample of female institutions most frequently offered vocational programs in clerical skills, cosmetology, and food service. The researchers also point to the dubious utility of these programs. They state, "it is ironic that many correctional institutions have provided vocational training programs in fields where licensing of ex-offenders has been denied" (Glick and Neto 1977: 73). This study reiterates the idea that prisons are not looking towards the future of their inmates. Inmates (both males and females) need job skills that will help "kick start" their resocialization back into society. Fewer opportunities in prison make the reality of successful resocialization for female inmates seem extremely challenging (Simon 1975, Sobel 1982).

Watterson (1996), for example, stated:

> When a woman gets out of prison, she's given $40, a coat, an address and told to go out and see if she can make it. Most women will return; they do so because of stress, fear, and the fact that they haven't learned the skills needed for living more effectively outside while they've been locked up (p. 204).

Research from the 1980s revealed that the number and variety of vocational programs for female offenders had increased compared to earlier decades (Arditi et al. 1973; Glick and Neto 1977). Ryan (1984) reported that 83 percent of the female facilities in his sample had at least one vocational program, with some states such as Texas and Pennsylvania offering 12 to 13 vocational programs. In addition, Crawford (1988) indicated that 90 percent of the female prisons in her sample offered some type of vocational program. Moreover, Weishet (1985) reported that 15 of the women's institutions in his sample offered non-traditional programming, whereas in 1973 none of his sample institutions had offered any type of non-traditional programming for females.

Some of the most current research by Morash et al. (1994) indicated that female inmates are still receiving fewer vocational programs than males and that those they receive tend to be gender stereotyped. Their survey revealed that about 20 percent of males and females were receiving some kind of vocational training. However, a significantly higher percentage of males were involved in auto repair, construction, and trade, while females were most likely to be involved in office training. The present study will build on the available information by examining whether the programs being offered to female inmates are not just equal but equitable in terms of non-traditional training.

WORK TRAINING AND PRISON INDUSTRIES

Through the 1900s, most correctional institutions have offered some type of industrial training, and work; however, past researchers have discovered that male prisons have enjoyed the upper hand in both the variety and number of industrial programs offered to inmates (Arditi et al, 1973; Glick Neto,

1977; Gabel, 1982; Pollack-Byrne 1990; Morash et al. 1994). In their 1973 sample of 47 male facilities, Arditi et al. revealed that programs were offered in the following areas: auto repair, bookbindery, cabinet making, cloth manufacturing, concrete, dairy, data processing, detergent manufacturing, farming, flag manufacturing, furniture manufacturing, heavy equipment operation, library, license plate, machine shop, metal shop, printing, road sign manufacturing, shoe manufacturing, engine repair, tailoring, twine manufacturing, and upholstery. Female inmates were only offered industrial programs in canning, food service, garment manufacturing, IBM keypunching, and laundry. It is apparent that a glaring disparity existed between the types and numbers of industrial programs offered to male and female inmates. The results revealed a male to female ratio of 23:5. This constitutes an almost five to one difference in the number of available prison programs.

Many other studies echo the previous findings. Glick and Neto (1977) reported that approximately 63 percent of their sample of female inmates worked while incarcerated. However, the majority (17.3 percent) were employed in food service, followed by sewing jobs (14.3 percent), housekeeping (8:4 percent), clerical (6.2 percent), laundry (5.5 percent), medical (4.2 percent), maintenance (3.4 percent), with 3.2 percent in other occupations. Gabel (1982) showed that 66 percent of the female inmates in her study were also assigned to traditional jobs in laundry, maintenance, food service, and clerical. Morash et al. (1994) revealed that 22.5 percent of the female inmates in their study cleaned and cooked, whereas only 16 percent of male inmates cleaned and cooked. They also showed that males worked more than females in farm, forestry, maintenance, repair, shop industries, textiles, and highway maintenance (Morash et al. 1994). Duncan's (1992) comprehensive study of female prison industries throughout the United States showed that the most commonly offered programs were sewing (25 states), data entry/data processing (16 states), furniture reupholstering and clerical (7 states), and telemarketing and microfilming (6 states). Duncan (1992) concluded that these programs were offering women experience in "real world" occupations, but that equality between male and female work opportunities still posed a problem. She also reported that 14 states had no plans to expand programming for women offenders due to a lack of space and money, while 36 states planned to expand to develop new programming for female inmates.

METHODS

As mentioned previously, existing research indicates that the disparity in correctional programming opportunities between male and female inmates seems to be shrinking. Although this research is informative, much of it is outdated and based on a small sample of institutions. This prison-level analysis provides a much-needed current examination of the educational and vocational programs available to inmates imprisoned during the 1990s. Moreover, it adds to a still somewhat small body of literature that examines programming opportunities inside prison walls.

To meet the goals of this study, all of the 50 states, plus Washington, D.C., were sent letters requesting information about the available academic and vocational programs at their state-run institutions during August of 1996. In addition to the program information, I also requested information about the gender make-up, population size, staff size, security level, and age of all of the institutions within each state. If this information was missing from state reports I acquired it from the 1996 American Correctional Association's Directory of Juvenile and Adult Correctional Department, Institutions, Agencies, and Paroling Authorities.

Each state was given about one month to respond. At about four, six, and ten weeks into the study, follow-up letters were sent to those institutions that failed to respond to the initial request for information. Those states that did not respond after ten weeks were then contacted by telephone. All in all, I received information from 30 states resulting in a sample of 474 institutions (417 male and 47 female).[1] Community correctional facilities, private facilities, co-educational and medical/intake facilities were excluded from the sample.

The dependent variables in this study consisted of 8 dichotomous variables indicating the presence or absence (0 = program not offered; 1 = program offered) of each particular program at each institution. In terms of academic programming, my two dependent variables were *general education* (i.e., adult basic education, GED, high school) and *college education* (i.e., associate or bachelors degree programs). As Table 22.1 suggests, approximately 51 percent of the sample institutions offered post-secondary educational programs, while almost 100 percent of the institutions offered some form of general academic programming.

Since there was such a variety of vocational/industrial programs at each of the institutions, each particular program was assigned to a career category as listed in the U.S. Census Bureau's Statistical Abstracts. These six career categories served as my dependent variables for availability of vocational programs: *managerial and professional; technical/sales/administrative support; service; production; operator/fabricator/laborer; and farm/forestry/fishing*. For example, if a particular institution offered a sewing program, then I would assign a "yes" to the operator/fabricator/labor program category, or if an institution offered automotive training, then I would assign a "yes" to the production category. Table 22.1 shows that 15 percent of the sample institutions offered managerial training programs, 36 percent offered technical sales programs, 72 percent offered service-work training, 54 percent offered production programs, some 42 percent offered operator/fabricator programming, 36

TABLE 22.1 VARIABLES, METRICS, AND DESCRIPTIVE STATISTICS (FULL SAMPLE)*

		Descriptives			
Variables	**Metrics**	**Mean**	**SD**	**Min.**	**Max.**
Dependent Variables					
General education	(0 = no, 1 = yes)	.99	.06	0	1
College	(0 = no, 1 = yes)	.51	.50	0	1
Managerial	(0 = no, 1 = yes)	.15	.36	0	1
Technical/Sales	(0 = no, 1 = yes)	.36	.48	0	1
Service	(0 = no, 1 = yes)	.72	.45	0	1
Production	(0 = no, 1 = yes)	.54	.49	0	1
Operator/fabricator	(0 = no, 1 = yes)	.42	.49	0	1
Farm/forestry/fishing	(0 = no, 1 = yes)	.36	.48	0	1
Explanatory Variables					
Gender	(0 = male, 1 = female)	.10	.30	0	1
Region	(0 = non-Southern, 1 = Southern)	.40	.49	0	1
Age of prison	(0 = before 1980; 1 = after 1980)	.53	.49	0	1
Minimum security	(0 = no, 1 = yes)	.19	.39	0	1
Medium security	(0 = no, 1 = yes)	.21	.41	0	1
Maximum security	(0 = no, 1 = yes)	.13	.33	0	1
Other security	(0 = no, 1 = yes)	.48	.50	0	1
Population size	(0 = less than 800; 1 = more than 800)	.54	.49	0	1
Staff size	(0 = less than 300; 1 = more than 300)	.58	.49	0	1

* The total sample size is 464.

percent of the institutions offered farm, forestry, and fishing program training.[2]

The key explanatory variables of interest here are the various structural characteristics of the prisons. *Gender* composition of the institution is a dummy variable coded (0 = male institution and 1 = female institution). Table 22.1 shows that approximately 10 percent (47) of the institutions in the sample were female institutions, while the rest (417) were male. *Age* of the institution is also a dichotomous variable indicating when the institution was built (0 = pre 1980; 1 = post 1980). Table 22.1 indicates that approximately 53 percent of the sample institutions were built after 1980, with some 47 percent built prior to 1980. *Security level* was measured with a series of four dummy variables (0 = no, 1 = yes) including minimum, medium, maximum, and other (i.e. mixed security level). Table 22.1 suggests that 19 percent of the institutions in the sample had a minimum security classification, 21 percent were medium security level, and 13 percent had a maximum security level. The majority of institutions in the sample (almost 48 percent) housed inmates of mixed security classifications.

In terms of size, *population size* is a dichotomous variable measuring the average daily population of the institution (0 = less than 800; 1 = more than 800).[3] Table 22.1 shows the majority of institutions (i.e. 54 percent) housed more than 800 prisoners. *Staff size* is also a dichotomous variable measuring the number of total staff (i.e. custodial and non-custodial) working full time at the institution on a daily basis (0 = less than 300; 1 = more than 300).[4] Again, Table 22.1 reveals that approximately 58 percent of the sample institutions have more than 300 full-time staff.

The final explanatory variable is a regional location variable. The variable *region* is a dummy variable (0 = non-Southern, 1 = Southern) measuring whether or not the institution was located in a Southern state as classified by the Bureau of Justice Statistics.[5] Table 22.1 shows that approximately 40 percent of the institutions in the sample were Southern. This variable was included because Southern institutions have a well-documented history of being the least progressive institutions in terms of academic and vocational program opportunities (Morash et al. 1994).

RESULTS

One of the foremost goals of this paper was to see if women's institutions were offering the same "types" of educational and vocational programs as men's institutions. Table 22.2 controls for gender of the institution and reveals the percentage of male and female institutions offering each type of academic and vocational program. In terms of general educational programs (i.e. GED and ABE), Table 22.2 shows that almost 100 percent of both the male

TABLE 22.2 AVAILABILITY OF PROGRAMS AT MALE AND FEMALE INSTITUTIONS

Program	Male Institutions[a]	Female Institutions[b]
General education	100.0%	100.0%.
College	51.1%	52.4%
Managerial	14.0%	23.4%
Technical/sales	33.4%	63.8%
Service	70.9%	80.9%
Production	55.0%	46.8%
Operator/fabricator	41.1%	46.8%
Farm/forestry/fishing	37.0%	31.9%

[a] 417 institutions
[b] 47 institutions

and female institutions offer some form of general education. These results run contrary to the previous work of the 1970s, which revealed that several states lacked any kind of general academic programming for women inmates (Arditi et al. 1973). These results indicate that the basic educational opportunities for female inmates have greatly increased in the past 30 years. It is possible that the years of legal battles pursued by female inmates to gain equal access to educational programs have succeeded in doing just that.

In terms of college program availability, Table 22.2 reveals that 52 percent of female institutions and 51 percent of male institutions offered some form of post-secondary education programs. However, this encouraging evidence of diminishing disparity is tempered by responses indicating that only about half of the institutions combined offered post-secondary education opportunities. It appears that once-thriving post-secondary correctional educational programs are now on the decline. This is very disheartening, because much research shows that post-secondary education works to reduce recidivism and increase self-esteem and employability (Knepper 1990; Harer 1995; Batiuk, Moke, and Rountree 1995).

Turning to vocational programming, Table 22.2 suggests that a much greater percentage of female institutions in comparison to male institutions still overwhelmingly offer training in technical/sales/administrative occupations (63.8 percent to 33.4 percent) and service occupations (80.9 percent and 70.9 percent). The technical/sales/administrative category includes vocational training for jobs such as medical assistants, sales associates, clerical/office staff, and telemarketing. The jobs within the service category include, food and laundry preparation, and other custodial duties. These findings are consistent with past research of Morash et al. (1994), which indicates that 85 percent of female institutions still offer gender-stereotyped "traditional" vocational programs.

Moreover, Table 22.2 shows that a greater percentage of male institutions offered occupational training in production (46.8 percent vs. 55 percent) and farm/forestry/fishing careers (31.9 percent vs. 37 percent). Some of the most common production courses offered were masonry, automotive, electronics, construction, graphic arts, and building trades (plumbing, electrical, etc.).

Despite this, the results from Table 22.2 also show improvements in program availability for female inmates. First, a greater percentage of the female institutions are offering vocational training in managerial and professional programs. This is a drastic improvement over past research, which indicated that during the 1970s females were offered no programs of this type and were only offered "typical" female jobs (Arditi et al. 1973). Also, Table 22.2 shows that more female institutions offer training in operator/fabricator/laborer programs (47 percent vs. 41 percent) than do male institutions. This finding is misleading because the occupation of sewing, which is a female-dominated occupation, fits into this job category. This finding suggests that females are receiving more training ill non-traditional occupations when they are actually being trained as seamstresses, a program traditionally offered to female inmates.

In order to discern whether the gendered nature of the institution accounts for specific program availability while also controlling for other prison-level variables, I next conducted logistic regression analysis. Specifically, I estimated the availability of academic education programs and college programs (l = yes; 0 = no), while controlling for prison characteristics. As is standard in logistic regression analysis, the exponentiated coefficients are also reported. These can be interpreted as indicating the odds of experiencing the dependent variable per unit change in an independent variable after subtracting the exponentiated coefficient from 1.0 and multiplying the absolute value by 100 (Neter, Wasserman, and Kutner 1989: 588).

Table 22.3 shows that gender composition of the institution did not significantly affect the likelihood of offering either type of academic programming. In fact, none of the prison variables were significant predictors of academic education program availability. However, Table 22.3 does indicate that several of the prison background variables were significant predictors of college program availability. Specifically, the exponentiated coefficient for the region variable indicates that Southern prisons are 77 percent (/1-.23/ X100) less likely to offer college programs than non-Southern institutions. This finding is consistent with the past research of Morash et al. (1994) and Rafter (1995), which indicate that Southern institutions are the least progressive in terms of program availability, while the Midwest and Northeast are the most progressive.

Moreover, Table 22.3 reveals that institutions built after 1980 are about 40 percent less likely to offer college programs than institutions built prior to 1980. This finding could reflect the "get tough" policies (three strikes and mandatory sentencing) associated with the 1980s war on drugs. Also, compared to institutions with mixed security levels, the more secure medium and maximum institutions are more likely to offer college programming (i.e., 113 percent, and 184 percent, respectively). Interestingly, staff size was not a statistically significant predictor of college program availability. Intuitively, it would seem that having more staff enables prisons to offer more programming opportunities. However, Arditi et al. (1973) found that larger staff size does not necessarily mean a greater number of educators, but rather more custodial (security) staff.

To further investigate the effects of gender composition on vocational program availability, I estimated logistic regression models of vocational program availability while controlling for the other prison background characteristics. Table 22.4 reveals that gender composition of the institution was a significant predictor of technical, service, and operator/fabricator/laborer program availability. Specifically, the exponentiated coefficients indicate that women's institutions are 604 percent more likely to offer technical/sales training (i.e., health assistants, clerical staff, and sales associates), 208 percent more likely to offer training in service occupations (i.e., cleaning and food service industries), and almost 100 percent more likely to offer training in the operator/fabricator/labor sector (i.e., sewing). This finding is consistent with past research of Morash et al. (1994), who indicate that women prisoners are likely to be disproportionately involved in cleaning and kitchen work while incarcerated.

TABLE 22.3 LOGISTIC REGRESSION COEFFICIENTS FOR ACADEMIC EDUCATION PROGRAM AVAILABILITY

	General Education			College		
Independent Variables	Coefficient	SE	Exp. (coeff)	Coefficient	SE	Exp. (coeff)
Intercept	4.34	1.84	76.90	.24	.30	1.27
Gender	9.62	160.30	15065.29	.41	.38	1.51
Region	−.44	1.64	.64	−1.48[a]	.24	.23
Age of prison	.62	1.56	1.86	−.49[a]	.23	.61
Minimum	9.44	126.17	12600.97	.59[b]	.33	1.81
Medium	7.86	103.41	2590.99	.76[a]	.29	2.13
Maximum	−2.05	1.67	.13	1.04[a]	.36	2.84
Population size	10.21	68.83	27223.77	.31	.27	1.36
Staff size	−.12	1.53	.89	.20	.30	.50

[a] $p<.05$
[b] $p<.10$

Not surprisingly, both the service and technical/sales jobs categories are the most female-dominated occupational categories outside of prison walls. In the United States, some 64 percent of the people employed in the technical/sales jobs are women, and 60 percent of the people employed in the service sector are women (U.S. Census Bureau 1997). These findings suggest that this abundance of traditional programming is preparing females to enter gender-stereotyped occupations in the real world, which are also among the most unstable, low paying jobs.

Moreover, Table 22.4 also shows that Southern prisons are 66 percent less likely to make managerial programs available to their inmates. They are also less likely to offer technical and service training programs. However, Southern institutions are 74 percent more likely to offer farm, forestry, and fishing programs.

In terms of the age of the prison, Table 22.4 shows that prisons built after 1980 do not offer more programming opportunities. However, the findings do indicate that newer prisons are about 82 percent more likely to offer managerial training. Overall, these results seem consistent with the get-tough policies of the 1980s.

In addition, the size of the prison, measured by the number of inmates, appears to have little effect on program availability. Specifically, Table 22.4 reveals that institutions with more than 800 inmates are more likely to offer production training programs (196 percent) and operator/fabricator programs (134 percent). Likewise, it would appear that institutions with a larger staff (i.e., more than 300) offer a greater variety of program opportunities.

Lastly, Table 22.4 indicates that when compared to prisons with mixed security levels, medium security prisons appear to offer the greatest variability in vocational training. Medium security institutions are more than 100 percent likely to offer every kind of vocational training program. In turn, minimum

TABLE 22.4 LOGISTIC REGRESSION COEFFICIENTS FOR VOCATIONAL PROGRAM AVAILABILITY

	Coefficient (Exp. Coeff.)					
Variables	Mang.	Tech.	Service	Prod.	Opert.	FFF
Constant	−3.02	−1.18	.13	−.91	−1.09	−1.84
	(.05)	(.31)	(1.14)	(.40)	(.33)	(.16)
Gender	1.35[a]	1.95[a]	1.12[a]	.34	.68[b]	.31
	(3.86)	(7.04)	(3.08)	(1.40)	(1.99)	(1.36)
Region	−1.07[a]	−.89[a]	−.67[a]	.02	−.04	.55[a]
	(.34)	(.41)	(.51)	(1.02)	(.96)	(1.74)
Age of prison	.60[a]	−.12	.06	−.04	−.52[a]	−.03
	(1.82)	(.88)	(1.07)	(.96)	(.59)	(.97)
Minimum	.51	.40	.75[a]	−.02	.00	.98[a]
	(1.67)	(1.49)	(2.12)	(.98)	(1.00)	(2.66)
Medium	.68[a]	.89[a]	1.19[a]	.92[a]	.60[a]	1.14[a]
	(1.97)	(2.44)	(3.31)	(2.53)	(1.83)	(3.13)
Maximum	1.28[a]	.32	.83[a]	.52	.35	.88[a]
	(3.56)	(1.38)	(2.29)	(1.67)	(1.42)	(2.42)
Population size	.42	.30	.26	1.08[a]	.85[a]	.25
	(1.52)	(1.35)	(1.30)	(2.96)	(2.34)	(1.28)
Staff size	.61	.55[b]	.78[a]	.40	.51[b]	.58[a]
	(1.84)	(1.73)	(2.18)	(1.49)	(1.67)	(1.78)

[a] $p<.05$
[b] $p<.10$

security facilities are more likely to offer service and farming programs, while maximum security facilities are more likely to offer managerial programs, service training, and farming programs.

DISCUSSION AND CONCLUSION

Several conclusions and policy implications flow from this paper. First, it appears that women's prisons are offering equal opportunities in basic education and post-secondary education programming. On the whole, this research indicates that general education programs are readily available across the United States, while post-secondary correctional educational programs are not quite as widespread. The results here showed that only about half of the institutions in the sample offered some type of post-secondary correctional programming. Specifically, the gender composition of the institution proved to be a non-significant predictor of college program availability.

Moreover, it seems that post-secondary programming opportunities are on the decline. In addition, prospects for reversing this trend do not look bright. New laws such as President Clinton's 1994 crime bill, which denied Pell Grant money to inmates, make it unlikely that most inmates will be able to afford post-secondary education while incarcerated. Furthermore, a few of the state officials I spoke to while collecting this data reported that they planned to cut all post-secondary educational opportunities within the next five years.

Second, the research indicates that prisons are offering a greater variety of vocational opportunities than ever before, but women's institutions are still more likely to offer gender-stereotyped vocational training. Specifically, the women's institutions in the sample were significantly more likely than male institutions to offer training in technical/sales/administrative occupations and service occupations (i.e., typical women's work). It is possible, as Pollock-Byrne (1990) suggests, that women's institutions and/or departments of correction are more comfortable relegating this type of service/technical work to females as opposed to male inmates.

Unfortunately, the majority of the jobs these women are being trained for are among the most underpaid and unstable jobs in society. A woman leaving prison with minimal skills, earning minimum wage, will not be able to support herself or her family, and thus may turn to the government for aid or recidivate and find herself back in prison. An in-depth study of incarcerated parents by Gabel and Johnston (1995) indicates that approximately 70 percent of incarcerated women are mothers. Moreover, they report that the majority of "incarcerated mothers plan to resume custody of all or some of their children upon release from prison" (Gabel and Johnston 1995: 26). Not only do these women face enormous stress in reunifying with children and families, but their burden is compounded because they have only been trained for low-paying, gender-stereotyped occupations.

Lastly, it appears that regional location and security level, as opposed to other prison-level characteristics, have strong predictive effects on post-secondary educational and vocational program availability. This calls into question the qualitative nature and philosophy of each state's correctional system. Future researchers may want to examine these qualitative differences to see how a state's punishment philosophy (i.e., rehabilitation, retribution, incapacitation, and deterrence) affects the structure and internal workings of prisons within that state. It would also be interesting to see how community sentiment affects punishment ideology and state legislation for prisoners.

Despite these results, there are several limitations to this research that should be noted. First, the sample only contained information from 30 states, and many larger states such as California were not included. Second, this sample did not include private prisons. Little research has been done on private prisons, and it appears to be an area where much future research is needed to recognize the similarities/differences between these and state/federal institutions.

Third, lumping together many programs into occupational categories may mask some of the unique programs being offered across the country. Many states are offering very progressive programs to inmates and this study did not fully recognize these. For example, Ohio offers a program called ONOW (Orientation to Non-Traditional Occupations for Women), which prepares women inmates for jobs in trade industries. It emphasizes training and information on plumbing, carpentry, electricity, math, physical fitness, employment skills, blueprint reading, job safety issues and sexual harassment issues. The supervisor of this program told me ONOW performs several functions for inmates: (1) it increases their self-esteem; (2) it eases the transition back into the community; (3) it provides inmates with job skills that enable them to be self-sufficient, productive members of the community, and (4) it lowers the recidivism rate of those who have completed the program. Most researchers tend to ignore females when exploring the links between programming and recidivism, employability, etc. As women continue to enter prison at a faster pace than males, future researchers must fully explore the success rates of these and other programs that women inmates are participating in. It appears that women inmates have reached some equality in terms of programming opportunities; however, the equitability of these programs still remains a question.

STUDY QUESTIONS

1. What are some of the traditional differences between programs for male and female inmates?
2. Do differences in programming still exist? What are they, and what are some reasons for these differences?
3. If you were able to design programs for female inmates, what would you include and why?

NOTES

1. The following states responded: Arkansas, District of Columbia, Florida, Louisiana, Oklahoma, South Carolina, Tennessee, Texas, West Virginia, Connecticut, Maine, Massachusetts, New Jersey, New York, Pennsylvania, Arizona, Colorado, Hawaii, Idaho, Montana, Oregon, Washington, Wyoming, Illinois, Michigan, Minnesota, Nebraska, North Dakota, Ohio, and Wisconsin.
2. I found that the five most available programs offered at women's institutions were: cosmetology, custodial/maintenance, food service preparation, horticulture, sewing, and construction trades. In contrast, the most available programs at male institutions were: automotive, agriculture/livestock, business, barber, building trades, computers, constructions, carpentry, culinary/baking, design/drafting, food service, furniture/upholstery, graphic arts, horticulture, HVAC, laundry, machining, metals, painting, printing, welding, and secretarial. All in all, male institutions offered a much wider variety of vocational programs than did female institutions.
3. If the documents from each state's department of corrections did not report the average daily population or if the information was outdated, then I acquired the information from the 1996 ACA Directory. This information is based on reported population as of June 30, 1995.
4. If the documents from each state's department of corrections did not report the average daily staff or if the information was outdated, then I acquired the information from the 1996 ACA Directory. This information is based on the reported number of staff as of June 30, 1995.
5. Regional assignments were based on information from the Bureau of Justice Statistic's report: Comparing Federal and State Prison Inmates, 1995. The Bureau of Justice Statistics classify the following states as Southern: Alabama, Arkansas, Delaware, District of Columbia, Florida, Georgia, Kentucky, Louisiana, Maryland, Mississippi,

North Carolina, Oklahoma, South Carolina, Tennessee, Texas, Virginia, and West Virginia.

REFERENCES

American Correctional Association. (1996). *Directory of Juvenile and Adult Correctional Department, Institutions, Agencies, and Paroling Authorities*. American Correctional Association.

Arditi, R., F. Goldberg, M. Hartle, J. Phelps. (1973). "The Sexual Segregation of American Prisons." *Yale Law Journal* 82:1229–1273.

Batiuk, M. E., P. Moke, and P. Wilcox Rountree. (1995). "Crime and Rehabilitation: Correctional Education as an Agent of Change—A Research Note." *Justice Quarterly* 14(1), 167– 180.

Bureau of Justice Statistics (1994). *Women in Prison*. Washington D.C.: U.S. Government Printing Office.

Bureau of Justice Statistics (1995). *Comparing Federal and State Prison Inmates, 1995*. Washington D.C.: U.S. Government Printing Office.

Bureau of Justice Statistics (1999). *Prisoners and Jail Inmates at Midyear, 1999*. Washington D.C.: U.S. Government Printing Office.

Crawford, J. (1988). *Tabulation of a Nationwide Survey of State Correctional Facilities for Adult and Juvenile Female Offenders*. College Park, MD: American Correctional Association.

Duncan, D. (1992). "ACA Survey Examines Industry Programs for Women Offenders." *Corrections Today* 54: 114.

Gabel, K. (1982). *The Legal Issues of Female Inmates*. Northhampton, MA: Smith College School for Social Work.

Gabel, K. and D. Johnston, M.D. (1995). *Children of Incarcerated Parents*. New York: Lexington Books.

Glick, R., and V. Neto. (1977). *National Study of Women's Correctional Programs*. National Institute of Law Enforcement and Criminal Justice. Washington DC: U.S. Government Printing Office.

Hare, Miles D. (1995). "Recidivism among Federal Prisoners Released in 1987." *Journal of Correctional Education* 46:98–128.

Knepper, P. (1990). "Selective Participation, Effectiveness, and Prison College Programs." *Offender Counseling, Services, and Rehabilitation* 14(2):109–35.

Morash, M., R. Haarr, and L. Rucker (1994). "A Comparison for Women and Men in U.S. Prisons in the 1980s." *Crime and Delinquency* 2: 197–221.

Neter, John, W. Wasserman, and M. H. Kutner (1989). *Applied Linear Regression Models*. 2nd ed. Homewood, IL: Irwin.

Pollock-Byrne, J. (1990). *Women, Prison, and Crime*. California: Brooks/Cole.

Rafter, N. (1995). *Partial Justice: Women, Prison, and Social Control*. 2nd ed. Boston: Northeastern University Press.

Ryan, T. (1984). *Adult Female Offenders and Institutional Programs: A State of the Art Analysis*. Washington D.C.: National Institute of Corrections.

Simon, R. (1975). *The Contemporary Woman and Crime*. Washington, D.C.: U.S. Government Printing Office.

Sobel, S. (1982). "Difficulties Experienced by Women in Prison." *Psychology of Women Quarterly* 82:107–117.

United States Census Bureau (1997). *Statistical Abstracts of the United States 1997*. 117th ed. Washington D.C.: U.S. Government Printing Office.

Watterson, K. (1996). *Women in Prison: Inside the Concrete Womb* Rev. ed. Boston: Northeastern University Press.

Weishet, R. (1985). "Trends in Programs for Female Offenders: The Use of Private Agencies as Service Providers." *International Journal of Offender Therapy and Comparative Criminology* 1: 35–42.

23

BEYOND CORRECTIONAL QUACKERY

PROFESSIONALISM AND THE POSSIBILITY OF EFFECTIVE TREATMENT

EDWARD J. LATESSA
FRANCIS T. CULLEN
PAUL GENDREAU

Despite the widespread advances that have been made in understanding criminal conduct and providing effective interventions, there are many who still practice correctional quackery. In this article, Latessa, Cullen, and Gendreau review four major sources of correctional quackery: failure to use research in designing programs, failure to use appropriate assessment tools, failure to use effective treatment models, and failure to evaluate. Some of the questionable theories they have come across include "treat them as babies and dress them in diapers," "give them a pet," and "put them in touch with their feminine side." The authors end by reviewing ways that agencies can improve correctional programming for offenders.

Long-time viewers of *Saturday Night Live* will vividly recall Steve Martin's hilarious portrayal of a medieval medical practitioner—the English barber, Theodoric of York. When ill patients are brought before him, he prescribes ludicrous "cures," such as repeated bloodletting, the application of leeches and boar's vomit, gory amputations and burying people up to their necks in a marsh. At a point in the skit when a patient dies and Theodoric is accused of "not knowing what he is doing," Martin stops, apparently struck by the transforming insight that medicine might abandon harmful interventions rooted in ignorant customs and follow a more enlightened path. "Perhaps," he says, "I've been wrong to blindly follow the medical traditions and superstitions of past centuries." He then proceeds to wonder whether he should "test these assumptions analytically through experimentation and the scientific method." And perhaps, he says, the scientific method might be applied to other fields of learning. He might even be able to "lead the way to a new age—an age of rebirth, a renaissance." He then pauses and gives the much-awaited and amusing punchline, "Nawwwwwww!"

The humor, of course, lies in the juxtaposition and final embrace of blatant quackery with the possibility and rejection of a more modern, scientific, and ultimately effective approach to medicine. For those of us who make a living commenting on or doing corrections, however, we must consider whether, in a sense, the joke is on us. We can readily see the humor in Steve Martin's skit and wonder how those in medieval societies "could have been so stupid." But even a cursory survey of *current* correctional practices yields the disquieting conclusion that we are a field in which quackery is tolerated, if not implicitly celebrated. It is not clear whether most of us have ever had that reflective moment in which we question whether, "just maybe," there might be a more enlightened path to pursue. If we have paused to envision a different way of doing things, it is apparent that our reaction, after a moment's contemplation, too often has been, "Nawwwwwwww!"

This appraisal might seem overly harsh, but we are persuaded that it is truthful. When intervening in the lives of offenders— that is, intervening with the expressed intention of reducing recidivism—corrections has resisted becoming a true "profession." Too often, being a "professional" has been debased to mean dressing in a presentable way, having experience in the field, and showing up every day for work. But a profession is defined not by its surface appearance but by its intellectual core. An occupation may lay claim to being a "profession" only to the extent that its practices are based on research knowledge, training, and expertise—a triumvirate that promotes the possibility that what it does can be effective (Cullen, 1978; Starr, 1982). Thus, medicine's professionalization cannot be separated from its embrace of scientific knowledge as the ideal arbiter of how patients should be treated (Starr, 1982). The very concept of "malpractice" connotes that standards of service delivery have been established, are universally transmitted, and are capable of distinguishing acceptable from unacceptable interventions. The concept of liability for "correctional malpractice" would bring snickers from the crowd—a case where humor unintentionally offers a damning indictment of the field's standards of care.

In contrast to professionalism, *quackery* is dismissive of scientific knowledge, training, and expertise. Its posture is strikingly overconfident, if not arrogant. It embraces the notion that interventions are best rooted in "common sense," in personal experiences (or clinical knowledge), in tradition, and in superstition (Gendreau, Goggin, Cullen, and Paparozzi, forthcoming). "What works" is thus held to be "obvious," derived only from years of an individual's experience, and legitimized by an appeal to custom ("the way we have always done things around here has worked just fine"). It celebrates being anti-intellectual. There is never a need to visit a library or consult a study.

Correctional quackery, therefore, is the use of treatment interventions that are based on neither (1) existing knowledge of the causes of crime nor (2) existing knowledge of what programs have been shown to change offender behavior (Cullen and Gendreau, 2000; Gendreau, 2000). The hallmark of correctional quackery is thus ignorance. Such ignorance about crime and its cures at times is "understandable"—that is, linked not to the willful rejection of research but to being in a field in which professionalism is not expected or supported. At other times, however, quackery is proudly displayed, as its advocates boldly proclaim that they have nothing to learn from research conducted by academics "who have never worked with a criminal" (a claim that is partially true but ultimately beside the point and a rationalization for continued ignorance).

Need we now point out the numerous programs that have been implemented with much fanfare and with amazing promises of success, only later to turn out to have "no effect" on reoffending? "Boot camps," of course, are just one recent and salient example. Based on a vague, if not unstated, theory of crime and an absurd theory of behavioral change ("offenders need to be broken down"—through a good deal of humiliation and threats—and then "built back up"), boot camps could not possibly have "worked." In fact, we know of no major psychological theory that would logically suggest that such humiliation or threats are components of effective therapeutic interventions (Gendreau et al., forthcoming). Even so, boot camps were put into place across the nation without a shred of empirical evidence as to their effectiveness, and only now has their appeal been tarnished after years of negative evaluation studies (Cullen, Pratt, Miceli, and Moon, 2002; Cullen, Wright, and Applegate, 1996; Gendreau, Goggin, Cullen, and Andrews, 2000; MacKenzie, Wilson, and Kider, 2001). How many millions of dollars have been squandered? How many opportunities to rehabilitate offenders have been forfeited? How many citizens have been needlessly victimized by boot camp graduates? What has been the cost to society of this quackery?

We are not alone in suggesting that advances in our field will be contingent on the conscious rejection of quackery in favor of an *evidence-based corrections* (Cullen and Gendreau, 2000; MacKenzie, 2000; Welsh and Farrington, 2001). Moving beyond correctional quackery when intervening with offenders, however, will be a daunting challenge. It will involve overcoming four central failures now commonplace in correctional treatment. We review these four sources of correctional quackery not simply to show what is lacking in the field but also in hopes of illuminating what a truly professional approach to corrections must strive to entail.

FOUR SOURCES OF CORRECTIONAL QUACKERY

FAILURE TO USE RESEARCH IN DESIGNING PROGRAMS

Every correctional agency must decide "what to do" with the offenders under its supervision, including selecting which "programs" or "interventions" their charges will be subjected to. But how is this choice made (a choice that is consequential to the offender, the agency, and the community)? Often, no real choice is made, because agencies simply continue with the practices that have been inherited from previous administrations. Other times, programs are added incrementally, such as when concern rises about drug use or drunk driving. And still other times—such as when punishment-oriented intermediate sanctions were the fad from the mid-1980s to the mid-1990s—jurisdictions copy the much-publicized interventions being implemented elsewhere in the state and in the nation.

Notice, however, what is missing in this account: The failure to consider the existing research on program effectiveness. The risk of quackery rises to the level of virtual certainty when nobody in the agency asks, "Is there any evidence supporting what we are intending to do?" The irrationality of not consulting the existing research is seen when we consider again, medicine. Imagine if local physicians and hospitals made no effort to consult "what works" and simply prescribed pharmaceuticals and conducted surgeries based on custom or the latest fad. Such malpractice would be greeted with public condemnation, lawsuits, and a loss of legitimacy by the field of medicine.

It is fair to ask whether research can, in fact, direct us to more effective correctional interventions. Two decades ago, our knowledge was much less developed. But the science of crime and treatment has made important strides in the intervening years. In particular, research has illuminated three bodies of knowledge that are integral to designing effective interventions.

First, we have made increasing strides in determining the *empirically established or known predictors* of offender recidivism (Andrews and Bonta, 1998; Gendreau, Little, and Goggin, 1996; Henggeler, Mihalic, Rone, Thomas, and Timmons-Mitchell, 1998). These include, most importantly: (1) antisocial values, (2) antisocial peers, (3) poor self-control, self-management, and prosocial problem-solving skills, (4) family dysfunction, and (5) past criminality. This information is critical, because interventions that ignore these factors are doomed to fail. Phrased alternatively, successful programs start by recognizing what causes crime and then *specifically design the intervention to target these factors for change*

(Alexander, Pugh, and Parsons, 1998; Andrews and Bonta, 1998; Cullen and Gendreau, 2000; Henggeler et al., 1998).

Consider, however, the kinds of "theories" about the causes of crime that underlie many correctional interventions. In many cases, simple ignorance prevails; those working in correctional agencies cannot explain what crime-producing factors the program is allegedly targeting for change. Still worse, many programs have literally invented seemingly ludicrous theories of crime that are put forward with a straight face. From our collective experiences, we have listed in Table 23.1 crime theories that either (1) were implicit in programs we observed or (2) were voiced by agency personnel when asked what crime-causing factors their programs were targeting. These "theories" would be amusing except that they are commonplace and, again, potentially lead to correctional quackery. For example, the theory of "offenders (males) need to get in touch with their feminine side" prompted one agency to have offenders dress in female clothes. We cannot resist the temptation to note that you will now know whom to blame if you are mugged by a cross-dresser! But, in the end, this is no laughing matter. This intervention has no chance to be effective, and thus an important chance was forfeited to improve offenders' lives and to protect public safety.

TABLE 23.1 QUESTIONABLE THEORIES OF CRIME WE HAVE ENCOUNTERED IN AGENCY PROGRAMS

- ✓ "Been there, done that" theory.
- ✓ "Offenders lack creativity" theory.
- ✓ "Offenders need to get back to nature" theory.
- ✓ "It worked for me" theory.
- ✓ "Offenders lack discipline" theory.
- ✓ "Offenders lack organizational skills" theory.
- ✓ "Offenders have low self-esteem" theory.
- ✓ "We just want them to be happy" theory.
- ✓ The "treat offenders as babies and dress them in diapers" theory.
- ✓ "Offenders need to have a pet in prison" theory.
- ✓ "Offenders need acupuncture" theory.
- ✓ "Offenders need to have healing lodges" theory.
- ✓ "Offenders need drama therapy" theory.
- ✓ "Offenders need a better diet and haircut" theory.
- ✓ "Offenders (females) need to learn how to put on makeup and dress better" theory.
- ✓ "Offenders (males) need to get in touch with their feminine side" theory.

Second, there is now a growing literature that outlines what does *not* work in offender treatment (see, e.g., Cullen, 2002; Cullen and Gendreau, 2000; Cullen et al., 2002; Cullen et al., 1996; Gendreau, 1996; Gendreau et al., 2000; Lipsey and Wilson, 1998; MacKenzie, 2000). These include boot camps, punishment-oriented programs (e.g., "scared straight" programs), control-oriented programs (e.g., intensive supervision programs), wilderness programs, psychological interventions that are non-directive or insight-oriented (e.g., psychoanalytic), and non-intervention (as suggested by labeling theory). Ineffective programs also target for treatment low-risk offenders and target for change weak predictors of criminal behavior (e.g., self-esteem). Given this knowledge, it would be a form of quackery to continue to use or to freshly implement these types of interventions.

Third, conversely, there is now a growing literature that outlines what *does* work in offender treatment (Cullen, 2002; Cullen and Gendreau, 2000). Most importantly, efforts are being made to develop principles of effective intervention (Andrews, 1995; Andrews and Bonta, 1998; Gendreau, 1996). These principles are listed in Table 23.2. Programs that adhere to these principles have been found to achieve meaningful reductions in recidivism (Andrews, Dowden, and Gendreau, 1999; Andrews, Zinger, Hoge, Bonta, Gendreau, and Cullen, 1990; Cullen, 2002). However, programs that are designed without consulting these principles are almost certain to have little or no impact on offender recidivism and may even risk increasing reoffending. That is, if these principles are ignored, quackery is likely to result. We will return to this issue below.

TABLE 23.2 EIGHT PRINCIPLES OF EFFECTIVE CORRECTIONAL INTERVENTION

1. Organizational Culture
Effective organizations have well-defined goals, ethical principles, and a history of efficiently responding to issues that have an impact on the treatment facilities. Staff cohesion, support for service training, self-evaluation, and use of outside resources also characterize the organization.

2. Program Implementation/Maintenance
Programs are based on empirically-defined needs and are consistent with the organizations values. The program is fiscally responsible and congruent with stakeholders' values. Effective programs also are based on thorough reviews of the literature (i.e., meta-analyses), undergo pilot trials, and maintain the staff's professional credentials.

3. Management/Staff Characteristics
The program director and treatment staff are professionally trained and have previous experience working in offender treatment programs. Staff selection is based on their holding beliefs supportive of rehabilitation and relationship styles and therapeutic skill factors typical of effective therapies.

4. Client Risk/Need Practices
Offender risk is assessed by psychometric instruments of proven predictive validity. The risk instrument consists of a wide range of dynamic risk factors or criminogenic needs (e.g., anti-social attitudes and values). The assessment also takes into account the responsivity of offenders to different styles and modes of service. Changes in risk level over time (e.g., 3 to 6 months) are routinely assessed in order to measure intermediate changes in risk/need levels that may occur as a result of planned interventions.

5. Program Characteristics
The program targets for change a wide variety of criminogenic needs (factors that predict recidivism), using empirically valid behavioral/social learning/cognitive behavioral therapies that are directed to higher-risk offenders. The ratio of rewards to punishers is at least 4:1. Relapse prevention strategies are available once offenders complete the formal treatment phase.

6. Core Correctional Practice
Program therapists engage in the following therapeutic practices: anti-criminal modeling, effective reinforcement and disapproval, problem-solving techniques, structured learning procedures for skill-building, effective use of authority, cognitive self-change, relationship practices, and motivational interviewing.

7. Inter-Agency Communication
The agency aggressively makes referrals and advocates for its offenders in order that they receive high quality services in the community.

8. Evaluation
The agency routinely conducts program audits, consumer satisfaction surveys, process evaluations of changes in criminogenic need, and follow-ups of recidivism rates. The effectiveness of the program is evaluated by comparing the respective recidivism rates of risk-control comparison groups of other treatments or those of a minimal treatment group.

Note: Items adapted from the Correctional Program Assessment Inventory—2000, a 131-item Questionnaire that is widely used in assessing the quality of correctional treatment programs (Gendreau and Andrews, 2001).

FAILURE TO FOLLOW APPROPRIATE ASSESSMENT AND CLASSIFICATION PRACTICES

The steady flow of offenders into correctional agencies not only strains resources but also creates a continuing need to allocate treatment resources efficaciously. This problem is not dissimilar to a hospital that must process a steady flow of patients. In a hospital (or doctor's office), however, it is immediately recognized that the crucial first step to delivering effective treatment is diagnosing or *assessing* the patient's condition and its severity. In the absence of such a diagnosis—which might involve the careful study of symptoms or a battery of tests—the treatment prescribed would have no clear foundation. Medicine would be a lottery in which the ill would hope the doctor assigned the right treatment. In a similar way, effective treatment intervention requires the appropriate assessment of both the risks posed by, and the needs underlying the criminality of, offenders. When such diagnosis is absent and no classification of offenders is possible, offenders in effect enter a treatment lottery in which their access to effective intervention is a chancy proposition.

Strides have been made to develop more effective classification instruments—such as the Level of Supervision Inventory (LSI) (Bonta, 1996), which, among its competitors, has achieved the highest predictive validity with recidivism (Gendreau et al., 1996). The LSI and similar instruments classify offenders by using a combination of "static" factors (such as criminal history) and "dynamic factors" (such as antisocial values, peer associations) shown by previous research to predict recidivism. In this way, it is possible to classify offenders by their level of risk and to discern the types and amount of "criminogenic needs" they possess that should be targeted for change in their correctional treatment.

At present, however, there are three problems with offender assessment and classification by correctional agencies (Gendreau and Goggin, 1997). First, many agencies simply do not assess offenders, with many claiming they do not have the time. Second, when agencies do assess, they assess poorly. Thus, they often use outdated, poorly designed, and/or empirically unvalidated classification instruments. In particular, they tend to rely on instruments that measure exclusively static predictors of recidivism (which cannot, by definition, be changed) and that provide no information on the criminogenic needs that offenders have. If these "needs" are not identified and addressed—such as possessing antisocial values—the prospects for recidivism will be high. For example, a study of 240 (161 adult and 79 juvenile) programs assessed across 30 states found that 64 percent of the programs did not utilize a standardized and objective assessment tool that could distinguish risk/needs levels for offenders (Matthews, Hubbard, and Latessa, 2001; Latessa, 2002).

Third, even when offenders are assessed using appropriate classification instruments, agencies frequently ignore the information. It is not uncommon, for example, for offenders to be assessed and then for everyone to be given the same treatment. In this instance, assessment becomes an organizational routine in which paperwork is compiled but the information is ignored.

Again, these practices increase the likelihood that offenders will experience correctional quackery. In a way, treatment is delivered blindly, with agency personnel equipped with little knowledge about the risks and needs of the offenders under their supervision. In these circumstances, it is impossible to know which offenders should receive which interventions. Any hopes of individualizing interventions effectively also are forfeited, because the appropriate diagnosis either is unavailable or hidden in the agency's unused files.

FAILURE TO USE EFFECTIVE TREATMENT MODELS

Once offenders are assessed, the next step is to select an appropriate treatment model. As we have suggested, the challenge is to consult the empirical literature on "what works," and to do so with an eye toward programs that conform to the principles of effective intervention. At this stage, it is inexcusable either to ignore this research or to implement programs that have been shown to be ineffective. Yet, as we have argued, the neglect of the existing research on effective treatment models is widespread. In the study of 240 programs noted above, it was reported that two-thirds of adult programs and over half of juvenile programs did not use a treatment model that research had shown to be effective (Matthews et al., 2001; Latessa, 2002). Another study—a meta-analysis of 230 program evaluations (which yielded 374 tests or effect sizes)—categorized the extent to which interventions conformed to the principles of effective intervention. In only 13 percent of the tests were the interventions judged to fall into the "most appropriate" category (Andrews et al., 1999). But this failure to employ an appropriate treatment approach does not have to be the case. Why would an agency—in this information age—risk quackery when the possibility of using an evidence-based program exists? Why not select effective treatment models?

Moving in this direction is perhaps mostly a matter of a change of consciousness—that is, an awareness by agency personnel that quackery must be rejected and programs with a track record of demonstrated success embraced. Fortunately, depending on the offender population, there is a growing number of treatment models that might be learned and implemented (Cullen and Applegate, 1997). Some of the more prominent models in this regard are the "Functional Family Therapy" model that promotes family cohesion and affection (Alexander et al., 1998; Gordon, Graves, and Arbuthnot, 1995), the teaching youths to think and react responsibly peer-helping ("Equip") program (Gibbs, Potter, and Goldstein, 1995), the "Prepare Curriculum" program (Goldstein, 1999), "Multisystemic Therapy" (Henggeler et al., 1998), and the prison-based "Rideau Integrated Service Delivery Model" that targets criminal thinking, anger, and substance abuse (see Gendreau, Smith, and Goggin, 2001).

FAILURE TO EVALUATE WHAT WE DO

Quackery has long prevailed in corrections because agencies have traditionally required no systematic evaluation of the effectiveness of their programs (Gendreau, Goggin, and Smith, 2001). Let us admit that many agencies may not have the human or financial capital to conduct ongoing evaluations. Nonetheless, it is not clear that the failure to evaluate has been due to a lack of capacity as much as to a lack of desire. The risk inherent in evaluation, of course, is that practices that are now unquestioned and convenient may be revealed as ineffective. Evaluation, that is, creates accountability and the commitment threat of having to change what is now being done. The cost of change is not to be discounted, but so too is the "high cost of ignoring success" (Van Voorhis, 1987). In the end, a professional must be committed to doing not simply what is in one's self-interest but what is ethical and effective. To scuttle attempts at program evaluation and to persist in using failed interventions is wrong and a key ingredient to continued correctional quackery (more broadly, see Van Voorhis, Cullen, and Applegate, 1995).

Evaluation, moreover, is not an all-or-nothing procedure. Ideally, agencies would conduct experimental studies in which offenders were randomly assigned to a treatment or control group and outcomes, such as recidivism, were measured over a lengthy period of time. But let us assume that, in many settings, conducting this kind of sophisticated evaluation is not feasible. It is possible, however, for virtually all agencies to monitor, to a greater or lesser extent, the *quality* of the programs that they or outside vendors are supplying. Such evaluative monitoring would involve, for example, assessing whether treatment services are being delivered as designed, supervising and giving constructive feedback to treatment staff, and studying whether offenders in the program are making progress on targeted criminogenic factors (e.g., changing antisocial attitudes, manifesting more prosocial behavior). In too many cases, offenders are "dropped off" in intervention programs and then, eight or twelve weeks later, are deemed—without any basis for this conclusion—to have "received treatment." Imagine if medical patients entered and exited hospitals with no one monitoring their treatment or physical recovery. Again, we know what we could call such practices.

CONCLUSION—BECOMING AN EVIDENCE-BASED PROFESSION

In assigning the label "quackery" to much of what is now being done in corrections, we run the risk of seeming, if not being, preachy and pretentious. This is not our intent. If anything, we mean to be provocative—not for the sake of causing a stir, but for the purpose of prompting correctional leaders and professionals to stop using treatments that cannot possibly be effective. If we make readers think seriously about how to avoid selecting, designing, and using failed correctional interventions, our efforts will have been worthwhile.

We would be remiss, however, if we did not confess that academic criminologists share the blame for the continued use of ineffective programs. For much of the past quarter century, most academic criminologists have abandoned correctional practitioners. Although some notable exceptions exist, we have spent much of our time claiming that "nothing works" in offender rehabilitation and have not created partnerships with those in corrections so as to build knowledge on "what works" to change offenders (Cullen and Gendreau, 2001). Frequently, what guidance criminologists have offered correctional agencies has constituted *bad* advice—ideologically inspired, not rooted in the research, and likely to foster quackery. Fortunately, there is a growing movement among criminologists to do our part both in discerning the principles of effective intervention and in deciphering what interventions have empirical support (Cullen and Gendreau, 2001; MacKenzie, 2000; Welsh and Farrington, 2001). Accordingly, the field of corrections has more information available to find out what our "best bets" are when intervening with offenders (Rhine, 1998).

We must also admit that our use of medicine as a comparison to corrections has been overly simplistic. We stand firmly behind the central message conveyed—that what is done in corrections would be grounds for malpractice in medicine—but we have glossed over the challenges that the field of medicine faces in its attempt to provide scientifically-based interventions. First, scientific knowledge is not static but evolving. Medical treatments that appear to work now may, after years of study, prove ineffective or less effective than alternative interventions. Second, even when information is available, it is not clear that it is effectively transmitted or that doctors, who may believe in their personal "clinical experience," will be open to revising their treatment strategies (Hunt, 1997). "The gap between research and knowledge," notes Millenson (1997, p. 4), "has real consequences...when family practitioners in Washington State were queried about treating a simple urinary tract infection in women, eighty-two physicians came up with an extraordinary 137 different strategies." In response to situations like these, there is a renewed evidence-based movement in medicine to improve the quality of medical treatments (Millenson, 1997; Timmermans and Angell, 2001).

Were corrections to reject quackery in favor of an evidence-based approach, it is likely that agencies would face the same difficulties that medicine encounters in trying base treatments on the best scientific knowledge available. Designing and implementing an effective program is more complicated, we realize, than simply visiting a library in search of research on program effectiveness (although this is often an important first step). Information must be available in a form that can be used by agencies. As in medicine, there must be opportunities for training and the provision of manuals that can be consulted in how *specifically* to carry out an intervention. Much attention has to be paid to implementing programs as they are designed. And, in the long run, an effort must be made to support widespread program evaluation and to use the resulting data both to improve individual programs and to expand our knowledge base on effective programs generally.

To move beyond quackery and accomplish these goals, the field of corrections will have to take seriously what it means to be a *profession*. In this context, individual agencies and individuals within agencies would do well to strive to achieve what Gendreau et al. (forthcoming) refer to as the "3 Cs" of effective correctional policies: First, employ *credentialed people*; second, ensure that the *agency is credentialed* in that it is founded on the principles of fairness and the improvement of lives through ethically defensive means; and third, base treatment decisions on *credentialed knowledge* (e.g., research from meta-analyses).

By themselves, however, given individuals and agencies can do only so much to implement effective interventions—although each small step away from quackery and toward an evidence-based practice potentially makes a meaningful difference. The broader issue is whether the *field* of corrections will embrace the principles that all interventions should be based on the best research evidence, that all practitioners must be sufficiently trained so as to develop expertise in how to achieve offender change, and that an ethical corrections cannot tolerate treatments known to be foolish, if not harmful. In the end, correctional quackery is not an inevitable state of affairs—something we are saddled with for the foreseeable future. Rather, although a formidable foe, it is ultimately rooted in our collective decision to tolerate ignorance and failure. Choosing a different future for corrections—making the field a true profession—will be a daunting challenge, but it is a future that lies within our power to achieve.

STUDY QUESTIONS

1. What are the four sources of correctional quackery identified by the authors?
2. What are the eight principles of effective correctional intervention?
3. What are the three Cs identified by the authors?

REFERENCES

Alexander, James, Christie Pugh, and Bruce Parsons. 1998. *Functional Family Therapy: Book Three in the Blueprints and Violence Prevention Series.* Boulder, CO: Center for the Study and Prevention of Violence, University of Colorado.

Andrews, D. A. 1995. "The Psychology of Criminal Conduct and Effective Treatment." Pp. 35–62 in James McGuire (ed.). *What Works: Reducing Reoffending.* West Sussex, UK: John Wiley.

Andrews, D. A., and James Bonta. 1998. *Psychology of Criminal Conduct,* 2nd ed. Cincinnati: Anderson.

Andrews, D. A., Craig Dowden, and Paul Gendreau. 1999. "Clinically Relevant and Psychologically Informed Approaches to Reduced Re-Offending: A Meta-Analytic Study of Human Service, Risk, Need, Responsivity, and Other Concerns in Justice Contexts." Unpublished manuscript, Carleton University.

Andrews, D. A., Ivan Zinger, R. D. Hoge, James Bonta, Paul Gendreau, and Francis T. Cullen. 1990. "Does Correctional Treatment Work? A Clinically Relevant and Psychologically Informed Meta-Analysis." *Criminology* 28:369–404.

Bonta, James. 1996. "Risk-Needs Assessment and Treatment." Pp. 18–32 in Alan T. Harland (ed.). *Choosing Correctional Options That Work: Defining the Demand and Evaluating the Supply.* Thousand Oaks, CA: Sage.

Cullen, Francis T. 2002. "Rehabilitation and Treatment Programs." Pp. 253–289 in James Q. Wilson and Joan Petersilia (eds.), *Crime: Public Policies for Crime Control.* Oakland, CA: ICS Press.

Cullen, Francis T. and Brandon K. Applegate, eds. 1997. *Offender Rehabilitation: Effective Correctional Intervention.* Aldershot, UK: Ashgate/Dartmouth.

Cullen, Francis T. and Paul Gendreau. 2000. "Assessing Correctional Rehabilitation: Policy, Practice, and Prospects." Pp. 109–175 in Julie Horney (ed.). *Criminal Justice 2000: Volume 3—Policies, Processes, and Decisions of the Criminal Justice System.* Washington, DC: U.S. Department of Justice, National Institute of Justice.

Cullen, Francis T. and Paul Gendreau. 2001. "From Nothing Works to What Works: Changing Professional Ideology in the 21st Century." *The Prison Journal* 81:313–338.

Cullen, Francis T., Travis C. Pratt, Sharon Levrant Miceli, and Melissa M. Moon. 2002. "Dangerous Liaison? Rational Choice Theory as the Basis for Correctional Intervention." Pp. 279–296 in Alex R. Piquero and Stephen G. Tibbetts (eds.), *Rational*

Choice and Criminal Behavior: Recent Research and Future Challenges. New York: Routledge.

Cullen, Francis T., John Paul Wright, and Brandon K. Applegate. 1996. "Control in the Community: The Limits of Reform?" Pp. 69–116 in Alan T. Harland (ed.), *Choosing Correctional Interventions That Work: Defining the Demand and Evaluating the Supply*. Thousand Oaks, CA: Sage.

Cullen, John B. 1978. *The Structure of Professionalism*. Princeton, NJ: Petrocelli Books.

Gendreau, Paul. 1996. "The Principles of Effective Intervention with Offenders." Pp. 117–130 in Alan T. Harland (ed.). *Choosing Correctional Options That Work: Defining the Demand and Evaluating the Supply*. Newbury Park, CA: Sage.

Gendreau, Paul. 2000. "1998 Margaret Mead Award Address: Rational Policies for Reforming Offenders." Pp. 329–338 in Maeve McMahon (ed.), *Assessment to Assistance: Programs for Women in Community Corrections*. Lanham, MD: American Correctional Association.

Gendreau, Paul and D. A. Andrews. 2001. *Correctional Program Assessment Inventory—2000*. Saint John, Canada: Authors.

Gendreau, Paul and Claire Goggin. 1997. "Correctional Treatment: Accomplishments and Realities." Pp. 271–279 in Patricia Van Voorhis, Michael Braswell, and David Lester (eds.), *Correctional Counseling and Rehabilitation*, 3rd edition. Cincinnati: Anderson.

Gendreau, Paul, Claire Goggin, Francis T. Cullen, and D. A. Andrews. 2000. "The Effects of Community Sanctions and Incarceration on Recidivism." *Forum on Corrections Research* 12 (May): 10–13.

Gendreau, Paul, Claire Goggin, Francis T. Cullen, and Mario Paparozzi. 2002. "The Common Sense Revolution in Correctional Policy." In James McGuire (ed.), *Offender Rehabilitation and Treatment: Effective Programs and Policies to Reduce Re-Offending*. Chichester, UK: John Wiley and Sons.

Gendreau, Paul, Claire Goggin, and Paula Smith. 2001. "Implementing Correctional Interventions in the 'Real' World." Pp. 247–268 in Gary A. Bernfeld, David P. Farrington, and Alan W. Leschied (eds.). *Inside the "Black Box" in Corrections*. Chichester, UK: John Wiley and Sons.

Gendreau, Paul, Tracy Little, and Claire Goggin. 1996. "A Meta-Analysis of the Predictors of Adult Offender Recidivism: What Works?" *Criminology* 34:575–607.

Gendreau, Paul, Paula Smith, and Claire Goggin. 2001. "Treatment Programs in Corrections." Pp. 238–263 in John Winterdyk (ed.), *Corrections in Canada: Social Reaction to Crime*. Toronto, Canada: Prentice-Hall.

Gibbs, John C., Granville Bud Potter, and Arnold P. Goldstein. 1995. *The EQUIP Program: Teaching Youths to Think and Act Responsibly Through a Peer-Helping Approach*. Champaign, IL: Research Press.

Goldstein, Arnold P. 1999. *The Prepare Curriculum: Teaching Prosocial Competencies*. Rev. ed. Champaign, IL: Research Press.

Gordon, Donald A., Karen Graves, and Jack Arbuthnot. 1995. "The Effect of Functional Family Therapy for Delinquents on Adult Criminal Behavior." *Criminal Justice and Behavior* 22:60–73.

Henggeler, Scott W., with the assistance of Sharon R. Mihalic, Lee Rone, Christopher Thomas, and Jane Timmons-Mitchell. 1998. *Multisystemic Therapy: Book Six in the Blueprints in Violence Prevention Series*. Boulder, CO: Center for the Study and Prevention of Violence, University of Colorado.

Hunt, Morton. 1997. *How Science Takes Stock: The Story of Meta-Analysis*. New York: Russell Sage Foundation.

Latessa, Edward J. 2002. "Using Assessment to Improve Correctional Programming: An Update." Unpublished paper, University of Cincinnati.

Lipsey, Mark W. and David B. Wilson. 1998. "Effective Intervention for Serious Juvenile Offenders." Pp. 313–345 in Rolf Loeber and David P. Farrington (eds.), *Serious and Violent*

Juvenile Offenders: Risk Factors and Successful Intervention. Thousand Oaks, CA: Sage.

MacKenzie, Doris Layton. 2000. "Evidence-Based Corrections: Identifying What Works." *Crime and Delinquency* 46:457–471.

MacKenzie, Doris Layton, David B. Wilson, and Suzanne B. Kider. 2001. "The Effects of Correctional Boot Camps on Offending." *Annals of the American Academy of Political and Social Science* 578 (November): 126–143.

Matthews, Betsy, Dana Jones Hubbard, and Edward J. Latessa. 2001. "Making the Next Step: Using Assessment to Improve Correctional Programming." *Prison Journal* 81:454–472.

Millenson, Michael L. 1997. *Demanding Medical Excellence: Doctors and Accountability in the Information Age*. Chicago: University of Chicago Press.

Rhine, Edward E. (ed.). 1998. *Best Practices: Excellence in Corrections*. Lanham, MD: American Correctional Association.

Starr, Paul. 1982. *The Social Transformation of American Medicine: The Rise of a Sovereign Profession and the Making of a Vast Industry*. New York: Basic Books.

Timmermans, Stefan and Alison Angell. 2001. "Evidence-Based Medicine, Clinical Uncertainty, and Learning to Doctor." *Journal of Health and Social Behavior* 42:342–359.

Van Voorhis, Patricia. 1987. "Correctional Effectiveness: The High Cost of Ignoring Success." *Federal Probation* 51 (March): 59–62.

Van Voorhis, Patricia, Francis T. Cullen, and Brandon K. Applegate. 1995. "Evaluating Interventions with Violent Offenders: A Guide for Practitioners and Policymakers." *Federal Probation* 59 (June): 17–28.

Welsh, Brandon C. and David P. Farrington. 2001. "Toward an Evidence-Based Approach to Preventing Crime." *Annals of the American Academy of Political and Social Science* 578 (November): 158–173.

PART

VI

REENTRY INTO THE COMMUNITY

Despite one's opinions about incarceration and punishment, the fact remains that the vast majority of offenders who are incarcerated will be released from prison. Some will complete all of their time and "max" out, while many others will be receiving some conditional release, traditionally called parole. Given the large number of offenders incarcerated in the United States, the number reentering society is staggering. Estimates are that over 700,000 offenders per year will exit prison for the foreseeable future.

Parole from prison, like the prison itself, is primarily an American innovation. It emerged from a philosophical revolution and a resulting tradition of penal reform established in the late eighteenth century in the newly formed United States. As with many other new ideas that emerged in early America, parole had its roots in the practices of English and European penal systems. Alexander Maconochie is usually given credit as being the father of parole. In 1840, Captain Maconochie was put in charge of the English penal colony in New South Wales at Norfolk Island, about 1,000 miles off the coast of Australia. To this colony were sent the criminals who were twice condemned. They had been shipped from England to Australia and then from Australia to Norfolk. Conditions were allegedly horrible, and it was under these conditions that Maconochie devised parole. Although the roots of parole spring from Australia, it was the prison reform movement in the United States that embraced the concept and developed and expanded its use.

Perhaps no aspect of the correctional system came under more attack than parole. Liberals questioned the secretiveness of the process and the arbitrariness of the release decision. Conservatives questioned both the wisdom of releasing offenders after only a portion of their sentence had been served and the effectiveness of parole supervision in protecting the public. Despite these attacks, parole has survived in many states and remains a vehicle for release and supervision of offenders in the community.

The failure of prisons to rehabilitate offenders has often been attributed to a lack of support and transitional care and services. One of the ways in which transition from prison to the community is made more effective is through community correctional facilities, often called halfway houses. Halfway houses have a long history in the United States and are considered by many to be essential to the reintegration of offenders into the community. Substance abuse treatment, housing, employment training, counseling, and family services are some of the programs that community correctional programs such as halfway houses provide. Giving support and assistance to those in need is only one role these programs play. Protecting the community and cost effectiveness are also critical aspects that need to be factored in when we consider the effectiveness of correctional programs such as halfway houses.

24

HOW TO PREVENT PRISONER REENTRY PROGRAMS FROM FAILING

INSIGHTS FROM EVIDENCE-BASED CORRECTIONS

SHELLEY JOHNSON LISTWAN
FRANCIS T. CULLEN
EDWARD J. LATESSA

The ever-pressing need to assist inmates reentering society makes it even more important that reentry programs follow the research on effective practices. Adhering to the principles of effective intervention helps ensure that the programs that are developed for inmates during reentry into society will result in the best results possible. In this discussion of the reentry process the authors discuss how to develop and implement reentry programs and warn us about the consequences of ignoring scientific research.

At one point in our history, nobody would have imagined releasing a prison inmate into society with little supervision or support. As Simon (1993) shows, well into the 1950s, such a practice would have been unthinkable. From the implementation of parole as a widespread correctional policy, a key component of release from prison was securing employment. It was assumed that offenders would be "disciplined"—kept under control—by the supervision and structured life inherent in holding a steady job. If no job could be found, then parole was seldom an option.

This model of "industrial parole," however, became increasingly suspect due to three interrelated developments. First, as the United States moved into a post-industrial economy, the availability of steady employment for those at society's bottom reaches—the stratum from which inmates are disproportionately drawn—gradually deteriorated. In Simon's view (1993, p. 65), there was a "decoupling of the labor market for low-skilled labor from the economy as a whole." Second, the growth of minority populations in prisons—again, a group most hard-hit by economic distress—further undermined the notion that all offenders could secure a job upon return to society. Third, the seven-fold overall rise in state and federal prison populations in the three decades after 1970 created a surplus population of tens of thousands of offenders that prisons could no longer afford to keep locked up, but who had dim prospects for employment.

In "post-industrial parole," the control or discipline over offenders thus shifted from a meaningful reintegration into the community to "supervision" by parole officers. This supervision has varied from

Excerpts from "How to Prevent Prisoner Reentry Programs from Failing: Insights from Evidence-Based Corrections" (2006), by Shelley Johnson Listwan, Francis T. Cullen, and Edward J. Latessa, *Federal Probation*, 70(3): 19–25.

a clinical model emphasizing rehabilitation to a policing model emphasizing deterrence. But in either case, parole had largely forfeited its former role of working with offenders to allow them to assume meaningful roles in the community upon their reentry (Simon, 1993).

Recently, however, there has been a growing recognition that it is irresponsible to simply release tens of thousands of inmates from prison and to place them into parole officer caseloads that are too high to allow for meaningful intervention and reentry. In a way, this has been corrections' "dirty little secret"—a practice that simply is indefensible from a public policy standpoint. Beyond lack of resources, there is no way to justify the unsystematic dumping of offenders back into society, since it jeopardizes both the successful reintegration of offenders and the protection of public safety. Fortunately, reacting to this public policy debacle is a movement to identify strategies to guide prisoner reentry.

In this article, we attempt to add our voice to this conversation. Although many persuasive ideas are being put forward and promising programs implemented, we are concerned that insufficient attention is being given to an important development in corrections: the increasing knowledge about "what works" to change offender conduct, knowledge that is based on the "principles of effective correctional intervention" (Cullen & Gendreau, 2000). Informed by this perspective, we attempt to outline how this knowledge base can help inform current attempts to design and implement efficacious reentry programs. We also caution that a failure to heed evidence-based correctional practice is likely to result in reentry programs that do not reach their full potential and, perhaps, simply do not work (MacKenzie, 2000; Latessa, Cullen, & Gendreau, 2002).

THE REENTRY CRISIS

There is little dispute that inmate reentry is a potentially serious social problem that can no longer escape attention. The sheer number of people involved is one factor precipitating a crisis in this area. At mid-year 2004, there were an estimated 2.1 million adults serving time in prison (Harrison & Beck, 2005). Of these, it is estimated that approximately 650,000 inmates are released back to the community each year (Travis, Solomon, & Wahl, 2001). While the number of adults on parole grew in 2003 by approximately 3 percent, 17 states saw increases of anywhere from 25 percent to 50 percent per year (Glaze & Palla, 2004).

Arguably, inmates reentering society are an especially unstable group. In a 15-state study, two-thirds of prisoners released in 1994 were arrested during a three-year follow-up period (Hughes, Wilson, & Beck, 2001; Langan & Levin, 2002). The process of reentry appears to have become more difficult for inmates, with just under half of parolees completing their parole supervision successfully, a 25 percent decrease from just 20 years ago (Glaze, 2002).

This may in part be due to many of the "get tough" strategies of the 1980s and 1990s. Increases in mandatory sentences, truth-in-sentencing policies, and the elimination of parole boards force many inmates to "expire" (or serve their full sentence in the institution) without any supervision or support in the community. As noted by Travis and Lawrence (2002), "in 1976, 65% of prison releases were discretionary, decided by the parole board. By 1999, the share of prison releases that were made by parole boards dropped to 24%" (p. 4). Without discretionary sentences, many inmates have little incentive for participating in rehabilitative services, such as educational opportunities, while in the institutions (Haney, 2002). The lack of incentive, coupled with the penal harm movement (see Clear, 1994), results in fewer inmates leaving prison fully equipped to handle the difficulties that will face them upon release.

The federal government appears to have recognized the crisis surrounding reentry through several important initiatives (e.g., The Serious and Violent Offender Reentry Initiative and the Federal Second

Chance Act). The current resources, however, seem minimal compared to the staggering costs to manage and deal with the large influx of prisoners reentering the community each year. For some states, such as Nevada, the money is used simply to establish services for a small segment of the serious and violent population returning to the community. For other states, such as Ohio, the money is used as "gap" dollars to fill in areas where services already exist. In both circumstances, as in many states across the country, the money only affects a small portion of the overall population reentering the community.

In the context of an era of "get tough" policies, the reentry movement represents an important effort to provide social services to offenders as they reintegrate into the community. The question that remains is whether the reentry programs being proposed and implemented are likely to be effective and with whom. The issue of effectiveness is complicated because the reentry process involves both the assumption of productive social roles and refraint from criminal behavior. The question we address is whether the reentry programs being proposed are likely to be successful. Specifically, are these programs and services properly designed to address the issues of these high-risk and high-need offenders?

THE PRINCIPLES OF EFFECTIVE CORRECTIONAL INTERVENTION

Current research supports the notion that rehabilitation can work for offenders (e.g., see Cullen & Gendreau, 2000). Research on the "principles of effective intervention" (see Gendreau, 1996) provides a framework for effective programming. In fact, research on rehabilitation programs in general finds that the ability to effectively change offenders' behavior varies based on whether certain principles are followed (Andrews, Zinger, Hoge, Gendreau, & Cullen, 1990; Lipsey, 1992; Izzo & Ross, 1990; Gendreau & Ross, 1987; Van Voorhis, 1997). Effective programs typically share certain features such as using behavioral and cognitive approaches, occurring in the offenders' natural environment, being multi-modal and intensive enough to be effective, encompassing rewards for pro-social behavior, targeting high-risk and high-criminogenic need individuals, and matching the learning styles and abilities of the offender (Allen, MacKenzie, & Hickman, 2001; Andrews & Bonta, 2003; Cullen & Gendreau, 2000; Gendreau, 1996; Lipsey, 1992; Lipsey & Wilson, 1998; Wilson, Bouffard, & MacKenzie, 2005).

In this regard, our premise is that to reach their full potential, reentry programs must incorporate the principles of effective correctional intervention. Although these principles are now widely discussed, they apparently have not achieved the status of common knowledge or accepted wisdom. As a result, although other sources can be consulted (e.g., Andrews & Bonta, 2003; Cullen & Gendreau, 2000; Gendreau, 1996), we will briefly discuss this perspective's three core principles: risk, needs, and responsivity.

The risk principle refers to identifying personal attributes or circumstances predictive of future behavior (Andrews, Bonta, & Hoge, 1990). What is often ignored in regard to this principle is the importance of risk to service delivery. Specifically, it indicates that our most intensive correctional treatment services should be geared towards our highest risk population (Andrews & Bonta, 2003; Andrews et al., 2002; Bonta, 2002; Gendreau, 1996; Lowenkamp & Latessa, 2005).

The second principle of effective classification refers to targeting the criminogenic needs that are highly correlated with criminal behavior. The most promising targets related directly to the most significant areas of risk: changing antisocial attitudes, feelings and values, attending to skill deficiencies in the area of poor problem-solving skills, self-management and self-efficacy, and impulsivity, poor self-control, and irresponsibility (Andrews & Bonta, 2003; Gendreau, 1996; Listwan, Van Voorhis, & Ritchey, in press; Van Voorhis, 1997). Programs should ensure that the vast majority of their interventions are targeting these factors.

The third principle of effective classification is responsivity. The responsivity principle refers to delivering an intervention that is appropriate and matches the abilities and styles of the client. A number of studies have found that the characteristics of the client may have an impact or be a barrier to treatment (see, Andrews & Bonta, 1998). Overall, the effectiveness of correctional interventions is dependent upon whether the services are varied based on risk, need, and responsivity factors of the individual.

EFFECTIVE CORRECTIONAL REENTRY

The development of services for those reentering society varies widely across the nation. While some jurisdictions or even states have spent considerable time and money developing services for parolees as they are released back into their communities, others are forced to rely on a more fragmented approach to service delivery. As Petersilia (2003) notes, for some jurisdictions reentry involves specific programs and services and for others it simply describes the process of parole. We still know relatively little about the overall effectiveness of parole, and even less about the effectiveness of the "newer" reentry programs.

In an ideal model, reentry programs should include three or more phases designed to transition the inmate into the community (Taxman, Young, & Byrne, 2003). The first phase would begin in the institution with service delivery congruent with the inmate's needs. The second phase would begin as the inmate is released from the institution. The inmate's risks and needs may change significantly as he or she enters the community context. Ideally, the individual would continue in treatment services and case plans would be updated as needed. The final phase is an aftercare or relapse prevention phase where clients would receive ongoing support and services to address their needs (Taxman et al. 2003). While this model may provide the overall structure necessary to implement an effective reentry program, the process and services offered by these programs are key to their success.

We will focus our attention on several specific areas: the assessment process, the targets for change, and relapse prevention or aftercare. The first area of concern is the assessment process, which clearly needs to begin while the inmate is still in prison. Two issues related to assessment are important for reentry programs: the process of selection and the identification of risk, need, and responsivity characteristics. Selection criteria should be developed with a clinical or legal rationale. Selection criteria allow organizations to screen out individuals who do not need intensive services as well as minimizing the risk of mixing populations (e.g., high risk/low risk, violent/non-violent, etc.). Simply relying on one factor, such as original charge, will produce an eclectic group of offenders, thereby making service delivery difficult if not ineffective.

The assessment results should guide service delivery (type and duration) and include dosage and matching as well as the measurement of change. The assessment and identification of criminogenic factors and client characteristics (including both risk/need and responsivity) is important for a variety of reasons. First, they identify factors related to the individual's specific need for use in his or her treatment plan. Those services should target key criminogenic factors or needs such as attitudes and beliefs, criminal associates, family dysfunction, addictions, and education and employment (Andrews & Bonta, 2003; Gendreau, Little & Goggin, 1996). Focused services on criminogenic needs are crucial in reducing future criminal behavior.

Assessment results also allow for service and treatment providers to screen out offenders who cannot succeed in a specific intervention. Responsivity factors such as motivation, personality, and intelligence can impact how individuals respond or their amenability to treatment (Andrews & Bonta,

2003; Listwan, Sperber, Spruance, & Van Voorhis, 2004; Van Voorhis, Cullen, & Applegate, 1995; Van Voorhis, Spruance, Ritchie, Listwan, Seabrook, & Pealer, 2002). For example, assessments can identify and screen out low-functioning offenders from services that require a normal range of cognitive functioning or those who are highly anxious from programs or staff that utilize confrontational strategies (Andrews et al., 1990; Palmer, 1974; Warren, 1983).

Programs should also reassess offenders to help determine whether a program had an impact on an offender's risk of future criminal behavior. The reassessment process should begin once the offender returns to the community and again while the offender is under supervision. The results should then ultimately guide any changes in the offender's treatment plan. Reassessment can also inform key stakeholders and providers as to whether the program or services had an impact on the offender's overall risk.

The difficulty experienced by any correctional program is how to proceed with the assessment results; specifically, which factors should be given priority. The principles provide an important blueprint for reentry programs. The core treatment services should be sufficiently intensive and structured around the individual needs of the client. The key targets mentioned above should be given priority. However, many correctional programs are forced to devote resources to crisis management. The immediate needs such as housing, medical, and transportation supersede more important core treatment needs that are likely to produce long-term change. In this next section we will discuss the core targets often faced by parolees and their importance for the reentry movement.

Securing legitimate employment can provide a buffer to crime and delinquency (Sampson & Laub, 1993; Solomon, Johnson, Travis, & McBride, 2004) and assist inmates as they are released. reentry programs often focus resources on employment, given its importance in allowing the offender to be a productive member of the community. The prison industries that exist in many prisons nationwide dovetail nicely with this goal. The prison may establish programs with local businesses that train inmates in the institution and provide them with employment once released.

Securing reasonable and sustainable employment is challenging for parolees reentering the community and programs may experience a number of barriers to fulfilling this particular need. For example, even when a prison has a particular job-training program available, the interest by inmates is often greater than the number of openings available. Those with felony records are less likely to find employment given their perceived risk and potential public fear. Finally, fewer than half of inmates report having been employed fulltime prior to their incarceration (Solomon et al., 2004), making them less marketable on their return to the community.

For many paroling offenders, education is an important first step in their reintegration process. Not surprisingly, research finds that many inmates are lacking basic educational skills. In fact, in 1997 only 40 percent of adult inmates had finished their high school education (Harlow, 2003). And while most states do offer educational services to their inmates, only half of adult inmates reported that they had participated in these services. Moreover, only 11 percent of inmates reported that they have participated in college-level or post-secondary vocational classes (Harlow, 2003).

Employment and education are clear needs exhibited by a significant portion of the reentering population. However, the focus on education and employment should not displace a sustained and informed effort to reduce recidivism. Studies find that programs that target education and employment are not as effective as those utilizing proven treatment strategies, namely those based on cognitive behavioral treatment models (Wilson, Bouffard, & MacKenzie, 2005; Wilson, Gallagher, & MacKenzie, 2000). Simply educating people without helping them understand the consequences of behavior and develop pro-social alternatives is likely to fall short.

An offender returning home to his or her family presents special considerations for reentry programs. Families represent an important support system for offenders both while incarcerated and in the community. Their absence can have a significant effect on the offender's family structure and the long-term risk of future criminal behavior by the offender's child, a particularly important consideration given that more than 1.5 million children have a parent in state or federal prison (Mumola, 1999). Youth with an incarcerated parent may feel they are more responsible for adult roles; they may feel stigmatized, or may have an increased risk of addiction or delinquency. Marital relationships are often strained and are more likely to end in divorce for a variety of reasons, including financial hardships, lack of emotional support, or simply the stress of having an absent spouse (Travis et al., 2003).

The increased risk of family breakdown for inmates is particularly important in light of the research on social support. Social support can help reduce strain and subsequent negative emotions, as well as produce higher levels of self-control and predictability (Cullen, Wright, & Chamlin, 1999; Colvin Cullen, & Vander Ven, 2002). Research has suggested that offenders who discontinue crime are often socially bonded to family, maintaining contact while within the institution (Hairston, 1998). Successful reunification of offenders with their families requires clear attention to their issues and concerns. In many circumstances families are not well equipped to handle the parolee and in some circumstances are considered high risk for criminal behavior themselves. The problem is further compounded when children are placed in out-of-home care due to the parent's criminal activity and child welfare agencies see the parent as a continued risk to the child (Maluccio & Ainsworth, 2003).

While many agencies recognize the importance of providing family-based therapy, most programs struggle with reunifying families. The families face immense structural problems such as poverty and inadequate living situations, or emotional and personal barriers to welcoming the person back into the family (Henggeler & Borduin, 1990; Hoffman, 1981; Klein, Alexander & Parsons, 1977). However, research clearly shows that family-based interventions can strengthen the family support network and provide the appropriate care needed by the offender. Moreover, family-based therapies that rely on behavioral and social learning models have been shown in the literature to be highly effective (Henggeler & Borduin, 1990; Gordon, Arbuthnot, Gustafsori, & McGreen, 1988; Patterson, Chamberlain, & Reid, 1982).

Community collaboration is another key component for many reentry programs. First, reentry involves the participation and collaboration of a host of community-based social service agencies. These agencies are often charged with providing services for inmates as they transition to the community. Services may include the core components discussed above, such as education, employment, housing, counseling and mental health services. But other key services exist as well, including medical, dental, clothing, and transportation services. These services require a great deal of planning for reentry personnel and can be quite costly.

Second, on a structural level, reentry for many offenders means reentering neighborhoods or reuniting with peers that may have originally contributed to their delinquency. On one hand, many reentry programs have been developed with the recognition that a collaborative effort of a number of agencies working to provide a variety of services to offenders is imperative to successful programming. However, the need to recognize how the structural and community factors contribute to delinquency is also an important factor.

Services need to be based on empirically validated treatment strategies if long-term change is expected. In this vein, the importance of using cognitive behavioral programs cannot be overstated. Numerous studies have demonstrated that cognitive behavioral programs reduce recidivism (Andrews et al., 1990; Antonowicz & Ross, 1994; Garrett, 1985; Izzo & Ross, 1990; Lipsey, 1992; Losel, 1995). Cognitive theory suggests that offenders possess limited problem-solving skills (Ross & Fabiano, 1985), have antisocial values and attitudes (Jennings, Kilkenny, & Kohlberg, 1983), and display thinking errors (Yochelson & Samenow, 1976). Cognitive behavioral therapies improve problem-solving skills and target offenders' thinking and problem-solving through a system of reinforcement, pro-social modeling, and role-playing (Michenbaum, 1977; Ross & Fabiano, 1985; Wilson, Bouffard, & MacKenzie, 2005).

This research is particularly important to the reentry movement. As suggested by Haney (2002), many inmates return home from prison suffering from psychological distress and maladaptive coping strategies. The offenders may have deeply entrenched antisocial attitudes and values. Many will require intensive treatment to change destructive and cyclical patterns of thinking.

Finally, another key initiative for reentry programming is intensive aftercare and relapse prevention services. Research on effective aftercare models indicates that aftercare should begin during the active treatment phase and should include frequent contacts and home visits (Altschuler & Armstrong, 1994). In addition, the offender's risk and needs should be reassessed to determine whether the appropriate services have been provided. The intensity and duration of aftercare should not be fixed, but depend on the risk and needs of the offenders. As part of this continuum of care, relapse prevention strategies offer tremendous promise. These strategies include teaching participants ways to anticipate and cope with high-risk situations. Programs that are based on cognitive or social learning strategies view relapse as a temporary setback that can be overcome through learning alternative responses (Dowden, Antonowicz, & Andrews, 2000).

For reentry programs, the aftercare phase represents an important point in the offender's relapse prevention. Inmates may begin their reentry process highly optimistic and with good intentions. With appropriate service delivery they may find reentry manageable and be quite successful in the early days and months. However, as the daily stressors and frustrations of fully assimilating back into neighborhoods, families, and workplaces are realized, the client may find it increasingly difficult to maintain a pro-social lifestyle. A well-designed reentry program should not only assist offenders in skill development but also see the aftercare phase as a time when clients are practicing newly acquired skills and behaviors. Without a formal and structured program in place that builds upon earlier treatment protocols, offenders may relapse when the services and social support dwindle.

CONCLUSION

The myriad of needs of the reentry population offer important targets for change. Careful attention to the criminogenic needs of offenders is key to effective correctional programming. Ultimately programs need to follow the empirical research on effective interventions. Programs that fail to develop clear goals and objectives, use effective classification systems, rely on appropriate theoretically relevant models, and plan for relapse will inevitably falter.

Parole-based programs can be measured for effectiveness in a number of ways. These may include long-term objectives such as reducing prison populations and arrest rates. However, they can include key intermediate objectives such as reducing numbers of substance abusers or increasing the number of participants who successfully complete treatment, obtain a GED or become gainfully employed. Other objectives may look at social indicators such as number of drug-free babies or the reunification of families and children. Finally, we can see increasing community collaboration or cost effectiveness as a measure of success. While it is true that successful reentry can be measured in more ways than just avoiding recidivism, such avoidance must be a core component given the nature of the population. The fear is that reentry programs that target a clearly difficult population (e.g., serious and violent offenders) will be judged negatively because of high recidivism rates and ultimately accused of compromising public safety. The programs and services will then be vulnerable to attack because they will appear not to work. Key stakeholders are ultimately concerned with two main issues: cost and impact. Programs that are not able to translate their "success" into these categories may face an uncertain future.

Importantly, if we ignore scientific evidence in the development and continued implementation of these programs, we are re-opening the door to punitive programs. The fear is that there will be a call for the discontinuation of these programs based on the notion that they "did not work" when in feet they were never effectively designed and implemented. Without careful planning and care, the popularity of this "new" reentry movement will likely falter and fall victim to another swing in the pendulum towards more punitive and retributive policies.

STUDY QUESTIONS

1. How has sentencing policy affected the reentry issue?
2. What changes have occurred in parole, and how does this affect prisoner reentry?
3. What is the crisis in reentry that the authors describe?
4. What are the principles of effective intervention, and why are they so important to reentry?
5. What are some of the solutions that are offered by the authors?

REFERENCES

Agnew, R. (1992). Foundation for a general strain theory of crime and delinquency. *Criminology*, 30, 47–87.

Allen, L. C., MacKenzie, D. L., & Hickman, L. (2001). The effectiveness of cognitive behavioral treatment for adult offenders: A methodological quality-based review. *International Journal of Offender Therapy and Comparative Criminology*, 45(4), 498–514.

Andrews, D. A., & Bonta, J. (2003). *The psychology of criminal conduct*. Cincinnati: Anderson.

Andrews, D. A., Zinger I., Bonta, J., Hoge, R. D., Gendreau, P., & Cullen, F. T. (1990). Does correctional treatment work? A psychologically informed meta-analysis. *Criminology*, 28, 369–404.

Antonowicz, D. H. & Ross, R. R. (1994). Essential components of successful rehabilitation programs for offenders. *International Journal of Offender and Comparative Criminology*, 38(2), 97–104.

Altschuler, D. M. & Armstrong, T. L. (1994). *Intensive Aftercare for High Risk Juveniles: A Community Care Model*. Washington D.C.: Office of Juvenile Justice and Delinquency Prevention.

Bauer, L. (2002). *Justice Expenditure and Employment in the United States*. U.S. Department of Justice. Bureau of Justice Statistics. Washington, D.C.

Bonta, J. (2002). Offender risk assessment: guidelines for use. *Criminal Justice and Behavior*, 29(4), 355–79.

Briere, J. & C. E. Jordan (2004). Violence against women: outcome complexity and implications for assessment and treatment. *Journal of Interpersonal Violence*, 19, 1252–1276.

Campbell, J. (2002). Health consequences of intimate partner violence. *The Lancet*, 359, 1331–1336.

Clear, T. (1994). *Harm in American Penology: Offenders, Victims, and Their Communities*. Albany, NY: State University of New York Press.

Cohen, S. & Wills, T. A. (1985). Stress, social support, and the buffering hypothesis. *Psychological Bulletin*, 98, 310–357.

Colvin, M. (2002). *Crime and Coercion: An Integrated Theory of Chronic Criminality*. New York: St. Martin's Press.

Colvin, M., Cullen, F. T., & Vander Ven, T. (2002). Coercion, social support, and crime: An emerging theoretical consensus. *Criminology*, 40, 19–42.

Cullen, F. T. (1994). Social support as an organizing concept for criminology: Presidential address to the academy of criminal justice sciences. *Justice Quarterly*, 11, 527–559.

Cullen, F. T., & Gendreau, P. (2000). Assessing correctional rehabilitation: Policy, practice, and prospects. In J. Homey (Ed.), *Criminal justice 2000: Vol. 3—Policies, processes, and decisions of the criminal justice system* (pp. 109–175). Washington, DC: U.S. Department of Justice, National Institute of Justice.

Cullen, F. T., Wright, J. P., & Chamlin, M. B. (1999). Social support and social reform: A progressive crime control agenda. *Crime & Delinquency*, 2, 188–207.

Dowden, C., Antonowicz, D., & Andrews, D. (1999). The effectiveness of relapse prevention with offenders: A meta analysis. *International Journal of Offender Therapy and Comparative Criminology*, 47, 516–528.

Garrett, C. (1985) "Effects of residential treatment on adjudicated delinquents: A meta-analysis." *Journal of Research in Crime and Delinquency*, 22(4), 287–308.

Gavranidou, M. & Rosner, R. (2003). The weaker sex? Gender and post-traumatic stress disorder. *Depression and Anxiety*, 17, 130–139.

Gendreau, P. (1996). The principles of effective intervention with offenders. *In Choosing Correctional Options That Work*, edited by A. Harland. Thousand Oaks, CA: Sage Publications, Inc., pp. 117–130.

Gendreau, P., Little, T., & Goggin, C. (1996). A meta-analysis of the predictors of adult offender recidivism: What works! *Criminology*, 34, 575–607.

Gendreau, P., & Ross, R. R. (1987). Revivification of rehabilitation: Evidence from the 1980's. *Justice Quarterly*, 4(3), 349–407.

Glaze, L. E. (2002). *Probation and Parole in the United States, 2002*. U.S. Department of Justice. Bureau of Justice Statistics. Washington, D.C. NCJ 205336.

Glaze, L. & Palla, S. (2004). *Probation and Parole in the United States, 2003*. Bureau of Justice Statistics Bulletin. Washington, DC: U.S. Department of Justice, Office of Justice Programs.

Gordon, D. A., Arbuthnot, J., Gustafson, K., & McGreen, P. (1988). Home-based behavioral-systems family therapy with disadvantaged juvenile delinquents. *American Journal of Family Therapy*, 16, 243–255.

Grove, W. & Meehl, P. (1996). Comparative efficacy of informal (subjective, impressionistic) and formal (mechanical, algorithmic) prediction procedures: The clinical statistical controversy. *Psychology, Public Policy, and Law*, 2(2), 293–323.

Haney, C. (2002). The Psychological Impact of Incarceration: Implications for Post Prison Adjustment. Paper prepared for the Urban Institute's Re-Entry Roundtable. Washington, D.C.

Harlow, C. W. (1996). *Profile of Jail Inmates*. U.S. Department of Justice. Bureau of Justice Statistics. Washington D.C. NCJ 164620.

Harlow, C. W. (2003). *Education and Correctional Populations*. Washington, DC: U.S. Department of Justice, Office of Justice Programs, Bureau of Justice Statistics. NCJ 195670.

Hairston, C. F. (1998). The forgotten parent: Understanding the forces that influence incarcerated fathers' relationships with their children. *Child Welfare*, 77, 617–638.

Harrison, P. M., & Beck, A. J. (2004). *Prison and Jail Inmates at Midyear 2004* (NCJ 208801). Washington, DC: U.S. Department of Justice, Office of Justice Programs, Bureau of Justice Statistics.

Henggeler, S. W., & Borduin, C. M. (1990). Family Therapy and Beyond: A Multisystemic Approach to Treating the Behavior Problems of Children and Adolescents. Pacific Grove CA: Brooks/Cole.

Hoffman, L. (1981). *Foundations of Family Therapy*. New York: Basic Books.

Hughes, T., Wilson, D., & Beck, A. (2001). *Trends in State Parole, 1990–2000*. Bureau of Justice Statistics Special Report. Washington D.C. NCJ 184735.

Izzo, R. & Ross, R. R. (1990). "Meta-analysis of rehabilitation programs for juvenile delinquents: A brief report." *Criminal Justice and Behavior*, 17,134–142.

Jennings, W., Kilkenny, R., & Kohlberg, L. (1983). "Moral development theory and practice for youthful and adult offenders." In W. Laufer and J. Day (eds.), *Personality Theory, Moral Development and Criminal Behavior.* Lexington, MA: Lexington Books.

Klein, N., Alexander, J., & Parsons, B. (1977). Impact of family systems intervention on recidivism and sibling delinquency: A model of primary prevention and program evaluation. *Journal of Consulting and Clinical Psychology,* 45, 469–474.

Koss, M. P., Bailey, J. A., Yuan, N. P, Herrara, V. M., & Lichter, E. (2003). Depression and PTSD in survivors of male violence: Research and training initiatives to facilitate recovery. *Psychology of Women Quarterly,* 27, 130–142.

Krupnick, J. L., Green, B., Stockton, P., Goodman, L., Corcoran, C., & Petty, R. (2004). Mental health effects of adolescent trauma exposure in a female college sample; exploring differential outcomes based on experiences of unique trauma types and dimensions. *Psychiatry: Interpersonal and Biological Processes,* 67, 264–279.

Lang, J., Rogers, C. S., Laffaye, C., Satz, L. E., Dresselhaus, T. R., & Stein, M. B. (2003). Sexual trauma, posttraumatic stress disorder, and health behavior. *Behavior Medicine,* 28, 150–158.

Langan, P. A. & Levin, D. J. (2002). Recidivism of Prisoners Released in 1994. U.S. Department of Justice. Bureau of Justice Statistics. Washington, D.C. NCJ 193427.

Latessa. E. J., Cullen, F. T. Cullen, & Gendreau, P. (2002). Beyond correctional quackery: Professionalism and the possibility of effective treatment. *Federal Probation,* 66, September, 43–49.

Lipsey, M. (1992). Juvenile delinquency treatment: A meta-analytic inquiry into the variability of effects. In *Meta-Analysis for Explanation: A Casebook,* edited by T. D. Cook, H. Cooper, D. S. Cordray, H. Hartmann, L. V. Hedges, R. J. Light, T. A. Louis, and F. Mosteller. New York, NY: Russell Sage Foundation.

Lipsey, M., & Wilson, D. (1998). Effective intervention for serious juvenile offenders: A synthesis of research. In *Serious and Violent Juvenile Offenders: Risk Factors and Successful Interventions,* edited by R. Loeber and D. P. Farrington. Thousand Oaks, CA: Sage Publications, Inc.

Listwan, S. J., Van Voorhis, P. & Ritchy, P. N. (2007). Personality, criminal behavior, and risk assessment: Implications for theory and practice. *Criminal Justice and Behavior.*

Listwan, Shelley J., Sperber, K. G., Spruance, L. M., & Van Voorhis, P. (2004). "High anxiety offenders in correctional settings: It's time for another look." *Federal Probation,* 68(3), 43–50.

Losel, F. (1995). Increasing consensus in the evaluation of offender rehabilitation? Lessons from the recent research synthesis. *Psychology, Crime & Law,* 2, 19–39.

Lowenkamp, C. T. & Latessa, E. J. (2005). Increasing the effectiveness of correctional programming through the risk principle: Identifying offenders for residential placement. *Criminology and Public Policy,* 4(2), 501–528.

Lynch, J. P. & Sabol, W. J. (2001). *Prisoner Reentry in Perspective,* Washington DC, The Urban Institute.

MacKenzie, D. L. (2000). Evidence-based corrections: Identifying what works. *Crime and Delinquency,* 4, 457–471.

Maluccio, A. & Ainsworth, F. (2003). Drug use by parents: A challenge for family reunification practice. *Children and Youth Services Review,* 25, 511–533.

Martin, S. S., Butzin, C. A., Saum, C. A., & Inciardi, J. A. (1999) "Three-year outcomes of therapeutic community treatment for drug-involved offenders in Delaware: From prison to work release to aftercare." *The Prison Journal,* 79(3), 294–320.

Meichenbaum, D. (1977). *Cognitive Behavioral Modification: An Integrative Approach.* New York: Plenum Press.

Mumola, C. J. (1999). *Incarcerated parents and their children.* U.S. Department of Justice: Bureau of Justice Statistics. Washington, D.C. NCJ 182335.

Nicolaidis, C., Curry, M., McFarland, B., & Gerrity, M. (2004). Violence, mental health, and physical symptoms in an academic internal medicine practice. *Journal of General Internal Medicine, 19,* 819–827.

Nishith, P., Resick P. A., & Mueser, K.T. (2001). Sleep difficulties and alcohol use motives in female rape victims with posttraumatic stress disorder. *Journal of Traumatic Stress,* 3,469–479.

Palmer, T. (1974). The youth authority's community treatment project. *Federal Pròbation,* 38(1), 3–13.

Parks, G. A. & Marlatt, G. A. (1999). Relapse prevention therapy for substance-abusing offenders: A cognitive-behavioral approach. In *What Works: Strategic Solutions: The International Community Corrections Association Examines Substance Abuse* edited by E. Latessa. Lanham, MD: American Correctional Association, p. 161–233.

Patterson, G. R., Chamberlain, P., & Reid, J. B. (1982). A comparative evaluation of a parent-training program. *Behavior Therapy,* 13, 638–650.

Petersilia, J. (2001). Prisoner reentry: Public safety and reintegration challenges. *The Prison Journal,* 81, 360–375.

Petersilia, J. (2003). *When Prisoners Come Home: Parole and Prisoner Re-Entry.* New York: Oxford University Press.

Ross, R. & Fabiano, E. A. (1985). *Time to Think.* Johnson City: Institute of Social Science and Arts, Inc.

Sampson, R. J., & Laub, J. H. (1993). *Crime in the making: Pathways and turning points through life.* Cambridge: Harvard University Press.

Simon, J. (1993). *Poor discipline: Parole and the social control of the underclass, 1890.* Chicago: University of Chicago Press.

Taxman, F. S., Young, D. & Byrne, J. M. (2003). *From Prison Safety to Public Safety: Best Practices in Offender Reentry.* National Institute of Justice: Washington, DC.

Travis, J., Chincotta, E. M., & Solomon, A. (2003). *Families Left Behind: The Hidden Costs of Incarceration and Re-Entry.* Washington, D.C.: The Urban Institute.

Travis, J., & Lawrence, S. (2002). *Beyond the prison gates: The State of Parole in America.* Washington, DC: The Urban Institute.

Travis J., Solomon, A., & Wahl, M. (2001). *From Prison to Home—The Dimensions and Consequences of Prisoner Reentry,* Washington DC: The Urban Institute.

Van Voorhis, P. (1987). Correctional effectiveness: The high cost of ignoring success. *Federal Probation* 51(l): 56–60.

Van Voorhis, P., Cullen, F. T., and Applegate, B. (1995). "Evaluating interventions with-violent offenders: A guide for practitioners and policymakers." *Federal Probation* 59(3): 17–28.

Van Voorhis, P., Spruance, L. M., Listwan, S. J., Ritchey, P. N., Pealer, J., & Seabrook, R. (2002). *The Georgia Cognitive Skills Experiment Outcome Evaluation Phase Two.* Technical Report submitted to the Georgia Board of Pardons and Parole.

Warren, M. (1983). Application of interpersonal maturity theory to offender populations. In W. Laufer & J. Day (Eds.), *Personality Theory, Moral Development, and Criminal Behavior.* Lexington, M.A.: Lexington Books.

Wexler, H. K., Melnick, G., Lowe, L., and Peters, J. (1999). "Three year reincarceration outcomes for amity in-prison therapeutic community and aftercare in California." *The Prison Journal,* 79(3), 321–336.

Wilson, D. B., Bouffard, L. A., & Mackenzie, D. L. (2005). Quantitative review of structured, group-oriented, cognitive-behavioral programs for offenders. *Criminal Justice and Behavior,* 32, 172–204.

Wilson, D. B., Gallagher, C. A., & MacKenzie, D. L. (2000). A meta-analysis of corrections based education, vocation, and work programs for adult offenders. *Journal of Research in Crime and Delinquency,* 37, 347–368.

Yochelson, S. & Samenow, S.E. (1976). *The Criminal Personality Volume 1: A Profile for Change.* New York: Jason Aronson.

25
HALFWAY HOUSES (UPDATED)*

EDWARD J. LATESSA
LAWRENCE F. TRAVIS III
CHRISTOPHER T. LOWENKAMP

There are many who believe that providing offenders who are released from prison with support and assistance can mean the difference between them remaining out of or returning to prison. No correctional program offers more reintegrative opportunities than community residential programs, often called halfway houses. Some halfway houses provide minimal services and support, such as a warm meal and a place to sleep, while others offer a wide range of services and treatment. Whether the program is considered "three hots and a cot" or a full-service facility, halfway houses play an important role in the supervision and rehabilitative efforts of the correctional system. For many years, proponents of halfway houses have argued that they were effective in reducing recidivism for offenders. Unfortunately, there was not much empirical evidence to support that contention, at least until recently. In the following article, Latessa, Travis, and Lowenkamp present the results from a major study of halfway houses that was conducted in Ohio. This study demonstrates that halfway houses can indeed reduce recidivism, provided that services and treatment are consistent with the principles of effective intervention.

WHAT'S IN A NAME?

Until recently, community corrections residential programs were subsumed under the general title of halfway houses. This label, however, has proven to be inadequate as a description of the variety of residential programs used with correctional populations today. The International Halfway House Association, founded in 1964, has itself changed its name to reflect more accurately the variety of purposes and persons served by residential programs.

The contemporary name given to such programs, community corrections residential facilities, is a broader title that reflects the role expansion of the traditional halfway house that has occurred in recent years. Rush (1991) defines a residential facility as "a correctional facility from which residents are regularly permitted to depart, unaccompanied by any official, for the purposes of using community resources, such as schools or treatment programs, and seeking or holding employment" (p. 265).

This definition is free of any reference to incarceration that was implicit in the term *halfway*. Further, it does not necessitate the direct provision of any services to residents within the facility, and clearly identifies the program with a correctional mission. Thus, unlike the traditional halfway house, the

Excerpts from and revisions to "Smart Sentencing: The Emergence of Intermediate Sections" by Edward J. Latessa and Lawrence F. Travis III. Revisions (2005) by Edward J. Latessa, Lawrence F. Travis III, and Christopher T. Lowencamp.

community residential facility serves a more diverse population and plays a broader correctional role. Traditional halfway houses are included within the category of residential facilities, but their ranks are swelled by newer adaptations, such as community corrections centers, prerelease centers, and restitution centers.

THE DEVELOPMENT OF COMMUNITY RESIDENTIAL PROGRAMS

Halfway houses as transitional programming for inmates released from prisons are not a new phenomenon (Latessa & Allen, 1982). Their origins can be traced at least as far back as the early nineteenth century in England and Ireland (Keller & Alper, 1970). In the United States, the exact origin of halfway houses is not clear, but one such program was started in New York City in 1845, the Isaac T. Hooper Home (Rush, 1991, p. 143). A halfway house for released female prisoners was opened in Boston, Massachusetts, in 1864. For nearly 100 years, halfway houses tended to be operated by charitable organizations for the benefit of released inmates. Halfway house programs did not begin a period of expansion until after World War II (Beha, 1977).

In the 1950s, specialized residential programs designed to deal with substance-abusing offenders were added to the traditional halfway house programs. Residential programs for alcoholic or drug addicted offenders opened and spread throughout this period, and into the 1960s. For typical criminal offenders, however, halfway house placements were rare.

In the middle 1960s, the President's Commission on [Law Enforcement] and Administration of Justice (1967) signaled a change in correctional philosophy toward the goal of reintegration. Reintegration placed increased emphasis on the role of the community in corrections, and on the value of keeping offenders in the community, rather than in prison, whenever possible. This ideology of community corrections supported the notion of residential placements for convicted offenders, and halfway houses began a period of unprecedented expansion, supported by federal funds from programs as diverse as the Office of Economic Opportunity and the Law Enforcement Assistance Administration (Hicks, 1987, p. 6).

During the early 1980s, however, support for halfway house programs dwindled. The effects of recession, demise of LEAA, and a general hardening of public attitudes toward offenders worked against the continued growth and development of halfway houses or other residential programs. This period of retrenchment was, however, short-lived. The same forces that temporarily halted the growth of residential programs soon added their weight to continued development.

In the last decade, community corrections residential facilities have grown in response to the crisis of prison crowding. Allen et al. (1978, p. 1) attribute an increased use of halfway houses with parole populations to three factors: the philosophy of reintegration, success with such programs in the mental health field, and the lower costs of halfway houses compared with prisons. To these was added the need to respond to prison crowding in the 1980s.

The lack of prison capacity, coupled with an increasing emphasis on risk control and retributive sentencing, spurred a search for intermediate sanctions. Over the last several years, a number of observers have called for the creation of penal sanctions that range in severity between incarceration and traditional probation supervision (McCarthy, 1987). They suggest that such sanctions will allow the correctional system to meet the punitive and risk-control goals of sentencing, especially with those persons diverted from prison or jail because of crowding.

The list of intermediate sanctions includes house arrest, electronic monitoring, and intensive supervision (*Federal Probation*, 1986; Petersilia, 1987). DuPont (1985) explicitly identifies a role for community residential facilities as an adjunct to traditional probation or parole supervision. Such facilities would serve to increase both the punitive severity and public safety of traditional community-based corrections.

In an era when both correctional costs and populations grow yearly, planners, practitioners, and policymakers have supported a wide range of correctional alternatives. As Guynes (1988) has observed, one effect of prison and jail crowding has been a dramatic increase in probation and parole populations. Further, Petersilia (1985), among others, suggests that these larger supervision populations are increasingly made up of more serious and more dangerous offenders. Community residential facilities have come to be seen as an important option for the management and control of these growing and more dangerous offender populations.

A result has been the redefinition of the role of community residential facilities. The traditional role of transitional placement for offenders, or as a response to special needs populations such as substance abusers, has been expanded. Residential placement has emerged as a correctional alternative in its own right.

Hicks (1987) observes that the use of residential placement as an alternative to incarceration or traditional community supervision has engendered some changes in operations and philosophy. She terms this a movement "toward supervision rather than treatment." Thus in many cases residential facilities provide little more than a place to live and access to community resources. The emphasis in these programs is upon custody and control rather than counseling and correction.

PRISON ON THE CHEAP?

Unable or unwilling to underwrite the costs of prison for large numbers of convicted offenders, several jurisdictions have supported community residential facilities. As Hicks (1987) notes, "Budget weary legislators often view halfway houses as an inexpensive lunch" (p. 7). Residential programs, they hope, will provide public safety as well as incarceration, but at a fraction of the cost. As substitute prisons, however, the atmosphere of these programs has changed. Traditional halfway houses, where staff and programs are designed for the provision of direct services to residents, still continue.

These programs provide counseling, substance abuse treatment, educational and vocational training, and a variety of social services. In other, newer programs, especially those operated by corrections departments, the atmosphere is closer to that of a minimum-security prison than a rehabilitative community.

This addition of residential programs as "bed space" to the traditional use of such programs as treatment modalities has led to a schizophrenic field of practice. In most facilities, rules and regulations are stricter, and enforcement more rigid, than in earlier days. Additionally, a number of "large" facilities, housing hundreds of residents, have been added. Typically "pre-release" centers, these larger facilities house prison inmates eligible for parole, or in the final months before their release.

The recent growth in community residential facilities has complicated the picture. These facilities serve a variety of clients, ranging from as-yet-unconvicted offenders diverted from court through prison inmates. Facility sizes range from those housing fewer than 10 residents to those with populations in the hundreds. Treatment services range from programs providing full services to those in which few, if any, direct services are available to residents. The one constant is that residents live in the facilities for a period of time, and are generally free to leave the facilities during approved hours, for approved purposes, without escort.

RESIDENTIAL FACILITIES IN CONTEMPORARY CORRECTIONS

As the foregoing discussion illustrates, it is not possible to describe the average residential facility. Diversity in population, program, size, and structure is the rule. It is, unfortunately, also not possible to know for certain how many such facilities are in operation today, or the number of offenders served by them. As Hicks (1987) observes, "There are no national figures, only educated guesses" (p. 1).

The International Halfway House Association published a directory of residential facilities in 1981 that lists almost 2,300 facilities with a combined capacity of nearly 100,000 beds (Gatz & Murray, 1981). Not all of these facilities, however, serve correctional populations. Five years earlier, Seiter et al. (1977) estimated that approximately 400 facilities existed that served correctional populations, with a capacity of about 10,000 beds. In 1978, a survey of parole authorities revealed the existence of nearly 800 facilities, with almost 15,000 inmates being paroled to halfway house placements. More recently, the National Institute of Corrections supported a survey that identified 641 community corrections residential facilities. The identification was based on the characteristics of residents as under correctional supervision, among other criteria.

While the methods and definitions employed in these different studies varied considerably, the results are fairly consistent. Given these admittedly incomplete data, it is possible to estimate that there are in excess of 600 residential facilities in operation today. Further, it appears that the number of facilities has grown as much as 50 percent in the last decade.

It is not possible to estimate the number of offenders served by these facilities with any certainty. Length of residence is typically short, on the order of three to four months, meaning that a facility with 50 beds may serve 150 to 200 individuals annually. Based on the probability that a halfway house would serve three to four times as many residents as it has beds in each year, Allen and his colleagues (1978, p. 2) estimate that roughly 10,000 beds equals 30,000 to 40,000 residents each year. Further, many of those in residential facilities are included in the totals of other correctional population counts, such as the number of prison inmates or persons under parole supervision. Still, it is clear that the total number of residents in these facilities each year is substantial.[1]

TYPES OF FACILITIES

The large number of facilities and their differing traditions, populations, and services render it difficult to assess the impact of residential programs. Beyond noting that these programs have played an important role in the provision of services to convicted offenders, and that their importance as alternatives to imprisonment has increased, the variety of facilities means that questions of effectiveness must be narrowly drawn.

Allen and his colleagues (1978), for example, have developed a four-class typology of halfway houses, using two dimensions to yield four possible types of facilities. Halfway houses can be either public or private, and they can be either interventive or supportive in program. Public or private, of course, relates to the organization of the facility as either a government entity or not. Program types are based on whether the services of the facility are designed to intervene in problem areas of the residents' lives, such as substance abuse counseling, or to provide a supportive environment in which residents use community resources.

This simple typology indicates that different facilities must be assessed differently. For example, a residential facility designed to provide supportive services would not be well evaluated on the basis of direct service provision. Similarly, a program aimed at intervention would not be well understood solely in terms of resident length of stay. Rather, the type of program offered in a facility must form an important base of any assessment effort.

WHAT DO WE KNOW ABOUT THE EFFECTIVENESS QUESTION?

Despite the long tradition of residential community correctional programs, until recently the research literature concerned with them was sparse and inconclusive. In 2002 however, the largest study of community correctional facilities was conducted (Lowenkamp & Latessa, 2002). This study included an examination of 38 halfway houses and over 6,400 offenders (3,200 each in the treatment and comparison groups). While results from this study showed that overall halfway houses did indeed reduce recidivism, not all programs were effective. Furthermore, programs had a much more pronounced effect on higher risk offenders, and higher quality programs performed better than low quality. Figure 25.1 shows the overall reductions in recidivism for the programs under study. These data indicate that most of the programs reduced recidivism. Figures 25.2 through 25.5 show the results based on the risk level of the offenders. These data indicate that while few programs were effective with lower risk offenders (those with a relatively low probability to recidivate in the first place), as the risk increased, so did the effects. For higher risk offenders, the vast majority of halfway houses showed substantial reductions in recidivism.

THE FUTURE OF RESIDENTIAL FACILITIES

What does the future hold for residential community correctional facilities? Residential facilities that evolved from traditional halfway houses are now becoming multiservice agencies.

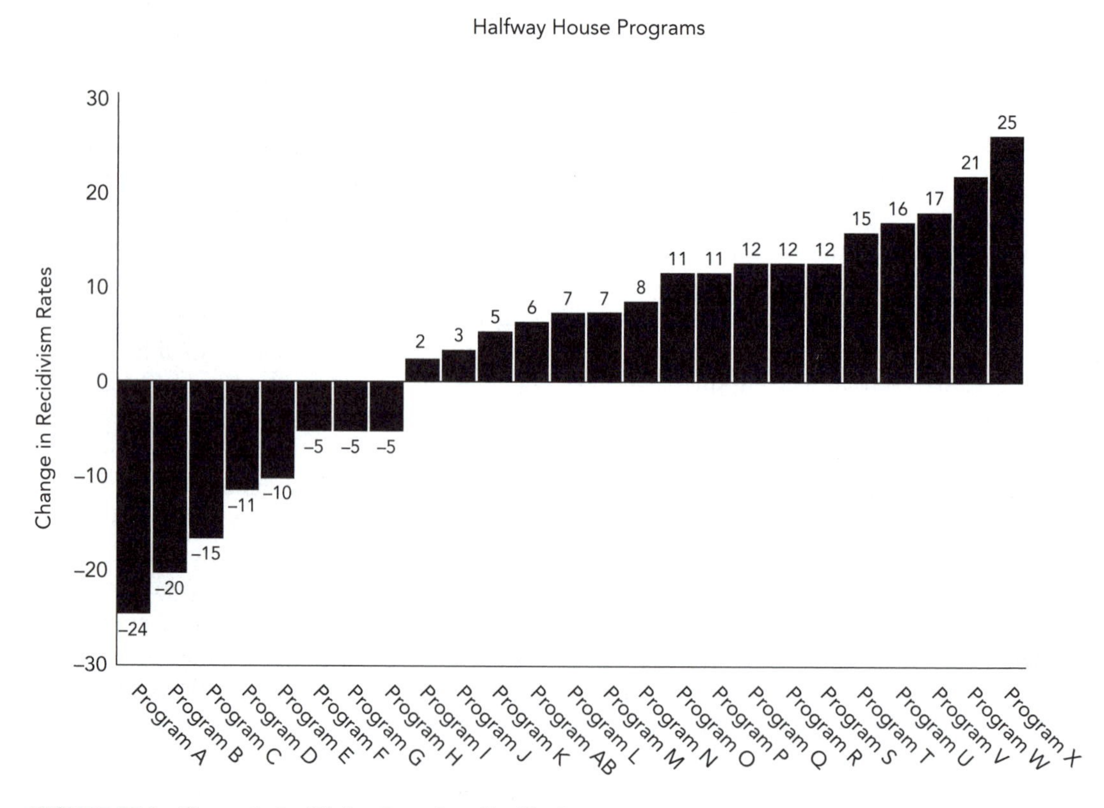

FIGURE 25.1 Change in Recidivism Rates for All Offenders

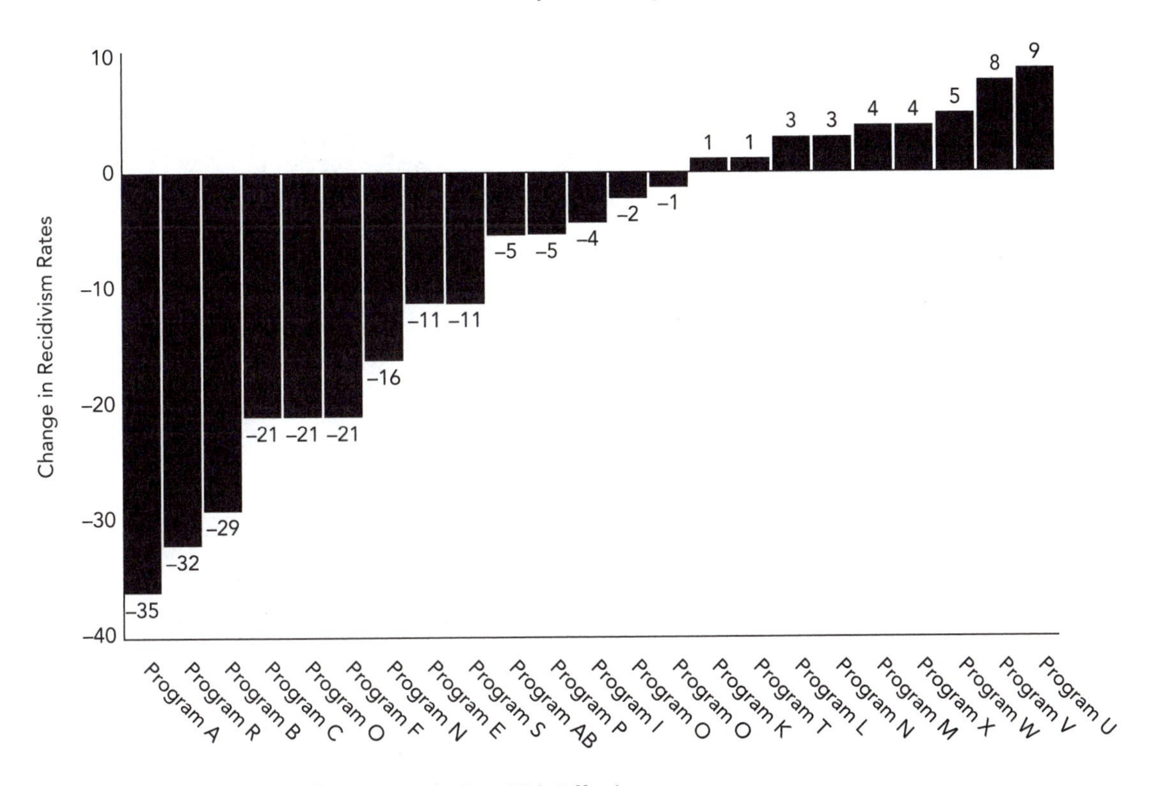

FIGURE 25.2 Change in Recidivism Rates for Low-Risk Offenders

Second, residential community correctional facilities will continue to grow and develop new programs. In large part this will be a response to the crowding of local and state correctional institutions. Many traditional residential facilities will seize the opportunity and will diversify and offer a wider range of programs and services, such as victim assistance programs, family and drug counseling, drunk driver programs, work release centers, and house arrest, electronic monitoring, and day programs for offenders.

Finally, while there has been an increase in public sector operation of residential facilities, particularly prerelease and reintegration centers, it will be the private sector that will continue to play a dominant role in the development and operation of residential correctional programs. A number of arguments support private provision of community-based correctional services. Principal among these is cost-effectiveness. Proponents argue that the private sector will contain costs and thus, for the same dollar amount, provide more, or at least better, service. Government agencies, it is suggested, cannot achieve the same level of cost-efficient operation as can private, especially for-profit, companies.

As Clear, Hairs, and Record (1982) succinctly summarize: "Due to 'domestication' (characterized by a lack of competition and critical self-assessment), corrections officials often are inadvertently rewarded by taking a budget-administration approach rather than a cost-management stance." The attraction of private involvement in community corrections is the promise of a free market, or, as Greenwood

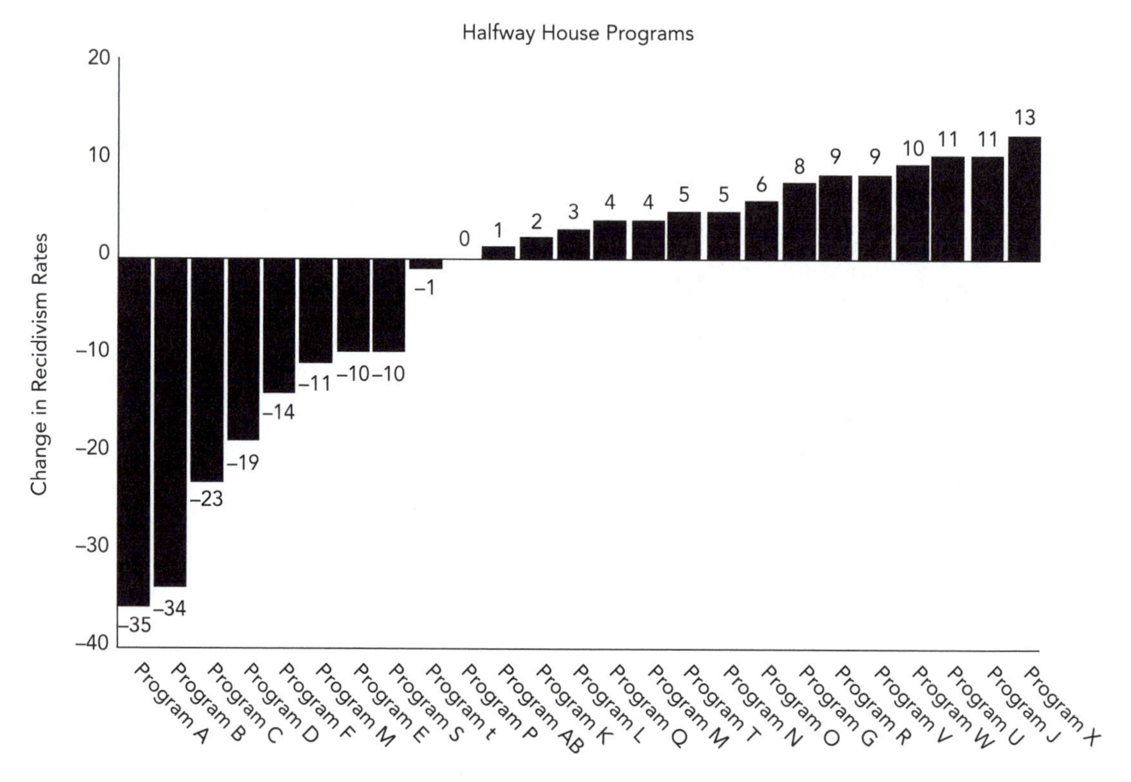

FIGURE 25.3 Change in Recidivism Rates for Low/Moderate-Risk Offenders

(1981) put it, "They would be free to innovate, to use the latest technology and management techniques as in any profit service industry."

Another, perhaps more compelling, reason for the continued development of private community residential programs is that they can offer what Gendreau and Ross (1987) call "therapeutic integrity." That is, because of their accountability to the contractor and the possibility of competition, privately operated programs may provide more intensive and higher-quality service provision than might government agencies. Indeed, many who have studied public community correctional agencies have lamented the increasingly bureaucratic role of the change agent (Clear & Latessa, 1989), noting the large number of staff who are simply "putting in time" for retirement or who are encumbered by paperwork and red tape. It often seems that organizational goals outweigh concerns about effective treatment and service delivery.

Of course, this is really an issue of accountability that involves some nonmonetary value questions. This is one of the fundamental differences between the private and public sectors. Private enterprise often measures outcome in terms of profit, while the public sector measures it in terms of social value and benefits. While there is no empirical evidence that the private sector is "better" at providing services, reducing recidivism, and so forth, there is a growing sentiment that it ought to at least be given a chance. Privately run facilities may also be in a better position to lobby for more services, staff, and programs. One need only look at the typical adult probation department, where caseloads range from 150 to 300, to see how ineffective they have been in garnering additional

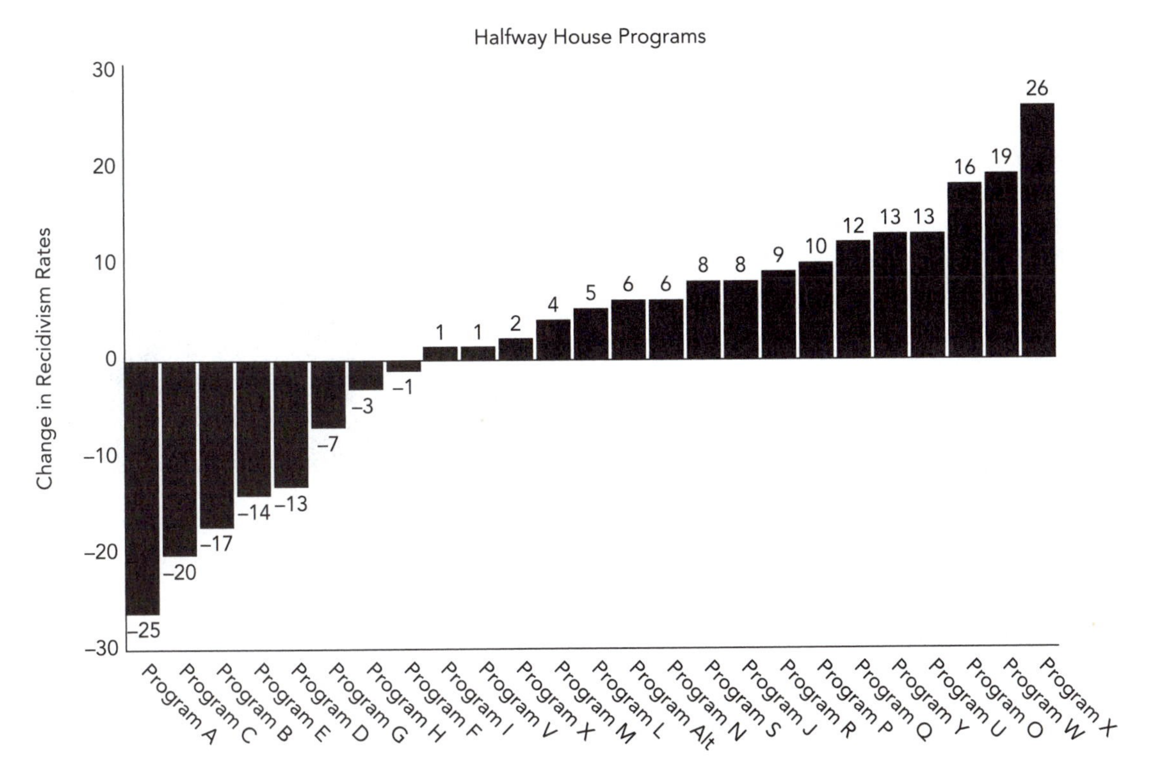

FIGURE 25.4 Change in Recidivism Rates for Moderate-Risk Offenders

resources. Private providers may, because of contractual agreements, be better able to advocate for additional support.

Of more importance than the simple dichotomy between public and private operation is the future evolution of the mission of community corrections residential facilities. The traditional halfway house had a charitable, quasi-volunteer, and service-oriented mission (Wilson, 1985). The contemporary multiservice community agency or department of corrections-operated facility is more formal, legalistic, and control oriented. As correctional agencies contract with both new private sector vendors and older, charitable programs, the emphasis in residential facilities may change from treatment to custody. Further, as the importance of correctional contracts for the support and spread of residential facilities grows, the "community" nature of these programs may increasingly be replaced by a more formal, governmental administrative style. That is, the forces that currently support the development of programs may ultimately change them in fundamental ways.

The traditional halfway house operated by a civic-minded reform group for the purpose of assisting offenders may be replaced by for-profit or nonprofit contractors working for the government. Thus, rather than a focus on the needs and interests of the community and the offender, the emphasis may be placed on the needs of the correctional system for bed space.

Of course, it is also entirely likely that the current confusion in residential programs will continue. There will continue to be traditional halfway houses focused on the needs of residents, with deep roots in the community. There will also be a variety of

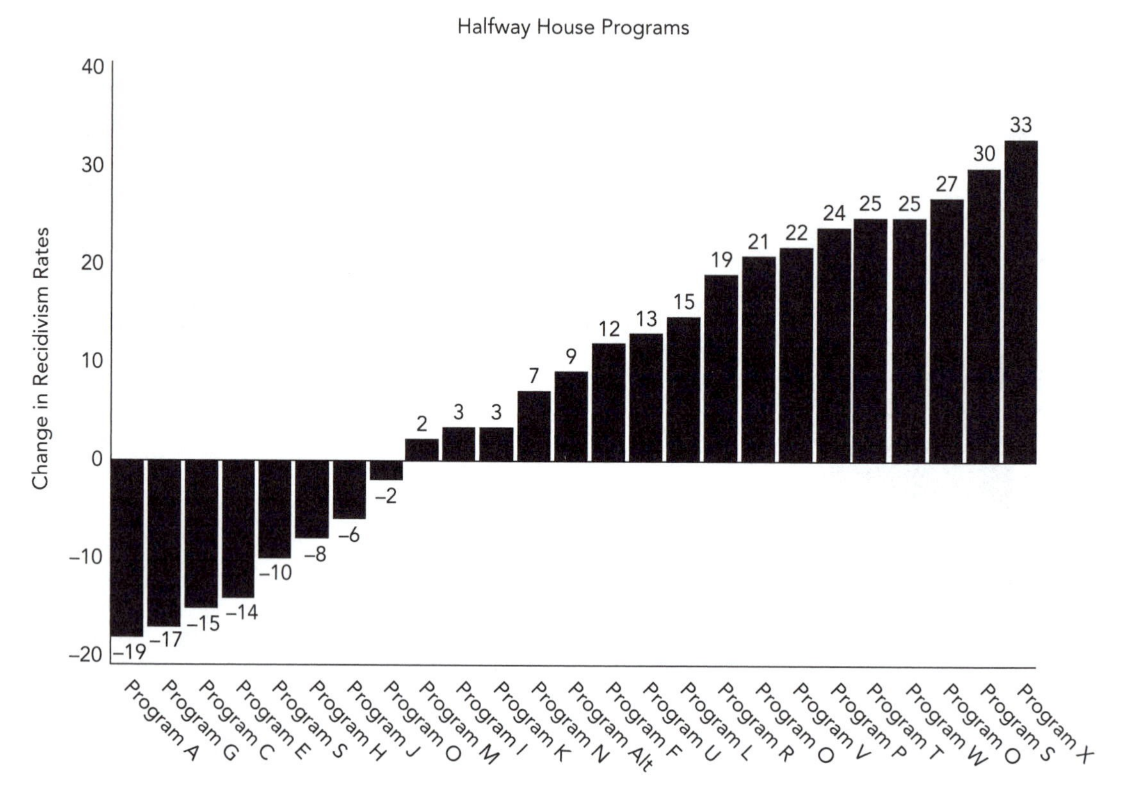

FIGURE 25.5 Change in Recidivism Rates for High-Risk Offenders

custody and crowding-control facilities designed to provide minimal direct services. Only time will tell what the future of community corrections residential facilities will be. The one thing that is clear is that some form of such facilities will exist in the future.

STUDY QUESTIONS

1. What are some of the possible reasons that halfway houses were more effective with higher risk offenders?
2. Trace the historical development of halfway houses.
3. What are the different types and models of halfway houses?
4. What are some of the differences between traditional halfway houses and more contemporary community residential centers?
5. What does the future hold for halfway houses?

AUTHORS' NOTE

*This is an updated version of "Residential Community Correctional Programs," first published in *Smart Sentencing: The Emergence of Intermediate Sanctions*, James M. Byrne, Arthur L. Lurigio, and Joan Petersilia (eds.). Copyright © 1992 by Sage Publications. New material on the effectiveness of halfway houses has been added to the original article.

NOTE

1. Estimating the size of the community corrections residential facility population is hazardous at best. In her 1987 article, however, Hicks reported interviews with representatives of California, Texas, and the Federal Bureau of Prisons. These officials estimated that by 1988, the combined total of offenders served in residential facilities for these three jurisdictions would exceed 7,000. Given that these numbers do not include probationers or misdemeanants in all three jurisdictions, a conservative extrapolation yields an estimated 70,000 offenders in residential facilities during 1988. This represents about 10 percent of the prison population for that year.

REFERENCES

Allen, H. E., Carlson, E. W., Parks, E. C., & Seiter, R. P. (1978). Program models: Halfway houses. Washington, DC: U.S. Department of Justice.

Beha, J. A. (1977). Testing the functions and effects of the parole halfway house: One case study. Journal of Criminal Law and Criminology, 67, 335–350.

Clear, T., Hairs, P. M., & Record, A. L. (1982). Managing the cost of corrections. Prison Journal, 53, 1–63.

Clear, T., & Latessa, E. J. (1989, March). Intensive surveillance versus treatment. Paper presented at the annual meeting of the Academy of Criminal Justice Sciences, Washington, DC.

DuPont, P. (1985). *Expanding sentencing options: A governor's perspective.* Washington, DC. National Institute of Justice.

Federal Probation. (1986). *Intensive probation supervision* [Special issue]. Vol. 50, No. 2.

Gatz, N., & Murray, C. (1981). An administrative overview of halfway houses. *Corrections Today,* 43, 52–54.

Gendreau, P., & Ross, R. R. (1987). Revivification of rehabilitation: Evidence from the 1980's. *Justice Quarterly,* 4, 349–407.

Greenwood, P. (1981). *Private enterprise prisons? Why not?* Santa Monica, CA: RAND Corporation.

Guynes, R. (1988). Difficult clients, large caseloads plague probation, parole agencies. Washington, DC: U.S. Department of Justice.

Hicks, N. (1987). A new relationship: Halfway houses and corrections. *Corrections Compendium,* 12(4), 1, 5–7.

Keller. O. J., & Alper, G. (1970). *Halfway houses: Community centered correction and treatment.* Lexington, MA: D. C. Heath.

Latessa, E. J., & Allen, H. E. (1982). Halfway houses and parole: A national assessment. *Journal of Criminal Justice,* 10(2), 153–163.

Latessa, E. J., & Travis, L. F. (1986, October). Halfway houses versus probation: A three year follow-up of offenders. Paper presented at the annual meeting of the Midwestern Criminal Justice Association, Chicago.

Lowenkamp, C. T., & Latessa, E. J. (2002). *Evaluation of Ohio's halfway houses and community-based correctional facilities.* University of Cincinnati.

McCarthy, B. R. (Ed.). (1987). *Intermediate punishments: Intensive supervision, home confinement, and electronic surveillance.* Monsey, NY: Criminal Justice Press.

Petersilia, J. (1985). Probation and felon offenders. Washington, DC: U.S. Department of Justice.

Petersilia, J. (1987). *Expanding options for criminal sentencing* (Publication No. R-3544-EMC). Santa Monica, CA: RAND Corporation.

President's Commission on Law Enforcement and Administration of Justice. (1967). *Taskforce report: Corrections.* Washington, DC: Government Printing Office.

Rush, G. E. (1991). *The dictionary of criminal justice* (3rd ed.). Guilford, CT: Dushkin.

Seiter, R. P., Carlson, E. W., Bowman, H., Grandfield, H., Beran, N. J., & Allen, H. E. (1977). *Halfway houses.* Washington, DC: Government Printing Office.

Wilson, G. P. (1985). Halfway house programs for offenders. In L. F. Travis (Ed.), *Probation, parole, and community corrections* (pp. 151–164). Prospect Heights, IL: Waveland.

26
WELCOME HOME?

EXAMINING THE "REENTRY COURT" CONCEPT FROM A STRENGTHS-BASED PERSPECTIVE

SHADD MARUNA
THOMAS P. LEBEL

As we have learned, the number of offenders returning to the community is at an all-time high and will only continue to grow. One of the new concepts for more effectively assisting these offenders is the reentry court. This innovation draws some of its elements from drug and mental health courts that have sprung up around the country. Reentry courts hold out the promise for bringing together various components of the community in an effort to reduce risk, address needs, and provide the support and supervision necessary to reintegrate offenders into the community.

In the book *After Prison—What?* Maud Booth writes, "When one thinks that this prejudice and marking of discharged prisoners robs them of any chance of gaining a living, and in many instances forces them back against their will into a dishonest career, one can realize how truly tragic the situation is" (119). That was written in 1903. According to Verne McArthur, in his book *Coming Out Cold: Community Reentry from a State Reformatory*, "The released offender confronts a situation at release that virtually ensures his failure" (1). That was written in 1974.

Unfortunately, the conditions faced by ex-convicts today have not improved much and may have even deteriorated since these conclusions were reached. Fast forwarding to the present, Jeremy Travis and Joan Petersilia (2001:301) write, "Prisoners moving through the high-volume, poorly designed assembly line (of corrections)... are less well prepared individually for their return to the community and are returning to communities that are not well prepared to accept them." Additionally, there has been a radical change in the scale of the reentry problem over the last 100 years. Nearly 600,000 individuals will be released from U.S. prisons this year (that is over 1,600 per day) compared to 170,000 in 1980 and only a few thousand at the turn of the century when Booth was writing.

In addition, largely due to new "tough on crime" approaches in paroling practice, reentering society has been made a more difficult and precarious transition than ever before. Of the 459,000 U.S. parolees who were discharged from community supervision in 2000, 42 percent were returned to incarceration—11 percent with a new sentence and 31 percent in some other way (Bureau of Justice Statistics 2001). In a recent study of 272,111 prisoners released in 15 states in 1994, 67.5 percent were rearrested within three years, as compared to an estimated 62.5 percent in a similar study of 1983 releases (Langan and Levin 2002). Because of the enormous growth of the prison population since the early 1980s, this small change translates into huge numbers. In 1980, 27,177 paroled ex-convicts were returned to state prisons. In 1999, this number was 197,606. As a percentage of all admissions to state prisons, parole violators more than doubled from 17 percent in 1980 to 35 percent in 1999. In California, a staggering 67 percent of prison admissions were parole failures (Hughes, Wilson, and Beck 2001). These figures indicate that the reentry problem is not only a product of the 1990's incarceration boom, but is actually a leading cause of the boom as well. It is no wonder then that former Attorney General Janet Reno (2000:1) referred to ex-convict reentry as "one of the most pressing problems we face as a nation."

As such, the broad new proposals for revamping reentry policy through a "jurisprudential lens" (Travis and Petersilia 2001: 291) that have emerged in recent years (e.g., Office of Justice Programs 1999; Travis 2000) could not be more welcome or better timed. Before leaving office, the Clinton Administration developed a series of relatively large-scale initiatives intended to address the reentry crisis through a scattering of experimental pilot programs. The Clinton Administration's reentry proposals (OJP 2001) were never fully implemented, but the Bush Administration has developed its own reentry project (OJP 2002), which borrows much of the content of its predecessor's plan.

Among the most significant of the new proposals[1] is the "reentry court" experiment, based on the drug court model, which would cast judges as "reentry managers" (Travis 2000:8). Whereas, the role of the judiciary typically ends after sentencing, the reentry court model would move the court system into a "sentence management" role, overseeing the convicted person's eventual return to the community.

A reentry court is a court that manages the return to the community of individuals being released from prison, using the authority of the court to apply graduated sanctions and positive reinforcement and to marshal resources to support the prisoner's reintegration, much as drug courts do, to promote positive behavior by the returning prisoner (OJP 1999:2).

The concept of the reentry court is very much still under development, and the pilot sites in California, Colorado, Delaware, Florida, Iowa, Kentucky, New York, Ohio, and West Virginia all differ significantly in their emphases and approaches. Still, the underlying premises are largely borrowed from drug treatment courts and other problem-solving courts. According to the Office of Justice Programs (1999:79), these core elements include:

- *Assessment and strategic reentry planning* involving the ex-offender, the judiciary, and other key partners—this sometimes involves the development of a contract or treatment plan.
- *Regular status assessment meetings* involving both the ex-offender and his circle of supporters or representatives from his family and community.
- *Coordination of multiple support services* including substance abuse treatment, job training programs, faith institutions, and housing services.
- *Accountability to community* through the involvement of citizen advisory boards, crime victims' organizations, and neighborhood groups.
- *Graduated and parsimonious sanctions* for violations of the conditions of release that can be swiftly, predictably, and universally applied.
- *Rewards for success,* especially by negotiating early release from parole after established goals are achieved or by conducting graduation ceremonies similar to those used in drug courts.

The working assumption is that "offenders respond positively to the fact that a judge is taking an interest in their success" (OJP 1999:6). In addition, "The frequent appearances before the court with the offer of assistance, coupled with the knowledge of predictable and parsimonious consequences for failure, assist the offender in taking the steps necessary to get his life back on track" (6). With the explicit intention of reducing recidivism and assisting ex-offenders, reentry courts clearly have the potential to embody the principles of therapeutic jurisprudence (Wexler 2001) in the same way that drug treatment courts often do (see Hora, Schma, and Rosenthal 1999). Reentry court advocates also hope that these courts will achieve the level of popular and political support that drug courts have enjoyed.

As with any transplantation of a model from one context to the next, however, one must be cautious about applying the drug court model to the reentry process. After all, the success of the drug court movement in many ways might be attributable to features unique to addiction recovery or to the population of clients participating in the programs (i.e., non-violent, drug-involved offenders). Pioneering drug court judge, Hon. Richard Gebelein (2000), makes a case to this effect in trying to explain the popularity of drug courts in an era in which there is allegedly little support for the rehabilitative ideal. Gebelein argues that drug courts have succeeded because, unlike previous failed rehabilitative efforts, the drug court movement has been able to provide a clear narrative of what is causing the criminal behavior of the drug court clients and what they need to get better. Drug court's "advantage over 'plain old' rehabilitation," Gebelein (2000:3) suggests, is "the focus on one problem (addiction) that is causally related to crime committed by one group of offenders (addicts)." He argues that the narrative that addiction is a disease and, as such, needs to be treated by professionals, is one that makes sense to the public and to policy makers at this point in history.

The critical question, then, is: *Is there a similar narrative for how and why reentry should work?* In this paper, we will argue that a new narrative, which we refer to as a strengths-based or "restorative" narrative, is emerging in multiple fields that would fit nicely with the reentry court concept. Unfortunately, the current reentry proposals do not seem to reflect an explicitly restorative agenda and therefore may suffer the same fate as previous efforts to improve offender reentry processes.

REENTRY: AN INITIATIVE IN NEED OF A NARRATIVE

> Bullets kill and bars constrain, but the practice of supervision inevitably involves the construction of a set of narratives which allows the kept, the keepers, and the public to believe in a capacity to control (crime) that cannot afford to be tested too frequently.
>
> —Jonathan Simon *(1993), Poor Discipline: Parole and the Social Control of the Underclass*

In his tremendous history of parole in the United States, Simon (1993:9) writes, "One of the primary tasks of an institution that exercises the power to punish is to provide a plausible account of what it does and how it does what it does." This might be particularly important for community corrections, which, as Fogel (1984:85) notes, lacks the "forceful imagery that other occupations in criminal justice can claim: police catch criminals, prosecutors try to get them locked up, judges put them in prisons, wardens keep them locked up, but what do probation officers do?" Simon argues that a good correctional narrative needs some rather obvious components. It needs, first, a plausible theory of criminogenesis (what causes people to commit crime?) and, second, a set of practices that appear capable of reversing this process.

Unlike the drug court model described by Gebelein, today's reentry system seems to have no such compelling narrative for what it does or how it works. In fact, Rhine (1997: 74) concludes that the lack of a "plausible narrative of community-based supervision" is "the most pressing and vexing problem facing probation and parole administrators today." The "growing conviction that the system no longer represents a credible response to the problem of crime" (Rhine 1997:71) has led to several new proposals to severely curtail or even abandon parole supervision[2] entirely (e.g., Austin 2001). One of the participants at a recent expert panel on the future of community corrections stated this matter quite bluntly: "Public regard for probation is dangerously low, and for the most part in most places, what passes for probation supervision is a joke. It's conceptually bankrupt and it's politically not viable.... We have to realize that we don't have broad public legitimacy" (Dickey and Smith 1998:3). Another participant described the public mood toward community corrections as a "malaise." He continued, "Even more importantly, there is a malaise in our own house [among probation professionals]" (Dickey and Smith 1998:5).

It is in this climate that the reentry court initiative has emerged with the promise of breathing new life into a much-maligned system of parole and community supervision. If instituted on a broad scale, the reentry court would represent a significant change in the structure of how the process of prison release works. It is not clear, however, that this important new policy initiative is being accompanied by a new policy *narrative*. In fact, the discourse around these new reentry initiatives may sound eerily familiar to those who have followed the history of parole in the U.S. According to Reno (2000:3):

> The reentry court is modeled on the... theory of a carrot and stick approach, in using the strength of the court and the wisdom of the court to really push the issue.... The message works with us: stay clean, stay out of trouble, and we'll help you get a job, we'll help you prepare in terms of a skill. But if you come back testing positive for drugs, if you commit a further crime, if you violate the conditions of your release, you're going to pay.

This description unfortunately makes the new reentry court initiative sound suspiciously like "simply another word for parole supervision, which many have tried to discredit and dismantle" (Austin 2001:314).

Indeed, Reno's stick and carrot are key symbols of the two reigning paradigms in parole practice over the last 100 years, which can be broken down into the familiar dichotomy of punishment and welfare (Garland 1985), monitor and mentor, or cop and social worker. We refer to these as "risk-based" and "need-based" narratives, respectively. Both are deficit models—that is, they emphasize convicts' problems—but they require very different technologies and connote different meanings.

Below, we briefly outline both narratives, discussing their plausibility as explanatory accounts and their internal coherence. In addition, using a therapeutic jurisprudence lens, we will also evaluate each narrative in terms of its fit with established psychological principles regarding sustained behavior change (see Wexler 2001), and the empirical evaluation research referred to as "what works" (Gendreau, Cullen, and Bonta 1994). Finally, whenever possible, we will try to present the convicted person's own interpretation of these narratives, as these subjective perceptions are also crucial in understanding the success or failure of correctional practice.

CONTROL NARRATIVES (RISK-BASED)

The February 2000 press release from U.S. Senator Joseph Biden's office announcing the "first-ever" reentry court in Delaware began with the macho headline "Biden Introduces Tough New Court Program for Released Inmates." Getting "tough" on those who have already "paid their debt" to society has become a standard, if not always coherent reentry narrative. The basic story, here, seems to be that ex-prisoners are dangerous, and they need to be watched carefully at all times. Indeed, this implication is clear in the new name given to the Reentry Initiative in the United States. Originally titled "Young Offender Reentry Initiative" (OJP 2001) under the Clinton Administration, the Bush Administration transformed the project into the "Serious and Violent Offender Reentry Initiative" (OJP 2002) and have toughened up the language of control substantially in their version of the proposal. Whereas the Clinton Administrations call for proposals emphasized the problems of substance abuse, mental illness, and stigmatization, the Bush Administration's reworking focuses on minimizing the risks posed by the "most predatory" ex-convicts.

This points out another important difference between drug courts and the reentry courts. Whereas drug courts explicitly exclude violent offenders, the reentry court plan would focus almost exclusively on persons thought to be at risk for violence. Peyton and Gossweiler (2001) found that of 212 reporting drug courts in their study, only seven of them include persons with violence in their criminal histories. Indeed, drug courts that receive federal funding are prohibited from admitting offenders with current violent charges or with prior convictions of violent felony crimes. Because of the different public and professional assumptions about the differences between persons convicted of violent versus nonviolent crime (and in particular, drug-related nonviolent crime), treatment of these two populations probably require different narratives.

Underlying the "risk management" approach to violence is the assumption that returning ex-convicts will respond best to the constant threat of sanctions (or, at any rate, if they do not, then they are too dangerous to be out of prison). In terms of policy prescriptions, this narrative suggests the need for an "electronic panopticon" (Gordon 1991) or "pee 'em and see 'em" (Cullen 2002) approach to reentry involving electronic monitoring, intensive supervision (i.e., additional home and office visits), random drug testing, home confinement, extensive behavior restrictions, strict curfews, and expanded lengths of supervision. The basic idea is that these forms of tough community controls can reduce recidivism by thwarting an offender's criminal instincts.

Empirically, these prototypically "tough" community sanctions—intensive community supervision in particular—have failed to live up to the promise of the control narrative. Petersilia and Turner's (1993) nine-state random-assignment evaluation found no evidence that the increased surveillance in the community deterred offenders from committing crimes. At the same time, their research quite conclusively showed that this additional control increased the probability that technical violations would be detected, leading to greater use of incarceration (and hence much higher costs).

Further, the control narrative has little support from the psychological literature on behavioral change. Specific deterrence in general has long been pronounced "dead" as a social scientific concept (see esp. McGuire 1995), and the literature is especially critical of the notion that prisons could serve as an effective deterrent. For instance, psychological research on effective punishment suggests that, to be effective, punishing stimuli must be immediate, predictable, and as intense as possible—none of which is possible in even the most Draconian correctional intervention (Gendreau, Goggin, and Cullen 1999).

Research on effective planned change similarly suggests that power-coercive strategies are the least likely to promote internalization and long-term change (Chin and Benne 1976). Kelman (1958), for instance, discusses three means of changing behavior: change via compliance, change via identification, and change via internalization. The first strategy, utilizing power-coercive means, may achieve instrumental compliance, Kelman says, but is the least likely of the three to promote "normative re-education" and long-term transformation once the "change agent" has been removed (see also Bottoms 2000). This hypothesis is empirically supported in MacKenzie and De Li's (2002) rigorous study of intensive supervision probation. They write:

> The disappointing factor is the possibility that the offenders may be influenced only as long as they are being supervised.... When probation is over,

> these offenders may return to their previous levels of criminal activity because the deterrent effect of arrest may wear off when they are no longer under supervision (37–38).

Heavy-handed control tactics can undermine the perceived legitimacy in paroling authorities among clients (see Tyler, Boeckmann, Smith, and Huo 1997). For instance, parole conditions that include prohibitions against associating with fellow ex-convicts or entering drinking establishments (both of which are nearly impossible to enforce) are often viewed as evidence that the entire parole process is a joke. Persons returning from the trauma of prison with few resources and little hope are likely to become "defiant" (Sherman 1993) at the "piling up of sanctions" (Blomberg and Lucken 1994) involved in such risk-based supervision. And constant threats that are not backed up can lead to a form of psychological inoculation. Colvin, Cullen, and Vander Ven (2002:22) write:

> Coercive interpersonal relations constitute the most aversive and negative forces individuals encounter. These are most likely to produce a strong sense of anger. The anger is only intensified if the individual perceives the coercive treatment as unjust or arbitrary. Instead of producing conformity, such coercive treatment creates greater defiance of authority.

Ex-convicts often feel they have paid their debt to society already and should therefore be left alone after release. Far from endorsing a "seamless" transition from prison control to community control, ex-convict academics Alan Mobley and Chuck Terry (2002) write, "No one wants the separation of prison and parole more urgently than do prisoners. When people 'get out,' they want to *be out*. Any compromise or half-measure, any 'hoops' or hassles placed in their path, breeds resentment." The extent of this resentment is apparent in the fascinating, and apparently somewhat widespread, phenomenon of convicts choosing to "max out" their sentences inside a prison rather than be released early and face high levels of supervision (see also Petersilia and Deschenes 1994).

Most importantly, however, the control narrative suffers from the "deeply entrenched view" that "equates punishment and control with incarceration, and that accepts alternatives as suitable only in cases where neither punishment nor control is thought necessary" (Smith 1984:171). Essentially, if parolees are such dangerous men and need so much supervision, then why aren't they still in prison? The average U.S. parole officer—who has a caseload of 69 parolees each averaging 1.6 face-to-face contacts per month (Camp and Camp 1997)—simply cannot compete with the iron bars, high walls and razor wire of the prison when it comes to securing constraint-based compliance (see Bottoms 2000:92–93). Colvin and his colleagues (2002:23) write, "Although in theory consistent coercion can prevent crime, it is highly difficult to maintain consistent coercion in interpersonal relations, which requires nearly constant monitoring to detect noncompliance." As a result, of course, those who truly support a risk-centered narrative traditionally oppose parole release altogether, supporting instead maximum use of incapacitation.

SUPPORT NARRATIVES (NEED-BASED)

The traditional counter to a risk-based parole system is a program of aftercare based on needs. Here the story is that ex-convicts are people with multiple deficits: some resulting from their incarceration (e.g., post-traumatic stress, disconnection from family, unfamiliarity with the world of work); some existing prior to incarceration (e.g., poor educational history, psychological problems, anger issues); and some attributable to societal forces outside of their control (e.g., discrimination, abuse, poverty, isolation). The most significant of these deficits, in the support narrative, are those deemed "criminogenic needs" or those problems that seem to be empirically related to offending (cognitive deficits are especially important here). In order to reduce crime, these needs must be "met" or at least "addressed." Specifically, released prisoners are thought to need access to programs in addiction counseling, cognitive therapy, life skills training, anger management, and the like.

Like the control narrative, this account has intuitive appeal. Yet, unlike in the case of coercive strategies of control, there is a well-known body of research (the so-called "What Works" literature) that supports the notion that rehabilitative interventions can marginally reduce recidivism rates when treatment is correctly matched to a client's criminogenic needs (see Gendreau et al. 1994). Moreover, in the few studies that ask returning prisoners themselves what would help to keep them "straight," basic "survival" needs (i.e., concerns like housing and employment) are almost always mentioned prominently (e.g., Erickson, Crow, Zurcher, and Connet 1973).

The support narrative, however, is a difficult sell politically. As everyone has needs, can it make sense for the state to prioritize the needs of persons who have recently been punished by the criminal justice system? As Bazemore (forthcoming) argues, "The notion of someone who has hurt another citizen... getting help or service without making amends for what has been damaged flies in the face of virtually universal norms of fairness." This was recently illustrated vividly in New York State, where gubernatorial candidate Carl McCall suggested that ex-convicts should receive help getting into college programs. During a discussion with homeless shelter residents who complained of difficulties receiving federal assistance for education because of their criminal records, McCall stated, "Just because you're an ex-offender, you should not be denied education aid. In fact, if you're an ex-offender I think you ought to get a preference." This simple statement of the support position set off an eruption of protest from his gubernatorial opponents, both Democratic and Republican, one of whom said, "Now he wants ex-convicts to get preference over hard-working students. No wonder Carl McCall was such a failure as president of the N.Y.C. Board of Education" (Nagourney 2002:B1).

Indeed, if the State ever really tried to meet all of the needs of ex-convicts (including financial, esteem, and self-actualization needs) and not just those needs deemed "criminogenic," the outpouring of generosity would surely contradict all principles of justice—let alone the controversial notion of "less eligibility." Who would not want to go to prison if the reward awaiting them upon release was that all their needs would be met? Of course, the needs of ex-convicts are rarely met in the 1.6 monthly meetings with a parole officer, referral or placement orders, and social service access that are at the heart of the casework model. "Needs" in correctional terms have come to connote something quite different than the way the word was defined by Maslow (1970), who left "procriminal attitudes" or "criminal associates" off his hierarchy. In their powerful essay contrasting criminogenic needs to human needs, Tony Ward and Claire Stewart (forthcoming:4) point out: "Even when the focus has been on offenders' needs, policy makers tend to be concerned with reducing further crimes or the incidence of disruptive behavior within prisons rather than the enhancement of their well being[3] and capabilities." In fact, needs have become synonymous with risk factors, and "meeting needs" can often equate to expanding the net of social control. So, for example, random mandatory drug testing for marijuana use gets framed as meeting a person's need to stop risky behaviors. It is unclear what is meant to represent the carrot in such treatment.

COMBINING CARROTS AND STICKS: AN ODD COUPLE?

The traditional, middle-ground position, which appeals to Reno and many of the contemporary reentry reformers, is to resolve the pendulous mentor-monitor debate by trying to do both. Basically, the idea is that if one combines a control approach (which does not really work, but is assumed to have public support) with a treatment approach (that works a little, but is thought to lack widespread support), the end result will be a program that is both popular and effective.

Instead, more often than not, the result of mixing such disparate goals is a "muddle" (Dickey and Smith 1998). David Fogel (1978:10–11) once quipped, "A parole officer can be seen going off to his/her appointed rounds with Freud in one hand and a .38 Smith and Wesson in the other.... Is Freud a backup to the .38? Or is the .38 earned to 'support' Freud?" The history of crime control in the 20th Century suggests that when both tools (the therapeutic and the punitive) are available, the latter will almost always win out or at least undermine the former (Garland 1985). Although parents and parental guardians are comfortable combining a disciplinary role with a social support role, this cop-and-counselor combination may not be possible in the much more limited relationship between the reentry court judge and the ex-convict or the parole officer and parolee. Indeed, more often than not, interventions premised on a combination-deficit model end up becoming "almost all stick and no carrot" (Prison Reform Trust 1999).

Theoretically, control strategies are intended to encourage instrumental compliance during the supervisory period, while the treatment strategies are designed to help participants internalize new, moral values. That is, the therapy or the job training is what is really going to work, but without the heavy coercion, the ex-prisoners will not show up for the treatment. And this hypothesis has some empirical support (MacKenzie and Brame 2001; Petersilia and Turner 1993). In particular, it has been well established that persons coerced into drug treatment programs fare equally as well as those who enter voluntarily (Farabee, Prendergast, and Anglin 1998).

Nonetheless, coercing compliance is one thing, but coercing good behavior is quite another. Consistent coercion may produce minimal levels of criminal behavior but it also produces very low levels of prosocial behavior (Colvin, Cullen, and Vander Ven 2002:28). Paul Gendreau and his colleagues (1999:89) argue this forcefully:

> Punishment only trains a person what not to do. If one punishes a behaviour what is left to replace it? In the case of high-risk offenders, simply other anti-social skills! This is why punishment scholars state that the most effective way to produce behavioural change is not to suppress "bad" behaviour, but to shape "good" behavior.

Carrot and stick models of reentry assign a largely passive role to the ex-prisoner and hence are unlikely to inspire intrinsically motivated self-initiative (Bazemore 1999). As such, critics argue that the operant conditioning implied in the carrot and stick metaphor confounds blind conformity with responsible behavior. Clark (2000:42) writes: "Compliance makes a poor final goal for drug courts. Obedience is not a lofty goal. We can teach animals to obey."

Moreover, coerced treatment is often resented by correctional consumers, who prefer self-help groups to state-sponsored reform programs (Irwin 1974; Mobley and Terry 2002). The eminent social psychologist George H. Mead (1918) explained the reason why combination control-support efforts are doomed to failure, almost a century ago:

> The two attitudes, that of control of crime by the hostile procedure of the law and that of control through comprehension of social and psychological conditions, cannot be combined. To understand is to forgive, and the social procedure seems to deny the very responsibility which the law affirms. On the other hand the pursuit by criminal justice inevitably awakens the hostile attitude in the offender and renders the attitude of mutual comprehension practically impossible (592).

In a process evaluation of the experimental Reentry Partnership Initiative, Faye Taxman and colleagues (2002:8) found telling evidence in support for this view. They write: "Program designers assumed offenders would be willing to be under additional community supervision in exchange for access to free community-based services on demand. They were surprised when almost no one took them up on the offer." The authors conclude that the offenders' past experiences with law enforcement, supervision agencies, and treatment providers had "left them dubious about the real intention of these agencies and staff." Therefore, the authors decide that any further "efforts to find fault, increase revocations, or speed a return to the justice system will only undermine the reentry goals" (8; see also Tyler et al. 1997).

Finally, the carrot and stick model of reentry fails to assign a meaningful role to the community. Although the process of reintegration has always had as much to do with the community as it has with the individual, carrot and stick reintegration models focus almost exclusively on the individual ex-prisoner. If reentry is to be a meaningful concept, presumably it implies more than physically reentering society, but also includes some sort of "relational reintegration" back into the moral community. Braithwaite and Braithwaite (2001:49) list four facets of what they call "reintegration":

- Approval of the person—praise
- Respectfulness
- Rituals to terminate disapproval with forgiveness
- Sustaining pride in having the offender included as a member of communities of care (families, the school, the law abiding community at large).

Reintegration, then, means full inclusion in and *of* a wider moral community. Social dependency and intensive supervision (or so-called carrots and sticks) seem to be the opposite of this sort of moral and social inclusion.

STRENGTHS-BASED REENTRY: AN EMERGING NARRATIVE?

Nobody makes the critical point: We need these people. The country is missing something because a huge bulk of its population is not a part of it. They have talents we need.

—Mimi Silbert, co-founder of Delancey Street
(cited in Mieszkowski 1998)

An alternative paradigm is emerging (actually reemerging) in social service areas related to corrections that may be useful in re-imagining reentry. For the sake of consistency (and not just to invent another new term), we will refer to this as a "strengths-based" paradigm[4] (see also Bazemore 1999; Nissen and Clark forthcoming; van Wormer 2001)—or else "restorative reentry."[5] Strengths-based or restorative approaches ask not what a person's deficits are, but rather what positive contribution the person can make. Nissen and Clark (forthcoming) caution that strengths (of youths, families, and communities) are believed to be the most commonly wasted resources in the justice system. Strengths need to be assessed and "targeted" in the same way that risks and needs traditionally have been. To do so, one simply asks "How can this person make a useful and purposeful contribution to society?" In Jeremy Travis's (2000:7) words: "Offenders are seen as assets to be managed rather than merely liabilities to be supervised." This shift represents a move away from the notion of entitlement to the principle of "social exchange" (Levrant, Cullen, Fulton, and Wozniak 1999:22) or to what Bazemore (1999) calls "earned redemption."

Importantly, we make no pretension to "discovering" (and most certainly not inventing) this paradigm. Strengths-based themes have been a staple of progressive criminal justice reforms at least since the time of Maconochie's Mark System. After a recent rejuvenation in the 1960s and 1970s under the guise of the "New Careers Movement"

(Cressey 1965; Grant 1968), however, this theme largely disappeared from correctional practice and rhetoric. The case being made in this section is only that there are signs that a strengths narrative seems to be coming back in multiple guises in the social services, and that this theme may be an appropriate one to introduce into the reentry debate.

In the reentry context, the strengths *narrative* begins with the assumption that ex-convicts are stigmatized persons, and implicitly that this stigma (and not some internal dangerousness or deficit) is at the core of what makes ex-convicts likely to reoffend. The "narrative of criminogenesis" that Simon (1993) calls for, then, is clearly based on a labeling/social exclusion story—on which, of course, the very idea of "reintegration" is also premised (Duffee and McGarrell 1990). Johnson (2002:319) writes, "released prisoners find themselves 'in' but not 'of' the larger society" and "suffer from a presumption of moral contamination." To combat this social exclusion, the strengths paradigm calls for opportunities for ex-convicts to make amends, demonstrate their value and potential, and make positive contributions to their communities. In the language of the New Careers movement, the goal is to "devise ways of creating more helpers" (Pearl and Riessman 1965:88). Strengths-based practice, like the New Careers movement before it, would seek "to transform receivers of help (such as welfare recipients) into dispensers of help; to structure the situation so that receivers of help will be placed in roles requiring the giving of assistance" (Pearl and Riessman 1965: 88–89).

These accomplishments are thought to lead to "a sense of hope, an orientation toward the future, and the willingness to take responsibility" (Richie 2001:385). Moreover, such demonstrations send a message to the community that the offender is worthy of further support and investment in their reintegration (Bazemore 1999). Ideally, these contributions can be recognized and publicly "certified" in order to symbolically "de-label" the stigmatized person (see Maruna 2001: chapter eight). Although this sort of reentry is always a challenge, it is far more likely to occur in a reciprocal situation: one needs "to do something to get something" (Toch 1994:71). A participant in the Rethinking Probation conference discussed the intuitive appeal of such a narrative:

> Let me put it this way, if the public knew that when you commit some wrongdoing, you're held accountable in constructive ways and you've got to earn your way back through these kinds of good works,... (probation) wouldn't be in the rut we're in right now with the public (Dickey and Smith 1998:36).

This symbolic appeal of transforming the probationer into a "giver rather than a consumer of help" is also evidenced by the enthusiasm around community service as a sanction in the 1970s, especially in Europe.

STRENGTHS-BASED PRACTICES: A GROWING TREND

Indeed, the narrative seems to have become somewhat contagious, at least among academics, over the last half-decade or so. Variations of strengths-based practice can now be found in every form of social work practice in the United States (Saleebey 1997) and are slowly making their way into traditional criminal justice practice (Clark 2000, 2001; Nissen and Clark forthcoming; van Wormer 2001). Identical paradigm shifts seem to be taking place across a variety of other disciplines including the focus on "positive psychology," developmental resilience, appreciative inquiry, wellness research, solution-focused therapy, assets-based community development, and narrative therapy. All of these new paradigms share an anti-pathologizing approach that focuses on building on strengths rather than correcting deficits.

In a criminal justice framework, strength approaches would ask not what needs to be done to a person in response to an offense, but rather what the person can accomplish to make amends for his or her actions (e.g., in the form of community service contributions). In the last 30 years, virtually every U.S. probation department has had some experience with community service as a sanction, and it has been widely viewed as a rare penal success story. Yet despite its origins as a rehabilitative panacea, community service is no longer uniformly justified using a strengths narrative. According to Bazemore and Maloney (1994:24), "punishment now appears to have become the dominant objective of service sanctions in many jurisdictions." Indeed, in the United Kingdom this shift has been made explicit by the relabeling of community service as a "community punishment order." When it is strengths-based, community service work is voluntarily agreed upon and involves challenging tasks that could utilize the talents of the offender in useful, visible roles (McIvor 1998).

Probation and parole projects in which offenders visibly and directly produce things the larger community wants, such as gardens, graffiti-free neighborhoods, less dangerous alleys, habitable housing for the homeless ... have also helped build stronger communities, and have carved channels into the labor market for the offenders engaged in them (Dickey and Smith 1998:35).

These volunteer activities could take place both inside as well as outside the prison. In a partnership program with Habitat for Humanity, convicts from 75 prisons (working alongside volunteers from the community) built over 250 homes for low income Americans in 1999 (Ta 2000). Prisoners in New York State have been involved in the crucial work of providing respite care to fellow inmates dying of AIDS and other illnesses in the prison system. In the year 2000, as part of a service learning curricula focused on "personal responsibility and reparation," prisoners in the state of Ohio performed more than 5 million hours of community service work, including rehabbing low-income homes, training pilot and companion dogs, and repairing computers to be donated to schools (Wilkinson 2001). Perhaps most impressive among the contributions made by prisoners is the little publicized but essential work that teams of prisoners have voluntarily undertaken in fighting the forest fires ravaging America's national parks. Prisoners are routinely sent into areas struck by flooding or other natural disasters to provide support to relief efforts.

Prisoners also have initiated parenting programs—like the Eastern Fathers' Group (EFG) that was created "by" and "for" incarcerated fathers at a maximum-security New York State prison (Lanier and Fisher 1990). Consisting of mutual support meetings, monthly educational seminars, and a certified parenting education course, the EFG served to heighten participants' sense of accomplishment and responsibility. At the same time it helped fathers work through the grief they experienced over the loss or deterioration of family bonds. Surveys of prisoners in the United States show that 55 percent of State and 63 percent of Federal prisoners have children under the age of eighteen, and almost half of those parents were living with their children at the time they were incarcerated (Bureau of Justice Statistics 2000). Active engagement in parenting while incarcerated is thought to provide a "stability zone" for offenders that "softens the psychological impact of confinement" (Toch 1975) and may help reduce recidivism and "transmit prosocial attitudes to a future generation" (Lanier and Fisher 1990:164).

Another characteristically strengths-based role is that of the "wounded healer" or "professional ex-" (Brown 1991:219), defined as a person who desists from a "deviant career" by "replacing it" with an occupation as a paraprofessional,[6] lay therapist, or counselor. Although it is impossible to measure the true extent of the "professional ex-" phenomenon, Brown (1991:219) estimated that around three-quarters of the counselors working in the over ten thousand substance abuse treatment centers in the United States are former substance abusers themselves. Describing female "wounded healers," Richie (2001:385) writes:

> Most services that are successful in helping women reintegrate into the community have hired (or are otherwise influenced by) women who have been similarly situated. The extent to which women have a peer and/or mentoring relationship with someone whom they perceive is "like them" is critical.

In addition to such professional work, thousands of former prisoners and addicts freely volunteer their time helping others in mutual aid groups like Bill Sands' Seventh Step organization. Indeed, the "twelve steps" of Alcoholics Anonymous (AA) and Narcotics Anonymous (NA) are premised around an explicit service orientation, codified in the Twelfth Step and the Fifth Tradition, which encourages those who find sobriety to assist others in taking this journey. According to O'Reilly (1997:128), "next to avoiding intoxicants," the therapeutic power of *helping* is "the major premise upon which (AA) is built." AA and NA members who have been sober for many years often remain with the organization, not so much because they need to *receive* any more counseling, but because the act of counseling *others* can itself be empowering and therapeutic. Members who stay connected to the program eventually take on the role of sponsors and become the mentors and teachers of the next generation of recovering addicts. AA's co-founder Bill Wilson said that he felt that his own sobriety was dependent upon his acting as a mentor in this way.

With little doubt, the best existing model for a strengths-based, mutual aid society for ex-convicts outside prison is the Delancey Street program based in San Francisco. Founded in 1971 by Mimi Silbert and ex-convict John Maher, Delancey Street has grown from an organization consisting of ten recovering addicts (and one criminal psychologist) living in an apartment to a thriving organization with 1,500 full-time residents in five self-run facilities, more than 20 businesses that double as training schools, and an annual operating budget of close to $24 million (Boschee and Jones 2000; Mieszkowski 1998). The program is self-supporting and has no professional staff. Instead, taking an "each one teach one" approach, older residents teach and train newer arrivals [who] then utilize these new skills to sustain the organization once the more senior residents "graduate" into private housing and independent careers. Silbert says residents "learn a fundamental lesson...that they have something to offer. These are people who have always been passive....But strength and power come from being on the giving end" (Boschee and Jones 2000:11).

Finally, in recent years there have been several attempts to coordinate the efforts and energies of a variety of such mutual aid groups in the name of creating lasting social change. In what is being called the "New Recovery Movement" (White 2001:16), wounded healers are also beginning to become "recovery activists," turning their "personal stories into social action" (19), and turning "recovery outwards" (19). Instead of working solely on their own addiction problems, recovering persons and their supporters would mobilize their strengths in order to change "the ecology of addiction and recovery" (White 2001:19). These and other mutual aid efforts are thought to help transform individuals from being part of the problem into being part of the solution as they give their time in the service of helping others.

THEORETICAL AND EMPIRICAL SUPPORT FOR THE "HELPER PRINCIPLE"

Although these activities can be justified on many grounds, one of the central theoretical premises all of these strengths-based practices share is some faith in the "helper principle" (Pearl and Riessman 1965). Promoted in the 1960s New Careers Movement, the helper principle simply says that it may be better (that is, more reintegrative) to give help than to receive it (see also Cullen 1994:543–544). The alleged benefits of assuming the role of helper include a sense of accomplishment, grounded increments in self-esteem, meaningful purposiveness, and a cognitive restructuring toward responsibility (Toch 2000). Rather than coercing obedience, strengths-based practices are thought to develop intrinsic motivations toward helping behaviors—what Nissen and Clark (forthcoming:70) call the "difference between compliance and growth." Clients are supposedly "turned on" to prosocial behavior through involvement with activities that utilize their strengths. In the words of Alexis de Tocqueville (1835/1956:197), "By dint of working for one's fellow-citizens, the habit and the taste for serving them is at length acquired." In addition, as part of a helping collective, the "wounded healer" or community volunteer is thought to obtain "a sense of belonging and an esprit de corps" (Pearl and Riessman 1965:83). According to the helper principle, all these experiences should be related to successful reintegration and social inclusion.

Recent research on desistance from crime might provide some indirect empirical support for this claim. For instance, as is well known, Sampson and Laub (1993) found that one-time offenders who were employed and took responsibility for providing for their spouses and children were significantly more likely to desist from crime than those who made no such bonds. A less well known finding of their research was that desistance was strongly correlated with assuming financial responsibility for one's aging parents or siblings in need as well (Sampson and Laub 1993:219–220). One way to interpret these findings might be to hypothesize that nurturing behaviors may be inconsistent with a criminal life-style. Indeed, Lynne Goodstein speculates that women's traditional responsibility for other family and community members may be one reason that females are so dramatically underrepresented in criminal statistics (cited in Cullen 1994).

Moreover, quasi-experimental evaluations of community service sentencing consistently show that it outperforms standard probation and other sanctions in reducing recidivism (Rex 2001; Schneider 1986). Further, McIvor (1998) found that people who viewed their experience of community service as "rewarding" had lower rates of recidivism than those who found it a chore, indicating that this impact is less about deterrence and more likely something to do with prosocial modeling or moral development (Van Voorhis 1985). McIvor (1998) writes, "In many instances, it seems, contact with the beneficiaries gave offenders an insight into other people, and an increased insight into themselves;...greater confidence and self-esteem;...(and) the confidence and appreciation of other people" (McIvor 1998:55–56; cited in Rex 2001).

More recently, longitudinal studies have tried to assess the long-term impact of volunteer work on life course trajectories. Uggen and Janikula (1999) investigated the question of whether involvement in volunteer work can induce a change in a person's likelihood of antisocial conduct. They found a robust negative relationship between volunteer work and arrest even after statistically controlling for the effects of antisocial propensities, prosocial attitudes, and commitments to conventional behavior. Uggen and Janikula (1999:355) conclude:

> What is it about the volunteer experience that inhibits antisocial behavior? We suggest that the informal social controls emphasized in social bond, social learning, and reintegrative theories are the mechanism linking volunteer work and antisocial behavior. Informal social controls are consonant with Tocquevillian conceptions of "self-interest, rightly understood," in which volunteers are gradually socialized or "disciplined by habit rather than will."

Finally, Maruna's (2001) research on the psychology of desistance from crime offers further evidence of a link between a "generative" identity and criminal reform. In a clinical comparison of successfully and unsuccessfully reformed ex-convicts, Maruna found that those who were able to "go straight" were significantly more care-oriented, other-centered and focused on promoting the next generation. They tried to find some meaning in their shameful life histories by turning their experiences into cautionary or hopeful stories of redemption, which they shared with younger offenders in similar situations. Whereas active offenders characterized themselves as being doomed or predestined to failure, reformed offenders had an almost overly optimistic sense of control over their future and strong internal beliefs about their own self-worth. In short, their personal narratives (the stories they told about how they were able to "go straight") resembled "strength narratives" far more than control or support narratives. Indeed, the latter seemed to characterize the narratives of active offenders.

None of this research is firm evidence in favor of the "helper principle." In particular, although these studies may suggest a basic incompatibility between helping activities and criminal lifestyles, they tell us little about how to "create more helpers." Indeed, the lack of research on mutual aid organizations, self-help groups, and informal mentoring and parenting among convicts and ex-convicts is rather startling considering how much research is funded each year to examine the impact of greater controls and, less frequently, treatment programming (see Uggen and Piliavin 1998:1421–1422). Still, as a narrative—that is, a theoretical premise—the restorative idea of "earned redemption" seems to have at least some plausibility from the limited research that exists.

A STRENGTHS-BASED REENTRY COURT

> Become future focused: the past, and the focus on past failures, can open the door to demoralization and resignation—hope is future based.
>
> —Michael D. Clark (2001:23)

Strengths-based practices and principles may be uniquely suited to the new reentry court idea. First, unlike traditional jurisprudence, reentry courts would presumably be future-oriented rather than focused on the past. Determining guilt and devising a fair response to a criminal act are responsibilities that belong to other courts. The reentry court's role might more reasonably be understood as dispensing "reintegration"—not release from prison or supervision (as is the traditional role of the parole board), but rather a release from the stigma of the original conviction. The work of reentry, then, would be the facilitation of opportunities to make amends for what one has done and the recognition of these contributions and accomplishments. True to its name, then, the reentry court could become a "court of redemption," through which a stigmatized person has the opportunity to formally "make good."

Rewarding positive achievements, rather than punishing violations, is an unusual role for the courts. Parole as it is currently practiced focuses almost entirely on detecting and punishing failure—even though the "what works" principles suggest that positive reinforcement should outweigh punishment by a 4:1 ratio (Gendreau et al. 1994). As conformity is all that is required of deficit-based parole, it makes little sense to commend or acknowledge persons simply for doing what they are supposed to and following the rules. Indeed, the primary "reward" available in parole today is to "get off" parole early, a particularly strange and unceremonious process.[7]

Alternatively, a strengths-based reentry court might be modeled on Braithwaite's (2001:11) notion of "active responsibility": "Passive responsibility means holding someone responsible for something they have done in the past. Active responsibility means the virtue of taking responsibility for putting things right for the future." The court would not be concerned with past offenses, misbehavior in prison or even violations of parole. All of these crimes and misdemeanors are properly punished by other authorities. The focus, instead, would be on monitoring, recording, and judging what the individual has done to redeem him or herself through victim reparation, community service, volunteer work, mentoring, and parenting.[8] Witnesses would be called, testimony would be offered, tangible evidence would be produced—not in the name of establishing guilt or innocence, but rather in order to assess the contribution being made by the returning prisoner both in prison and afterwards. The reentry court could then be the setting for a "public recognition ceremony" acknowledging these contributions and accomplishments as "a milestone in repaying (one's) debt to society" (Travis 2000:9).

With no powers to punish, a strengths court, then, would be more a challenge to returning ex-convicts than a threat. That is, the ex-offender would be given an opportunity to be publicly and formally reintegrated if they were willing to pay a debt to society in terms of their service and contribution. Winick (1991:246) refers to this as "harnessing the power of the bet":

> Many people do not respond well when told to do so. Unless they themselves see merit in achieving the goal, sometimes even when the costs of non-compliance are high, they may well resent pressure imposed by others and refuse to comply or may act perversely in ways calculated to frustrate achievement of the goal. By contrast, the offer to wager can be accepted or rejected. The choice is up to the individual. The law strongly favors allowing such choice, rather than attempting to achieve public or private goals through compulsion.

Winick (1991:247) argues that, unlike coerced compliance, this challenge model is likely to mobilize "the self-evaluative and self-reinforcing mechanisms of intrinsic motivation" and effect "lasting attitudinal and behavioral change in the individual."

The notion of rewarding success, of course, is a key component of the reentry court idea. In drug treatment courts,[9] "applause is common" and "even judicial hugs are by no means a rare occurrence" (Wexler 2001:21). Travis (1999:133) asserts that "the court should use positive judicial reinforcement by serving as a public forum for encouraging pro-social behavior and for affirming the value of individual effort in earning the privilege of successful reintegration." In the experimental Reentry Partnership Initiatives, successful "reentry graduates" may eventually move from being "recipients of services" to acting as role models and "guardians" for newly released offenders just entering the structured reentry phase of the process (Taxman et al. 2002: 18; similar recommendations were proposed by Erickson et al. 1973:103–105). Among other program requirements, each participant in Richland County, Ohio's new reentry court is required to complete 300 hours of community service work that commences upon incarceration (Wilkinson 2001). Finally, all reentry courts are required to outline milestones in the reentry process (such as the completion of this sort of volunteer work) that would trigger recognition and an appropriate reward (Office of Justice Programs 1999).

A strengths approach would probably take this further, and following Johnson (2002:328) would recast the reentry court process as "a mutual effort at reconciliation, where offender and society work together to make amends—for hurtful crimes and hurtful punishments—and move forward."

Braithwaite and Braithwaite (2001:16) have argued that praise may work in the exact opposite form that shaming does. That is, while it is better to shame an individual act and not the whole person, it may be better to praise the whole person than the specific act.

> So when a child shows a kindness to his sister, better to say "you are a kind brother" than "that was a kind thing you did"....(P)raise that is tied to specific acts risks counter productivity if it is seen as an extrinsic reward, if it nurtures a calculative approach to performances that cannot be constantly monitored....Praising virtues of the person rather than just their acts...nourishes a positive identity (Braithwaite and Braithwaite 2001:16).

According to Makkai and Braithwaite (1993:74), such praise can have "cognitive effects on individuals through nurturing law-abiding identities, building cognitive commitments to try harder, encouraging individuals who face adversity not to give up . . . and nurturing belief in oneself."

As such, the strengths-based reentry court would need to go beyond the occasional rewarding of specific acts of service and instead build gradually to a more holistic "earned redemption" of the participant's character and reputation. This might take the shape of a "status elevation ceremony" that could "serve publicly and formally to announce, sell, and spread the fact of the Actor's new kind of being" (Lofland 1969: 227). In such rituals, "Some recognized member(s) of the conventional community must publicly announce and certify that the offender has changed and that he is now to be considered essentially non-criminal" (Meisenhelder 1977:329). These need not be once-off occasions. Just as Braithwaite and Braithwaite (2001) propose that reintegration ceremonies may need to occur more than once, multiple certification rituals may be needed in multiple domains in order to counteract the stigma faced by former prisoners. If endorsed and supported by the same social control establishment involved in the "status degradation" process of conviction and sentencing, this public redemption might carry considerable social and psychological weight for participants and observers (Maruna 2001: chapter eight).

Most importantly, the reward would also involve the "expiration" of the individual's criminal history—allowing the person freedom from having to declare previous convictions to potential employers, licensing bodies, or other authorities and to resume full citizenship rights and responsibilities.[10] The ultimate prize, then, for (proactive) "good behavior" would be permission to legally move on from the past and wipe the slate clean. This, it seems, may better represent the definition of "reintegration."

STUDY QUESTIONS

1. What are the core elements of problem-solving courts such as reentry courts?
2. Briefly describe the risk- and needs-based approaches outlined in the article.
3. What are some of the "carrots and sticks" referred to in the article?
4. What is a strengths-based approach to reentry courts? Give some examples.

NOTES

1. The original Clinton agenda also involved a substantial new project referred to as the Reentry Partnership Initiative (RPI), which is beyond the scope of this paper, although similar in many ways to the reentry court. For instance, the stated goal of the RPI initiative is to "improve risk management of released offenders ... by enhancing surveillance, risk and needs assessments, and pre-release planning" (RPI Report 2000:1; see also Taxman, Young, Byrne, Holsinger, and Anspach 2002).
2. These should be seen as distinct from previous efforts to abolish parole release structures, which largely left post-incarceration supervision intact.
3. Even in the most progressive versions of the support narrative, this level of need-fulfilment is difficult to achieve. For instance, Sullivan and Tifft (2001) point out that although there is much talk in restorative justice circles about "meeting the needs" of offenders as well as victims, the two are seen as significantly different. While crime victims are thought to need understanding, support and love from those around them, offenders are said to need a job, clothing, and shelter. Sullivan and Tifft (2001:83) write, "By focusing on this level of needs alone, we do not show the same level of concern for them as we do for those who have been harmed."
4. This of course is an umbrella term that encompasses approaches that go by many other names (most notably Restorative Justice, the New

Careers movement, relational rehabilitation, and the New Recovery Movement).

5. "Restorative Reentry" is the preferred phrase of the Open Society Institute's remarkable array of strengths-based, advocacy projects sponsored as part of the After Prison Initiative (see <http://www.soros.org/crime/CJIGuidelines.htm#tapi>).
6. Interestingly, the Clinton Administration's original Young Offender Initiative (OJP 2001:12) stated: "Applicants are encouraged to use ex-offenders as staff and those with a history of substance abuse or mental illness. Having some staff with these backgrounds helps the therapeutic process and builds the community's capacity to continue services after the grant ends." There is no mention of utilizing the strengths of ex-offenders in this way in the Bush Administration's initiative.
7. When one of this paper's authors earned his freedom after 56 months of parole supervision, he was offered not so much as a "congratulations" or a "good luck" from the officer who had such power over his life. In fact, he only found out that he had been released from parole supervision when he called his PO to get a travel pass to visit family out of state. The memorable dialog proceeded something as follows: "So, does that mean I'm free?" "Yes, you don't need to report anymore." "Do I have all of my rights back?" "I don't know anything about that." "Thanks."
8. Research in the substance abuse field by Petry, Tedford, and Martin (2001:34) suggests that prosocial activity reinforcement (that is, rewarding positive behaviors) is more effective than reinforcement that is purely directed toward the absence of negative behaviors (e.g., drug abstinence). For instance, they found that prosocial activity reinforcement may result in improvements in psychosocial functioning (employment, medical, family problems) that are not apparent when drug abstinence alone is reinforced.
9. At their best, drug courts can epitomize the ideals of therapeutic jurisprudence, a clearly strengths based approach (see Hora, Schma, and Rosenthal 1999). Still, these ideals are not always realized in practice and one should be careful about exaggerating the role of praise in the actual practice of problem-solving courts. Ethnographers report that participants who successfully complete one large-scale drug court program, for instance, receive only "a congratulatory remark from the judge along with a T-shirt and key chain, claiming they are now '2 smart 4 drugs'" (Miethe, Lu, and Reese 2000:536). Burdon and colleagues (2001:78) write: "Descriptions of actual drug court operations reveal that most drug courts emphasize sanctions for noncompliance and few routinely use reinforcement of positive, desired behavior. (When used) rewards tend to be intermittent and, in contrast to sanctions, less specific, not immediately experienced, and based on a subjective evaluation of a defendants progress in treatment."
10. Like many other observers, we would argue that ex-convicts should retain their full civil rights (voting, jury membership, etc.) regardless of reentry court participation. These rights are entitlements and should not be used as "rewards" even in a reciprocity based reentry program.

REFERENCES

Austin, James. 2001. "Prisoner Reentry: Current Trends, Practices, and Issues." *Crime and Delinquency* 47:314–334.

Bazemore, Gordon. 1999. "After Shaming, Whither Reintegration: Restorative Justice and Relational Rehabilitation." Pp. 155–194 in *Restorative Juvenile Justice: Repairing the Harm of Youth Crime,* edited by G. Bazemore and L. Walgrave. Monsey, NY: Criminal Justice Press.

Bazemore, Gordon. 2004. "Reintegration and Restorative Justice: Toward a Theory and Practice of Informal Social Control and Support."

In *Ex-Offender Reintegration: Desistance from Crime After Prison,* edited by S. Maruna and R. Immarigeon. Albany, NY: SUNY Press.

Bazemore, Gordon and Dennis Maloney. 1994. "Rehabilitating Community Service: Toward Restorative Service Sanctions in a Balanced Justice System." *Federal Probation* 58:24–35.

Blomberg, Thomas and Karol Lucken. 1994. "Stacking the Deck by Piling Up Sanctions: Is Intermediate Punishment Destined to Fail?" *The Howard Journal* 33(l):62–80.

Booth, Maud B. 1903. *After Prison—What?* New York: Fleming H. Revell Company.

Boschee, Jerr and Syl Jones. 2000. "Recycling Excons, Addicts and Prostitutes: The Mimi Silbert Story." [Online], Available: www.socialent.org/pdfs/MimiSilbertStory.pdf.

Bottoms, Anthony E. 2000. "Compliance and Community Penalties." Pp. 87–116 in *Community Penalties: Change and Challenges,* edited by A. Bottoms, L. Gelsthorpe, and S. Rex. Cullompton: Willan.

Braithwaite, John. 2001. "Intention Versus Reactive Fault." Pp. 345–357 in *Intention in Law and Philosophy,* edited by N. Naffine, R. Owens, and John Williams. Aldershot, UK: Ashgate.

Braithwaite, John and Valerie Braithwaite. 2001. "Part One." Pp. 3–69 in *Shame Management Through Reintegration,* edited by E. Ahmed, N. Harris, J. Braithwaite, and V. Braithwaite. Cambridge: University of Cambridge Press.

Brown, David J. 1991. "The Professional Ex-: An Alternative for Exiting the Deviant Career." *The Sociological Quarterly* 32:219–230.

Burdon, William M., John M. Roll, Michael L. Prendergast, and Richard A. Rawson. 2001. "Drug Courts and Contingency Management." *Journal of Drug Issues* 31:73–90.

Bureau of Justice Statistics. 2000. *Incarcerated Parents and Their Children* (NCJ 182335). Washington, DC: U.S. Department of Justice.

Bureau of Justice Statistics. 2001, August 28. *Probation and Parole in the United States, 2000—Press Release* (NCJ 188208). Washington, DC: U.S. Department of Justice.

Camp, Camille G. and George M. Camp. 1997. *The Corrections Yearbook.* South Salem, NY: Criminal Justice Institute, Inc.

Chin, Robert and Kenneth D. Benne. 1976. "General Strategies for Effecting Changes in Human Systems." Pp. 22–44 in *The Planning of Change,* 3rd ed., edited by W. G. Bennis, K. D. Benne, R. Chin, and K. Corey. New York: Holt, Rinehart and Winston.

Clark, Michael D. 2000. "The Juvenile Drug Court Judge and Lawyer: Four Common Mistakes in Treating Drug Court Adolescents." *Juvenile and Family Court Journal* 51(4):37–46.

Clark, Michael D. 2001. "Influencing Positive Behavior Change: Increasing the Therapeutic Approach of Juvenile Courts." *Federal Probation* 65(1): 18–27.

Colvin, Mark, Francis T. Cullen, and Thomas M. Vander Ven. 2002. "Coercion, Social Support, and Crime: An Emerging Theoretical Consensus." *Criminology* 40:19–42.

Cressey, Donald R. 1965. "Social Psychological Foundations for Using Criminals in the Rehabilitation of Criminals." *Journal of Research in Crime and Delinquency* 2:49–59.

Cullen, Francis T. 1994. "Social Support as an Organizing Concept in Criminology: Presidential Address to the Academy of Criminal Justice Sciences." *Justice Quarterly* 11:527–559.

Cullen, Francis T. 2002. "Rehabilitation and Treatment Programs." Pp. 253–289 in *Crime: Public Policies for Crime Control,* edited by J. Q. Wilson and J. Petersilia. Oakland, CA: Institute for Contemporary Studies.

Dickey, Walter J. and Michael E. Smith. 1998. *Dangerous Opportunity: Five Futures for Community Corrections: The Report from the Focus Group.* Washington, DC: U.S. Department of Justice, Office of Justice Programs.

Duffee, David E. and Edmund F. McGarrell. 1990. *Community Corrections: A Community Field Approach.* Cincinnati, Ohio: Anderson.

Erickson, Rosemary J., Wayman J. Crow, Louis A. Zurcher, and Archie V. Connet. 1973. *Paroled But Not Free.* New York: Human Sciences Press.

Farabee, David, Michael Prendergast, and M. Douglas Anglin. 1998. "The Effectiveness of Coerced Treatment for Drug-abusing Offenders." *Federal Probation* 62(1):3–10.

Fogel, David. 1978. "Foreword." Pp. 7–15 in *Dangerous Men: The Sociology of Parole* by Richard McCleary. Beverly Hills, CA: Sage Publications.

Fogel, David. 1984. "The Emergence of Probation as a Profession in the Service of Public Safety: The Next Ten Years." Pp. 65–99 in *Probation and Justice: Reconsideration of Mission*, edited by P. D. McAnany, D. Thompson, and D. Fogel. Cambridge, MA: Oelgeschlager, Gunn, and Hain.

Garland, David. 1985. *Punishment and Welfare: A History of Penal Strategies.* Brookfield, VT: Gower Publishing Company.

Gebelein, Richard S. 2000. *The Rebirth of Rehabilitation: Promise and Perils of Drug Courts.* Papers from the Executive Sessions on Sentencing and Corrections (NCJ 181412). Washington, DC: U.S. Department of Justice, National Institute of Justice.

Gendreau, Paul, Francis T. Cullen, and James Bonta. 1994. "Intensive Rehabilitation Supervision: The Next Generation in Community Corrections?" *Federal Probation* 58:173–84.

Gendreau, Paul, Claire Goggin, and Francis T. Cullen. 1999. *The Effects of Prison Sentences on Recidivism.* A Report to the Corrections Research and Development and Aboriginal Policy Branch, Solicitor General of Canada, Ottawa.

Gordon, Diana. 1991. *The Justice Juggernaut: Fighting Street Crime, Controlling Citizens.* New Brunswick, NJ: Rutgers University Press.

Grant, J. Douglas. 1968. "The Offender as a Correctional Manpower Resource." Pp. 226–234 in *Up from Poverty: New Career ladders for Nonprofessionals,* edited by F. Riessman and H.L. Popper. New York: Harper and Row.

Hora, Peggy F., William G. Schrna, and John T. A. Rosenthal. 1999. "Therapeutic Jurisprudence and the Drug Treatment Court Movement: Revolutionizing the Criminal Justice Systems Response to Drug Abuse and Crime in America." *Notre Dame Law Review* 74:439–537.

Hughes, Timothy A., Doris. J. Wilson, and Allen J. Beck. 2001. *Trends in State Parole, 1990–2000.* Washington, D.C.: U.S. Department of Justice, Bureau of Justice Statistics: Special Report.

Irwin, John. 1974. "The Trouble with Rehabilitation." *Criminal Justice and Behavior* 1(2): 139–149.

Johnson, Robert. 2002. *Hard Time,* 3rd ed. Belmont, CA: Wadsworth.

Kelman, Herbert C. 1958. "Compliance, Identification and Internalization: Three Processes of Opinion Change." *Journal of Conflict Resolution* 2:51–60.

Langan, Patrick A. and David J. Levin. 2002. *Recidivism of Prisoners Released in 1994* (NCJ 193427). Washington, D.C.: U.S. Department of Justice, Bureau of Justice Statistics.

Lanier, Charles S. and Glenn Fisher. 1990. "A Prisoners' Parenting Center (PPC): A Promising Resource Strategy for Incarcerated Fathers." *Journal of Correctional Education* 41:158–165.

Levrant, Sharon, Francis T. Cullen, Betsy Fulton, and John F. Wozniak. 1999. "Reconsidering Restorative Justice: The Corruption of Benevolence Revisited?" *Crime and Delinquency* 45:3–27.

Lofland, John. 1969. *Deviance and Identity.* Englewood Cliffs, NJ : Prentice-Hall.

MacKenzie, Doris L. and Robert Brame. 2001. "Community Supervision, Prosocial Activities, and Recidivism." *Justice Quarterly* 18(2): 429–448.

MacKenzie, Doris L. and Spencer De Li. 2002. "The Impact of Formal and Informal Social Controls on the Criminal Activities of Probationers." *Journal of Research in Crime and Delinquency* 39:243–276.

Makkai, Toni and John Braithwaite. 1993. "Praise, Pride and Corporate Compliance." *International Journal of the Sociology of Law* 21: 73–91.

Maruna, Shadd. 2001. *Making Good: How Ex-convicts Reform and Rebuild Their Lives.* Washington, DC: American Psychological Association Books.

Maslow, Abraham H. 1970. *Motivation and Personality,* 2nd ed. New York: Harper and Row.

McArthur, Veme A. 1974. *Coming Out Cold: Community Reentry from a State Reformatory.* Lexington, MA: Lexington Books.

McGuire, James. 1995. "The Death of Deterrence." In *Does Punishment Work? Proceedings of a Conference Held at Westminster Central Hall*, London, UK, edited by J. McGuire and B. Rowson. London: ISTD.

McIvor, Gillian. 1998. "Pro-social Modelling and Legitimacy: Lessons from a Study of Community Service." In *Pro-social Modelling and Legitimacy: The Clarke Hall Day Conference*, edited by S. Rex and A. Matravers. Cambridge: Institute of Criminology, University of Cambridge.

Mead, George H. 1918. "The Psychology of Punitive Justice." *American Journal of Sociology* 23: 577–602.

Meisenhelder, Thomas. 1977. "An Exploratory Study of Exiting from Criminal Careers." *Criminology* 15:319–334.

Mieszkowski, Katherine. 1998. "She Helps Them Help Themselves." *Fast Company* 15:54–56.

Miethe, Terrance D., Hong Lu, and Erin Reese. 2000. "Reintegrative Shaming and Recidivism Risks in Drug Court: Explanations for Some Unexpected Findings." *Crime and Delinquency* 46:522–541.

Mobley, Alan and Charles Terry. 2002. *Dignity, Resistance and Re-Entry: A Convict Perspective.* Unpublished manuscript.

Nagourney, Adam. 2002, June 20. "McCall Urges Giving Help on Tuition to Ex-convicts." *New York Times*, B1.

Nissen, Laura B. and Michael D. Clark. Forthcoming. *Power of the Strengths Approach in the Juvenile Drug Court—Practice Monograph.* Washington, DC: U.S. Department of Justice, Office of Justice Programs, Juvenile Drug Court Programs Office.

O'Reilly, Edmund B. 1997. *Sobering Tales: Narratives of Alcoholism and Recovery.* Amherst, MA: University of Massachusetts Press.

Office of Justice Programs. 1999. *Reentry Courts: Managing the Transition from Prison to Community, A Call for Concept Papers.* Washington, DC: U.S. Department of Justice, Office of Justice Programs.

Office of Justice Programs. 2001. *Young Offender Initiative: Reentry Grant Program.* Washington, DC: U.S. Department of Justice, Office of Justice Programs.

Office of Justice Programs. 2002. *Serious and Violent Offender Reentry Initiative—Going Home.* Washington, DC: U.S. Department of Justice, Office of Justice Programs.

Pearl, Arthur and Frank Riessman. 1965. *New Careers for the Poor: The Nonprofessional in Human Service.* New York: The Free Press.

Petersilia, Joan and Elizabeth P. Deschenes. 1994. "What Punishes? Inmates Rank the Severity of Prison vs. Intermediate Sanctions." *Federal Probation* 58:38.

Petersilia, Joan and Susan Turner. 1993. "Intensive Probation and Parole." Pp. 281–335 in *Crime and Justice: An Annual Review of Research, Vol. 19*, edited by M. Tonry. Chicago, IL: University of Chicago Press.

Petry, Nancy M., Jacqueline Tedford, and Bonnie Martin. 2001. "Reinforcing Compliance with Nondrug-related Activities." *Journal of Substance Abuse Treatment* 20:33–44.

Peyton, Elizabeth A. and Robert Gossweiler. 2001. *Treatment Services in Adult Drug Courts: Report on the 1999 National Drug Court Treatment Survey* (NCJ 188085). Washington, DC: U.S. Department of Justice, Office of Justice Programs.

Prison Reform Trust. 1999. *Prison Incentives Scheme.* London: Prison Reform Trust.

Reentry Partnerships Initiative Report 2000. "Reducing the Threat of Recidivism." *RPI Report: Newsletter of the Reentry Partnerships Initiative* 1:12.

Reno, Janet. 2000. *Remarks of the Honorable Janet Reno on Reentry Court Initiative*, John Jay College of Criminal Justice, New York, February 10, 2000.

Rex, Sue. 2001. "Beyond Cognitive-Behaviouralism? Reflections on the Effectiveness Literature." In *Community Penalties: Change and Challenges*, edited by A. E. Bottoms, L. Gelsthorpe, and S. Rex. Cullompton, UK: Willan.

Rhine, Edward E. 1997. "Probation and Parole Supervision: In Need of a New Narrative." *Corrections Management Quarterly* 1(2):71–75.

Richie, Beth 2001. "Challenges Incarcerated Women Face as They Return to Their Communities: Findings from Life History Interviews." *Crime and Delinquency* 47:368–389.

Saleebey, Dennis. 1997. The *Strengths Perspective in Social Work Practice,* 2nd ed. New York: Longman.

Sampson, Robert J. and John Laub. 1993. *Crime in the Making: Pathways and Turning Points Through Life.* Cambridge, MA: Harvard University Press.

Schneider, Anne L. 1986. "Restitution and Recidivism Rates of Juvenile Offenders: Results from Four Experimental Studies." *Criminology* 24: 533–552.

Sherman, Lawrence W. 1993. "Defiance, Deterrence, and Irrelevance: A Theory of the Criminal Sanction." *Journal of Research in Crime and Delinquency* 30:445–473.

Simon, Jonathan. 1993. *Poor Discipline: Parole and the Social Control of the Underclass, 1890–1990.* Chicago: The University of Chicago Press.

Smith, Michael E. 1984. "Will the Real Alternatives Please Stand Up?" *New York University Review of Law and Social Change* 12:171–97.

Sullivan, Dennis and Larry Tifft. 2001. *Restorative Justice: Healing the Foundations of Our Everyday Lives.* Monsey, NY: Willow Free Press.

Ta, Christine. 2000, October. "Prison Partnership: It's About People." *Corrections Today* 62(6): 114–123.

Taxman, Faye S., Douglas Young, James M. Byrne, Alexander Holsinger, and Donald Anspach. 2002. *From Prison Safety to Public Safety: Innovations in Offender Reentry.* University of Maryland, College Park, Bureau of Government Research.

Toch, Hans. 1975. *Men in Crisis: Human Breakdowns in Prisons.* Chicago: Aldine.

Toch, Hans. 1994. "Democratizing Prisons." *Prison Journal* 73:62–72.

Toch, Hans. 2000. "Altruistic Activity as Correctional Treatment." *International Journal of Offender Therapy and Comparative Criminology* 44:270–278.

Tocqueville, Alexis. 1835/1956. *Democracy in America.* New York: Knopf. (Original work published in 1835).

Travis, Jeremy. 1999. "Prisons, Work and Re-entry." *Corrections Today* 61(6): 102–33.

Travis, Jeremy. 2000. *But They All Come Back: Rethinking Prisoner Reentry, Research in Brief-Sentencing and Corrections: Issues for the 21st Century* (NCJ 181413). Washington, D.C.: U.S. Department of Justice, National Institute of Justice.

Travis, Jeremy and Joan Petersilia. 2001. "Reentry Reconsidered: A New Look at an Old Question." *Crime and Delinquency* 47:291–313.

Tyler, Tom R., Robert J. Boeckmann, Heather J. Smith, and Yuen J. Huo. 1997. *Social Justice in a Diverse Society.* Denver, CO: Westview Press.

Uggen, Christopher and Jennifer Janikula. 1999. "Volunteerism and Arrest in the Transition to Adulthood." *Social Forces* 78:331–362.

Uggen, Christopher and Irving Piliavin. 1998. "Asymmetrical Causation and Criminal Desistance." *Journal of Criminal Law and Criminology* 88:1399–1422.

Van Voorhis, Patricia. 1985. "Restitution Outcome and Probationers' Assessments of Restitution: The Effects of Moral Development." *Criminal Justice and Behavior* 12:259–287.

van Wormer, Katherine. 2001. *Counseling Female Offenders and Victims: A Strengths-Restorative Approach.* New York: Springer.

Ward, Tony and Claire Stewart. 2004 "Criminogenic Needs and Human Needs: A Theoretical Model." *Psychology, Crime and Law.*

Wexler, David, B. 2001. "Robes and Rehabilitation: How Judges Can Help Offenders 'Make Good " *Court Review* 38:18–23.

White, William L. 2001. *The Rhetoric of Recovery Advocacy: An Essay on the Power of Language.* [Online]. Available: http://www.bhrm.org/advocacy/recovadvocacy.htm.

Wilkinson, Reginald A. 2001. "Offender Reentry: A Storm Overdue." *Corrections Management Quarterly* 5(3):46–51.

Winick, Bruce J. 1991. "Harnessing the Power of the Bet: Wagering with the Government as a Mechanism for Social and Individual Change." Pp. 219–290 in *Essays in Therapeutic Jurisprudence,* edited by David B. Wexler and Bruce J. Winick. Durham, NC: Carolina Academic Press.

27

PAROLE VIOLATIONS AND REVOCATIONS IN CALIFORNIA

ANALYSIS AND SUGGESTIONS FOR ACTION[1]

RYKEN GRATTET
JOAN PETERSILIA
JEFFREY LIN
MARLENE BECKMAN

No state has faced a more daunting task in reining in its correctional system than California. Once seen as the model for corrections, California now exemplifies all that is wrong with the correctional system. This problem is exacerbated by the high number of offenders that are released from prison, revoked on technical violations, and returned to prison. The authors discuss the results of a three-year study of the causes and consequences of parole violations in California and offer some practical solutions to this revolving door of incarceration.

The debate about the costs and benefits of imprisonment is taking place all across the United States, but the stakes are highest in California. California's 173,000 prisoners constitute the largest prison population of any state. One in seven state prisoners in the United States is incarcerated in California, and between 1980 and 2007, California's prison population increased over sevenfold, compared with a fourfold increase nationally. And, despite a 2003 vow by Governor Arnold Schwarzenegger to reduce the states prison population, California's prison population continues to grow; recent projections predict a prison population of 191,000 in the next five years.[2]

California's prison expenditures are also among the highest in the nation—per inmate, per staff, and as a share of the overall state budget. In 2006–2007, the average annual cost of housing a California prisoner in was $43,287, 1.6 times higher than the national average of about $26,000. At the beginning of the prison building boom in the early 1980s, adult and youth corrections accounted for four percent of California's general fund expenditures at $1 billion per year. Today, California's budget for state corrections is over $10 billion a year, and growing at a rate of seven percent annually—the fastest-growing segment of the states criminal justice expenditures. State correctional costs now account for approximately ten percent of total state spending—nearly the same amount the state spends on higher education. Even after adjusting for inflation, general fund expenditures to support California Department of Corrections and Rehabilitation (CDCR) operations increased 50 percent between 2001–2002 and 2008–2009.[3]

Central to California's debate over its prison system are the topics of parole violations and

Excerpts from "Parole Violations and Revocations in California: Analysis and Suggestions for Action," 2009, Ryken Grattet, Joan Petersilia, Jeffrey Lin, and Marlene Beckman, in *Federal Probation*, 73(1): 2–11.

revocations (returns to prison). In September 2005, the National Institute of Justice (NIJ) funded the authors to undertake a three-year comprehensive study of the causes and consequences of parole violations and revocations in California. The study was supported fully by CDCR, the agency that oversees all of California state corrections. Their cooperation was essential to access and understand the extensive data that our project required. The project represents the largest, most comprehensive, and most rigorous study of parole violations and revocations ever conducted.

UNDERSTANDING CALIFORNIA CORRECTIONS AND THE IMPORTANCE OF PAROLE VIOLATIONS

California's recidivism rate, as measured by the return-to-prison rate, is 66 percent, compared to a 40 percent national average. Sixty-six percent of all parolees in California returned to prison within three years, 27 percent for a new criminal conviction and 39 percent for a technical or administrative violation (which can result from new crimes or violations of the conditions of parole).[4] On any given day, six out of ten admissions to California prisons are returning parolees.[5]

Part of the explanation for California's anomalously high parole return rate is its unique sentencing and parole system. California, for the most part, has a *mandatory* parole release system. California moved from an indeterminate to a determinate sentencing system in the late 1970s, and as a result, most offenders are released after they have served their original court-imposed sentence, less any accumulated good time credit. California's Determinate Sentencing Law (DSL) allows offenders to earn, with some exceptions, day-for-day good time, which can result in a 50 percent reduction in the amount of time they must serve. For about 80 percent of prisoners in California, there is no appearance before a parole board to determine whether they are fit to return to the community; instead, they are *automatically* released. Once released, nearly all prisoners are placed on formal parole supervision, usually for three years. California is virtually alone in this practice of combining determinate sentencing *and* placing all released prisoners on parole. Most other states either have an indeterminate sentencing system, where a discretionary parole board determines release dates, or reserve parole for only their most serious or risky offenders.

The state's growing prison population, combined with its universal parole practices and lengthy parole terms, has resulted in California supervising far more parolees than any other state. The Bureau of Justice Statistics reports that in 2007, California supervised about 120,000 parolees on any given day, accounting for 15 percent of all parolees in the country.[6]

California's parole population is now so large and its parole agents so overburdened that parolees who represent serious threats to public safety often are not watched closely, and those who wish to go straight often cannot get the help they need. About 80 percent of all California parolees have fewer than two 15-minute face-to-face meetings with a parole agent each month, and nearly all of these meetings take place in the parole agent's office. It is estimated that two-thirds or more of all California parolees have substance abuse problems and nearly all of them are required to be drug tested.[7] Yet few of them will participate in appropriate treatment while in prison or on parole. California's recent Expert Panel on Adult Offender Recidivism found that 50 percent of exiting state prisoners did not participate in *any* rehabilitation or work program, nor did they have a work assignment during their *entire* prison stay. Many did not get the help they needed on parole either: 56 percent of parolees did not participate in any formal program while under parole supervision.[8]

Clearly, this low level of supervision and service provision has not prevented crime. As noted above, two-thirds of all California parolees return at least once to a California prison within three years. Due to their high failure rate, parolees account for the bulk of prison admissions in California; in 2006, nearly two-thirds (64 percent) of all persons admitted to California prisons were parole violators. Parole revocations have been rising nationally over the last 20 years, but California's have increased more. Over the last 20 years, the number of parole revocations has increased about six-fold nationally. In California, the number of parole revocations has increased 30-fold.[9]

California's unique decision-making process partly explains its high parole revocation rate. The decision to send a parole violator back to prison is often not made by a judge, but by a politically appointed deputy commissioner at the Board of Parole Hearings. Criminologists have coined the term "back-end sentencing" to describe how the parole revocation process centers on parole board practices.[10] Not only are back-end sentences determined by correctional officials instead of judges in California, but the standard of evidence used (preponderance of the evidence) is much lower than is required in a court of law (beyond a reasonable doubt). This more lenient standard is deemed appropriate because in California, prisoners remain in the legal custody of the CDCR while on parole. Parole in California is not a reward for good behavior, as it might be in an indeterminate sentencing state, but rather an extension of a felons sentence and a period of extended surveillance after prison. As such, if parolees do not abide by the imposed parole conditions, the state has the legal right to revoke their parole terms and return them to prison.

California's parole revocation process is also unique in another way. The maximum term for a parole violation in California is 12 months in prison. If a parolee is sentenced to that maximum term, there is usually a day-for-day credit for time served in prison or in jail awaiting case disposition, assuming no prison rule infractions. This means that a parole violator who is not convicted of a new crime by a criminal court—totaling nearly 70,000 prison commitments in 2006—will only spend, on average, slightly more than four months in custody. Naturally, not everyone receives the maximum 12-month sentence; California's Rehabilitation Strike Team found that of all parolees returned to a prison in 2004, 20 percent (one in five parole violators) served less than one month in a California prison.[11]

This system of "catch and release" makes little sense in terms of deterrence, incapacitation, treatment, and cost. Parolees quickly learn that being revoked from parole does not carry serious consequences, undercutting the deterrent effect of serving prison time; the resources of the police, the parole board, and parole officers, who have to reprocess the same individuals over and over again, are also wasted. The constant churning of parolees also disrupts community-based treatment, since parolees who are enrolled in community treatment programs are constantly having that treatment disrupted for what, in the treatment providers' views, are predictable and minor rule violations (e.g., testing positive for drug use). Churning also encourages the spread of prison gang culture into the communities where inmates are discharged. Finally, given California's overcrowding crisis in prisons, there is the high opportunity cost of occupying a limited number of prison beds that, in some cases, could be used for offenders who pose a greater risk to public safety.

Policymakers and practitioners agree that an overhaul of California's parole system is urgently needed. In fact, more than a dozen reports published since 1980 have recommended changes in California's parole revocation procedures.[12] Unfortunately, California's parole violation process is so complex and involves decisions by so many parties, including the police, prosecutors, judges, parole agents and parole board commissioners, that it is unclear exactly what needs to be done to fix the problem.

STUDY RESEARCH QUESTIONS AND DATA

To better understand the complexities of the parole violation process and the characteristics of parolees who are returned to prison, we needed to unpack the "black box" of the parole violation and revocation process. We needed to study not only characteristics of parolees, but also characteristics of the supervising agency, parole agents, and the communities to which parolees return. We needed to identify the key decision points that ultimately lead to parole revocation and prison returns, and also how characteristics of the parole agent, caseload type, and variations in community characteristics impact the processes of violation and revocation.

We also had to better understand the critical role of Board of Parole Hearings (BPH), which has the ultimate responsibility for deciding which parole violators are returned to prison and which are allowed to remain in the community. In the mid-1990s, California adopted a "zero-tolerance" policy for "serious" and "violent" parolees (as defined in the Penal Code), such that parole agents are required to report *every* offender originally convicted of these crimes who violates *any* condition of parole to BPH for disposition. BPH is a politically appointed body with a history, especially in recent years, of returning to prison most parolees who come before it. BPH may be the most important gatekeeper of using prison for the sanctioning of parole violations, and yet its role and impact have gone virtually unnoticed and unstudied.

We assembled an extraordinarily large and complex database that tracked every adult on parole in California at any point during the calendar years 2003 and 2004. The resulting study sample consisted of 254,468 individuals. These parolees were responsible for 151,750 parole violations that made it to the court or BPH hearing level (thousands more were terminated at the parole unit level) over the two study years. These parole violation and revocation incidents were a central focus of our study. In addition to recording the details of each parolees behavior on a weekly basis during the two-year study period, we also merged data about each parolee, reflecting their personal characteristics and criminal histories, the nature and types of supervision to which they were subjected, the characteristics of agents who supervised them, and (using their addresses) the communities to which they returned. Using other statewide and national databases, we then collected information on "host" communities (e.g., services available, demographic and political characteristics of residents). The combined database allowed us to analyze the way in which three clusters of factors—characteristics of the parolee, the agency, and the community—interact to produce variations in parole outcomes.

We also investigated the major aspects of California's sentencing and parole system that we believe impact parole revocations and prison returns. Because California releases nearly all prisoners subject to the Determinate Sentencing Law (DSL), with no opportunity to retain even the most likely recidivists, and then places all of them on parole supervision, the state's parole agents end up supervising some individuals who pose a far more serious threat to society than the typical parolee in a state with discretionary release policies.[13] In states that use discretionary release, these high-risk prisoners can be denied parole and kept in prison. Parole officers in California often point out that the high revocation rates are caused by the behavior of parolees who were almost certain to reoffend and should not have been released from prison in the first place.

On the other hand, since California law allows minor technical parole violators to be returned to prison (whereas some states do not), and these prisoners are also eventually released to parole supervision, California parole caseloads also include many less serious offenders as well. This point is critical to understanding parole violations in California: California parole caseloads likely contain an unusually high proportion of offenders at both extremes of the seriousness continuum—offenders who probably would not be on parole in other states, either because they are too serious to have been released from prison in the first place by parole boards operating in indeterminate states, or because they are such low-risk offenders that they would not have been assigned to post-prison parole supervision at release.

California's DSL not only changed the way in which prisoners automatically got released and required all prisoners to serve a post-prison parole term, but it also simultaneously and significantly increased both the length of the initial parole supervision term imposed and the length of the prison term that could be subsequently imposed if the parolee violated parole conditions. Before the passage of the law in 1977, prisoners released to parole were subject to a one-year period of parole. But DSL *tripled* the length of time on parole for most prisoners. Equally important, DSL also doubled the length of prison time that can be imposed upon parole revocation from six months to one year.[14] And under California law, when a person is returned to prison for a parole violation, the "clock stops" on the time owed for parole supervision. So, when a person leaves prison after serving time for a parole violation, he still faces the remaining supervision time he owed the state before he went back to prison for the violation. In this way, parole supervision can stretch out for years for some individuals. Offenders often call it "doing a life sentence on the installment plan," since they go in and out, never able to formally discharge from parole supervision.

In addition to changes in sentencing policy and the structure of parole in the last decade, the discretion held by California parole agents in the handling of violations has substantially eroded. In 1994, BPH implemented new regulations, referred to as the "Robin Reagan rules," that significantly added to the list of parole violations the Division of Adult Parole Operations (DAPO) is required to refer to the parole board, thereby exposing more parolees to BPH decisions to return them to prison. These regulations were adopted as a result of a heinous murder committed by a parolee.

Whereas parole agents and supervisors once wielded discretion about how to handle many violations, now much of that authority has shifted to BPH. DAPO estimated that 85 percent of parole violations, including technical violations, were subject to mandatory referral policies in 2005. This means that parole agents and their supervisors have very little discretion in the handling of these cases and these offenders. BPH makes a decision about whether to return the parole violator to prison, and the vast majority of cases that go before BPH result in a return to prison. In 1993, about 65 percent of parolees referred to BPH for parole violations were returned to prison and 35 percent were continued on parole. By 2007, however, about 90 percent of parolees were returned to prison by BPH and only 10 percent were continued on parole. Whether these mandatory referral rules are appropriate or not is a political determination, but one thing is clear: parole agents, parole supervisors and DAPO retain discretionary decision-making power over a declining percentage of violations.

Like the role of discretion in California's sentencing system, discretion in parole has shifted from corrections professionals to legislative and regulatory bodies that are politically elected or appointed. This change has occurred with virtually no discussion or public input, but the consequences are critically important. For one, it means that the extent to which changes in parole agent recruitment, training, or culture can reduce the number of parolee returns to prison is often overestimated. The parole agent recommends the disposition for the violation (e.g., to prison or not), but ultimately, the parole board has the sole authority to return a parolee to custody. These and other legal and procedural constraints are important to understanding the very complicated processes of prison release, parole supervision, and all too often, return to prison.

The growth of California's prison population—combined with the policy of placing *all* exiting prisoners on parole supervision for three years, simultaneously reducing the discretion of parole agents to handle minor violations for an increasing proportion of parolees, and increasing the prison time served for violations—provides the requisite conditions for the growing contribution of parole violators to the state prison population. No other state has created this hybrid system (shifting simultaneously to fixed-term prison release *and* universal parole supervision) while at the same time reducing parole agent discretion and lengthening parole terms and prison terms upon revocation.

Our hope is that the empirical data analyzed in this report will permit policymakers in California to devise sounder parole supervision and revocation policies that better balance public safety and public resources. Importantly, such research should help advise policymakers on the "seriousness" of parole violators being returned to prison, which in turn can greatly influence the prison capacity discussion.

DATA AND ANALYTIC APPROACH

Our statistical models separately investigate the prediction of *parole violations,* which are largely behavioral events, and the prediction of *parole revocations,* which reflect system responses to that behavior. We relied solely on official records rather than offender self-reports, even though we recognized that not all (or even most) parole violations came to the attention of authorities. Our database consisted of detailed information about every adult on parole in California at any point during 2003 and 2004. The resulting sample comprises 254,468 separate individuals. Some individuals were already on parole at the start of our study (January I, 2003), whereas others were either free or in prison at the start of our study, but were released to parole at some time during the two-year study period. Study subjects were observed for two years (January 1, 2003 to December 31, 2004). However, since many subjects were already on parole at the start of the study period, we were able, through various methods of statistical estimation, to analyze violation and revocation patterns over longer periods of time.

We assembled a detailed personal and parole supervision profile for each parolee's in the sample, consisting of their demographic characteristics and criminal records, the type(s) of parole supervision to which they were assigned, and all new technical and criminal recidivism events that occurred during the study period. We also recorded information about each parolee's supervising parole agent (e.g., age, race, gender, job tenure) and, using the parolee's address, characteristics of the community to which the parolee returned upon release from prison. Data were merged from over a dozen different state and national databases to create as comprehensive a profile as possible for each subject.

With the databases assembled and merged, we were then able to conduct our statistical analyses. In terms of parole *violations,* we structured the data for survival analysis—a multivariate method that examines both the likelihood and timing of violations. Violations were tracked on a weekly basis for each parolee throughout 2003 and 2004. The data format allowed us to construct multivariate survival models predicting the likelihood and timing of different types of violation behavior.

For our analyses of parole revocations, we created a dataset documenting every parole violation case heard in criminal court and/ or by BPH. These data, reflecting 151,750 violation reports, were used to estimate logistic regression models predicting revocation outcomes of interest—specifically, whether criminal violation cases were successfully prosecuted in court as opposed to being referred to the parole board, and whether cases heard by BPH were returned to prison or continued on parole. Thus, we were able to assess the relative impact of individual, organizational, and community-level measures on numerous parole outcomes. In all of our analyses, we investigated the likelihood (i.e., probability) as well as the severity of the outcome. In addition to the administrative data we compiled, we also collected extensive qualitative information from field observations, staff interviews, and reviews of agency directives and policy memos.

WHAT PREDICTS PAROLE VIOLATIONS?

Nearly half (49 percent) of the parolees in our sample had at least one formal parole violation report during our study period, and 24 percent had multiple parole violation reports. Each report could contain multiple violations of any type (e.g., criminal, technical). Together, these parolees were responsible for 296,958 violation reports. CDCR tracks 247 different types of prohibited parolee behavior, ranging from violations of the parole process, usually referred to as technical violations, to serious and violent criminal offenses like robbery, assault with deadly weapons, and homicide.

Over a third (35 percent) of all the recorded parole violations were for noncriminal, or "technical," violations. Two-thirds of technical violations were for absconding supervision, meaning that the parolee missed an appointment and/or his or her whereabouts were unknown. Other technical violations include weapons access, psychological endangerment, and various violations of the parole process such as violations of special conditions of parole imposed by a parole agent or deputy commissioner. Interestingly, the parole violation reports that pertained to drug use or drug sales (over 110,000 of them) accounted for over a third of all parole violation reports (37 percent) during our study period.

Two-thirds (65 percent) of all parole violations were for criminal behavior. Thirty-nine percent of the criminal violations were classified, according to the CDCRs internal coding system, as Type I (the least serious—mostly drug use and possession); 17 percent were classified as Type II (moderately serious—e.g., forgery, drug sales, burglaries, battery without serious injury, driving violations); and 10 percent—nearly 29,000 violation reports—were classified as Type III (the most serious—e.g., major assaults, major drug crimes, robberies, rapes, and homicides).

In terms of the timing of violations among parolees in the study, the risk of all types of violations was highest during the first 180 days following release from prison, and declined thereafter. A major factor behind this declining risk pattern was that the most risk-prone parolee's tended to violate early and be returned to prison. We theorized that the remainder were probably more compliant, less likely to violate, and more likely to successfully complete their parole period. Indeed, after 360 days on parole, a "surviving" parolee's risk of violation had dropped 70 percent from what it was during the first two months of parole. From 360 to 900 days, a parolee's risk only dropped another 10 percent. In other words, after about 360 days, a parolee's risk of violation, while not zero, had substantially leveled off.

In terms of demographic and other personal characteristics, the youngest parolees (ages 18 to 30) posed the greatest risk of all kinds of violations except Type I criminal violations (the least serious). Male parolees posed significantly higher risks for all types of violations except absconding. Black parolees posed the same risks as nonblack parolees for technical violations but much greater risks than parolees from other racial backgrounds for the most serious and violent criminal violations. Parolees with a record of mental health problems had higher risks for all types of violations, and they had particularly elevated risks for the most violent criminal violations.

The best predictor of a parolee's violation risk was the number of prior adult prison incarcerations in California. For all violation types, an offender coming out on his or her second release from prison had a 20 percent higher risk of violation than an offender on his or her first release. After a third release, an offender had a 39 percent higher risk of violation than an offender on first release. By the ninth release, an offender had a 124 percent higher risk of violation than an offender on first release.

In general, the extent of prior criminal record had more predictive value than the seriousness of prior record, but certain "seriousness indicators" did exhibit relationships to violation risk. Age at first adult commitment to a California prison, for example, predicted Type III (the most serious) criminal violations. For every additional year older a parolee was at his or her first prison commitment, the risk of a Type III violation decreased by 2.5 percent. However, parolees who were older when first committed to California prisons tended to present higher risks for technical violations and Type I criminal violations. This latter group may have been largely composed of drug offenders who had substance dependence driving their offending, and as a result of drug use, were prone to generating technical and Type I criminal violations, but were less likely to be involved in more serious criminal behavior.

The seriousness of the current commitment offense, while exhibiting a relationship to violation risk, did not predict violations in the ways that policymakers often assume. Parolees committed for violent and sex offenses, overall, had lower risks for most violations than those offenders committed for property and drug crimes. However, those who had been committed for violent offenses did show elevated risk for violent criminal violations and serious sexual violations.

Sex offender registrants posed lower risk for violations than other types of offenders for several types of violations (e.g., having any violation, absconding. Type I criminal violations). Sex offender registrants were no more likely to commit the most violent violations than other offenders.

Policymakers arc particularly interested in the threat that paroled sex offenders pose to their communities, so we investigated these outcomes separately. We found that sex offender parolees were significantly more likely to be violated for sex crimes, but it is critical to note that these sexual violations were very rare—during the study period, reoffending sex offenders accounted for 1.5 percent of all violations and in about two-thirds of the cases, the offenses were victimless (i.e., the paroled sex offenders failed to register as required by California Penal Code section 290). The majority of sexual violations, including the most serious violations involving rape, sexual assault, and child molestation, were committed by parolees who were *not* registered sex offenders. Setting aside the violations involving failure to register, of the 1,528 sexual violations committed during 2003 and 2004, just 25 percent were committed by sex offender registrants. The vast majority of sexual violations, including 78 percent of the most serious Type III sexual violations, were committed by paroled offenders who had not been previously sentenced for sex-related crimes.

INTENSITY OF SUPERVISION, PAROLE AGENT CHARACTERISTICS, AND PAROLE ORGANIZATION

California parolees are assigned to one of five levels of supervision, with the assigned level determining the frequency and degree of oversight provided by parole agents. Twenty-three percent of parole supervision performed during 2003 and 2004 was classified as "minimum service," with the requirement that parolees see their parole agents only twice a year. Most contact between agents and parolees under minimum service supervision occurs through the mail; that is, parolees periodically mail a postcard to their agents to check in. Another 43 percent of supervision during our study period was classified as "control service"; parolees supervised at this level see a parole officer once every six weeks. These two classifications—in which relatively little supervision or programming is actually applied to parolees—accounted for 65 percent of the total supervision applied to parolees in 2003 and 2004.

Given that these offenders are placed in low-risk categories because they are not expected to be likely recidivists, a question to be considered is whether the effort expended to provide cursory oversight to so many former inmates is an effective use of resources. This issue is particularly pressing because California loses track of so many of its parolees; perhaps greater intensity of supervision or services for higher-risk parolees could help prevent new crimes, or the resources expended on low-risk parolees could be better used to locate those whose whereabouts are unknown. On any given day, nearly 17 percent of all California parolees—more than 20,400 people—are "parolees-at-large," meaning they have absconded supervision. This is the highest rate of absconding in the nation and is far above the national average of seven percent.[15]

We found that, consistent with prior research, supervision intensity affected the risk of reported violations.[16] More intensive parole supervision increased the risk of all violations, holding constant the offenders personal attributes, offense background, and community conditions. The biggest differences in the effects of supervision on violation risk were found between minimum service supervision and active supervision (i.e., supervision at all other levels). Parolees who were on minimum service caseloads, which involved infrequent face-to-face or collateral contact, monthly mail correspondence, and no narcotics testing, had significantly lower risks for all kinds of violations than those parolees who were more actively supervised.

The differences in violation risk between parolees on minimum service supervision and active supervision were most pronounced among the most discretionary violations—technical violations not involving absconding and Type I criminal violations (the least serious, mostly involving drug use and possession). Compared to minimum-service parolees, actively supervised parolees had between two and three times the risk of technical and Type I criminal violations. Active supervision parolees also had consistently higher risks of absconding, Type II, Type III, and violent criminal violations, although the differences were not as great as among the more discretionary violation types. What became clear from the contrast between parolees on active supervision and those on minimum supervision was that more closely supervised parolees did not seem to be deterred from engaging in behavior that could result in parole revocation.

We also detected differences in violation risks among active supervision categories, but these differences were not as pronounced as those between active supervision and minimum service supervision. In general, parolees in more intensive supervision categories posed higher risks for violations.

California is subdivided into four parole regions, each supervising roughly one-fourth of the California parole population. The regions are understood to have differences in their organizational cultures and in the types of parolees they supervise. Region 3, which comprises Los Angeles County, is perceived to be the most overstretched part of the parole system, overseeing the supervision of the most serious parolees in the state. As a result, some believe that there is a lower rate of reporting of less serious violations in Region 3, as they have more serious criminal violations to contend with.

We found little support for regional differences in parole outcomes. Once the characteristics of parolees and communities were statistically controlled, Region 3 reported violations in a manner similar to the other three regions. Region 3 did report fewer drug use and possession violations (Type I criminal violations), but its reporting patterns for technical violations—both absconding and violations of the parole process—were no different from those of other regions. Nor was the risk that a parolee in Region 3 would be cited for a Type II or Type III criminal violation different from that of other regions.

We also explored the extent to which differences in parole outcomes were traceable to parole agent characteristics, and were able to detect some relationships between agent characteristics and violation risk. We found that female agents (who performed 28 percent of parole supervision during 2003–2004) appeared to exercise discretion in ways more "forgiving" of low-level criminal violations (i.e., Type I, mostly drug use and possession). Male agents, on the other hand, appeared to adopt a more lenient approach toward absconding than female agents. No gender differences were found in the reporting of the more serious Type II and III criminal violations.

Some research on black judges and black police officers suggests that, as a group, black parole agents might have more tolerance for violations.[17] During our study, 32 percent of all supervision was done by black agents, 25 percent by Hispanic agents, 35 percent by white agents, and the rest was performed by Asian agents and those from other racial categories. We might theorize that black agents, like blacks in the rest of American society, may be more likely to have friends or family members who have had contact with the criminal justice system.[18] As a result, they might be more sensitive to the conditions that foster criminal behavior and more wary of the effectiveness of system responses. Therefore, black agents might show more tolerance for less serious violations. Whether or not the theorized explanation is correct, our results supported this result. Parolees supervised by black agents had lower risks of technical violations and Type I criminal violations. But parolees with black agents were no different from other parolees in terms of their risks for Type II and III criminal violations.

Nearly half (48 percent) of parole supervision during 2003–2004 was done by parole agents with less than three years of job experience as a parole agent. Thirty percent of supervising agents were under age 40 and 83 percent of agents had previously worked in a CDCR correctional institution. We were told that older agents and those who have not worked in the prison system as correctional officers are more likely to see "shades of gray," and thus tolerate some parolee behavior that other agents would elect to violate. Contrary to expectations, parolees assigned to agents with prior employment experience in a prison actually had an eight percent *lower* risk of the least serious Type I criminal violations than parolees assigned to agents with no prior prison employment. Prior employment in a prison did not affect the risks for any other type of criminal or technical violation. Moreover, neither parole agent age nor tenure on the job as a parole agent was significantly related to any type of criminal or technical violation.

CDCR announced a number of significant parole policy changes during 2003 arid 2004. One policy, referred to as the "New Parole Model," was announced with much fanfare in February 2004, before being scaled back significantly in April 2005. The New Parole Model proposed the greater use of intermediate sanctions for parole violators and the adoption of a parole violation matrix to standardize the handling of violations. We found no evidence that this announced policy change had any observable impact on parole decision-making or case processing outcomes at the aggregate level.

COMMUNITY CONDITIONS AND REENTRY ENVIRONMENTS

Research suggests that community characteristics can have criminogenic or reintegrative effects on parolee behavior. In other words, neighborhood factors can either promote or discourage illicit activities. The following are common hypotheses made about the relation between neighborhood factors and parolee behavior:

Communities with greater financial resources may be able to fund more rehabilitation and work programs, which can provide parolees with pathways out of criminal lifestyles.

Communities with more progressive political views may have more tolerance for minor rule violations.

Less socioeconomically disadvantaged communities may provide better informal social supports that suppress criminal activity (i.e., increased residential stability).

On the other hand, socially disorganized (i.e., disadvantaged) communities may not be able to fund many alternatives to prison, and may exhibit other conditions that are conducive to criminal behavior.

Politically conservative communities may have less tolerance for illicit behavior, and may exhibit an increased propensity to violate parolees.

To explore these ideas, we used parolee address records to link individuals to data about their communities. We mapped parolee addresses to U.S. census tracts to compile measures of poverty, unemployment, and public assistance. As a measure of service availability in parolees' reentry environments, we drew data from the United States Substance Abuse and Mental Health Services Administration, listing the addresses of all substance abuse and mental health treatment providers in California that accept clients from criminal justice agencies.

We found modest support for the above hypotheses as they relate to an understanding of parole violations in California. Parolees who lived in neighborhoods that scored highly on socioeconomic disadvantage were at greater risk to abscond than parolees who lived in less disadvantaged environments. However, parolees residing in disadvantaged neighborhoods did not pose a greater risk to commit other kinds of violations than those from less disadvantaged neighborhoods.

Importantly, we found some evidence of the correlation between substance abuse and mental health treatment services on the one hand and lower risk of Type I (the least serious) criminal violations—which mainly involved drug use, drug possession, and misdemeanor violations of the law. If there is a cause/result relationship, it may be attributable to the effectiveness of these programs, but it may also have been due to a "parole agent effect"; that is, parole agents may have been less likely to violate parolees for low-level violations when they perceived that there were program opportunities that presented alternatives to initiating the formal violation and revocation process. Given that there were few alternatives to prison during 2003–2004, this observed effect is important and might be strengthened if more programs were in existence.

WHAT PREDICTS PAROLE REVOCATIONS AND RETURN TO PRISON?

There are two ways parolees experience revocation: through county criminal courts and through the parole board (BPH). Courts only handle criminal violations—those that result from an arrest by a police officer or parole agent. BPH handles technical violation cases, as well as criminal violation cases that county courts do not successfully prosecute. The process by which cases are sorted through one venue versus the other, as well as the reasons that some parole violators are returned to custody while others are allowed to remain in the community, are not well understood.

The parolees in our study sample generated 151,750 parole violation cases in 2003 and 2004 that were processed either through the criminal court system or through the BPH. Eighty-four percent (127,742) of these cases involved new criminal violations. These criminal violation cases were heard first in criminal court; if a conviction could not be obtained in court, they were referred for assessment by the parole board. Sixteen percent (24,008) of all cases involved only technical violations, and these cases were heard by the parole board. Importantly, the board operates under a more lenient standard of evidence than the courts, and may return a parole violator to prison for no more than 12 months.

Of the 127,742 criminal violation cases reported during 2003 and 2004, 25 percent (31,417 eases) resulted in a new prison term delivered in criminal court. The other 75 percent (96,325 cases) were referred to the parole board. Among these referred criminal violation cases, the board elected to return 73 percent to prison. Not surprisingly, more serious criminal charges were more likely to result in a prison return. Type III criminal violation cases—the most serious—resulted in prison return 88 percent of the time. Moderately serious criminal cases (Type II) resulted in return almost as frequently; these parole violators were returned 80 percent of the time. The least serious criminal cases (Type I) only resulted in return to prison 52 percent of the time. Thus, when moderately serious and very serious criminal parole violations are evaluated by the board, the certainty of return is extremely high. The board appears to exercise greater discretion over cases involving Type I crimes—most of which involve drug use and possession violations.

A small but significant number of violent crimes such as homicide, robbery, and rape were processed through the parole board.[19] These crimes carry lengthy prison terms when they are prosecuted in courts of law. However, when handled through the parole board, the maximum return time is capped at 12 months. Even though the proportion of homicide, robbery, and rape cases constituted a very small share of the total number of criminal parole violations returned to custody through the board, the fact that such cases were pursued in this arena is significant. The board was clearly not a venue that exclusively dealt with "small-time" criminal cases. Further, because the board operates under a more lenient standard of evidence, there is a greater possibility that factually innocent criminal parole violators might be returned to custody.

Adding together the criminal violation cases that resulted in a new term through criminal courts and those criminal violation cases that resulted in a return to prison through the parole board, we found that among the 127,742 criminal violation cases officially recorded in 2003 and 2004, over three-quarters (77 percent) resulted in some form of prison return, either through the courts or through the board.

In addition to criminal violation cases referred from courts, the parole board also heard 24,008 technical violation cases (16 percent of all cases)—many of which involved absconding. Like criminal violation cases, technical violation cases heard by the parole board exhibited a high rate of prison return. About 85 percent of these technical violation cases resulted in a return to custody. Those cases involving technical charges (without absconding) were returned 79 percent of the time. Cases involving absconding (without other technical charges) were returned 85 percent of the time. Cases involving *both* technical and absconding charges were returned 91 percent of the time. Overall, the board returned 75 percent of all violation cases it heard.

We next turned to understanding the patterns and logic of the parole revocation process through multivariate statistical analyses (logistic regression). Our analysis was designed to answer two interrelated questions: What factors affected the sorting of violation cases through the courts versus through the parole board, and, once in front of the parole board, what affected the chances that a parolee would be returned to custody, as opposed to being continued on parole? As with our multivariate analysis of parole violations, we examined how parolee characteristics, organizational factors, and community characteristics correlated with and may have impacted revocation decision-making. We also investigated the relationship between case characteristics—such as the number and severity of violation charges—and revocation outcomes.

CASE AND INDIVIDUAL CHARACTERISTICS

Violation case characteristics were critical to determining whether or not criminal violation cases were processed through criminal courts or through the parole board. They also influenced whether a case processed by the parole board resulted in a return to prison. As expected, cases involving more charges, and more serious charges, were likely to receive harsher treatment. In court decisions, the number of criminal charges contained in a case was not related to decisions to re-imprison, but the severity of those charges did predict court sanctioning decisions. Board decisions were, for the most part, driven by both the number and severity of charges involved in violation cases.

In terms of individual factors, parolees with longer, and more serious, histories of criminal behavior were likely to be considered public safety risks by court and board decision-makers, and their cases were treated accordingly. Irrespective of the seriousness of their current parole violations, parolees' histories of imprisonment, for example, were significantly predictive of harsher treatment in both decision venues. Those who had served more adult prison spells (both for new court-ordered terms and returns to custody on parole violations) in California were more likely to be sent back to custody by both the court and the board. Parolees on their "second strike" were also significantly more likely to be returned through the court than parolees without such status, and when their cases were referred to the board, they were significantly more likely to be re-incarcerated in cases involving criminal violations.

Statutorily-defined serious and violent offenders were actually less likely than others to experience court return to prison, but when their criminal violation cases were referred to the parole board, they were more likely to be returned to custody. Similarly, registered sex offenders were less likely than others to be returned to prison through court, but they were treated more severely by the board. One explanation for these findings is that the criminal violation cases of serious and violent offenders, as well as sex offender registrants, may have been unappealing to court decision-makers because they tended to lack compelling evidence. However, court decision-makers may have also referred these cases because they felt that the board, using a lower standard of evidence, could act quickly and decisively to reincarcerate parolees who were perceived as particularly threatening to public safety. The board sanctioned these types of parolees especially severely in low-level (Type I) criminal violation cases—the type allowing for the most discretion. It appears that low-level criminal activity, much of which is detected through parolee drug testing, was a crucial mechanism by which the parole board reincarcerated "high-profile" parole violators. Note that the criminal courts could not legally impose very harsh sanctions for these low-level crimes, and so they seemed to opt, through case referral, for the greater certainty of punishment that the board was able to provide.

Demographic characteristics were also somewhat predictive of case outcomes. Parolee age affected criminal court decisions, but not board decisions. Courts were inclined to prosecute the criminal violation cases of the youngest parolees (ages 18–30). Black parolees were more likely to have their cases referred to BPH—the more discretionary venue—and when their cases were heard by BPH, they were more likely to be incarcerated for criminal violations. Asian and Hispanic parolees were the most likely to be successfully prosecuted in criminal court, and Hispanics were also among the most likely to be returned to custody in criminal violation cases. White parolees, who had the lowest likelihood of court conviction, also had the lowest likelihood of return through BPH for criminal violation cases (although they were among the most likely to be returned when they absconded). These findings suggest that there may be observable or unobservable traits associated with parolees of different demographic groups that affect their case outcomes.

ORGANIZATIONAL FACTORS

Over and above case- and parolee-specific characteristics, organizational factors also affected revocation decisions by the court and the parole board. Los Angeles County (Region 3) appeared distinct in its treatment of parole violators. Criminal violations in Los Angeles were more likely to result in reincarceration through the court. Board decisions were also uniquely patterned in Los Angeles. Technical parole violators were more likely to be returned to custody by the board in this region, while absconders were less likely to be returned by the board. These findings could have been due to many factors: differences in organizational culture across parole regions, unmeasured variation in local parolee populations that affected sanctioning decisions (e.g., gang affiliation, addiction and employability), or the effectiveness of policing practices in different regions.

Practical constraints on decision-making also appeared to play a role in violation case outcomes. A key practical constraint was available custodial space. We found that when available space in prison reception centers decreased, for example, the parole board was more likely to continue cases on parole, as opposed to returning parolees to prison. Moreover, in courts, workload pressures (measured as the ratio of felony cases to district attorneys in each county) were linked to an increased likelihood of case referral to the parole board. As felony court caseloads increased, courts were inclined to refer more criminal parole violation cases.

COMMUNITY FACTORS

To generate a county-level measure of the "punitiveness" of different communities, we collected information on the results of ballot proposition voting and party registration from the Secretary of State. We selected data reflecting voting patterns of ballot propositions that pertained directly to state correctional practices—for example, Proposition 36, which allows some nonviolent drug offenders to receive treatment instead of incarceration for parole violations, and Proposition 66, which proposed a scaling back of California's "three strikes" law. Our hypotheses were that community conditions and attitudes, as well as the availability of treatment, would be related to parole practices. Our statistical models showed that, net of all other measured factors, some characteristics of parolees' communities were related to the treatment of parole violations in court and before the parole board. For example, more "punitive" counties—as measured by political party affiliation and electoral ballot voting—were more likely to return criminal parole violators through the court, and in violation cases heard by the board, these counties were more likely to return parolees to prison, regardless of whether the case involved a criminal violation, absconding, or other technical violations.

Community characteristics can also serve as cues to decision-makers that reflect something about individual parolees themselves. The extent of "racial threat" in a community, which has been examined in prior sentencing research, is illustrative of this point.[20] Racial threat refers to the hypothesis that sanctioning officials may be sensitive to the prevalence of threatening minority groups in communities, and therefore punish offenders from these communities more harshly. Census tracts with higher proportions of black residents, and those with higher black unemployment rates, may be perceived as particularly unstable or crime-ridden, and parolees that live in these communities may be penalized by decision-makers because they come from, and are therefore representative of, these disadvantaged environments. In our models, parolees who came from communities that had a higher proportion of black residents, and higher black unemployment rates, were more likely to be returned by the court with a new term, as opposed to being referred to the parole board. When their cases were heard by the parole board, these parolees were generally more likely to be returned to prison, especially for criminal violations.

However, while community characteristics can have a stigmatizing effect on case outcomes, they can also have the opposite effect. For example, census tracts with more mental health and substance abuse services in close proximity were associated with more lenient outcomes among criminal violation cases and technical violation cases (not involving absconding) decided by the parole board. This may have been due to the fact that decision-makers had more treatment options in these communities, and therefore more opportunities to keep parole violators out of prison, or that parolees from service-rich communities somehow appeared less threatening than parolees from communities that lack services.

A central implication of our analyses of revocations is that the response of criminal justice institutions does not totally derive from, and is not necessarily proportionate to, the extent of parolees' criminal behavior, as is often assumed by policymakers, government officials and the public. While case characteristics matter in terms of court and board outcomes, so too do the characteristics of the individual, the organizations handling that individual's case, and the community that the person comes from.

POLICY AND RESEARCH IMPLICATIONS

Our findings suggest a number of policy and research implications, the most important of which are:

1. *Concentrate supervision and services on the first six months.* Parole should front-load services and surveillance to focus on a parolees first six months after release, when the risk of recidivism is the highest.
2. *Expand use of early and earned discharge.* Parolees are most at risk of all kinds of violations during the first six months on parole. Parolees that make it to the sixth month without violation pose significantly lower risks than parolees who do not. The duration of the imposed parole term should be closely linked to an offender's risk level or accomplishment of individual benchmarks. Low-risk offenders might not be assigned parole supervision at all, or those who adjust well to parole could be released after six months of supervision. Moderate-risk offenders might be assigned a year or two of parole, whereas high-risk offenders might serve two years or more, and very high-risk offenders might be assigned lifetime parole.
3. *Align parolee risk and supervision levels.* Parole services and surveillance should be primarily risk-based rather than offense-based. CDCR needs to assign parole caseloads and supervision levels so that offenders are matched to types of surveillance and services that are most appropriate for them. Resources should be more heavily focused on higher-risk parolees, and very intensive (and expensive) programs should be reserved for those whose risk and need profiles suggest they will likely benefit from program participation.
4. *Employ a parole violation matrix.* The parole division and the parole board should adopt policy-driven approaches to parole violations using a decision-making matrix and graduated community-based sanctions. This tool would allow parole officials to respond consistently to parole violations, using a well-developed range of intermediate sanctions. The response should reflect the original risk level of the parolee coupled with a proportionate response to the seriousness of the violation. Every major study on California's prison system published since the 1980s has recommended the use of such a tool, but it has never been implemented, even though such instruments are used in over 20 other states.[21] California is currently developing such an instrument and plans to pilot test it in winter 2009.
5. *Expand intermediate sanctions options.* CDCR should implement additional intermediate sanction programs, particularly for drug-involved parolees. Current program offerings are woefully inadequate for appropriately dealing with the wide range of parole violations. CDCR cannot do this alone, as the most effective reentry programs and intermediate sanctions require community engagement and collaboration. The expansion of evidence-based intermediate sanctions should both reduce recidivism and save expensive prison beds for the most violent criminals.
6. *Encourage criminal prosecution.* Parolees who commit new crimes should be prosecuted in criminal courts whenever possible. California's "back-end sentencing" system allows some very serious criminals to evade the more severe criminal penalties that would have been imposed had their cases been criminally prosecuted as opposed to handled by the parole board, where the maximum term imposed was only 12 months.

Further, we found some evidence that stresses on the capacity of California's justice system—as measured by jail and prison overcrowding and district attorney caseloads—resulted in greater likelihoods that BPH would handle criminal violation cases. While case and offender characteristics are appropriate criteria for board referral decisions, system capacity should not affect these decisions.

7. *Track extralegal factors affecting revocation.* CDCR should develop better evaluation methods to reduce the influence of extralegal factors—particularly parolee race—on violation case outcomes. We found that black parole violators were more likely to experience referral to the parole board, and more likely to be returned by the board for certain types of violations. We also found effects related to age, gender, and mental health status. The state must explore the causes and consequences of the influences of demographic and personal characteristics on sanctioning decisions.
8. *Expand substance abuse and mental health programs.* Substance abuse-related violations and the violations of parolees with mental health problems make up a large share of all violations. These populations are not well-served by short returns to prison, where the few available services and sanctions are of insufficient duration to improve their outcomes. CDCR should expand intermediate sanctions specifically for these populations, so as to allow for community-based and in-custody treatment in a non-prison environment for sufficient time periods to address these criminogenic needs.

CONCLUSION

This study is just the first step toward a better understanding of California's parole violation and revocation process. The data we collected were primarily administrative; other types of data, such as systematic interviews with parolees about their parole experiences, would highlight issues of discretion and sanctioning that are difficult to capture through quantitative analyses of official records alone. Future research on parole outcomes could also benefit from improvements to data quality. Some of our variables were underspecified (e.g., the community variables and parole agent characteristics). Other factors that may be related to parole outcomes, such as addiction and employability of parolees, were beyond the scope of our data collection effort. Data on the extent and type of programs parolees participated in could also expand on what we have done here. Given that many parolees are violated for program noncompliance, and that others may benefit from work and educational programming, it would be useful to know the degree to which parolees are engaged in assigned programming. Future studies might also address parole policies more specifically. Our research has generated many insights that can inform certain policies, such as early discharge from parole and the timing of service delivery.

It is important to note that our data is from 2003–2004 and California's parole system is currently undergoing the most significant changes in its procedures since the late 1970s. Currently, California is implementing a new, evidence-based, parole violation decision-making instrument (PVDMI) to help agents and BPH assess risk and needs in determining sanctions. PVDMI was specifically designed for California parolees using another new instrument, the California Static Risk Assessment (CSRA). CSRA uses the offender's past criminal history and characteristics such as age and gender to predict the likelihood that they will reoffend.

CSRA, combined with the severity ranking of all parole violations, has been incorporated into PVDMI, which results in a score that designates the appropriate violation response level. The response levels range from least intensive (e.g., community programs) to most intensive responses (in-custody drug treatment or return to prison recommendations). PVDMI is designed to focus California's prison resources on higher-risk parolees while targeting less serious parole violators for community-based alternatives that address the root sources of their problems. DAPO is acquiring or redirecting treatment resources to plan for the expanded use of community-based sanctions in responding to parole violations in California. PVDMI was developed with the full participation and support of BPH and it is anticipated that the instrument will impact BPHs decision-making as well. Implementation of PVDMI will be evaluated by the University of California Irvine Center for Evidence-Based Corrections.[22]

As these and other parole reforms move forward and parole data systems and knowledge about parole outcomes improve, it should be easier to implement studies that focus specifically on the potential effectiveness of various policy choices. We hope that this research will provide guidance for future research efforts and for the important discussions that will be taking place over the next several years about parole in California and the United States.

STUDY QUESTIONS

1. Briefly sketch the California prison system. Why are the stakes so high to reduce revocations?
2. What predicts parole violations in California?
3. Why does intensive parole supervision often lead to increased violations and revocation?
4. How did the race of parole officers affect the rates of technical violations of parolees?
5. What are the policy and research implications outlined by the authors?

NOTES

1. This article is based on Grattet, R., Petersilia, J., & Lin, J. (2008). *Parole violations and revocations in California*, final report for National Institute of Justice, grant number 2005-IJ-CX-0026, Washington, DC: National Institute of Justice. (NCJRS, NCJ 224521). The complete report is available on the NCJRS Web site at http:// www.ncjrs.gov/pdffilesl/nij/grants/224521.pdf and the UCI's Center for Evidence-Based Corrections Web site at http://ucicorrections.seweb.uci.edu/pubs.
2. Petersilia, J. (2008). California's correctional paradox of excess and deprivation. In M. Tonry (Ed.), *Crime and justice: A review of research (Crime and Justice, Vol. 37)* (pp. 207–278). Chicago, IL: University of Chicago Press.
3. Legislative Analyst's Office (2008). *Judicial & Criminal Justice: 2007–08 Analysis*, Sacramento, CA.
4. Fischer, R. (2005). *Are California's recidivism rates really the highest in the Nation? It depends on what measure of recidivism you use.* Irvine, CA: UCI Center for Evidence-Based Corrections.
5. Petersilia, J. (2006). *Understanding California corrections.* Berkeley, California: California Policy Research Center. Report available online at http:// ucicorrections.seweb.uci.edu/pubs.
6. Glaze, L., & Bonczar, T. (2007). *Probation and Parole in the United States. 2006.* Washington, DC: Bureau of Justice Statistics. (NCJRS, NCJ 220218).
7. U.S. General Accounting Office (1991). *Drug treatment: State prisons face challenges in providing services.* Report to the Committee on Government Operations, House of Representatives, Washington, DC: U.S. Congress. More estimates can also be found in Bloom, B., Owen, B. & Covington, S. (2003). *Gender-responsive strategies—Research, practice and Guiding principles for women offenders.* Washington, DC: National Institute of Corrections. Report available online at http:// archive.gao.gov/t2pbat7/145135.pdf.
8. California Expert Panel on Adult Offender Recidivism Reduction Programming (2007). *A roadmap for effective offender programming in California: Report to the California State Legislature.* Sacramento, CA: California Department of Corrections and Rehabilitation.
9. Travis, J. (2003). *Parole in California. 1980–2000: Implications for reform.* Washington, DC: Urban Institute.

10. Travis, J. (2005). *But they all come back: Facing the challenges of prisoner reentry.* Washington, DC: Urban Institute.
11. Glaze & Bonczar, *Probation and Parole in the United States, 2006* (see note 6).
12. For a listing of these reports, see California Expert Panel on Adult Offender Recidivism Reduction Programming, *A roadmap for effective offender programming in California* (note 8). Several of these reports were conducted by the Little Hoover Commission and are available at http://www.lhc.ca.gov/lhcdir/crime.html.
13. Indeterminate sentencing, with a hearing before the parole board, is reserved for California prisoners who have been sentenced to life in prison with the possibility of parole. About 20,000 prisoners (12 percent) in the California prison population have been sentenced to life with the possibility of parole. In 2006, 98.5 of all released California prisoners were placed on post-prison parole supervision.
14. See California Department of Corrections and Rehabilitation (2006). *Department Operations Manual,* Chapter 8: Adult Parole Operations. Available online at http://www.cdcr.ea.gov/Regulations/Adult_Operations/docs/DOM/Ch_8_Printed_Final_DOM.pdf.
15. Petersilia, California's correctional paradox of excess and deprivation (see note 2).
16. Petersilia, J. and Turner, S. (1993). Intensive probation and parole. In M. Tonry (Ed.), *Crime and justice: An annual review of research (Crime and Justice. Vol. 17)* (pp. 281–335). Chicago, IL: University of Chicago Press.
17. Welch, S., Combs, M., & Gruhl, J. (1988). Do Black judges make a difference? *American Journal of Political Science, 32* (1). 126–136. Sherman, L. (1980). Causes of police behavior: The current state of quantitative research. *Journal of Research in Crime and Delinquency, 17.* 69–100.
18. Costello, M., Chiricos, T., Burianek, J., Gertz, M., & Maier-Katkin, D. (2002). The social correlates of punitiveness toward criminals: A comparison of the Czech Republic and Florida. *Justice System Journal, 23.* 191–220. Wilson, G., & Dunham, R. (2001). Race, class, and attitudes toward crime control: The views of the African-American middle class. *Criminal Justice and Behavior, 28.* 259–278.
19. In 2003 and 2004, the Board returned parolees for 246 homicides, 1,006 robberies, and 691 crimes involving rape or sexual assault—together accounting for 1.5 percent of all criminal violation cases during this time.
20. Helms, R. & Jacobs, D. (2002). The political context of sentencing: An analysis of community and individual determinants. *Social Forces, 81*: 577–604. Stolzenberg, L., D'Alessio, S., & Eitle, D. (2004). A multilevel test of racial threat theory. *Criminology,* 42. 673–698.
21. See Martin, B., & Van Dine, S. (2008). *Examining the impact of Ohio's progressive sanction grid,* final report for National Institute of Justice, grant number 2005-IJ-CX-0038, Washington, DC: National Institute of Justice (NCJRS, NCJ 224317).
22. The details of PVDMI and CSRA are available from the California Department of Corrections and Rehabilitation Web site, http://www.cdcr.ca.gov/News/2008_Press_Releases/Oct_3.html.

28
PUTTING PUBLIC SAFETY FIRST

13 STRATEGIES FOR SUCCESSFUL SUPERVISION AND REENTRY

PEW CENTER ON THE STATES

The PEW Center has provided a concise and practical roadmap for successful offender supervision and reentry. By following these 13 strategies, states can improve supervision and build a system that increases the likelihood that offenders will be reintegrated successfully into their communities after they are released from prison.

EXECUTIVE SUMMARY

More than five million people are under community supervision—either probation or parole—on any given day in the United States. Success rates among these offenders are not high: more than 40 percent of probationers and more than half of parolees do not complete their supervision terms successfully. In fact, parole violators account for almost 35 percent of admissions to state prisons, and nearly half of local jail inmates were on probation or parole when they were arrested.

High failure rates, the continued rise in prison costs, the release each year of more than 700,000 persons from confinement, and the mounting economic downturn—all of these trends present policy makers and corrections executives with a rare opportunity, even an imperative, to reform probation and parole in ways that will keep communities safe and save scarce public funds. Fortunately, decades of learning in the field and a growing research base has led to a consensus among many corrections professionals about what needs to be done to achieve better results.

That consensus is reflected in the 13 strategies presented here—strategies that can reduce recidivism and hold offenders accountable for their actions while also cutting substance abuse and unemployment, and restoring family bonds. Even modest reductions in recidivism will result in fewer crimes, fewer victims, and budget savings for states and localities. Given the sheer numbers of people on probation and parole and the cost to society of new crimes they commit, solid execution of these strategies by community supervision agencies could dramatically improve public safety and free corrections dollars for other pressing public priorities.

1. DEFINE SUCCESS AS RECIDIVISM REDUCTION AND MEASURE PERFORMANCE

Probation and parole agencies—like all agencies—should define their mission, be clear about criteria for success, and set benchmarks for performance. Most practitioners would agree that public safety is, and always has been, an important goal of their agencies. But the typical strategies employed to accomplish that goal tend to focus on catching offenders when they do something wrong—"trail 'em, nail 'em and jail 'em," as the saying goes.

Failing to define success as recidivism reduction, and holding supervision officers accountable to that standard, will result in a continued emphasis on "outputs" (such as the number of contacts probation officers have with their probationers), at the expense of the public safety outcomes that matter most. In order to accomplish their public safety mission, parole and probation agencies should adopt risk reduction and behavior change strategies and measure their performance against the standard of recidivism reduction, substance abuse, employment, victim restitution, and other reintegration outcomes.

2. TAILOR CONDITIONS OF SUPERVISION

Probationers and parolees are often subject to a long, generic list of conditions of supervision that may be unrealistic for any individual to meet, let alone those struggling to hold a job, support their families, and stay sober. Many in the field agree that conditions of release should instead reflect what Carl Wicklund, executive director of the American Probation and Parole Association, refers to as the "three R's" of supervision conditions: Parole and probation conditions should be Realistic, Relevant, and Research-based. Realistic conditions are few in number and attainable, and include only those rules for which the agency is prepared to consistently hold supervisees accountable. Relevant conditions are tailored to the individual risks and needs most likely to result in new criminal behavior. Research-based conditions are supported by evidence that compliance with them will change behavior and result in improved public safety or reintegration outcomes.

3. FOCUS RESOURCES ON HIGHER RISK OFFENDERS

Research has demonstrated that evidence-based interventions directed towards offenders with a moderate to high risk of committing new crimes will result in better outcomes for both offenders and the community. Conversely, treatment resources targeted to low-risk offenders produce little, if any, positive effect. In fact, despite the appealing logic of involving low-risk individuals in intensive programming to prevent them from graduating to more serious behavior, numerous studies show that certain programs may actually worsen their outcomes. By limiting supervision and services for low-risk offenders and focusing on those who present greater risk, parole and probation agencies can devote limited treatment and supervision resources where they will provide the most benefit to public safety.

4. FRONTLOAD SUPERVISION RESOURCES

Research clearly identifies the period immediately following release from prison and jail as a particularly high-risk time for offenders. Not only is the risk of new crimes greatest during this period, but offenders often have a heightened need for substance abuse treatment, mental health, housing, and other services as well. Parole and probation agencies should respond by concentrating resources in the first few days and weeks of supervision, including reaching into correctional institutions to begin the case planning process for those who will be supervised after release.

Frontloading resources has the obvious benefit of providing oversight and treatment when it is most needed. It also helps identify the cases that warrant enhanced supervision and those that do not. Offenders who consistently meet parole and probation conditions may require less supervision later on, thus offsetting the cost of shifting resources upfront. Simply increasing surveillance without a strategy for addressing offenders' criminal risk factors, however, will most likely lead to finding more violations without affecting behavior change or preventing crime.

5. IMPLEMENT EARNED DISCHARGE

Providing incentives for meeting case-specific goals of supervision is a powerful tool to enhance individual motivation and promote positive behavior change. Many experts recommend a system of earned discharge whereby lower risk probationers and parolees can earn their way off supervision by adhering to specific goals and strict guidelines. An opportunity to reduce a term of supervision can be a strong incentive for offenders to meet supervision requirements, find and retain a job, stay sober or in treatment, and participate in the programs most likely to reduce recidivism. It also further helps supervision agencies frontload and concentrate their resources on higher-risk offenders.

6. SUPERVISE OFFENDERS IN THEIR COMMUNITIES

In a system of place-based supervision, parole and probation officers have geographically-based caseloads and may have "satellite" offices located in the communities in which high concentrations of their supervisees live and work. By supervising offenders where they live, fostering relationships with those who know them best, and becoming familiar with local resources and high-risk areas, parole and probation officers are much better positioned to manage their caseloads. Further, organizing caseloads by neighborhood efficiently allocates scarce resources and reduces costly and time-consuming officer travel. This model contrasts sharply with the conventional model of "fortress" supervision, in which officers hunker down in large, centrally located headquarters and see offenders only from across a desk in the office environment.

7. ENGAGE PARTNERS TO EXPAND INTERVENTION CAPACITY

Given the substantial treatment, health, housing, education, and employment needs of parolees and probationers, it is essential for supervision agencies to partner with other organizations such as community health care providers, housing authorities, substance abuse treatment providers, mental health service providers, workforce development boards, faith-based organizations, and other community organizations. Jails and prisons also are critical partners, as they typically gather information, assessments and program intervention information that will be critical to successful supervision. Greater coordination between such organizations will enhance the capacity of supervision agencies to help keep offenders crime- and drug-free.

8. ASSESS CRIMINAL RISK AND NEED FACTORS

Supervision agencies should use reliable assessment instruments to identify both risk and need factors and link the results to a supervision case plan. Assessment instruments analyze offenders' criminal histories in combination with their responses during structured interviews and produce a score that indicates whether they are at low, medium, or high risk of reoffending. Research has shown that once these tools are scientifically validated for the specific offender populations to be supervised, they are far better than individual judgment at identifying risk levels and the attitudes and behaviors that drive offenders' criminal activity.

There is broad agreement among experts that such instruments should be used to determine the intensity of supervision and types of services that offenders receive. Some jurisdictions are beginning to use assessment tools prior to sentencing. This allows judges to use the instruments' predictive power to help make decisions about whether to sentence a defendant to incarceration or what conditions of probation to set. By identifying high-risk offenders, as well as those who may require minimal monitoring and intervention, assessment instruments serve as a guide for the efficient use of resources.

9. BALANCE SURVEILLANCE AND TREATMENT IN CASE PLANS

Case plans should reflect individual criminal risk factors and treatment needs in addition to surveillance requirements and obligations to meet with the probation or parole officer. Research has repeatedly shown that a combination of surveillance and treatment is more effective at reducing recidivism than a singular reliance on monitoring and control alone. Cognitive-behavioral interventions, and certain community-based drug treatment, and education and job assistance programs have been proven to contribute to lower recidivism rates and should be considered in the development of supervision plans.

Ideally, supervision case plans will be built on empirical risk and need assessments, incorporate offender goals, enhance individual motivation, and consider the input of stakeholders such as corrections officials, law enforcement, victims, family members, and community-based service organizations. Assessment and case planning for offenders returning from prisons and jails should begin shortly after admission and be carefully coordinated with community supervision staff to assure more successful reentry.

10. INVOLVE OFFENDERS IN THE SUPERVISION PROCESS

Supervision should evolve from a contact-driven system to a behavioral management model in which the individual being supervised is an active participant in the development of the case plan. The results of the risk assessment will identify the key components of the plan, and the supervision officer is responsible for ensuring it protects the public and holds offenders accountable. But parolees and probationers also may have valuable input, especially on the sequencing of goals and the roles of family or clergy. As active participants in the process, they will feel an increased sense of accountability and motivation, resulting in better outcomes and greater public safety.

In this model, the routine interaction between parole and probation officers and their charges is itself an intervention. Officers can enhance offenders' engagement in the process of behavior change by clearly communicating conditions of supervision, reviewing assessment information and developing case plans with offenders, working with them to update and modify goals and supervision case plans as appropriate, and explaining the reasoning behind such adjustments.

11. ENGAGE INFORMAL SOCIAL CONTROLS

Only a small fraction of an offender's time is spent interacting with his parole or probation officer, even under the most intensive supervision regimes. Practitioners and academics alike have long known that relationships with family, friends, and employers are more effective than formal legal controls in promoting positive behavior change and reducing recidivism. In recognition of this, parole and probation officers should be encouraged to incorporate offenders' support networks into the assessment, case planning, and supervision process, and to be trained to recognize where these networks exist and how to engage them.

12. USE INCENTIVES AND REWARDS

Research indicates that positive reinforcement, incentives, and rewards are powerful tools in the supervision process. By employing them for progress, along with sanctions for violations, parole and probation officers can enhance offender motivation, support positive behavior change, and reduce recidivism. Focusing on the gains that offenders have made can promote adherence to supervision conditions and encourage positive responses. Examples of incentives and rewards include awarding certificates of achievement, reducing reporting requirements, deferring a monthly payment, removing conditions (such as home detention or curfew), or asking the offender to be a "mentor" to others. Just as with sanctions, incentives and rewards should be provided with certainty and in a timely fashion to have the greatest impact on behavior change.

13. RESPOND TO VIOLATIONS WITH SWIFT AND CERTAIN SANCTIONS

Many parolees and probationers are sent to prison for technical violations of their supervision conditions, such as failing to attend drug treatment, rather than for committing a new criminal offense. Many of these violators can be held accountable in the community without compromising public safety, thus conserving prison beds for violent, serious and persistent offenders.

High-risk offenders who present a threat to the community should be returned to prison when they commit a serious violation or new crime. However, there are many probationers and parolees whose minor violations would be better and more cost-efficiently met with responses that are both proportional lo the seriousness of the violation and address the situations that may have led to the behavior. Many jurisdictions have established guidelines that set out clear penalties—low intensity interventions like community service for minor violations and more restrictive options such as very short jail stays for serious infractions. The deterrent impact of the sanctions will be enhanced if they are imposed as quickly as possible after they are detected. For appropriate violations, certain, swift and graduated sanctions can be more effective at preventing relapse and future offending (and at the same time be less expensive) than revocation to prison.

CONCLUSION

The 13 strategies presented here illustrate what evidence, research, and practitioner expertise suggest probation and parole supervision should look like. Community supervision agencies may not be able to implement all of the strategies in the short run. Nor can agencies accomplish them on their own. They will need the support of leaders in the executive, legislative, and judicial branches of government, as well as allied agencies, law enforcement, and community organizations.

But getting supervision right requires a willingness to apply the 13 strategies through a multi-year effort. Adopted alone, each strategy will produce a positive but limited impact on recidivism and other key performance measures. Implemented together, they have the potential to yield valuable cost savings and transform community supervision into a powerful force for public safety.

STUDY QUESTIONS

1. According to PEW, when should reentry begin?
2. How can states improve offender supervision?
3. What are some of the informal social controls that are recommended?
4. What are some incentives and rewards that are recommended?
5. Why is it important to respond quickly to violations?

PART

VII

CONTEMPORARY ISSUES

The final part highlights three important aspects of the U.S. correctional system: prison population growth, the "war on drugs," and the death penalty. A great deal of media attention was paid to the PEW Center on the States' report "1 in 100," the first reading in this part, which revealed many startling features of current correctional practice. Most notably, the incarceration rate in the United States has exceeded 1 in 100 adults for the first time in history. Despite many policy changes and program implementations, America's prison population continues to grow, presenting many states with budgetary crises and other unintended consequences. Related to prison population growth, the "war on drugs" may go down in history as the most influential criminal justice policy in the twentieth century. The second article presents a critical analysis of this controversial policy. Finally, the death penalty is explored through an investigation into specifically how correctional officers perform a modern-day execution. While the U.S. Supreme Court has dealt with many issues related to the death penalty in the past, technological advances in the area of DNA evidence and other efforts that have revealed miscarriages of justice are likely to keep the debates surrounding the death penalty in the forefront of policy makers' collective minds.

29
ONE IN 100

BEHIND BARS IN AMERICA IN 2008

PEW CENTER ON THE STATES

In February 2008 the The PEW Center on the States published a report titled "One in 100: Behind Bars in America 2008." Almost immediately after its release the report garnered a great deal of media attention, as it highlighted an important—and unfortunate—milestone in correctional practice in the United States. For the first time in history, the incarceration rate exceeded 1 out of 100 adults in America. The following excerpt from this PEW report details important demographic trends in the U.S. prison population and also shows how states and regions across the country vary in terms of correctional practices. States that have experienced the highest rates of growth are highlighted, as is the folly that higher incarceration rates lead automatically to safer communities. Also discussed in this piece is the relative cost that comes with ever-increasing prison populations. The cost factor is particularly relevant in light of how many states are experiencing grave budgetary crises. In some cases, other priorities—such as education and healthcare—also become strained because of necessary increases in correctional budgets.

EXECUTIVE SUMMARY

> There isn't a person in public office that's not sensitive to the accusation of being soft on crime. But you don't have to be soft on crime to be smart in dealing with criminals.
>
> —OH Gov. Ted Strickland (D), *The Columbus Dispatch*, January 26, 2008

Three decades of growth in America's prison population has quality nudged the nation across a sobering threshold: for the first time, more than one in every 100 adults is now confined in an, American jail or prison. According to figures gathered and analyzed by the Pew Public Safety performance Project, the number of people behind bar in the United States continued to climb in 2007, saddling cash-strapped states with soaring costs they can ill afford and failing to have a clear impact either on recidivism or overall crime.

For some groups, the incarceration numbers are especially startling. While one in 30 men between the ages of 20 and 34 is behind bars, for black males in that age group the figure is one in nine. Gender adds another dimension to the picture. Men still are roughly 10 times more likely to be in jail or prison, but the female population is burgeoning at a far brisker pace. For black women in their mid- to late-30s, the incarceration rate also has hit the 1-in-100 mark. Growing older, meanwhile, continues to have a dramatic chilling effect on criminal behavior. While one in every 53 people in their 20s is behind bars, the rate for those over 55 falls to one in 837.

While the national incarceration trend remains on the rise, some states report a flattening of growth, or even a decline, figures from January 1 of this year show. Texas' count dropped slightly over the previous year, but with California's massive system dipping by 4,068 inmates, Texas has become the nation's imprisonment leader. New York and Michigan, also among the country's biggest systems, reported declines as well.

There is reason to suspect those states may soon have lots of company. Prison costs arc blowing holes in state budgets but barely making a dent in recidivism rates. At the same time, policy makers are becoming increasingly aware of research-backed strategies for community corrections—better ways to identify which offenders need a prison cell and which can be safely handled in the community, new technologies to monitor their whereabouts and behavior, and more effective supervision and treatment programs to help them stay on the straight and narrow. Taken together, these trends are encouraging policy makers to diversify their states' array of criminal sanctions with options for low-risk offenders that save tax dollars but still hold offenders accountable for their actions.

POLICY CHOICES DRIVE GROWTH

> There's a shift away from the mindset of lock them up and throw away the key. That cannot sustain itself.
>
> —OH State Rep. John J. White (R-Kettering), *Dayton Daily News*, February 11, 2007

In exploring such alternatives, lawmakers are learning that current prison that current growth is not driven primarily by a parallel increase in crime, or a corresponding surge in the population at large. Rather, it flows principally from a wave of policy choices that are sending more lawbreakers to prison and, through popular "three-strikes" measures and other sentencing enhancements, keeping them there longer. Overlaying that picture in some states has been the habitual use of prison stays to punish those who break rules governing their probation or parole. In California, for example, such violators make up a large proportion of prison admissions, churning in and out of badly overloaded facilities. Nationally, more than half of released offenders are back in prison within three years, either for a new crime or for violating the terms of their release.[1]

Few doubt the necessity of locking up violent criminals and those who repeatedly threaten community safety. And policy makers understandably are moved to act by especially heinous crimes or victims seeking justice in the name of a loved one.

Increasingly, however, states are discovering that casting such a wide net for prisoners creates a vexing fiscal burden—especially in lean times. Finding enough dollars to house, feed, and provide a doctor's care to a low-risk inmate is a struggle besetting states from Arizona to Vermont. In the absence of tax hikes, lawmakers may find themselves forced to cut or limit other vital programs—from transportation to education and healthcare—to foot the incarceration tab.

That tab, meanwhile, is exploding, fueled in part by staff overtime expenses and a steep rise in inmate healthcare costs. In 1987, the states collectively spent $10.6 billion of their general funds—their primary pool of discretionary tax dollars—on corrections. Last year, they spent more than $44 billion, a 315 percent jump, data from the National Association of State Budget Officers show. Adjusted to 2007 dollars, the increase was 127 percent. Over the same period, adjusted spending on higher education rose just 21 percent.

TAKING A DIFFERENT TACK

Faced with the mushrooming bills, many states are confronting agonizing choices and weathering bitter divisions in their legislatures. But lawmakers are by no means powerless before the budget onslaught. Indeed, a rising number of states already are diversifying their menu of sanctions with new approaches that save money but still ensure that the public is protected and that offenders are held accountable. And some already are reaping encouraging results.

Kansas and Texas are well on their way. Facing daunting projections of prison population growth, they have embraced a strategy that blends incentives for reduced recidivism with greater use of community supervision for lower-risk offenders. In addition, the two states increasingly are imposing sanctions other than prison for parole and probation violators whose infractions are considered "technical," such as missing a counseling session. The new approach, born of bipartisan leadership, is allowing the two states to ensure they have enough prison beds for violent offenders while helping less dangerous lawbreakers become productive, taxpaying citizens.

No policy maker would choose this path if it meant sacrificing public safety. But gradually, some states are proving that deploying a broad range of sanctions can protect communities, punish lawbreakers and conserve tax dollars for other pressing public needs.

A SNAPSHOT OF PRISON GROWTH

The United States incarcerates more people than any country in the world, including the far more populous nation of China. At the start of the new year, the American penal system held more than 2.3 million adults. China was second, with 1.5 million people behind bars, and Russia was a distant third with 890,000 inmates, according to the latest available figures. Beyond the sheer number of inmates, America also is the global leader in the rate at which it incarcerates its citizenry, outpacing nations like South Africa and Iran. In Germany, 93 people are in prison for every 100,000 adults and children. In the U.S, the rate is roughly eight times that, or 750 per 100,000.[2]...

To produce a fresh portrait of incarceration levels at the start of 2008, Pew conducted a survey of inmate counts from the states and the federal government. Our finding: the U.S. prison population rose by more than 25,000 inmates in 2007—a 1.6 percent rate of growth that brought the national prison census to 1,596,127. Although the 2007 expansion didn't match the 3.1 percent hike during 2006, the growth tracks projections[3] and continues a pattern of steady expansion that has characterized the U.S. penal system for more than 30 years.

1 IN 100 ADULTS BEHIND BARS

The consequences of that upward trend are many, but few can rival this: more than 1 in 100 adults is now locked up in America. With 1,596,127 in state or federal prison custody, and another 723,131 in local jails, the total adult inmate count at the beginning of 2008 stood at 2,319,258. With the number of adults just shy of 230 million, the actual incarceration rate is 1 in every 99.1 adults.

That statistic masks far higher incarceration rates by race, age, and gender. A separate analysis of midyear 2006 data from the U.S. Department of Justice shows that for Hispanic and black men, for instance, imprisonment is a far more prevalent reality than it is for white men.[4] The young, meanwhile, are disproportionately more likely to wind up in prison than their elders. While one in every 15 black males

PRISON COUNT PUSHES UP

Between 1987 and 2007, the national prison population has nearly tripled.

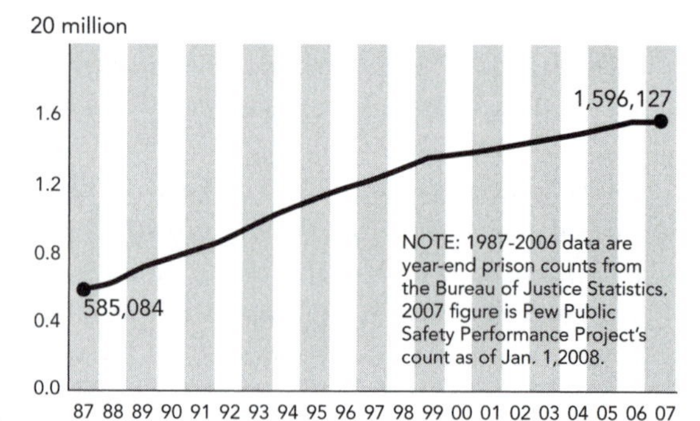

Sources: Bureau of Justice Statistics, Pew Public Safety Performance Project.

FIGURE 29.1 Prison Count Pushes Up.

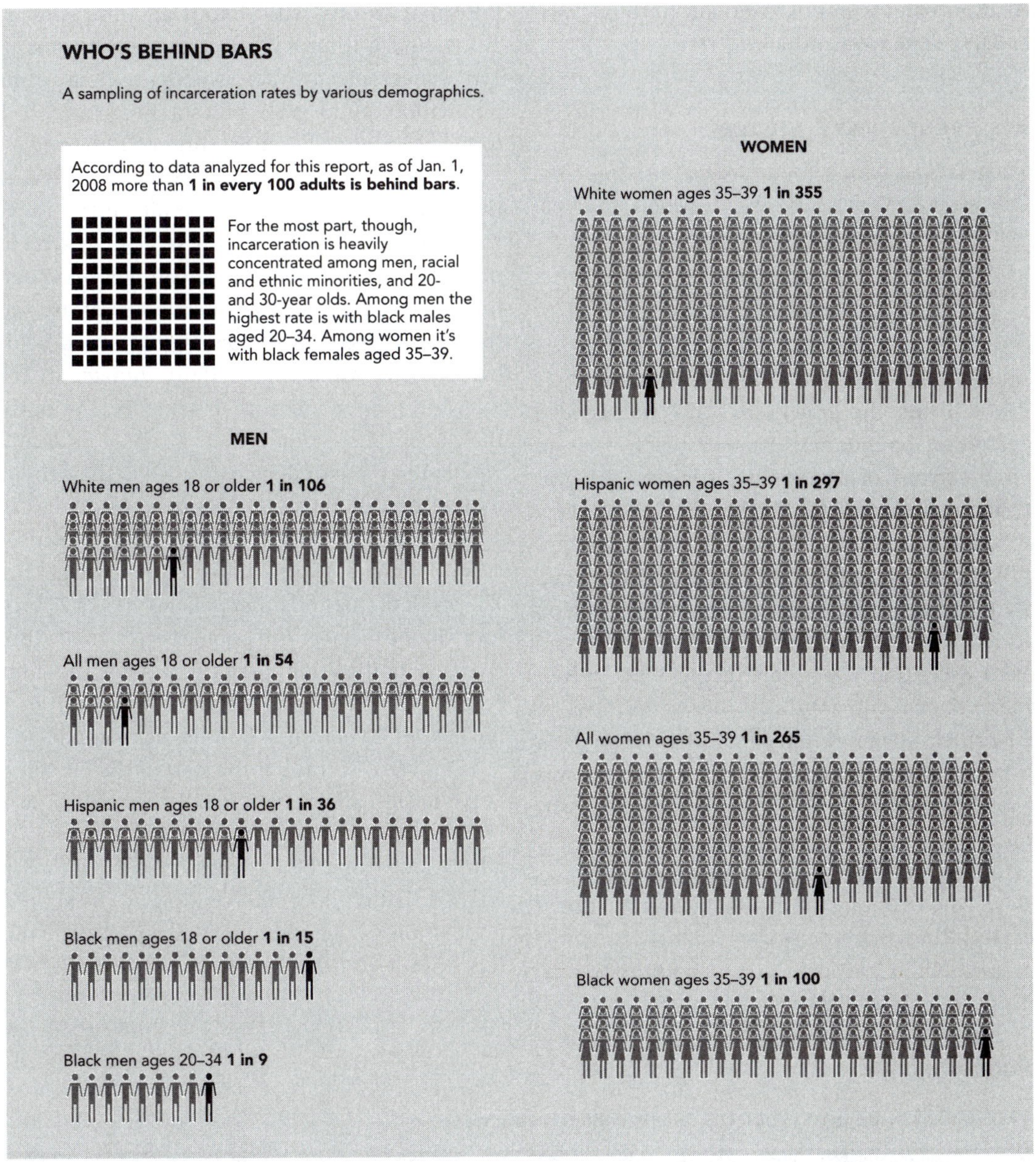

WHO'S BEHIND BARS

A sampling of incarceration rates by various demographics.

According to data analyzed for this report, as of Jan. 1, 2008 more than **1 in every 100 adults is behind bars**.

For the most part, though, incarceration is heavily concentrated among men, racial and ethnic minorities, and 20- and 30-year olds. Among men the highest rate is with black males aged 20–34. Among women it's with black females aged 35–39.

MEN

White men ages 18 or older **1 in 106**

All men ages 18 or older **1 in 54**

Hispanic men ages 18 or older **1 in 36**

Black men ages 18 or older **1 in 15**

Black men ages 20–34 **1 in 9**

WOMEN

White women ages 35–39 **1 in 355**

Hispanic women ages 35–39 **1 in 297**

All women ages 35–39 **1 in 265**

Black women ages 35–39 **1 in 100**

Sources: Analysis of "Prison and Jail Inmates at Midyear 2006," published June 2007 by the U.S. Department of Justice, Bureau of Justice Statistics. All demographic statistics, with exception of "1 in every 100 adults" are midyear 2006, not 2008 figures.

FIGURE 29.2 Who's Behind Bars.

aged 18 or older is in prison or jail, for black men over 55, the rate is one in 115....

STATE TRENDS VARY WIDELY

> "I don't think we're getting the worst drug lords into the prisons. We're just getting the people who went out and got caught. It's the low-hanging fruit."
> —KY State Justice Secretary J. Michael Brown, Testimony to KY Senate Judiciary Committee, *Lexington Herald-Leader,* January 24, 2008

Look beneath the national incarceration numbers and you'll find the growth in 2007 transcended geographical boundaries. A majority of states in all four regions of the country finished the year with more prisoners than they housed at the start. The South led the way, with its population jumping from 623,563 to 641,024—a rise of 2.8 percent. Only three of the 16 states in the southern region reported a drop in inmates, while nine experienced growth exceeding 4 percent. In the West, meanwhile, Arizona outpaced all other states, and in the Northeast, New Hampshire's population grew the fastest. Among Midwestern states, Iowa was the growth leader, expanding its inmate count by 6.1 percent.

All told, 36 states reported higher numbers as 2008 dawned. Among the eight largest correctional agencies—those with more than 50,000 inmates—four grew (Ohio, Florida, Georgia, and the Federal Bureau of Prisons) while four (New York, Michigan, Texas, and California) saw their populations dip. Ten states, meanwhile, experienced an inmate population jump of 5 percent or greater, a list topped by Kentucky, with a surge of 12 percent.

Kentucky and Nevada are two states with relatively small correctional systems hit hard by growth. In Kentucky, an indeterminate sentencing structure means the parole board has broad powers to determine when a prisoner is suitable for release—and thus, to a large degree, how big the crowd behind bars will be. Guidelines require inmates to serve a certain proportion of their sentence, but beyond that, board discretion comes into play in deciding whether to grant or deny parole. Over the past year, under new appointees to the board, the parole grant rate declined and the prison population increased as more inmates stayed locked up for a longer time. The result of this and other policies was a 12 percent jump in the incarcerated population in 2007. Absent a change of direction, projections show the inmate count will continue to rise to nearly 31,000—an increase of 40 percent—over the next decade.

Out West, Nevada at the start of the 2007 legislative session also faced a rapidly expanding prison population, fueled by an unexpected jump in prison admissions from the Las Vegas area. New forecasts warned that without intervention by the state, the population would continue its steep ascent, climbing from 13,000 prisoners to more than 18,000

DOING THE MATH

The calculation behind the **1 in 100 U.S. adults behind bars** statistics.

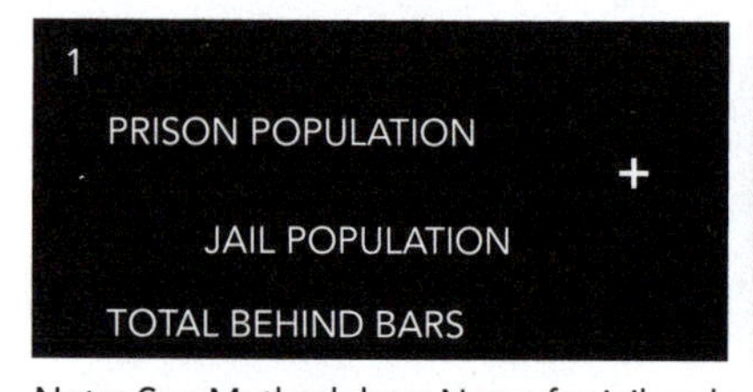

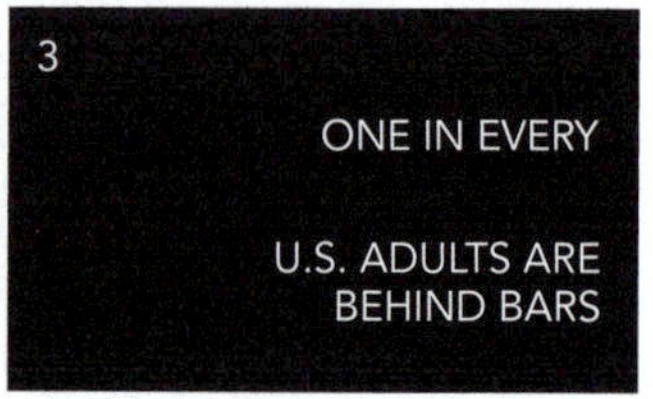

Note: See Methodology Notes for jail and adult population estimates. Source: Pew Public Safety Performance Project.

FIGURE 29.3 Doing the Math.

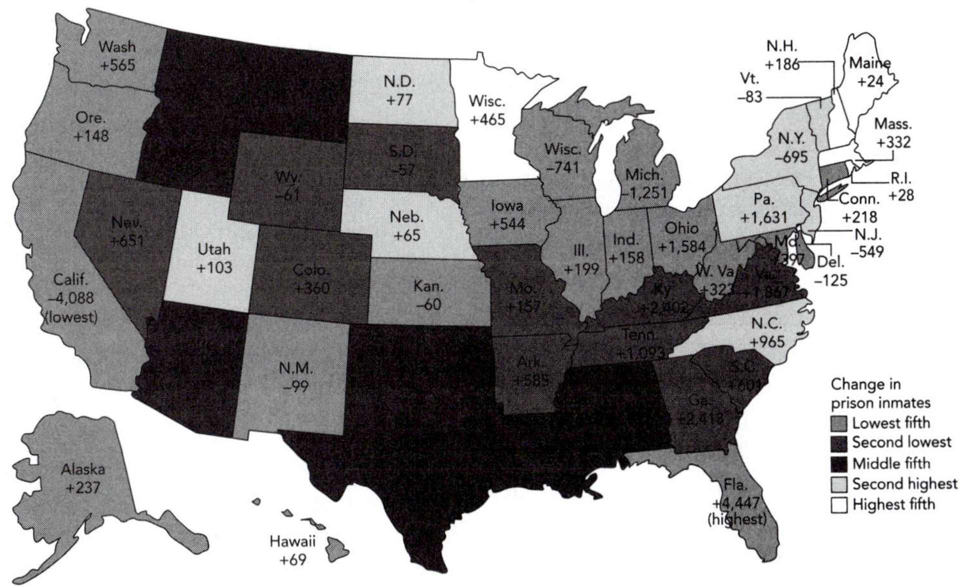

FIGURE 29.4 Wide Variance in Prison Growth.

over the next 10 years. The fiscal consequences were alarming. Among other things, the growth forced prisoners from Washington and Wyoming who were housed in Nevada back to those states. That meant both lost revenue and new appropriations from the state general fund. At the beginning of 2008, Nevada's jails and prisons held 13,552 inmates, a 5 percent jump over the number incarcerated in the Silver State at the end of 2006.

FLORIDA: A CASE STUDY IN GROWTH

For policy makers keen on understanding the dynamics of prison growth, Florida serves as a compelling case. Between 1993 and 2007, the state's inmate population has increased from 53,000 to over 97,000. While crime and a growing resident population play a role, most of the growth, analysts agree, stemmed from a host of correctional policies and practices adopted by the state.

One of the first came in 1995, when the legislature abolished "good time" credits and discretionary release by the parole board, and required that all prisoners—regardless of their crime, prior record, or risk to recidivate—serve 85 percent of their sentence. Next came a "zero tolerance" policy and other measures mandating that probation officers report every offender who violated any condition of supervision and increasing prison time for these "technical violations." As a result, the number of violators in Florida prisons has jumped by an estimated 12,000.[5] Crime in Florida has dropped substantially during this period, but it has fallen as much or more in some states that have not grown their prison systems, or even have shrunk them, such as New York.

Without a change of direction, Florida is expected to reach a peak of nearly 125,000 inmates by 2013. Based on that projection, the state will run out of prison capacity by early 2009 and will need to add another 16,500 beds to keep pace.[6]

THE COSTS—HIGH AND CLIMBING FAST

Prisons and jails are "24-7" operations. They require large, highly trained staffs. Their inhabitants are troubled, aging, and generally sicker than people outside prison walls. Even absent continued growth, the cost of keeping the nation's lock-ups running safely is staggering. Total state spending on corrections—including bonds and federal contributions—topped $49 billion last year, up from $12 billion in 1987. By 2011, continued prison growth is expected to cost states an additional $25 billion.[7]

The primary catalyst behind the increase is obvious: prison growth means more bodies to feed, clothe, house, and supervise. While figures vary widely by state, the average per prisoner operating cost was $23,876 in 2005, the most recent year for which data were available. Rhode Island spent the most per inmate ($44,860) while Louisiana had the lowest per inmate cost, $13,009.[8] While employee wages and benefits account for much of the variance among states, other factors—such as the inmate-to-staff ratio—play a role as well. Capital expenses, meanwhile, are difficult to estimate, but researchers cite $65,000 per bed as the best approximation for a typical medium security facility.[9]

CALIFORNIA: $8.8 BILLION AND GROWING

> "We are jammed up with this situation right now because we have fallen in love with one of the most undocumented beliefs: That somehow you get safer if you put more people in jail."
> —CA Senate President Pro Tem Don Perata (D-East Bay), *Associated Press*, December 8, 2007

Remarkably, 13 states now devote more than $1 billion a year in general funds to their corrections systems. The undisputed leader is California, where spending totaled $8.8 billion last year. Even when adjusted for inflation, that represents a 216 percent increase over the amount California spent on

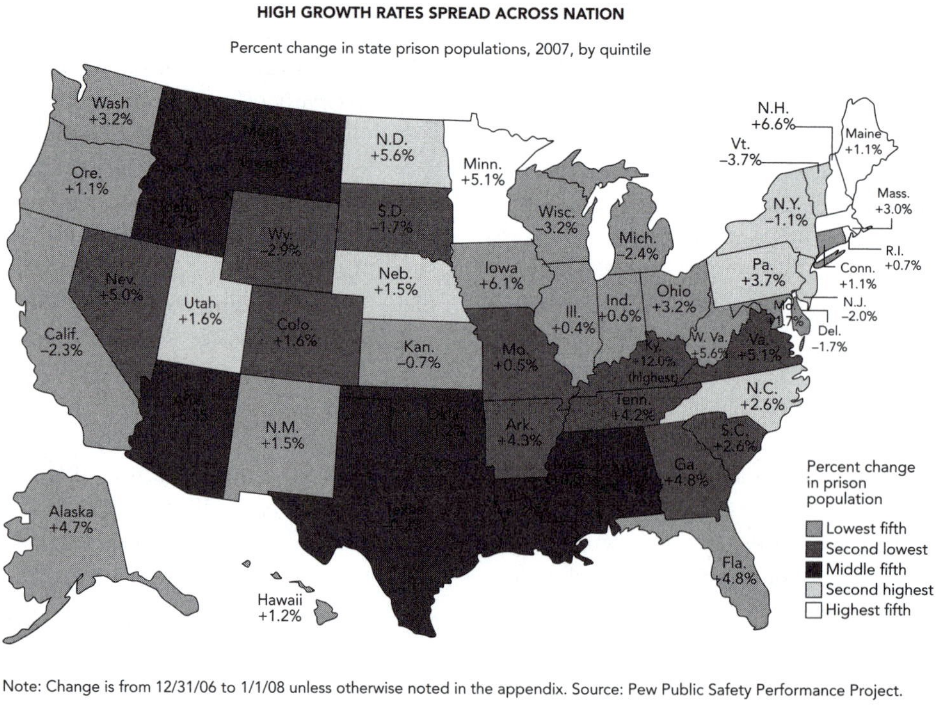

HIGH GROWTH RATES SPREAD ACROSS NATION

Percent change in state prison populations, 2007, by quintile

Note: Change is from 12/31/06 to 1/1/08 unless otherwise noted in the appendix. Source: Pew Public Safety Performance Project.

FIGURE 29.5 High Growth Rates Spread Across Nation.

corrections 20 years earlier. And last year, the governor signed a bill authorizing another $7.9 billion in spending, through lease revenue bonds, for 53,000 more prison and jail beds. Texas, with a slightly larger number of inmates, ranks a distant second in spending, investing roughly $3.3 billion last year.

California vividly symbolizes the financial perils of the state prison business. On top of the perennial political tug-of-war, the state's whopping corrections budget is shaped by a bevy of court settlements that make predicting and controlling spending tricky. Following successful lawsuits by prisoner plaintiffs, California now is subject to court oversight of inmate medical and dental care, mental health services, its juvenile offenders, and the treatment of disabled inmates. Even its parole revocation system is controlled by a legal settlement, and thereby subject to judicial orders that influence spending.

Healthcare costs have been affected more than any other category. In FY 2000–01, California spent $676 million on such costs. By FY 2004–05, after the state settled a lawsuit alleging negligent and insufficient medical care, spending had soared to $1.05 billion, an increase of 55 percent.[10] And that was before a judge appointed a federal receiver to run prison healthcare, a move that is driving such spending up even more dramatically. It now stands at $2.1 billion annually, a 210 percent increase since 2000.

HEALTH CARE, GERIATRICS DRIVE COSTS

As California has learned, medical care is one of the principal cost drivers in corrections budgets today. From 1998 to 2001, healthcare spending in state prisons grew 10 percent annually, a 2004 report by the Council of State Governments found. At the time of the study, medical care costs totaled $3.7 billion annually and accounted for about 10 percent of correctional spending.[11]

Under the 1976 U.S. Supreme Court ruling *Estelle v. Gamble*, states are compelled to provide a constitutionally adequate level of medical care, or care that generally meets a "community standard." Beyond that mandate, the rise in medical outlays largely stems from mushrooming costs associated with special needs populations, including HIV-positive prisoners and geriatric inmates.

Communicable diseases are a particular concern, spreading quickly in a crowded prison environment where risky behaviors such as tattooing and piercing, unprotected sex, fighting, and intravenous drug use are not uncommon.[12] Hepatitis C, a blood-borne, life-threatening disease, is the biggest worry. The latest Hepatitis C treatments cost as much as $30,000 per inmate annually. At one California prison, in Vacaville, the chief medical officer estimates that half of the 3,200 inmates have been infected with Hepatitis C.[13] Other states put the in-prison prevalence at between 25 and 40 percent.[14]

Increasingly, the graying of the nation's prisons is causing costs to swell. While crime remains overwhelmingly a young man's game, between 1992 and 2001, the number of state and federal inmates aged 50 or older rose from 41,586 to 113,358, a

TWENTY YEARS OF RISING COSTS

Between fiscal years 1987 and 2007, total state general fund expenditures on corrections rose 315 percent.

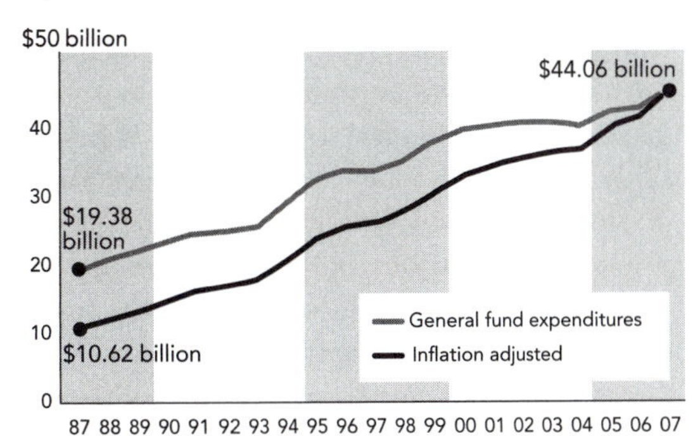

Note: These fi gures repre-sent state general funds. They do not include federal or local government corrections and typically do not include fund-ing from other state sources.
Source: National Association of State Budget Offi cers, "State Expenditure Report" series. Infl ation adjusted fi gures are based on a reanalysis of data in this series.

FIGURE 29.6 Twenty Years of Rising Costs.

staggering jump of 173 percent, a 2004 National Institute of Corrections report found.[15] And older inmates are gradually making up a larger proportion of the overall count. In the federal prisons, for example, about one-quarter of the population was over 50 in 1989. By 2010, that proportion is forecast to grow to one-third. On the state level, Oklahoma recently found that 16 percent of newly admitted inmates were over 45 years old—more than double the rate in 1990.[16]

While aging decreases criminal activity, it brings a multitude of challenges in a prison setting. Because they are often preyed upon by younger, stronger inmates, older convicts may require special housing.[17] Hearing and visual impairments, incontinence, dietary intolerance, depression, and the early onset of chronic diseases are other complicating management factors. As a result, the average cost associated with an older prisoner is $70,000—two to three times that of a younger prisoner.[18]

The bottom line: Some crimes are so heinous they warrant a lifetime behind bars. But states are spending more and more on inmates who are less and less of a threat to public safety.

STAFF VACANCIES, OVERTIME SPIKE

Another key cost driver is compensation for the officers who patrol cellblocks.

In 2006, the most recent year for which data were available, there were approximately 4.25 million state government employees. About 11 percent of them—or one in nine—worked in corrections,[19] but prisons are struggling mightily to keep a full complement of officers on staff. The result—the extensive use of overtime—is one of the biggest budget busters confronting states.

In Wisconsin, for instance, overtime rose 27 percent between 2005 and 2006, largely due to an unanticipated 1,200-inmate jump in the prison population.[20] California's overtime costs, meanwhile, exploded by 35 percent between 2005 and 2006, as the state struggled to keep its 33 prisons staffed despite nearly 4,000 vacancies. Overtime costs in California topped half a billion dollars in 2006, with 15 percent of the corrections workforce earning at least $25,000 in overtime that year. Six employees even earned more than the $212,179 annual salary set aside for Gov. Arnold Schwarzenegger.[21]

The economic picture is so dire in California, where a budget deficit of $14.5 billion is predicted for the coming fiscal year, that the Republican governor has proposed releasing more than 22,100 inmates before their terms are up. Eligibility would be limited to nonviolent, non-serious offenders, and the plan excludes sex offenders and those convicted of 25 other specific crimes. Governor Schwarzenegger says the state would save $1.1 billion through his proposal, but so far it has received a cool reception from both parties in the legislature.

RESTITUTION, CHILD SUPPORT, TAX PAYMENTS LAG

> "Our policy and funding decisions need to be based on good data and the latest research. Unless we have that foundation, I'm not confident we're doing everything we can to fight crime effectively and to be efficient with taxpayer dollars."
> —AZ State Sen. John Huppenthal (R-Phoenix), press release, February 6, 2007

While overtime and healthcare costs show up vividly in budget documents, the nation's reliance on incarceration for many low-risk offenders inflicts economic hardship in many other, less obvious ways. If they have a job at all, prisoners are typically unable to earn more than a very low wage, making it unlikely they will pay much, if anything, in child support, victim restitution, or taxes. National statistics on such impacts are scarce. But a few state-level reports document the difference incarceration can make.

In a 2001 study, Massachusetts found that more than three-quarters of the state's prison population had paid none of its mandated child support in the previous 12 months. During the same timeframe, more than two-thirds of parolees with child support obligations managed to make at least partial payments. Overall, the average prisoner paid only $206 over the previous year for child support obligations, while the average amount paid by parolees was $1,538—more than seven times as much.[22]

In Florida, meanwhile, statistics show that offenders under supervision in the community make substantial restitution payments to victims. In FY 2004–2005, one study showed, Florida probationers paid more than $37.3 million in restitution under mandatory financial obligation agreements established at the onset of their supervision.[23]

CROWDING OUT OTHER PRIORITIES

Year by year, corrections budgets are consuming an ever larger chunk of state general funds, leaving less and less in the pot for other needs. Collectively, correctional agencies now consume 6.8 percent of state general funds, 2007 data show.[24] That means one in every 15 dollars in the states' main pool of discretionary money goes to corrections. Considering all types of funds, corrections had the second fastest rate of growth in FY 2006. With a 9.2 percent jump, it trailed transportation but outpaced increases in spending on education and Medicaid.[25]

Some states spend an even larger proportion of their budgets on corrections. Oregon, for example, directed one in every 10 dollars to corrections, while Florida and Vermont spent one in 11. Minnesota and Alabama are at the other extreme, spending less than 3 percent of their general fund dollars on corrections. Over the past 20 years, corrections spending took up a larger share of overall general fund expenditures in 42 states.

Some policy makers are questioning the wisdom of devoting an increasingly large slice of the budget pie to incarceration, especially when recidivism rates have remained discouragingly high. Are we getting our money's worth? Is our investment in this system returning sufficient dividends for victims, taxpayers and society at large?

In fiscal year 2007, an estimated 1 in every 15 state general fund dollars was spent on corrections.

State	Corrections as a percentage of total general fund expenditures, 2007	1987–2007 percentage point change
Oregon	10.9%	+4.6
Florida	9.3%	+3.6
Vermont	9.3%	+5.2
Colorado		+5.1
California		+3.8
Texas		+4.2
Arizona		+0.8
Montana		+2.4
Oklahoma		+4.1
Arkansas		+5.1
Maryland	7.6%	–1.5
Louisiana		+1.7
Missouri		+3.7
Delaware		+1.9
Ohio		+2.5
South Dakota		+3.1
Idaho		+3.8
Utah	3.9%	+2.5
South Carolina	6.7%	+0.8
Virginia	6.7%	–8.1
Wisconsin	6.7%	+4.0
New Hampshire		+2.5
Nevada	6.4%	–2.1
Pennsylvania		+4.1
Iowa		+2.6
Washington		+2.4
North Carolina		+0.9
Kansas		+1.3
Tennessee	5.6%	–2.0
Georgia	5.4%	–0.5
Mississippi	5.4%	+1.5
Alaska	5.3%	+2.0
Indiana	5.3%	+0.3
North Dakota	6.3%	+3.7
Illinois	6.2%	+0.8
Kentucky	6.2%	+1.8
Nebraska	5.2%	+1.1
Massachusetts	6.1%	+1.9
New York	5.1%	–2.0
New Jersey	4.9%	+0.7
Rhode Island		+1.4
West Virginia		+3.3
Connecticut		+2.0
New Mexico	4.2%	–0.5
Maine		+0.4
Wyoming		+0.1
Hawaii		+1.3
Minnesota		+1.0
Alabama	2.6%	–2.4
National average	6.8%	+1.8

States in bold *saw a decrease in the percentage of their general fund dedicated to corrections.*

Note: Michigan does not have a comparable figure because of the state's general fund definition. See Jurisdictional Notes.
Source: National Association of State Budget Officers, "State Expenditure Report" series. Percentage point increases are based on a reanalysis of data in this series.

FIGURE 29.7 Taking a Bigger Cut.

On average, corrections is the fifth-largest state budget category, behind health, elementary and secondary education, higher education, and transportation. But nearly all corrections dollars come from the states' own coffers; healthcare, by contrast, draws a majority of funding from the federal government, primarily through Medicaid. For some public officials, that distinction highlights the effect of corrections spending on other priorities.

OF BOOKS AND BARS

Between 1987 and 2007, the amount states spent on corrections more than doubled while the increase in higher education spending has been moderate.

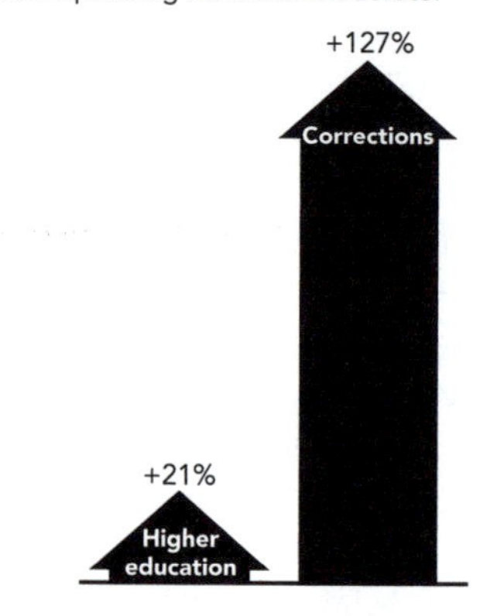

Source: National Association of State Budget Officers, "State Expenditure Report" series. Inflation adjusted general fund figures are based on a reanalysis of data in this series.

FIGURE 29.8 Of Books and Bars.

PRE-K, HIGHER ED FUNDING LAGS

> "If we don't change the course now, we will be building prisons forever and ever—prisons we can't afford."
>
> —TX State Senator John Whitmire (D-Houston), Chair, Senate Criminal Justice Committee, *Austin-American Statesman*, January 31, 2007

Higher education is of particular concern. Higher education spending accounts for a roughly comparable portion of state expenditures as corrections, and other than tuition is paid for almost entirely out of state rather than federal funds. States don't necessarily make explicit choices between higher education and corrections funding, but they do have to balance their budgets. So, unlike the federal government, a dollar spent in one area is unavailable for another.

In 1987, states collectively spent $33 billion of their general funds on higher education. By 2007, they were spending $72.88 billion, an increase of 121 percent. Adjusted to 2007 dollars, the increase was 21 percent. Over the same timeframe, inflation-adjusted corrections spending rose 127 percent, from $10.6 billion ($19.4 billion in 2007 dollars) to more than $44 billion.

Some regional differences were more dramatic. While inflation-adjusted prison spending rose 61 percent in the Northeast in the last 20 years, higher education spending went the other way, dropping by 5.5 percent. In the West, meanwhile, the number of dollars allocated to prisons skyrocketed by 205 percent. At the same time, higher education spending rose just 28 percent.

Corrections spending also competes with the funding many states want to devote to early childhood education, one of the most proven crime prevention strategies. Research shows that attending a high-quality pre-kindergarten influences a child's success both in school and in life. One rigorous study that followed severely disadvantaged children into adulthood showed that participation in pre-kindergarten dramatically reduced participation in juvenile and adult crime, and increased high school graduation, employment, and earnings, with a total benefit-cost ratio of 16 to 1.[26]

Backed with such evidence of success, states have substantially increased support for high-quality, voluntary pre-kindergarten. New state pre-k funding exceeded $525 million in FY 2008, an increase of more than 12 percent over FY07 expenditures, bringing total state investments in early education across the country to $4.8 billion.[27]

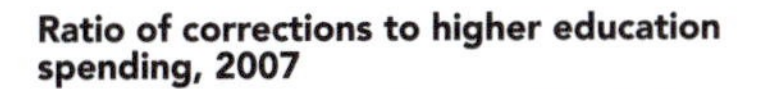

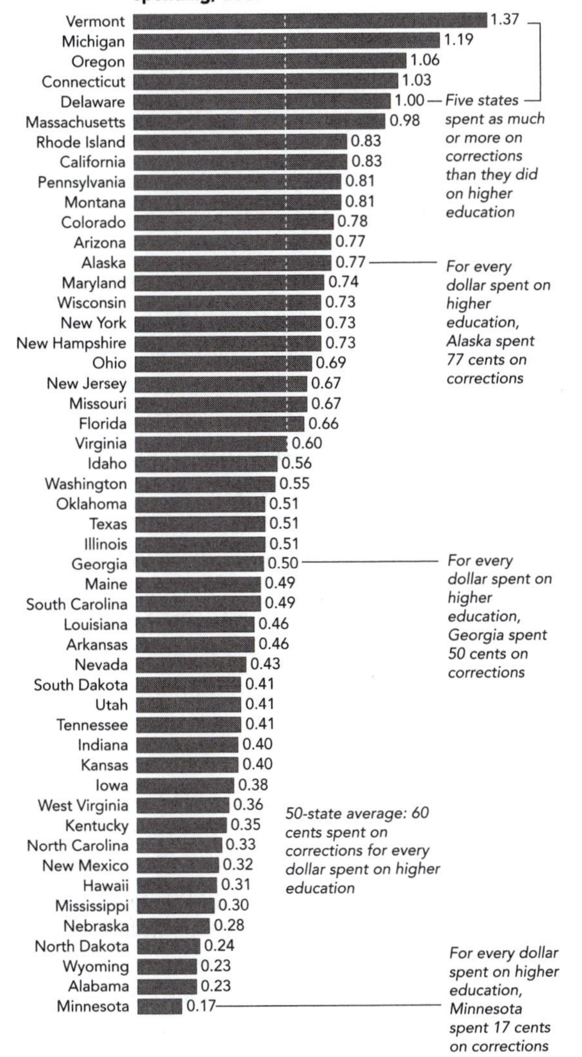

FIGURE 29.9 Making Decisions Where to Spend.

Increasingly, state policy makers are finding that a dollar spent for pre-k classes now can forestall many more dollars for prison beds down the road.

> It's not good public policy to take all of these taxpayer dollars at a very tough time, and invest it in the prison system when we ought to be investing it in the things that are going to transform the economy, like education and diversifying the economy.
> —MI Gov. Jennifer Granholm (D), *Associated Press*, December 12, 2007

STUDY QUESTIONS

1. What policies and interventions have been employed to aid states that have experienced the highest growth in prison populations?
2. What appears to be the cause of the rapid growth in the prison population as a whole?
3. What programs and/or strategies have been put in place in areas where prison growth has been dealt with successfully?
4. What implications does rapid prison growth have for any state correctional system (i.e., what are the unintended consequences of increasing incarceration rates)?
5. Why doesn't increasing incarceration rates automatically lead to safer communities?

NOTES

1. Langan, Dr. Patrick A., and Dr. David J. Levin, *Recidivism of Prisoners Released in 1994*, U.S. Department of Justice, Bureau of Justice Statistics (Washington, D.C.: June 2002)
2. International incarceration rates from International Centre for Prison Studies at King's College, London, "World Prison Brief." www.kcl.ac.uk/depsta/rel/icps/worldbrief/world_brief.html
3. State projections were reported in *Public Safety, Public Spending: Forecasting America's Prison*

Population, 2007–2011, Public Safety Performance Project, The Pew Charitable Trusts (Washington, D.C.: February 2007).

4. Sabol, Dr. William J., et al, *Prison and Jail Inmates at Midyear 2006*. U.S. Department of Justice, Bureau of Justice Statistics (Washington, D.C.: June 2007) All incarceration rates for subpopulations in this report are derived from this and other Bureau of Justice Statistics reports.
5. The number of offenders sentenced to prison for technical violations increased 7.1 percent in FY 2004–05, 4.3 percent in FY 2005–06, and 5.8 percent in FY 2006–07.
6. Workpapers of the Criminal Justice Estimating Conference, October 8, 2007. Tallahassee, FL: EDR.
7. *Public Safety, Public Spending, p. ii.* These cost estimates are cumulative, including operating and capital expenditures from 2007 to 2011.
8. *Public Safety, Public Spending*, p. 33.
9. *Public Safety, Public Spending*, p.22.
10. Office of California State Controller Steve Westly, *California Department of Corrections and Rehabilitation, Review Report: Healthcare Delivery System* (Sacramento, CA: August, 2006).
11. Council of State Governments, Trends Alert, Information for State Decision-Makers, *Corrections Health Care Costs*, by Chad Kinsella, January 2004.
12. *Ibid.*
13. Prison's Deadliest Inmate, Hepatitis C, Escaping: Publichealth Workers Warn of Looming Epidemic of 'Silent Killer,' *Associated Press* (Vacaville, CA: March 14, 2007).
14. Fox, Rena K. et al, "Hepatitis C Virus Infection Among Prisoners in the California State Correctional System," *Clinical Infectious Diseases* (June 2005).
15. Anno, Jaye B., et al, *Addressing the Needs of Elderly, Chronically Ill, and Terminally Ill Inmates*, U.S. Department of Justice, National Institute of Corrections, Criminal Justice Institute (Middleton, CT: February, 2004).
16. Turley, Jonathan, George Washington University Law School professor. Testimony before the House Judiciary Committee, Dec. 6, 2007.
17. *Addressing the Needs of Elderly, Chronically Ill, and Terminally Ill Inmates*
18. *Ibid.*
19. U.S. Census Bureau, State Government Employment and Payroll data: http://www.census.gov/govs/www/apesst.html. For more, see Appendix A-5.
20. Marley, Patrick, "Prison officers rack up overtime," Milwaukee Journal Sentinel, December 12, 2007.
21. Chorneau, Tom, "$500 million in OT at state prisons," San Francisco Chronicle, July 15, 2007
22. Thoennes, Dr. Nancy, *Child Support Profile: Massachusetts Incarcerated and Paroled Parent*, Center for Policy Research, (Denver, CO: May 2002).
23. Florida Department of Corrections, *Restitution and Other Monetary Obligations Collected from Offenders Under Supervision in FY 2004–05*, available online at http://www.dc.state.fl.us/oth/ccmyths.html.
24. National Association of State Budget Officers, "State Expenditure Report FY 2006," December 2007. http://www.nasbo.org/Publications/PDFs/fy2006er.pdf
25. *Ibid.*
26. Schweinhart, L. J., Montie, J., Xiang, Z., Barnett, W. S., Belfield, C. R., & Nores, M. (2005). *Lifetime effects: The High/Scope Perry Preschool study through age 40.* (Monographs of the High/Scope Educational Research Foundation, 14). Ypsilanti, MI: High/Scope Press.
27. Prek Now, *Votes Count, Legislative Action on Prek Fiscal Year 2008* (Washington, D.C.: September 2007). www.preknow.org.
28. In the latest Gallup Poll, only 2 percent of Americans volunteered "crime" as the most important problem facing the country. In March 1977, by contrast, 15 percent of Americans polled by Gallup volunteered "crime" as the most important problem facing the country.

Cited in Sam Roberts, "All Crime Is Local In '08 Politics," The New York Times, Sept. 16, 2007.

29. For more detail on Texas and the legislators who helped advance this legislation, see the following reports: Council of State Governments Justice Center, *Justice Reinvestment State Brief: Texas*, and Public Safety Performance Project, The Pew Charitable Trusts, *Changing Direction: A Bipartisan Team Paves a New Path for Sentencing and Corrections in Texas*.
30. Vera Institute of Justice, *Managing State Prison Growth: Key Trends in Sentencing Policy* (New York, January 2008).
31. *Prison and Jail Inmates at Midyear 2006*
32. *Ibid*.
33. For more detail on Kansas and a national discussion of the issues surrounding parole violators, see the following reports: Council of State Governments Justice Center, *Justice Reinvestment State Brief: Kansas*, and Public Safety Performance Project, The Pew Charitable Trusts, *When Offenders Break the Rules: Smart Responses to Parole and Probation Violations*.
34. Vera Institute of Justice, Reconsidering Incarceration: New Directions for Reducing Crime, by Don Stemen (New York: January 2007).

30

SOCIAL CONSEQUENCES OF THE WAR ON DRUGS

THE LEGACY OF FAILED POLICY

ERIC L. JENSEN
JURG GERBER
CLAYTON MOSHER

The "war on drugs" that many regard as having officially started during the Reagan administration may be the most influential policy position of the criminal justice system in the last fifty years. The law enforcement, court processes, and correctional innovations resulting from this war have all been the subject of evaluative research, but the authors here take a more comprehensive approach to the issue. A broad overview of the war on drugs provides a critical analysis of its social consequences, and readers will see how this "get tough" policy may ultimately have done more harm than good in terms of the U.S. drug/crime nexus. In relation to what has come to be known as the "prison industrial complex," drug offenders (particularly African-American men) have been disproportionately disenfranchised. Finally, the authors reveal that the "war" is far from over—and even if it ended today, the negative consequences would likely remain with us for decades to come.

The current "war on drugs" has radically transformed the criminal justice system. Although criminologists are aware of the multitudes of problematic justice system outcomes associated with this war, the widespread social, economic, health, political, and human costs of the current antidrug crusade have not been studied extensively by criminologists. The objective of this study is to bring attention to the broader societal costs of this war.

In a previous article, we argued that "the 1986 War on Drugs has resulted in some of the most extensive changes in criminal justice policy and the operations of the justice system in the United States since the due process revolution of the 1960s" (Jensen & Gerber, 1996, p. 421). This most recent in a series of drug wars in the United States has now lasted almost 17 years. Although huge amounts of economic resources, $18.8 billion by the federal government in fiscal year 2002 alone, personnel, and massive prison construction have been hurled at the problem, the drug war has failed to eliminate illegal drug use. In fact, the Household Survey of Drug Abuse shows that illegal drug use was declining substantially in the 6 to 7 years before the drug war was declared by President Reagan and continued this downturn for the next 6 years with fluctuations

Excerpts from "Social Consequences of the War on Drugs: The Legacy of Failed Policy" by Eric L. Jensen, Jurg Gerber, and Clayton Mosher. *Criminal Justice Policy Review*, Volume 15, Number 1, March 2004.

occurring since the early 1990s (Jensen & Gerber, 1998; *Sourcebook of Criminal Justice Statistics*, 2001). Given this seemingly natural downturn—which was occurring in Canada also—the drug war seems to have had no effect on illegal drug use.

The war on drugs and its influences on the criminal justice system have received a great deal of attention from criminologists and other social scientists. Prison populations have exploded with persons convicted of drug offenses. Between 1980 and 2001, the number of persons in state and federal prisons for drug offenses increased by approximately 1,300% (www.ojp.usdoj.gov/bjs/prisons.htm). Incarceration and prison construction have become major industries; in part replacing the old rust belt industries that were the economic backbone of America for decades (Christie, 2000). Law enforcement personnel are being redirected away from handling other types of crimes in favor of drug offenses (Mast, Benson, & Rasmussen, 2000). Criminal courts are so overloaded with drug cases that special drug courts have been created to more speedily handle the burdensome caseloads (Inciardi, McBride, & Rivers, 1996). For the first time in American history much harsher sentences are required for one form of an illegal drug (crack) than another form of the same substance (powder cocaine) (Belenko, 1993). Attempts have been made to criminalize the behavior of pregnant women by charging them with delivery of drugs to a minor (Beckett, 1995; Sagatun-Edwards, 1998). If these charges fail—as they most often do—child protection services have been used to remove the baby from its mother.

The drug war has also spread over into the civil arena. This pandemic spillover of state intrusion into the civil arena in the name of controlling crime represents a rapid and drastic slide down the slippery slope of reducing what heretofore were considered the due process rights of Americans. The most pervasive example of crime control absent due process is the civil forfeiture of assets in drug-related cases (Blumenson & Nilsen, 1998; Jensen, 2000). Law enforcement agencies seized nearly $7 billion in allegedly drug-related assets from fiscal year 1985 through 1999 (Jensen, 2000; *Sourcebook of Criminal Justice Statistics*, 2001). When law enforcement is partially self-financed, it becomes less accountable to the public.

Public school students are required to take drug tests in an increasing number of schools even when drugs have not been shown to be a serious problem in the school (see Crowley, 1998). Drug-sniffing dogs are frequently used in schools and school parking lots to uncover illegal drugs without search warrants.

The U.S. drug war is becoming global. The federal government is attempting to influence the governments of other nations throughout the world to deal with drug issues as the U.S. government sees fit. This international arm twisting and cajoling interferes with the sovereignty of foreign governments (Bouley, 2001; Bullington, Krebs & Rasmussen, 2000; del Olmo, 1993; Denq & Wang, 2001; Garcia, 1997; Ryan, 1998).

Although criminologists are aware of this multitude of problematic justice system outcomes associated with the War on Drugs, we must now begin to consider the widespread social, economic, health, political, and human costs of the current antidrug crusade. The objective of this article is to bring attention to these broader societal costs of the drug war. Drug policy has become a major force in the lives of millions of persons caught in the justice system; the same holds true for millions of their family members, relatives, and friends; and the inner-city communities that suffer as a result of the policies emanating from this state-constructed moral panic.

What does the future hold for the millions of young men—disproportionately African American—who will come out of prison to face a new life stigmatized as ex-convicts and drug addicts? Will they find living-wage jobs and form stable families or return to the destructive lifestyles of their youth? How is the legitimate political influence of African Americans being influenced by the loss of the right to vote of millions of young, Black men who are convicted felons? How have repressive policies regarding syringes led to the spread of HIV/AIDS? The prison construction boom of the 1980s and 1990s may lead to the need for continued, expanded wars on crime when the cohorts of young men are smaller in the future—capacity causes utilization. Crime control is now a basic industry in the United States. The benefits of medical cannabis use for the chronically ill may not be realized due to the active federal intervention to stop state initiatives that allow it. These are the broader issues that we will begin to draw attention to in this article.

PRISON CAPACITY: IF YOU BUILD IT, THEY MUST COME

It has been argued by some criminologists that the creation of prison capacity generates the prisoners to fill this capacity (see Coates, Miller, & Ohlin, 1978); others assert that limited prison capacity acts as a constraint on prison populations. In the late 1960s, criminologists and other analysts of criminal justice system trends, perhaps deluded by the increased use of alternative sanctions such as probation, predicted a leveling-off, or even declines in the overall level of imprisonment in the United States (e.g., Blumstein & Cohen, 1973; Rothman, 1971). The President's Commission on Law Enforcement and Administration of Justice (1967, pp. 4–5) predicted that the increased use of community programs would curtail institutional growth: "the population projection for the prison system shows the smallest aggregate increase of any of the correctional activities." In addition to the impact of alternative sanctions on prison populations, some held that judicial decisions on prison overcrowding in the 1970s, which prevented corrections officials in some states from receiving new inmates and even ordered some facilities closed, presaged a decline in the use of incarceration (Zimring & Hawkins, 1991).

As early as 1971, however, the American Friends Service Committee (1971, p. 172) argued that the result of providing new cell space was "inevitable: the coercive net of the justice system will be spread over a larger number of people, trapping them for longer periods of time." Similarly, a 1980 study sponsored by the National Institute of Justice (1980), while indicating that the data were only "suggestive," asserted that

> as a matter of history, this study has found that state prison populations were more likely to increase in years immediately following construction than at any other time, and that increases in the numbers of inmates closely approximates the change in capacity. (pp. 138–139)

Between 1990 and 1999, the total number of inmates in state and federal prisons increased 75%. State prisoners increased by 71% and federal prisoners by 127%. States with the largest increases in prison populations during this time were Texas (173%), Idaho (147%), West Virginia (126%), and Hawaii (124%) (Bureau of Justice Statistics, 2000b). California has built 21 new prisons in the last 20 years and increased its inmate population eightfold. As Schlosser (1998) has noted, the number of drug offenders imprisoned in California in 1997 was more than twice the number imprisoned for *all* crimes in 1978.

During the mid-1990s, an average of three 500-bed prison facilities have opened *each week* in the United States (Schlosser, 1998). Christie (2000), in his provocatively titled book *Crime Control as Industry,* refers to low-level offenders as the "raw material" for prison expansion. He suggests that the prison industry needs inmates just as the paper industry needs trees—the key difference, however, is that trees may well turn out to be a finite resource.

And of course, the war on drugs has led to unprecedented racial disproportions in our prison population. Donzinger (1996) estimated that if current growth rates continue for the next 10 years, by the year 2020 more than 6 in 10 African American males between the ages of 18 and 34 will be incarcerated, with the total prison population topping 10 million. And once built at an average cost of $100,000 per cell, these prison beds must be occupied.

Significant developments in the 1980s and into the 1990s would appear to indicate that the incredible recent growth rates in incarcerated populations will not soon abate; although the rate of growth in prison populations slowed somewhat from 1999 through 2001 (Bureau of Justice Statistics, n.d.). Consider, in this context, the rising rates of juvenile incarceration and the continual calls for transferring more juveniles to adult court. There is also the issue of the increasing involvement of private companies in the imprisonment business (Quittner, 1998); the globalization of the economy, whereby companies that are unwilling or unable to obtain cheap labor in Third World countries are making increased use of prison labor (Overbeck, 1997; Robinson, 1998; Wright, 1998), and the growing interest of rural communities in securing prisons as a means of economic development (McDonald, 1997). As a prison liaison group chair in a rural Michigan jurisdiction noted, "this is going to mean more jobs and more money to the community... there's no possible way for those guys to get out, so we just reap the benefits" (as cited in Julien, 1998).

There is of course a very cruel irony in all these developments. As state governments take funds from education and social programs to expand their prison systems, citizens are less able to compete in an increasingly competitive marketplace. Skills will be low, employment opportunities limited, and more people will live in poverty. Such conditions are criminogenic, but instead of investing in programs to prevent criminal activity, "the government spends dollars on the final result of the poverty circle" (McDonald, 1997).

As Schlosser (1998) recently pointed out, there are several similarities between the emergent prison-industrial complex and the military-industrial complex that it appears to have superseded. Although crime has replaced communism as the external evil that can be exploited by politicians, the most striking similarity between the two is the need to create policies that are more concerned with the economic imperatives of the industry than the needs of the public it allegedly serves. In addition, the policies allegedly create significant employment opportunities in the communities where prisons locate, thereby tying the economic prosperity of literally millions of people to the growth of the crime control industry. Finally, both the military and prison industries have an internal logic that allows them to benefit regardless of whether their policies succeed or fail. As Donzinger (1998) notes,

> if we lose a war, we need more weapons to win the next one; if we win a war, we need more weapons so we can keep on winning; if crime is up, we need more prisons to lower crime, if crime is down, we need more prisons so it stays down.

The importance of labor market conditions was also emphasized by Sellin (1976, p. vii) who argued that "the demands of the labor market shape(d) the penal system and determined its transformation over the years, more or less unaffected by the theories of punishment in vogue." Similarly, Rusche and Kirchheimer (1939) in their classic historical-comparative study of prisons, noted that compared to European countries, the United States was characterized by a shortage of labor in the early industrial period, with the result that convict labor needed to be productive. However, this position has been critiqued for its tendency to economic reductionism (Greenberg, 1980; see also Zimring & Hawkins, 1991). In a recent comparative study of the influences on rates of imprisonment from 1955–1985, Sutton (2000) found that significant predictors of growth in prison populations in the United States were higher rates of unemployment, the right-party (Republican) domination of the cabinet, and declines in welfare spending.

DIMINISHED LIFE CHANCES: INCARCERATION, JOBLESSNESS, AND WEAK SOCIAL BONDS

Between 1980 and 2001, the number of persons incarcerated in state prisons in the United States grew by 316% (Bureau of Justice Statistics, n.d.a.).

Furthermore, the number of incarcerated persons per 100,000 population rose from 139 in 1980 to 470 in 2001 (Bureau of Justice Statistics, n.d.a.). Interestingly, "tough on crime" policies implemented during the Clinton administration resulted in the largest increases in federal and state prison populations of any president in American history (Feldman, Schiraldi, & Ziedenberg, 2001).

Incarceration is concentrated among young, uneducated males; particularly African Americans. In 1999, over 44% of the number of inmates in state and federal prisons and local jails were Black, and 11% of Black males in their 20s and early 30s were either in prison or jail in 1999 (Bureau of Justice Statistics, 2000a). In the mid-1990s, one out of every three young Black males was under some form of state supervision (Western & Beckett, 1999).

A growing proportion of prison inmates has been convicted of nonviolent drug offenses. In 1979, 6% of state prison inmates were convicted of nonviolent drug offenses, whereas in 1998 the proportion had increased to nearly 21%, nearly a fourfold increase (Bureau of Justice Statistics, n.d.b; Western & Beckett, 1999). In 1985, before the declaration of a new war on drugs and the passage of harsh federal antidrug legislation, 34% of federal prisoners were incarcerated for drug offenses. By 1998, 58% of federal prisoners had been sentenced for drug offenses (Bureau of Justice Statistics, 2000a).

Furthermore, sentences for drug offenses are long in comparison to other crimes. In 2000, mean times served for selected federal offenses were as follows: drug offenses 41 months, violent crimes 54 months, fraudulent property crimes 15 months, and other property crimes 19 months (*Sourcebook of Criminal Justice Statistics*, 2001). Thus, average times served for drug offenses were closer to those for violent crimes than for property offenses.

It has also been found that African Americans are more likely than Whites to be in prison for drug offenses (Irwin & Austin, 2001; Maguire & Pastore, 1998, p. 505). This disproportionality of incarceration by race is exacerbated by the infamous 100:1 sentencing ratio for crack offenses. In 1996, 86% of federal convictions for crack offenses were Black whereas only 5% were White (Maguire & Pastore, 1998, p. 415). In addition, the median sentence for Blacks convicted of a federal drug offense was 84 months—2 years longer than the average sentence for a violent crime—whereas it was 46 months for Whites (Maguire & Pastore, 1998, p. 396). Thus, Blacks experience the brunt of these extremely harsh crack sanctions.

In sum, the end result of these changes in penalties and prosecution of drug offenses is a large number of young, Black males in prison for such offenses. Additionally, they are serving long prison terms in comparison to many other inmates. Although the effects of this change in patterns of imprisonment for the criminal justice system are intuitively obvious, we must turn our attention to the long-term effects on society, specifically the unemployment and further marginalization of these men once they are released from prison.

Research has clearly shown that the likelihood of unemployment increases as a result of incarceration (Sampson & Laub, 1993; Western & Beckett, 1999). Western and Beckett (1999, pp. 1048–1051) found that incarceration has large negative effects on the employment of ex-prisoners, which decay 3 to 4 years after release. Changes in public policies since the Reagan Administration years have exacerbated this problem. As Petersilia (2003a, p. 4) has recently pointed out, "dozens of laws were passed restricting the kinds of jobs for which ex-prisoners can be hired, easing the requirements for their parental rights to be terminated, restricting their access to welfare benefits and public housing, disqualifying them from a host of job training programs" (see also Jensen, in press). In addition, the ability to find and retain employment are key factors in forming bonds to the conventional society and desistance from criminal behavior (Elliott & Voss, 1974; Sampson & Laub, 1993).

Employment, and the lack thereof, is related to marriage. Studies cited by Wilson (1996, p. 96) found that 20% to 25% of the decline in marriage rates of African Americans is due to the joblessness of Black males. This is particularly problematic for young Black males. In addition, these studies were of general samples of African Americans and not specific to the low-income communities from which most drug prisoners are sentenced. The effect of the explosion in joblessness in inner cities combined with the obstacles faced by ex-prisoners finding employment can be expected to produce larger negative outcomes in these communities.

Research by Sampson (1995, p. 249) found that both the total sex ratios and the employment prospects of Black men had independent effects on the structure of Black families in cities in the United States: "this race-specific interaction clearly supports Wilson's (1987) hypothesis regarding the structural sources of black family disruption." In this earlier work, Wilson proposed that the ratio of employed men per 100 women of the same age and race influenced marital stability. With the decline in the number of economically stable Black men, Black female-headed households increased (Wilson, 1987). More specifically, Sampson (1995) also found strong independent effects of sex ratios and employment on family disruption among those families in poverty. That is, "the lower the sex ratio and the lower the male employment rate, the higher the rate of female-headed families with children in poverty" (Sampson, 1995, p. 250).

Furthermore, one of the strongest predictors of urban violence is family structure. With other factors controlled, "in cities where family disruption is high the rate of violence is also high" (Sampson, 1995, p. 249). Based on his earlier work, the author states that this causal connection appears to be based in patterns of community social ties and informal networks of social control (see Sampson & Groves, 1989; see also Hagan, 1994).

The causal chain between incarceration, joblessness, and weak social bonds is therefore long and complex. As stated by Sampson and Laub (1993),

> job stability and marital attachment in adulthood were significantly related to changes in adult crime—the stronger the adult ties to work and family, the less the crime.... We even found that strong marital attachment inhibits crime and deviance regardless of the spouse's own deviant behavior, and that job instability fosters crime regardless of heavy drinking. Moreover, social bonds to employment were directly influenced by State sanctions—incarceration as a juvenile and as an adult had negative effects on later job stability, which in turn was negatively related to continued involvement in crime over the life course. (p. 248)

Thus, the binge of imprisonment for drug offenses has substantial negative outcomes for society and inner-city African American communities in particular. The incarceration of large numbers of young Black men for drug offenses has created an artificially low unemployment rate in the United States in recent years.

In 2002 alone, nearly 600,000 people were released from prison. This puts hundreds of thousands of young Black men with the stigma of ex-convict back into primarily low-income urban communities each year (see Petersilia, 2003a). The obstacles they face in finding employment that provides a living wage and related marital stability should be focal points of public concern and social policy in the immediate future. As they currently exist, the punitive justice policies so popular in the United States today simply continue to fuel the social disorganization and decline of the most disadvantaged segments of our society.

HIV/AIDS—"INVISIBLE, EXTRAJUDICIAL EXECUTIONS?" (GREEN, 1996)

Two percent to 3% of state and federal prisoners are HIV-positive or have AIDS—a rate five times higher than that of the general population (Petersilia,

2003a). The number of confirmed AIDS cases among prisoners increased by nearly 400% between 1991 and 1997 (Bureau of Justice Statistics, 1999). Additionally, it is estimated that 22% of female and 13% of male inmates in New York City jails are HIV-positive (Aids in Prison Project, 1997). Marquart, Brewer, Mullings, and Crouch (1999) note that in the New York, California, and Texas prison systems, AIDS is now the leading cause of death. In 1997, about one in every five deaths of prisoners was attributable to AIDS-related causes (Bureau of Justice Statistics, 1999). The rate of mortality for HIV-infected prisoners is at least three times the rate of mortality of HIV-patients in non-prison communities (Center for HIV Information, 1997).

In addressing the issue of HIV in prisons, it is important to take into account the comparatively high rates of assault and sexual assault that can facilitate the spread of the virus. An earlier Federal Bureau of Prisons study reported that 30% of federal prison inmates engaged in homosexual activity while incarcerated (Nacci & Kane, 1984). Although no national studies of the extent of sexual assault in prisons have been conducted, based on projections from a number of studies, it is estimated that there were 530,000 male rape victims behind bars in the United States (Stop Prisoner Rape; www.igc.org/spr). A substantial proportion of these rapes occur in local and county jails, where over half the inmate population has not been convicted of an offense. There are, of course, other HIV-risk factors for prison inmates such as the frequent incidents of interpersonal violence in these settings involving lacerations and bites, which has been exacerbated by the double celling of inmates. The use of needles for tattooing and body piercing, and sharing of syringes for IV drug use in prisons are also of great concern.

Unfortunately, federal and state prison authorities have been slow to develop policies to deal with this crisis. In an international survey of 19 countries prepared for the World Health Organization, the United States was listed as one of four countries that did not have a national policy for HIV management in prison (Center for HIV Information, 1997). And although an increasing number of inmates in state and federal prisons are HIV-positive, the number of effective HIV prevention programs in these facilities is declining. In 1990, 96% of all state and federal prisons had AIDS education programs in at least one prison—by 1994, that rate had dropped to 75% ("HIV Prevention Programs," 1996). Green (1996), discussing the situation in California prisons and noting the disproportional concentration of HIV infection among minority inmates, asserts that

> considering the history of genocide in this country, imprisoning targeted groups in an epidemic situation and then withholding treatment and education to stop the spread of the diseases sounds like giving smallpox-contaminated blankets to the Native Americans.

Given recent history, it seems unlikely that state or federal governments will implement progressive policies such as making condoms, bleach, methadone, and sterile injection equipment available to prisoners, as the World Health Organization has suggested (Jurgens, 1996).

Although many Americans and policy makers currently view prisoners as unworthy of compassion, there is a far greater threat posed by the spread of HIV in prison populations. The overwhelming majority of prison inmates will be released at some time, and as Marquart et al. (1999) in a study of women prisoners in the state of Texas note,

> Recent drug control policies, grounded in deterrence and based on harsh legal penalties, have led to the incarceration of numerous offenders who are low criminal risks but represent major public health risks on release. Criminal justice policies penalizing drug users may be contributing to the spread of HIV infection in the wider society. (p. 82)

Are there any signs that any of this will end soon? It is perhaps notable that an overly optimistic and misleading press release from the Office of National Drug Control Policy (ONDCP) was titled "FY 2000 Drug Control Budget Builds on Success—Budget Provides $17.8 Billion for Demand and Supply Reduction." A perusal of the fine print of this press release reveals that, similar to drug control policy in the last two decades in the United States, two thirds of the money is devoted to supply reduction, the bulk of which is composed of additional monies for law enforcement. Only one third of the money is devoted to "demand reduction."

MEDICINAL MARIJUANA—REEFER MADNESS AGAIN

The ONDCP (1997), in its statement on the use of marijuana for medical purposes, asserted that state-level initiatives to allow the use of medical marijuana had

> sent a confusing message to our children that could not have come at a worse time. In recent years, we have seen drug use by our young people increase at an alarming rate. Among 8th graders, the use of illicit drugs, primarily marijuana, has tripled. This increase has been fueled by a measurable decrease in the proportion of young people who perceive marijuana to be a dangerous substance.

Aside from the fact that this statement conveniently neglects the reality that levels of illicit drug use by youth were considerably higher in the late 1970s, it is even more curious in the context of ONDCP's contention in the same document that the "foremost objective" of the office "is to create a national drug control strategy based on *science* rather than *ideology*" [italics added].

In critiquing California's medical marijuana legislation, President Clinton's "drug czar," General McCaffrey, noted that the wording of California's Proposition 215 led to a situation whereby "any other illness" would include "recalling forgotten memories, cough suppressants, and writer's cramp." McCaffrey continued, "this is not medicine. This is a Cheech and Chong show" (Mundell, 1998). In response to the California initiative, the Clinton government threatened to prosecute doctors who prescribed marijuana to their patients.

Interestingly, as Grinspoon and Bakalar (1995) pointed out in an editorial published in *the Journal of the American Medical Association*, the Drug Enforcement Administration's (DEA's) own administrative law judge, Francis Young, asserted in 1988 that marijuana in its natural form fulfilled the legal requirements of currently accepted medical use in treatment in the United States. Young added that marijuana was "one of the safest therapeutically active substances known to man" (as cited in Grinspoon & Bakalar, 1995 p. 1875). Interestingly, Young's order that marijuana be reclassified as a Schedule II drug was overruled, not by any medical authority, but by the DEA itself.

There is also evidence that the National Institute of Drug Abuse was instrumental in suppressing a 1997 World Health Organization report suggesting that marijuana was far less harmful than alcohol and tobacco ("The report the WHO tried to hide," 1998). However, the evidence for marijuana's medical uses is mounting. The substance is effective in treatment of more than 100 separate illnesses or diseases (http://www.medicalmarijuana.org), with studies demonstrating marijuana's usefulness in reducing nausea and vomiting, stimulating appetite, promoting weight gain, and diminishing intraocular pressure associated with glaucoma (Zimmer & Morgan, 1997). And despite the contention of ONDCP and other federal drug agencies that similar effects are possible with synthetic tetrahydrocannabinal (THC) or Marinol, studies suggest that smoked marijuana is more effective because it delivers THC to the bloodstream more quickly. In addition, some evidence suggests that the psychoactive side effects of Marinol may actually be more intense than those that are associated with smoking marijuana (Zimmer & Morgan, 1997).

ONDCP and other federal drug agencies have also attempted to dismiss studies of marijuana's effectiveness by claiming that the research is lacking in scientific standards. However, as Grinspoon and Bakalar (1995) note, although it is certainly true that many of the studies examining medical marijuana are not consistent with FDA standards, this is primarily because of the bureaucratic, legal, and financial obstacles that are put in place by this same federal agency.

It appears as though federal drug agencies have a vested interest in keeping marijuana illegal. Since 1970, approximately 13.5 million Americans have been arrested for marijuana possession, and in 1999 alone, there were 708,480 marijuana-related arrests (Charbeneau, 1998; U.S. Department of Justice, n.d.). Despite popular belief then, there is little question that marijuana is the main focus of the drug warriors. It is worth noting, however, that the federal government's strict prohibitionist position with respect to marijuana is opposed by the American Public Health Association, the Federation of American Scientists, the Physicians' Association for AIDS Care, the Lymphoma Foundation of America, and national associations of prosecutors and criminal defense attorneys. *The New England Journal of Medicine* has supported marijuana's use as medicine, the *Journal of the American Medical Association* published the previously mentioned editorial by Grinspoon and Bakalar, which delivered essentially the same message (Morgan & Zimmer, 1997), and based on a review of the research the Senate Special Committee on Illegal Drugs (2002) in Canada recently concluded that cannabis can be a beneficial therapy for the treatment of specified medical conditions. Despite the fact that 11 states and the District of Columbia have passed legislation allowing for medicinal marijuana, the legal status of using the substance for these purposes is unclear given the federal resistance to recognize the new state policies.

THE WAR ON DRUGS AND DISENFRANCHISEMENT

One of the unanticipated consequences of the war on drugs is the disenfranchisement of a particular segment of society. Although most Americans will not be unduly disturbed by the prospect of convicted felons being unable to vote, the disproportionate impact of felony disenfranchisement on African Americans should be cause for concern.

Historically, the United States limited the right to vote to relatively few, primarily affluent White males, and excluded women, African Americans, and the poor. One other category, convicted felons, were unable to vote as a result of the United States's adopting the European practice of declaring convicted offenders "civilly dead" on conviction (Fellner & Mauer, 1998). The felony disenfranchisement laws gained some additional currency after the Civil War when White Southerners sought to limit Black suffrage with the aid of supposedly race-neutral laws (e.g., grandfather clauses).

Depending on state legislation, convicted felons may not lose the right to vote; or lose it while in prison, on probation, on parole, or even *for life.* Maine, for instance, does not disenfranchise convicted felons; Idaho disenfranchises incarcerated felons; California felons in prison or on parole; Georgia felons in prison, on parole, and on probation; and Alabama, similar to Georgia, also disenfranchises ex-felons (i.e., felons are disenfranchised *for life*) (Fellner & Mauer, 1998). The numbers of disenfranchised people are exceptionally large, but the proportions of certain categories of people are even more disturbing:

- 3.9 million adults are currently or permanently disenfranchised as a result of a felony conviction;
- Florida and Texas have each disenfranchised more than 600,000 people;
- 73% of the disenfranchised are not in prison but are on probation, on parole, or have completed their sentences;
- In Alabama and Florida, 31% of all Black men are permanently disenfranchised;
- 13% of all adult Black men are currently disenfranchised;
- 1.4 million Black men are disenfranchised compared to 4.6 million Black men who voted in 1996 (Fellner & Mauer, 1998).

An important study by Uggen and Manza (2002) recently concluded that felon disenfranchisement may have altered seven recent U.S. Senate elections and at least one presidential election.

> Assuming that Democrats who might have been elected in the absence of felon disenfranchisement had held their seats as long as the Republicans who narrowly defeated them, we estimate that the Democratic Party would have gained parity in 1984 and held majority control of the U.S. Senate from 1986 to the present.... In examining the presidential elections, we find that the Republican presidential victory of 2000 would have been reversed had just ex-felons been allowed to vote. (p. 794)

Unfortunately, if current trends continue, the situation will become worse. Mandatory minimum sentence laws, "three strikes" laws, and the war on drugs will increase the number of disenfranchised people and, most likely, increase the racial disparity in this practice. The long-term consequence of this will be the further attenuation of African American political power. More than a decade ago, Wilson (1987) spoke of *The Truly Disadvantaged.* Not only is work disappearing (see also Wilson, 1996), what little political clout existed has eroded. Urban areas have traditionally been strongholds of minority politicians and politicians sympathetic to minority issues. The disenfranchisement of some of their supporters will lead to a political restructuring of the city. In turn, this will lead to even fewer programs for these populations. Instead, politicians will likely heed the calls for more "law and order" emanating from the remaining electorate. And the vicious spiral will continue.

CONCLUSIONS

Few scholars who study the war on drugs are not aware of some of the problems this war entails for the criminal justice system. In fact, even professionals in the field echo some of the concerns of academicians. Former federal drug czar Barry McCaffrey spoke of "America's internal gulag" when referring to the seemingly ever-growing number of drug offenders in prisons ("Prison boom," 1999, p. 12). The irony of such a development must be overwhelming for Christie, should he be aware of McCaffrey's label.

Some positive developments are occurring at the state level, however. Since late 2000, Republican governors in at least seven states, including George Pataki in New York, Gary Johnson in New Mexico, and Dirk Kempthorne in Idaho, have called for placing more drug offenders into treatment and fewer in prison—although the previous year Governor Kempthorne advocated and passed longer sentences for methamphetamine offenses. Although these developments can be viewed in a positive light, it is important not to lose sight of the opposition of many criminal justice officials in the states where these changes have been suggested and of recent developments at the federal level.

In Arizona and California, citizen initiatives have passed that provide drug treatment instead of prison for persons convicted of first- and second-time drug possession offenses when no violent crime is present. Although these laws have faced criticism by prosecutors, police, and judges who assert that the law does not give criminal justice authorities enough power to force offenders into treatment, the research shows that these laws are diverting tens of thousands of persons convicted of possession from incarceration into treatment (www.drugpolicyalliance.com, www.prop36.org).

In the November 2002 elections, the voters of the District of Columbia passed a measure similar to those in Arizona and California. This initiative requires that persons convicted of drug possession for a nonviolent offense receive treatment instead of incarceration. The law contains no funding for implementation of this policy, however.

Recent appointments to key positions in the federal government by President George W. Bush indicate that the war may not yet be over. Former Senator John Ashcroft, appointed U.S. Attorney General, has supported revoking the driver's license of anyone arrested for marijuana possession, even if they were not driving at the time. He also supported evicting entire families from public housing if one of their members was suspected of using or selling drugs, even when the other family members were not involved. Ashcroft also opposes devoting funds to demand-side programs believing that a government that shifts resources to drug treatment and prevention programs instead of police and prisons "is a government that accommodates us at our lowest and least" (as quoted in Lindesmith Center, 2001). President Bush also appointed John Walters to the position of federal drug czar, leading Smith (2002, p. 121) to comment "Walters' appointment is the clearest sign yet that the Bush administration is committed to a punishment approach to the problems caused by illegal drugs." In 1996, Walters indicated that he opposed needle exchange programs on moral grounds (Smith, 2002); he also fervently opposes the decriminalization of marijuana. Walters actively campaigned against a marijuana initiative in the state of Nevada and in response to a proposal for decriminalization of marijuana in Canada, stated "If Canada wants to become the locus for that kind of activity, they're likely to pay a heavy price" (Bailey, 2003). As Stroup and Armentano (2002, p. 223) suggest, "many of Mr. Walters more egregious claims about cannabis appear to have been lifted straight from the 1936 propaganda film [Reefer Madness]."

The rhetoric in recent federal documents might lead one to believe that there have been some changes, however. Witness, for example, the relative prominence that the prevention and treatment of drug abuse received in the 2001 Annual Report of the National Drug Control Policy,

> Preventing drug abuse in the first place is preferable to addressing the problem later through treatment and law enforcement....There are approximately five million drug abusers who need immediate treatment and who constitute a major portion of domestic demand....Accordingly, the *Strategy* focuses on treatment. Research clearly demonstrates that treatment works.... Providing access to treatment for America's chronic drug abusers is a worthwhile endeavor. It is both compassionate public policy and sound investment (Office of National Drug Control Policy, 2001, pp. 4–6).

Unfortunately for the harm reduction effort, such rhetoric is offset by the reality of budgetary appropriations. An overview of the proportions of the budgets devoted to law enforcement and drug treatment during the decade of the 1990s indicates that there have not been major redistributions (Office of National Drug Control Policy, 2001, p. 119). Although there have been some increases in the percentage devoted to treatment, any declarations that the drug war is over are clearly premature.

However, it might be interesting to speculate how the end of the war on drugs would affect the consequences that we identified in this article. Although it seems highly improbable that we will witness such an event, it is theoretically possible that the war will be ended with the stroke of a few legislative, judicial, and executive pens. Even if this were to occur, such an event would not fundamentally change the adverse long-term consequences that have cumulated during the last 17 years. Only a comprehensive and vigorously enforced affirmative action–like program aimed at overcoming the negative consequences of the war would do so.

Incarceration provides one example. The mean time served for a federal drug sentence for a drug offense is 41 months. Even if the war ended today, the most recently admitted convicts would remain in prison an average of well over 3 years. The only escape from this situation would be large-scale pardons for drug offenders. Obviously this will not happen. Furthermore, the internal logic of prison expansion would also necessitate new "raw material" for the cell space that exists. If nothing else, states must pay off the long-term debts that have been encumbered for this unprecedented wave of prison construction. A new war on some other outlawed, or yet to be outlawed, behavior would likely be the end result.

Postconviction employment would continue to be problematic for ex-offenders. Given that the average time served is over 3 years and that employment difficulties are most pronounced for the first 3 to 4 years after release, employment difficulties would be with us for almost a decade after the end of the war on drugs. The problems associated with unemployment, such as marital instability and family violence would also exist, and their effects would be passed on to yet another generation.

All of the other negative consequences that we have identified in this study, the growth in HIV/AIDS rates, the prohibition of cannabis for medical uses, and the attenuation of the political power of targeted subordinate racial and ethnic groups, would also continue to exist. Whereas the end of the war might stop the further acceleration of the spread of HIV infection by not sending drug users to prisons, ex-inmates would still be infected and potentially spread the virus to their sexual partners and those with whom some will share needles. Similarly, ex-offenders would still be without franchise in many states, but there would be fewer newly disenfranchised felons and ex-felons. The only remedy for such adverse consequences would be the passage of legislation such as the Civic Participation and Rehabilitation Act of 1999. This bill, along with others not yet filed, could reverse some of these adverse consequences. For this to happen, though, powerful interest groups that lobby on behalf of offenders would have to emerge; a scenario that seems highly unlikely in the United States.

Most criminologists have paid little attention to the societal consequences of the war on drugs to date. We see this article as a wake-up call for the discipline. Social scientists interested in race relations, family issues, political participation, labor force issues, and health care policy have studied the areas we have identified as societal consequences of the war on drugs. Most criminologists, however, have limited their inquiries to Sutherland's traditional definition of criminology: the making of law, the breaking of law, and the societal response to the breaking of law. We would argue that criminologists cannot afford to ignore the societal consequences of the last dimension of Sutherland's definition. Doing so will make us "enablers." Limiting our studies to the making and breaking of law, and its societal responses, will reify the "drug problem" (or more broadly, "the crime problem") as nothing more than that. If we expand our inquiry, however, to the study of the societal consequences of public policies, we begin the process of challenging the assumptions underlying our (society's) proposed solutions.

STUDY QUESTIONS

1. As far as "get-tough" policies go, in what ways does the war on drugs differ from other policies (e.g., three-strikes legislation or mandatory minimum sentencing)?
2. Explain how the relationship between disenfranchisement, joblessness, marital strain, and violence works, according to the authors.
3. Speculate as to the reasons why policy makers avoid implementing progressive policies that might prevent HIV/AIDS within the context of the offender population.
4. Should marijuana (and/or the prospect of medicinal marijuana) pose an exception to the war on drugs? Why or why not?
5. Are there any "corrective" policies that should be implemented in light of the failures of the war on drugs that have been identified by these authors?

REFERENCES

American Friends Service Committee. (1971). Struggle for justice: A report on crime and punishment in America. New York: Hill and Wang.

Bailey, E. (2003, February 2). The drug war refugees. *Los Angeles Times*. Retrieved from http://www.latimes.com.

Beckett, K. (1995). Fetal rights and "crack moms": Pregnant women in the War on Drugs. *Contemporary Drug Problems*, 22, 587–612.

Belenko, S. R. (1993). *Crack and the evolution of anti-drug policy.* Westport, CT: Greenwood.

Blumenson, E., & Nilsen, E. (1998). Policing for profit: The drug war's hidden economic agenda. *University of Chicago Law Review, 65,* 35–114.

Blumstein, A., & Cohen, J. (1973). A theory of the stability of punishment. *Journal of Criminal Law and Criminology, 64,* 198–207.

Bouley, E. E., Jr. (2001). The drug war in Latin America: Ten years in a quagmire. In J. Gerber & E. L. Jensen (Eds.), *Drug war, American style: The internationalization of failed policy and its alternatives* (pp. 169–195). New York: Garland.

Bullington, B. H., Krebs, C. P., & Rasmussen, D. W. (2000). Drug policy in the Czech Republic. In A. Springer & A. Uhl (Eds.), *Illicit drugs: Patterns of use—patterns of response* (pp. 73–88). Innsbruck, Austria: StudienVerlag.

Bureau of Justice Statistics, (n.d.a.). Retrieved from http://www.ojp.usdoj.gov/bjs.

Bureau of Justice Statistics, (n.d.b). Number of sentenced inmates incarcerated under state and federal jurisdictions per 100,000, 1980–1999. Retrieved from http://www.ojp.usdoj.gov/glance/incrt.txt.

Bureau of Justice Statistics. (1999, November). *HIV in prisons, 1997.* Washington, DC: U.S. Department of Justice.

Bureau of Justice Statistics. (2000a, April). *Prison and jail inmates at midyear 1999.* Washington, DC: U.S. Department of Justice.

Bureau of Justice Statistics. (2000b, August). *Prisoners in 1999.* Washington, DC: U.S. Department of Justice.

Butterfield, F. (2001, February 12). California lacks resources for law on drug offenders, officials say. *The New York Times.* Retrieved from http://www.nytimes.com.

Center for HIV Information. (1997). Aids and HIV infection in prisoners. Retrieved from http://hivinsite.ucsf.edu/akb/1997/01pris.

Charbeneau, T. (1998). *Might as well face it we're addicted to lies.* Retrieved from www.marijuananews.com.

Christie, N. (2000). *Crime control as industry: Towards GULAGS, western style* (3rd ed.). New York: Routledge.

Coates, R. B., Miller, D. D., & Ohlin, L. E. (1978). *Diversity in a youth correctional system: Handling delinquents in Massachusetts.* Cambridge, MA: Ballinger.

Crowley, D. W. (1998). Drug testing in the Rehnquist era. In E. L. Jensen & J. Gerber (Eds.), *The new War on Drugs: Symbolic politics and criminal justice policy* (pp. 123–139). Cincinnati, OH: Anderson/Academy of Criminal Justice Sciences.

del Olmo, R. (1993). The geopolitics of narcotrafficking in Latin America. *Social Justice, 20,* 1–23.

Denq, F., & Wang, H. (2001). The war on drugs in Taiwan: An American model. In J. Gerber & E. L. Jensen (Eds.), Drug war. *American style: The internationalization of failed policy and its alternatives* (pp. 149–167). New York: Garland.

Donzinger, S. (1996). *The real war on crime.* New York: Harper.

Donzinger, S. (1998). Fear, crime, and punishment in the United States. *Tikkun, 12,* 24–27.

Elliott, D.S. & Voss, H. L. (1974). *Delinquency and dropout.* Lexington, MA: Lexington.

Feldman, Lisa; Schiraldi, Vincent and Jason Ziedenberg. (2001) Too Little Too Late: President Clinton's Prison Legacy. *Center on Juvenile and Criminal Justice.* Retrieved from http://www.cjcj.org/pubs/clinton/clinton.html.

Fellner, J. & Mauer, M. (1998). Losing the vote: the impact of felony disenfranchisement laws in the United States. Retrieved from www.hrw.org/reports98/vote.

Garcia, A. F. (1997). Harm reduction at the supply side of the drug war: the case for Bolivia. In P.G. Erickson, D.M. Riley, Y.W. Cheung, & P. A. O'Hare (Eds.) *Harm reduction: a new direction for drug policies and programs* (pp. 99–115) Toronto, ON: The University of Toronto Press.

Green, C. (1996). *HIV+ and in prison: the shadow of death row.* Retrieved from www.igc.apc.org/justice.

Greenberg, D. F. (1980). Penal sanctions in Poland: A test of alternative models. *Social Problems, 28,* 194–204.

Grinspoon, L., & Bakalar, J. (1995). Marijuana as medicine: A plea for reconsideration. *Journal of the American Medical Association, 273,* 1875–1876.

Hagan, J. (1994). *Crime and disrepute.* Thousand Oaks, CA: Pine Forge Press.

HIV prevention programs in prisons on the decline. (1996, May 16). *Reuters.* Retrieved from http://www.reuters.com.

Inciardi, J. A., McBride, D. C., & Rivers, J. E. (1996). *Drug control and the courts.* Thousand Oaks, CA: Sage.

Irwin, J., & Austin, J. (2001). *It's about time: America's imprisonment binge* (3rd ed.). Belmont, CA: Wadsworth.

Jensen, E. L. (2000). The civil forfeiture of assets: Harms inherent within U.S. policy. In A. Springer & A. Uhl (Eds.), *Illicit drugs: Patterns of use—Patterns of response* (pp. 31–45). Innsbruck, Austria: Studien Verlag.

Jensen, E. L. (in press). Non-criminal sanctions for drug offenses in the U.S.A. In S. Scheerer (Ed.), *Drug prohibition regimes: International perspectives.* Onati, Spain: International Institute of the Sociology of Law.

Jensen, E. L., & Gerber, J. (1996). The civil forfeiture of assets and the War on Drugs: Expanding criminal sanctions while reducing due process protections. *Crime and Delinquency, 42,* 421–434.

Jensen, E. L., & Gerber, J. (1998). The social construction of drug problems: An historical overview. In E. L. Jensen & J. Gerber (Eds.), *The new war on drugs: Symbolic politics and criminal justice policy.* Cincinnati, OH: Anderson/Academy of Criminal Justice Sciences.

Julien, R. (1998, February 27). Lapeer supports thumb prison expansion. *Michigan Live* (Flint ed.). Retrieved from http://www.mlive.com.

Jurgens, R. (1996). *HIV/AIDS in prison.* Canadian Aids Society. Ottawa: Health Canada.

Lindesmith Center. (2001, January 22). *Judiciary committee to vote on Ashcroft.* Retrieved from www.drugpolicy.org.

Maguire, K., & Pastore, A. L. (Eds.). (1998). *Sourcebook of criminal justice statistics—1997.* Washington, DC: Government Printing Office.

Marquart, J., Brewer, V., Mullings, J., & Crouch, B. (1999). The implications of crime control policy on HIV/AIDS-related risk among women prisoners. *Crime and Delinquency, 45,* 82–98.

Mast, B. D., Benson, B. L., & Rasmussen, D. W. (2000). Entrepreneurial police and drug enforcement. *Public Choice, 104,* 285–308.

McDonald, P. (1997). The lockdown of higher education. *Westchester County Weekly.* Retrieved from http://www.westchesterweekly.com.

Mundell, E.J. (1998, August 5). Legal expert supports medical marijuana. *Reuters.* Retrieved from http://www.reuters.com.

Nacci, P., & Kane, T. (1982). *Sex and sexual aggression in federal prisons.* Washington, DC: Federal Bureau of Prisons.

National Institute of Justice. (1980). *American prisons and jails* (Vol. 1). Washington, DC: Government Printing Office.

Nevada secretary of state questions drug czar's failure to comply with law. (2002, December 5). *Drug Policy Alliance Newsletter.* Retrieved from http://actioncenter.drugpolicy.org/news.

Office of National Drug Control Policy. (1997). *ONDCP statement on marijuana for medical purposes.* Washington, DC: Government Printing Office.

Office of National Drug Control Policy. (2001). *The national drug control strategy: 2001 Annual Report.* Washington, DC: Government Printing Office.

Overbeck, C. (1997). *Prison factories: Slave labor for the New World Order?* Retrieved from http://www.parascope.com/articles/0197/prison.html.

Petersilia, J. (2003a, March/April). Prisoner reentry and criminological knowledge. *Criminologist,* pp. 1, 3, 4–5.

Petersilia, J. (2003b). *When prisoners come home: Parole and prisoner reentry.* New York: Oxford University Press.

President's Commission on Law Enforcement and Administration of Justice. (1967). *Task force report: Corrections.* Washington, DC: Government Printing Office.

Prison boom expected to go on for a generation, officials say. (1999, March 7). *Houston Chronicle,* p. 12A.

Quittner, J. (1998, April 22). The incarceration industry: Teeming prison rolls bode well for private jails. *Fox News.* Retrieved from http://www.ipmet.org/prison/news.

The report the WHO tried to hide. (1998, February 21). *New Scientist.* Retrieved from http://www.newscientist.com.

Robinson, M. (1998). *The new money machine.* Retrieved from http://accnt.ashcc.uky.edu.

Rothman, D. (1971). *The discovery of the asylum: Social order and disorder in the new republic.* Boston: Little, Brown.

Rusche, G., & Kirchheimer, O. (1939). *Punishment and social structure.* New York: Columbia University Press.

Ryan, K. (1998). Globalizing the problem: The United States and international drug control. In E. L. Jensen & J. Gerber (Eds.), *The new War on Drugs: Symbolic politics and criminal justice policy* (pp. 141–156). Cincinnati, OH: Anderson/Academy of Criminal Justice Sciences.

Sagatun-Edwards, I. J. (1998). Crack babies, moral panic, and the criminalization of behavior during pregnancy. In E. L. Jensen & J. Gerber (Eds.), *The new War on Drugs: symbolic politics and criminal justice policy* (pp. 107–121). Cincinnati, OH: Anderson/Academy of Criminal Justice Sciences.

Sampson, R. J. (1995). Unemployment and imbalanced sex ratios: Race-specific consequences for family structure and crime. In M. B. Tucker & C. Mitchell-Kernan (Eds.), *The decline in marriage among African Americans: Causes, consequences, and policy implications* (pp. 229–254). New York: Russell Sage.

Sampson, R. J., & Groves, W. B. (1989). Community structure and crime: testing disruption. *American Journal of Sociology, 94,* 774–802.

Sampson, R. J., & Laub, J. H. (1993). *Crime in the making: Pathways and turning points through life.* Cambridge, MA: Harvard University Press.

Schlosser, E. (1998, December). The prison-industrial complex. *Atlantic Monthly.* Retrieved from http://www.theatlantic.com.

Sellin, T. (1976). *Slavery and the penal system.* New York: Elsevier.

Senate Special Committee on Illegal Drugs. (2002, September). *Cannabis: Our position for a Canadian public policy* (Summary report).

Smith, A. (2002). America's lonely drug war. In M. Gray (Ed.), *Busted: Stone cowboys, narco-lords and Washington's War on Drugs* (pp. 121–124). New York: Thunder's Mouth Press/Nation Books.

Sourcebook of Criminal Statistics. (2001). Retrieved from http://albany.edu/sourcebook.

Stroup, K., & Armentano, P. (2002). The problem is pot prohibition. In M. Gray (Ed.), *Busted: Stone cowboys, narco-lords and Washington's War on Drugs* (pp. 223–224). New York: Thunder's Mouth Press/Nation Books.

Sutton, J. R. (2000). Imprisonment and social classification in five common-law democracies, 1955–1985. *American Journal of Sociology, 106,* 350–386.

Uggen, C., & Manza, J. (2002) Democratic contraction? Political consequences of felon disfranchisement in the United States. *American Sociological Review, 67,* 777–803.

U.S. Department of Justice, (n.d). *Uniform Crime Reports.* Retrieved from http://www.ojp.usdoj.gov.

Western, B., & Beckett K. (1999). How unregulated is the U.S. labor market? The penal system as a labor market institution. *American Journal of Sociology, 104,* 1030–1060.

Wilson, W. J. (1987). *The truly disadvantaged: The inner city, the underclass, and public policy.* Chicago: University of Chicago Press.

Wilson, W. J. (1996). When work disappears: The world of the new urban poor. New York: Vintage.

Wright, P. (1998). *Business behind bars.* Retrieved from http://www.speakeasy.org/wfp/29/prisonl.html.

Zimmer, L., & Morgan, J. P. (1997). *Marijuana myths, marijuana facts.* New York: Linde-smith Center.

Zimring, F. E., & Hawkins, G. (1991). *The scale of imprisonment.* Chicago: University of Chicago Press.

31
"THIS MAN HAS EXPIRED"

WITNESS TO AN EXECUTION

ROBERT JOHNSON

Capital punishment is another long-touted solution to the problem of violent crime. After a decade-long moratorium that ended with the execution of Gary Gilmore in 1977, capital punishment moved into full swing in the 1980s and 1990s. However, a period of readjustment followed the moratorium, during which most death-sentence cases resulted in life sentences. At that time, the process of review was very slow, but in recent years the likelihood of a death sentence actually being carried out has increased. Reversals are less frequent, and cases are moving along at a more rapid pace. There are currently over 3,000 inmates awaiting execution on death rows across the United States. In the following article, the work of an execution team described by Robert Johnson has just begun.

The death penalty has made a comeback in recent years. In the late sixties and through most of the seventies, such a thing seemed impossible. There was a moratorium on executions in the U.S., backed by the authority of the Supreme Court. The hiatus lasted roughly a decade. Coming on the heels of a gradual but persistent decline in the use of the death penalty in the Western world, it appeared to some that executions would pass from the American scene [cf Commonweal, January 15, 1988], Nothing could have been further from the truth.

Beginning with the execution of Gary Gilmore in 1977, over 100 people have been put to death, most of them in the last few years. Some 2,200 prisoners are presently confined on death rows across the nation. The majority of these prisoners have lived under sentence of death for years, in some cases a decade or more, and are running out of legal appeals. It is fair to say that the death penalty is alive and well in America, and that executions will be with us for the foreseeable future.

Gilmore's execution marked the resurrection of the modern death penalty and was big news. It was commemorated in a best-selling tome by Norman Mailer, *The Executioner's Song.* The title was deceptive. Like others who have examined the death penalty, Mailer told us a great deal about the condemned but very little about the executioners. Indeed, if we dwell on Mailer's account, the executioner's story is not only unsung; it is distorted.

Gilmore's execution was quite atypical. His was an instance of state-assisted suicide accompanied by an element of romance and played out against a backdrop of media fanfare. Unrepentant

Excerpts from "'This Man Has Expired': Witness to an Execution" by Robert Johnson. *Commonweal Foundation,* 66 (1): 9–15.

and unafraid, Gilmore refused to appeal his conviction. He dared the state of Utah to take his life, and the media repeated the challenge until it became a taunt that may well have goaded officials to action. A failed suicide pact with his lover staged only days before the execution, using drugs she delivered to him in a visit marked by unusual intimacy, added a hint of melodrama to the proceedings. Gilmore's final words, "Let's do it," seemed to invite the lethal hail of bullets from the firing squad. The nonchalant phrase, at once fatalistic and brazenly rebellious, became Gilmore's epitaph. It clinched his outlaw-hero image, and found its way onto tee shirts that confirmed his celebrity status.

Befitting a celebrity, Gilmore was treated with unusual leniency by prison officials during his confinement on death row. He was, for example, allowed to hold a party the night before his execution, during which he was free to eat, drink, and make merry with his guests until the early morning hours. This is not entirely unprecedented. Notorious English convicts of centuries past would throw farewell balls in prison on the eve of their executions. News accounts of such affairs sometimes included a commentary on the richness of the table and the quality of the dancing. For the record, Gilmore served Tang, Kool-Aid, cookies and coffee, later supplemented by contraband pizza and an unidentified liquor. Periodically, he gobbled drugs obligingly provided by the prison pharmacy. He played a modest arrangement of rock music albums but refrained from dancing.

Gilmore's execution generally, like his parting fete, was decidedly out of step with the tenor of the modern death penalty. Most condemned prisoners fight to save their lives, not to have them taken. They do not see their fate in romantic terms; there are no farewell parties. Nor are they given medication to ease their anxiety or win their compliance. The subjects of typical executions remain anonymous to the public and even to their keepers. They are very much alone at the end.

In contrast to Mailer's account, the focus of the research I have conducted is on the executioners themselves as they carry out typical executions. In my experience executioners—not unlike Mailer himself—can be quite voluble, and sometimes quite moving, in expressing themselves. I shall draw upon their words to describe the death work they carry out in our name.

DEATH WORK AND DEATH WORKERS

Executioners are not a popular subject of social research, let alone conversation at the dinner table or cocktail party. We simply don't give the subject much thought. When we think of executioners at all, the imagery runs to individual men of disreputable, or at least questionable, character who work stealthily behind the scenes to carry out their grim labors. We picture hooded men hiding in the shadow of the gallows, or anonymous figures lurking out of sight behind electric chairs, gas chambers, firing blinds, or, more recently, hospital gurneys. We wonder who would do such grisly work and how they sleep at night.

This image of the executioner as a sinister and often solitary character is today misleading. To be sure, a few states hire freelance executioners and traffic in macabre theatrics. Executioners may be picked up under cover of darkness and some may still wear black hoods. But today, executions are generally the work of a highly disciplined and efficient team of correctional officers.

Broadly speaking, the execution process as it is now practiced starts with the prisoner's confinement on death row, an oppressive prison-within-a-prison where the condemned are housed, sometimes for years, awaiting execution. Death work gains momentum when an execution date draws near and the prisoner is moved to the death house, a short walk from the death chamber. Finally, the process culminates in the death watch, a twenty-four-hour period that ends when the prisoner has been executed.

This final period, the death watch, is generally undertaken by correctional officers who work as a team and report directly to the prison warden. The warden or his representative, in turn, must by law preside over the execution. In many states, it is a member of the death watch or execution team, acting under the warden's authority, who in fact plays the formal role of executioner. Though this officer may technically work alone, his teammates view the execution as a shared responsibility. As one officer on the death watch told me in no uncertain terms: "We all take part in it; we all play 100 percent in it, too. That takes the load off this one individual [who pulls the switch]." The formal executioner concurred. "Everyone on the team can do it, and nobody will tell you I did it. I know my team." I found nothing in my research to dispute these claims.

The officers of these death watch teams are our modern executioners. As part of a larger study of the death work process, I studied one such group. This team, comprised of nine seasoned officers of varying ranks, had carried out five electrocutions at the time I began my research. I interviewed each officer on the team after the fifth execution, then served as an official witness at a sixth electrocution. Later, I served as a behind-the-scenes observer during their seventh execution. The results of this phase of my research form the substance of this [chapter].

THE DEATH WATCH TEAM

The death watch or execution team members refer to themselves, with evident pride, as simply "the team." This pride is shared by other correctional officials. The warden at the institution I was observing praised members of the team as solid citizens—in his words, country boys. These country boys, he assured me, could be counted on to do the job and do it well. As a fellow administrator put it, "an execution is something [that] needs to be done and good people, dedicated people who believe in the American system, should do it. And there's a certain amount of feeling, probably one to another, that they're part of that—that when they have to hang tough, they can do it, and they can do it right. And that it's just the right thing to do."

The official view is that an execution is a job that has to be done, and done right. The death penalty is, after all, the law of the land. In this context, the phrase "done right" means that an execution should be a proper, professional, dignified undertaking. In the words of a prison administrator, "We had to be sure that we did it properly, professionally, and [that] we gave as much dignity to the person as we possibly could in the process.... If you've gotta do it, it might just as well be done the way it's supposed to be done—without any sensation."

In the language of the prison officials, "proper" refers to procedures that go off smoothly, "professional" means without personal feelings that intrude on the procedures in any way. The desire for executions that take place "without any sensation" no doubt refers to the absence of media sensationalism, particularly if there should be an embarrassing and undignified hitch in the procedures, for example, a prisoner who breaks down or becomes violent and must be forcibly placed in the electric chair as witnesses, some from the media, look on in horror. Still, I can't help but note that this may be a revealing slip of the tongue. For executions are indeed meant to go off without any human feeling, without any sensation. A profound absence of feeling would seem to capture the bureaucratic ideal embodied in the modern execution.

The view of executions held by the execution team members parallels that of correctional administrators but is somewhat more restrained. The officers of the team are closer to the killing and dying, and are less apt to wax abstract or eloquent in describing the process. Listen to one man's observations:

> It's a job. I don't take it personally. You know, I don't take it like I'm having a grudge against this person and this person has done something to me. I'm

> just carrying out a job, doing what I was asked to do....This man has been sentenced to death in the courts. This is the law and he broke this law, and he has to suffer the consequences. And one of the consequences is to put him to death.

I found that few members of the execution team support the death penalty outright or without reservation. Having seen executions close up, many of them have lingering doubts about the justice or wisdom of this sanction. As one officer put it:

> I'm not sure the death penalty is the right way. I don't know if there is a right answer. So I look at it like this: if it's gotta be done, at least it can be done in a humane way, if there is such a word for it....The only way it should be done, I feel, is the way we do it. It's done professionally, it's not no horseplaying. Everything is done by documentation. On time. By the book.

Arranging executions that occur "without any sensation" and that go "by the book" is no mean task, but it is a task that is undertaken in earnest by the execution team. The tone of the enterprise is set by the team leader, a man who takes a hard-boiled, no-nonsense approach to correctional work in general and death work in particular. "My style," he says, "is this: if it's a job to do, get it done. Do it and that's it." He seeks out kindred spirits, men who see killing condemned prisoners as a job—a dirty job one does reluctantly, perhaps, but above all a job one carries out dispassionately and in the line of duty.

To make sure that line of duty is a straight and accurate one, the death watch team has been carefully drilled by the team leader in the mechanics of execution. The process has been broken down into simple, discrete tasks and practiced repeatedly. The team leader describes the division of labor in the following exchange:

> The execution team is a nine-officer team and each one has certain things to do. When I would train you, maybe you'd buckle a belt, that might be all you'd have to do....And you'd be expected to do one thing and that's all you'd be expected to do. And if everybody does what they were taught, or what they were trained to do, at the end the man would be put in the chair and everything would be complete. It's all come together now.
>
> So it's broken down into very small steps....
>
> *Very small*, yes. Each person has *one* thing to do.
>
> I see. What's the purpose of breaking it down into such small steps?
>
> So people won't get confused. I've learned it's kind of a tense time. When you're executin' a person, killing a person—you call it killin', executin', whatever you want—the man dies anyway. I find the less you got on your mind, why, the better you'll carry it out. So it's just very simple things. And so far, you know, it's all come together, we haven't had any problems.

This division of labor allows each man on the execution team to become a specialist, a technician with a sense of pride in his work. Said one man,

> My assignment is the leg piece. Right leg. I roll his pants' leg up, place a piece [electrode] on his leg, strap his leg in...I've got all the moves down pat. We train from different posts; I can do any of them. But that's my main post.

The implication is not that the officers are incapable of performing multiple or complex tasks, but simply that it is more efficient to focus each officer's efforts on one easy task.

An essential part of the training is practice. Practice is meant to produce a confident group, capable of fast and accurate performance under pressure. The rewards of practice are reaped in improved performance. Executions take place with increasing efficiency, and eventually occur with precision. "The first one was grisly," a team member confided to me. He explained that there was a certain amount of fumbling, which made the execution seem interminable. There were technical problems as well: The generator was set too high so the body was badly burned. But that is the past, the officer assured me. "The ones now, we know what we're doing. It's just like clockwork."

THE DEATH WATCH

The death-watch team is deployed during the last twenty-four hours before an execution. In the state under study, the death watch starts at 11 o'clock the night before the execution and ends at 11 o'clock the next night when the execution takes place. At least two officers would be with the prisoner at any given time during that period. Their objective is to keep the prisoner alive and "on schedule." That is, to move him through a series of critical and cumulatively demoralizing junctures that begin with his last meal and end with his last walk. When the time comes, they must deliver the prisoner up for execution as quickly and unobtrusively as possible.

Broadly speaking, the job of the death watch officer, as one man put it, "is to sit and keep the inmate calm for the last twenty-four hours—and get the man ready to go." Keeping a condemned prisoner calm means, in part, serving his immediate needs. It seems paradoxical to think of the death watch officers as providing services to the condemned, but the logistics of the job make service a central obligation of the officers. Here's how one officer made this point:

> Well, you can't help but be involved with many of the things that he's involved with. Because if he wants to make a call to his family, well, you'll have to dial the number. And you keep records of whatever calls he makes. If he wants a cigarette, well, he's not allowed to keep matches so you light it for him. You've got to pour his coffee, too. So you're aware what he's doing. It's not like you can just ignore him. You've gotta just be with him whether he wants it or not, and cater to his needs.

Officers cater to the condemned because contented inmates are easier to keep under control. To a man, the officers say this is so. But one can never trust even a contented, condemned prisoner.

The death-watch officers see condemned prisoners as men with explosive personalities. "You don't know what, what a man's gonna do," noted one officer. "He's liable to snap, he's liable to pass out. We watch him all the time to prevent him from committing suicide. You've got to be ready—he's liable to do anything." The prisoner is never out of at least one officer's sight. Thus surveillance is constant, and control, for all intents and purposes, is total.

Relations between the officers and their charges during the death watch can be quite intense. Watching and being watched are central to this enterprise, and these are always engaging activities, particularly when the stakes are life and death. These relations are, nevertheless, utterly impersonal; there are no grudges but neither is there compassion or fellow-feeling. Officers are civil but cool; they keep an emotional distance from the men they are about to kill. To do otherwise, they maintain, would make it harder to execute condemned prisoners. The attitude of the officers is that the prisoners arrive as strangers and are easier to kill if they stay that way.

During the last five or six hours, two specific team officers are assigned to guard the prisoner. Unlike their more taciturn and aloof colleagues on earlier shifts, these officers make a conscious effort to talk with the prisoner. In one officer's words, "We just keep them right there and keep talking to them—about anything except the chair." The point of these conversations is not merely to pass time; it is to keep tabs on the prisoner's state of mind, and to steer him away from subjects that might depress, anger, or otherwise upset him. Sociability, in other words, quite explicitly serves as a source of social control. Relationships, such as they are, serve purely manipulative ends. This is impersonality at its worst, masquerading as concern for the strangers one hopes to execute with as little trouble as possible.

Generally speaking, as the execution moves closer, the mood becomes more somber and subdued. There is a last meal. Prisoners can order pretty much what they want, but most eat little or nothing at all. At this point, the prisoners may steadfastly maintain that their executions will be stayed. Such bravado is belied by their loss of appetite. "You can see them going down," said one officer. "Food is the last thing they got on their minds."

Next the prisoners must box their meager worldly goods. These are inventoried by the staff, recorded on a one-page checklist form, and marked for disposition to family or friends. Prisoners are visibly saddened, even moved to tears, by this procedure, which at once summarizes their lives and highlights the imminence of death. At this point, said one of the officers, "I really get into him; I watch him real close." The execution schedule, the officer pointed out, is "picking up momentum and we don't want to lose control of the situation."

This momentum is not lost on the condemned prisoner. Critical milestones have been passed. The prisoner moves in a limbo existence devoid of food or possessions; he has seen the last of such things, unless he receives a stay of execution and rejoins the living. His identity is expropriated as well. The critical juncture in this regard is the shaving of the man's head (including facial hair) and right leg. Hair is shaved to facilitate the electrocution; it reduces physical resistance to electricity and minimizes singeing and burning. But the process has obvious psychological significance as well, adding greatly to the momentum of the execution.

The shaving procedure is quite public and intimidating. The condemned man is taken from his cell and seated in the middle of the tier. His hands and feet are cuffed, and he is dressed only in undershorts. The entire death watch team is assembled around him. They stay at a discrete distance, but it is obvious that they are there to maintain control should he resist in any way or make any untoward move. As a rule, the man is overwhelmed. As one officer told me in blunt terms, "Come eight o'clock, we've got a dead man. Eight o'clock is when we shave the man. We take his identity; it goes with the hair." This taking of identity is indeed a collective process—the team makes a forceful "we," the prisoner their helpless object. The staff is confident that the prisoner's capacity to resist is now compromised. What is left of the man erodes gradually and, according to the officers, perceptibly over the remaining three hours before the execution.

After the prisoner has been shaved, he is then made to shower and don a fresh set of clothes for the execution. The clothes are unremarkable in appearance, except that velcro replaces buttons and zippers, to reduce the chance of burning the body. The main significance of the clothes is symbolic: they mark the prisoner as a man who is ready for execution. Now physically "prepped," to quote one team member, the prisoner is placed in an empty tomblike cell, the death cell. All that is left is the wait. During this fateful period, the prisoner is more like an object "without any sensation" than like a flesh-and-blood person on the threshold of death.

For condemned prisoners, like Gilmore, who come to accept and even to relish their impending deaths, a genuine calm seems to prevail. It is as if they can transcend the dehumanizing forces at work around them and go to their deaths in peace. For most condemned prisoners, however, numb resignation rather than peaceful acceptance is the norm. By the accounts of the death-watch officers, these more typical prisoners are beaten men. Listen to the officers' accounts:

> A lot of 'em die in their minds before they go to that chair. I've never known of one or heard of one putting up a fight.... By the time they walk to the chair, they've completely faced it. Such a reality most people can't understand. Cause they don't fight it. They don't seem to have anything to say. It's just something like "Get it over with." They may be numb, sort of in a trance.

> They go through stages. And, at this stage, they're real humble. Humblest bunch of people I ever seen. Most all of 'em is real, real weak. Most of the time you'd only need one or two people to carry out an execution, as weak and as humble as they are.

These men seem barely human and alive to their keepers. They wait meekly to be escorted to their deaths. The people who come for them are the warden and the remainder of the death watch team, flanked by high-ranking correctional officials. The warden reads the court order, known popularly as a death warrant. This is, as one officer said, "the real deal," and nobody misses its significance. The condemned prisoners then go to their deaths compliantly, captives of the inexorable, irresistible momentum of the situation. As one officer put it, "There's no struggle.... They just walk right on in there." So too, do the staff "just walk right on in there," following a routine they have come to know well. Both the condemned and the executioners, it would seem, find a relief of sorts in mindless mechanical conformity to the modern execution drill.

WITNESS TO AN EXECUTION

As the team and administrators prepare to commence the good fight, as they might say, another group, the official witnesses, are also preparing themselves for their role in the execution. Numbering between six and twelve for any given execution, the official witnesses are disinterested citizens in good standing drawn from a cross-section of the state's population. If you will, they arc every good or decent person, called upon to represent the community and use their good offices to testify to the propriety of the execution. I served as an official witness at the execution of an inmate.

At eight in the evening, about the time the prisoner is shaved in preparation for the execution, the witnesses are assembled. Eleven in all, we included three newspaper and two television reporters, a state trooper, two police officers, a magistrate, a businessman, and myself. We were picked up in the parking lot behind the main office of the corrections department. There was nothing unusual or even memorable about any of this. Gothic touches were notable by their absence. It wasn't a dark and stormy night; no one emerged from the shadows to lead us to the prison gates.

Mundane considerations prevailed. The van sent for us was missing a few rows of seats so there wasn't enough room for all of us. Obliging prison officials volunteered their cars. Our rather ordinary cavalcade reached the prison but only after getting lost. Once within the prison's walls, we were sequestered for some two hours in a bare and almost shabby administrative conference room. A public information officer was assigned to accompany us and answer our questions. We grilled this official about the prisoner and the execution procedure he would undergo shortly, but little information was to be had. The man confessed ignorance on the most basic points. Disgruntled at this and increasingly anxious, we made small talk and drank coffee.

At 10:40 p.m., roughly two-and-a-half hours after we were assembled and only twenty minutes before the execution was scheduled to occur, the witnesses were taken to the basement of the prison's administrative building, frisked, then led down an alleyway that ran along the exterior of the building. We entered a neighboring cell block and were admitted to a vestibule adjoining the death chamber. Each of us signed a log, and was then led off to the witness area. To our left, around a corner some thirty feet away, the prisoner sat in the condemned cell. He couldn't see us, but I'm quite certain he could hear us. It occurred to me that our arrival was a fateful reminder for the prisoner. The next group would be led by the warden, and it would be coming for him.

We entered the witness area, a room within the death chamber, and took our seats. A picture window covering the front wall of the witness room offered a clear view of the electric chair, which was about twelve feet away from us and well-illuminated. The chair, a large, high-back solid oak structure with imposing black straps, dominated the death chamber. Behind it, on the back wall, was an open panel full of coils and lights. Peeling paint hung from the ceiling and walls; water stains from persistent leaks were everywhere in evidence.

Two officers, one a hulking figure weighing some 400 pounds, stood alongside the electric chair. Each had his hands crossed at the lap and wore a forbidding, blank expression on his face. The witnesses gazed at them and the chair, most of us scribbling notes furiously. We did this, I suppose, as much to record the experience as to have a distraction from the growing tension. A correctional officer entered the witness room and announced that a trial run of the machinery would be undertaken. Seconds later, lights flashed on the control panel behind the chair indicating that the chair was in working order. A white curtain, opened for the test, separated the chair and the witness area. After the test, the curtain was drawn. More tests were performed behind the curtain. Afterwards, the curtain was reopened, and would be left open until the execution was over. Then it would be closed to allow the officers to remove the body.

A handful of high-level correctional officials were present in the death chamber, standing just outside the witness area. There were two regional administrators, the director of the Department of Corrections, and the prison warden. The prisoner's chaplain and lawyer were also present. Other than the chaplain's black religious garb, subdued grey pinstripes and bland correctional uniforms prevailed. All parties were quite solemn.

At 10:58 the prisoner entered the death chamber. He was, I knew from my research, a man with a checkered, tragic past. He had been grossly abused as a child, and went on to become grossly abusive of others. I was told he could not describe his life, from childhood on, without talking about confrontations in defense of a precarious sense of self—at home, in school, on the streets, in the prison yard. Belittled by life and choking with rage, he was hungry to be noticed. Paradoxically, he had found his moment in the spotlight, but it was a dim and unflattering light cast before a small and unappreciative audience. "He'd pose for cameras in the chair—for the attention," his counselor had told me earlier in the day. But the truth was that the prisoner wasn't smiling, and there were no cameras. The prisoner walked quickly and silently toward the chair, an escort of officers in tow. His eyes were turned downward, his expression a bit glazed. Like many before him, the prisoner had threatened to stage a last stand. But that was lifetimes ago, on death row. In the death house, he joined the humble bunch and kept to the executioner's schedule. He appeared to have given up on life before he died in the chair.

En route to the chair, the prisoner stumbled slightly, as if the momentum of the event had overtaken him. Were he not held securely by two officers, one at each elbow, he might have fallen. Were the routine to be broken in this or indeed any other way, the officers believe, the prisoner might faint or panic or become violent, and have to be forcibly placed in the chair. Perhaps as a precaution, when the prisoner reached the chair he did not turn on his own but rather was turned, firmly but without malice, by the officers in his escort. These included the two men at his elbows, and four others who followed behind him. Once the prisoner was seated, again with help, the officers strapped him into the chair.

The execution team worked with machine precision. Like a disciplined swarm, they enveloped him. Arms, legs, stomach, chest, and head were secured in a matter of seconds. Electrodes were attached to the cap holding his head and to the strap holding his exposed right leg. A leather mask was placed over his face. The last officer mopped the prisoner's brow, then touched his hand in a gesture of farewell.

During the brief procession to the electric chair, the prisoner was attended by a chaplain. As the execution team worked feverishly to secure the condemned man's body, the chaplain, who appeared to be upset, leaned over him and placed his forehead in contact with the prisoner's, whispering urgently. The priest might have been praying, but I had the impression he was consoling the man, perhaps assuring him that a forgiving God awaited him in the next life. If he heard the chaplain, I doubt the man comprehended his message. He didn't seem comforted. Rather, he looked stricken and appeared to be in shock. Perhaps the priest's urgent ministrations betrayed his doubts that the prisoner could hold himself together. The chaplain then withdrew at the warden's request, allowing the officers to affix the death mask.

The strapped and masked figure sat before us utterly alone, waiting to be killed. The cap and mask dominated his face. The cap was nothing more than a sponge encased in a leather shell with a metal piece at the top to accept an electrode. It looked decrepit and resembled a cheap, ill-fitting toupee. The mask, made entirely of leather, appeared soiled and worn. It had two parts. The bottom part covered the chin and mouth, the top the eyes and lower forehead. Only the nose was exposed. The effect of a rigidly restrained body, together with the bizarre cap and the protruding nose, was nothing short of grotesque. A faceless man breathed before us in a tragicomic trance, waiting for a blast of electricity that would extinguish his life. Endless seconds passed. His last act was to swallow, nervously, pathetically, with his Adam's apple bobbing. I was struck by that simple movement then, and can't forget it even now. It told me, as nothing else did, that in the prisoner's restrained body, behind that mask, lurked a fellow human being who, at some level, however primitive, knew or sensed himself to be moments from death. The condemned man sat perfectly still for what seemed an eternity but was in fact no more than thirty seconds. Finally the electricity hit him. His body stiffened spasmodically, though only briefly. A thin swirl of smoke trailed away from his head and then dissipated quickly. The body remained taut, with the right foot raised slightly at the heel, seemingly frozen there. A brief pause, then another minute of shock. When it was over, the body was flaccid and inert.

Three minutes passed while the officials let the body cool. (Immediately after the execution, I'm told, the body would be too hot to touch and would blister anyone who did.) All eyes were riveted to the chair; I felt trapped in my witness seat, at once transfixed and yet eager for release. I can't recall any clear thoughts from that moment. One of the death watch officers later volunteered that he shared this experience of staring blankly at the execution scene. Had the prisoner's mind been mercifully blank before the end? I hoped so.

An officer walked up to the body, opened the shirt at chest level, then continued on to get the physician from an adjoining room. The physician listened for a heartbeat. Hearing none, he turned to the warden and said, "This man has expired." The warden, speaking to the director, solemnly intoned: "Mr. Director, the court order has been fulfilled." The curtain was then drawn and the witnesses filed out.

THE MORNING AFTER

As the team prepared the body for the morgue, the witnesses were led to the front door of the prison. On the way, we passed a number of cell blocks. We could hear the normal sounds of prison life, including the occasional catcall and lewd comment hurled at uninvited guests like ourselves. But no trouble came in the wake of the execution. Small protests were going on outside the walls, we were told, but we could not hear them. Soon the media would be gone; the protesters would disperse and head for their homes. The prisoners, already home, had been indifferent to the proceedings, as they always are unless the condemned prisoner had been a figure of some consequence in the convict community. Then there might be tension and maybe even a modest disturbance on a prison tier or two. But few convict luminaries are executed, and the dead man had not been one of them. Our escort officer offered a sad tribute to the prisoner: "The inmates, they didn't care about this guy."

I couldn't help but think they weren't alone in this. The executioners went home and set about their lives. Having taken life, they would savor a bit of life themselves. They showered, ate, made love, slept, then took a day or two off. For some, the prisoner's image would linger for that night. The men who strapped him in remembered what it was like to touch him; they showered as soon as they got home to wash off the feel and smell of death. One official sat up picturing how the prisoner looked at the end. (I had a few drinks myself that night with that same image for company.) There was some talk about delayed reactions to the stress of carrying out executions. Though such concerns seemed remote that evening, I learned later that problems would surface for some of the officers. But no one on the team, then or later, was haunted by the executed man's memory, nor would anyone grieve for him. "When I go home after one of these things," said one man, "I sleep like a rock." His may or may not be the sleep of the just, but one can only marvel at such a thing, and perhaps envy such a man.

STUDY QUESTIONS

1. Describe the execution process, including the work of the death watch team.
2. What functions are served by the elaborate and impersonal procedures used, and how are they carried out?
3. Do you believe that this impersonal process is more civilized than previous forms of executions (e.g., stoning or hanging)? Would you expect this type of execution to be more or less effective as a form of retribution and deterrence than previous methods?